'Down to Weymouth town by Ridgeway'

Prehistoric, Roman and later sites along the Weymouth Relief Road

by Lisa Brown, Chris Hayden and David Score

with contributions by
Leigh Allen, Edward Biddulph, Sheila Boardman, Anwen Cooper, John Cotter, Michael Donnelly, Vix Hughes, Lynne Keys, Ian Scott, Mark Gibson, Louise Loe, Peter Northover, Ruth Shaffrey, Elizabeth Stafford, Daniel Stansbie, Lena Strid and Helen Webb

Illustrations by
Magdalena Wachnik, Julia Collins, Mark Gridley, Hannah Kennedy, and Georgina Slater

Dorset Natural History and Archaeological Society Monograph Series: No. 23

2014

Edited and prepared for publication by Lisa Brown

Proceedings of Dorset Natural History and Archaeological Society. Hon. Editor: Paul Lashmar

ISBN 978-0-900341-59-5

This book is one of a pair of monographs about the excavations along the route of the Weymouth Relief Road. The companion volume is *'Given to the Ground'*: *A Viking Age Mass Grave on Ridgeway Hill, Weymouth* (L. Loe, A. Boyle, H. Webb and D. Score), DNHAS Monograph Series 22 (2014)

Designed and typeset by Production Line, Oxford
Printed in Great Britain by Berforts Information Press, Eynsham, Oxford

Dorset County Museum, High West Street, Dorchester DT1 1XA
Oxford Archaeology, Janus House, Osney Mead, Oxford OX2 0ES

Great Things

Sweet cyder is a great thing,
A great thing to me,
Spinning down to Weymouth town
By Ridgeway thirstily,
And maid and mistress summoning
Who tend the hostelry:
O cyder is a great thing,
A great thing to me!

an extract, by Thomas Hardy

Contents

Chapter 1: Introduction

Chapter 2: Neolithic, Early Bronze Age and later activity at Ridgeway Hill
by Chris Hayden

Chapter 3: The Finds from Ridgeway Hill

Contents

Chapter 6: The Finds from Southdown Ridge

Chapter 7: Discussion of Southdown Ridge *by Lisa Brown*

Chapter 8: Excavations and Survey at Redlands and Bincombe Valley

List of Figures

List of Tables

Summary

The construction of the Weymouth Relief Road presented an opportunity to investigate archaeologically a transect across a landscape of intricately varied geology that preserves a wealth of archaeological and historical remains dating from the Palaeolithic to the post-medieval periods. Remains of prehistoric and Roman date are particularly extensive in this area, and the variety and extent of this resource make it one of the richest and most important cultural landscapes in England.

The northern end of the Relief Road encroaches on the South Dorset Ridgeway, a stretch of land within which lie at least 500 recognised archaeological monuments, and which includes one of the densest concentrations of Bronze Age round barrows in Britain. The visible remains of several other periods have been identified along and in the lee of the Ridgeway and southwards towards the coastal plain to Weymouth. One of the best recognised of these monuments is the Iron Age hillfort of Maiden Castle, which excavation demonstrated to have a Neolithic precursor in the form of a causewayed enclosure. The adjacent site of Poundbury and the Romano-British town of *Durnovaria*, modern Dorchester, have also been the subject of frequent and extensive examination.

This volume presents the results of archaeological investigations undertaken by Oxford Archaeology (OA) during 2008-2009, prior to the construction of the Weymouth Relief Road. At two sites, Ridgeway Hill and Southdown Ridge, large scale excavation was undertaken in the light of the evaluation and assessment results. At the southern stretch of the road scheme at Redlands the previously discovered remains of a Roman settlement produced a requirement for small-scale excavation. This revealed further limited evidence of Romano-British activity in the form of boundary ditches and a possible trackway, and the investigations also defined the eastern extent of settlement. Limited investigations at Two Mile Coppice and Lorton Meadows, located either side of Redlands, produced no archaeological discoveries, and geophysical survey along the route of Littlemoor Road also revealed nothing of note.

Evaluation and earthworks survey were carried out at Bincombe Valley on the Ridgeway Fault just to the south of the Ridgeway Hill site. The site was selected for investigation because of the presence of previously recognised, well preserved strip lynchets, hypothesised as examples of possible Anglo-Saxon features. Whilst the results of OA's work demonstrated a general sequence for the lynchets, it was not possible to confirm their date or whether they were deliberately constructed.

The most significant archaeological findings were at Ridgeway Hill and Southdown Ridge. At Ridgeway Hill a sequence of early, middle and late Neolithic pits was investigated and dated using radiocarbon determinations, small collections of pottery and spatial analysis. Several groups of early Bronze Age inhumation and cremation burials in pits and cists were also excavated. Although heavily truncated, the evidence suggests that these were probably originally associated with barrows, and a programme of radiocarbon dating revealed important information about their chronology. Several of the burials were associated with well preserved Beakers, and the excavation also produced an important collection of flints. Two Bronze Age ring ditches, a possible Roman field system and several Roman and Anglo-Saxon burials were also examined, along with a row of undated empty 'graves', a post-medieval stone building and trackway.

At Southdown Ridge the partial remains of a settlement that emerged during the late Bronze Age/early Iron Age transition were discovered lying adjacent to a truncated cross-ridge dyke and a set of early Iron Age field enclosures. The evidence suggests that the early inhabitants were engaged in shale-working as well as agriculture. After a possible interruption in occupation during the middle Iron Age, the settlement area was extensively remodelled during the late Iron Age, when the occupants continued working shale into armlets within a complex of stone built structures. The settlement was abandoned during the late Iron Age or early post-conquest period and the field boundaries were converted into a burial ground. Several individuals were interred here in accordance with the distinctive south Dorset burial tradition, which included the offering of grave goods. Three coffined burials in keeping with Roman customs indicated continuing funerary activity into the early Roman period. Around this time the area previously occupied by the settlement was converted to agricultural use by wholesale levelling with midden-like material, including pottery, that derived from the earliest phases of occupation. The only traces of post-medieval activity were a small collection of pottery, a poorly dated limestone quarry and a set of field drains.

Acknowledgements

Oxford Archaeology was employed by Skanska Civil Engineering, the Main Contractor building the Weymouth Relief Road on behalf of Dorset County Council, who funded the work, and the central part played by these organisations is gratefully acknowledged. The project was managed for Dorset County Council by Matthew Piles and Oxford Archaeology would like to extend their appreciation to him and his team and in particular Kerry Hall, DCC Public Relations Officer for the enthusiastic and positive way in which they supported the archaeological works. Their proactive approach to promoting and disseminating the results of the work was very refreshing and enriched the archaeological experience for all concerned. A special mention is due to Steve Wallis, Dorset County Archaeologist, who monitored the works on behalf of the Planning Authority, for his sound advice and guidance and constantly cheerful disposition. Thanks are due also to Mick Rawlings, RPS Consulting, Skanska's archaeological consultant, who produced the original project specification and provided additional valuable input during the works. Oxford Archaeology would also like to acknowledge Willie McCormick, Project Manager, Skanska, and his project team for the efficient way in which they facilitated our work on site, and in particular Helen Jenkins, Environment Manager, Skanska, who was directly responsible for overseeing our work on the project. The ground works on the scheme were undertaken by Walters UK Ltd, and thanks are due to Paul Baker, Contracts Manager, and Kevin Davies, Works Manager and their excellent site staff for providing plant and other attendances and ensuring that our excavations ran smoothly.

The project was managed for Oxford Archaeology by David Score and the excavation was directed by Project Officer Vix Hughes, who was assisted by many other Oxford Archaeology field staff, including Alistair Zochowski, Neville Redvers-Higgins, Bron Pihlwret, Mattias Pihlwret, Robin Maggs, Mike Harris, Mark Gibson and Laura King. The survey work was carried out by Conan Parsons. The finds were processed by Kay Proctor under the management of Leigh Allen, and environmental work supervised by Rebecca Nicholson. The archive was organised by Nicola Scott, and the post-excavation assessment stage of the project co-ordinated by Alex Smith.

The following Oxford Archaeology specialists have contributed advice and reports to this monograph: Leigh Allen (worked bone), Sheila Boardman (charred plant remains and wood charcoal), Lisa Brown, Anwen Cooper, Edward Biddulph and John Cotter (pottery), Michael Donnelly (flint and chert), Mark Gibson, Louise Loe and Helen Webb (human remains), Ian Scott (metalwork and glass), Ruth Shaffrey (shale and worked stone), Dan Stansbie (fired clay), Elizabeth Stafford (molluscs) and Lena Strid (animal bone). External expert Lynne Keys reported on the iron slag and high temperature debris, and Peter Northover analysed and reported on the socketed axe.

Several individuals from Oxford Archaeology have greatly assisted with the production of this monograph, which was overseen by Anne Dodd. The illustrations were drawn by Magdalena Wachnik, Hannah Kennedy, Julia Collins, and Georgina Slater and objects photographed by Magdalena Wachnik, who oversaw all the graphics work. Mark Gridley is gratefully acknowledged for the reconstruction drawing (Fig. 4.3). Lisa Brown, who edited and co-ordinated the production of this volume, is grateful for the dedicated, swift and efficient work of typesetting carried out by Charlie Webster (Production Line, Oxford).

The authors are indebted to Richard Bradley, who kindly read and commented on the original drafts of the Ridgeway Hill and Southdown Ridge reports. Oxford Archaeology is also grateful to Paul Lashmar of DNHAS, who advised on the format, summary and cover design. The monograph has benefited greatly from their input but any remaining shortcomings are the responsibility of the authors and editor.

Chapter 1: Introduction

GENERAL INTRODUCTION

This report presents the results of archaeological investigations undertaken by Oxford Archaeology (OA) during 2008-2009, prior to the construction of the Weymouth Relief Road (Fig. 1.1). The work entailed extensive excavation at two sites – Ridgeway Hill (WEY08) and Southdown Ridge (WESR09) and a small-scale excavation – Redlands (WEROM09). An earthworks survey and evaluation were carried out at Bincombe Valley (BIVA08) and evaluations were also carried out at Two Mile Coppice (WETPM09) and Lorton Meadows (WELM08). Additionally, geophysical survey was undertaken along the route of Littlemoor Road and a scheme-wide watching brief was carried out on all ground works affected by the scheme.

The most significant archaeological findings were at Ridgeway Hill and Southdown Ridge. At Ridgeway Hill a sequence of Neolithic pits was investigated, along with several groups of early Bronze Age inhumation and cremation burials in pits and cists. The evidence indicates that the burials were originally associated with barrows, and important information about the chronology of the burials was obtained through a programme of radiocarbon dating. Two Bronze Age ring ditches, a (probably) Roman field system and several Roman and Anglo-Saxon burials were also found. A stone building and a trackway dating to the post-medieval period may have been associated with the railway that ran below the site.

The excavations at Southdown Ridge revealed a late Bronze Age/early Iron Age settlement associated with a cross-ridge dyke and an agricultural enclosure system. Following a period of limited action during the middle Iron Age, the settlement area was remodelled during the late Iron Age, when the occupants undertook activities including shale-working within a complex of stone built structures and pathways. During the late Iron Age the abandoned settlement and the surrounding enclosures were converted into a burial ground in which several individuals were interred according to the distinctive south Dorset Durotrigian burial rites. Three coffined supine burials testify to continuing funerary activity into the early Roman period. At some point during the transition between the late Iron Age and early Roman period the area

previously occupied by the settlement was levelled and consolidated using midden-like deposits associated with the earliest phases of settlement activity, and with stone robbed from later Iron Age structures. A poorly dated limestone quarry, recorded in a small machine trench, was almost certainly exploited during the post-medieval period, and field drains of that period transected the site.

The Redlands site was selected for excavation because the remains of a 1st-2nd century Roman settlement, including a stone building and an infant burial, were exposed in the Redlands Sports Ground (Valentin 1999) to the west of the railway. The remains of a metalled surface and a scatter of Roman pottery had been found during the excavation of a drainage ditch in the same area (Boulter and Squib 1980). The evaluation to the east of the railway had indicated the presence of Roman features (Wessex Archaeology 2004; GSB 2004), and these proved to be Roman midden-like deposits, a ditched trackway and ditches that predated the midden.

In the course of the earthworks survey at Bincombe a sequence of probable lynchets were examined, with inconclusive results. It was not possible to be certain whether their construction was deliberate or simply a by-product of a particular pattern of ploughing, and no clear evidence of structures or other deliberate construction was identified. However, the deposits that formed the positive lynchets suggested the presence of a boundary feature that prevented sediments from continuing downslope. Pottery of 17th-18th century date suggests that the earthworks were quite recent features, and the RCHM(E) (1970, 23) notes that they remained in use into the 19th century. However, evidence that they had gradually spread could indicate that they formed over a period of unknown length.

LOCATION, GEOLOGY AND TOPOGRAPHY

The sites investigated in advance of construction of the road are located to the north of the city of Weymouth along the route of the A354 relief road (Figs 1.1-1.2). Ridgeway Hill lies on the South Dorset Ridgeway at NGR SY 672 857. The site extended from the summit of the Ridgeway down

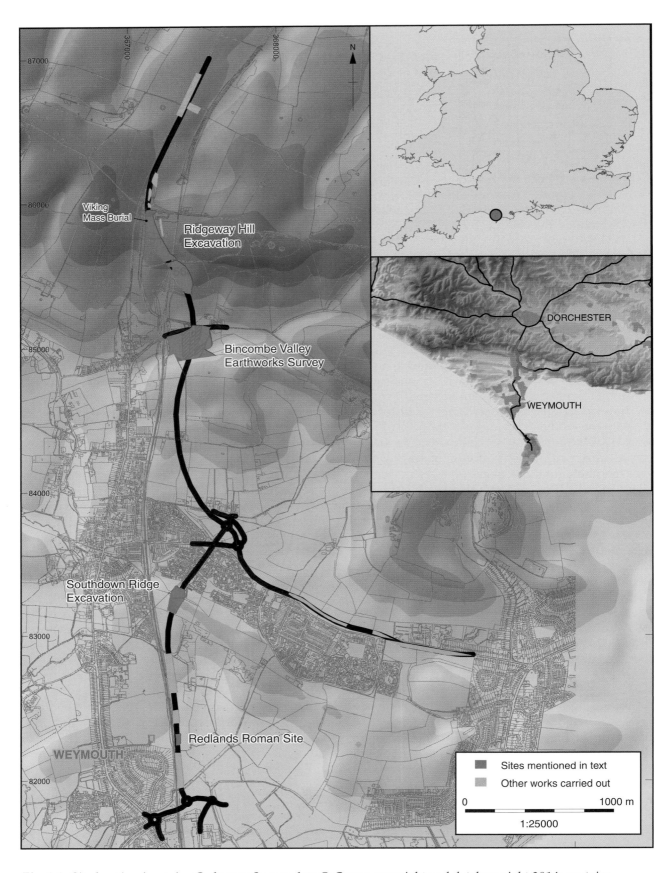

Fig. 1.1: Site location (contains Ordnance Survey data © Crown copyright and database right 2014; contains Ordnance Survey data © Crown copyright 2014 Ordnance Survey 100005569)

the southern slopes, dropping from 140m aOD at the northern end to 95m at the southern end (Fig. 1.3). It was bounded to the west by the A354, to the north by the lane from Down Farm to Broadmayne, and to the east and south by fields. The South-West Coastal Path cut across the site in an area that was not excavated. This area was largely under arable cultivation prior to the excavation, although the southern-most, and most steeply sloping fields were under pasture.

Bincombe is centred at NGR SY 675 850, and extends across the Bincombe Valley (Hellwell Bottom) to the south of the Upwey to Bincombe road, from the railway line at the west to the south of West Farm to the east. The bottom of the valley in this area lies at around 60m OD, and the land rises towards the Ridgeway to the north and to the Knoll to the south. The land was being used as pasture at the time of the survey.

Southdown Ridge lies some 2.5km south of Ridgeway Hill, between Littlemoor Road and Lorton Lane, on a spur of land at NGR SY 673 832. The majority of the Relief Road route was set to grass, and has historically been used predominantly for agricultural purposes. The southern length of the route lies within a Nature Reserve managed by the Dorset Wildlife Trust.

The Redlands site lay immediately to the east of the railway line, Greenway Road and the Redlands Sports Centre, and just to the north of Two Mile Coppice, at NGR SY 673 823. The area was covered by young oak trees prior to excavation.

Geology

The geology of the coastal plain around Weymouth is dominated by clay, but outcrops of Oolitic and Purbeck limestone create some relief (Fig. 1.4; (http://mapapps.bgs.ac.uk/geologyofbritain/home.html). The solid strata encountered along the line of the road scheme are predominantly clay formations and interbedded limestones, mudstones, siltstones and sandstone groups, with the northern end of the route intersecting chalk.

In the southern part of the route the basal geology consists of formations of Jurassic date. To the east of Manor Roundabout, in the northern Redlands sector of the city, the land is fairly flat, lying at about 5-10m aOD. Here and on the lower slopes of Southdown Ridge the underlying solid geology is Oxford Clay. Southdown Ridge itself represents a narrow band of Corallian Limestone, which rises gently to *c* 60m aOD. The lowest (Nothe) formation of the Corallian Group comprises interbedded sandstones and mudstones. Gravelly sands and clays with thin beds of limestone were encountered in exploratory boreholes close to the

boundary with the underlying Oxford Clay at the southern edge of Southdown Ridge. Overlying the Nothe Formation the Osmington Oolite Formation and the Clavellata Formation, limestones distinguished by the presence of oolites and shelly fossils, were encountered in boreholes and trial pits from the top of Southdown Ridge and as far north as the boundary with the Littlemoor development (Fig. 2.2). A review of 19th-century Ordnance Survey maps indicates that lime manufacture, using a kiln, was taking place at some point in the vicinity of Southdown Ridge.

To the south the land falls gently as it approaches the sea, whilst the northern face of the ridge is a pronounced scarp slope. The Redlands site lies in an area of gently sloping ground, which falls from 45m aOD at the west to 22m aOD at the east. The local geology is composed of Kimmeridge and Oxford Clays overlying the Kellaways Formation.

To the north of Southdown Ridge the land dips away to *c* 30m aOD at Littlemoor Road, and here the road scheme crosses over Kimmeridge Clay. The route rises northwards to approximately 80m aOD over the western flank of The Knoll, which is an outcrop of Purbeck and Portland Limestone Groups. The route then dips again into the Lower Bincombe Valley where it crosses over narrow bands of Wealden and Oxford Clays at *c* 60m aOD. The Bincombe area spans the 'Ridgeway Fault', and the underlying geology here varies across the valley, crossing bands of mudstone of the Ridgeway Member, sandstone of the Portland Sand Formation and limestone of the Portland Cherty Member, the Portland Freestone Member and the Mupe Member, which are covered by bands of Wealden and Oxford Clays.

The route then climbs up the southern slope of the Ridgeway, which is composed of Upper Chalk of Cretaceous date. It crosses the Ridgeway at *c* 140m aOD and then descends gently towards Dorchester. The Upper Chalk of the Ridgeway Hill site was overlain by a 0.3m thick ploughsoil, with a diffuse boundary between the two due to ploughing activity.

PROJECT BACKGROUND

Planning background

The excavations were carried out in 2008–2009 as part of a wider set of investigations (Loe *et al.* 2014) which were undertaken prior to the construction of the Weymouth Relief Road. The new road was constructed in 2008-2011 by Skanska Civil Engineering and Owen Williams, designed to replace a 7km stretch of the A354 running from the Ridgeway to the Manor Roundabout, Redlands,

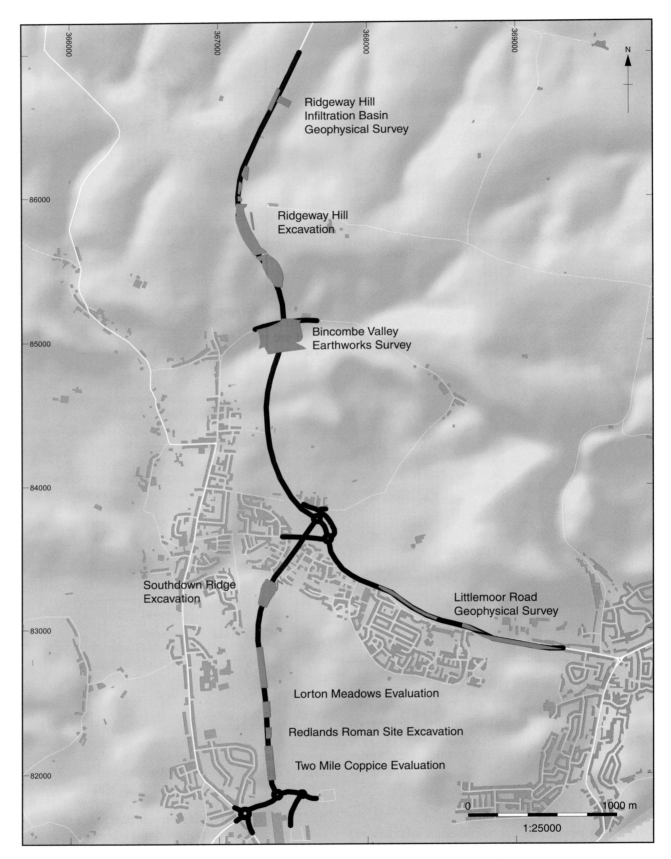

Fig. 1.2: All works carried out (contains Ordnance Survey data © Crown copyright 2014 Ordnance Survey 100005569)

Fig. 1.3 Aerial view taken from above the Ridgeway looking south over the Ridgeway Hill excavation

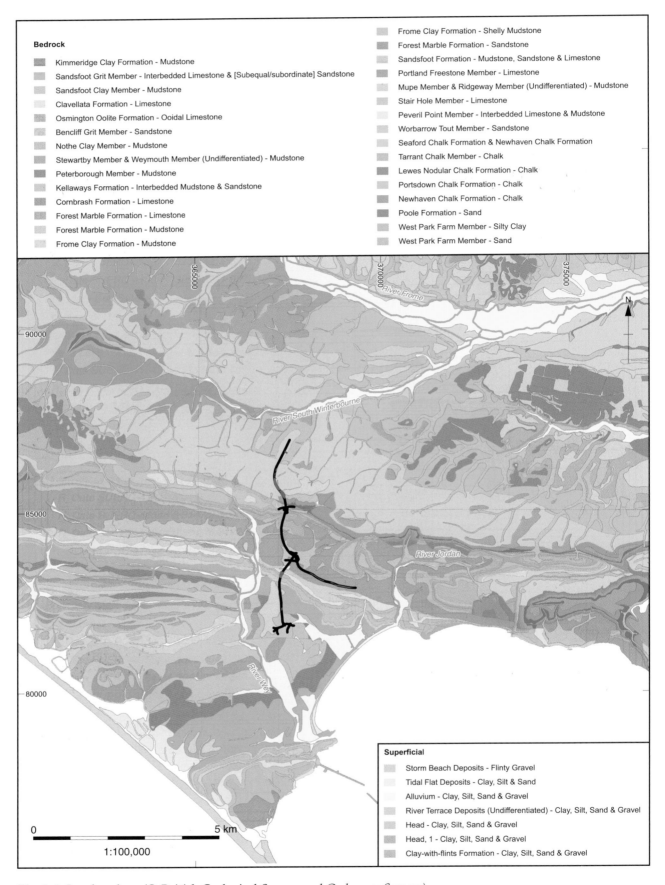

Bedrock

- Kimmeridge Clay Formation - Mudstone
- Sandsfoot Grit Member - Interbedded Limestone & [Subequal/subordinate] Sandstone
- Sandsfoot Clay Member - Mudstone
- Clavellata Formation - Limestone
- Osmington Oolite Formation - Ooidal Limestone
- Bencliff Grit Member - Sandstone
- Nothe Clay Member - Mudstone
- Stewartby Member & Weymouth Member (Undifferentiated) - Mudstone
- Peterborough Member - Mudstone
- Kellaways Formation - Interbedded Mudstone & Sandstone
- Cornbrash Formation - Limestone
- Forest Marble Formation - Limestone
- Forest Marble Formation - Mudstone
- Frome Clay Formation - Mudstone

- Frome Clay Formation - Shelly Mudstone
- Forest Marble Formation - Sandstone
- Sandsfoot Formation - Mudstone, Sandstone & Limestone
- Portland Freestone Member - Limestone
- Mupe Member & Ridgeway Member (Undifferentiated) - Mudstone
- Stair Hole Member - Limestone
- Peveril Point Member - Interbedded Limestone & Mudstone
- Worbarrow Tout Member - Sandstone
- Seaford Chalk Formation & Newhaven Chalk Formation
- Tarrant Chalk Member - Chalk
- Lewes Nodular Chalk Formation - Chalk
- Portsdown Chalk Formation - Chalk
- Newhaven Chalk Formation - Chalk
- Poole Formation - Sand
- West Park Farm Member - Silty Clay
- West Park Farm Member - Sand

Superficial

- Storm Beach Deposits - Flinty Gravel
- Tidal Flat Deposits - Clay, Silt & Sand
- Alluvium - Clay, Silt, Sand & Gravel
- River Terrace Deposits (Undifferentiated) - Clay, Silt, Sand & Gravel
- Head - Clay, Silt, Sand & Gravel
- Head, 1 - Clay, Silt, Sand & Gravel
- Clay-with-flints Formation - Clay, Silt, Sand & Gravel

0   5 km

1:100,000

Fig. 1.4 Local geology (© British Geological Survey and Ordnance Survey)

removing the hairpin bend in the A354 and providing a bypass for Redlands, Broadwey and Upwey.

Skanska Civil Engineering commissioned OA to undertake a programme of archaeological works to mitigate the impact of the scheme on archaeological remains. Owen Williams (part of Amey PLC) built the road in partnership with Skanska and commissioned additional archaeological consultancy services and advice from RPS Planning and Development. The programme of archaeological work was required by Condition 15 of the planning consent for the road scheme imposed by the County Planning Authority.

Prior to the commencement of the archaeological works the route was subject to several phases of archaeological assessment, including desk-based assessment, walk-over survey, test-pitting, geophysical survey, earthwork survey, fieldwalking and auger survey (Dorset County Council 2005). These investigations were designed to evaluate archaeological potential, and this culminated in the preparation of an Environmental Statement to support the planning application for the scheme. The route corridor was designed to avoid, as far as possible, significant archaeological sites and was carried out in accordance with an approved Written Scheme of Investigation (WSI) for the project produced by RPS Planning and Development (Rawlings 2007). This was designed to mitigate the impact of the scheme where significant archaeological remains would be affected.

The archaeological interventions are presented in Table 1.1.

The mitigation works included a scheme-wide watching brief along the entire route, geophysical survey at intervals along the Littlemoor Road, evaluation excavations at Two Mile Coppice and Lorton Meadows and an evaluation and earthworks survey at Bincombe Valley. Major excavations were undertaken at Ridgeway Hill and Southdown Ridge and a smaller excavation at Redlands.

Table 1.1 Archaeological works along the Relief Road

Site Code	Site name	Archaeological action
WEY 08	Ridgeway Hill	Geophysical survey and excavation
WESR 09	Southdown Ridge	Excavation
WEROM 09	Redlands Roman Site	Excavation
WETM 09	Two Mile Coppice	Evaluation
WELM 08	Lorton Meadows	Evaluation
BIVA 08	Bincombe Valley	Topographic survey and evaluation
WRR 08	Weymouth Relief Road	Scheme-wide watching brief

The results of the Ridgeway Hill and Southdown Ridge excavations are presented in Chapters 2-7 of this volume, while the results of the excavation at Redlands and the earthworks survey at Bincombe Valley form Chapter 8. Significant discoveries at the Watching Brief area to the north of Ridgeway Hill are included with the main excavation report for that site in Chapter 2.

Mention of the relatively minor results of evaluation at Lorton Meadows and Two Mile Coppice is confined to this section of the report, summarised here: Two Mile Coppice is located immediately to the south of the Roman site at Redlands, centred at NGR SY 673 821. A total of eight evaluation trenches produced no significant results, only the discovery of a single fragment of post-medieval brick from the topsoil of Trench 2. The Lorton Meadows site is located to the north of Redlands, centred at NGR SY 672 825. No archaeological remains were discovered at this location.

Archaeological background

The Relief Road lies in one of the richest and best-known prehistoric landscapes in Britain, an area that preserves visible remains of several periods, of which the best-recognised are Maiden Castle, the adjacent site of Poundbury and the Romano-British town of *Durnovaria*, modern Dorchester (Fig. 1.5). Remains dating to the Bronze Age and Roman periods are particularly prolific in the area between Dorchester and Weymouth, but evidence of past activity for almost every other archaeologically defined period has also been recorded. The route of the road was thoroughly researched when the road was planned, and this summary makes use of the records of that research (Wessex Archaeology 2003).

The Palaeolithic period is not well-represented in the Weymouth area, but the Southern Rivers Palaeolithic Archaeology Project, which plotted all known Lower and Middle Palaeolithic finds, shows a sparse distribution of Palaeolithic findspots in the Dorchester region. These include handaxes from Maiden Castle and Came Farm, Winterbourne Came (Wessex Archaeology 1994). The Mesolithic period is also poorly-represented in the vicinity of the route, but there is some material from the wider region. Mesolithic groups utilised the local chert for tool production on the Isle of Portland and along the Fleet, and chert implements probably of Mesolithic date have also been found inland, as noted in the South Dorset Ridgeway Survey (Woodward 1991, 127-9). Closer to the road scheme, possible Mesolithic flakes and blades were found just east of Bincombe Barn and Upwey and a Portland chert core of Mesolithic type was noted from Ridgeway Hill (Wymer 1977, 67; 75).

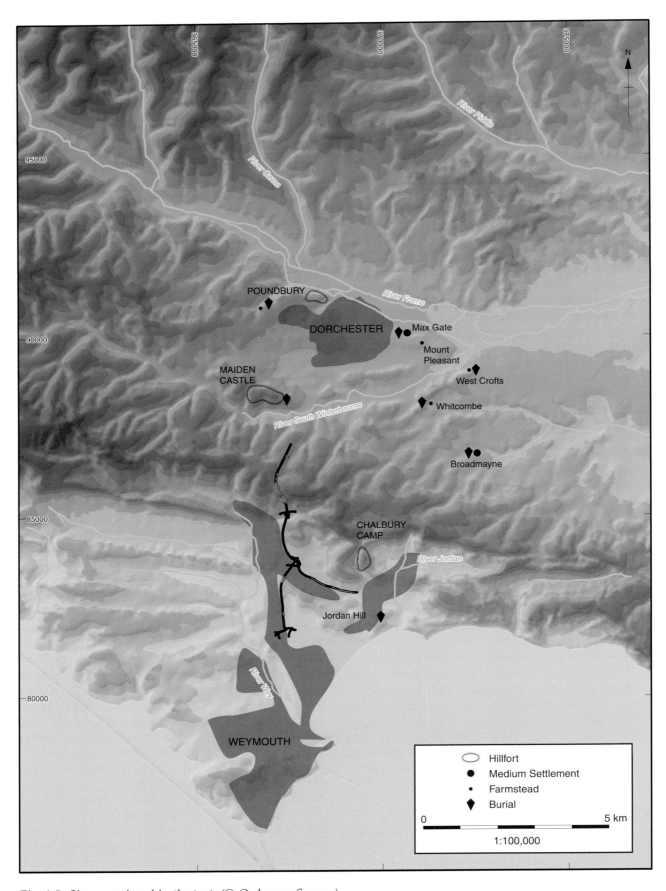

Fig. 1.5 Sites mentioned in the text (© Ordnance Survey)

The area immediately around Dorchester was a focus of activity during the earlier and later Neolithic, and there are monuments dating from both phases. A Neolithic causewayed enclosure lies within the Iron Age hillfort at Maiden Castle, a little over 2km north of Ridgeway Hill, and late Neolithic enclosures were also discovered during the construction of the Dorchester bypass. Several earlier and later Neolithic sites have been examined close to the town at Alington Avenue, Mount Pleasant, Thomas Hardye School, Maumbury Rings, Greyhound Yard, Middle Farm and Poundbury (Woodward 1991). Small Neolithic settlement sites in the area, often represented by single pits, include one discovered at Sutton Poyntz (Farrar 1958). Neolithic stone artefacts have a wide distribution in the area, as reflected in the South Dorset Ridgeway Survey (Woodward 1991).

One of the densest concentrations of Bronze Age round barrows in Britain lies along the Dorset Ridgeway. In this location, within an area only one mile wide, some 40 barrows have been identified (Woodward 1991, 426-7), a density matched in England only around Avebury and Stonehenge in Wiltshire. These sites, and the development of the landscape, are the subject of a number of syntheses (Woodward 1991; Woodward and Woodward 1996; Grinsell 1959 and 1982, Webster 2008; Gale 2003).

The Ridgeway Hill site crosses the part of the Ridgeway occupied by the R8 Ridgeway Hill group of barrows (RCHM(E) 1970). Here, a more or less diffuse line of barrows extends along the top of the Ridgeway to the east and west of the site, and there are examples also to the south and, in greater numbers, to the north. Most of them appear to have been bowl barrows, but a probable pond barrow (Weymouth 406) lies to the north-west of the site, and one of the excavated sites was a bell barrow (Bincombe 25). Most of the barrows were probably constructed during the early Bronze Age, although cremation burials were sometimes inserted in these older monuments during the middle Bronze Age, and some may have been constructed during that period. Several barrows in the vicinity of the site which have been excavated or otherwise investigated are discussed in detail in the context of the site narrative (Chapter 2).

The middle Bronze Age saw the introduction of large-scale field systems, but these are difficult to date without excavation as field systems of Iron Age and Romano-British date are also known. The RCHM(E) distinguishes only between 'Celtic fields', this designation including 'all fields of regular shape laid out before the Saxon Conquest', and later fields, characterised by strip lynchets and ridge and furrow (RCHM(E) 1970, 622). Traces of ancient fields above Bincombe Tunnel on Ridgeway Hill, numbered as Ancient Field Group 7 by the RCHM(E) (1970, 627), may be of middle Bronze Age or later date. Although the middle Bronze Age also saw the emergence of recognisable farmstead settlements, such as one excavated at Shearplace Hill, Sydling St. Nicholas, north-west of Dorchester (Rahtz 1962), none was encountered in the vicinity of the Relief Road. Flat cremation burial cemeteries are also a feature of this period, and one of the type sites for this tradition was at Rimbury, just to the south-west of Ridgeway Hill, where more than 100 urns containing cremation burials were revealed during the excavation of a reservoir.

There is some evidence for late Bronze Age settlement in the immediate area of the route. An excavation by Wessex Archaeology at Coburg Road, Dorchester, produced pottery probably belonging to the latest stages of the Bronze Age (Smith *et al.* 1992), and the Iron Age hillfort of Chalbury, north-west of Preston, was probably first enclosed during the late Bronze Age (Whitley 1943).

Several other Iron Age hillforts lie within the vicinity of the excavations. Maiden Castle and Poundbury, located *c* 2km from the northern end of the scheme, are amongst the most extensively excavated (Wheeler 1943; Green 1987; Sharples 1991). With the more distant Hod Hill to the north-east (Richmond 1968), and Eggardon (Wells 1979) and Abbotsbury Castle to the west (Beavis 1974), these sites formed an important network of hillfort sites within the tribal area of the Durotriges, serving complementary functions as agricultural, distribution and occupation centres.

Early Iron Age settlements, some of them enclosed, have also been identified in the Dorchester area. At Waddon near Portesham, just north of Weymouth, an enclosed early Iron Age settlement was represented by a series of roundhouses constructed on low stone foundations (Hirst 2000). A small-scale Iron Age farmstead at Pins Knoll, Litton Cheney, 14km to the west of Dorchester (Bailey 1967), appears to have originated during the early Iron Age and been more or less continually occupied to the Roman period. Although apparently unenclosed and on a smaller scale than the hillfort, the pottery from a farmstead at Quarrey Lodden, Bincombe, (Bailey and Flatters 1972) suggests that occupation may have continued to the Roman period, long after Chalbury was abandoned (Sharples 1991, 258-60).

During the middle Iron Age, settlement activity intensified at Maiden Castle and Poundbury, and contemporary occupation has been recognised at Alington Avenue, Whitcombe and Fordington Bottom near the route of the Dorchester bypass (Smith 1997). Several other Iron Age settlements sited beside the River Frome seem to have emerged only during the late Iron Age, when settlement activity associated with Maiden Castle dispersed. Field systems, unknown in the area around Maiden Castle during the zenith of middle Iron Age hillfort construction, also developed during the late Iron Age, perhaps indicating a breakdown of communal ownership of land at this stage. It has been suggested that the focal point of Dorchester was akin to an *oppidum* during the late Iron Age (Green 1987).

Several inhumation burials and cemeteries have been found in the south Dorset area. The Durotrigian burial tradition is distinguished by the crouched position of the bodies and accompanying grave goods. Durotrigian burials are grouped into cemeteries at Maiden Castle and Jordan Hill (Woodward 1992) and Whitcombe, Portesham, near Weymouth (Fitzpatrick 1997). Burials associated with settlement activity have also been identified at Broadmayne, Max Gate and West Crofts to the east of Dorchester and, further afield, at Tolpuddle to the north-east of the city.

The major known features of the Romano-British landscape in the area are the town of *Durnovaria* (Dorchester), the temples at Maiden Castle and Jordan Hill, a harbour settlement in the Radipole area, a villa at Preston, and the road between *Durnovaria* and the Radipole settlement (RCHM(E) 1970, 643). Roman finds are, however, more widespread than this, and occur close to the line of the Roman road at several points along its length. A field system of possible Roman date recorded by the RCHM(E) as Ancient Field Group 7 fell partially within the Ridgeway Hill excavation

No finds of definite Saxon date had previously been noted in the immediate vicinity of the route, but there is evidence of settlement at Dorchester from at least the 8th century, and the town gave its name to the shire. Records of a royal residence of this period seem to place it at Fordington, just outside Dorchester (Keen 1984, 2207-8). Saxon burials of 7th century date have been found at Maiden Castle and at Wareham House, Mount Pleasant (Green 1985, 149-52), and a settlement of 5th–7th century date is known at Poundbury (Green 1987). The settlements established by the later Middle Ages are largely those still in existence today (RCHM(E) 1970). Medieval strip lynchets and ridge and furrow are visible over large areas both within and around the Relief Road, along with limited traces of (probably) post-medieval narrow rig (RCHM(E) 1970, 622).

The construction of the railway at Weymouth was completed in 1857. It runs in a tunnel below Ridgeway Hill, from which a ventilation shaft emerges just to the west of the southern part of the excavation, and a short distance to the north of the point where the railway line emerges from its tunnel. A building and associated features found nearby may have been associated with the construction of the tunnel.

METHODOLOGY

The archaeological work was undertaken in accordance with the WSI and OA's standard fieldwork methodologies (Wilkinson 1992). The works were monitored throughout by Steve Wallis, the Senior Archaeologist for Dorset County Council and Mick Rawlings of RPS.

The topsoil was stripped under archaeological supervision using 360° tracked excavators with toothless buckets. The spoil was removed from the site to other areas within the scheme under controlled conditions to ensure removal and stockpiling without this traffic impacting upon the archaeological horizon. Mechanical excavation ceased at either undisturbed natural deposits or when archaeological features were identified. After stripping, the sites were cleaned and all features and deposits were digitally planned, issued with unique context numbers, then excavated by hand and recorded in accordance with established OA practice. A stratigraphic matrix was compiled to record the relationships of the archaeological features and deposits encountered.

Data-capture for site plans was by a combination of electronic distance measurement and GPS. Data-capture for site plans is, as standard, capable of reproduction at a scale of 1:100. More complex features or areas were recorded at greater resolution for reproduction at 1:10, 1:20, or 1:50, as necessary. The site grid was established relative to the Ordnance Survey National Grid and all levels taken were relative to Ordnance Datum. All excavated features were drawn in plan at 1:20 for most features, but 1:10 for burials, and sections at 1:20. Digital and black and white slide photographs were taken of all excavated features. Work carried out during the watching brief was monitored by an archaeologist and features discovered were excavated and recorded in the same way as those found in the main excavation.

All pits and graves were completely excavated. A 50% sample of one of the ring ditches at the Ridgeway Hill site was excavated in sections 2m wide. Other ditches at all sites were sampled to varying degrees, but in general a minimum of 20% of prehistoric and Roman features and 10% of post-medieval features were excavated, generally including the terminals. The large Roman quarry pits at Ridgeway Hill were sampled to varying degrees, but in each case at least one section was cut across the whole feature and either a quarter or half of the rest of the feature was excavated. The post-medieval quarry at Southdown Ridge was investigated in a single machine trench.

The generic environmental sampling strategy included the routine sampling of undisturbed, securely dated deposits for charred plant macrofossils, molluscs, animal and human bone. A strategy developed in consultation with OA's environmental manager involved the examination of contexts associated with the round barrow, the quarry pits, burials, and linear features, undertaken in line with current English Heritage Guidelines (Environmental Archaeology: A guide to the theory and practice of methods, from sampling and recovery to post-excavation, Centre for Archaeology Guidelines 2002/01).

Soil samples for the recovery of charred plant remains, charcoal and molluscs, generally of 40 litres, were taken from the Neolithic pits at Ridgeway Hill, from selected areas of the burials and, where appropriate, from other features. Incremental samples of 2 litres were taken from the ring ditch fills and from one of the Roman quarry pits at Ridgeway Hill. Monoliths for pollen analysis were taken from a Neolithic pit, but contained too little pollen to merit analysis.

Artefacts were treated in accordance with UKIC guidelines, First Aid for Finds (1998). Finds were sorted by material type, bagged and labelled according to the individual deposit from which they were recovered, ready for later cleaning and analysis. Flints were individually bagged to prevent damage. All registered finds were processed and packaged according to standards of good practice. In accordance with the procedures outlined in MAP2 and current English Heritage guidelines, iron objects and a selection of non-ferrous artefacts, including coins, were submitted for X-radiography and stabilisation where appropriate.

The human remains and articulated animal remains encountered during fieldwork were cleaned with minimal disturbance prior to recording and removal. Investigation and excavation of human remains was undertaken by, or under supervision of, suitably experienced specialist staff and in accordance with IFA Guidelines (Roberts & McKinley 1993; Brickley & McKinley 2004).

Radiocarbon dating was carried out by the Scottish Universities Environmental Research Centre AMS Facility. The dates have been calibrated using OxCal v.4.1 (Bronk Ramsey 2009) using the IntCal09 (Reimer *et al.* 2009) calibration data.

THE ARCHIVE

The project archive is currently stored at the offices of OA South and will be transferred to the Dorset County Museum.

STRUCTURE OF THE VOLUME

The results of the two major excavations, Ridgeway Hill and Southdown Ridge, are each presented in three parts: site narrative, specialist reports and discussion. These form Chapters 2-7. Two minor sites, an excavation at Redlands and valley contour survey at Bincombe, have been combined and presented in full in Chapter 8.

Chapter 2: Neolithic, Early Bronze Age and Later Activity at Ridgeway Hill

by Chris Hayden

INTRODUCTION

The Ridgeway Hill site was a roughly rectangular area centred at NGR SY 672 857. It measured around 630m north-south and up to 110m east-west (although generally around 75m), with an area of *c* 5.1ha. The northern part of the site was under arable cultivation prior to excavation, but the southern-most, steeply sloping, fields were under pasture (Fig. 2.1). The site lies adjacent to the boundary between the parishes of Bincombe and Weymouth.

The most significant features revealed at Ridgeway Hill were a sequence of Neolithic pits and several groups of early Bronze Age burials. The pits include examples that date from the early, middle and late Neolithic and the Beaker period, but others cannot be so precisely dated. The early Bronze Age burials include inhumation and cremation burials in pits and cists, which may originally have been associated with barrows. Although they had all suffered more or less severely from truncation, a large number of radiocarbon dates obtained from them provide significant insights into their chronology.

Smaller numbers of Roman, Anglo-Saxon and post-medieval features were found. The Roman features consist of a row of three, probably late Roman, burials cut across an early Bronze Age

Fig. 2.1 View of the site before excavation, looking south

13

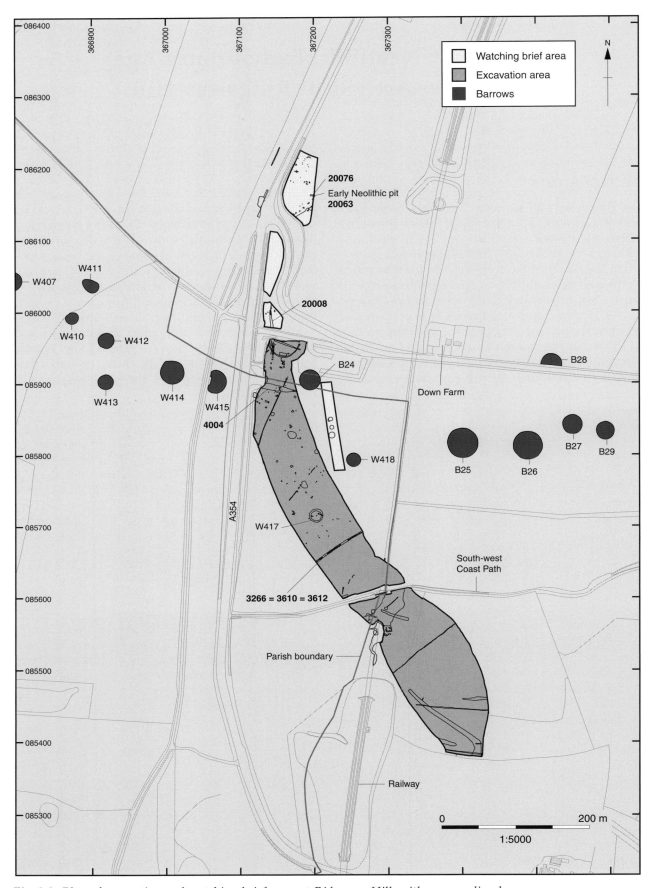

Fig. 2.2 Plan of excavation and watching brief areas at Ridgeway Hill, with surrounding barrows

barrow, ditches which may have formed part of a Roman field system, and a series of probably Roman chalk quarry pits. Two Anglo-Saxon graves contained the remains of three individuals dating from the 7th-8th centuries AD. A Roman chalk quarry pit which lay immediately adjacent to the site, and which contained a mass burial of decapitated Vikings dating from the 10th to 11th century, is described in a separate monograph (Loe *et al.* 2014). No evidence contemporary with the Viking burials was found in the Ridgeway Hill excavation. The post-medieval features were a small building, a drain and sump, and a quarry pit, which may have been related to the construction of the railway tunnel that runs below the site.

R8 Ridgeway Hill barrows

The site crosses the area of the Ridgeway occupied by the R8 Ridgeway Hill group of barrows (RCHM(E) 1970) (Fig. 2.2). A more or less diffuse string of barrows extends along the top of the Ridgeway to the east and west of the site, although there are examples also to the south and, in greater numbers, to the north. Most of these appear to have been bowl barrows, but a probable pond barrow (Weymouth 406) lies to the north-west of the site, and one of the excavated sites was a bell barrow (Bincombe 25).

A number of barrows in the vicinity of the site have been excavated or otherwise investigated, although the published records are of varying quality. One of the excavated barrows (Bincombe 27), which lies just to the east of the site, was reported to lie on an occupation site which included pits, coarse Beaker pottery and tools of Portland chert (Best 1965, 103; RCHM(E) 1970, 511, 456).

The Bincombe barrow (Bincombe 24) lies immediately adjacent to the northern end of the site to the east (Payne 1943, with earlier references). The barrow was excavated after it had been partially destroyed by a farmer removing stones. Its construction comprised a dry stone wall up to 0.9 m tall with a diameter of 7.6m. It is unclear if this wall originally formed a kerb for the barrow or was an internal structure. The primary burials, below the ground surface, were of two adult males, one of them associated with a Beaker bowl. The secondary burials included four inhumations. One of these was a boy with a handled Beaker, but one of the others was associated with what is described as an Iron Age vessel. The published accounts make no mention of an associated ditch.

Slightly further to the east, an excavated bell barrow (Bincombe 25) was again associated with a wall, 0.6 m tall and with a diameter of 9.1m, which

is interpreted as having formed a kerb (Best 1965). The barrow itself consisted of a cairn covered by a turf stack with a chalk capping. The primary burials were of an adult female inhumation associated with a Beaker and a copper alloy awl in a central cist, a satellite burial of a child in a cist and a pit containing a cremation burial. Four secondary cremation burials were found within the mound, one of which was contained within an Enlarged Food Vessel.

Further east still, along the crest of the Ridgeway, the bowl barrow (Bincombe 27) covering the possible occupation site again consisted of a cairn covered by a turf stack and capped with chalk (Best 1965, 103). The primary burials consisted of an inhumation associated with a Beaker in a central cist and a satellite burial consisting of a child in a cist. The secondary burials were of six inhumation burials, one of which was in a cist associated with a Food Vessel at the bottom of a very deep shaft grave. This cist is described as having been constructed using some of the stones associated with the primary cist. Another of the secondary inhumation burials was associated with a wooden 'slat', which is interpreted as having been part of a bow.

To the west of the excavation, again at the northern end of the site along the crest of the Ridgeway, two further barrows have been investigated. Fragments of an Enlarged Food Vessel and very fragmented human remains, including a molar from an individual probably 15 to 25 years old, were recovered from a plough damaged bowl barrow (Bincombe 36) just to the east of the site (Calkin and Putnam 1970). Just to the west of that barrow, a further bowl barrow is reported to have probably contained two inhumation burials (RCHM(E) 1970, 456).

Radiocarbon dates

A total of 22 radiocarbon dates obtained from the Neolithic pits, early Bronze Age burials and one of the Anglo-Saxon burials were calibrated using OxCal v.4.1 (Bronk Ramsey 2009), using the IntCal09 (Reimer *et al.* 2009) calibration data (Table 2.1).

PREHISTORIC FEATURES

The prehistoric features consisted of pits dating from the early, middle and late Neolithic and the late Neolithic/early Bronze Age, and a number of early Bronze Age burials, mostly in groups which may, originally, have been associated with small bowl barrows (Fig. 2.3). Only one grave was, however, associated with a ring ditch.

The Neolithic and Late Neolithic/Early Bronze Age Pits

The Neolithic and late Neolithic/early Bronze Age pits were distributed widely across the northern half of the site, some occurring as isolated features, others in small groups or pairs (Fig. 2.3). The largest group of pits (Set 3) was found scattered in a band around 25m wide, which ran east-west across the middle of the site, to the south of all of the early Bronze Age burials.

The pits were dated by a small number of radio-

Table 2.1 Summary of radiocarbon dates

Lab no.	Set	Feature/ Grave	Fill/ Skeleton	Grave/ feature type	Material	Uncal date BP
Middle Neolithic pits						
SUERC-41527	1	3091	3090	pit	hazel nutshell	4450±30
SUERC-41530	3	3330	3329	pit	hazel nutshell	4355±30
Late Neolithic pit						
SUERC-41528	2	3373	3431	pit	aurochs humerus	4465±30
Late Neolithic/early Bronze Age pit						
SUERC-41529	3	3544	3590	pit	cattle patella	4050±30
Early Bronze Age burials						
Start burials						
Start Set 7						
SUERC-41531	7	3227	3334	LIP1	right human femur	3750±30
SUERC-41532	7	3227	3307	LIP2	right human femur	3525±30
SUERC-41536	7	3227	3228	LIPs	right human femur	3665±30
SUERC-41537	7	3200	3211	SIP	human femur	3580±30
SUERC-41538	7	3223	3231	SIP	human humerus	3475±30
Span Set 7						
End Set 7						
Start Set 9						
SUERC-41549	9	3315	3316	LIP	left human femur	3685±30
SUERC-41550	9	3232	3279	LIC	left human femur	3655±30
End Set 9						
Span Set 9						
Start Set 6						
SUERC-41542	6	3147	3520	LIP1	right human femur	3715±25
SUERC-41546	6	3147	3193	CC/LIP2	cremated human long bone fragments	3585±30
SUERC-41547	6	3147	3192	SIC/LIP3	human femur	3590±30
SUERC-41548	6	3155	3220	CC	cremated human long bone fragments	3430±30
End Set 6						
Span Set 6						
Start Set 4						
SUERC-41540	4	3036	3037	SIP	right human femur	3625±30
SUERC-41539	4	3046	3048	SIC	left human femur	3585±30
SUERC-41541	4	3044	3045	SIP	human long bone	3580±30
SUERC-28559	4	3067	3084	LIP	human bone	3575±30
End Set 4						
Span Set 4						
SUERC-41551	8	3208	3205	SCC	cremated human long bone fragments	3580±30
SUERC-41552	10	3033	3034	SCP	cremated human long bone fragments	3390±30
End burials						
Span Burials						
Anglo-Saxon burial						
SUERC-41556		3615	3616	grave	left human fibula	1305±25

carbon dates, the pottery they contained, and, in the absence of such evidence, on the basis of their spatial associations in groups. Unfortunately, although the only pottery recovered from the pits in the central band (Set 3) is Beaker, radiocarbon dates show that the band contained pits dating from both the middle Neolithic and the late Neolithic/early Bronze Beaker period. Most of the pits in this band did not contain pottery, nor were other chronologically diagnostic artefacts recovered. In the absence of such evidence, although it seems likely that the pits in this band date from either the middle

$\delta^{13}C$ (‰)	$\delta^{15}N$ (‰)	*Unmodelled calibrated dates*		*Modelled dates*	
		68.40%	*95.40%*	*68.40%*	*95.40%*
-25.5	-	3320-3020	3340-2940		
-22.5	-	3010-2910	3010-2910		
-23.2	5.7	3330-3030	3340-3020		
-23.9	5.1	2620-2490	2840-2470		
				2250-2090	2400-2060
				2150-2040	2260-2030
-21.4	10.0	2210-2050	2280-2030	2090-2030	2200-2020
-21.3	9.6	1910-1770	1940-1750	1920-1780	1950-1770
-21.5	9.5	2130-1970	2140-1950	2130-1970	2140-1950
-21.2	9.8	1970-1880	2030-1780	1970-1890	2030-1870
-21.4	9.4	1880-1740	1890-1690	1890-1790	1890-1740
				180-300	150-400
				1850-1720	1880-1640
				2150-2030	2220-1980
-21.4	10.1	2140-2020	2200-1960	2120-1980	2140-1970
-21.5	9.8	2130-1970	2140-1940	2120-1970	2130-1950
				2110-1920	2130-1770
				0-150	0-370
				2140-2040	2240-1990
-21.2	9.7	2190-2030	2200-2030	2090-2030	2150-1970
-23.9	-	1980-1890	2030-1880	2020-1920	2030-1900
-21.2	10.3	2010-1890	2030-1880	1950-1880	2010-1820
-25.1	-	1770-1680	1880-1630	1880-1730	1890-1690
				1870-1690	1880-1630
				220-410	170-550
				2020-1920	2090-1900
-21.9	10.4	2030-1940	2120-1890	1980-1910	2020-1890
-21.3	10.4	1980-1890	2030-1870	1970-1900	2020-1880
-21.5	10.0	1970-1880	2030-1780	1970-1900	2020-1880
	-	1960-1880	2030-1780	1960-1900	2020-1880
				1950-1870	2010-1790
				0-100	*0-240*
-25.5	-	1970-1880	2030-1780	1970-1880	2030-1780
-21.6	-	1740-1630	1760-1600	1750-1660	1870-1620
				1730-1590	1830-1450
				420-650	290-860
-20.2	9.9	cal AD 660-770	cal AD 650-780		

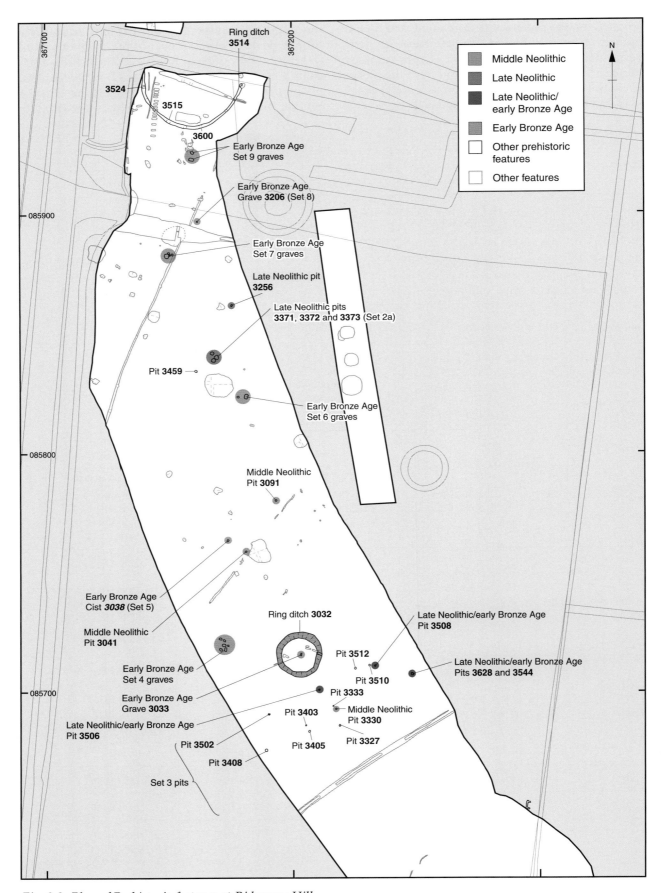

Fig. 2.3 Plan of Prehistoric features at Ridgeway Hill

Neolithic or the late Neolithic/early Bronze Age, the date of most of them remains uncertain.

One further complication affecting the dating of the pits is raised by a middle Neolithic radiocarbon date obtained for one of the pits (3373) assigned to the late Neolithic. The pit contained pottery in a shelly fabric which only occurs elsewhere on the site in pits (including pits in the same spatial group: Set 2a) in which the pottery was clearly identifiable as Grooved Ware. The radiocarbon date of 3340-3020 cal BC (95.4% confidence) and probably 3330-3030 (68.2% confidence; SUERC-41528: 4465±30) is not, however, consistent with the chronology of Grooved Ware elsewhere (Garwood 1999). The radiocarbon date was obtained from a large aurochs humerus weighing 655 g. Whilst this was the only aurochs bone from the pit, it was associated with a quite large group of cattle bone. It was originally thought

that the large size of the bone and the association with the cattle bone indicated that the bone formed part of a deliberate deposit, and was unlikely to have been residual. Clearly, however, either the aurochs bone must be regarded as residual or the pottery as intrusive. It is suggested below that it is most likely that the aurochs bone was residual, or became deposited in a context that was significantly more recent than the bone itself for whatever other reason, and that the pottery and spatial association of the pit are more reliable indicators of the date of the pit. Some uncertainty must, however, remain.

The early Neolithic pits

The only early Neolithic feature was a large oval pit (20063) found in the watching brief area at the northern end of the site, on the northern

Table 2.2 Summary of dimensions and form of Neolithic and late Neolithic/early Bronze Age pits

Pit	Max width (m)	Depth (m)	Plan	Sides	Base
Early Neolithic					
20063	2.10	0.88	subrect/oval	vertical/irregular	flat/irregular
Middle Neolithic					
3041	0.60	0.12	circular	steep	flat
3091	0.68	0.15	circular	steep	irregular - 8 'stakeholes' in base
3330	0.66	0.42	circular	irregular, asymmetric	V-shaped
Late Neolithic					
3256	1.86	0.16	oval	asymmetric sloping	concave
3371	1.60	0.94	circular	near vertical	flattish
3373	1.50	0.75	circular	near vertical	flattish
3372	1.70	0.45	subtriangular/circular	asymmetric steep/vertical	flattish
Late Neolithic/early Bronze Age					
3508	0.55	0.22	oval	shallow curved	irregular concave
3544	1.22	0.36	circular	steep curved	flat
3628	0.84	0.29	oval? (cut away by 3544)	steep curved	flat
3506	0.64	0.35	irregular oval	V-shaped profile	pointed
Undated					
3459	0.95	0.15	circular	bowl-shaped	
3403	0.58	0.46	almond-shaped	Y-shaped profile	flat base cut by a 'posthole' 0.30 x 0.18 m wide by 0.16 m deep
3405	0.74	0.30	circular	Y-shaped profile	irregular; cut by three 'postholes' (diams 0.11, 0.09 & 0.16 m)
3333	0.48	0.14	irregular, almond-shaped	irregular bowl-shaped	
3510	0.69	0.24	circular	bowl-shaped	
3408	1.25	0.24	oval	bowl-shaped	flat
3327	0.90	0.17	ogival	bowl-shaped	-
3512	0.76	0.35	oval	steep	concave
3502	0.96	0.20	subsquare/circular	shallow curved	irregular, cut by 4 'postholes' (3462: 0.25 m deep; 3464: 0.48 m wide x 0.30 m deep; 3472: 0.35 m wide x 0.30 m deep; 3474: 0.28 m wide x 0.24 m deep;

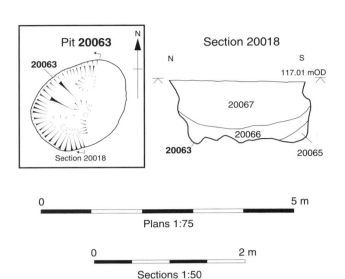

Plans 1:75

0 — 5 m

0 — 2 m

Sections 1:50

Early Neolithic pit 20036

Fig. 2.4 Early Neolithic pit 20063

facing slope of the Ridgeway (Figs 2.2 and. 2.4). It has been dated to the early Neolithic on the basis of the large quantity of Plain Bowl pottery it contained.

The dimensions of the pit – 2.1m by 1.6m across and 0.9m deep – are large compared to many other early Neolithic pits, although not outside the range of the largest such pits elsewhere (Table 2.2). Although the pit had broadly vertical sides and a flat base, both aspects were very irregular. Despite its irregularity, its form and the pattern of fills does not suggest that it was a tree-throw hole (cf. Moore and Jennings 1992).

Three fills were distinguished, although the first section cut through the pit was recorded as just one context (20064). The primary fill (20065) consisted of a sterile chalky layer, probably derived from the collapse of the sides of the pit. The two upper fills consisted of dark and mid brown clayey silt (20066 and 20067).

Large assemblages of Plain Bowl pottery (102 sherds / 560g) and worked flint (447 pieces) were recovered from the two upper fills of the pit (Table 2.3). Although the flint was mostly flakes, chips and irregular waste, it included a large number of other types (see below). Samples taken for charred plant

Table 2.3 Summary of finds from Neolithic and late Neolithic/early Bronze Age pits

Pit	Fills	Pot (no. sherds/weight g)	Flint (no.)	Animal bone (no. frags/weight g)
Early Neolithic				
20063	20064: (equivalent to 20067 and 20066)	97/502*	160	
	20067: mid brown silty clay			
	20066: dark brown clay silt		149	
	20065: grey white chalk		138	
Middle Neolithic				
3041	3043: mid orange brown silty clay	2/9	54	61/8
	3042: limestone slabs around edge of pit			
3091	3090: dark brown clay silt	12/45	40	
3330	3328: mid dark brown silty loam	5/6	65	
	3329: mid brown silty loam	1/1	41	
Late Neolithic				
3256	3254: mid brown silt	16/20	6	
	3255: light greyish brown silt	11/17	1	
Set 2a				
3371	3419: mid brown silty clay		25	
	3418: white chalk rubble			

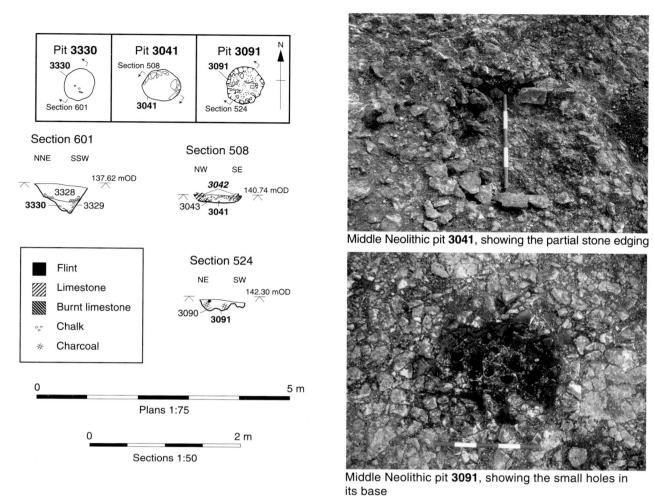

Flint

Limestone

Burnt limestone

Chalk

Charcoal

Middle Neolithic pit **3041**, showing the partial stone edging

Middle Neolithic pit **3091**, showing the small holes in its base

Fig. 2.5 *Middle Neolithic pits*

Animal bone details	Shell (no. frags/weight g)	Charred plant remains	Charcoal (> 2 mm)	Other
		HNS +	+	
pig tooth 12/3; indet 49/5	1/1		+++	
		HNS +++	+++++	Fe fragment
		HNS +++	++	
		HNS +	+++	
		HNS +++	++	
		HNS +++	++	
		grain + Vicia/pisum +		

Table 2.3 (continued)

Pit	Fills	Pot (no. sherds/weight g)	Flint (no.)	Animal bone (no. frags/weight g)
	3417: dark brown silty clay		4	7/0
	3416: white chalk rubble			
	3415: mid brown silty loam with chalk rubble		2	
	3414: red brown silt			2/0
3372	3442: dark brown silty clay	6/8	34	3/11
	3443: white grey silty loam with chalk rubble	4/5	8	16/91
	3444: mid grey brown silty loam		6	41/29
	3445: white chalk rubble			16/22
3373	3433: dark red brown silty loam		17	5/296
	3432: light grey brown silty loam	1/1		
	3431: white chalk rubble	9/7	7	8/687
	3430: red brown silty loam		29	13/4

Late Neolithic/early Bronze Age

Pit	Fills	Pot (no. sherds/weight g)	Flint (no.)	Animal bone (no. frags/weight g)
3506	3505: mid dark brown clayey silt	21/26	5	
3508	3507: mid dark brown clayey silt	51/99	32	
3544	3543: mid dark brown clayey silt	3/5	80	291/307
	3590: mid dark brown clayey silt		27	781/919
3628	3614: light mid orange brown clayey silt and gravel		55	249/285

Undated

Pit	Fills	Pot (no. sherds/weight g)	Flint (no.)	Animal bone (no. frags/weight g)
3459	3460: dark brown silt		25	
3403	3332: dark brown clayey silt		1	
3405	3404: mid dark brown clayey silt		3	
3333	3331: mid dark brown silt		22	
3510	3509: mid dark brown clayey silt		1	
3408	3406: mid dark brown clayey silt		5	1/28
	3407 (bone at base of pit)			25/34
3327	3326: mid dark brown silty loam		6	
3512	3511: mid dark brown clayey silt		7	
	3523: dark brown clay silt with charcoal lenses			
3502	3461: dark brown clayey silt		36	
	3463: dark brown clayey silt		25	
	3471: dark brown clayey silt		10	
	3473: mid dark brown clayey silt	7/2	15	

* combined figures for all contexts in pit

remains contained only a single hazelnut shell and very small quantities of charcoal from context 20067. Waterlogged plant remains recovered from the uppermost fill (20065) included clearly modern seeds and do not suggest that any waterlogged Neolithic material was preserved. Samples taken for pollen analysis contained very little pollen.

The middle Neolithic pits

Three pits (3330, 3041 and 3091) were assigned to the middle Neolithic on the basis of radiocarbon dates and the presence of Peterborough Ware sherds (Fig. 2.5). The pits were filled with deposits of brown silty clay of varying hues, all containing charcoal flecks.

Pit 3330 lay within the band of pits near the centre of the site (Set 3). A radiocarbon date of 3090-2900 cal BC (95.4%; 3010-2910 cal BC at 69.2%; SUERC-41530: 4355±30) was obtained from hazelnut shells (part of a large group recovered from the pit) from the lowermost fill (3329). The other two pits (3041 and 3091) lay around 60m and 70m to the north, c 25m apart. A radiocarbon date again on hazelnut shell forming part of a larger group from the single fill (3090) of one of these pits (3091), gave a slightly earlier date of 3340-2940 cal BC (95.4%; 3320-3020 cal BC at 68.2%; SUERC-41527: 4450±30). These two dates fail a χ^2 test (T=5.01 (5% = 3.8); 1 df)

Animal bone details	Shell (no. frags/weight g)	Charred plant remains	Charcoal (> 2 mm)	Other
amphib and small mam		grain + HNS ++	++	glass fragment
				glass fragment
small mam		grain +	+	
indet.	1/1			
cattle tooth; large mam rib; indet.			flecks	
indet; large mam long bone; small mam	3/4			
deer tooth; indet.				chalk 1 crem bone 1/1
cattle pelvis; indet.		grain + HNS +		
		grain + HNS +		human bone 12/4?
aurochs humerus; cattle humerus & mandible; indet.	1/4		flecks	
cattle tooth; deer metacarpal; indet; small mam			++	human bone: 25/3? worked bone
		HNS ++	+	
		HNS +++	++	
see Table 3.35	43/42		flecks	
see Table 3.35	48/69		flecks	
see Table 3.35	33/37			
	5/51	HNS ++	++	
		HNS +++	++++	
		HNS ++	+	
		HNS ++	+	
	1/1		+	
cattle tooth			flecks	
		Grain +	++++	
		HNS +	flecks	
			+	
			flecks	
			flecks	CBM 1/1
			flecks	
			flecks	

indicating that they were significantly different in date, and thus that the pits represent at least two distinct episodes of middle Neolithic activity.

The two northern pits (3041 and 3091) were both small features (Table 2.2), measuring 0.6-0.7m wide by *c* 0.15m deep; the southern pit (3330) was of similar width (0.6m) but was slightly deeper (0.4m). All of the pits were circular in plan, but they varied in profile (Fig. 2.5). The southern pit (3330) had an irregular, V-shaped profile. The two northern pits had steep sides but, whilst pit 3041 had a flat base, pit 3091 had an irregular base which was cut by eight small holes of varying sizes distributed with no obvious order. Comparable but slightly larger features were found in the bases of three of the undated pits, but otherwise such features were absent from the other pits on the site. The origin of these small holes is uncertain. Whilst it is possible that they were deliberately cut features, perhaps cut to hold posts which might have been related to a light superstructure (cf. Butler 1936), it seems more likely that they were natural root holes, solution holes or animal burrows. One of the northern pits (3041) was distinguished by the presence of limestone slabs (3042) set around the edges of the northern and south-eastern sides. They measured up to 0.2m by 0.15m by 0.1m and showed no clear signs of having been shaped.

To some extent the contrasts between the finds recovered from these pits correspond to those found amongst the larger groups of later pits (Table 2.3). As in the later pits, the clearest contrast is in the food remains. Pits 3091 and 3330 both contained quite large groups of charred hazelnut shells but no animal bone, whilst pit 3043 contained no charred plant remains but did contain a small quantity of animal bone, amongst which the only identifiable fragment was a pig tooth. Pit 3043 also contained a fragment of mussel shell.

Unlike the later pits, however, in which pottery tended to be associated with plant remains, and flint with animal bone, there is little indication of associations between the plant and animal remains and other categories of finds. Pottery was recovered from all of the pits. The quantities were generally small, however, and whilst the largest assemblage of pottery, from pit 3091, was associated with a large group of hazelnut shells, the large group of hazelnut shells in pit 3330 was associated with only a small group of pottery. Furthermore, this pit contained the largest assemblage of flint, rather than pit 3041, which contained the only animal bone. Flint was also recovered from all of the pits. These assemblages were all dominated by flakes, but chisel and oblique arrowheads were recovered from both pits 3041 and 3330, serrated flakes from the same pits, cores and a microdenticulate from pit 3330 and scale flaked knife from pit 3091. All of the pits also contained charcoal but this occurred in much greater quantities in pit 3091 than in the others. Pit 3043 contained a quite large quantity of burnt stone. A small fragment of iron recovered from pit 3091 clearly indicates that the pit has suffered from some disturbance, although there is no indication that this had significantly affected the feature.

The late Neolithic pits

Four pits were assigned to the late Neolithic on the basis of the presence of Grooved Ware in three of them (Fig. 2.6). The lack of consistency between the chronology suggested by the pottery in pit 3373 and a radiocarbon date on an aurochs humerus from the same pit has been discussed above. Three of the pits formed a group (Set 2a) which lay around 125m from the northern end of the excavation. The fourth pit (3256) lay around 20m to the north of this pit group. Grooved Ware was recovered from two of the pits (3372 and 3373) in the group and from the isolated pit (3256).

The isolated pit (3256) was a quite shallow, wide, oval feature, 1.86m wide by 0.16m deep (Table 2.2). The three pits forming the group were of similar widths (1.5m to 1.7m), but varied in depth (from 0.5m to 1.0m), although all were deeper than the isolated pit. The pits in the group all had steep sides and flat bases, and were approximately circular in plan. Like the early Neolithic pit, these late Neolithic pits are large, and, in particular, deep compared to many pits of this period.

The deeper pits belonging to the pit group contained sequences of up to six distinct fills. There were clear contrasts in these fills. Most consisted of brown silty clay or loam deposits, the shade of which varied from dark red brown to light grey brown, reflecting in part the proportion of chalk they contained. These brown deposits, however, contrasted more or less clearly with white deposits consisting primarily of chalk rubble. Pit 3371 contained four layers of fill consisting of brown silty loam or clay layers alternating with chalk rubble. The chalk layers were sterile, all of the small number of finds having been recovered from the brown layers. In this case it could be argued that the chalk was deposited in the pits to cover the deposits containing artefacts. This pattern was not apparent, however, in the other pits. In pit 3373 the second layer of fill (3431) consisted predominantly of chalk rubble but also contained a quite large quantity of animal bone as well as small quantities of pottery, flint and shell.

Although the late Neolithic pits were larger than the middle Neolithic pits, they generally contained smaller quantities of finds. To some extent, however, the patterning amongst the finds is similar. The clearest distinction amongst the finds assemblages is between pits which contained animal bone and those which contained charred hazelnut shells, and occasionally also grain and, in one case, charred pea or bean (Table 2.3). There was only one case where animal bone and charred plant remains occured together in the same context (3433), the uppermost fill of pit 3373, which also contained a large assemblage of animal bone, but only a very small number of hazelnut shells and very little charred grain. This is not only the only context where charred plant remains and animal bone occurred, it is also the only pit where the two categories were represented. In the other pits, the patterns of deposition of animal bone and charred plant remains were consistent throughout the sequence of deposits. Thus, pit 3256 contained hazelnut shells in both its layers of fill and pit 3372 contained animal bone in all four of its fills. Pit 3371 contained very few finds in any of its fills, although a small quantity of charred hazelnut shells were recovered from a middle fill.

Much of the animal bone could not be identified, but included cattle and deer teeth in pit 3372, and a cattle pelvis, humerus and mandible, a deer metacarpal and the aurochs humerus (from which the middle Neolithic date was obtained) in pit 3373 (see below). A range of rodent and amphibian bones

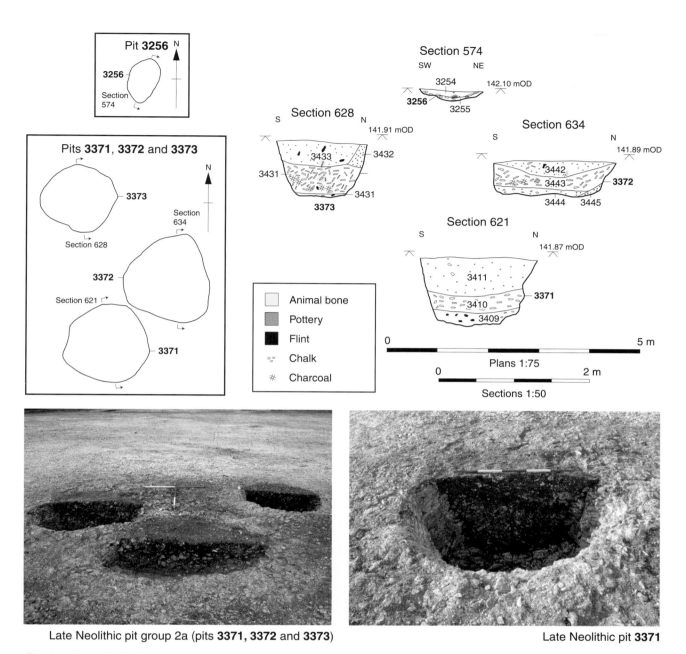

Late Neolithic pit group 2a (pits **3371**, **3372** and **3373**)

Late Neolithic pit **3371**

Fig. 2.6 Late Neolithic pits

was recovered from all of the pits in the pit group, and may derive from disturbance or be chance inclusions in the pits. The entire small group of animal bone recovered from pit 3371 consisted of rodent or amphibian bones. Two small fragments of glass were recovered from this pit, providing evidence that it had suffered from limited disturbance. Two of the pits that produced animal bone also contained small numbers of marine shells: a limpet in pit 3373, and a cockle and a mussel in pit 3372 (Table 2.3).

Unlike the middle Neolithic pits, there were some more or less clear relationships between the plant and animal remains and other categories of finds.

The closest associations were between pottery and plant remains on the one hand, and between flint and animal bone on the other. Although these associations are far from perfect, the two largest groups of hazelnut shells, in pit 3256, were both associated with the largest assemblages of pottery. Similarly, the largest groups of animal bone, in pits 3373 and 3372, occurred with quite large groups of flint, although there were also large groups of flint which were not associated with any animal bone. The flint consisted largely of flakes, but pit 3373 also contained a few blades and a bladelet, and a chisel arrowhead, a microdenticulate, a crested blade and a few blade-like flakes were recovered from pit 3372.

The late Neolithic/early Bronze Age pits

Four pits, all forming part of the band of pits (Set 3) scattered across the centre of the site, were dated to the late Neolithic/early Bronze Age (Fig. 2.7). Three of them (3506, 3508 and 3544) contained Beaker pottery. A radiocarbon date of 2840-2470 cal BC (95.4%; 2620-2490 cal BC at 68.2%; SUERC-41529: 4050±30) was obtained from a cattle patella from the lowest fill (3590) of one of these pits (3544). The bone formed part of a large assemblage, which is discussed in more detail below. This date is very early for Beaker pottery (Needham 2005), and it is perhaps worth noting that just a single sherd of Beaker pottery weighing 3g was recovered from this pit, and that this sherd came from the uppermost fill (3543), above the layer that contained the cattle bone. Furthermore, pit 3544 cut the fourth pit (3628), which also contained animal bone, and it is possible that some of the bone, including the dated piece, recovered from pit 3544, was originally deposited in the earlier pit. Whilst there is thus some uncertainty about the association of this date with the pottery, and perhaps with the pit, the date should nonetheless provide a good estimate for the large deposit of animal bone. Clearly, although this single date cannot give any indication of the length of the period over which the Beaker pits in this area were in use, it does suggest that at least some of the activity related to the pits preceded the earliest burials on the site.

Pit 3508 might have formed a pair with pit 3510, but given that the other late Neolithic/early Bronze Age pits do not appear to have belonged to similar pairs or groups, it is difficult to have confidence that 3508 and 3510 were contemporaneous on this basis alone.

The pits were all quite small, measuring between around 0.5m and 1.2m wide and from around 0.2 to 0.4m deep (Table 2.2). Although their exact outlines were often rather irregular, most were roughly circular in plan. Pits 3508, 3544 and 3628 had more or less irregular profiles, with rounded sides and more or less flat bases. Pit 3506, in contrast, had a more V-shaped profile. All of the pits contained only single fills, except for pit 3544, in which two fills were distinguished. The fills consisted of more or less dark brown silty loam or clayey silt deposits, almost all of which were flecked with charcoal. The only exception was the fill of pit 3628, which consisted of a lighter, more orangey clayey silt.

The broad contrast seen in the Neolithic pits between those containing charred plant remains and those containing animal bone was again the most marked contrast in the finds from the late Neolithic/early Bronze Age pits. The two pits near the eastern edge of the excavation (3544 and 3628) contained large assemblages of animal bone and, as discussed above, it is possible that at least some of the bone in the later pit (3544) derived from the earlier pit. These two pits also contained quite large groups of marine shells, consisting of limpets,

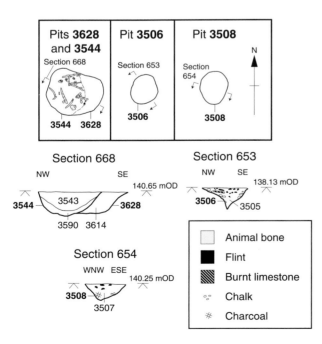

Late Neolithic/early Bronze Age pit **3544**, showing the deposit of animal bone and marine shell

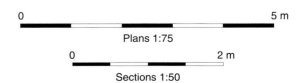

Fig. 2.7 Late Neolithic/early Bronze Age pits

periwinkles and single examples of scallop, mussel, oyster and possibly razorshell.

The animal bone in these pits consisted primarily of cattle and pig bone, although sheep/goat was also represented, as well as a fragment of antler and some possibly intrusive small mammal bones. Differing parts of the cattle and pig skeletons were represented (see below). The cattle bone consisted predominantly of skull, mandible and teeth and probably also vertebrae and ribs, which can, however, only be identified as large mammal bones. Cattle long bones were represented only by one small ulna fragment, and there were only small quantities of cattle bone representing the phalanges, patella and sacrum. The pig bones, in contrast, consisted predominantly of long bone fragments from the forelimbs (humerus, radius, and ulna) and from the feet, although skull fragments and teeth were also represented, and ribs may have been. Sheep/goat was represented primarily by fragments from the hind limbs (femur and tibia). The other two pits both contained assemblages of hazelnut shells and a little charcoal.

Associations between animal bone and flint, and between charred plant remains and pottery, similar to those seen in the late Neolithic pits, were again apparent in the late Neolithic/early Bronze Age pits. The two pits that contained the only large groups of animal bone (3544 and 3628) were associated with some of the largest groups of flint and contained little pottery. The only large groups of pottery, in contrast, were recovered from the other two pits (3508 and 3506), which contained sizeable groups of hazelnut shells.

The flint assemblages from all of the pits were dominated by flakes. Not surprisingly, however, given the very different sizes of the assemblages, the flint from the pits associated with animal bone was much more diverse than that from the pits associated with plant remains. Although pit 3508 contained a scraper and a core, the remaining flint from this pit and from pit 3506, both of which were associated with plant remains, consisted of flakes, chips and irregular waste. Pit 3544, in contrast, which contained the largest group of animal bone, contained blades and bladelets, fabricators, serrated flakes, a scale flaked knife, a microdenticulate, a scraper, a piercer and cores. The smaller assemblage from pit 3628 also included blades, a bladelet and a serrated flake.

Undated, probably Neolithic or early Bronze Age pits

A total of nine pits probably date from the Neolithic or early Bronze Age, but cannot be more precisely dated. Of these, eight lay in the band of pits that ran across the centre of the site (Set 3). The remaining

example (3459) lay near the group of late Neolithic pits (Set 2a). Although the date of all of these pits is uncertain, a number of arguments can be used to narrow the range of plausible dates. It seems likely, for example, on the basis of its location around 7m from the group of late Neolithic pits (Set 2a), that pit 3459 dated from the late Neolithic. Similarly, on the basis of the dated examples, it seems likely that the pits distributed in the central band (Set 3) date from either the middle Neolithic or the late Neolithic/ early Bronze Age. Within the band some of the pits appeared to form pairs, and it seems likely that these pairs were of similar date. The undated pit (3333) lay just over 1m from pit 3330 which is dated to the middle Neolithic. Similarly undated pit 3510 lay just over 1.5m from pit 3508, dated to the late Neolithic/early Bronze Age on the basis of the Beaker pottery it contained. Unfortunately, the remaining pits either formed pairs in which both pits are undated (3403 and 3405 which lay just over 2m apart) or were isolated features which lay at distances of between 5m to 20m from the other pits.

The dimensions of these undated pits were similar to those of most of the dated examples. They were all smaller than the early and late Neolithic pits, all but one of them having widths less than 1m and depths less than 0.5m. Although some were quite irregular in plan, they were all approximately circular or oval. Most also had simple, shallow bowl-shaped profiles. A few, however, had more distinctive forms. The two undated pits forming a pair (3403 and 3405) had Y-shaped profiles. The base of one of these pits (3403) was cut by a small, 'posthole' 0.30 m across and 0.16 m deep. The base of the second (3405) was irregular and was cut by three similar 'postholes' with diameters of between 0.09m and 0.16m (Fig. 2.8). One of the isolated pits (3502) was bowl-shaped in profile, but its base was cut by three 'postholes' between 0.28m and 0.48m wide and up to 0.30m deep. As has been argued above, with reference to similar features in the base of middle Neolithic pit 3091, the interpretation of these 'postholes' is uncertain, and whilst the possibility that they were anthropogenic cannot be excluded, it seems most likely that they were natural in origin.

All but one of the pits contained only single fills. The exception was pit 3512, which contained two fills. The fills, like those of the more certainly dated pits, consisted of more or less dark brown silty loam or clayey silt deposits, almost all of which were flecked with charcoal. The two layers in pit 3512 were distinguished only by a slight difference in colour.

The finds from the undated pits are consistent with the broad distinction between assemblages containing animal bone and those that contained charred plant remains noted in the better dated pits.

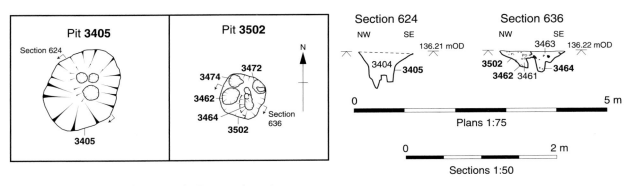

Fig. 2.8 Undated Neolithic or early Bronze Age pits

Table 2.4 Summary of late Neolithic/early Bronze Age burials

(SIP = small inhumation pit; LIP = large inhumation pit; CC = cremation cist; SIC = small inhumation cist; LIC = large inhumation cist; SCC = small cremation cist; SCP = small cremation pit)

Probable order by date	Strati-graphic position	Grave	Grave type	Skeleton no.	Age category	Age range	Sex	Completeness %
Set 7								
5		3223	SIP	3231	Older child	7.5-8.5 yrs	/	<25
4	2	3227	LIP	3307	Older child	11.25-13	/	26-50
3		3200	SIP	3211	Adolescent	11-18 yrs	/	<25
2	3	3227	LIP	3228	Adult		/	stray bones
1	1	3227	LIP	3334	Mature adult	36-45 yrs	M	51-75
not dated		3225	SIP	3264	Young child	1.25-2.75 yrs	/	<25
not dated	1	3227	LIP	3335	Adult		/	stray bones (probably part of 3334)
Set 6								
4		3155	CC	3220	Adult			crem - 918.5g
3	3	3147 (3149)	CC (LIP)	3192	Young child	4.5-5.5 yrs	/	<25
2	2	3147 (3210)	CC (LIP)	3193	Older child or adolescent	7.5 to 13 yrs		crem - 253.2g
1	1	3147	LIP	3520	Young adult	20-25 yrs	?M	>76
Set 4								
4		3067	LIP	3084	Young adult	18-25 yrs	?	26-50
3		3044	SIP	3045	Adolescent	10.75-14.5yrs	/	<25
2		3046	SIC	3048	Prime adult	26-35 yrs	?M	51-75
1		3036	SIP	3037	Adult	>18yrs	?	<25
not dated		3087	SIP	3088	Adolescent	9.5-15 yrs	/	<25
Set 9								
2		3232	LIC	3279	Older child	10.5-12.5 yrs	/	51-75
1		3315	LIP	3316	Mature adult	35-39 yrs	?F	>76
Set 8								
not dated	2?	3206	SCC	3205	Young child	1-2 yrs	/	teeth only
	1	3206	SCC	3205	Adult			crem - 1297.5g
Set 10								
not dated	2?	3033	SCP	3035	Infant	1-5 mths	/	teeth only
	1	3033	SCP	3034	Adult (older)		?M	crem - 1462.5g

28

Only one of these pits (3408), however, contained animal bone, and of that the only identifiable piece was a cattle tooth. Hazelnut shells were recovered from four of the other pits (3403, 3405, 3333 and 3512), but only 3403 produced large numbers. Pit 3327 contained a small quantity of charred grain. Charcoal was generally associated with the assemblages of charred plant remains. Pit 3459, which contained hazelnut shells, also contained a small group of marine shells: three fragments of scallop shell, one of oyster and one of mussel. The only other fragment of marine shell recovered was a fragment possibly of limpet shell from pit 3510

Not surprisingly, given that none of these pits contained pottery, there is little indication of the further, albeit weaker associations noted in some of the other pits between flint and animal bone, and pottery and charred plant remains. The largest group of flint was recovered from pit 3333, which also contained hazelnut shells. Pit 3408, which produced the only animal bone, contained only a modest assemblage of flint. Overall, the flint assemblage was again dominated by flakes, but scrapers were recovered from pits 3459 and 3502, cores from pits 3327 and 3502, and blades and bladelets from pits 3459, 3327, 3408, 3502 and 3333. Pit 3502 also yielded an awl and pit 3333 a microdenticulate. The lack of any further clear associations is underlined by the fact that a pebble used as a rubber was found in pit 3408, where it was associated with a small group of animal bone rather than charred plant remains.

The early Bronze Age burials

Introduction

A total of 16 early Bronze Age graves – either simple pits or stone cists set in pits – containing the remains of 21 individuals were found at Ridgeway Hill (Table 2.4). Only one of these graves, a badly truncated cremation burial (Set 10), containing also some uncremated bones from a child, at the centre of ring ditch 3032, was directly associated with a ring ditch. The remaining burials mostly formed small groups (Sets 4, 6, 7 and 9; Figs 2.9-2.13) consisting of between 2 and 5 graves, which were distributed across the northern half of the site to the north of the late Neolithic/early Bronze Age pits forming Set 3 (see above, Fig. 2.3). However, two isolated burials (Sets 5 and 8) were also exposed (Figs 2.14-2.15). Although none of these other burials was associated with a ring ditch there is some evidence to suggest that they may originally have been associated with small bowl barrows, which have been completely levelled, presumably by ploughing and the ensuing erosion.

Some very fragmented remains of a child were also recovered from a natural fissure (3325) in the chalk which lay near the Set 9 burials. The fissure also contained an iron nail and pieces of worked flint, and it seems likely that the finds are intrusive. Rather than being a deliberate burial, the remains of the child, which consisted only of fragments of the cranial vault and four teeth, may have derived from disturbance of another grave nearby. The fragmentary remains derive from a child of 7-8 years. They probably did not derive from the nearby cist grave 3232, which contained the remains (3279) of a slightly older child (10.5 to 12.5 years old). The fragmentary remains in the fissure therefore suggest the existence of another grave, which has been completely destroyed. It is worth noting that both upper and lower molars were present, suggesting that the fragments had not been moved very far from their original position. It is quite possible that all archaeological trace of further graves elsewhere had also been removed by truncation, including any secondary burials which may have been contained within the putative barrows. The fragmentary remains found in the fissure are included in the osteological report below, but have not been included in the analysis of the burials presented in this section of the report.

The preservation of the burials was very varied, but many consisted of very shallow graves in which only very fragmentary remains had survived. Radiocarbon dates were, however, obtained from all of the burials (Table 2.1) that appeared to be well enough preserved to provide a viable sample. Although five burials remain undated, the dates nonetheless provide a clear picture of the chronology and order of the burials. The dates show that the burials associated with the ring ditch (Set 10) were probably later than the other burials.

The truncation of the graves may have had a significant effect on our understanding of the burials. Not only may some graves have been removed entirely but, as will become apparent below, the deepest graves, described below as large inhumation pits, appear to be characterised by a number of other attributes, including sequences of burials and graves goods. It is clear, however, that in the case of the shallower graves any such features would probably have been destroyed by truncation.

Radiocarbon dates

A total of 17 radiocarbon dates were obtained for the late Neolithic/early Bronze Age burials, each date representing a different individual (Table 2.1; Fig. 2.16). The aim was to provide as comprehensive a set of dates for the burials as was possible in order to answer a series of questions:

- when did burial begin and end?
- when did burial in each set begin and end and for how long was each set in use?
- were different sets in use at the same time or did they form a sequence?
- what was the chronological relationship between the burials within each set, including burials deposited in stratigraphic sequences, and in what order were they deposited?
- were there any chronological differences between the different types of graves or burials (inhumation vs cremation) – and, in particular, were the large inhumation pits chronologically primary burials?

To answer these questions, the dates have been incorporated into a Bayesian model using OxCal (v.4.1; Bronk Ramsey 2009). The structure of the model is shown in Fig. 2.16. The dates have been included within a single phase, from which the start and end dates of burial overall were obtained. Within this phase, each set of burials has also been repre-

sented as a phase, excluding the sets which contain only one burial. Within these phases, the stratigraphic sequences of burials in Sets 6 and 7 (graves 3147 and 3227 respectively) have been represented as sequences, within which the order of the burials can be used to constrain the modelled date ranges. As is discussed in more detail below, in the case of grave 3227 in Set 7, the stratigraphic order of the burials is incompatible with the dates obtained for the bones (reflected in low agreement indices). It is clear from the dates that the poor agreement between the modelled and original dates is caused by the fact that the stratigraphically latest sample was obtained from a small group of bones (3228) which was, in fact, probably close in date to the earliest burial in the sequence (3334) and earlier than the burial (3307) which lay stratigraphically between the two. This sample has, therefore, been excluded from the model (ie has not been used to calculate the modelled dates), although the date is still shown in relevant figures.

The dates were all obtained from skeletal remains and thus are directly associated with the burials. It

Table 2.5 Summary of size and form of late Neolithic/early Bronze Age burials (by grave type)

Set	Feature	Width (m)	Length (m)	Depth (m)	Profile	Plan
Large inhumation pit						
Set 6	3147	1.8	2.4	0.4	steep sides, flat base	irreg oval
Set 7	3227	1.7	1.9	0.6	vertical sides, flat base	oval
Set 9	3315	1.2	2.0	0.4	steep sides, flat base	reniform
Set 4	3067	0.8	1.9	0.3	bowl, uneven base	subrect
Inhumation cist						
Set 9	3232	1.2	1.3	0.5	steep sides, flat base	irreg oval
Set 4	3046	1.1	1.5	0.1	saucer, undulating base	oval
Cremation cist						
Set 5	3038	0.6	1.0	0.3	steep sides, uneven base	subrect/trapez
Set 6	3155	0.8	1.0	0.3	steep sides, flattish base	irreg oval
Set 6	3149 (in 3147)	0.5	0.8	0.3	steep sides, base, dips down to much deeper section	rect/trapez
Small inhumation pit						
Set 7	3223	0.6	0.9	0.1	steep sides, undulating base	irreg subrect
Set 4	3087	0.6	0.7	0.1	saucer, undulating base	irreg oval
Set 4	3044	1.0	1.1	0.1	saucer, undulating base	oval
Set 4	3036	0.8	1.2	0.1	saucer, undulating base	reniform
Set 7	3225	0.4	0.8	0.1	irreg, saucer	reniform
Set 7	3200	0.6	0.9	0.1	irreg, saucer	reniform
Small cremation cist						
Set 8	3206	0.5	0.5	0.1	Steep sides, flat base	circ
Small cremation pit						
Set 10	3033	0.5	1.1	0.1	Saucer	reniform
Pit						
Set 4	3106	1	1.3	0.2	saucer, undulating base	oval

is also assumed that where only single individuals were contained within a grave the burials were deposited soon after the grave was cut and that they thus provide a good date for the grave itself. In the case of multiple burials the same assumption is made for the earliest burials, all of which lay on the bases of the graves concerned.

The types of burials

The burials have been divided into six types (Table 2.4), according to the form (pit vs cist) and size of the grave, and the type of burial: inhumation – all crouched where skeletons were well enough preserved to tell – cremation, or isolated uncremated remains. Further analysis shows that certain types of burials, and most notably the large inhumation pits, were associated more or less clearly with other attributes, such as the presence of grave goods and multiple burials, chalk fills, and that they were almost always the earliest burials in their groups.

The types are:

large inhumation pits
small inhumation pits
large inhumation cists
small inhumation cists
cremation cists
small cremation cists
small cremation pits

The size of the graves

There were clear contrasts in the size of the grave cuts, the clearest of which was amongst the pits containing inhumation burials (Fig. 2.17). These clearly fall into two groups, the largest pits measuring around 1.9 to 2.4m across and from 0.3 to 0.6m deep, whilst the small pits measured only 0.7 to 1.2m across and all were very shallow, measuring less than 0.1m deep (Table 2.5). It is the shallowness of these small pits which provides one reason for

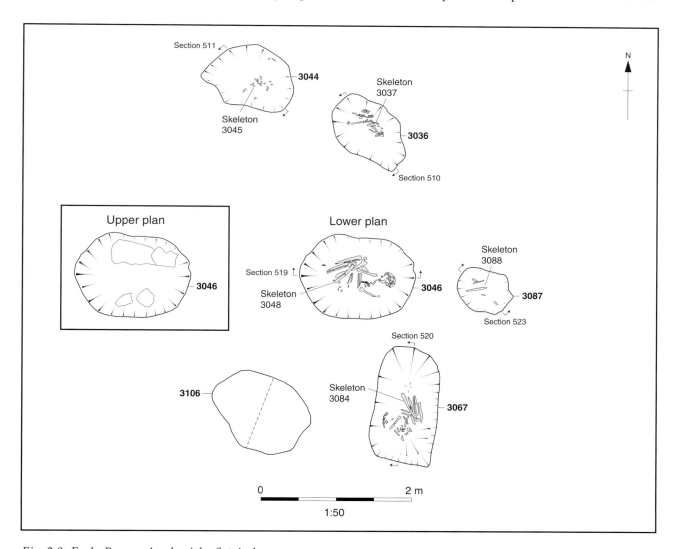

Fig. 2.9 Early Bronze Age burials: Set 4 plan

31

thinking that these burials were originally cut through a barrow and would thus have been covered by a greater depth of soil or chalk. A similar contrast – between large and small features – can perhaps be seen between large and small cists containing inhumation burials, although, since only two such burials were found, it is impossible to be certain that this distinction formed part of a recurrent pattern.

The cists containing cremation burials were mostly of very similar sizes, generally measuring around 0.9m wide and 0.3m deep. The one exception to this was a smaller isolated cist (Set 8), which measured just 0.5m across and 0.1m deep. The central burial (Set 10) associated with the ring ditch stands out from these wider patterns. It was the only cremation burial to be found in a pit rather than a cist, and the pit was of similar size to the small inhumation pits, measuring 1.1m across and 0.1m deep.

The form of the features

All of the large inhumation pits, except for that in Set 4 (grave 3067; Figs 2.9-2.10), had vertical or steep sides and flat bases, and were roughly oval in plan, although grave 3315 in Set 9 (Fig. 2.13) was more elongated in form than the others. The large inhumation pit (3067) in Set 4, in contrast, was bowl shaped in profile and had an uneven base. It was also closer to subrectangular in shape than the other large inhumation pits. No indications were observed in either the form of the pits or their fills to suggest that the large inhumation pits had contained wooden structures.

The small inhumation pits consisted largely of shallow, bowl-shaped features with undulating bases. They were less regular in plan, but most were irregular oval-shaped in plan or tended towards being kidney-shaped. Their irregularity in plan and their bowl-shaped profiles are probably largely a product of truncation. They may originally have had steeper sides and were perhaps more regular in plan at the surface.

Although most of the cists had suffered from some disturbance, their original form was clear. Most of the cists containing cremation burials consisted of roughly rectangular or trapezoidal arrangements of thin limestone slabs, set on end around the edges of pits cut into the chalk (Fig. 2.11). Although in most cases each side of the cist was formed by a single, principal slab, in many cases further slabs had been added, in the case of cist 3155 (Set 6) forming two layers of stones on each side. The bases of the pits were formed of the natural chalk and were slightly irregular. There was little indication that the cists had originally been covered by further stones. A single slab was found lying within cist 3155 (Set 6), which might have formed part of a cover (Fig. 2.11, upper plan). It was too small to have covered all of the cist, but did lie directly over the deposit of cremated remains. It is possible that it was used simply to cover that deposit rather than the cist as a whole. The only other indication that the cists might have been covered was provided by a large number of fragments of limestone which lay within cist 3038 (Set 5), but it is impossible to be certain that they did not derive from the upper parts of stones which had lined the sides of the pit (Fig. 2.14).

The small cist (3206), containing a cremation burial which forms Set 8, may have been constructed in a slightly different way (Fig. 2.15). This feature was preserved to a depth of only 0.1m, so probably only the bottom of the structure survived. The base was formed by a flat slab, from which other slabs sloped upwards slightly towards the sides of the pit.

The two cists associated with inhumations were preserved to differing extents. Cist 3232 (Set 9) was the best preserved and consisted of a roughly oval arrangement of thin limestone slabs set on end on the chalk base of the pit around the edges of the pit (Fig. 2.13). Grave 3046 (Set 4) survived to a depth of only 0.14m, and the cist within it was only poorly preserved (Figs 2.9-2.10). Just four slabs survived, two along the north side of the grave and two along the south, lying next to, and partially above, the skeleton. It seems, likely, however, that these stones were the partial remains of an originally more extensive arrangement of stones which lined the sides of the pit. The original arrangement could, then, have been similar to that in the other cist (3232) associated with an inhumation burial.

Limestone does not occur naturally within the area of the excavation, but does occur just a short distance to the south, where it outcrops today, and appears to erode naturally into slabs which are quite similar to those used to construct the cists. Most of the limestone slabs were quite thin, often no more than 0.03m thick, although they reached lengths of up to 0.6m. The slabs did not show any clear signs of having been worked, although they were presumably either roughly shaped into the appropriate shape and size or were selected from their source because they were of an appropriate shape or size.

The associations of grave types

As has been mentioned, most of the burials fall into spatial groups (Sets 4, 6, 7 and 9), although there was also one isolated burial (Set 8), an isolated cist which did not contain any human remains (Set 5),

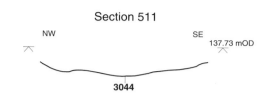

Section 511

NW   SE
                              137.73 mOD

3044

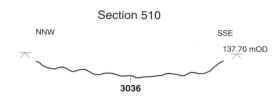

Section 510

NNW   SSE
                              137.70 mOD

3036

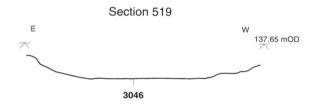

Section 519

E   W
                              137.65 mOD

3046

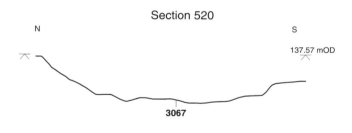

Section 520

N   S
                              137.57 mOD

3067

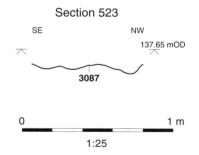

Section 523

SE   NW
              137.65 mOD

3087

0   1 m

1:25

*Fig. 2.10 Early Bronze Age burials:
Set 4 sections and photographs*

Set 4, grave **3046,** skeleton 3048, prime adult, small inhumation cist

Set 4, grave **3036**, skeleton 3037, adult, small inhumation pit

Set 4, grave **3044**, skeleton 3045, adolescent, small inhumation pit

Set 4, grave **3067**, skeleton 3084, young adult, large inhumation pit

Set 4, grave **3087**, skeleton 3088, adolescent, small inhumation pit

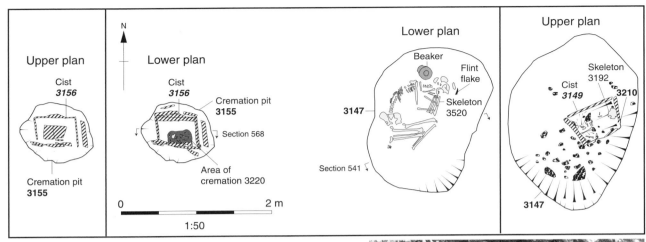

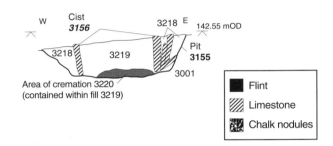

Section 568

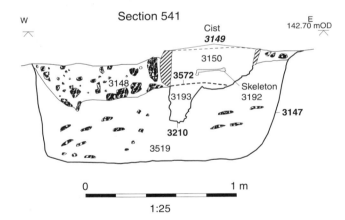

Section 541

| Flint |
| Limestone |
| Chalk nodules |

Set 6, grave **3155**, skeleton 3220, adult, cremation cist

Set 6, grave **3147** (3149), skeleton 3192, young child, cremation cist in large inhumation pit

Set 6, grave **3147**, skeleton 3520, young adult in large inhumation pit

Set 6, grave **3147 (3210)**, skeleton 3193, older child or adolescent, cremation cist in large inhumation pit

Fig. 2.11 Early Bronze Age burials: Set 6

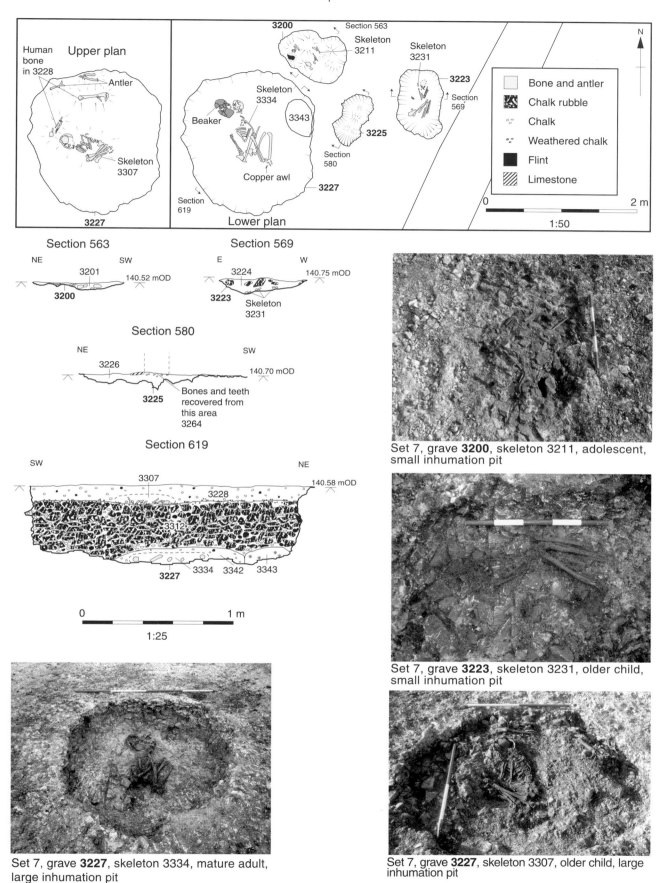

Set 7, grave **3200**, skeleton 3211, adolescent, small inhumation pit

Set 7, grave **3223**, skeleton 3231, older child, small inhumation pit

Set 7, grave **3227**, skeleton 3334, mature adult, large inhumation pit

Set 7, grave **3227**, skeleton 3307, older child, large inhumation pit

Fig. 2.12 Early Bronze Age burials: Set 7

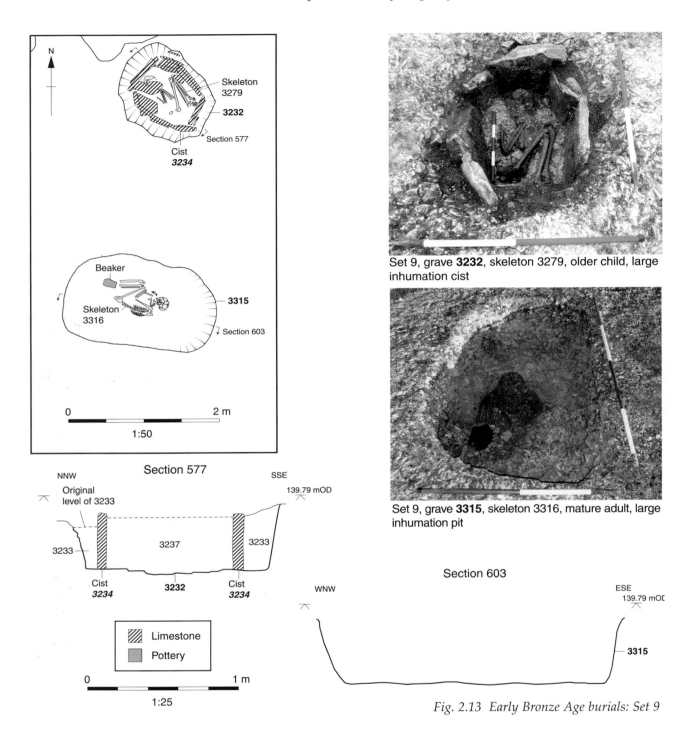

Set 9, grave **3232**, skeleton 3279, older child, large inhumation cist

Set 9, grave **3315**, skeleton 3316, mature adult, large inhumation pit

Fig. 2.13 Early Bronze Age burials: Set 9

and the central burial (Set 10) associated with a ring ditch.

The types of graves that made up each group varied, and there was little apparent order in this variation (Table 2.6). Set 7 consisted of four graves, one of which was a large inhumation pit, the others all being small inhumation pits (Fig. 2.12). Set 4 had the same composition but included also a small cist containing an inhumation. Set 6 consisted of a single large inhumation pit and two inhumation cists, one of which (3149), however, had been

constructed within the large inhumation pit (3147; Fig. 2.11). Set 9 consisted of just two burials: a large inhumation pit and a large cist containing an inhumation.

The chronology of the sets of graves and grave types

Overall, the radiocarbon dates suggest that burial began at Ridgeway Hill between 2410 and 2060 cal BC (95.4%) and probably between 2250 and 2090 cal BC (68.2%), and ended between 1830 and 1460 cal

Table 2.6 Summary of associations of late Neolithic/early Bronze Age grave types in sets (Number of graves (number of individuals represented))

	Large inhumation pit	Small inhumation pit	Inhumation cist	Cremation cist	Small cremation cist	Small cremation pit	Total no. graves	Total no. of individuals represented
Set 6	1 (3)			2 (2)*			2	4
Set 7	1 (3)	3 (3)					4	6
Set 9	1 (1)		1 large (1)				2	2
Set 4	1 (1)	3 (3)	1 small (1)				5	5
Set 8					1 (2)		1	2
Set 10						1 (2)	1	2
Total	4 (9)	6 (6)	2 (2)	2 (2)	1 (2)	1 (2)	15	21

*1 cremation cist was constructed within a large inhumation pit and the individuals it contained are entered in this table as having been present in both the cist and the inhumation pit

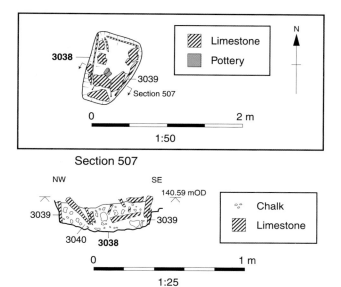

Set 5, 'grave' **3038,** empty, cist

Fig. 2.14 Early Bronze Age burials: Set 5

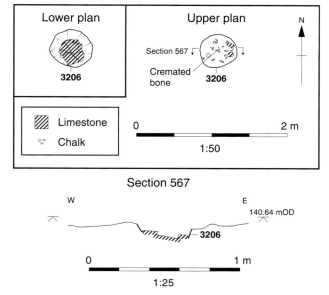

Set 8, grave **3206**, skeleton 3205, adult, small cremation cis

Fig. 2.15 Early Bronze Age burials: Set 8

OxCal v4.1.6 Bronk Ramsey (2010); r:5 Atmospheric data from Reimer et al (2009);

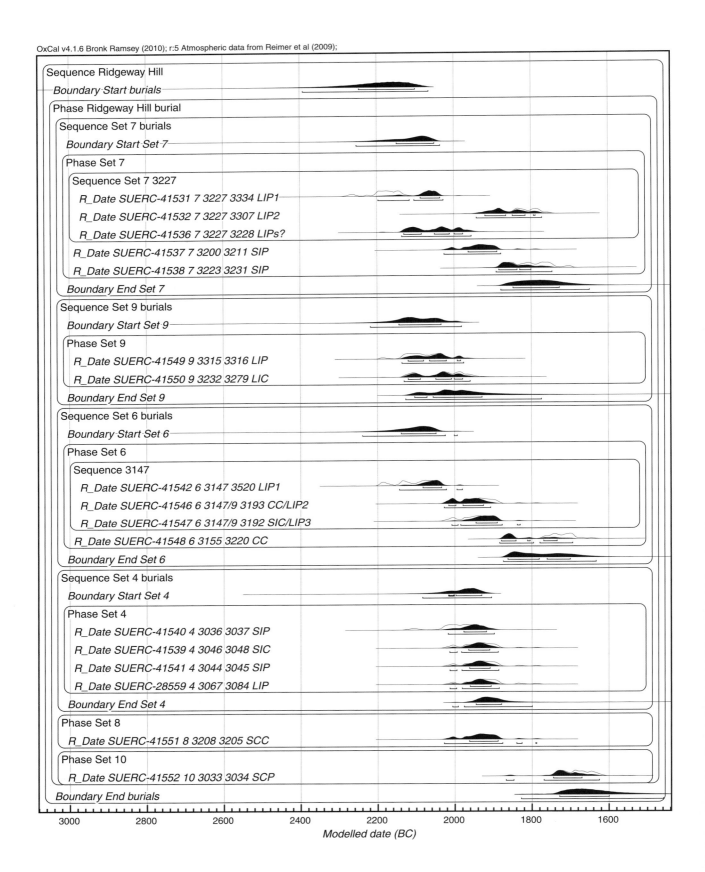

Fig. 2.16 Radiocarbon dates for early Bronze Age burials: overall model by burial group

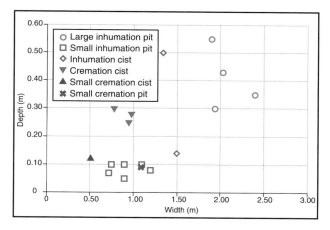

Fig. 2.17 Size and the categories of early Bronze Age burials

BC (95.4 %) and probably between 1730 and 1600 cal BC (68.2%; Fig. 2.18). The dates suggest that burial extended over a period of between 290 and 880 years (95.4%) and probably between 420 and 650 years. The periods over which the sets of burials were made within this overall period were, however, quite varied (Fig. 2.19). The burials in Sets 6 and 7 appear to have been made over quite long periods: Set 6 over a period of between 170 and 550 years (95.4%) and probably over a period of between 210 and 410 years, 68.2%), and Set 7 over a period of 150 and 400 years (95.4%) and probably of between 180 and 300 years. In contrast, the burials in Sets 4 and Set 9, which includes only two burials, were made over shorter periods. The burials in Set 4 were made over a period of less than 240 years

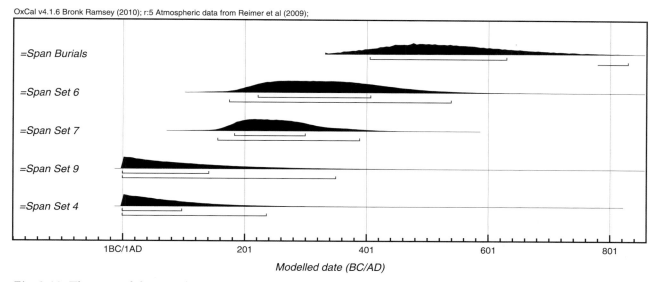

Fig. 2.18 The span of the periods over which burials were made in each set

Table 2.7 Probable order of the dates at which burial in different sets began and ended

The probabilities in the table express the chance that the events listed on the left occurred before the events listed on the top (ie there is a probability of 0.57 that Set 7 began before Set 6). Cases where it is likely that the event on the left preceded that at the top are shown in bold and italics. The events are listed in the most probable order.

Order	Start Set 7	Start Set 6	Start Set 9	End Set 9	Start Set4	SUERC-41551 8 3208 3205 SCC	End Set 4	End Set 7	End Set 6	SUERC-41552 10 3033 3034 SCP
Start Set 7	-	0.57	*0.61*	**0.94**	**0.97**	**1.00**	**1.00**	**1.00**	**1.00**	**1.00**
Start Set 6	0.43	-	0.55	**0.93**	**0.96**	**1.00**	**1.00**	**1.00**	**1.00**	**1.00**
Start Set 9	0.39	0.45	-	**1.00**	**0.94**	**0.99**	**1.00**	**1.00**	**1.00**	**1.00**
End Set 9	0.06	0.07	0.00	-	0.53	*0.72*	*0.81*	**0.95**	**0.95**	**0.98**
Start Set 4	0.03	0.04	0.06	0.47	-	*0.79*	**1.00**	**1.00**	**1.00**	**1.00**
SUERC-41551 8 3208 3205 SCC	0.00	0.00	0.01	0.28	0.21	-	*0.69*	**0.99**	**0.98**	**1.00**
End Set 4	0.00	0.00	0.00	0.19	0.00	0.31	-	**0.97**	**0.96**	**0.99**
End Set 7	0.00	0.00	0.00	0.05	0.00	0.01	0.03	-	0.51	0.80
End Set 6	0.00	0.00	0.00	0.05	0.00	0.02	0.04	0.49	-	0.74
SUERC-41552 10 3033 3034 SCP	0.00	0.00	0.00	0.02	0.00	0.00	0.01	0.20	0.26	-

OxCal v4.1.6 Bronk Ramsey (2010); r:5 Atmospheric data from Reimer et al (2009);

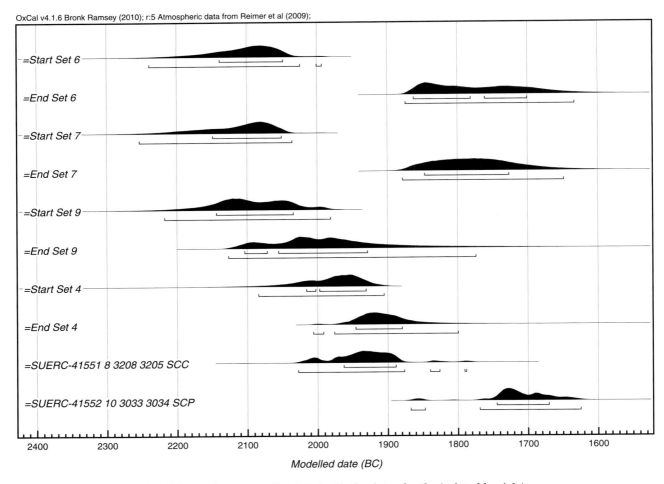

Fig. 2.19 The start and end dates of each set of burials (with the dates for the isolated burials)

(95.4%) and probably less than 100 years (68.2%). The two burials in set 9 were made over a period of less than 370 years (95.4%), but probably less than 150 years (68.2%). It should be borne in mind that whilst almost all of the burials were dated, a small number – 1 in Set 7 (3225) and 2 in Set 4 (3087 and 3106), as well as the stray uncremated bones in Set 8 and 10 (graves 3206 and 3033) – were not, and it is possible that these estimates would be extended further if dates could be obtained for the remaining burials.

It is possible that Set 7, beginning in the period 2260-2030 cal BC (95.4%), and probably in the period 2150-2050 cal BC (68.2%), was the set which began earliest (Table 2.7; Fig. 2.12). However, the estimates for the start of Sets 6 and 9 are very close to that for Set 7, Set 6 probably having begun in the period 2240-1980 cal BC (95.4%) and probably in the period 2140-2040 cal BC (68.2%), and Set 9 probably having begun in the period 2220-1980 cal BC (95.4%) and probably in the period 2150-2030 cal BC (68.2%). What is clear, however, is that Set 4 began appreciably later (in the period 2090-1900 cal BC, 95.4%, and probably in the period 2020-1930 cal BC,

68.2%). Indeed, burial in Set 9 may have come to an end (2130-1770 cal BC, 95.4%, and probably 2110-1920 cal BC, 68.2%) at roughly the same time that burial was beginning in Set 4. In Sets 6 and 7, however, burials continued to be made to a later date, both ending in similar periods, Set 7 in the period 1880-1640 cal BC (95.4%), and probably in the period 1850-1720 cal BC (68.2%), and Set 6 in the period 1880-1630 cal BC (95.4%) and probably in the period 1870-1700 cal BC (68.2%).

The isolated cremation cist (3208) forming Set 8 was probably constructed within the same period as the burials in Set 4, c 2030-1820 cal BC (95.4%), and probably 1970-1880 cal BC (68.2%). The small cremation pit at the centre of the ring ditch almost certainly post-dated the burial activity in all of the other sets. It is dated to 1870-1620 cal BC (95.4%), and probably 1750-1660 cal BC (68.2%).

The radiocarbon dates suggest that the differences between the grave types can be understood in chronological terms only to a limited extent (Fig. 2.20). As has just been noted, the only example of a small cremation pit (3033, Set 10), which formed the central burial associated with a ring ditch, was the

40

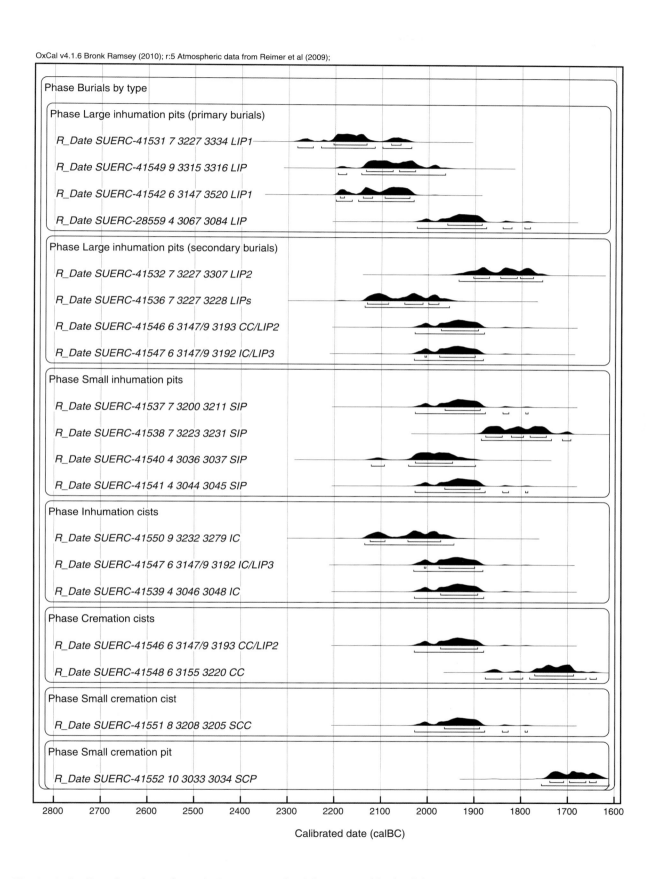

Fig. 2.20 Radiocarbon dates for early Bronze Age burials arranged by burial type

latest burial, and thus stands out chronologically from the others. Aside from this, the only clear suggestion of chronological patterning involves the large inhumation pits. Three of these, 3227, 3315 and 3147 in Sets 7, 9 and 6 respectively, were amongst the earliest graves, with date ranges falling largely before 2000 cal BC (3334 in Set 7: 2200-2020 cal BC, 95.4% and 2090-2030 cal BC, 68.2%; 3520 in Set 6: 2150-1970 cal BC, 95.4% and 2090-2030, 68.2%; 3316 in Set 9: 2140-1970 cal BC, 95.4% and 2120-1980 cal BC, 68.2%). The large inhumation pit (3067) in Set 4 did not conform to this pattern, falling near to the middle of the period in which the burials were made (2020-1880 cal BC, 95.4% and 1960-1900 cal BC, 68.2%). As is discussed in more detail below, this pit differed from the other inhumation pits in other ways too. Most of the other burials – the secondary burials in the large inhumation pits, the small inhumation pits and most of the cremation cists – in contrast, largely date from after 2000 cal BC. There is little indication of chronological differentiation amongst these burials. Nor is there any clear indication that, overall, cists were later than pits. The date

range for the earliest cist (3232, Set 9: 2130-1950 cal BC, 95.4% and 2120-1970 cal BC, 68.2%), which contained an inhumation burial, is not much later than those for the large inhumation pits. Whilst other cists associated with cremations do not occur at such an early date, overall there is a large overlap between the date ranges for cremation burials and inhumations. It will be suggested below, however, that once the age of the burials is taken into account, some chronological trends are apparent and, in particular, that there may have been a change in the treatment of adult burials, from inhumation in large pits to cremation burial in cists and, finally perhaps, to cremation in small pits. No similar trend in the treatment of children is apparent.

The age and sex of the burials

The burials fall into three types: crouched inhumations, cremation burials and stray, uncremated remains. All of the small inhumation pits and the cremation cists contained the remains of only single individuals. The large inhumation pits, with the exception of grave 3067 in Set 4 – which, as has been noted, was also exceptional in other ways – were distinguished from the other burials by the presence of additional burials and, in one case, by the presence of stray bones. The exceptional small cremation cist (Set 8) and the central cremation burial in a small pit associated with the ring ditch (Set 10) were also distinguished from the other burials by the presence of stray uncremated bones from second individuals, in addition to the main deposit of cremated remains.

Unfortunately many of the skeletons, especially those in small inhumation pits, were very poorly preserved, and, like the cremation burials, their age and sex could not be determined (Table 2.4). The burials to which an age could be attributed comprised roughly equal numbers of children (including adolescents: 11 in total) and adults (10 in total; Fig. 2.21). Partly, no doubt, the high proportion of children simply reflects the relatively small size of the population represented within the excavation. It is, however, consistent with wider patterns. Garwood's (2007b) analysis of early Bronze Age burials in Dorset showed that burials of children were most common in his period 2 (*c* 2150-1800 cal BC), within which almost all of the child burials at Ridgeway Hill would also fall, and a number of other sites from this period have high proportions of children (ibid., 74). It is also worth noting, firstly that the distribution of burials of different ages was not uniform, and secondly, that there were quite clear distinctions in the way in which burials of different ages were treated (Table 2.8).

Most of the sets contained only a single adult burial. In cases such as Sets 8, 9 and 10, which

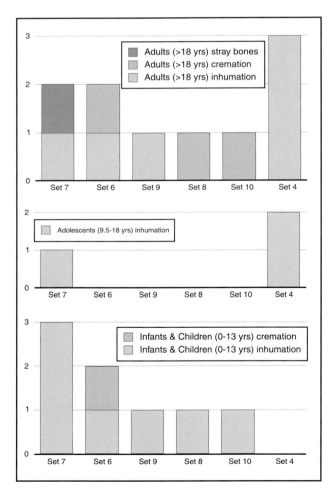

Fig. 2.21 Numbers of late Neolithic/early Bronze Age burials by age category

Table 2.8 Summary of ages of burials by grave type

Age category	LIP	SIC	CC	SCC	SCP	SIP	LIC	LIP secondary	SCC secondary	SCP secondary	Total
Infant										1 (stray)	1
Young child						1		1	1 (stray)		3
Older child						1	1	2			4
Adolescent						3					3
Young adult	2										2
Prime adult		1									1
Mature adult	2										2
Older adult					1						1
Adult			1	1		1		1 (stray)			4
Total	4	1	1	1	1	6	1	4	1	1	21

contained the remains of two individuals only, one of the burials was of an adult and the other of a child. In Set 7, excluding a small group of adult bones consisting of fragments of rib, humerus and femur, only the first burial was of an adult, the remaining four individuals all being children or adolescents. A similar pattern occurred in Set 6, where the first burial was of an adult and two subsequent burials were of children, although a cremation cist in this group did contain the remains of an adult. The clearest exception to this pattern was Set 4, which contained the remains of three adults, the remaining two burials being adolescents. As has been mentioned above, Set 4 was also exceptional in a number of other ways.

With the exception of the stray adult bones mentioned above, all of the adults were either buried singly (ie were the only remains in the grave) or formed the primary burial in a sequence of burials. Adult skeletons were most commonly found as the primary burials in large inhumation pits, where in two cases they formed the first burial in sequences. Adult skeletons were, however, also recovered from the small inhumation cist (3048) in Set 4, from cremation cists (large and small) in Sets 6 (3155) and 8 (3206) and from the central burial (3033) in Set 10. In the case of both the central burial (3033) in Set 10 and the cremation cist (3206) in Set 8, the presence of further stray uncremated bones suggests that the cremation burials might have been the primary burials, although since both were shallow, disturbed features, it is impossible to determine the chronological relationship between the cremation burials and the stray, uncremated bones.

In contrast, at least half of the infants and children had been deposited as secondary burials in sequences (Table 2.8). Three of these burials occurred in large inhumation pits, which are particularly associated with sequences of burials, but other uncremated remains of children were found with possibly earlier cremation burials. A single inhumation burial of a child was, however, found alone in the large inhumation cist (3232) in Set 9. Two further child inhumation burials were found in small inhumation pits. This type of grave, however, was particularly associated with burials of adolescents. All three of the burials of adolescents found at Ridgeway Hill were associated with this type of grave. A single adult was also found in this type of grave.

Overall, although not perfect, this patterning (Table 2.8) suggests that age was an important criterion influencing the type of burial which individuals received.

Unfortunately, the results from Ridgeway Hill can provide little similar information with respect to gender. Since the burials included many children, cremation burials, and very poorly preserved skeletal remains, it is not surprising that it has been possible to determine the sex of only a small number of them (Table 2.4). Four of the skeletons were male or probably male. These skeletons included probable examples forming the cremation burial (3034) in the small pit (3033, Set 10) at the centre of the ring ditch, and the inhumation burial (3048) in the small cist (3046) in Set 4. It is notable, given the patterning found at barrow burials elsewhere (Petersen 1972; Mizoguchi 1993) that the primary burials in two of the large inhumation pits (skeleton 3520 in grave 3147 in Set 6, and skeleton 3334 in grave 3227 in Set 7) were male. The primary burial in the large inhumation pit (3315) in Set 9, however, was female (skeleton 3316). Whilst the data is, therefore, insufficient to suggest clearly that the primary burials in large inhumation pits were usually adult males, it is noticeable that the female example, unlike the male burials, was not associated with a sequence of later burials. As is discussed in the next section, the female burial in Set 9 also lacks the clear chronological priority of the male examples.

Sequences of burials within single graves

Four graves contained the remains of more than one individual. It is possible that further evidence for the deposition of more than one individual in a grave has been removed by truncation. The two graves providing the clearest evidence for sequences of burials were both large inhumation pits, the deepest graves found on the site. It is quite clear that if these graves had been truncated to the extent that the small inhumation pits may have been, almost all of the evidence for burials other than the first would have been removed. It is worth recalling that in many of the small inhumation pits, the surviving evidence for what is taken to be the first or only burial in these graves was very partial and fragmentary.

The other two graves containing the remains of more than one individual consisted of very shallow features in which the second individual was represented by very small groups of bone fragments and teeth. Such evidence could easily have been removed entirely from other shallow features.

Uncremated remains with cremation burials.

Two cremation burials – one (3034) in the small cremation pit (3033, Set 10) at the centre of the ring ditch, and one (3205) in the small cremation cist (3206) in Set 8 – also contained small numbers of uncremated remains from a second individual. In one case (3035, in pit 3033, Set 10) the uncremated remains belonged to an infant 1 to 5 months old; in the second they belonged to a young child of 1 to 2 years of age. The cremation burial in pit 3033 was probably of an adult; the age of that in cist 3206 could not be determined. The small groups of uncremated bones consisted of nothing more than a few bone fragments and teeth in both cases. Both features were shallow and had clearly suffered from truncation. It is possible that in both cases, the unburnt fragments derived from secondary burials which have been almost entirely removed by this truncation.

Sequences of burials in large inhumation pits

Grave 3147 (Set 6)

Of the two large inhumation pits that contained sequences of burials, grave 3147 in Set 6 contained the most complex sequence (Fig. 2.11). The first burial was a probably male, young adult inhumation (3520) which lay on the base of the pit. This burial was covered with a layer of chalk (3519). The sequence after this point is ambiguous. The chalk layer was cut by a pit (3210) which contained the cremated remains (3193) of a child or adolescent aged 7.5-13 years. The pit was P-shaped in profile. Most of the base was rounded, and lay at a depth of up to 0.3m deep. Towards it western side, however, the base became much deeper, and descended steeply to a depth of 0.5m. The cremated remains lay primarily in the deeper part of the pit, but also extended across the shallower part. On the very edges of this pit, a stone cist (3149) had been constructed.

The ambiguity concerns whether the pit was cut first, and the cist then constructed around it, or the cist was constructed first and the pit then cut within it. The cist was surrounded by a silty clay deposit (3148). There were no clear indications of a cut for the cist within this deposit, so it seems likely that it was deposited after the cist had been constructed. The bottom of the stones forming the cist lay precisely at the edges of the pit (3210) on the surface of the underlying chalk deposit (3519), and there was thus no stratigraphic relationship between the pit and the upper silt clay fill (3148). The fact that the cist was constructed directly upon the chalk deposit (3519) covering the first burial, without any indication that any silt or chalk had accumulated, and the absence of any indication of a cut for the cist in the upper silt (3148), all suggest that the cist was constructed quite soon after the chalk (3519) covering the first inhumation had been deposited. It also suggests that the pit had been completely cleared out to a certain depth, leaving no trace of a recut, before the cist was constructed, or that the cist was constructed quite soon after the first inhumation burial had been covered, but that pit 3210 was cut through the cist, again leaving no clear trace of a recut, at a later date. The radiocarbon dates discussed below suggest that the period between the first and second burials may have been quite long, and hence the second or third options appear the most likely.

The cremation deposit in pit 3120 was covered by a further silty deposit (3150) which contained the remains of the third burial – the poorly preserved, partial remains of the skeleton of a second child of 4.5 to 5.5 years.

Radiocarbon dates were obtained for all three of the burials in this grave, and they allow us to estimate the intervals between each burial, and over how long a period overall, the burials were made. In this case, the stratigraphic order of the burials corresponds well to the dates obtained. The model thus places all of the burials in a sequence, and uses the stratigraphic information to constrain the dates for the burials (Fig. 2.16).

Table 2.9 Intervals between the burials

Interval	68.2%		95.4%	
Set 6				
@3520 LIP1 to 3193 CC2	50	180	10	240
@3193 CC2 to 3192 SIC3	-10	60	-10	120
@3192 SIC3 to 3220 CC	20	220	10	270
Set 7				
@3334 LIP1 to 3307 LIP2	160	360	120	420
@3307 LIP2 to 3228 LIPs	-270	-110	-350	-50
@3334 LIP1 to 3228 LIPs	-50	170	-80	230
@3228 LIPs to 3200 SIP	50	200	-40	250
@3200 SIP to 3307 LIP2	10	150	-50	220
@3307 LIP2 to 3223 SIP	-40	90	-100	160
Set 4				
@3037 to 3048	-20	40	-60	100
@3048 to 3045	-30	30	-70	80
@3045 to 3084	-30	30	-70	80
Set 9				
@3316 LIP to 3279 LIC	-40	80	-90	160

Overall, the radiocarbon dates suggest that the burials in grave 3147 were made over a period of between 70 and 300 years (95.4%) and probably between 100 and 220 years (68.2%). The estimates of the intervals between the burials at 95.4% probability are not very precise (Table 2.9), ranging from -10 years (the negative value implying that the stratigraphically later burial was actually slightly older than the burial below) to 240 years. Whilst, however, the interval estimates suggest that the burials could all have been deposited with only short intervening periods, clearly this possibility is not consistent with the burials having been made over a period of more than 70, and probably more than 100, years. The more precise but less certain estimates at 68.2% probability suggest that it is more likely that a longer interval had elapsed between the first and second burial (between 50 and 180 years) than between the second and the third (-10 to 60 years).

Grave 3227 (Set 7)

A second sequence of burials was found in grave 3227 in Set 7 (Fig. 2.12). The first burial (3334) in this large inhumation pit was again of a male adult of 36 to 45 years, who lay on the base of the pit. A Beaker was placed behind the head, and a small deposit of dark brown silt around 0.5m across, possibly the remains of decayed organic material, lay on the base of the pit near its western edge. This deposit, the Beaker and the inhumation burial were covered by a deposit of silty clay (3342) similar to that which filled the Beaker (3335). The silty clay layer was

covered by a deposit of chalk (3312), and on top of this chalk a second inhumation burial (3307), of a child of 11 to 13 years, was deposited. A small number of further bones, consisting of a fragmented femur and fragments of rib, humerus and more femur from an adult were found in the layer (3228) which covered the second inhumation.

Radiocarbon dates were obtained from both of the inhumation burials (3334 and 3307) and the stray adult bones at the top of the grave in context 3228. The results obtained for the three dated individuals are not consistent with their stratigraphic order: the stray adult bones (3228) at the top of the grave being older than the child (3307) below and close in date to the first burial (3334) below that (Fig. 2.16). Since the two inhumations consisted of more or less well-preserved, articulated burials which appear to have remained *in situ*, it seems likely that the small group of adult bones (3228) was redeposited some time after the individual which they represent had died. There are two possible explanations for this chronological anomaly. It is possible that the small group of bones (3228) represents an earlier secondary burial, deposited after the first burial (3334), which was then disturbed by the insertion of what now appears to have been the second burial (3307).

The second possibility is that the small group of bones was originally buried or in some other way stored elsewhere and was then buried in grave 3227, perhaps deliberately, a long time after death. There was no indication of a recut in the fills of the pit that might have been associated with the deposition of the second inhumation burial (3307), which perhaps argues against the first suggestion. As was the case for grave 3147, the fact that the second inhumation burial (3307) lay directly upon the chalk covering the first burial (3334), and the absence of any evidence that silt had accumulated after that burial, suggests that the second inhumation (3307) followed the first (3334) quite quickly. In fact, however, the radiocarbon dates suggest again that a quite long interval of between 120 and 420 (95.4%), and probably of between 160 and 360 years (68.2%), elapsed between the first and second inhumation burials (Table 2.9). This long interval suggests that the second possibility – that the grave was cleaned out to the top of the surviving chalk is the most plausible interpretation.

Overall, the radiocarbon dates suggest that burials were made in grave 3227 over a period of between 120 and 420 years (95.4%) and probably between 160 and 330 years (68.2%). Although it is likely that the small group of bones (3228) were later in date than the first inhumation (3334), the possible interval between them can be estimated only as between -80 years and 230 years (95.4%) and probably between -50 and 170 years (68.2%), the minus figure again implying that it is possible that the small group was in fact earlier than the first inhumation. A long interval of between 50 and 350 years (95.4%), and probably of between 110 and 270 years (68.2%), elapsed between the stray bones (3228) and the second inhumation burial (3307). As is discussed below, it is likely that one of the burials in a small inhumation pit (3200) was made during this interval.

Sequence of burials within sets

The radiocarbon dates provide the means not only of looking at the intervals between burials within single graves, but also within the sets as wholes. They thus provide a means of examining the question of whether the sequence of burials in the large inhumation pits occurred before burials were placed in other types of graves around the large inhumation pits, or whether burials were deposited in both contexts over the same period. It is also possible to examine the intervals of time that elapsed between burials of all kinds within sets, and examine whether there were significant hiatuses in deposition, or if burials were interred more or less

regularly. It is important to note in this context that, where stratigraphic information has been used in a Bayesian model to refine the dates of particular burials in relation to each other, the dates involved are constrained by the model to fall into a particular order. The high probabilities of one burial following another in these cases are a product of the stratigraphic information included in the model rather than the radiocarbon dates themselves, although in all but one case the dates are consistent with the stratigraphic order. It is also important to note that not only were a small number of burials not dated, but that, given the shallow depth of many of the graves, other burials have not survived. Any further burials could, of course, extend the periods over which the sets of burials formed and make the periods between burials within sets shorter.

The first contrast revealed by this analysis (Table 2.10), however, is between groups of graves in which burials were made over relatively long periods, in which the order of the burials can be determined with considerable certainty, and groups of graves in which burials were made over quite short periods and in which it is, as a result, impossible to determine the order of the burials with any certainty.

Table 2.10 Order of late Neolithic/early Bronze Age burials within sets

The figures show the probability that the burial on the column to the left preceded the burial listed in the row along the top (eg there is a probability of 0.64 that burial 3036 preceded burial 3046). The burials are arranged from left to right and from top to bottom in the most probably order. Probabilities of greater than 0.66 are in **bold**.

Order Set 4	SUERC-41540 4 3036 3037 SIP	SUERC-41539 4 3046 3048 SIC	SUERC-41541 4 3044 3045 SIP	SUERC-28559 4 3067 3084 LIP
SUERC-41540 4 3036 3037 SIP	-	0.64	0.66	0.67
SUERC-41539 4 3046 3048 SIC	0.36	-	0.52	0.54
SUERC-41541 4 3044 3045 SIP	0.34	0.48	-	0.52
SUERC-28559 4 3067 3084 LIP	0.33	0.46	0.48	-

Order Set 9	SUERC-41549 9 3315 3316 LIP	SUERC-41550 9 3232 3279 LIC
SUERC-41549 9 3315 3316 LIP	-	0.61
SUERC-41550 9 3232 3279 LIC	0.39	-

Order Set 6	SUERC-41542 6 3147 3520 LIP1	SUERC-41546 6 3147/9 3193 CC/LIP2	SUERC-41547 6 3147/9 3192 SIC/LIP3	SUERC-41548 6 3155 3220 CC
SUERC-41542 6 3147 3520 LIP1	-	**1.00**	**1.00**	**1.00**
SUERC-41546 6 3147/9 3193 CC/LIP2	0.00	-	**1.00**	**1.00**
SUERC-41547 6 3147/9 3192 SIC/LIP3	0.00	0.00	-	**0.98**
SUERC-41548 6 3155 3220 CC	0.00	0.00	0.02	-

Order Set 7	SUERC-41531 7 3227 3334 LIP1	SUERC-41536 7 3227 3228 LIPs	SUERC-41537 7 3200 3211 SIP	SUERC-41532 7 3227 3307 LIP2	SUERC-41538 7 3223 3231 SIP
SUERC-41531 7 3227 3334 LIP1	-	**0.85**	**1.00**	**1.00**	**1.00**
SUERC-41536 7 3227 3228 LIPs	0.15	-	**0.94**	**1.00**	**1.00**
SUERC-41537 7 3200 3211 SIP	0.00	0.06	-	**0.90**	**0.97**
SUERC-41532 7 3227 3307 LIP2	0.00	0.00	0.10	-	**0.69**
SUERC-41538 7 3223 3231 SIP	0.00	0.00	0.03	0.31	-

Sets 4 and 9 belong to the latter group. For the burials in Set 4, the probability of any burial preceding another does not exceed 0.67. Thus, whilst the dates suggests that it is more likely that small inhumation pit 3036 was the first, followed by small inhumation cist 3046, small inhumation pit 3044 and then large inhumation pit 3067, this order is still very uncertain. (Small inhumation pit 3087 was not dated and is therefore not included in this order.) This uncertainty is reflected in the estimates of the intervals between burials (Table 2.9), which range from -70 to 100 years (at 95.4%), the minus figure again implying that the first burial was in fact later than the second. At 68.2% probability the estimates are typically around -30 to 30 years. This is consistent with the overall estimate of the duration of the period over which burials were made in this group, which suggests that the group was used for a relatively short period (of less than 120 years (95.4%) and probably less than 60 years (68.2%)) compared to the other groups of burials. The most probable order of these graves differs from that suggested in the other groups, both in terms of the kinds of graves involved and the age of the individuals involved. Given the low probabilities involved in this sequence, however, little weight can be attached to this result. It is also worth recalling that, unlike all of the other sets of burials, this set was dominated by burials of adults and adolescents and included no children. This unusual (for the Ridgeway Hill burials) composition in terms of age may have been related to the lack of a clear sequence which, in the other groups, involves primarily the burial of children and adolescents after adults.

Set 9 contained only two burials, which again seem to have buried at relatively close dates. Again, although it is more likely that large inhumation pit 3315 preceded the large inhumation cist (3232), the probability is only 0.61, and the estimate of the interval between the two is very broad: -90 to 160 years at 95.4% confidence and -40 to 80 at 68.2%.

In contrast to these two groups, the order of the burials in Sets 6 and 7 can be established with much greater certainty, the probabilities involved usually exceeding 0.9, although in part this reflects the stratigraphic relationships between some of the burials. The simplest sequence was in Set 6. In this set, the first burial was the primary inhumation (3520) in the large inhumation pit. This was followed by the cremation burial (3193) and the second inhumation (3192) in the same pit, as described above. The final burial (3220), in cremation cist 3155, was made after all of the burials in the large inhumation pit. The intervals between the burials in the large inhumation pit have already been discussed above. There is likely to have also

been an appreciable interval of between 10 and 270 years (95.4%) and probably 20 to 220 years (68.2%) between the last burial in the large inhumation pit (3192) and the burial in the cremation cist (3220).

The most probable order of the burials in Set 7 suggests that, in this case, the sequence of burials in the large inhumation pit discussed above occurred over a period in which at least one burial was made in a small inhumation pit. The earliest burial in this group was again the primary inhumation burial (3334) in the large inhumation pit (3227). As has been discussed above, the next burial by age was the small group of bones in context 3228 which, however, occurred stratigraphically as the third burial within the large inhumation pit (3227), above a burial (3307) which was actually more recent by date. By date, the third burial in the sequence was a burial (3200) in a small inhumation pit, which almost certainly preceded in date the second inhumation burial (3307) which was placed in the large inhumation pit. This second inhumation (3307) was probably close in date to another burial (3231) in another small inhumation pit (3223).

Although there appear to have been significant intervals between the burials in the large inhumation pit (3227), and although the overall sequence of burials is clear, the intervals between all of the dated burials in this group, taken as a single sequence, need not have been so large. The estimates of the intervals in this single sequence at 95.4% all range from negative values of between -30 and -100 years to positive values of between 160 and 250 years. At 68.2% probability, the estimates suggest that the largest interval, of at least 50 years, may have occurred between the first inhumation burial (3334) or the stray bones (3228) in the same grave (3227) and the burial (3211) in small inhumation pit 3200. Another appreciable gap of at least 10 years (at 68.2%) probably occurred between the burial (3211) in the small inhumation pit (3200) and the second inhumation burial (3307) in the large inhumation pit (3227).

Although overall the burials may have been interred in a sequence which does not contain any very long hiatuses, it is worth noting that the sequence implies that the cremated child remains (3307) were interred (and presumably the cist which contained them constructed) after the barrow mound had been built over the large inhumation burial (3227) in which they occurred. This conclusion follows from the suggestion that the shallow depth of the small inhumation pit (3200, containing burial 3211) reflects the fact that it was a secondary burial cut through the barrow mound.

The inhumation burial (3264) in inhumation pit 3225 was not dated and thus does not form part of this sequence.

A striking feature of the sequences of burials in all of the sets where the order can be established by radiocarbon dates with some plausibility, or strati-graphically, is that the sequence always begins with an adult burial. This first burial is followed by burials which consist almost entirely of children and adolescents. As has been discussed above, the only exceptions to this are the burials in Set 4 – the order of which cannot be established with any certainty, the burial of an adult (3220) in cremation cist 3155 in Set 6, and the small group of bone (3228) in grave 3227 in Set 7.

The grave fills

The fills of the graves can be divided into two types. Almost all of the fills consisted of mid or dark brown or orange brown silty clay or silty loam deposits, presumably derived from the natural soil on the site. The second type of fill consisted of chalk rubble. Although all of the burials had been cut into chalk, chalk backfill appeared to have been used only to cover the first inhumation burials in large inhuma-tion pits. Such deposits were found only in the large inhumation pits 3147, 3227 and 3315 in Sets 6, 7 and 9. In graves 3147 and 3315 the chalk (3519 and 3318) lay directly upon the burial, whilst in grave 3772 there was a thin layer of silty clay over the burial upon which the chalk lay. The chalk layers varied in thickness, from around 0.25m deep in grave 3315 and 0.3m in grave 3227 to around 0.5m deep in grave 3147. In all cases, however, it is clear that more chalk had been removed from the grave than had been put back in. It is possible that the extra chalk had been retained to form part of the barrow mounds that

may have covered these burials, perhaps being used to form a chalk capping.

The interpretation of the deposits of chalk is, however, complicated by the fact that in both graves 3147 in Set 6 and grave 3227 in Set 7, later burials were deposited directly upon the chalk layer, in a pit cut into the chalk in the case of grave 3147 (Fig. 2.11), and simply on the surface of the chalk in the case of grave 3227 (Fig. 2.12) without any indication of further sediment having been deposited in the pits, and despite the evidence which suggests that appreciable periods had elapsed between the first and second burials. This span was possibly between 50 and 180 years (68.2% probability) in the case of grave 3147 and probably between 160 and 360 years in the case of grave 3227. These long periods suggest that the pits were re-opened and cleaned out down to the surviving surface of the chalk without leaving any trace of a recut. It is possible, then, that the chalk fills in these pits were originally deeper than suggested by the state they were found in when excavated.

The position of the burials

It was generally only in the large inhumation pits and in the cists containing inhumations that the skeletons were sufficiently well preserved for their posture to be clear. The remains in the small inhuma-tion pits were generally too poorly preserved for the posture to be clear, although enough survived of the skeleton in grave 3223 (Set 7) to suggest that it was crouched and oriented like most of the better preserved skeletons in the larger pits and cists (Fig. 2.12). In the case of the better preserved skeletons,

Table 2.11 Orientation of burials with other attributes

Probable order by date	Strati-graphic position	Grave	Grave type	Skeleton no.	Burial facing	Burial side	Burial head to	Age category	Age range	Sex
Set 7										
5		3223	SIP	3231	E? (truncated - uncertain)	?L	N?	Older child	7.5-8.5 yrs	/
4	2	3227	LIP	3307	S	R	W	Older child	11.25-13	/
1	1	3227	LIP	3334	NE	L	NW	Mature adult	36-45 yrs	M
Set 6										
1	1	3147	LIP	3520	E	L	N	Young adult	20-25 yrs	?M
Set 4										
4		3067	LIP	3084	NE	R	SE	Young adult	18-25 yrs	?
2		3046	SIC	3048	N	R	E	Prime adult	26-35 yrs	?M
Set 9										
2		3232	LIC	3279	NE	L	NW	Older child	10.5-12.5 yrs	/
1		3315	LIP	3316	N	R	E	Mature adult	35-39 yrs	?F

the burials were all crouched, with the back more or less curved forward, the legs generally tightly contracted, the knees drawn up towards the face, and the arms either also tightly contracted or at least bent, with the hands near the face.

The orientation of the burials appeared to vary in a more or less systematic way, although the reasons for the variation remain obscure (Table 2.11). All but one of the inhumation burials faced either north, north-east or east. Some of the burials, however, lay on their right sides and some on the left, and the heads thus lay either to the east or south-east (for burials on their right sides) or to the north or north-west (for burials on their left sides). The one exception was the second inhumation burial (3307) in grave 3227, which faced towards the south and lay on its right side with the head to the west.

Although the orientation of the burials thus seems not have been random, there are no obvious correlations between the orientation and other attributes of the burials. Four of the inhumations for which the orientation could be determined could also be sexed. The one probably female example lay facing north, on her right side, with the head to the east, in the same position as one of the male burials. The two other male burials both lay with the heads to the north/north-east, on their left sides, with the heads to the north/north-west. There is thus no clear relationship with the sex of the burials. Nor is there are clear relationship with age or the type of grave (Table 2.11).

The composition of the cremation burials

Most of the cremation burials consisted of quite large deposits of cremated remains, the largest weighing 1.4kg, although the smallest, of a child, weighed only 0.25kg (Table 2.4). McKinley (2000a) indicates the cremated remains of an adult usually weigh between 1.0 and 2.4kg (with a mean weight of 1.6kg). The relatively large size of the deposits from Ridgeway Hill, despite the evidence that most of the burials had suffered from truncation and the fact that they contained only very small quantities of charcoal, suggests that the cremated remains were picked very carefully and thoroughly from the pyre debris.

Of the four cremation burials, three were placed in stone cists, two in Set 6, and one in Set 8 (Figs 2.11 and 2.15). The remaining cremation was placed in a small pit, and formed the burial at the centre of the ring ditch (Fig. 2.22). Although none of the earliest burials had been cremated, the chronology of the cremation burials overlaps to a large degree with that of the inhumations. The latest burial (3034), in the pit (3033) at the centre of the ring ditch, had been cremated, but even in this case the cremated remains were associated with a small number of uncremated bones from a child. One of the cremation burials (3220 in grave 3155) in Set 6 was the latest burial in that set, and one of the latest burials on the site. It may well, however, have been close in date to the latest of the inhumation burials (eg 3307 in grave 3227 or 3223 in grave 3231, both in set 7). The burials from Ridgeway Hill thus underline the extent to which the two forms of burial were in use at the same time, rather than indicating any clear trend over time. It is, however, worth noting that in the sequence of burials, the earliest examples (in graves 3227 in Set 7 and grave 3147 in Set 6) both began with inhumation burials, whereas the later examples of burials which may have formed sequences (grave 3206 in Set 8 and grave 3033 at the centre of the ring ditch) both appear to have begun

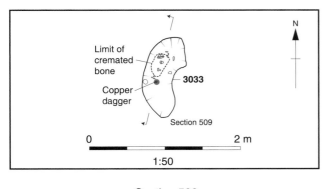

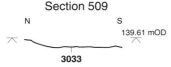

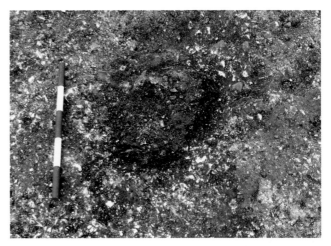

Set 10, grave **3033**, skeleton 3034, Adult (older), small cremation pit

Fig. 2.22 Central burial 3033 (Set 10)

with cremation burials. Thus, whilst the two forms of burial clearly overlapped chronologically to a large degree, there is some evidence to suggest that the use of the differing forms of burial in relation to the status of individuals changed over time.

Grave goods

The early Bronze Age burials were associated with few grave goods or other artefacts, and what grave goods were recovered were almost all associated with the primary burials in the large inhumation pits. Alongside what appear to have been deliberately deposited grave goods, a range of other finds was recovered. Many of these were small flint chips, which do not appear to have been deliberately deposited. There are also some more ambiguous cases, including one case in which animal bone may have been deposited in a grave, but was in a layer not directly associated with a burial.

Three of the primary burials in large inhumation pits were associated with grave goods – 3334 in grave 3227, Set 7; 3520 in grave 3147, Set 6; and 3316 in grave 3315, Set 9 (Figs 2.11, 2.12, 2.13). The only exception was the slightly later large inhumation pit (3067) in Set 4 which differed from the other large inhumation pits in other respects as well. The range of grave goods in the large inhumation pits was small, and was similar in each case. Two of the burials (3334 and 3316) were associated with a single Beaker and a small copper alloy awl. The third example, 3520, contained a Food Vessel and possibly a large side trimming flake.

There appears to have been some patterning in the positioning of these grave goods, although as was the case with the orientation of the graves, it is difficult to relate this patterning to other attributes of the burials (Table 2.12). In grave 3227, the Beaker was placed behind the head and the awl by the feet (Fig. 2.12). In grave 3315, however, this positioning was reversed, with the Beaker lying by the feet and the awl by the skull (Fig. 2.13). The awl was recovered from an environmental sample and its precise

Table 2.12 Location of grave goods

Set	Grave	Skeleton	Artefact	Location in relation to body	Location in relation to cardinal points
7	3227	3334	Beaker	behind head	NW
			Cu alloy awl	by feet	SE
9	3315	3316	Beaker	by feet	NW
			Cu alloy awl	by head	E
6	3147	3520	Food Vessel	behind head	N
			Flint flake	in front of head	NE

location is, therefore, uncertain. It is, however, worth noting that although both of these burials faced NNE, the inhumation in grave 3315 lay on her right side and with her head to the east, whilst the inhumation in grave 3227 lay on his left side with his head to the west. Thus, although the locations of the grave goods was inverted with respect to the body, they were similar with respect to the cardinal points, that is both Beakers lay at the north-west of the grave, and both awls lay at the east/south-east.

In grave 3147, the Food Vessel again lay behind the head (Fig. 2.11). The primary inhumation burial (3520) in this grave lay facing the east on his left side with his head to the north. The position of the Food Vessel is, therefore, consistent with that of grave 3227 if the side on which the burial lay is given precedence (even though the orientation of the burial in relation to the cardinal points differs slightly). The other artefact which may have been deliberately deposited as an offering in this burial was a large side trimming flake, 88mm long. It lay close to the hands, in front of the face of the inhumation.

It is worth noting that the awls recovered from graves 3227 and 3315 were very small, fine examples, and it is possible that other examples may not have survived. Blue spots were noted on all of the deposits of cremated remains 3220, 3193, 3205 and 3034 in graves 3155, 3147, 3206 and 3033 in Sets 6, 8 and 10, which might have derived from copper alloy objects which have not survived.

The only other object that appears to have been deliberately deposited with a burial was the tip of a copper alloy dagger found on the base of grave 3033 adjacent to the deposit of cremated remains (3034). This grave had clearly suffered from truncation and it is quite possible that any other grave goods, like the rest of the dagger, had not survived.

Fragments of Beaker pottery were also recovered from the cist (3038) which formed Set 5. The cist did not contain any cremated or other human remains, but it is possible that the Beaker sherds were originally a deliberate grave offering which has only partially survived.

A localised dark brown silty deposit (3343) containing a little charcoal was found in grave 3227 (Set 7) near the eastern side of the grave, adjacent to the legs of the inhumation burial (Fig. 2.12). This deposit was quite distinct from the rest of the fill around the burial, which consisted of a light brown silty clay. Although no artefacts were recovered from it, it is possible that this dark deposit marked the location of decayed organic grave goods. The recent discoveries of organic remains in a cist at Whitehorse Hill, Dartmoor (Jones *et al.* 2012), which probably dates from the 19th to the 17th centuries cal BC, and may thus have been contemporary with the later burials at Ridgeway Hill, suggest that organic objects may have been present in many more of the burials at Ridgeway Hill.

Other probably deliberately deposited finds

Alongside the objects discussed above which appear to have been deliberately deposited in association with a burial as grave goods, there were two contexts in which other objects were recovered from the graves which appear to have been deliberately deposited but which were not so clearly associated with a burial. The first example consisted of three fragmented antlers, probably from roe deer, recovered from the silty upper fill (3228) of grave 3227 in Set 7. This deposit covered the second inhumation burial (3307) and the small group of adult bones. The antlers lay near the NNW edge of the grave, to the north of the small group of adult bones (Fig. 2.12). The second was a fragmentary cattle pelvis recovered from the silty clay fill (3148) which surrounded the cist (3149) in grave 3147 in Set 6. Its chronological relationship with the later burials is, therefore, uncertain, though this layer clearly post-dated the construction of the cist.

Other finds recovered from the graves

The other finds recovered from the graves, which do not appear to have been deliberately deposited, consist of animal bone, flint and pottery. Aside from the cattle pelvis and antler discussed above, almost all of the animal bone recovered from the graves was from small mammals or, in a few cases, amphibians. All of these bones are likely to have been either intrusive or natural occurrences. Especially large assemblages of such bones were recovered from the cremation deposit (3193) in grave 3147 in Set 6 and the fill (3335) of the Beaker in grave 3227 in Set 7. The only other bones were small fragments of a cattle tooth, a large mammal mandible and a medium-sized mammal long bone in the fill (3237) of the inhumation cist (3232) in Set 9. Whilst these bones might have been part of a partially preserved grave offering, they were recovered not from the layer covering the burial, but from the layer above that, and were not therefore, directly associated with the burial.

Small numbers of pieces of flint were recovered from almost all of the graves. Almost all of this consisted of chips and flakes, or natural or burnt unworked fragments. The only exceptions were bladelets in graves 3044 (context 3003) and 3227 (context 3228) and a serrated flake in grave 3147 (context 3148). Graves 3044 in Set 4, 3149 in Set 6

and 3227 in Set 7 contained the largest number of pieces.

Aside from the Beakers and Food Vessel deposited with burials, very little pottery was recovered from the graves. Two small Beaker sherds were, however, recovered, one from grave 3327 (Set 7; context 3342), the other from grave 3149/3147 (Set 6; context 3150). The remaining pottery consisted of two small residual sherds, one probably middle Neolithic, from grave 3046 (Set 4; context 3050), the other a larger sherd, probably of Grooved Ware, from grave 3315 (Set 9; context 3317).

The ring ditches

Two ring ditches were exposed within the site (Fig. 2.3). The first (3032) lay near the middle of the site and was almost certainly associated with grave 3033, which lay at its centre. It seems likely, therefore, that this ring ditch was associated with a barrow which had been entirely ploughed out. A second, larger ring ditch (3514) lay only partially with the excavated area at the northern end of the site. It is less clear that this feature was also related to a barrow. Its diameter of around 38m is large for such a monument, and no burials were found within it, although any central burial might have been removed by a Roman ditch. Furthermore, it was penannular, with a narrow entrance to the east. None of these features excludes the possibility that it was related to an early Bronze Age barrow, although they would make it rather atypical. It was associated with few finds, which do not give any clear indication of its date. Although its date and purpose remain uncertain, there are few other obvious alternative interpretations, and it is, therefore, described here.

The first ring ditch (3032) had an internal diameter (ie within the ring ditch) of 13.7m (Figs. 2.23-2.24). A total of 13 sections, generally 2m wide, were cut at 2m intervals around the ring ditch, giving a total sample of around 50%.

The ditch varied in width around its perimeter, from 1.4m at its narrowest point to 3.5m at the widest (mean = 2.3m). This variation, however, is likely to have been largely the product of differences in the extent to which the sides of the ditch have collapsed. The profile of the ditch varied considerably. In several sections, however, the ditch had a Y-shaped profile (Fig. 2.23), which is similar to that found at the Overton experimental earthwork after the upper part of the profile had collapsed (Bell *et al.* 1996, figs 7.5–6). It seems likely, therefore, that the ring ditch was originally narrower than these measurements suggest. In other sections, the profile was irregular, had stepped sides, or more regular sides which sloped at around 45°. The depth

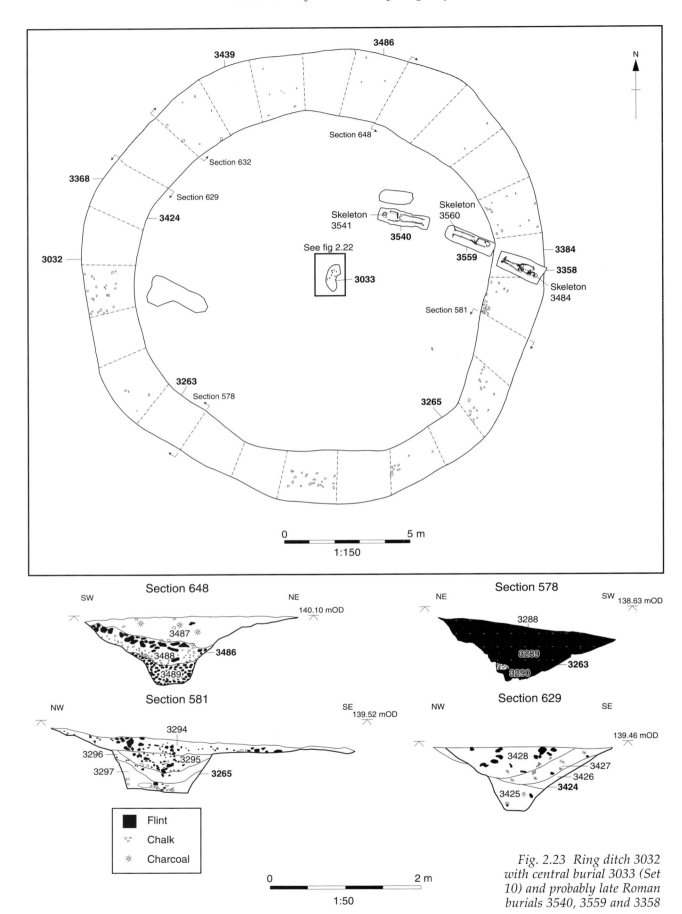

Section 648

Section 578

Section 581

Section 629

Flint

Chalk

Charcoal

0   2 m

1:50

Fig. 2.23 Ring ditch 3032 with central burial 3033 (Set 10) and probably late Roman burials 3540, 3559 and 3358

Fig. 2.24 Ring ditch 3032 from the north-west

of the ditch was much more consistent, generally falling between 0.75 and 0.95m, although at its deepest point it was 1.2m deep, and the base of the ditch was generally flat.

The ditch was filled with more or less complex sequences of fills largely consisting either of red, orange or yellow brown silty clay or of deposits of chalk (Fig. 2.25). Most of the deposits contained some chalk, which often formed 30% or more of the deposit. Other than the fact that many of the primary fills consisted of chalk deposits, there was little apparent order in the sequences of deposition, nor was there any clear indication that the ditch had preferentially filled from one side from, for example, an internal mound.

The quantities of finds recovered from the ring ditch were small, and much of what was recovered lay within the upper fills. Most of the pottery was Roman, and came almost exclusively from the uppermost preserved fills, although six later prehistoric or Roman sherds were recovered from a slightly lower fill (3388) in section 3384. Only three Beaker sherds were recovered from the ring ditch, two of these again retrieved from uppermost fills (3390 in cut 3384 and 3397 in cut 3368). In cut 3265,

however, a single Beaker sherd was found in the second layer of fill. A single probably middle Neolithic sherd was also recovered from an upper fill (3289) in cut 3263.

Much of the small assemblage of flint was also recovered from upper fills, although in a few cuts, especially on the northern side of the ring ditch, small numbers of pieces of worked flint were found in most layers of fill (cuts 3424, 3439, 3486 and 3384). The flint consisted again largely of flakes, but a wide range of other types was also recovered: blades, bladelets, a scale flaked knife, denticulates, a serrated flake, end scrapers and a side scraper, awls, a piercer and a borer, a chisel arrowhead and an arrowhead blank, and a flint sphere.

The small assemblages of animal bone and charred plant remains were also all recovered from upper fills. The animal bone comprised only a single sheep tooth, two horse teeth, and unidentified fragments. The charred plant remains consisted of a few charred cereal grains and hazelnut shells.

The second possible ring ditch (3514) lay only half within the excavated area (Fig. 2.3). As was mentioned above, it would have had an internal diameter of around 38m, and was penannular, with

Fig. 2.25 Section 632 across ring ditch 3032

an entrance 2.3m wide, on the eastern side. A total of 10 sections were cut across it, at intervals of between 12 and 13m.

In all of the sections the profile was Y-shaped or stepped, suggesting that like the other ring ditch, the width has been exaggerated by the collapse of the sides of the ditch. The width varied from just 0.8m to 1.3m (mean = 1.1m), but the ditch was originally probably narrower. The depth of the ditch was again more consistent, varying from 0.5 to 0.65m. In all of the cuts it had a flat base. The fills again consisted either of brown, grey brown or red brown silty clay or of deposits of chalk. Most of the chalk deposits occurred as primary fills, although there were also a few chalk fills higher up the stratigraphic sequence. The other fills also contained varying quantities of chalk.

The quantities of finds recovered from this ring ditch were even smaller than those from 3032. Almost all came from cut 3515 (Fig. 2.3). The finds from this cut included two Roman sherds from the uppermost fill (3516), 20 pieces of worked flint, consisting largely of flakes but including a piercer, a core and a bladelet, a few charred cereal grains and charcoal, and a fragment of an unidentified animal tooth. The flint, charcoal, and charred plant remains were spread throughout the whole sequence of fills. The only other finds were seven pieces of worked flint including a serrated flake and an end scraper from the uppermost fill (3528) in cut 3524, and some unidentified fragments of animal bone and charcoal from the primary fill (3601) in cut 3600.

The later Bronze Age and Iron Age

After the early Bronze Age, there appears to have been a hiatus in activity throughout the rest of the Bronze Age and throughout most, at least, of the Iron Age. The only possible evidence of activity in this period was provided by a feature, either a pit or the end of a ditch (20076), measuring 0.9m wide and 0.45m deep, which was found in the watching brief to the north of the main excavation (Fig. 2.2). This feature contained two small sherds (3g) which may date from the late Bronze Age, although clearly they are insufficient to provide certain evidence for the date of the feature.

ROMAN ACTIVITY

The next phase of activity was marked by the establishment of a field system (Fig. 2.26). The date of the ditches forming this field system cannot be established very precisely. They contained few finds, but what was recovered included Roman and possibly later prehistoric pottery. It seems likely, therefore, that it dated either from the late Iron Age or, more likely, given the quantities of pottery involved, the Roman period.

Sometime after the establishment of the field system, a dispersed series of large pits was cut across the site. Two of them cut ditches which formed part of the field system. Roman pottery, as well as residual prehistoric material, was recovered from the lower fills of several of these pits. The finds from the upper fills included post-medieval

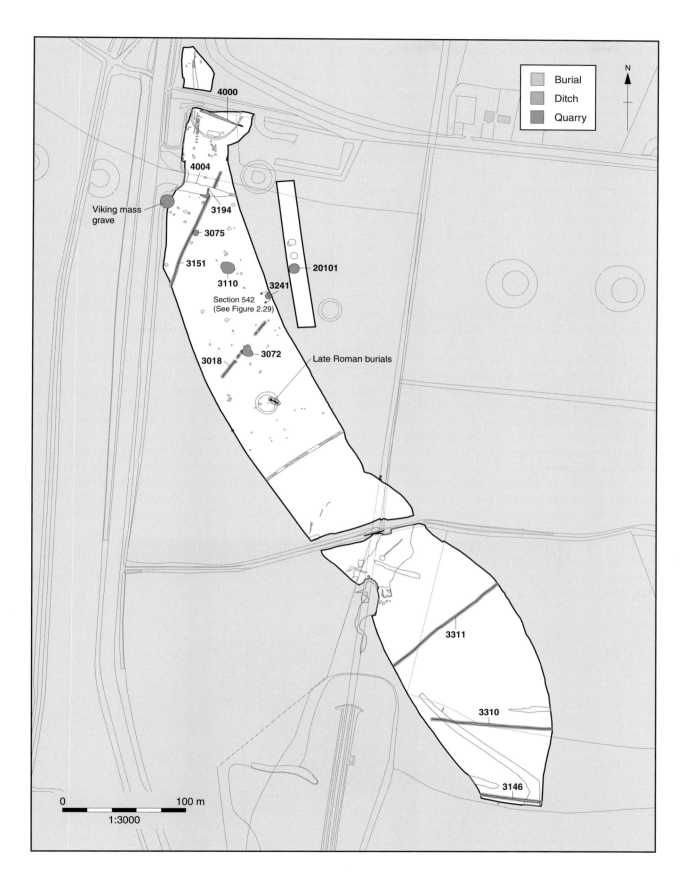

Fig. 2.26 *Plan of late Iron Age or Roman field system, Roman quarry pits, and probably late Roman burials*

material, including fragments of clay pipe. Although the use of these pits remains uncertain, perhaps the most plausible suggestion is that they were chalk quarries. The mass burial, probably of Vikings, which is reported on separately (Loe *et al.* 2014), was contained within the upper part of a quarry pit similar to those described here, which lay just to the east of the site.

Alongside these pits and ditches, which suggest that the site was now used in a more mundane way than it had been in the early Bronze Age, a row of three probably late Roman inhumation burials were inserted within and across the ring ditch near the centre of the site. This suggests that the funerary monuments on the site had some significance for the Romans.

The field system

The field system was defined by at least four ditches (4000, 3151, 3018 and 3311) in the northern half of the site (Fig. 2.26). A further two ditches (3310 and 3146) in the southern part of the site may also have formed part of the system. However, their alignment differed from that of the other ditches and they contained no finds. Their date and relationship with the Roman ditches is, therefore, uncertain.

The Roman ditches appear to have defined a more or less rectilinear system of fields. Since, however, they were clearly aligned with respect to the contours of the site, in plan the system was slightly skewed. The most northerly ditch (4000) extended for 48m and was aligned roughly parallel to the crest of the Ridgeway. The ditches to the south (3151, 3018 and 3311) lay almost at right angles to the first, and ran roughly at right angles to the contours, though their alignments differed slightly as a result of the way in which the hillside sloped. The spacing between the three latter, roughly parallel ditches varied. The first two (3151 and 3018) lay only around 80m apart, but the latter two (3018 and 3311) were separated by a distance of around 280m. The remaining two undated ditches (3310 and 3146), in contrast, lay roughly parallel to the contours.

All but one of the ditches were very shallow features, less than 0.25m deep. They appeared to have suffered from a significant degree of truncation, especially in the case of ditch 3108, only segments of which were preserved. It is possible that the gap at the northern end of ditch 3151 was also the result of truncation, rather than having been an entrance. The ditches were preserved in profile only as more or less irregular bowl-shaped features. Their widths generally averaged only 0.5 to 0.7m. although ditch 4000 reached a maximum width of 2.2m. The one exception to this general pattern was ditch 3311, which was preserved to an average depth of 0.38m and in one place to a depth of 0.94m. Where it was best preserved, it had a steep-sided profile, with either a flat or a V-shaped base.

The two undated ditches to the south (3310 and 3146) were, like most of the Roman ditches, shallow features with more less regular bowl-shaped profiles less than 0.25m deep, but slightly wider than the Roman ditches, at around 1m wide.

Fig. 2.27 Roman quarry pit 3075

Fig. 2.28 Roman quarry pit 3075

Given their shallow depth, it is not surprising that few finds were recovered from the ditches. Ditch 4000 contained no finds and ditch 3018 contained only residual worked flint. Residual flint was also recovered from ditches 3311 and 3151, but these ditches both also contained pottery. This pottery included a small residual Beaker sherd in ditch 3311, but consisted largely of probably later prehistoric and Roman pottery, to which a more precise date cannot be attributed. A Roman *terminus ante quem* for the ditches is provided by the chalk quarry pits described below, one (3072) of which cut ditch 3011 whilst another (3075) cut ditch 3151. The two southern, undated ditches contained no finds.

The Roman chalk quarry pits

A total of six Roman chalk quarry pits were identified within the excavation and watching brief areas. A seventh example, which contained the Viking mass burial, lay immediately to the west of the site (Loe *et al.* 2014). These pits were scattered with little apparent order at intervals of around 40 to 60m across the northern half of the site.

They were all more less irregular circular or oval features (Fig. 2.26). They appear to have been cut without a great deal of attention to their final form or profile, but generally had steep or stepped sides and flattish bases (Figs 2.27-2.29). Their size varied. The largest measured over 12m across and the smallest

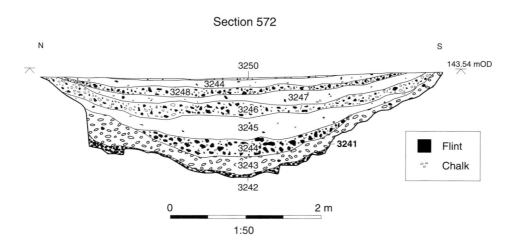

Fig. 2.29 Section of Roman quarry pit 3241

Fig. 2.30 Location of burials within ring ditch 3032. The three Roman inhumation burials lie in a row to the left; the Bronze Age burial in the centre of the ring ditch. (The body to the right marks a natural feature.)

only around 5m, but most were around 7 to 8m in diameter. Their depth was slightly more consistent, generally being around 1.0 to 1.5m deep. They contained more or less complex sequence of fills, which consisted largely of deposits of brown silty clay and white chalk-rich layers, although some more clay-like or more sandy layers were also distinguished.

Given their size, they contained quite small assemblages of finds. The most significant of these for the chronology of the pits were sherds of Roman pottery recovered in quite small quantities, from the lower fills of most of the pits (3072, 3075, 3110 and 3241), if not from the primary fills. Additionally, they produced small quantities of Roman brick or tile, residual flint, animal bone, including horse, cattle, sheep/goat, pig and dog bone, fragments of fish bone, including an eel vertebra and post-temporal fragment, and small quantities of charred grain and charcoal. The uppermost layers of the quarry pits contained a small range of later finds, including clay pipe in pits 3241 and 3110 and glass, indicating that the features survived as hollows until quite recently.

As well as cutting two of the ditches of the probably Roman field system, one of the quarry pits (3194) was cut by what seems to have been a post-medieval trackway (4004).

The Romano-British burials

A row of three probably late Romano-British inhumation burials, aligned end to end, roughly WNW-ESE, was found near the centre of the site

(Fig. 2.30). The western most grave (3540) lay within a ring ditch (3032), the middle burial (3559) just cut the inner edge of the ring ditch, and the third (3358) was cut almost entirely into the fills of the ring ditch.

The graves were all rectangular features, which measured around 2m long and from 0.6 to 0.8m wide, and all were filled with brown silty clay. Their depth, however, varied. The grave (3540) nearest the centre of the ring ditch was just 0.14m deep, the middle grave (3559) 0.32m and the grave across the ring ditch (3358) 1.0m deep (Fig. 2.31). The difference in depth could be accounted for if the barrow associated with the ring ditch was still extant when the graves were cut, grave 3540 having been cut through the tallest part of the barrow and grave 3358 having been dug entirely beyond it. The ring ditch itself had clearly largely silted up by the time the graves 3559 and 3358 were cut.

The two deeper graves (3358 and 3559) had steep sides and flat bases. All that was preserved of the shallower grave (3540) was the bottom of the sides where they curved towards the flat base, and the shape of the original profile is unclear.

Each grave contained a single inhumation burial. The two eastern-most graves both contained women of over 45 years of age in the case of grave 3358 and of 18 to 25 years in the case of grave 3559. Not surprisingly, the skeleton from the shallow grave near the centre of the ring ditch was the least well preserved. The individual was also younger than the others, less than 18 years old, and of indeterminate sex.

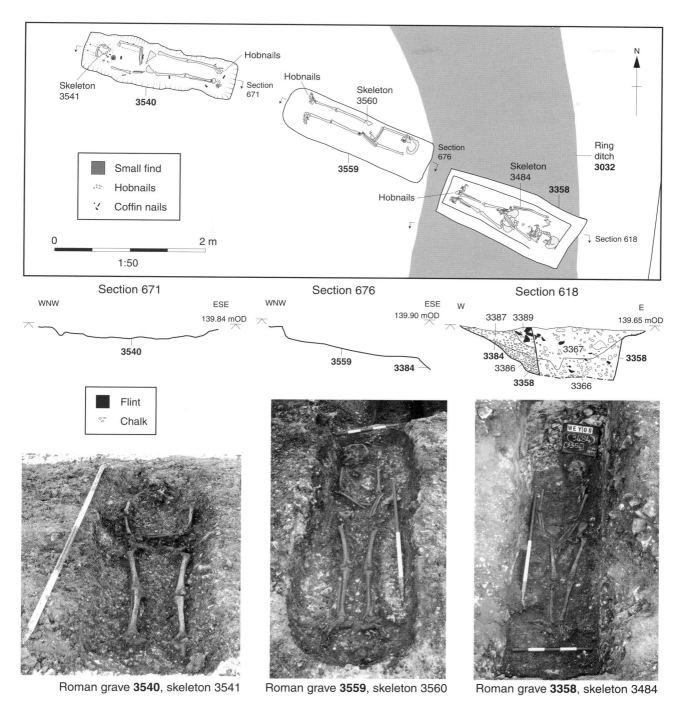

Roman grave **3540**, skeleton 3541 | Roman grave **3559**, skeleton 3560 | Roman grave **3358**, skeleton 3484

Fig. 2.31 The probably late Roman burials associated with ring ditch 3032

All three of the burials were supine. Two lay with their heads to the east, the other (3541 in grave 3540) to the west. Aside from this, there were only slight variations in their postures. In two cases (skeleton 3541 in grave 3540 and skeleton 3484 in grave 3358) the head was resting on its left side; in the other it was resting on the right. The arms generally lay down the sides of the body, but the position of the hands varied slightly, lying on the stomach, pelvis or upper leg. In each case the grave fitted quite neatly around the skeleton.

In each grave hobnails were found close to the feet, suggesting that the shoes or boots of which the nails formed part, were being worn when the individuals were interred. The number of hobnails varied. Graves 3540 and 3559 contained large numbers of hobnails (135 and 97 respectively), but grave 3358 contained only six.

Other nails found in the graves indicated the presence of wooden coffins, and a small fragment of mineralised wood was recovered from grave 3540.

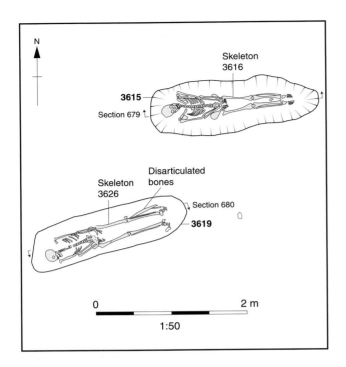

Section 679

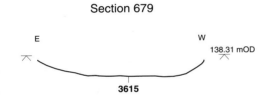

Section 680

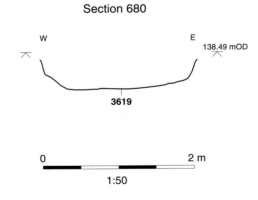

Anglo-Saxon grave 3615, skeleton 3616

Anglo-Saxon grave 3619, skeleton 3626
with disarticulated remains

Anglo-Saxon grave 3619, disarticulated
remains below skeleton 3626

Fig. 2.32 The Anglo-Saxon burials

The number of coffin nails varied only slightly, from 29 in grave 3559 to 36 in grave 3358. The position of the nails gives little clear indication of the forms of the coffins. The nails were found distributed around the skeletons, but clearly, as the coffins decayed, the nails had moved from their original positions.

Few other artefacts were recovered. A small number of tiny fragments of thin copper alloy sheet from an unidentified object were recovered from grave 3559, and an iron spike was recovered from grave 3540. A possibly shaped, small sandstone ball was found in grave 3358, along with a fossilised shark's tooth, but these fossils occur naturally in the chalk and it was, therefore, not necessarily deliberately deposited.

THE ANGLO-SAXON BURIALS

Following the Roman activity, there appears to have been another, shorter hiatus in activity until the 7th or 8th century, when two graves, containing three skeletons, were cut (Fig. 2.32). One of these (3616 in grave 3615) has been radiocarbon dated to cal AD 650-780 (95.4% confidence; SUERC-41556: 1305±25 BP; and 660-770 at 68.2%).

The two graves lay at the northern end of the site, near its western edge (Fig. 2.33), just under 1m apart, one grave (3619) lying to the south-west of the other. Both were oriented close to east-west. The only finds recovered from the graves were a small number of residual flint chips and flakes.

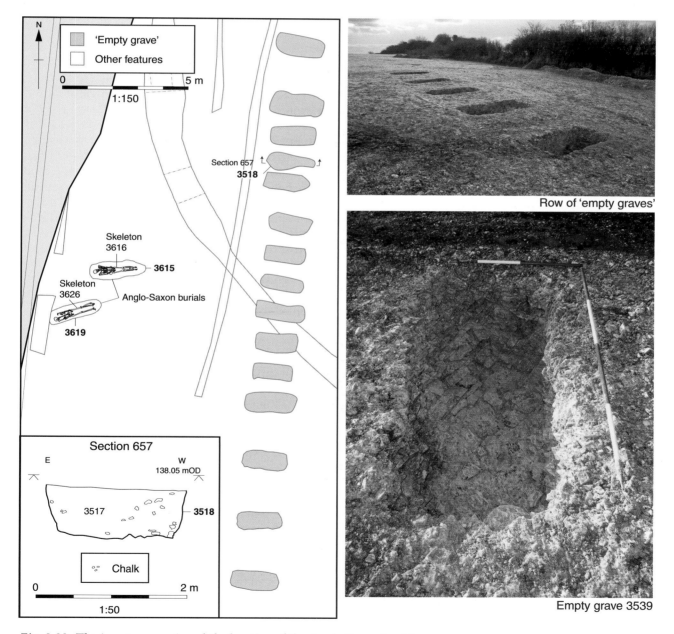

Row of 'empty graves'

Empty grave 3539

Fig. 2.33 The 'empty graves', and the location of the Anglo-Saxon burials

61

The graves were roughly subrectangular in plan, although grave 3615 was rather irregular. In profile the graves differed: grave 3619 had quite steep sides and a flat base, whilst grave 3615 had more gently sloping sides, again with a flat base. The graves were both around 2.2m long, but grave 3619, measuring 0.6m across, was slightly narrower than grave 3615, which was 0.8m wide. Both graves were around 0.3m deep.

Grave 3615 contained a single inhumation burial of a 20-23 year-old male. The skeleton lay supine, with its head to the west. The upper arms lay down the side of the body with the hands meeting on the pelvis.

Grave 3619 contained two individuals. One was a supine inhumation of a 19 year-old male, who lay in a position very similar to skeleton 3615. The fill of the grave contained the disarticulated remains a second older male 45 years or more old. The bones of this second individual were dispersed throughout the fill, some lying above the other skeleton, some below (Fig. 3.32). The bones that lay below the later burial were found mostly on the northern side of the grave; the bones above were scattered mostly around the edges of the grave. The parts of the skeleton were widely spread through the grave, with little indication that they had retained any of their original articulated order. The upper mandible, for example, was found at the eastern end of the grave whilst the lower mandible was at the west. It seems likely, therefore, that the original fill of the grave, including the skeleton, had been mostly removed from the feature, probably when the second burial was interred, although it seems that some of the original deposit was pushed to the north side of the grave. Once the second burial had been placed in the grave, it was backfilled with the original fill, including parts of the first inhumation burial. This scenario seems more likely than the possibility that the disarticulated remains were retrieved from a third grave and then used to backfill the new grave.

THE EMPTY 'GRAVES'

Just under 5m to the east of the Anglo-Saxon burials, a row of 15 rectangular or subrectangular pits was found (Fig. 2.33). These pits contained no finds apart from two flint flakes and a small, unworked fragment of purple slate, and their date and purpose are unknown. Their size and shape are suggestive of graves, but all appear to have been simply backfilled, probably with the material dug from them, quite soon after they had been cut.

The pits were all aligned east-west, and formed a north-south aligned row 23m long. The spacing between the pits varied. At the southern end of the row some of them were nearly 2m apart, but near the northern end, a couple were separated by less then 0.2m. Most of them, however, lay 0.4 to 0.6m apart.

Of the 15 examples, eight were excavated. In profile they all had steep sides and flat bases. Their length and width were quite consistent, the length varying from 1.7 to 2.0m (mean = 1.85m) and the width from 0.65 to 0.9m (mean = 0.75m). The depth, however, was much more varied, ranging from 0.35 to 1.05m (mean = 0.65m). The pits were filled with single deposits of mixed chalk and brown silt, probably a mixture of the soil and chalk which was dug from the pits. There was no indication that a primary fill had begun to form before they were backfilled, suggesting that they were filled soon after they were cut.

POST-MEDIEVAL FEATURES

A range of post-medieval features were found, scattered predominantly in the southern part of the site. The most striking of these was the remains of a small building which lay just upslope of a ventilation shaft for the railway tunnel (Figs 2.34-2.35). Near the building, the remains of a post-medieval drain and a large pit were found. The remaining features consist of probable trackways and wheel ruts (Fig. 2.26). One of these trackways (3266, 3610 and 3612) ran east-west, 130m to the north of the building. The second (4004) also ran roughly east-west, but lay near the northern end of the site. The final example (20008) ran north-south, within the watching brief area to the north of the site.

The post-medieval building, drain and quarry

The building had been constructed on a terrace cut into the chalk hillside, which sloped upwards to the east. Although it had been largely demolished, the eastern and southern sides were better preserved, up to a height of 1.2m, where they had been protected by the slope of the hill, than the western side. The northern side had been removed entirely. The structure was rectangular, measuring 6.9m east-west, in which direction the whole width of the structure was preserved, and over 7.0m north-south. There was a doorway, 1.34m wide through the western wall. The walls were of roughly coursed, crudely squared chalk and limestone blocks, bonded with a sandy mortar. The internal faces of the walls were rendered. A compact deposit of black ashy silt and charcoal (3402) had been used to form the floor, or the base of the floor. Within the building, on the east and southern walls, small rectangular structures (3412 and 3413) made of limestone and chalk blocks and unfrogged brick extended from, and were bonded into, the walls. The eastern example (3412) extended 0.65m from the wall, was 1.25m wide, and was preserved to a height of 0.36m. The southern example (3413) extended 1.7m from the wall, was 1.7m wide, and was preserved to a height of 0.7m. The bricks at the top of this structure appeared to form a flue, which extended through the wall. The bricks forming this flue were covered in soot. The building was covered with a layer of chalk, tile and mortar rubble, mixed with ash and grey silt, up to 1m thick, which presumably derived from the building's demolition. A further deposit of demolition debris was found to the south-east of the building.

The building was associated with a range of iron objects, which included nails, bolts, spikes, clamps, punches or chisels, fragments of a bar, of sheets and plates, and a coal shovel blade. The only remaining finds were fragments of roof tile and a rib from a medium-sized mammal. Although the exact use of the metal items remains obscure, along with the flue, they suggest that the building may have had a light industrial role, perhaps connected to the construction of the railway.

What appears to have been a sump (3570) connected to a drainage channel was found 23m to the north of the building. The sump consisted of an oval pit, 3.8 by 4.1m across and 0.8m deep, with a bowl-shaped profile. The channel extended for 20m to the north-east. It contained no finds. Although the date of this feature is, therefore, uncertain, its location suggests that it may have been related to the building.

Thirteen metres to the west of the sump lay an irregular pit (3568), up to 5m across. It was filled with orange-brown clay loam, and contained a 19th- or 20th-century table knife with a bone handle and a corroded whittle tang blade.

The post-medieval trackways

Three post-medieval trackways ran across the site (Fig. 2.3). The most southerly example (3266=3610= 3612) ran SW-NE across the southern part of the site, around 100m to the north of the building. It consisted of a linear hollow, around 2.6m wide, the

Fig. 2.34 Post-medieval building 3400

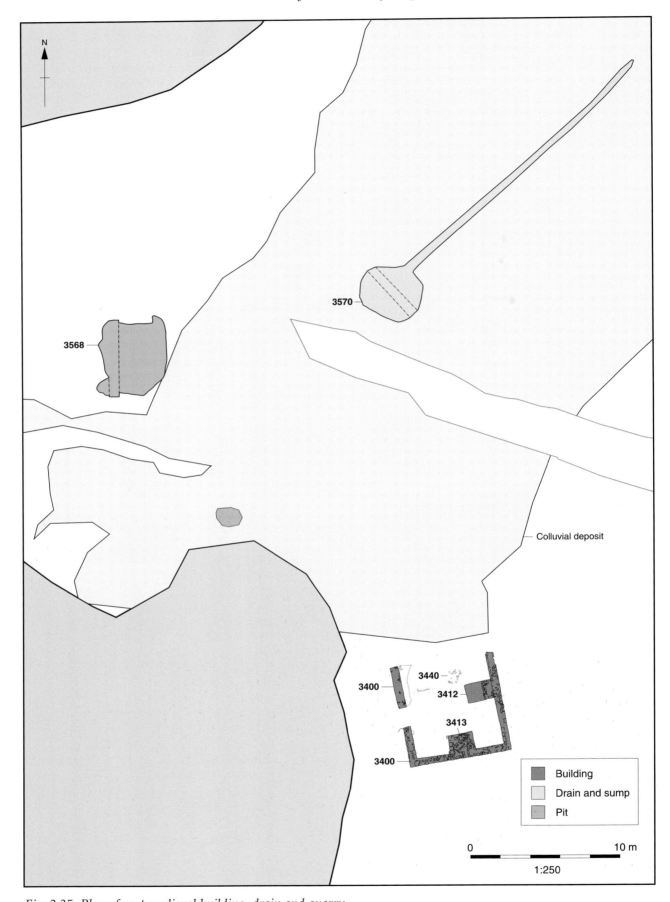

Fig. 2.35 Plan of post-medieval building, drain and quarry

Fig. 2.36 Post-medieval trackway 3266

edges of which were marked by ruts up to 0.25m deep (Fig. 2.36). At certain points the feature had been truncated so that only the deeper ruts on either side survived. It was filled with varying deposits of grey, yellow or red brown silty clay, which contained no finds.

Near the northern end of the excavation, the second trackway (4004) ran roughly east-west across the site. It cut across a Roman quarry pit (3194) and one of the ditches (3151) which formed part of the probably Roman field system. It again consisted of a shallow, linear hollow, up to 9.4m wide and 0.45m deep, which was cut by ruts. At the eastern end, these deeper ruts were all that survived of the feature. The ruts were around 1.3m apart, and ranged in width from 0.35 to 0.65m and in depth from 0.1 to 0.4m. The trackway was filled with compact silt and chalk deposits, and contained a small range of finds, including a fragments of clay pipe, of post-medieval brick or tile and of iron, which suggest that it was of quite recent date. Two residual flint flakes were also recovered from it.

The third trackway (20008) ran north-south, for a distance of around 30m, petering out to the north, in the watching brief area to the north of the excavation. It also consisted of a linear hollow, up to 3.3m wide, which was cut by wheel ruts. At the northern end, the hollow petered out, leaving only the three ruts, which in turn, had been truncated away only a few metres further to the north. Unlike the other trackways, this example had been paved with a layer of siltstone slabs. These stone slabs had been laid after the trackway had already begun to silt up. They lay immediately above a layer of crushed chalk, which in turn lay above two layers of brown silt. The stone slabs were covered by a layer of darker brown clayey silt. The only find recovered from this trackway was a sherd of yellow-glazed post-medieval pot.

UNDATED AND NATURAL FEATURES

A large number of probably natural features were found, scattered widely across the excavation and watching brief areas. It was not always easy to distinguish between these natural features and anthropogenic features. A small number of features which appear more likely to have been anthropogenic, but for which no there was no dating evidence, were also found.

Many of the natural features consisted of hollows and fissures in the chalk. Such features were scattered quite widely across the site. One example (3225), an irregular 'channel' near to Beaker grave 3227 (Set 9) at the northern end of the site, contained an iron nail and bone from a 7-8 year old child which may have derived from a disturbed Beaker burial. No finds were recovered from the other examples.

A total of 29 features were identified as tree-throw holes. Although these features were scattered widely over the northern half of the site, in the same broad area as the Neolithic and late Neolithic/early Bronze Age features, none of them contained any finds, and their date is unknown.

The undated features were eight possible pits, and three possible postholes. The only finds recovered from these features were a flint blade and a flake from a possible posthole, an isolated feature which lay to the east of Roman quarry pit 3072, and a few fragments of animal bone from a wide, shallow pit, measuring 3m across and 0.2m deep, found in the watching brief area to the west of the site.

Chapter 3: The Finds from Ridgeway Hill

PREHISTORIC POTTERY
by Lisa Brown

Introduction

A total of 554 sherds (2742g) of earlier prehistoric pottery was recovered from the excavation at Ridgeway Hill. An additional 99 sherds (547g) of this date, most from pit 20063, were found during the watching brief. The assemblage dates from the early Neolithic period to the early Bronze Age, with the exception of half a dozen sherds of possible Iron Age date. Almost all of the early Neolithic material came from pit 20063. The period best represented is the early Bronze Age, and includes three substantially complete Beakers and a Food Vessel associated with graves.

Methodology

The pottery was recorded on an Access Database. Fabrics were identified with the aid of a hand lens and binocular microscope at 20x and 10x magnification, and classified using an alpha-numeric dominant inclusion code, further subdivided on size and frequency of inclusions, following the recommended guidelines of the Prehistoric Ceramics Research Group (PCRG 1997).

All sherds were counted and weighed by rim, body and basal fragments within each context. The following characteristics were recorded: fabric, form, surface treatment, decoration, degree of abrasion, type and position of residue and date. Abrasion was classified as (3) high-surface survival minimum, breaks heavily eroded; (2) moderate – surface somewhat preserved but clearly worn; (1) slight – little indication of wear apparent.

Of the 573 contexts yielding prehistoric pottery, some 214 (37%) produced only one sherd, and 234 (77%) produced up to five sherds. This allowed little scope for statistical analysis of stylistic or fabric progression, so selection for illustration focussed on reflecting the typological range rather than a chronological ceramic sequence. Key feature assemblages are highlighted where possible in the illustrated catalogue, but these generally include few diagnostic sherds.

Condition

The condition of the assemblage from the main excavation is variable, in part reflecting the good preservation of the funerary vessels. Even so, the average sherd weight for this group is only 5g and almost 40% of sherds are highly abraded. The condition of the pottery from the watching brief is generally poor. The assemblage has an average sherd weight of only 5.5g and almost half of the material was highly abraded (factor 3).

Fabrics

The earlier prehistoric pottery range includes 15 individual fabrics within six ware groups, defined on the basis of principal inclusions (Table 3.1).

F Predominantly flint temper

F1 – Fine smooth clay with a slightly soapy fill containing sparse, ill-assorted calcined white and grey flint pieces mostly < 4mm. Typically a middle Neolithic fabric.

F2 – Fine sandy clay incorporating moderate, ill-assorted very coarse calcined flint pieces up to 5mm in size. Typically a middle Neolithic fabric.

F3 – Fine sandy, slightly micaceous fabric with rare white chips of flint <2mm. Single sherd (1g). May be later prehistoric.

Table 3.1 Quantification of prehistoric pottery fabrics

Fabric	No. Sherds	Weight (g)
F1	13	31
F2	3	36
F3	1	1
G1	13	14
G2	82	43
G3	313	1816
G4	94	776
O1	1	5
Q1	7	5
SH1	9	5
SH2	12	40
SH3	4	4
SH4	16	56
SH5	68	395
V1	17	19

V Vesicular fabric

V1 – Fine smooth or slightly sandy fabric with abundant vesicules representing leached shell and/or small limestone pieces. Middle Neolithic and early Bronze Age.

G Predominantly grog temper

G1 – Soapy fabric containing sparse-moderate inclusions of grey and red grog and rare small chips of flint 1-2mm in size. Typically an early Bronze Age fabric.

G2 – Fine sandy fabric incorporating sparse-moderate grey and red grog pieces and rare small limestone pieces <3mm in size. Typically an early Bronze Age fabric.

G3 – Fine soapy fabric with small inclusions of grey and red grog, no additional inclusions visible. Exclusively an early Bronze Age fabric.

G4 – Soapy fabric incorporating a moderate quantity of coarse grog inclusions 2-5mm in size, along with rare small limestone fragments. Exclusively an early Bronze Age fabric.

SH Predominantly fossil shell temper

SH1 – Fine sandy fabric containing rare rounded quartz pieces and rare small chips of fossil shell. Late Neolithic fabric.

SH2 – Fine to medium sandy clay with a moderate quantity of fossil shell pieces 1-2mm in size. Early and late Neolithic fabric.

SH3 – Clay incorporating medium grade rounded quartz sand and abundant quantities of small crushed fossil shell pieces, and rare ooliths. Late Neolithic fabric.

SH4 – Soapy fabric with sparse fine shell and red and grey grog. Early Neolithic fabric.

SH5 – Slightly micaceous, very finely sanded fabric, somewhat soapy feel, incorporating moderate to common very coarse shell, when leached has an overall 'corky' appearance. Early Neolithic fabric.

O Predominantly oolite temper

O1 – Medium grade rounded translucent quartz sand fabric with abundant ovoid vesicules representing leached oolites, rare fragments of calcined flint up to 4mm. Early Neolithic fabric.

Q Predominantly quartz sand

Q1 – Medium grade sandy, slightly micaceous fabric, silver mica, incorporating rounded quartz, rare black ferrous pellets, sparse to moderate small calcite inclusions (<2mm), some probably 'beef' calcite, and angular black mineral (rock). May be later prehistoric, probably late Bronze Age or Iron Age.

The absence of exotic components amongst the rather restricted range of raw materials identified amongst the Ridgeway Hill prehistoric fabrics indicates local or near-local production. All the required materials could have been procured within a short distance of the site. The naturally occurring inclusions of fossil shell (including oolite) are components of the Jurassic formations that outcrop immediately to the south at Southdown Ridge, which is itself made up of a band of Corallian Limestone. The Kimmeridge and the porous Oxford Clays, both fossil-bearing, good quality potting clays, lie immediately to hand to the south of Ridgeway Hill. The Purbeck Beds, and specifically those in the Poxwell district east of Weymouth, may have been the source of the minor beef calcite component of the assemblage (Brown 1991, 186). The flint inclusions in the (mostly Neolithic) flint-tempered fabrics no doubt derived from flint bands within the Cretaceous Upper Chalk of the Ridgeway crossing south of Dorchester.

Neolithic

Early Neolithic

The only early Neolithic pottery from the site came from pit 20063 in the Watching Brief to the north of the main site. Some 97 sherds (502g) were recovered, about 80% of them from a lower fill (20066). Most of the sherds are in shell-tempered fabrics, predominantly SH5, and eight sherds in vesicular ware V1 had no doubt incorporated shell, subsequently leached. A single oolitic-tempered body sherd and a tiny (1g) flint-tempered (F1) sherd were also present.

Over 40 of the sherds in 'corky' fabric SH5 appear to belong to a single fragmented Plain Bowl vessel scattered within fills 20064 and 20066. The pot was unreconstructable, apart from the rim, due to the 'shredded' quality of the sherds (Fig. 3.1, no. 1). Charred organic residue adhering to the outer surface suggested that it had been used for cooking. Five other vessels, all probably Plain Bowls, three in fabric SH5, one in SH4 and another in SH2, were found in fill 20066 (Fig. 3.1, nos 2-6). These were represented only by very small sherds or sherd groups, none amounting to more than 80g in weight, and so further distinction within the broad 'Plain Bowl' category was not possible. Pottery of a similar date has been recovered from the Dorchester area, including the long barrow at Allington Avenue (Davies *et al.* 2002) and from a group of pits at Flagstones (Smith *et al.* 1997).

Middle Neolithic

Only 32 sherds (77g) of pottery was classified as middle Neolithic. Most of this material came from three pits (3041, 3091 and 3330), the remainder was residual in later features. The best preserved decorated sherds are Peterborough Ware, but the very fragmentary nature of this material precluded assigning it to substyles within this broad tradition.

Pit 3041 produced two sherds (8g), including a rim of Peterborough Ware in fabric F1 in a very abraded condition (Fig. 3.1, 7). Pit 3091 was more productive, yielding 10 abraded sherds (39g). Six grog-tempered sherds and a single sherd in fabric

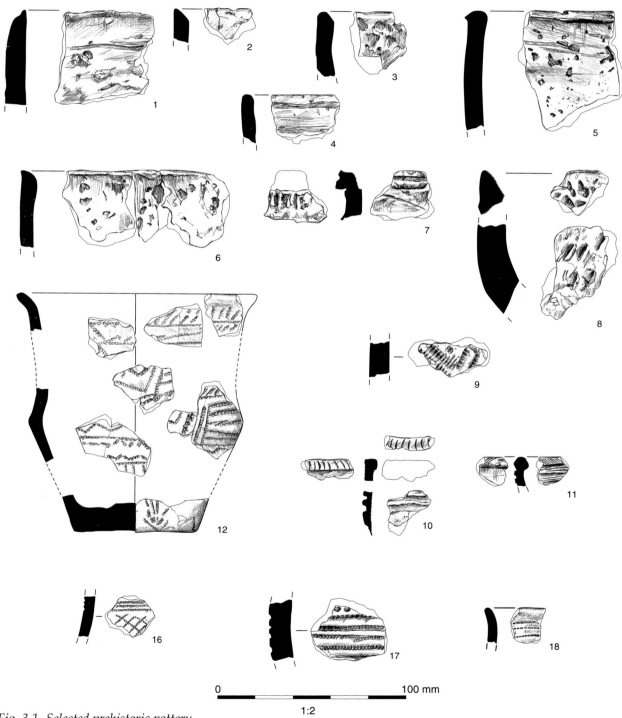

Fig. 3.1 *Selected prehistoric pottery*

F1 are undecorated, but a small rim fragment (6g) in F2 decorated with bird bone impressions and two fingernail-impressed sherds (30g) in the same fabric probably belonged to a single thick-walled vessel (Fig. 3.1, no. 8).

The pottery from pit 3330, six joining sherds in fabric V1, weighing only 5g, is so fragmentary that it could not be precisely dated. Also, the pit was a different shape and depth to the other two, but a radiocarbon determination of 3090-2900 cal BC places the fill, if not the pottery, in the middle Neolithic period.

Fill 3183 of Roman chalk quarry pit 3072 contained eight sherds (16g) of Peterborough Ware in fabric F1. Two joining sherds bear faint traces of narrow wedge-shaped impressions (Fig. 3.1, no. 9). A single 4g, undecorated sherd from fill 3263 of ring ditch 4042 is in the same fabric. Two small fragments in fabric V1 and one in F1 from the fill an early Bronze Age inhumation burial may be residual Peterborough ware sherds, but they are small fragments together weighing 3g and could not be precisely classified.

Late Neolithic

Just 22 sherds (17g) of pottery could be confidently dated to the late Neolithic period. All are in shell-tempered fabrics, and several fragments belong to Grooved Ware vessels. The pottery was recovered from three pits: 3372 and 3373 (in Set 2a) and 3256. The Grooved Ware vessel from pit 3373 was represented by eight small, abraded fragments (4g) in fabric SH1, with a fingernail-impressed rim (Fig. 3.1, no. 10). Pit 3372 yielded nine small sherds (9g), including a sherd in SH2 with a slashed rim (Fig. 3.1, no. 11).

Bronze Age

Early Bronze Age

A total of 496 sherds weighing 2647g of early Bronze Age pottery was identified. All are in grog-tempered fabrics G1-G4, the majority in the relatively fine variety, G3. Sherds representing 14 individual vessels were classifiable, of which 13 are Beakers and one a Food Vessel.

Pottery from burials

Four vessels, placed as grave goods, are complete or nearly complete.

A fragmented Beaker (66 sherds/126g) in fabric G3 was recovered from the fill of Set 5 cist grave 3038 (context 3040). The vessel was probably a grave offering, although no human bone survived (and therefore no radiocarbon date is available). Although incomplete, the profile was recon-

13

0   100 mm

1:2

Fig. 3.2 The Beaker from grave 3315

structable. The size of this Beaker is such that it can be easily held in an adult hand, marking it out from the other burial pots out as a very 'individualised' vessel. The shape corresponds to the British Low-Carinated Beaker type (Needham 2005, 183-8), decorated with a complex, somewhat chaotically arranged, comb-stamped pattern, covering the entire surviving surface (Fig. 3.1, no.12). Beakers of broadly similar low-carinated type found at British sites in Wiltshire, Hampshire and Oxfordshire are associated with human bone radiocarbon dated to as early as 2500 cal BC (Needham 2005, 185).

The near complete Beaker accompanying the primary inhumation burial of a female in Set 9 Grave 3315 (context 3317/3318; SF10024) most closely resembles the rather heterogenous group of Weak-Carinated Beakers (Needham 2005, 188-91). Recovered in 94 fragments (776g), it was made from a coarse grog and limestone-tempered fabric (G4), unique to this vessel. The Beaker is decorated with quite crudely executed incised triangles, infilled with diagonal and vertical lines (Fig. 3.2., no. 13). The quality of the surface finish is relatively poor, and the wall thickness greater than that of the other Beakers. The pot lay at the feet of the skeleton, and an awl close to the head. The skeleton produced a radiocarbon date of 2140-1970 cal BC (modelled). Other radiocarbon dated examples of British Weak-Carinated Beakers focus on a date range of 2200-1900 cal BC (Needham 2005, 189), easily accommodating this vessel.

The primary inhumation burial (skeleton 3334) of three in Set 7 Grave 3227 was a male adult accompanied by a Long-Necked Beaker (SF 10327; Fig. 3.3, no. 14). The Beaker is complete but broken into 113 sherds (855g). It is 220mm high, very well made, in fabric G3, with a thin wall, highly smoothed surface, with complex zoned decoration of parallel, comb-impressed lax chevron tracks infilled with carefully spaced fingernail impressions. The motif is stretched over the entire profile. A radiocarbon date of 2200-2020 cal BC (modelled) was obtained from the skeleton. This date corresponds well to an observed pattern of use of Long-Necked beakers in burial contexts starting during, or slightly before, the 22nd century BC at other British sites (Needham 2005, 195-8). Both the radiocarbon date and the complex decorative scheme indicate that the Ridgeway Hill vessel belongs to the earlier rather than later end of the Long-Necked Beaker tradition, the latter more typically associated with rusticated and/or non-combed stamped motifs.

Grave 3147 (Set 6) produced the only certain example of a Food Vessel from the site (SF 101600; Fig. 3.4, no. 15). It is almost complete, in 58 sherds

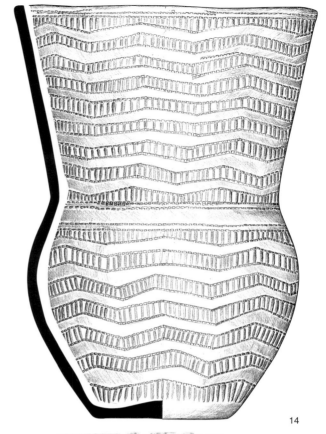

14

Fig. 3.3 The Beaker from grave 3227

0   100 mm

1:2

71

(706g). The fabric is similar to G3, the most common of the grog-tempered wares, but very poorly fired. The form is a little unusual for a Food Vessel, with a simple, unexpanded flat rim and a hollowing just below the rim. Rusticated decoration covers all but the curve at the base, and was executed quite precisely by pinching up the clay between thumb and forefinger. The vessel lay behind the head of the primary burial of this grave, skeleton 3520, which produced a date of 2200-2030 cal BC (unmodelled), 2150-1970 cal BC (modelled). The use of Food Vessels as grave offerings is known elsewhere in the Weymouth region, including to the northeast of Ridgeway Hill at bowl barrow sites at Bincombe (Best 1965, 103; Calkin and Putnam 1970).

Boast (1995, 78) has commented that a lower investment of effort in the fabric of burial Beakers, with a corresponding higher investment of finish and decorative embellishment, have been observed in many cases. However, the Ridgeway Hill Beakers do not fit this model particularly well. The Long-Necked Beaker from Grave 3227, in the finest of the grog-tempered fabrics, has extremely well finished surfaces and complex and painstakingly applied decoration. The small, hand-sized Beaker from Grave 3038 is in the same fabric, the pattern complex but rather carelessly executed. By contrast, the Beaker from Grave 3315 was produced in the coarsest of fabrics (G4), thick-walled, the surface poorly finished, and the decoration rather crude.

Other early Bronze Age pottery

Several other small fragments of early Bronze Age pottery, all probably from Beakers, were recovered from Set 3 pits 3506, 3508 and 3544. All are in fabric G3, suggesting they were contemporary and produced at the same location.

Only pit 3544 had an associated radiocarbon date (2840-2470 cal BC unmodelled). A single 3g body sherd (SF 10231) decorated with a comb-impressed lattice design was recovered from fill 3543 (Fig. 3.1, no. 16). Pit 3506 produced a single Beaker body

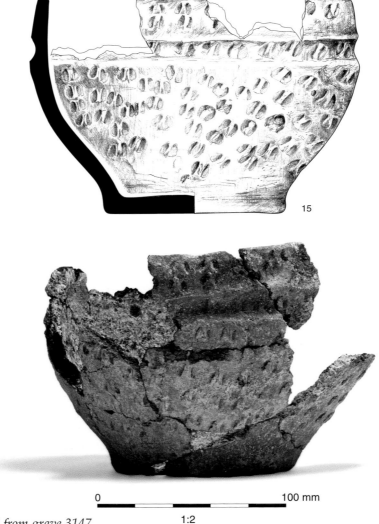

Fig. 3.4 The Food Vessel from grave 3147

15

0   100 mm

1:2

sherd (13g) decorated with deep comb-impressed decoration running in close horizontal rows (Fig. 3.1, no. 17). Fill 3507 of pit 3508 contained 35 tiny, abraded sherds (28g), some recovered from sieving. These included two comb-impressed sherds (Fig. 3.1, no. 18) and a 1g fragment that had faint traces of cord impressions.

The fill of a Roman grave (3544) cut into Bronze Age ring ditch 3032 yielded a 1g sherd of fingernail rusticated Beaker or Food Vessel, also in Fabric G3. This fragment no doubt derived from the early Bronze Age activity associated with the barrow.

Later prehistoric

The pottery evidence indicates an absence, or near absence of later Bronze Age and Iron Age activity on the site. A poorly defined feature (20076) located in the watching brief to the north of the main excavation contained two small oxidised sherds (3g), the only pottery in fabric Q1, a sandy clay incorporating beef calcite. Another five sherds (3g) in this fabric were recovered from the fill of late Roman burial 3358 in the main excavation area. The fibrous 'beef' calcite is a common product of burial diagenesis of organic-rich shales that contain calcium carbonite, and easily attributable to clays local to Weymouth.

Fabrics containing beef calcite formed a small proportion of the early Neolithic pottery assemblage from Maiden Castle (Cleal 1991, 173). However, this mineral was also identified in significant proportions of Iron Age grog-tempered and limestone-tempered wares from the site, with Poxwell, east of Weymouth proposed as a likely source (Brown 1991, 186). Bearing in mind that none of the early Neolithic fabrics from Ridgeway Hill contained beef calcite, but that it was identified in several of the Iron Age fabrics from Southdown Ridge and in late burial 3358, the pottery in this fabric is more likely to be Iron Age than earlier prehistoric.

Illustrated catalogue

Fig. 3.1

1. Early Neolithic Plain Bowl. Fabric SH5. Pit 20063 (20064/20066)
2. Early Neolithic Plain Bowl. Fabric SH4. Pit 20063 (20066)
3. Early Neolithic Plain Bowl. Fabric SH5. Pit 20063 (20066)
4. Early Neolithic Plain Bowl. Fabric SH5. Pit 20063 (20066)
5. Early Neolithic Plain Bowl. Fabric SH5. Pit 20063 (20066)
6. Early Neolithic Plain Bowl. Fabric SH2. Pit 20063 (20066)
7. Peterborough Ware rim. Fabric F1. Pit 3041 (3043)
8. Middle Neolithic thick-walled vessel decorated with

bird bone and fingernail impressions. Fabric F2. Pit 3091 (3090)
9. Peterborough Ware fragment decorated with wedge-shaped impressions. Fabric F1. Quarry 3072 (3183)
10. Grooved Ware rim with fingernail-impressed decoration. Fabric SH1. Pit 3373 (3431)
11. Grooved Ware rim with slashed decoration. Fabric SH2. Pit 3372 (3443)
12. Low-Carinated Beaker with comb-impressed decoration. Fabric G3. Cist grave 3038 (3040)
16. Beaker fragment with comb-impressed decoration. Fabric G3. Pit 3544 (3543)
17. Beaker fragment with comb-impressed decoration. Fabric G3. Pit 3506 (3505)
18. Beaker rim with comb-impressed decoration. Fabric G3. Pit 3508 (3507)

Fig. 3.2

13. Weak-Carinated Beaker decorated with incised triangles. Fabric G4. Grave 3315 (3317/3318)

Fig. 3.3

14. Well finished Long-Necked Beaker with complex zoned decoration. Fabric G3. Grave 3227 (3261)

Fig. 3.4

15. Food Vessel with rusticated decoration. Fabric G3. Grave 3147 (3519)

IRON AGE AND ROMAN POTTERY
by Edward Biddulph and Lisa Brown

Introduction

Only 176 sherds (826g) of Iron Age and Roman pottery were recovered. The assemblage was recorded using standard OA methods (Booth nd), and quantified by sherd count, weight, minimum number of vessels based on rim count (MV) and estimated vessel equivalents (EVE), which record the percentage of rim circumference that survives (Table 3.2).

The assemblage spans the Iron Age to late Roman period. Many context groups could not be dated precisely within this range, but an emphasis on the Iron Age and early Roman periods was clear. The condition of the pottery was generally poor, most sherds very fragmentary and abraded, consistent with deposition in quarry and barrow deposits.

Assemblage composition

The eight body sherds of shelly ware (E40; Southdown Ridge equivalent SH) are likely to have belonged to vessels produced during the Iron Age. The fabric is a uniform handmade ware, oxidised externally and with a black or dark grey interior surface. At Tolpuddle Ball, some 25km north of Weymouth, all occurrences of shelly ware in an assemblage spanning the Iron Age and Roman period were dated to the early Iron Age, although

Table 3.2 *Quantification of Iron Age, Roman and post-medieval pottery*

Ware	Sherds	Weight (g)	MV	EVE
B11 – Dorset black-burnished ware	142	513	10	0.63
E20 – Iron Age fine sand-tempered ware	2	6		
E40 – Iron Age shelly ware	8	15		
F51 – Oxford red colour-coated ware	1	11	1	0.04
F53 – New Forest colour-coated ware	1a	1	6	
O10 – Fine oxidised ware	2	45		
O20 – Sandy oxidised ware	6	22		
R30 – Medium sandy grey ware	1	2		
S20 – South Gaulish samian ware	1	3		
S30 – Central Gaulish samian ware	2	2		
Z30 – Post-medieval wares	10	201		
Total	176	826	11	0.67

Table 3.3 *Pattern of Roman pottery deposition*
MSW = mean sherd weight (weight/no. sherds)

Feature	Sherds	Weight (g)	MSW
Quarry	76	327	4
Barrow ditch	60	171	3
Pit	9	44	5
Layer	8	166	21
Ditch	8	42	5
Burial cremation	6	9	2
Burial inhumation	5	25	5
Natural feature	2	33	17
Posthole	1	2	2
Building	1	7	7
Total	176	826	71

there the fabrics were entirely unoxidised (Laidlaw 1999, 115). At Maiden Castle similar quantities of Jurassic shell-tempered wares were present in all phases of activity, typically forming 3% to 8% of each phase group, from the early Iron Age to the early 1st century AD, although some proportion was undoubtedly residual (Brown 1991, 188; table 66).

Nonetheless, in common with most Iron Age pottery assemblages from sites in the Dorset region, the Ridgeway Hill late Iron Age and Roman group was dominated by distinctive sandy wares with a source in the Wareham-Poole Harbour area of Dorset, confirmed by a tourmaline rich heavy mineral suite (Williams 1977) and by kiln evidence (Hearne and Smith 1991). Within the Iron Age pottery assemblage from Southdown Ridge this fabric is classed as QU1. The range produced at the Wareham-Poole Harbour production site during the Roman period is commonly referred to as South-East Dorset Black-burnished ware 1, registered by Tomber and Dore (1998) as DOR BB 1, and here classified as fabric B11. This category is quite general, encompassing a range of hard, reduced fabrics that contained abundant well sorted quartz. As the fabric had a long history (Laidlaw 1999, 117), sherds lacking such diagnostic elements as rim and decoration cannot be dated more closely than Iron Age or Roman. Nonetheless, the few classifiable forms were probably all deposited during the Roman period.

A bead-rimmed jar and a cooking jar with an everted, almost upright, rim dated fill 3183 of quarry 3072 to the mid-late 1st century AD. A beaker or small cooking pot is likely to belong to the later 1st or 2nd century, and a straight-sided bowl with flanged rim (Gillam 1976, 70; 73) from fill 3117 of quarry 3110 is a type probably exclusively confined to the 2nd century. Bowls with dropped flanges date to the late Roman period.

Roman-period pottery other than Black-burnished ware was poorly represented. Indeed, the fabric with the most occurrences (sandy oxidised ware O20) is likely to be an oxidised version of fabric B11 (Table 3.2). The remaining pottery does, however, support the view that activity in the area continued to some extent throughout the Roman period. A body sherd in South Gaulish samian ware (S20) was from a Drag. 27 cup imported during the later 1st or very early 2nd century. A possible sherd of Central Gaulish samian ware (S30) arrived during the 2nd century. The New Forest (F53) and Oxford (F51) colour-coated wares date to the late Roman period (AD 250-400), and the sherd in fabric F51 is a rim from a bead-rimmed dish or hemispherical bowl (Young 1977, type C45 or C55), dated to c 240-400.

Spout fragments from two funnels, one recovered from fill 3397 of ring ditch 3032, the other from fill 3549 of quarry 3110, are of particular interest (Fig. 3.5). Both are in fairly fine oxidised wares, but the fabrics are not identical. Funnels were generally rare in the province, although widespread. They were not chronologically specific, and so no precise dating for the pieces here can be offered.

Deposition

Most of the pottery was recovered from quarry and barrow-ditch deposits (Table 3.3). It is not unusual to find deliberately selected Roman pottery in significant prehistoric monuments, like barrows, as, for example, at Ascott-Under-Wychwood (Biddulph *et al.* 2007), but such selection cannot be clearly demonstrated in this case. Accompanying mean sherd

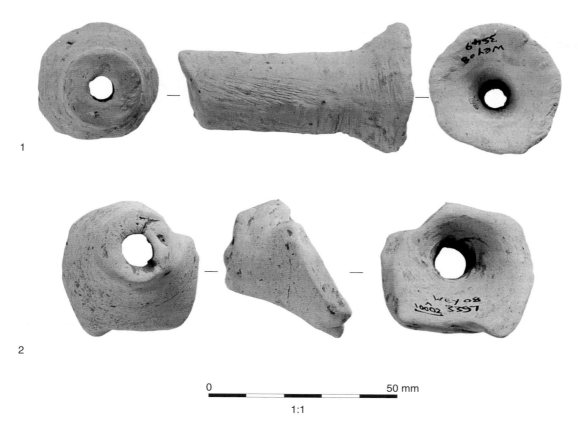

Fig. 3.5 Roman ceramic funnels

weights indicate that the pottery consisted of very small fragments, which were uniformly distributed across all features. This uniformity suggests that the pottery had been subject to a similar sequence of discard and disturbance before final deposition. The small amount of pottery from layers and natural features suggests that here too pottery deposition was incidental to the process of filling.

Illustrated catalogue (Fig. 3.5)

1. Funnel spout. Fabric O10. Ring ditch 3032 (3397)
2. Funnel spout. Fabric O10. Quarry 3110 (3549)

WORKED FLINT AND CHERT
by Michael Donnelly

Introduction

A total of 1475 flints was recovered from the excavations, and a further 583 pieces from the watching briefs (including the Viking mass burial pit; Table 3.4). Most of the chipped stone originated from pits, burials and ring ditches of Neolithic or Bronze Age date and were probably contemporary with these features. Several later features including the Roman quarry pits also contained large residual assemblages.

Methodology

The artefacts were catalogued according to OA South's standard system of broad artefact/debitage type (Bradley 1997). Additional information on the condition (rolled, abraded, fresh and degree of cortication) and state of the artefacts (burnt, broken, or visibly utilised) was also recorded. Retouched pieces were classified according to standard morphological descriptions (eg Bamford 1985, 72-77; Healy 1988, 48-9; Bradley 1997). Metrical and technological attribute analysis of butt type (Inizan *et al.* 1993), termination type, flake type (Harding 1990) and hammer mode (Onhuma and Bergman 1982) was undertaken, and the presence of platform edge abrasion and dorsal blade scars was recorded. Metrical analysis was undertaken using standard methods for recording length, breadth and thickness (Saville 1980).

Primary technology

Overall the assemblage is flake-based. The cores largely display flake scars. Many of the flake cores have multiple platforms. Despite the scarcity of blade cores, blade forms made up 18% of the blanks (including some quite long examples, up to 75mm). Narrow bladelets (<12mm wide), perhaps failed removals from a blade-based industry rather than

Table 3.4 The flint assemblage

Category type	Relief road excavation	Watching briefs	Total
Flake	908	309	1217
Blade	47	51	98
Bladelet	35	27	62
Blade-like	77	35	106
Irregular waste	56	26	82
Chip	2		2
Sieved chips 10-4mm	128	21	149
Sieved chips 4-2mm	92	19	111
Rejuvenation flake core face/edge	3		3
Rejuvenation flake core tablet		1	1
Crested blade or flake	3	4	7
Core opposed platform blades	2		2
Core single platform flake	1		1
Core multi platform flake	6	4	10
Core keeled non-discoidal	3		3
Core on a flake	2	2	4
Core fragment		2	2
Core tested module	3		3
Scraper end	20	11	31
Scraper side	4	2	6
Scraper end & side	3	1	4
Scraper disc	1		1
Scraper thumbnail		1	1
Scraper other	3	2	5
Arrowhead chisel	4		4
Arrowhead oblique	2		2
Arrowhead unfinished	1		1
Axe		2	2
Awl	4	2	6
Piercer	5	2	7
Other borer	1		1
Denticulate	6		6
Microburin*	1	1	2
End truncated blade		1	1
Fabricator	2		2
Ground implement flake*	1		1
Knife backed	1	1	2
Knife scale flaked	4		4
Knife plano-convex	1		1
Knife other*		2	2
Microdenticulate/serrated flake**	25	36	61
Notch		5	5
Hammerstone*	1		1
Retouch other	4	2	6
Retouched blade	2	4	6
Retouched flake	17	7	24
Total	1475	583	2058
No. flint (exc. chips) (%)	839/1255 (66.85%)	522/543 (96.13%)	1361/1798 (75.70%)
No. portland chert (exc. chips) (%)	412/1255 (32.83%)	21/543 (3.87%)	433/1798 (24.08%)
No. chert, quartz (exc. chips) (%)	4/1255 (0.32%)		4/1798 (0.22%)
Burnt unworked flint No./g	53/1886g	1/37g	54/1923g
No. burnt (exc. chips) (%)	36/1255 (2.87%)	14/543 (2.58%)	50/1798 (2.78%)
No. broken (exc. chips) (%)	178/1255 (14.18%)	75/543 (13.81%)	253/1798 (14.07%)
No. retouched (exc. chips) (%)	110/1255 (8.76%)	75/543 (13.81%)	185/1798 (10.29%)

* not retouched, one of each utilised   ** not all retouched, five utilised

Mesolithic forms, were also present. Two blade cores with opposed platforms are, however, likely to be Mesolithic. A core tablet and four core rejuvenation flakes testify to the care of the knappers.

All stages of core reduction were represented in the flake and blade assemblages (Table 3.5). Preparation flakes formed nearly 9% of the assemblage. Inner blade forms were by far the most common (54%), perhaps indicating that blade cores were pre-shaped elsewhere or that finished blade forms were brought to the site.

One definite axe-working flake was identified, and the presence of a broken polished flint axe and a probable rough-out in Portland chert suggests that many more axe-working flakes may have been present.

Most of the bulbs (45%) were produced with a hard hammer (Table 3.6), with just 11% being the product of a soft hammer, although a higher proportion of blades had soft-hammer bulbs. Many of the tools were found on hard-hammer struck pieces (58%), and although blade tools were common, few of them had soft-hammer bulbs (9%). Early Neolithic pit 20063 was, however, an exception, containing a much higher proportion of soft-hammer tools.

Plain platforms dominated the assemblage (54%; Table 3.7). Faceted, dihedral and punctiform platforms formed much smaller proportions, but reflect the mixed character of the assemblage overall (including a small Mesolithic component).

Terminal types (Table 3.8) were categorised as fine/feathered (61%), plunging (15%), hinged (15%) or stepped (10%). Many of the microdenticulates and serrated flakes were fashioned on pieces with plunging terminals types as they often form a natural curved edge, often concave, which forms a sickle-shaped piece suitable for plant processing.

Table 3.5 The lithic assemblage by blank type

Category type	Preparation	Distal trimming	Side trimming	Misc trimming	Inner	Axe working
Flakes	122	178	192	371	357	1
percentage	10.00%	14.58%	15.72%	30.38%	29.24%	0.08%
Blade forms	6	34	47	38	146	
percentage	2.21%	12.55%	17.34%	14.02%	53.87%	
Totals	128	212	239	409	513	1
percentage	8.52%	14.12%	15.91%	27.23%	34.16%	0.06%

Table 3.6 The lithic assemblage by hammer mode

Category type	Hard-hammer		Indeterminate		Soft-hammer	
	n	%	n	%	n	%
Flakes	532	48.28%	472	42.83%	98	8.89%
Blade and bladelets	28	19.44%	78	54.17%	38	26.39%
Blade-like flakes	27	28.72%	49	52.13%	18	19.15%
Tools	101	57.71%	59	33.71%	15	8.58%
Totals	688	45.41%	658	43.43%	169	11.16%

Table 3.7 The lithic assemblage by platform type

Category type	cortical	plain	dihedral	faceted	linear	punctiform	shattered	other
Flakes	60	610	59	165	145	11	36	18
percentage	5.43%	55.25%	5.34%	14.97%	13.13%	0.99%	3.26%	1.63%
Blade forms	6	129	6	29	40	6	21	3
percentage	2.50%	53.75%	2.50%	12.08%	16.67%	2.50%	8.75%	1.25%
Tools	6	84	15	47	11	2	4	3
percentage	3.49%	48.84%	8.72%	27.33%	6.40%	1.16%	2.32%	1.74%
Totals	72	823	80	241	196	19	61	24
percentage	4.75%	54.29%	5.28%	15.90%	12.93%	1.25%	4.02%	1.58%

Table 3.8 The lithic assemblage by terminal type

Category type	fine/ feathered	hinge	step	plunging	modified
Flakes	730	183	109	134	1
percentage	63.15%	15.83%	9.43%	11.59%	na
Blade forms	134	30	29	56	
percentage	53.82%	12.05%	11.65%	22.49%	
Tools	58	12	14	36	57
percentage	48.33%	10.00%	11.67%	30.00%	na
Totals	922	225	152	226	(58)
percentage	60.46%	14.75%	9.97%	14.82%	na

Secondary technology

There were 185 retouched tools alongside a hammer-stone, a flake from a polished implement and two microburins. Five microdenticulates/serrated flakes and one knife may have only been utilised rather than retouched; use damage has obscured the retouched edge. The most common tool type was serrated flakes/microdenticulates (61 examples plus six denticulates), followed by scrapers (48 examples including 31 end scrapers alongside, side, side and end, disc, thumbnail and other types). Awls, piercers and borers were also well represented (14 examples) and there were numerous retouched flakes (24), blades (6) and other retouch (6). Five notches were present and there was also one end truncated blade of probable Mesolithic to early Neolithic date. A similar date is likely for the notches, while the two microburins are Mesolithic in date. Two backed knives were present as well as four scale flaked, two simple and a single plano-convex fragment. These are mostly of late Neolithic-early Bronze Age date. Also dated to that period were four chisel and two oblique arrowheads and a chisel blank. An unfinished Portland chert axe rough-out and a utilised and broken polished flint axe were present alongside a flake from a polished implement. Two fabricators and a flint hammerstone were also found.

Table 3.9 The flint assemblage from early Neolithic pit 20063

Category type		Contexts		Total Pit 20063
	20064	20066	20067	
Flake	90	60	65	215
Blade	16	13	8	37
Bladelet	5	14	5	24
Blade-like	10	9	9	28
Irregular waste	7	4	12	23
Sieved chips 10-4mm		9	12	21
Sieved chips 4-2mm		11	8	19
Crested blade or flake	1	3		4
Core multi platform flake	2			2
Core fragmentary	2			2
Core on a flake	1		1	2
Scraper end			1	1
Scraper side	2			2
Scraper other		1	1	2
Axe		1	1	2
Awl			1	1
Piercer			1	1
Notch	1			1
End truncation			1	1
Knife other	1		1	2
Microdenticulate/serrated flake	20	12	3	35
Other retouch	1			1
Retouched blade		2	1	3
Retouched flake	1	4		5
Totals	160	143	131	434
No. flint (exc. sieved chips)	157/160 (98.12%)	121/123 (98.37%)	110/111 (99.1%)	388/394 (98.48%)
No. Portland chert (exc. sieved chips)	3/160/ (1.88%)	2/123 (1.63%)	1/111 (0.9%)	6/394 (1.52%)
No. burnt (exc. sieved chips)	1/160 (0.62%)	4/123 (3.25%)	6/111 (5.41%)	11/394 (2.79%)
No. broken (exc. sieved chips)	18/160 (11.25%)	14/123 (11.38%)	19/111 (17.12%)	51/394 (12.94%)
No. retouched (exc. sieved chips)	25/160 (15.63%)	19/123 (15.45%)	11/111 (9.91%)	55/394 (13.96%)

Overall, other than the single Mesolithic microburin, all the tools could belong to the Neolithic to early Bronze Age and most are likely to be of late Neolithic-early Bronze Age date.

Early Neolithic pit 20063 (Table 3.9)

Pit 20063 contained one of the largest assemblages, consisting of 434 pieces. The assemblage was almost entirely fashioned from flint, with only five flakes and an axe rough-out in Portland chert. The assemblage had a high blade index of 29%, which is consistent with the early Neolithic date indicated by the associated pottery. It also contained many blade tools, as well as a slightly larger number of tools on flakes.

Despite numerous samples, only 40 pieces of fine knapping waste (9%) were recovered, suggesting that the assemblage was moved from its point of origin, perhaps as a cache. Cores were rare and included two multiplatform cores, a core on a flake and two core fragments. All displayed flake scars, but are almost certainly the final use of the cores, and they may have been initially geared towards blade production. Four crested pieces – a blade, a blade-like flake and two flakes- were present in the assemblage, supporting the suggestion of initial blade production. Many of the blades have a distinctive pattern in their corticated surfaces, indicating that they were probably from the same core.

The tool assemblage includes a wide variety of types. In total, 51 retouched pieces were present, amounting to 13% of the assemblage. These included a large number of microdenticulates/ serrated flakes (35) in a variety of single and double-edged forms. Simple retouched flakes were the next most common type (5), followed by end scrapers (4) and retouched blades (3). The range of tools included many other scraper forms, awls, a piercer, a notch, backed knives and two axes. One of the axes was a pre-form or rough-out in Portland chert while the other was a broken polished flint axe butt.

The key difference between the pits fills (20066 upper, 20067 lower; in the first section cut through the pit these two fills were both recorded as context 20064) is the dominance of microdenticulates and simple retouched flakes and blades in the upper fill alongside more crested pieces and cores, whilst the lower fill has a more mixed tool assemblage, and only one core related product. Micro-debitage was probably absent from fill 20064 because it was not sampled.

The middle Neolithic pits (Table 3.10)

Three pits have been dated to the middle Neolithic, one (3330) in the band of pits across the centre of the site, and two (3041 and 3091) further to the north. The two more northern pits (3041 and 3091) contained small, similar assemblages, together totalling 41 lithics. There were, however, marked contrasts between these assemblages and the large group of 101 pieces recovered from the central pit (3330).

The lithics from the northern pits consisted almost entirely of flint, and contained just two pieces of Portland chert, as well as a single possibly worked quartz fragment. In contrast, nearly two thirds (61%) of the assemblage from the central pit (3330) consisted of Portland chert. The assemblages from the two northern pits were dominated by flakes, which account for 94% of all removals, with just 6% consisting of blade forms, whilst the assemblage from the central pit contained a higher proportion of blade forms (22%) and a correspondingly lower proportion of flakes (78%). The northern pits lacked any cores or core curation pieces, but these were quite well represented in the central pit, which contained one opposed platform blade core, a keeled non-discoidal core, a tested nodule and two core rejuvenation faces/edges.

There were more similarities in the retouched tools. The northern pits contained four retouched tools, consisting of a chisel arrowhead, a British oblique arrowhead, a scale-flaked knife and serrated flake. The central pit contained a similar range of types as well as a piercer.

The late Neolithic pits (Table 3.11)

Of the four pits dated to the late Neolithic, three formed a group – 3371, 3372 and 3373. The fourth (3256) was an isolated pit which lay a short distance from the group. None of the pits contained very large assemblages of lithics – the number of pieces ranging from 6 to 35 – and there were few clear contrasts in the composition of the assemblages.

The proportions of flint in relation to Portland chert varied, the smaller assemblages in pits 3256 and 3373 consisting entirely of flint, whilst the larger groups in pits 3371 and 3372 consisted of 17% and 41% of Portland chert respectively. The proportion of blade forms is quite high (20%), although flakes still dominate. Pit 3373 had a particularly high proportion (33%) of blade forms. The incidence of blade forms was further highlighted by a crested blade in pit 3372, although the only core recovered was flake-orientated. The tools from the late Neolithic pits included a chisel arrowhead, four microdenticulates, including two near refitting examples from pit 3372, and an end scraper.

Fine knapping waste and larger irregular waste was present in all of the pits. Levels of retouch breakage and burning were around the norm for the assemblage as a whole although there was some variation between individual pits.

Table 3.10 The lithic assemblages from middle Neolithic pits

Category type	Pit 3041	3091	3330	Total
Flake	17	13	57	87
Blade	1		6	7
Bladelet			2	2
Blade-like		1	8	9
Irregular waste	4	1	6	11
Sieved chips 10-4mm			6	6
Core rejuvenation face/edge			2	2
Core opposed platform blades			1	1
Core keeled non-discoidal			1	1
Core tested nodule			1	1
Arrowhead chisel	1		1	2
Arrowhead oblique	1		1	2
Piercer			1	1
Knife scale flaked		1	1	2
Microdenticulate/serrated flake	1		4	5
Retouched flake			3	3
Totals	25	16	101	142
No. flint	23/25 (92.0%)	15/16 (93.75%)	37/95 (38.95%)	75/136 (55.15%)
No. Portland chert	1/25 (4.0%)	1/16 (6.25%)	58/95 (61.05%)	60/136 (44.12%)
No. quartz	1/25 (4.0%)	-	-	1/136 (0.74%)
No. burnt	4/25 (16.0%)	-	6/95 (6.32%)	10/136 (7.35%)
No. broken	4/25 (16.0%)	2/16 (12.5%)	13/95 (13.68%)	19/136 (13.97%)
No. retouched	3/25 (12.0%)	1/16 (6.25%)	11/95 (11.58%)	15/136 (11.03%)

Table 3.11 The flint assemblage from late Neolithic pits

Category type	Contexts 3256	3371	3372	3373	Total
Flake	2	8	23	8	41
Blade			1	3	4
Bladelet				1	1
Blade-like		1	4		5
Irregular waste		2			2
Sieved chips 10-4mm		7	1	2	10
Sieved chips 4-2mm	3	1		1	5
Crested blade			1		1
Core single platform flake	1				1
Scraper end		1			1
Arrowhead chisel			1		1
Microdenticulate/serrated flake			4		4
Totals	6	20	35	15	76
No. flint (exc. sieved chips)	3/3 (100%)	10/12 (83.33%)	20/34 (58.82%)	12/12 (100.0%)	45/61 (73.77%)
No. Portland chert (exc. sieved chips)		2/12 (16.67%)	14/34 (41.18%)		16/61 (26.23%)
No. burnt (exc. sieved chips)				4/12 (33.33%)	4/61 (6.56%)
No. broken (exc. sieved chips)		1/12 (8.33%)	5/34 (14.71%)	5/12 (14.67%)	11/61 (18.03%)
No. retouched (exc. sieved chips)		1/12 (8.33%)	4/34 (11.76%)		5/61 (8.20%)

Table 3.12 The flint assemblages from late Neolithic/early Bronze Age pits

Category type	Contexts				
	3506	3508	3544	3628	Total
Flake	2	11	51	40	104
Blade			3	2	5
Bladelet			3	1	4
Blade-like			6	6	12
Irregular waste		1	3	4	8
Sieved chips 10-4mm		1	2	30	33
Sieved chips 4-2mm			9	31	40
Core multi platform flake		2	2		4
Core tested nodule			1		1
Scraper end		4	1		5
Piercer			1		1
Fabricator			2		2
Knife scale flaked			1		1
Microdenticulate/serrated flake			2	1	3
Other retouch			1		1
Retouched flake			2		2
Totals	2	19	90	115	226
No. flint (exc. sieved chips)	2/2 (100.0%)	18/18 (100.0%)	53/79 (67.09%)	52/54 (96.30%)	125/153 (81.70%)
No. Portland chert (exc. sieved chips)			26/79 (32.91%)	2/54 (3.70%)	28/153 (18.30%)
No. burnt (exc. sieved chips)	1/2 (50.0%)	1/18 (5.56%)	4/79 (5.06%)	2/54 (3.70%)	8/153 (5.23%)
No. broken (exc. sieved chips)			6/79 (7.59%)	5/54 (9.26%)	11/153 (7.19%)
No. retouched (exc. sieved chips)		4/18 (22.22%)	10/79 (12.66%)	1/54 (1.85%)	15/153 (9.80%)

Table 3.13 The flint assemblages from undated pits

Category type	Pit					
	3327	3408	3512	3333	3459	3502
Flake	2	6	6	8	17	49
Blade	1			1		1
Bladelet		1			1	2
Blade-like					3	6
Irregular waste	2				1	1
Chip					1	
Sieved chips 10-4mm			1	4	1	11
Sieved chips 4-2mm				7		5
Core multi platform flake	1					1
Core keeled non-discoidal						2
Scraper end						2
Scraper side					1	
Awl						1
Knife backed						1
Microdenticulate/serrated flake		1		1		
Other retouch						1
Retouched flake				1		1
Totals	6	8	7	22	25	84
No. flint (exc. sieved chips)	3/6 (50.0%)	2/8 (25.00%)	5/6 (83.33%)	2/11 (18.18%)	21/24 (87.50%)	22/68 (32.35%)
No. Portland chert (exc. sieved chips)	3/6 (50.0%)	6/8 (75.00%)	1/6 (16.67%)	9/11 (81.82%)	3/24 (12.50%)	46/68 (67.65%)
No. burnt (exc. sieved chips)	1/6 (16.67%)			1/11 (9.09%)	2/24 (8.33%)	3/68 (4.41%)
No. broken (exc. sieved chips)	1/6 (16.67%)	1/8 (12.5%)	1/6 (16.67%)	1/11 (9.09%)	3/24 (12.50%)	13/68 (19.12%)
No. retouched (exc. sieved chips)		1/8 (12.5%)		2/11 (18.18%)	1/24 (4.17%)	6/68 (8.82%)

Table 3.14 The flint assemblage from Burial Sets 4 and 6

Category type	3044 & 3046	3067 & 3106	Contexts 3147	3149	3210	Total
Flake	13	2	3	8	1	27
Blade			1			1
Bladelet	1					1
Blade-like				2		2
Chip				1		1
Sieved chips 10-4mm	8	1		7	2	18
Sieved chips 4-2mm					2	2
Microdenticulate/serrated flake			1			1
Totals	22	3	5	18	5	53
No. flint (exc. sieved chips)	13/14 (92.86%)		5/5 (100.0%)	10/11 (90.91%)	1/1 (100%)	29/33 (87.88%)
No. Portland chert (exc. sieved chips)	1/14 (7.14%)	2/2 (100.0%)		1/11 (9.09%)		4/33 (12.12%)
No. burnt (exc. sieved chips)						
No. broken (exc. sieved chips)	2/14 (14.29%)			1/11 (9.09%)		3/33 (9.09%)
No. retouched (exc. sieved chips)			1/5 (20.0%)			1/33 (3.03%)

The late Neolithic/early Bronze Age pits (Table 3.12)

A total of 226 pieces of worked stone was recovered from the four pits dated to the late Neolithic/early Bronze Age. This total, however, includes 61 sieved chips from pit 3628 and smaller numbers from two of the other pits. The assemblages recovered from particular pits were very different in size. Pits 3506 and 3508 contained just two and 19 pieces of worked flint whilst pits 3544 and 3628 contained 90 and 115 pieces respectively.

The proportion of flint and Portland chert again varied. The small assemblages from pits 3506 and 3508 consisted entirely of flint, and just 4% of the large assemblage from pit 3628 consisted of Portland chert. In contrast, a third of the assemblage from pit 3544 consisted of Portland chert.

The proportion of blade forms also varied. The small assemblages, not surprisingly, contained no blades, but blade forms made up 19% and 18% respectively of the larger assemblages from pits 3544 and 3628. The four cores were all flake orientated. The two pits containing cores (3508 and 3544) contained small numbers of chips and irregular waste. The largest group of fine waste was recovered from pit 3628 (which contained no cores).

The ranges of tools also varied. The only example from the larger assemblage in pit 3628 was a serrated flake. The small assemblage from pit 3508 contained four end scrapers. The only large group of tools, comprising an end scraper, a piercer, two fabricators, a scale flaked knife and two microdenticulates, was recovered from pit 3544.

Table 3.15 The flint assemblage from Burial Sets 7, 8 and 9

Category type	3200	3223	Contexts 3227	3206	3232
Flake	1	4	10		2
Bladelet			1		
Blade-like			1		
Sieved chips 4-2mm			2	2	3
Totals	1	4	14	2	5
No. flint (exc. sieved chips)	1/1 (100%)	4/4 (100%)	11/12 (91.67%)		2/2 (100%)
No. Portland chert (exc. sieved chips)			1/12 (8.33%)		
No. burnt (exc. sieved chips)					
No. broken (exc. sieved chips)			2/12 (16.67%)		1/2 (50%)
No. retouched (exc. sieved chips)					

Table 3.16 The flint assemblage from Ring Ditch 3032, (part 1)

CATEGORY TYPE	Contexts					
	3496	3424	3384	3368	3439	Total
Flake	127	38	27	19	13	260
Blade	2	1	1	2		10
Bladelet	1				1	3
Blade-like	4	3		2		10
Irregular waste			2		1	4
Sieved chips 10-4mm				1		1
Sieved chips 4-2mm			4			5
Crested blade						1
Core rejuvenation face/edge	1					1
Scraper end	4			2		7
Scraper side		1				1
Arrowhead chisel					1	1
Arrowhead blank						1
Awl	1				1	3
Piercer						1
Borer						1
Denticulate	1	1	1			4
Knife scale flaked						1
Microdenticulate/serrated flake	2		1			3
Other retouch						1
Retouched flake	2	1		2		6
Totals	145	45	36	28	17	325

No. flint (exc. sieved chips)	135/145 (93.10%)	37/45 (82.22%)	30/32 (93.75%)	21/27 (77.78%)	9/17 (52.94%)	249/319 (78.06%)
No. Portland chert (exc. sieved chips)	10/145 (6.90%)	8/45 (17.78%)	2/32 (6.25%)	6/27 (22.22%)	8/17 (47.06%)	70/319 (21.94%)
No. burnt (exc. sieved chips)		1/45 (2.22%)		1/27 (3.70%)	1/17 (5.88%)	3/319 (0.94%)
No. broken (exc. sieved chips)	5/145 (3.49%)	3/45 (6.67%)	2/32 (6.25%)	2/27 (7.41%)	3/17 (17.65%)	26/319 (8.15%)
No. retouched (exc. sieved chips)	10/145 (6.90%)	3/45 (6.67%)	2/32 (6.25%)	4/27 (14.81%)	2/17 (11.76%)	30/319 (9.40%)

Undated pits (Table 3.13)

Chipped stone recovered from six of the pits probably dates from the Neolithic or early Bronze Age but could not be more precisely dated. Most of

	3315	Total
	1	18
		1
		1
	1	7
		27
	1/1 (100%)	19/20 (95.0%)
		1/20 (5.0%)
		3/20 (15.0%)

these pits contained only small assemblages of flint, the only large group (of 84 pieces) coming from pit 3502. The proportion of Portland chert was very variable. Around two thirds of the large assemblage from pit 3502 consisted of Portland chert, as did high proportions of most of the small assemblages.

All of these assemblages were dominated by flakes, although small numbers of blade-based forms were also present in most. Of the larger assemblages, those from pits 3459 and 3502 contained notably high proportions of blade forms (19% and 16% respectively). Most of the pits also produced small numbers of pieces of irregular waste and chips. Pits 3502 and 3327 were, however, the only pits that produced contained cores. Few tools were recovered from these pits. The only large group, including two end scrapers, an awl and a backed knife, came from pit 3502. The remaining pits contained a side scraper, microdenticulates and a retouched flake.

Table 3.17 The flint assemblage from Ring Ditch 3032 (part 2)

CATEGORY TYPE	Contexts					
	burial 3382	3263	3008	3265	others	Total
Flake	6	7	8	5	10	260
Blade		1		2	1	10
Bladelet					1	3
Blade-like					1	10
Irregular waste			1			4
Sieved chips 10-4mm						1
Sieved chips 4-2mm			1			5
Crested blade			1			1
Core rejuvenation face/edge						1
Scraper end					1	7
Scraper side						1
Arrowhead chisel						1
Arrowhead blank					1	1
Awl		1				3
Piercer					1	1
Borer					1	1
Denticulate		1				4
Knife scale flaked	1					1
Microdenticulate/serrated flake						3
Other retouch					1	1
Retouched flake					1	6
Totals	7	10	11	7	19	325
No. flint (exc. sieved chips)	1/7 (14.29%)	6/10 (60.0%)	4/10 (40.0%)		6/19 (31.58%)	249/319 (78.06%)
No. Portland chert (exc. sieved chips)	6/7 (85.71%)	4/10 (40.0%)	6/10 (60.0%)	7/7 (100.0%)	13/19 (68.42%)	70/319 (21.94%)
No. burnt (exc. sieved chips)						3/319 (0.94%)
No. broken (exc. sieved chips)	2/7 (28.57%)	1/10 (10.0%)	3/10 (30.0%)	1/7 (14.29%)	4/19 (21.05%)	26/319 (8.15%)
No. retouched (exc. sieved chips)	1/7 (14.29%)	2/10 (20.0%)			6/19 (31.58%)	30/319 (9.40%)

Table 3.18 The flint assemblage from Ring Ditch 3514

CATEGORY TYPE	Contexts			
	3515	3533	3537	Total
Flake	8	5	5	18
Bladelet	1			1
Blade-like	1			1
Sieved chips 10-4mm	1			1
Core on a flake			2	2
Scraper end		1		1
Piercer			1	1
Microdenticulate/serrated flake		1		1
Totals	11	7	8	26
No. flint (exc. sieved chips)	10/10 (100.0%)	4/7 (57.14%)	8/8 (100.0%)	22/25 (88.0%)
No. Portland chert (exc. sieved chips)		3/7 (42.86%)		3/25 (12.0%)
No. burnt (exc. sieved chips)				
No. broken (exc. sieved chips)	2/10 (20.0%)			2/25 (8.0%)
No. retouched (exc. sieved chips)		2/7 (28.57%)	1/8 (12.50%)	3/25 (12.0%)

The early Bronze Age burials

Burial Sets 4 and 6 (Table 3.14)

Burial Sets 4 and 6 produced 25 and 28 flints from four and three contexts respectively. None of the burials had what might be considered formal lithic grave goods, with the possible exception of a serrated flake and a large utilised blade, both from context 3147 in Set 6. Given the high number of flints in later features, however, it is more likely that these finds were residual. Much of the remainder of the assemblages consisted of fine knapping waste (40%). This is probably due to the numerous samples taken. Some of the smaller material could be accidental or could simply reflect the high levels of fine shatter present in the background scatter. The bulk of the assemblage consisted of unmodified flakes and included a few blade forms (13%). Most of the assemblage was of flint (88%). None of this material was burnt and there were low levels of breakage and retouch.

Burial Sets 7, 8 and 9 (Table 3.15)

Burial Sets 7, 8 and 9 also contained very sparse assemblages with no retouched forms or burnt examples. They were heavily biased towards flint, and contained many pieces of fine shatter, again probably a product of the extensive sampling. Context 3227 contained the largest assemblage with 14 pieces, including a bladelet and a blade-like flake. It also, however, contained 20 natural fragments (not included in Table 3.4). The flints recovered from these burials are almost certainly residual.

Ring ditch 3032 (Tables 3.16-3.17)

Ring ditch 3032 contained numerous pieces, but very few pieces of finer knapping waste. In total, 325 flints were recovered from 43 fills from 16 cuts, including 319 non-sieved chips. There were nine major interventions with assemblages ranging from 145 down to 7 pieces, alongside seven very minor assemblages.

Table 3.19 The flint assemblage from Roman Quarry pits 3072, 3075, 3110 and 3194

| | Contexts | | | | |
Category type	3072	3075	3110	3194	Total
Flake	41	10	74	5	130
Blade	3	1	8	1	13
Bladelet	1		4		5
Blade-like	1	2	8		11
Irregular waste	7	1	4		12
Sieved chips 10-4mm				1	1
Sieved chips 4-2mm				2	2
Crested blade	1				1
Core opposed platform blades				1	1
Core tested nodule			1		1
Scraper end	1		1		2
Scraper side			2		2
Scraper end + side			1		1
Scraper other			2		2
Knife plano-convex			1		1
Piercer			1		1
Microburin			1		1
Microdenticulate/serrated flake	1		4		5
Ground implement flake	1				1
Denticulate			1		1
Hammerstone			1		1
Other retouch				1	1
Retouched blade			1		1
Retouched flake	2		1		3
Totals	59	14	116	11	200
No. flint (exc. sieved chips)	28/59 (47.46%)	12/14 (85.71%)	54/116 (46.55%)	4/8 (50.0%)	98/197 (49.75%)
No. Portland chert (exc. sieved chips)	31/59 (52.54%)	2/14 (14.29%)	62/116 (53.44%)	4/8 (50.0%)	99/197 (50.25%)
No. burnt (exc. sieved chips)	3/59 (5.08%)		1/116 (0.86%)		4/197 (2.03%)
No. broken (exc. sieved chips)	12/59 (20.34%)		21/116 (18.10%)	3/8 (37.5%)	36/197 (18.27%)
No. retouched (exc. sieved chips)	4/59 (6.78%)		14/116 (12.07%)	1/8 (12.5%)	19/197 (9.64%)

Flint dominated the assemblage by 78% to 22% for Portland chert, but in some contexts, the percentage of flint was over 93%. Conversely, some of the smaller assemblages favoured Portland chert.

Flakes were by far the most common product, accounting for 261 of 285 flakes and blade forms, giving a flake to blade ratio of 92% to 8%, a very low blade-form percentage for these assemblages. Many of the flakes were very squat and hard-hammer technology was dominant (60%), with only a very few soft hammer bulbs (5%), often on residual blade forms. Plain platforms were also very common (60%), but there were still many faceted (15%), linear (7%) and cortical (7%) examples.

Much of the assemblage is typically later prehistoric in character. The tools reflect this with a dominance of piercing tools, end scrapers, crude denticulates and simple retouched flakes. Neolithic or earlier activity is indicated by pieces such as the arrowheads, microdenticulates/serrates, the scale-flaked knife and some of the

finer scrapers as well as many flat flakes with faceted platforms related to tool manufacture. These probably originated from the barrow and reflect the intensity of lithic activity here during the Neolithic.

Ring ditch 3514 (Table 3.18)

The lithics from ring ditch 3514 were quite similar to those from ring ditch 3032, although the assemblage was far smaller (26 pieces). It maintained the dominance of flint (88%) over Portland chert (12%), was dominated by hard-hammer mode (61%) and flakes (90%) and also displayed a marked lack of fine knapping waste.

The two cores on small flakes displayed thick chalk cortex and had heavily irregular platform margins with prominent spurs. They are typically later prehistoric in appearance but are quite small at around 30g in weight. These probably represented the expedient use of chalk nodules from the barrow mound, either quarried into or found as

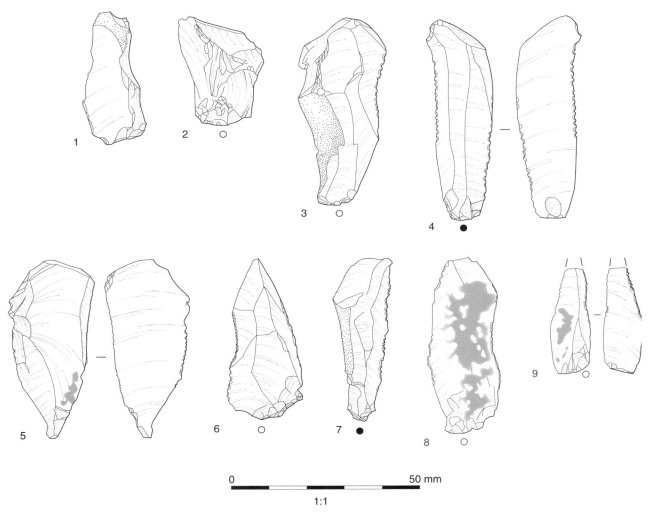

Fig. 3.6 Early Neolithic pit 20063: crested pieces, microdenticulates and serrated flakes

material slumped into the ring-ditch. The tool assemblage also reflected a mix of dates with a fine serrated flake with a faceted platform reflecting a Neolithic component, alongside a damaged scraper and a chunky piercer, pieces more typical of later prehistoric activity.

Roman quarry pits 3072, 3075, 3110 and 3194 (Table 3.19)

This group of features yielded considerable amounts of residual flintwork that must have represented activity prior to the quarrying. Rather oddly, the assemblages show a balance between flint (50%) and Portland chert (50%) that is not apparent in other residual assemblages.

Blade percentages amounted to 18%, indicating that much of the background scatter here dated to early prehistoric times. This was also hinted at by lower levels of hard-hammer technology (44%) and higher incidences of soft-hammer knapping (18%) than for other residual assemblages, such as those from the ring ditches.

Quarry pit 3110 contained the largest assemblage at 110 pieces. It contained a significant blade component (21%) alongside large numbers of flakes, many of which were from various stages of core shaping. Others were regular and thin and probably early. The tools included several microdenticulates, a microburin and some elongated tools such as scrapers and a piercer that appeared to be early. Other scrapers and some less well fashioned tools

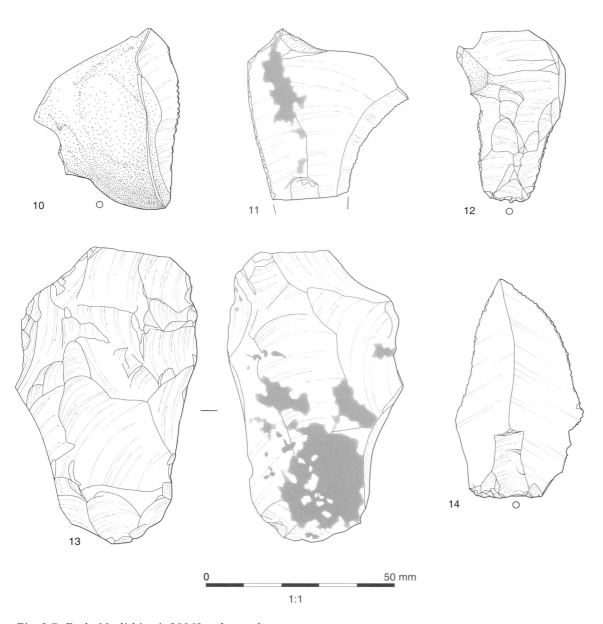

0   50 mm

1:1

Fig. 3.7 Early Neolithic pit 20063: other tools

may date to any period, but at least one scraper looked like a large, well made Neolithic horseshoe example, whilst a plano-convex knife fragment dated to the late Neolithic-early Bronze Age. Cores were rare, with only a single example of a tested nodule.

Quarry pit 3072 had the second largest assemblage at 59 pieces. This consisted of many flakes and some blade forms, often struck using soft-hammer technology (21%). The tools present included an end of blade scraper and two fine serrated pieces. These could date to either the Mesolithic or early Neolithic, while a flake from a polished object is likely to be Neolithic. Two retouched flakes round off the assemblage.

Many of these tools had faceted platforms, suggesting a Neolithic rather than a Mesolithic date.

Quarry pit 3075 contained a small assemblage of 14 pieces, none of which was fine waste. It included a massive blade as well as two blade-like flakes and some thin regular flakes. Much of the assemblage is apparently of Mesolithic or early Neolithic date. Quarry pit 3194 also contained material that was distinctly early in character. This included a fine blade tool, a combination end scraper and side denticulate as well as a blade and an opposed platform blade core of probable Mesolithic date.

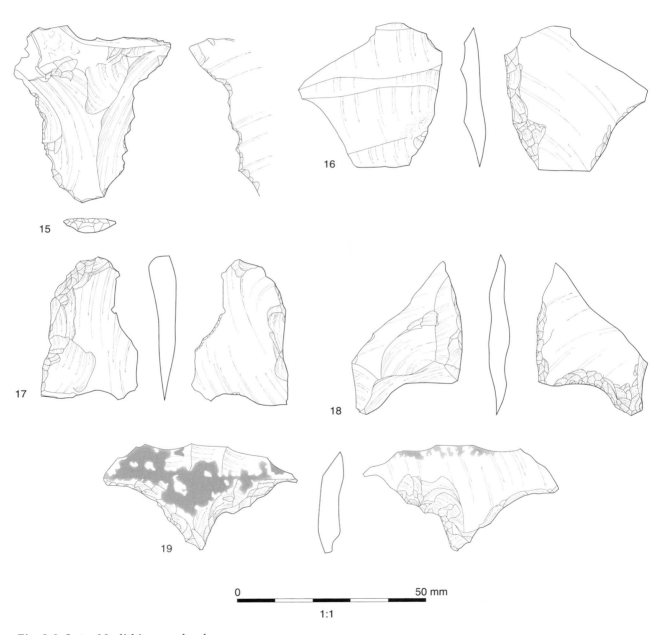

0   50 mm

1:1

Fig. 3.8 Later Neolithic arrowheads

Catalogue of illustrated flint (Figs 3.6-3.10)

Early Neolithic pit 20063

Crested pieces

1. Crested blade, single crest, flint. (20066). Early Neolithic, cat 1663
2. Crested flake, bi-directional, flint. (20066). Early Neolithic, cat 1649
3. Microdenticulate on crested blade, single crest, flint. (20064). Early Neolithic, cat 1499

Microdenticulates and serrated flakes

4. Double edged microdenticulate on inner blade, flint. (20066). Early Neolithic, cat 1607
5. Double edged microdenticulate on inner blade, flint. (20066). Early Neolithic, cat 1533
6. Microdenticulate on inner blade, flint. (20064). Early Neolithic, cat 1464
7. Microdenticulate on side trimming blade, flint. (20066). Early Neolithic, cat 1674
8. Microdenticulate on inner blade, flint. (20064). Early Neolithic, cat 1536
9. Microdenticulate on inner bladelet, flint. (20064). Early Neolithic, cat 1589

Other Tools

10. Serrate on preparation flake, flint. (20066). Early Neolithic, cat 1658
11. Serrate on snapped distal trimming flake, flint. (20066). Early Neolithic, cat 1729
12. Serrate on miscellaneous trimming flake, blunted upper right, flint. (20066). Early Neolithic, cat 1614
13. Axe rough-out, Portland chert. (20067). Early Neolithic, cat 1593
14. Simple knife on inner flake, flint. (20067). Early Neolithic, cat 1751

Later Neolithic

Later Neolithic arrowheads

15. Arrowhead blank, faceted platform flake off levallois core, Portland chert. Ring ditch 3032, (3217), cut 3212. Later Neolithic, cat 260
16. Chisel arrowhead, unfinished?, flint. Middle Neolithic pit 3330 (3328). Later Neolithic, cat 335
17. Oblique arrowhead, Portland chert. Middle Neolithic pit 3330 (3329). Later Neolithic, cat 415
18. British oblique arrowhead, flint. Middle Neolithic pit 3041 (3043). Later Neolithic, cat 1071

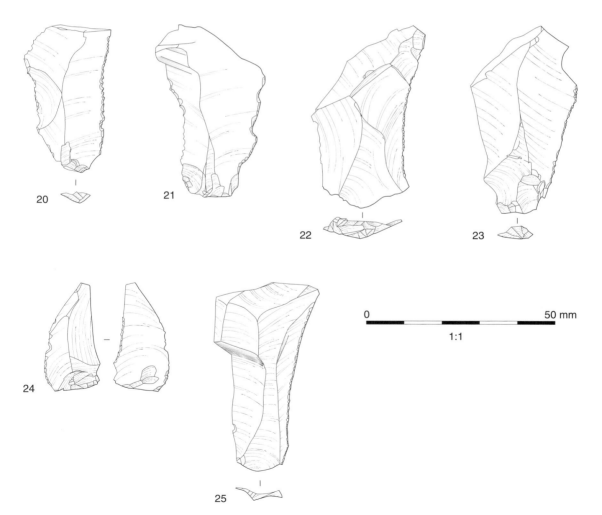

Fig. 3.9 Later Neolithic microdenticulates and serrated flakes

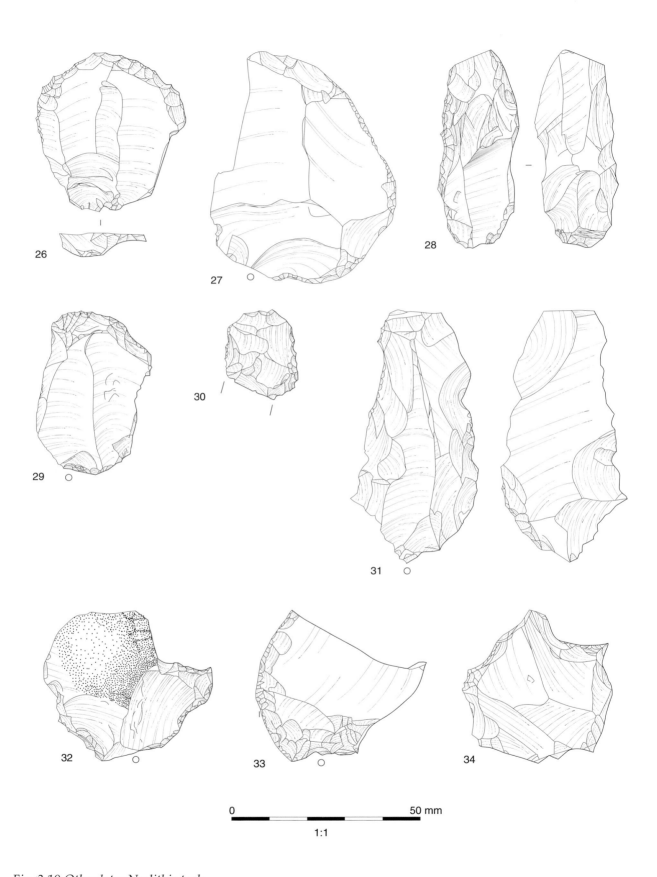

Fig. 3.10 Other later Neolithic tools

19. Chisel arrowhead, flint. Late Neolithic pit 3372 (3443). Later Neolithic, cat 645

Microdenticulates and serrated flakes

20. Microdenticulate on blade-like flake, faceted platform, Portland chert. Roman quarry pit 3110 (3119). Later Neolithic, cat 181
21. Microdenticulate on blade-like flake, flint. Late Neolithic/early Bronze Age pit 3544 (3543). Later Neolithic, cat 946
22. Microdenticulate on blade-like flake, faceted platform, Portland chert. Undated pit 3333 (3331). Later Neolithic, cat 409
23. Serrate on inner flake, Portland chert. Middle Neolithic pit 3330 (3328). Later Neolithic, cat 362
24. Serrate on inner flake, Portland chert. Ring ditch 3032 (3500), cut 3496. Later Neolithic, cat 1261
25. Microdenticulate on inner blade, Portland chert. Middle Neolithic pit 3330 (3329). Neolithic, cat 391

Other tools

26. End scraper on inner flake, faceted platform, Portland chert. Ring ditch 3032 (3501), cut 3501. Late Neolithic-early Bronze Age, cat 880
27. Side scraper on inner flake, flint. Undated pit 3459 (3460). Later Neolithic, cat 678
28. Fabricator, flint. Late Neolithic/early Bronze Age pit 3544 (3543). Later Neolithic, cat 928
29. End scraper on inner flake, flint. Late Neolithic/early Bronze Age pit 3508 (3507). Later Neolithic, cat 893
30. Knife fragment, heavy invasive retouch, plano-convex?, Portland chert. Ring ditch 3032 (3217), cut 3212. Later Neolithic/early Bronze Age, cat 160
31. Fabricator, Portland chert. Late Neolithic pit 3544 (3543). Later Neolithic, cat 961
32. Piercer on inner flake, flint. Ring ditch 3514 (3516), cut 3515. Middle-late Bronze Age, cat 910
33. Knife, scale flaked, Portland chert. Late Neolithic/early Bronze Age pit 3544 (3543). Later Neolithic, cat 1278

34. Piercer on inner flake, Portland chert. Late Neolithic/early Bronze Age pit 3544 (3590). Later Neolithic, cat 991

METALWORK *by Ian Scott*

Metalwork from Beaker and Bronze Age burials

Two small awls were recovered from Beaker inhumation burials and the tip of a blade from a fill (3035) of cremation burial 3033 in the centre of ring ditch 3032.

1. Awl, very small. Both ends taper, are pointed and circular in section. The middle of the awl measures 2mm wide and 1.7mm thick and is rectangular in section. Cu alloy. L: 37mm. Grave 3227 (3342). Sf 10068. Inv 262.
2. Awl, very small. Both points taper, are pointed and circular in section. The middle is 2mm wide and 1.3 mm thick and rectangular in section. Cu alloy. L: 31.5mm. Grave 3315 (3318), from soil around skull of skeleton 3316 (soil sample 1083). Inv 261.

Small awls are regularly found in Beaker and early Bronze Age burials. They are assumed to have been used for metalworking, and in particular for the fine working of gold ornaments (Taylor 1985, 184-86; Clarke *et al.* 1985, 86)). The Knocknague hoard, Co. Galway, Ireland contains three awls (Clarke *et al.*, 176, 304, no. 149, and illustration 5.11). Comparable awls have been recovered from primary inhumation burials in bowl barrow Preshute G.1 (a) ('The Manton Barrow'; Annable and Simpson 1964, 47 and 101, no 207) and bowl barrow Winterbourne Stoke G.8 (ibid., 52 and 107, no. 304).

3. Blade tip, possibly from a dagger of early Bronze Age date. The small fragment has a double convex cross section with a slight flattening in the middle, suggesting a flat blade with bevelled edges, but this

0   40 mm

2:1

Fig. 3.11 Blade tip (1) from grave 3033 (Set 10) and copper awls from graves 3227 (2) and 3315 (3)

Table 3.20 Late Roman inhumation burials: nails, hobnails and other metal finds

Grave	Context	Cu alloy Sheet fragts	Iron Nails	Nails or spikes	Hobnails	Mineralised wood	Undiagnostic fragts	Total
	3364		33	1	3		*	37
3358	3484				3			3
	Total		33	1	6		*	40
	3541		2		34			36
3540	3542		18	1	77	1	*	97
	Total		20	1	111	1	*	133
	3560		7		91		*	98
3559	3561	1	18		6			24
	Total	1	25		97		*	123
Total		1	78	2	214	1	*	296

is far from certain. The fragment is quite narrow. Cu alloy. L: 21.3mm; W: 10.9mm; Th: 1.4mm. Burial 3033 (3035). Sf 10012. Inv 259.

The identification of this fragment as the tip of an early Bronze Age dagger is not certain. Early daggers generally have short broad blades, but it could be comparable to the small knife-dagger from the primary inhumation in barrow Amesbury G.56 (Annable and Simpson 1964, 55, 111 no. 355). Too little of the blade survives to be certain of the cross section of the dagger blade, which might have helped to date the fragment.

Metalwork from later Roman inhumation burials

The three later Roman burials (graves 3358, 3540 and 3559) which cut across a Bronze Age ring ditch all contained a number of nails, presumably coffin nails. Two (3540 and 3559) also contained numerous hobnails, indicating the presence of nailed footwear.

Coffin nails

All three graves produced substantial numbers of coffin nails (Table 3.20). Two thirds of the nails in grave 3358 (n = 22/Total = 33) are complete or near complete and could be measured. Only three nails out of a total of 20 from grave 3540 are complete, and from grave 3559 there are 11 complete nails from a total of 25.

Numbers and lengths of nails

The 36 measured nails range in length from 38mm to 75mm, but 29 fall in the range 50mm to 70mm. The sample is too small – too few graves and too small a sample of complete nails – to treat statistically.

Table 3.21 Late Roman inhumation burials: numbers and lengths of complete nails

Length	Count	Median value	Av. length	Range
Grave 3358				
38	1			
50	3			
53	1			
54	1			
55	4			
57	1	59.5mm	58.9mm	32mm
62	2			
64	1			
65	3			
67	3			
70	2			
Count	22			
Grave 3540				
47	1			
60	1	60mm	60.66mm	28mm
75	1			
Count	3			
Grave 3559				
45	3			
50	1			
53	1			
55	1			
60	1	55mm	55.9mm	27mm
62	1			
63	1			
65	1			
72	1			
Count	11			
Total count	36			

However, the average length of nails from the graves is between 55.9mm and 60.66mm. In all three graves there is a substantial difference between the lengths of the shortest and longest nails (the 'range', Table 3.21). There are no extremely long nails from these graves, although both grave 3358 and 3540 produced long spikes or possible nail stems. The spike (sf 10132) from grave 3358 was 105mm long and the example (sf 10208) from grave 3540 measured 85mm in length. Both spikes are longer than the longest nail in each grave. The purpose of the long spikes is unclear.

Positions of nails and evidence for coffin construction

Grave 3358 produced 33 nails, 22 of which are complete or near complete. The plan of the grave shows the positions of only nine nails, all located adjacent to the coffin stain. The marked nails were located on the north long side, at the narrow foot of the coffin and on part of the south long side of the coffin adjacent to the foot end. The distribution of the nails confirms that they are coffin nails but does not provide detailed evidence for coffin construction.

Grave 3559 contained 25 nails, 11 of which are complete or near complete. There is no detailed information on the positioning of the nails in the grave. They are presumably coffin nails, but there is no evidence for the construction of the coffin.

Grave 3540 produced only three complete nails, although 20 nail fragments were also found in this grave. The grave plan shows nails positioned around the body, but again there is insufficient evidence to indicate the construction of the coffin.

Hobnails

There are 111 hobnails (148 fragments) from grave 3540 and 97 hobnails (102 fragments) from grave 3559 (Table 3.22). In both cases there are sufficient hobnails to indicate the presence of pairs of nailed footwear. The hobnails were concentrated by the

Table 3.22 Late Roman inhumation burials: hobnail counts

Grave	Hobnails (count)	Total
3358	Count	6
	Fragt Count	7
3540	Count	111
	Fragt Count	148
3559	Count	97
	Fragt Count	102
Total	Count	214
	Fragt Count	257

soles of the feet, strongly suggesting that in each grave the deceased was buried with shoes on their feet. No nailing patterns were discerned in either grave. By contrast grave 3358 contained only six hobnails (seven fragments), and on this evidence it seems unlikely that nailed footwear was present in the grave.

THE HUMAN REMAINS

Inhumation burials *by Mark Gibson and Louise Loe*

Introduction

This report describes only the inhumation burials. A total of 21 skeletons was recovered, as well as disarticulated human bone representing a further three individuals. The assemblage consists of seven adults and 10 juveniles dating from the early Bronze Age, three probably late Roman adults and three Anglo-Saxon adults. A more detailed version of this report is contained in the site archive.

Methodology

Osteological analysis was undertaken in accordance with published guidelines (Brickley and McKinley 2004). The information recorded for each skeleton included preservation status (McKinley 2004), an inventory of the bones, joints and teeth present and, where preservation allowed, an estimation of age (for adults: Scheuer and Black 2000; Brooks and Suchey 1990; Lovejoy *et al.* 1985; Buckberry and Chamberlain 2002; Iscan and Loth 1986a, 1986b; Meindl and Lovejoy 1985; for juveniles: Moorees *et al.* 1963; Scheuer and Black 2000) and sex (for adults: Phenice 1969; Bass 1987; Buikstra and Ubelaker 1994; but not juveniles: Brickley 2004, 23), scoring the presence and absence of non-metric traits (Mays 1998; Berry and Berry 1967; Finnegan 1978), and a full record of pathological lesions observed (Aufderheide and Rodríguez-Martín 1998; Ortner 2003; Resnick 1995a; Stuart-Macadam 1991, 101-113; Lewis 2004, 90; Boocock *et al.*, 1995; Rogers and Waldron 1995, 43-44; Brothwell's 1981, 155; Ogden's 2008, 293). Due to poor preservation the metric data which could be gathered was very limited. No cranial indices could be taken and there were few long bones sufficiently complete to provide estimates of stature or robusticity.

The early Bronze Age inhumation burials
(Table 3.23)

Preservation and completeness

Most of the early Bronze Age inhumations (11) were categorised as less than 25% complete. Only

Table 3.23 Summary early Bronze Age inhumation burials

Grave	Skeleton no.	Age category	Likely age range	Sex	Completeness %	Fragmentation	Surface condition (McKinley 2004, 16)
3223	3231	Older child	7.5-8.5 yrs	/	<25	High	4
3227	3307	Older child	11.25-13	/	26-50	High	4
3200	3211	Adolescent	11-18 yrs	/	<25	High	4
3227	3228	Adult		/	stray bones		
3227	3334	Mature adult	36-45 yrs	M	51-75	Med	3
3225	3264	Young child	1.25-2.75 yrs	/	<25	High	5
3227	3335	Adult		/	stray bones (prob. part of 3334)		
3147 (3149)	3192	Young child	4.5-5.5 yrs	/	<25	High	3
3147	3520	Young adult	20-25 yrs	?M	>76	Medium	4
3067	3084	Young adult	18-25 yrs	?	26-50	High	5
3044	3045	Adolescent	10.75-14.5yrs	/	<25	High	5
3046	3048	Prime adult	26-35 yrs	?M	51-75	High	5
3036	3037	Adult	>18yrs	?	<25	High	5
3087	3088	Adolescent	9.5-15 yrs	/	<25	High	5
3232	3279	Older child	10.5-12.5 yrs	/	51-75	Low	3
3315	3316	Mature adult	35-39 yrs	?F	>76	Medium	3
3206	3205	Young child	1-2 yrs	/	stray bones	High	2
3033	3035	Infant	1-5 mths	/	stray bones	High	2

two skeletons were over 75% complete, with the remaining five examples falling in between. Most of the skeletons were also highly fragmented, and many had suffered from significant erosion of the bone. The extent to which the skeletons had survived was clearly related to the depth of the graves that contained them. The best preserved skeletons were all recovered from large inhumation pits – the deepest graves on the site. Many of the other graves were extremely shallow, and it is clear that the poor preservation of the skeletons was in large part due to the severe truncation of the graves.

Disarticulated remains

It is reasonable to suppose that despite their poor preservation most of the skeletons originally consisted of complete inhumation burials. This may be true even of the juveniles represented only by teeth which were associated with cremated remains in graves 3033 and 3205. There was, however, at least one group of human bone that may have been deposited already disarticulated. This group consists of a highly fragmented and incomplete right adult femur, a fragment of a rib shaft, a

fragment of a femoral condyle and the shaft of a humerus, all of which were recovered from the upper fill (3228) of grave 3227. Radiocarbon dates show that the disarticulated bones were older than the inhumation burial which lay stratigraphically below them. The disarticulated bones may have derived from an earlier burial which was disturbed when the inhumation burial was interred, but it is also possible that they were curated bones which were buried long after the individual they represent had died.

The proximal half of a left 5th metacarpal was found within the Beaker (3335) in the same grave. Whilst this could be seen as a second example of the burial of disarticulated remains, the Beaker also contained a group of small mammal bones, and it is likely that the metacarpal derived from the primary inhumation burial (3334) in the grave, which, although generally well preserved, was missing some bones, including the left 5th metacarpal.

Demography

Table 3.24 shows the age and sex distribution of the assemblage. Of the 17 individuals, seven were adult

Skeletal pathology	No. teeth	No. AMTL	No sockets	Caries	Calculus	EH	Periodontitis	Periap. cavities
None observed	35	0	35	0	0	-	0	0
Cribra orbitalia	35	0	6	0	2	-	0	0
None observed	14	0	0	0	0	-	0	0
Kidney stones, osteochondritis dissecans	32	0	21	1	9	2	0	0
None Observed	12	0	0	0	0	-	0	0
None observed	29	0	5	0	2	-	0	0
Schmorl's nodes, partial sacralisation of LV5	27	0	16	0	6	3	0	0
None observed	17	0	0	0	3	1	0	0
None observed	32	0	0	0	0	-	0	0
Cribra orbitalia, vertebral body osteophytosis	27 1	5	5	9	4	0	1	
None observed	0	0	3	0	0	-	0	0
None observed	21	0	0	0	0	-	0	0
None observed	21	0	9	1	12	-	0	0
Cribra orbitalia, spondylosis deformans, spinal OA, vertebral body marginal osteophytosis, hand phalanx fracture	34	0	21	5	27	-	9	1
None observed	13	0	0	0	0	-	0	0
Cribra orbitalia	3	0	0	0	0	-	0	0

Table 3.24 Age and sex distribution of early Bronze Age burials

	Male	Female	Indet.	Total
Preterm				
Neonate				
Infant (1 month-1 year)			1	1
Young child (1-5 years)			3	3
Older child (6-12 years)			3	3
Adolescent (13-17 years)			3	3
Young adult (18-25 years)	1		1	2
Prime adult (26-35 years)	1			1
Mature adult (36-45 years)	1	1		2
Older adult (> 45 years)				
Adult (unspec.)			2	2
Total	2	2	13	17

and 11 were juvenile. The sex of only four of the adults could be determined, and of these three were male and one female. The single female was assessed as a probable female, one of the males as a definite male, whilst the other two were probable males. In the adult assemblage, only two skeletons could not be assigned an age more specific than older than 18 years. All of the juvenile skeletons could be assigned to more specific ages.

Non-metric traits

Table 3.25 gives the true prevalence rates (TPR) for non-metric traits within the adult sample. A range of six cranial and four post-cranial traits were observed. The most frequently observed cranial trait was the accessory supra-orbital foramen. Cranial non-metric traits can be used to support the idea of family ties within a skeletal assemblage (McKinley 2008, 69) and it could be inferred that the high TPR of the cranial traits indicates strong familial links within the cemetery. However, given the small sample size for most of these traits it seems more likely that the sample size is skewing the data.

Of the post-cranial traits, the double anterior calcaneal facet (L=50.00%, R=66.67%) was most frequently observed. Hypotrochanteric fossas of the femur, a vertical groove in the superior posterior part of the femoral shaft, between the gluteal muscle attachments and the lateral margin (L=40.00%, R=33.33%), were the next most common trait.

Table 3.25 Comparison of true prevalence rates for non-metric traits within the adult early Bronze Age burials

	Sk 3048		Sk 3084		Sk 3316		Sk 3334		Sk 3520		TPR %	
Cranial trait												
Metopism	1		/		0		0				0 25.00 (1/4)	
Ossicle at lambda	0		/		1		/				0 33.33 (1/3)	
	L	R	L	R	L	R	L	R	L	R	L	R
Parietal foramen	0	0	/	/	0	0	0	0	1	0	25.00 (1/4)	25.00 (1/4)
Accessory infraorbital foramen	/	/	/	/	0	0	/	/	/	1	0.00 (0/1)	50.00 (1/2)
Supraorbital foramen	0	0	/	/	0	0	1	0	0	0	0.00 (0/4)	25.00 (1/4)
Accessory supraorbital foramen	1	1	/	/	0	0	0	1	0	0	50.00 (2/4)	25.00 (1/4)
Post-cranial trait												
Femur – Hypotrochanteric fossa	0	/	1	1	0	/	0	0	1	0	40.00 (2/5)	33.33 (1/3)
Tibia – lateral squatting facet	/	/	/	/	0	/	0	/	1	/	33.33 (1/3)	0.00 (0/0)
Lateral talar extension	/	/	/	/	0	/	0	0	1	0	33.33 (1/3)	0.00 (0/2)
Calcaneus – double anterior facet	/	/	/	/	1	1	/	1	0	0	50.00 (1/2)	66.67 (2/3)

Palaeopathology

Adult dental health

Table 3.26 provides a summary of dental disease rates within the early Bronze Age inhumation burials. Carious lesions were observed in three of five of the adult dentitions, periodical cavities in two of six adult jaws, periodontal disease in two, ten of 130 teeth displayed dental enamel hypoplasia, and all of the dentitions had calculus deposits. These are generally high rates but the sample is too small for any significance to be attached to the figures. Only one of the adult jaws, however, had suffered from antemortem tooth loss, and that involved only one tooth.

One dental anomaly was recorded: one individual (skeleton 3048) exhibits a slight shovelling of the maxillary canines. Shovelling is more commonly seen in the maxillary incisors than the canines (Hillson 1996, 86) and is most frequent amongst Native Americans and Asians (>90%) and lowest amongst Europeans (Carbonell 1963)

Juvenile dental health

Not surprisingly, the dental health of the juveniles (Table 3.27) was better than that of the adults. Caries was observed in one juvenile dentition and calculus affected three, but no dental enamel hypoplasia, periapiceal cavities or antemortem tooth loss were observed. Two dental anomalies were observed in

Table 3.26 True and crude prevalence rates for dental pathology in the adult Bronze Age assemblage from Ridgeway Hill

| Sk number | No. teeth | No. crowns observable | No. sockets | Caries | Calculus | No. crowns/sockets with | | | |
						Dental enamel hypoplasia	Peridontitis	Periapiceal cavity	Ante-mortem tooth loss
3037	0	0	3	0	0	0	0	0	0
3048	27	26	5	5	9	4	0	1	1
3084	17	17	0	0	3	1	0	0	0
3316	30	30	21	5	27	0	2	1	0
3334	32	32	31	1	9	2	0	0	0
3520	27	25	16	0	6	3	0	0	0
Total	133	130	76	11	54	10	2	2	1
TPR %				8.46 (11/130)	41.53 (54/130)	7.69 (10/130)	2.63 (2/76)	2.63 (2/76)	1.32 (1/76)
CPR %				60.00 (3/5)	100.00 (5/5)	80.00 (4/5)	33.33 (2/6)	33.33 (2/6)	16.67 (1/6)

Table 3.27 True and crude prevalence rates for dental pathology in the juvenile Bronze Age assemblage from Ridgeway Hill

Sk number	No. Crowns observable		No. sockets observable	No. crowns/sockets with			
	Permanent	Deciduous		Caries		Calculus	
				Permanent	Deciduous	Permanent	Deciduous
3035	0	3	0	0	0	0	0
3045	30	2	0	0	0	0	0
3088	21	0	0	0	0	0	0
3192	11	15	5	0	0	0	2
3205	1	12	0	0	0	0	0
3211	14	0	0	0	0	0	0
3231	24	11	0	0	0	0	0
3264	3	9	0	0	0	0	0
3279	21	0	9	0	1	12	0
3307	31	4	6	0	0	2	0
3324	4	0	0	0	0	0	0
TOTAL	170	56	20	0	1	14	2
TPR %				0.00 (0/170)	1.79 (1/56)	8.24 (14/170)	3.57 (2/56)
CPR %				0.00 (0/11)	9.09 (1/11)	18.18 (2/11)	9.09 (1/11)

adolescent skeleton 3211. Enamel pearls were exhibited on the mesial and distal sides of the root of the right maxillary 1st molar and the right maxillary lateral incisor was slightly shovelled. The maxillary 1st molar is an unusual tooth for an enamel pearl. They are more common on teeth with fused roots, such as the maxillary 2nd or 3rd molars, the 1st molar more commonly having an enamel extension, where a tongue of enamel extends from the crown to run between the roots (Hillson 1996, 97-8).

Skeletal pathology

Table 3.28 shows the proportions of the assemblage affected by differing categories of disease. Metabolic disorders were the most frequently observed type of pathology, followed by spinal joint disease. This differs from other sites, where extra-spinal joint disease is often the most frequently recorded condition (Rogers 2000, 163).

Circulatory pathology

One mature adult male (skeleton 3334) had osteochondritis dissecans. A small subcircular lytic lesion was observed on the anterior surface of the right

Table 3.28 Crude prevalence rates of pathological conditions by disease category

	Adults (n=7)	Juveniles (n=10)
Circulatory	1	-
Metabolic disorders	3	2
Spinal joint disease	3	-
Trauma	1	-
Congenital/developmental	1	-

humeral trochlea. This is the third most common site for lesions associated with osteochondritis dissecans after the femoral condyle and talus, with the right side generally having a greater involvement than the left (Aufderheide and Rodríguez-Martín 1998, 82-3).

Metabolic disorders

In total four individuals had cribra orbitalia, of which two were juveniles. Calculi were represented by 23 rounded nodular concretions which were found with mature adult male skeleton 3334. They ranged from 5mm to 17mm in diameter and were primarily a light yellowish brown in colour. Where visible it was noted that the inside of the calculi were a dense white 'chalky' structure. Whilst these bore more similarity to kidney stones, it cannot be said for certain which type of stone this individual had. It should, however, be noted that today bladder stones are more commonly seen in young males in poor agricultural environments, whilst kidney stones are seen in adults in more affluent industrialised societies (Steinbock 1989).

Spinal joint disease

Of the individuals with observable vertebrae three of five exhibited lesions of joint disease (Table 3.29). Only a single individual (mature adult female skeleton 3316) had spinal osteoarthritis involving the apophyseal joints and/or the articular facets for the ribs. The cervical spine was only affected region. Marginal osteophytosis was observed in three adults. The thoracic spine, followed by cervical spine was the region most affected (Table 3.29). A third of adults in the assemblage had Schmorl's

Table 3.29 TPR's of spinal joint disease, showing distribution by spinal region

Spinal region	Osteo-arthritis TPR% (n/N)	Schmorl's nodes TPR% (n/N)	Marginal osteo-phytosis TPR% (n/N)	Spondylosis deformans TPR% (n/N)
Cervical	0.00 (0/17)	0.00 (0/12)	16.67 (2/12)	8.33 (1/12)
Thoracic	15.38 (4/26)	8.33 (1/12)	25.00 (3/12)	0.00 (0/12)
Lumbar	0.00 (0/17)	60.00 (6/10)	10.00 (1/10)	0.00 (0/10)
Total	6.67 (4/60)	20.59 (7/34)	17.65 (6/34)	2.94 (1/34)

(N=total number of observable vertebral arches with observable apophyseal joint facets; for all other conditions N=total number of observable vertebral bodies)

nodes (two of five adults with observable vertebral bodies). Of the seven vertebrae exhibiting Schmorl's nodes, the vast majority were of the lumbar, followed by thoracic spine, which is the reverse of what is most commonly observed (Rogers and Waldron 1995, 27). No Schmorl's nodes were observed in the cervical spine.

Trauma

The only trauma was on skeleton 3316. Two bones exhibited healed fractures: an intermediate and a distal hand phalanx which appear to have been crushed at the interphalangeal joint and became ankylosed during the healing process with the distal phalanx becoming angulated on the lateral plane.

Congenital/developmental anomalies

Congenital abnormalities were observed in one individual, a young adult male (skeleton 3520) who exhibited vertebral border shifting, in which the morphology of the affected vertebra mimics that of another type of vertebra. In this case, sacralisation had occurred, with the 5th lumbar vertebra partially taking the form of the first sacral vertebra. Transitional vertebrae occur in three-five percent of the population, two-thirds of which are complete or partial sacralisation of the 5th lumbar (Lopez-Duran 1995).

Discussion

The ratio of juveniles to adults was noticeably high amongst the early Bronze Age inhumation burials from Ridgeway Hill. Whilst other contemporary sites do have relatively high percentages of juveniles (33% in the Barnack assemblage and 36% in the Barrow Hills assemblage), they are far lower than that of the Ridgeway Hill assemblage (10 of out of 17; 59%). All of these exceed the period average of 28% (Roberts and Cox 2003, 75). The higher proportion of juveniles at Ridgeway Hill is unlikely to be due to illness or other forms of stress during childhood, and probably simply reflects the small size of the overall sample of burials. It is worth noting, also, that if the cremation burials are included the ratio at Ridgeway Hill is closer to that found at some other early Bronze Age sites.

The pathologies expressed by the Ridgeway Hill assemblage were generally unremarkable. However the rates of pathological lesions was somewhat unusual, most notably the complete absence of extra-spinal joint disease and non-specific inflam-mation/infection, two of the most common patho-logical categories found on archaeological populations (Rogers 2000, 163). The high fragmen-tation and poor surface condition of much of the assemblage is in part to blame for this, as is the high proportion of juveniles, which would have limited expression of disease.

The only pathology of particular note is the 23 calculi found with skeleton 3334. Whilst further investigation would be needed to confirm their exact aetiology, they appear to most closely resemble kidney stones. Given that kidney stones tend to be seen in more affluent industrialised societies rather than agricultural environments (Steinbock 1989) they could be of particular signifi-cance regarding this individual's status and diet. People with a diet that is high in meat protein and low in fibre run greater risk of developing kidney stones and have a greater tendency to get them repeatedly (ibid. 1989; Prien 1979). This indicates that this individual is more likely to have had a protein rich diet, something that is supported by the lack of CO in the orbits of skeleton 3334, if that protein was in the form of red meat. With regards to this individual's status it is worthy of note that skeleton 3334 was one of only two inhumations in this assemblage interred with a beaker (Sf 10036) and a copper alloy awl. It is, however, also worth noting that the ^{15}N level for this individual was no higher than that of many of the other burials. Indeed, overall, there was little variation in ^{15}N levels (Table 3.23).

Romano-British inhumation burials

Skeletons 3484, 3541 and 3560 were recovered from east-west aligned graves cut into barrow 3032. The skeletons lay in a supine position with both hands on their pelvis or stomach region. Iron nails were recovered from the soil surrounding all three individuals, indicating that they had been interred within coffins.

Skeletons 3484 and 3560 were 50-75% complete, and although all regions of the skeleton were present, ribs, vertebrae and pelvis were more or less poorly represented, and the condition of the remains was poor (grade 4 on McKinley's 2004, 16, scale). Skeleton 3541 was less well preserved, only 25-50% complete, with only the limb bones being well represented. The condition of the bone was very poor (grade 5 on McKinley's scale).

Because of its poor state, the sex and age, beyond being adult, of skeleton 3541 could not be established. On the basis of features of the skull, the sciatic notch (and in the case of skeleton 3484, the preauricular sulcus and measurements on the glenoid cavity and femoral head), the other two skeletons appear to be female. Degenerative changes on the partial auricular surfaces and single partial pubic symphysis indicate that skeleton 3484 was an older adult of 45 years or more. Neither the pubic symphysis nor the auricular surfaces survived in the case of skeleton 3560, and an estimated age of 18-25 years is based on dental attrition alone.

No metrical data could be obtained from skeletons 3541 and 3560, but based upon the maximum length of the left femur, it is estimated that skeleton 3484 was 1.51m tall, with an error margin of 327mm.

Various non-metric traits were recorded. Skeleton 3484 had a supra-orbital foramen on the left orbit and the mastoid foramen was extrasutural on the right side (left side was sutural). Post-cranially a hypotrochanteric fossa was present on both femoral shafts. Whilst it is generally thought that non-metric traits of the cranium are more likely to be genetically induced (Torgersen 1951a,b, 1954; Sjøvold 1984), it is thought that post-cranial non-metric traits may be under greater environmental control (Tyrell 2000). The bilateral hypotrochanteric fossas may, therefore, indicate a more physically active individual, especially with respect to actions that involve the gluteal muscles.

Three cranial non-metric traits were recorded in the case of skeleton 3560. A parietal foramen was present on the right parietal bone, but absent on the left, a supra-orbital foramen was present above the left orbit, but the notch remained unbridged on the right and the mastoid foramen was extrasutural bilaterally. The only post-cranial non-metric traits observed were bilateral double anterior calcaneal facets. The latter was the only trait observed in the case of skeleton 3541.

Several pathological conditions were noted. In the case of skeleton 3484 these included spinal and extra-spinal joint disease, metabolic disorders, non-specific inflammation/infection and a developmental anomaly. A Schmorl's node was present on the superior surface of the 1st sacral vertebra. Both

of the glanoid fossas exhibited slight porosity and osteophytosis on and adjacent to their margins. Iron deficiency anaemia was indicated by cribra orbitalia (type 3 after Stuart-Macadam 1991, 109) in both orbits. Non-specific inflammation/infection was indicated by pathological changes in two locations on this skeleton. The first was new bone grown in the right maxillary sinus indicating sinusitis (Boocock *et al.* 1995). The second was a small patch of healed periostitis on the medial midshaft of the left tibia. One of the pedal sesamoids had a bifurcation line, giving it a lobed appearance with two distinct articular facets for the head of the 1st metatarsal. The bifuraction line was regular and smooth indicating that the sesamoid had formed from two ossification centres, rather than the usual single centre (www.wheelessonline.com/ortho/sesamoid_fractures).

All of the tooth sockets/locations of the skeleton were present except for the left maxillary 3Rd molar and the right mandibular central incisor, both of which teeth were absent. Six teeth were missing post-mortem, and the left mandibular 3Rd molar was absent, probably due to agenesis. Calculus, periodontal disease, caries and AMTL were also observed on the dentition. Calculus was present on most teeth as was periodontitis (inflammation and resorption of the bone in the gum line). Caries was present on five teeth, mostly mandibular. They were all small, except in the case of the left mandibular 1st molar were it was gross and had destroyed all of the tooth crown. Six teeth were lost ante-mortem, all of them in the maxilla.

The only pathological lesions observed on skeleton 3560 were those associated with cribra orbitalia. The lesions were in the form of scattered foramina in both orbits (type 2 after Stuart-Macadam 1991,109) indicating iron deficiency anaemia (ibid., 109).

Calculus, periodontal disease, caries and AMTL were observed on the dentition. Calculus was present on most mandibular teeth and two of the maxillary and periodontitis was present on four tooth locations. Caries was present on five teeth, with two small carious lesion present on the left mandibular 1st molar. Four teeth were lost ante-mortem, all of them in the maxilla. All of the tooth sockets/locations of the skeleton were present except for the left mandibular lateral incisor, where the tooth was also absent. Four teeth were missing post-mortem, and both mandibular 3Rd molars were absent, probably due to agenesis.

No pathological conditions were observed on skeleton 3541. Both caries and calculus were, however, present on the dentition, as were some dental anomalies. A single carious lesion was found on the right mandibular 1st molar, and slight calculus was found on four teeth, all of them molars. No tooth sockets/locations were recovered with this skeleton.

Discussion

Osteological analysis revealed three adults, two females (a younger and an older adult) and one adult whose sex and age category could not be determined due to underrepresentation and fragmentation of diagnostic elements. The stature of the older adult female (skeleton 3484) was below average for the period, which is reported as 1.59m by Roberts and Cox (2001, 163).

Pathological lesions were present on both of the aged and sexed individuals, though unsurprisingly none were present on the more fragmentary unsexed adult. The young female exhibited only cribra orbitalia, whilst the older female had cribra orbitalia and a number of other conditions, including osteoarthritis and Schmorl's nodes. Both of these conditions are linked with age as well as activity, and it is, therefore, hardly surprising that they are present on the older but not the younger individual (Lovell 1997, 159; Rogers and Waldron 1995, 32; Roberts and Manchester 1995, 106). Whilst cribra orbitalia is not an unusual or rare condition, it may be worth noting that it was observed in both the orbits of both of the females, albeit in not very extensive or gross form (types 2 and 3 after Stuart-Macadam 1991,109), and that only 10% of individuals in Roman Britain usually exhibit this lesion (Roberts and Cox 2003, 141). Whilst this could just be a factor of the Ridgeway Hill Romano-British assemblage being so small, it could also be an indication of a systemic lack of iron in the diet of this population.

Anglo-Saxon inhumation burials

Three skeletons were recovered from two adjacent east-west grave cuts at the northern end of the site. Skeleton 3616 was in a single occupancy grave and lay in a supine position with its head at the west end and both hands laid upon the pelvis. Skeletons 3618 and 3626 were recovered from the same grave. Skeleton 3626 was buried in a supine position, also with its head at the west, its right hand on its pelvis and its left by its side. Disarticulated skeleton 3618 was recovered from the fill both above and below skeleton 3626. This suggests that skeleton 3618 was the first interment within this grave and was later disturbed during the interment of the later individual. A radiocarbon date (SUERC-41556: 1305±25 BP) indicates that skeleton 3616 dates from the Anglo-Saxon period (AD 650-780 at 95.4% confidence, and 660-770 at 68.2%).

Skeletons 3616 and 3626 were both nearly complete and had suffered very little post-mortem damage or fragmentation. Not surprisingly, the disarticulated remains (3618) were much more fragmented and less complete (25-50%).

On the basis of cranial and pelvic features and metrical data all three of the skeletons appear to have been male.

The pubic symphyses and auricular surfaces indicate that both skeletons 3616 and 3626 were young adults (Suchey-Brooks 1990; Lovejoy *et al.* 1985; Buckberry and Chamberlain 2002). The incomplete fusion of the ischial tuberoisty epiphyses in both skeletons confirms this and reduces the age range to between 20 and 23 years old at time of death for skeleton 3616. For skeleton 3626 the iliac crest and thoracic vertebral annular rings indicate an age of 19 years old at time of death (Scheuer and Black 2000). Multiple age indicators suggested that skeleton 3618 was an older adult, aged 45+ years. Greatest weight was placed on the auricular surface (Buckberry and Chamberlain 2002; Lovejoy 1985) and the pubic symphysis (Brooks and Suchey 1990) when arriving at this estimate.

Due to post-mortem damage and fragmentation no cranial metrics could be taken from skeletons 3616 and 3626, but most of the post-cranial ones were. Using the maximum length of the left femur, it was estimated that skeleton 3616 was approximately 1.75m (+/- 32.7mm) tall and that skeleton 3626 was approximately 1.77m (+/- 32.7 mm). In the case of skeleton 3618 no long bones were complete enough to allow a stature estimation to be made.

Non-metric traits observed in skeleton 3616 included a right accessory infraorbital foramen (left could not be observed) and extrasutural mastoid foramina bilaterally in the cranium. Post-cranially, an accessory sacral facet was observed on the right ilium/sacrum (absent on the left) as well as bilateral femoral hypotrochanteric fossa and double anterior facets of talus and calcaneus.

In the case of skeleton 3626, ossicles were observed at lambda and in the left and right lambdoid sutures. Postcranially, there was a bilateral hypotrochanteric fossa on the femora and there was a double anterior facet on the left calcaneus (only a single one was observed on the right). Some locations for both cranial and post-cranial non-metric traits could be observed on skeleton 3618, but only a hypotrochanteric fossa on the right femur was present.

A small number of pathologies were observed. In the case of skeleton 3616, the right neural arch of the 5th lumbar vertebrae had fractured and failed to reunite with the rest of the vertebrae just inferior to the superior articulation, and the left arch has partly fractured at the same point indicating unilateral spondylolysis. MSMs were noted bilaterally on the clavicles (costoclavicular ligament and corocoid),

100

humerii (pectoralis major and deltiod attachments) and femora (linea asperia). These, along with the spondylolysis and femoral hypotrochanteric fossa give the overall impression of an individual who led an active, physically demanding lifestyle.

In the case of skeleton 3626 pathological changes observed include evidence of spinal joint disease, trauma, a developmental anomaly and a condition of unknown aetiology. Spinal joint disease was evidenced solely in the form of Schmorl's nodes, which were present on the superior and inferior surfaces of seven thoracic and four lumbar vertebrae. The trauma was a healed fracture of the posterior tubercle of the left talus, which is likely to have been caused by forced plantar flexion of the foot trapping the posterior tubercle between the calcaneus and the posterior margin of the tibia (Galloway 1999, 210). Both condyles of the mandible were unusually formed. The medial half of both articular surfaces was depressed and flattened in comparison to the lateral sides. This is likely to be no more than a developmental anomaly and may have gone completely unnoticed in life. Both orbits also exhibited a boney spicule on the medial sides of the frontal bone portion of the orbit where the superior oblique muscle of the eyeball attaches.

The only skeletal pathology observed on skeleton 3618 was vertebral body osteophytes which was found on the margins of the 5th lumbar and 1st sacral vertebrae.

There was general little dental pathology. All three skeletons had calculus and a single canine of skeleton 3626 exhibited DEH in line form, indicating an arrest in enamel formation between the ages of 2.5 and 3.5 years. Skeleton 3618, however, had calculus, periodontal disease, caries and DEH of a line form which again indicates an arrest in the formation of enamel between the ages

of 2.5 and 3.5 years. Skeleton 3616 had an edge to edge bite.

Osteological analysis revealed three adult males, two young and one older. Pathological conditions were present on all three individuals, mostly in the form of dental pathology, though none of them had any dental conditions worthy of particular attention. There was no sign of dietary stress or deficiency on any of the skeletons, except a slight hypoplastic defect on a canine on both skeleton 3618 (older adult male) and 3626 (young adult male), the appearance of which was judged to have happened when the individuals were between 2.5 and 3.5 years old. Other factors, such as illness or environmental stress could have also caused these defects (Hillson 1996, 166). It was clear, however, from the musculo-skeletal stress markers that skeleton 3616 had led an active and physically demanding lifestyle. The only other sign of physiological stress on these individuals was in the form of a single fracture to the posterior tubercle of the talus on skeleton 3626.

Early Bronze Age cremation burials *by Helen Webb*

Introduction

Cremated bone was recovered from 10 contexts. A number of the contexts were related, for example, fills surrounding a main cremation deposit were taken as soil samples to recover cremated bone that had become mixed between the contexts by bioturbation, ploughing etc.. If the related contexts are considered as single deposits, the actual number of cremation deposits recovered is six (Table 3.30). Of these, four (3034, 3193, 3220 and 3205) were considered to be deliberate cremation deposits, comprising moderate to substantial bone weights. The other two

Table 3.30 Summary of contexts containing cremated human bone

Context number	Context description	Grouping/overall deposit number
3193	Cremation deposit in pit cist 3149	3193
3150	Backfill of cist 3149, overlies cremation deposit 3193	
3148	Backfill surrounding cist 3149	
3220	Cremation deposit in cist 3156	3220
3219	Backfill of cist 3156, overlies cremation deposit 3220	
3205	Cremation deposit in cist 3206	3205
3034	Cremation deposit in pit 3033 (in centre of ring ditch 3032)	3034
3035	Backfill of pit 3033, overlies cremation deposit 3034	
3050	Backfill of grave 3046, overlies inhumation 3048	3050
3445	Lower fill of pit 3372	3445

(3050 and 3445) comprised very small bone amounts which may have been residual and which could not be positively identified as human. All six cremation deposits underwent full osteological analysis.

All of the deliberate cremation deposits were of early Bronze Age or early to middle Bronze Age date. Three were associated with stone cist structures, the fourth with a small pit in the centre of ring ditch 3032.

Disturbance and truncation

The cists associated with cremation deposits 3220 and 3205 were truncated to some extent by plough action. However, the cremation deposits were concentrated at the base of the cist structures and were largely unaffected. The quantities of bone present, therefore, are probably representative of the whole amounts originally deposited. Cremation deposit 3193, also associated with a cist, was unaffected by plough truncation but the presence of micromammal bones, as well as the presence of two small cremated bone fragments in the backfill (3148) surrounding the cist structure, indicate some disturbance through animal burrowing.

The central cremation burial (3034) within ring ditch 3032 appeared to have suffered more significant truncation. The overall depth of the pit was only 0.1m and, whilst the cremated bone was concentrated at the base of the pit, some was present at the top of the feature. It is impossible to estimate how much bone may have been lost due to ploughing.

Methodology

In accordance with recommended practice (McKinley 2004, 9) contexts comprising or containing cremated bone were subject to whole-earth recovery. The deposits were wet sieved and sorted into fractions of >10mm, 10 – 4mm and 4 – 2mm. The bone from the >10mm and 10 – 4mm fractions were separated from the extraneous material, which included flint and chalk fragments. Where 4-2mm fractions comprised large total weights, bone weights within these fractions were estimated by separating the bone from 50g samples, and calculating the proportion present. Three deposits (3193, 3205 and 3034) also had unsorted 2-0.5mm residues. Visually, these appeared to contain proportions of cremated bone similar to the unsorted 4-2mm fractions. As such, the proportions calculated for the 4-2mm fractions were also applied to the residues in order to estimate the bone weights within them.

The bone was assessed for colour, weight and maximum fragment size. Each fraction was examined for identifiable bone elements and the presence of pyre and grave goods. An attempt was made to estimate the minimum number of individuals (MNI) present and their age and sex. The MNI was estimated on the basis of the identification of repeated elements. Age estimations were based upon dental development (Moorees et al. 1963), epiphyseal fusion (Scheuer and Black 2000) and the overall degree of cranial suture closure (Meindl and Lovejoy 1985), although the latter is recognised as one of the less reliable ageing methods (Cox 2000, 66-68). Estimation of sex was possible in only one deposit. This was based on the observation of a sexually dimorphic trait of the skull (Buikstra and Ubelaker 1994).

Results

A summary of the skeletal elements represented and the weight of bone present per fraction size is given in Table 3.31.

Condition and fragmentation

In general, the cremated bone was very fragmented, with a large proportion of fragments under 10mm. Significant proportions of the bone weights were, however, accounted for by the >10mm fractions. Unsurprisingly, given the general thickness of the cortex, the largest fragments observed were femoral shaft. In general, the 4-2mm fractions comprised comparatively small proportions of the total weights.

Weight of deposits

The MNI represented in each of the cremation deposits was one (see below). The four main deposits comprised fairly large to moderate bone weights. Cremation deposit 3034, the only deposit potentially having been affected by significant truncation, comprised the greatest bone weight, at 1462.5g, followed by deposit 3205, at 1297.5g. Both of these weights are within the range observed in modern adult cremations (McKinley 2000a, 269). The weight of cremation deposit 3220 fell just below the lower end of the range, at 918.5g. The lowest weight (253.2g) was observed in deposit 3193 (the remains of a juvenile).

Skeletal elements

Trabecular bone was poorly represented within all deposits. The vast majority of bone fragments were cortical bone, with cranial and long bone shaft fragments being the most frequent. McKinley (2004, 11) highlights the fact that the distinctive appearance of parts of the skull, even as small fragments, invariably leads to a bias in the amount of skull identified. This was evident in the Ridgeway Hill

Table 3.31 Summary of skeletal elements represented and weights of bone present in early Bronze Age cremation burials

Deposit	Skeletal region	> 10 mm frags	> 10 mm weight	10-4 mm frags	10-4 mm weight	4–2 mm frags	4–2 mm weight	Total weight per skeletal region	2-0.5 mm unsorted residue (est. bone weight)	Total deposit weight (inc. est weights)
3193	Skull	Vault, mand, petrous	18.0 g	Vault, mand condyle, orbit, tooth roots	28.4 g	Tooth roots	0.2 g	46.6 g	2.8 g	253.2 g
	Axial	Rib, CV arch, ilium	1.7 g	Rib, vert arch, CV2 arch, ilium	15.9 g	Rib frags	0.3 g	17.9 g		
	Upper limb	Dist hum, hum shaft, rad shaft, clav, phal	6.9 g	Rad/uln shaft, hum shaft, phal	11.8 g	Phal	0.1 g	18.8 g		
	Lower limb	Dist fem, fem, tib + fib shaft	16.0 g	Fem, tib + fib shaft, dist fib epiph	9.4 g		-	25.4 g		
	Unid long bone		12.3 g		27.0 g		0.3 g	39.6 g		
	Unid hand/foot		-		2.9 g		0.1 g	3.0 g		
	Unid joint surface		-		1.8 g		-	1.8 g		
	Unid other		7.2 g		58.6 g		31.5 g (est.)	97.3 g		
	Total weight (inc. est. weights)		62.1 g		155.8 g		32.5 g			
3220	Skull	Vault, mand, max	82.0 g	Vault, mand, max, zygo, tooth roots	49.2 g		-	131.2 g	0.0 g	918.5 g
	Axial	Rib, vert arch, LV5/SV1 frag; ilium	31.9 g	Rib, vert arch, ilio-pubic ramus frag	23.7 g		-	55.6 g		
	Upper limb	Hum, rad + ulna shaft, scap spine	63.0 g	Hum shaft, rad/ulna shaft	16.8 g		-	79.8 g		
	Lower limb	Fem, tib + fib shaft, MT1 frag	107.2 g	Fem, tib + fib shaft	39.2 g		-	146.4 g		
	Unid long bone		43.4 g		45.7 g		-	89.1 g		
	Unid hand/foot		-		0.3 g		-	0.3 g		
	Unid joint surface		2.9 g		1.8 g		-	4.7 g		
	Unid other		21.7 g		322.9 g		66.8 g (est.)	411.4 g		
	Total weight (inc. est. weights)		352.1 g		499.6 g		66.8 g			
3205	Skull	Vault, petrous, mand, mand condyle, max, zygo, tooth roots	135.6 g	Vault, mand, max, zygo, tooth roots	45.5 g		-	181.1 g	48.6 g	1297.5 g
	Axial	Rib, vert arch	41.9 g	Rib, vert arch	25.8 g	Rib	0.1 g	67.8 g		
	Upper limb	Hum shaft, rad/ulna shaft, scap, phals, MC, carpals	113.3 g	Hum shaft, rad/ulna shaft, phals, carpal, MC	11.8 g		-	125.1 g		
	Lower limb	Fem, tib + fib shaft, ?tarsal	154.0 g	Fem + tib shaft, phal	13.8 g		-	167.8 g		
	Unid long bone		77.2 g		35.3 g		-	112.5 g		
	Unid hand/foot		6.0 g		2.8 g		-	8.8 g		
	Unid joint surface		8.3 g		8.8 g		-	17.1 g		
	Unid other		64.5 g		393.0 g		111.2 g (est.)	568.7 g		
	Total weight (inc. est. weights)		600.8 g		536.8 g		111.3 g			

Table 3.31 (continued)

Deposit	Skeletal region	> 10 mm frags	> 10 mm weight	10-4 mm frags	10-4 mm weight	4–2 mm frags	4–2 mm weight	Total weight per skeletal region	2-0.5 mm unsorted residue (est. bone weight)	Total deposit weight (inc. est weights)
3034	Skull	Vault, mand, max	88.1 g	Vault, occip condyle, petrous, max, mand, mand condyle, tooth roots	55.0 g	-		143.1 g	278.8 g	1462.5 g
	Axial	Rib, vert arch	6.3 g	Rib, vert arch, CV1 + dens frags, ilium, acetab frag	16.2 g	-		22.5 g		
	Upper limb	Scap, hum shaft, rad head frag, rad/ulna shaft	19.8 g	Hum shaft, rad/ ulna shaft, rad head frag, prox ulna, phals, carpals	31.3 g	-		51.1 g		
	Lower limb	Fem shaft, dist fem, tib + fib shaft, calc, talus	52.1 g	Fem, tib + fib shaft, calc, sesamoid, cuneiform, phals	41.4 g	-		93.5 g		
	Unid long bone		26.2 g		94.4 g	-		120.6 g		
	Unid hand/foot		0.6 g		13.1 g	-		13.7 g		
	Unid joint surface		4.2 g		15.4 g	-		19.6 g		
	Unid other		6.5 g		487.4 g	225.7 g (est.)		719.6 g		
	Total weight (inc. est. weights)		203.8 g		754.2 g	225.7 g				
3050	Unid		-		0.1 g	-			0.0 g	0.1 g
	Total weight		-		0.1 g	-				
3445	Unid		-		<0.1 g	-			0.0 g	<0.1 g
	Total weight		-		<0.1 g	-				

NB: The deposit numbers given are the 'grouped' numbers from Table 1. The weights given include the bone weights from associated contexts.

Key: occip = occipital; mand = mandible; max = maxilla; zygo = zygomatic; scap = scapula; clav = clavicle; hum = humerus; rad = radius; MC = metacarpal; acetab = acetabulum; fem = femur; tib = tibia; frag = fragment; phal = phalanx; MT = metatarsal; calc = calcaneus; CV = cervical vertebra; LV = lumbar vertebra; SV = sacral vertebra; prox = proximal; dist = distal; epiph = epiphysis; est = estimated

cremations, with skull fragments comprising the highest proportion of identified fragments in three (3193, 3205 and 3034) of the four main cremation deposits.

Of the skull bones identified, vault fragments were unsurprisingly most frequent in all deposits. Fragments of the petrous portion of the temporal bone were observed in 3034, 3205 and 3193, and zygomatic fragments in 3205. Mandible and maxilla fragments were present in all four deposits, as were tooth roots. The tooth roots were generally incomplete, but incisors, canines, premolars and molars were all identified. In the case of juvenile cremation deposit 3193, the presence of an incompletely formed premolar (probably first) root allowed for a more precise estimation of age than the other bone fragments provided (see below).

Rib fragments were frequent in all four of the deposits. As with skull fragments, this is probably in part due to the relatively distinctive appearance of rib bones, and the subsequent ease in identifying even small fragments. Vertebral fragments were also identified in all four deposits. With the exception of a fifth lumbar or first sacral vertebral body fragment in deposit 3220, and an odontoid peg in 3034, only vertebral arch fragments were observed. Pelvis fragments were comparatively few, but where identified, ilium fragments were most common. That said, a small fragment of acetabulum was present in deposit 3034, and a probable ilio-pubic ramus fragment was identified in deposit 3220.

Fragments of all of the long bones – humerus, radius and ulna, femur, tibia and fibula – were identified in each of the deposits. The proximal articular surface of the radius was noted in deposits 3032, 3205 and 3193. However, in no case was the radial head complete so that a measurement could be taken for use in sex estimation. Carpals were identified in two deposits. Partial hamate, lunate and scaphoid bones were present in deposit 3034, and in 3205 fragments of hamate, trapezium, pisiform, lunate and triquetral were identified. Tarsals were identified only in deposit 3034. Partial talus, calcaneus and medial cuneiform bones were identified, as well as a sesamoid bone.

Metacarpal and metatarsal fragments were present in all four of the main deposits, but it was generally difficult to distinguish between them given the small size of most of the fragments. It was also difficult to distinguish between many of the small fragments of hand and foot phalanges, although a significant number could be identified due to their distinctive form. Hand phalanges were observed in deposits 3193, 3032 and 3205. The latter two deposits also contained identifiable foot phalanges.

As a result of the high fragmentation levels, unidentified bone fragments within the four main deposits were numerous. In all four of the main cremation deposits, just over half of the total bone weights were unidentified bone. Where possible, unidentified bone fragments were placed into one of three subcategories: unidentified long bone, unidentified joint surface or unidentified hand/foot. Unsurprisingly, unidentified long bone categories yielded the greatest bone weights, although the proportions of unidentified bone fragments that could not be categorised at all were highest.

Demography

None of the cremation deposits appeared to comprise more than one individual (no repeated elements were observed). Cist burials 3205 and 3220 and central ring ditch burial 3034 comprised the remains of adults. Aside from the general size and surface texture of bone fragments in these deposits, the presence of completely fused epiphyses (radial, humeral, phalangeal), and completed tooth root apices, confirmed the presence of adult remains. Only in one case, 3034, was a more precise age tentatively estimated. A number of cranial fragments in this deposit exhibited areas of suture which appeared significantly closed or obliterated, possibly indicating an older individual. The presence of marginal osteophytes in the hand phalanges of this individual was also suggestive of an older adult. Deposit 3193 contained the remains of a juvenile. The presence of an unfused distal fibula epiphysis, unfused phalangeal epiphyses, and an incompletely formed premolar root, suggested that this was an older child, or possibly an adolescent, 7.5-13 years.

Because of the high fragmentation levels and the subsequent paucity of sexually dimorphic skeletal elements, sex could be estimated for only one of the cremation deposits. However, the possible older adult represented in deposit 3034 was tentatively classified as male based upon the presence of two adjoining occipital (skull) fragments. These exhibited a notably large, prominent nuchal crest, indicative of a male individual. An estimation of sex based on a single cranial feature only should, however, be treated with caution.

Pathology

Lesions of pathology were observed in two of the cremation deposits. A cranial fragment from deposit 3193 (juvenile) comprised a partial orbit (eye socket). The roof of the orbit exhibited fine, scattered porous lesions, consistent with cribra orbitalia. In deposit 3034, osteophytes (new bone) were observed around the proximal margins of three distal hand phalanges.

Non-metric traits

Two non-metric traits were observed amongst the cremation deposits. A loose wormian bone was present within deposit 3205. Variations in the sutures of the skull have proven to be under significant genetic control (Torgersen 1951a,b, 1954; Sjøvold 1984, 1987).

In deposit 3034, a fragment of mandible exhibited a small, smooth, bony protrusion, adjacent to the alveolar margin. Such lesions are known as mandibular tori, and have been linked with high levels of masticatory stress (Roberts and Manchester 1995, 54). It is, of course, impossible to comment on the level of dental attrition in the present case, given the absence of dental crowns.

Colour of the cremated bone

All four of the main cremation deposits exhibited high proportions of buff white coloured fragments, indicative of complete oxidation of the majority of bones. The three cist cremation deposits (3193, 3205 and 3220) comprised between *c* 90% and 99% white fragments. Perhaps significantly, deposit 3034 from the centre of ring ditch 3032, comprised a slightly smaller proportion of white fragments (*c* 80%). The non-white fragments from all four deposits were largely light grey or blue-grey in colour (incompletely oxidised), with fewer black (charred) fragments. As may be expected, the grey and black colours were seen on areas such as the endocranium and medullary surfaces of long bones. However, in deposits 3193, 3220 and 3034, the darker blue-grey and black colours were more frequently observed on fragments of vertebral arch, including spinous processes.

A small number of bone fragments within all four of the main deposits exhibited small spots of turquoise-blue staining. The staining was dissimilar to the colours achieved through heat alteration, in that it appeared in discrete spots on the bone surfaces. These stains were distributed across various skeletal elements, that is, they were not clustered or confined to a specific skeletal region in any one of the deposits. For example, in deposit 3220, blue spots were noted on skull, rib and long bone fragments, and in deposit 3193, fragments of skull, femur and a metacarpal/metatarsal exhibited the staining. On a few fragments, the internal surfaces (as well as external surfaces) were affected.

Similar blue staining has been observed on cremated bone fragments from a Bronze Age cemetery at Eaglestone Flat, Curbar, Derbyshire (Barnatt 1994, 293), in a late Iron Age/early Roman cremation deposit from London Gateway (Webb forthcoming) and on the cremated bones from a Bronze Age urned burial from Findhorn, Moray in Scotland (Shepherd and Shepherd 2001, 121). It is probable that such staining is the result of the bone being in contact with copper alloy. In the Findhorn example, the stains were investigated using X-ray fluorescence spectrometry, which revealed that they consisted of copper compounds (ibid., 121). In the absence of such an object within a cremation deposit, and where staining is localised to certain parts of the body, it is suggested that the object may not have been deposited at all, but was removed from the pyre debris after the cremation (McKinley 1994b, 339). Where a range of bones and bone surfaces are involved, as in the Ridgeway Hill cremation deposits and both comparative examples noted above, it is more likely that contact with the object occurred after the cremation process, within the burial environment. Such stains are usually interpreted as deriving from the total decay of a small bronze artefact (Shepherd and Shepherd 2001, 121).

Small cremation deposits

Very small amounts of burnt bone were recovered from two contexts. The backfill (3050) of inhumation grave 3046 (Set 4) yielded two small fragments (0.1g). A single fragment (<0.g) was recovered from context 3445, the basal deposit in late Neolithic pit 3372. So small were the amounts of bone recovered from these contexts that they could not be identified as either animal or human. It would be unwise to classify these cases as intentional cremation deposits as it is possible that the bone fragments were washed or blown into the feature fills, or represent intrusions via bioturbation or ploughing.

Discussion

The four larger cremation deposits represent intentional burials of cremated individuals. Three were

adult (3220, 3205 and 3034), one of which (3034) may have been male, and one of which (3193) was a juvenile, c 7.5-13 years of age. The presence of single individuals within each of the cremation deposits is in keeping with other Bronze Age cremation burials. On average, only 5% of cremation burials comprise the remains of two individuals, and a far smaller proportion contain three (McKinley 1997, 130). The weights of bone within each of the deposits were also in keeping with the range observed in other Bronze Age cremation burials (ibid., 139). It has been noted that primary Bronze Age barrow burials consistently produce high bone weights (ibid., 142). In keeping with this pattern, central barrow burial 3034 produced the highest weight of all four deposits (1462.5g). This weight is very close to the average bone weight recorded for primary Bronze Age barrow cremation deposits (1525.7g; ibid., 142).

All three of the adult cremation deposits comprised bone weights that were within or just below the range of weights observed in modern adult cremations. This, along with the representation of all skeletal regions within the deposits, indicates that most of the cremated remains were collected from the pyre and buried. It is of course more difficult to comment on the weight of the juvenile cremation deposit (3193), but there was no evidence for intentional selection of specific skeletal regions for burial, and all skeletal elements were represented.

No burnt animal bone or artefacts were identified in any of the cremation deposits. This indicates that either pyre goods were not included in the cremations of these individuals or, if they were, that they were removed prior to the burial of the cremated remains. Animal bone is the most commonly found pyre offering, but has been recovered from only 16 % of Bronze Age cremation burials in England (McKinley 1997, 137). The only animal remains identified within the deposits were unburnt rodent bones and teeth (in deposit 3193), indicative of post-burial animal disturbance. Only cremation deposit 3034 had an associated artefact, in the form of a dagger or knife tip. This had been placed on the base of the pit, prior to the deposition of the cremated bone and had not been burnt. The blue staining on the bones may indicate the presence of other, decayed copper alloy grave goods. If this is indeed the case, it is interesting that all four of the cremation burials exhibited stains.

It appears as though a fairly high efficiency of cremation had been achieved in all four cremations, with the vast majority of bone being white in colour. In general, Bronze Age cremated bone shows more uniform burning than burials of later time periods, such as Roman (McKinley 2000c, 66). That said, a small proportion of the bone fragments within each of the deposits was non-white. It was noted that some of the darkest (less burnt) fragments in deposits 3193, 3220 and 3034 were vertebral arches. This pattern may be used to infer the position of the bodies on the pyre. If the bones of the spine were less heat affected than other regions of the skeleton, it seems reasonable to suggest that these were furthest from the heat source. Assuming that the bodies were laid on top of the pyre, as may have been the norm (McKinley 1997, 132), the lesser heat changes on the spine would suggest that the bodies were prone. This may be unusual, given that McKinley's (1997, 132) review of archaeological and ethnographic evidence for cremation indicates that a supine position was the norm.

THE ANIMAL BONE *by Lena Strid*

Introduction

The animal bone assemblage consisted of a total of 1910 refitted fragments from securely dated contexts. Of these, 1465 fragments (77%) derived from sieved soil samples. Despite the large number of sieved bones, only 155 (8%) were identifiable to taxa, almost half of which were microfauna. The assemblage ranges from the middle Neolithic to the Roman period, although the majority of the bones derive from the late Neolithic/early Bronze Age. A full record of the assemblage can be found in the site archive.

Methodology

The bones were identified at Oxford Archaeology South using comparative skeletal reference collections, in addition to osteological identification manuals. All animal remains were counted and weighed and, where possible, identified to species, element, side and zone. Sheep and goat were identified to species where possible, using Boessneck *et al.* (1964) and Prummel and Frisch (1986). They were otherwise classified as 'sheep/goat'. Ribs and vertebrae, with the exception of atlas and axis, were classified by size: 'large mammal' representing cattle, horse and deer; 'medium mammal' representing sheep/goat, pig and large dog; 'small mammal' representing small dog, cat and hare; and 'microfauna' representing animals such as frog, rat and mice.

The condition of the bone was graded on a 6-point system (0-5). Grade 0 representing very well preserved bone, and grade 5 indicating that the bone had suffered such structural and attritional damage as to make it unrecognisable.

The minimum number of individuals (MNI) was calculated based on the most frequently occurring bone for each species using Serjeantson's (1996) and Worley's (Strid 2012) zoning guides and taking into account left and right sides, as well as epiphyseal fusion and tooth wear. For the calculation of the number of identified fragments per species (NISP) all identifiable fragments were counted, although bones with modern breaks were refitted. The weight of bone fragments has been recorded in order to give an idea of their size and to provide an alternative means of quantification.

For ageing, Habermehl's (1975) data on epiphyseal fusion was used. Three fusion stages were recorded: 'unfused', 'in fusion', and 'fused'. 'In fusion' indicates that the epiphyseal line is still visible. Tooth wear was recorded using Grant's tooth wear stages (Grant 1982), and correlated with tooth eruption (Habermehl 1975). In order to estimate an age for the animals, the methods of Halstead (1985), Payne (1973) and O'Connor (1988) were used for cattle, sheep/goat and pig respectively.

Sex estimation was carried out on morphological traits on cattle pelves and pig canine teeth, using data from Schmid (1972) and Vretemark (1997). Further, the presence/absence of antler were used to sex roe deer remains.

Measurements were taken according to von den Driesch (1976), using digital callipers with an accuracy of 0.01mm. Large bones were measured using an osteometric board, with an accuracy of 1mm.

Preservation

The bones were generally poorly preserved, regardless of time period. Most bones show little preserved surface, rendering it difficult to observe pathologies, butchery marks and gnaw marks. The early Bronze Age and Roman assemblages showed the greatest variety in bone preservation, although since the two best preserved categories consist exclusively of teeth and microfauna bones, the apparent variety in bone preservation could be a taphonomic bias, rather than an actual difference in bone disposal practices.

Gnaw marks from a carnivore were found on a single bone in the late Neolithic/early Bronze Age assemblage. The scarcity of gnaw marks is probably directly related to the poor bone preservation. Burnt bones, ranging from partially charred to calcined, were recovered in relatively small numbers from features dating to the middle Neolithic, late Neolithic and Roman periods. In contrast, almost 20% of the bones from the late Neolithic/early Bronze Age assemblage were calcined or charred.

Overview of the assemblage

The prehistoric assemblage derives from a single middle Neolithic pit (3041), three closely situated late Neolithic pits (3371, 3372 and 3373), two pits (3544 and 3628) from the late Neolithic/early Bronze Age, one cremation burial and four inhumation burials (3067, 3232. 3147 and 3227) from the early Bronze Age. One ring ditch (3032) probably dated from the end of the early Bronze Age or the beginning of the middle Bronze Age period but the second ring ditch (3514) could not be clearly dated. The Roman assemblage comes from a probably late Roman inhumation (3041) and a quarry pit (3110).

The species present include cattle (*Bos taurus*), sheep/goat (*Ovis aries/Capra hircus*), pig (*Sus domesticus*), horse (*Equus caballus*), dog (*Canis familiaris*), red deer (*Cervus elaphus*), roe deer (*Capreolus capreolus*), aurochs (*Bos primigenius*), wood mouse (*Apodemus sylvaticus*), water vole (*Arvicola terrestris*), bank vole (*Myodes glareolus*), field vole (*Microtus agrestis*), common shrew (*Sorex araneus*) and frog/toad (*Rana* sp./*Bufo* sp.). The assemblage also included remains from red/roe deer, unidentified bird, mouse and shrew (Table 3.32).

The presence of microfauna in archaeological contexts is often problematic. Many of these taxa are burrowers and may, therefore, be intrusive. However, it cannot be excluded that the bones represent animals from these periods, and may, therefore, reflect the local environment in the past. Microfauna are often commensal (ie they live in the vicinity of human settlements and benefit from this, whereas the humans receive no benefit from the presence of the microfauna). Occasionally, evidence is found that microfauna were exploited by humans, for example, water voles from the Danish Neolithic settlement Muldbjerg I exhibited cut marks on the skulls, indicating utilisation of their fur (Noe Nygaard 1995). The microfauna from Ridgeway Hill show no such indications of human utilisation. They were found at all levels in the features.

The microfauna from the late Neolithic and early Bronze Age assemblages – house mouse, water vole, bank vole, field vole and common shrew – live in a wide variety of habitats, of which grasslands and

Table 3.32 Number of identified bones/taxon by chronological phase (MNI within parentheses)

	MN	LN	LN/EBA	EBA	EBA/MBA	Roman	Late Roman
Cattle		6 (1)	22 (2)	2 (2)		4 (1)	1 (1)
Sheep/goat			5 (2)		1 (1)	24 (2)	
Pig	12 (1)		51 (2)			3 (1)	2 (1)
Horse					2 (1)	9 (2)	
Dog						3 (1)	
Canid						7	
Red deer		3 (1)	1 (1)				1 (1)
Roe deer				3 (2)			
Deer sp.			2				
Aurochs		1 (1)					
Indet. bird						1	
Wood mouse				1 (1)			
Mouse sp.			2	1			
Water vole				3 (1)		2 (1)	
Bank vole/field vole		4		3		4	
Bank vole				1 (1)			
Field vole				17 (4)		31 (1)	
Rodent		5	1	14		34	1
Common shrew				2 (1)			
Shrew sp.		1		2			
Amphibian		1		1			
Microfauna		8	6	47		17	
Small mammal		1	1		1	4	
Medium mammal			44	1		20	
Large mammal		14	30	2	2	8	
Indeterminate	49	68	1158	12	7	67	1
Total	61	112	1321	112	13	237	6
Identified to species	12	15	78	32	3	77	4
Weight (g)	8	1140	1511	176	63	892	69

open woods are common. The bank vole and water vole prefer wetter habitats, while the field vole prefers dry pastures (Bjärvall and Ullström 1995). The local microfauna, therefore, indicate a local environment of pastures and crop growing fields as well as wetland. The predominance of field vole over bank vole in the Roman assemblage suggests that by that time the landscape was predominantly used for crop growing and animal pasture.

Middle Neolithic

The middle Neolithic assemblage comprised 61 bones from pit 3041 (Table 3.32). The pig remains consisted solely of tooth fragments, of which a single maxillary molar could be identified. Due to great fragmentation an age-at-death could not be discerned.

Late Neolithic

The late Neolithic assemblage came from three closely situated pits, 3371, 3372 and 3373. The animal bones derive from cattle, red deer, aurochs and commensal microfauna. Several fragments from large mammal long bones were also present (Table 3.33).

Pit 3371 contained only bones and teeth from microfauna and a rib fragment from a small mammal. It is, therefore, unlikely that the pit was used for disposal of butchery waste or cooking waste.

The faunal remains from pit 3372 comprised cheek teeth from cattle and red deer, microfauna long bones and several small fragments from indeterminate taxa. As a game animal, red deer may have held special significance related to the social

Table 3.33 Number of identified bones/taxon in the late Neolithic pits

	3371	3372	3373
Cattle		2	4
Red deer		2	1
Aurochs			1
Bank vole/field vole	1	2	1
Rodent	2		3
Shrew sp.			1
Amphibian	1		
Microfauna	5		3
Small mammal	1		
Large mammal		13	1
Indeterminate		57	11
Total	10	76	26
Weight (g)	0	153	987

activity of hunting and its implied status. However, since ritual deposits rarely include loose teeth, the presence of the molars could be accidental.

Pit 3373 contained three bone yielding fills. The shallow primary fill (3430) included a very small fragment from a red deer metatarsal. The second fill (3431) contained more animal bone, among them the distal half of an aurochs humerus and fragments of a cattle humerus shaft and a cattle mandible. While none of the bones displayed gnaw marks, their fragmented nature suggests that at least the cattle bones represent kitchen waste. The aurochs on the other hand may have held a different status in Neolithic society as a wild game animal and even if the humerus was not complete, the deposit of such bone may have held special significance. A radiocarbon date indicates that the humerus was middle Neolithic in date and may already have been old when deposited in the pit. The top fill (3433) included an almost complete right half of a cattle pelvis. The bone surface was in a poor condition, making it difficult to ascertain whether any cut marks from filleting or disarticulation were present. Complete meat-bearing bones from cattle are rare in the Ridgeway Hill assemblage, suggesting that the pelvis may have been deposited as part of a closing ritual for the pit.

Cattle are the only domestic species present in the assemblage. On late Neolithic sites in southern Britain pig is generally the most common species, followed by cattle and sheep. This is in stark contrast to sites from the preceding and succeeding time periods, including late Neolithic/early Bronze Age sites, where cattle is the most common taxon (Serjeantson 2011, 15-18). It has been suggested that the predominance of pig in the late Neolithic was associated with increased woodland for pannage or with a biased sample of sites, with more ceremonial and feasting sites targeted for excavation than in other periods (Albarella and Serjeantson 2002, 35).

Hunting is indicated by the presence of the aurochs humerus and a metacarpal and two mandibular teeth from red deer. As has been noted, however, the aurochs humerus may have been residual and, as the assemblage is small, it is impossible to ascertain to what extent hunting contributed to the diet. Domestic mammals generally dominate late Neolithic assemblages (Pollard 2006, 142-143), which suggests that hunting was an occasional pastime, possibly mainly a social event rather than purely utilitarian.

Bones from aurochs and cattle have been found on several Neolithic and Bronze Age sites in Britain and continental Europe. Isotopic analyses suggest that the two species occupied different habitats, aurochs probably feeding primarily on wetlands and cattle feeding on dryer pastures (Lynch *et al.*

2008). While aurochs may have occupied the flood-plains of the river Frome, red deer would have preferred a forested habitat. The archaeobotanical analyses indicate the presence of mature oak and hazel in the local area, although it is difficult to ascertain the extent of woodlands, particularly for regions further away from the settlement.

Late Neolithic/early Bronze Age

The late Neolithic/early Bronze Age assemblage comprises faunal remains from two pits (3544 and 3628). The faunal remains from the pits are dominated by pig bones (Table 3.34), in contrast to contemporary sites in southern Britain, where cattle dominate (Serjeantson 2011, 17). The majority of the pig remains comes from a single pit (3544), which could favour the hypothesis that a predominance of pig bones is connected to ceremonial and feasting deposits (Albarella and Serjeantson 2002,

Table 3.34 Number of identified bones/taxon in late Neolithic/early Bronze Age pits

	Pit 3544	Pit 3628
Cattle	16	6
Sheep/goat	4	1
Pig	40	11
Deer sp.	2	
Mouse sp.	1	
Rodent	1	
Microfauna	5	1
Small mammal	1	
Medium mammal	39	5
Large mammal	29	1
Indeterminate	934	224
Total		
Weight (g)	1226	285

Table 3.35 Elements of cattle and pig skeletons represented in late Neolithic/early Bronze Age pits

	Pit 3544		Pit 3628
	Fill 3543	Fill 3590	Fill 3614
Cattle Head	8	4	1
Axial skeleton		2	1
Front limb		1	
Hind limb		1	
Feet (including carpals and tarsals)			4
Pig Head	18	10	7
Axial skeleton			
Front limb		1	2
Hind limb		1	
Feet (including carpals and tarsals	9	1	1
Unidentified long bone (juvenile)			1

35). However, given the small size of the Ridgeway Hill assemblage, such interpretation must remain tentative.

The deer remains comprise two small antler fragments, too small for identification to species.

The skeletal element distribution is different in the two pits. The cattle remains in the upper fill (3543) of pit 3544 derive exclusively from the head, whereas the pig remains from this fill included elements from head and feet. In contrast the cattle and pig remains from the lower fill (3590) came from a wider variety of elements. The bone assemblage from the single fill (3614) of pit 3628 is much smaller than the one from pit 3544. The cattle remains comprise elements from head, neck and feet and the pig remains come from head, front limb and feet (Table 3.35). This suggests that the pits may mainly have been used for deposits of primary butchery waste, although a small amount of kitchen waste was deposited in fill 3590 and fill 3614. A single pig ulna indicates an animal of *c* 3.5 years of age upon death.

Early Bronze Age

The faunal remains in two of the early Bronze Age inhumation burials (3147 and 3227; Table 3.36) include fragments of a cattle pelvis and three roe deer antlers. These are the only animal bones which appear to have been deliberately deposited in the graves, although neither was directly associated with a burial, the pelvis having been recovered from

Table 3.36 Number of identified bones/taxon in early Bronze Age burials

	Inhumation 3067	Cremation 3210	Inhumation 3232	Inhumation 3147	Inhumation 3227
Cattle				1	1
Roe deer					3
Wood mouse		1			
Mouse sp.		1			
Water vole	3				
Bank vole/field vole		3			
Bank vole		1			
Field vole		17			
Rodent	2	10	1		1
Common shrew					2
Shrew sp.					2
Amphibian					1
Microfauna		44			3
Medium mammal			1		
Large mammal			2		
Indeterminate		7	4		1
Total					
Weight (g)	0	0	12	43	121

the fill (3148) around a cist (3149 in grave 3146 in Set 6), and the antler from upper fill (3228) of grave 3227 (Set 7), which covered the second inhumation burial in this grave (although it did also contain a small group of disarticulated human remains). The cattle pelvis fragment from inhumation (3147) is small, weighing only 43g, but could have formed a part of a portion of meat intended as grave goods, or remains from a funeral feast. The three roe deer antlers, one of which was shed, were found above and to the side of crouched inhumation burial 3227. The *in situ* position of the unshed antlers suggests that they derive from the same skull. None of the three antlers is worked, and their presence in the grave could represent raw material, hunting trophies and/or have a symbolic significance connected to the social status of the deceased.

The majority of the remaining faunal remains come from commensal microfauna (Table 3.36). While it cannot be excluded that microfauna were used as grave goods, they are more likely to be accidental inclusions. Indeed, none of the animal bones from the cremation burial are burnt, suggesting that they are intrusive.

Early to middle Bronze Age

Only a very small assemblage of animal bone was recovered from ring ditch 3032. Although the ring ditch itself dates from the early to middle Bronze Age, most of the animal bone was recovered from its upper fills, which contained Roman pottery. Sheep/goat and horse were present as well as unidentified small and large mammal. Two horse teeth are an unusual find for the early to middle Bronze Age. Remains of domestic horse became progressively more common in southern Britain from the early Bronze Age and by the late Bronze Age are present in small numbers in almost all assemblages (Bendrey 2010, 10-12). The examples here, however, could be of Roman date.

Roman

The Roman assemblage from quarry pit 3110 contains a great variety of taxa, although the amount of bones per species is low. Sheep/goat is the most numerous taxon, followed by horse (Table 3.32). Other species present include cattle, pig, dog, water vole and field vole. However, the majority of the sheep/goat remains are teeth (n: 21), which suggests that the assemblage might have been subjected to particular disposal practices or have suffered from poor bone preservation. The pig, horse and dog remains are mainly post-cranial, albeit in a poor condition, suggesting that bone preservation may have been the main reason for the

predominance of teeth from sheep/goat and cattle.

In Dorchester, as well as in rural settlements near the town, sheep/goat and cattle are found in similar abundance (Bullock and Allen 1997; Grimm 2008; Rielly 1997). While sheep/goat were more common in rural Iron Age settlements (Bullock and Allen 1997), an increase in the number of cattle bones during the Roman period is found in large areas of Roman Britain, and may have been associated with the increased need for draught oxen and food provisioning for towns and military forts.

The predominance of sheep/goat in the Roman assemblage could indicate that the inhabitants may have focussed on sheep husbandry, whether for meat, milk products or wool. However, the frequency of sheep bones may have been inflated by trade in cattle livestock to the urban markets in Dorchester. Zooarchaeological remains from a plethora of Roman urban sites show that beef formed the main part of the urban meat diet (King 1999, 179). In Dorchester, sheep/goat and cattle are found in similar abundance, which probably reflects the suitability for sheep grazing on the downlands.

Late Roman

Only a small assemblage of animal bone was recovered from a probably late Roman grave (3541). With the exception of a red deer antler tine and a cattle hyoid (tongue bone), the faunal remains (pig lateral metapodial, pig styloid, rodent incisor) are more suggestive of accidental inclusions in the grave fill than deliberate deposits. The cattle hyoid could derive from a food offering, whereas the antler tine might be a tool or could symbolise material for antler working in the afterlife.

CHARRED PLANT REMAINS AND WOOD CHARCOAL *by Sheila Boardman*

Introduction

Following a detailed assessment of 114 bulk soil samples by Smith and Nicholson (2011), 31 samples were selected for further investigation, 30 of these for charred plant remains and 13 for wood charcoal. The deposits investigated for charred plant remains range in age from the middle Neolithic to the Roman period, and for wood charcoal from the middle Neolithic to the early Bronze Age.

Methodology

The samples were processed at OA using a modified Siraf-type water separation machine. The flots were collected in a 250µm mesh and the heavy residues in a 500µm mesh. Flots and residues were sorted using a low power binocular microscope at magnifications of x10 to x20, for cereals grains, chaff, seeds and other quantifiable remains. Wood charcoal greater than 2mm in size was removed. Charcoal fragments were fractured by hand and sorted into groups based on features observed in transverse section at x10 to x40 magnifications. The fragments were then sectioned longitudinally along their radial and tangential planes and examined at magnifications of up to x250 using a Metam P1 metallurgical microscope. Identifications of the wood charcoal were made with reference to Schweingruber (1990), Hather (2000), Gale and Cutler (2000) and Clifford (in Godwin 1956, 385). All wood greater than 4mm in size was examined, together with a selection of the material in the 2-4mm size range.

Identifications of the charred grains, chaff and seeds were carried out at magnifications of x10 to x40, using standard morphological criteria for the cereals (eg Jacomet 2006) and other plants (eg Berrgren 1969; 1981), and by comparison with modern reference material. Classification and nomenclature of plant material follows Stace (2010).

Results

Wood charcoal

There is little clear sign of change over time in the charcoal recovered from the Neolithic pits (Table 3.37). The samples derive from two middle Neolithic pits, two late Neolithic pits and five Neolithic/early Bronze Age pits.

Hazel (*Corylus*) fragments were dominant in almost all of the samples. Oak (*Quercus*) and hawthorn group (Pomoideae) charcoal also occurred in all of the samples. Although these two usually formed relatively small proportions of the charcoal overall, oak (consisting of both heartwood and sapwood) was particularly common in three samples – one from the middle Neolithic, one from the late Neolithic and one from the late Neolithic/early Bronze Age – emphasising the general similarity of the samples from different phases.

Most of the other, less frequently occurring species had a similar chronological distribution

Table 3.37 Summary of wood charcoal

		1007	1018	1103	1104	1077
Sample No		1007	1018	1103	1104	1077
Context No		3043	3090	3442	3460	3326
Sample vol. (litres)		20	40	36	40	41
Feature type		Pit	Pit	Pit	Pit	Pit
Set		1	1	2a	2?	3
Period		MN	MN	LN	LN	LN/EBA
Taxaceae						
Taxus baccata		22				3
Fagaceae						
Quercus	oak	34hs	10	48hs	2	3
Betulaceae						
Corylus avellana	hazel	21	85	53	95	49
Rosaceae						
Prunus avium/padus type	wild/bird cherry	2	6		2	14
Prunus spinosa type	blackthorn					2
Prunus sp.	cherry/blackthorn		1			7
Pomoideae* (see key below)	syn. Maloideae	19	8	7	17	11
cf. Pomoideae		3				
Aceraceae						
Acer campestre	field maple					
Oleaceae						
Fraxinus excelsior	ash	2				
Total Identified Fragments		103	110	115	119	89
Indet. charcoal fragments		4	9	7	3	6

KEY Symbols used in fragment counts: h - includes heartwood s - includes sapwood r - includes roundwood

*Pomoideae (syn. Maloideae) includes: *Pyrus* (pear) *Malus* (apple), *Crataegus* (hawthorn), *Sorbus* (rowan, service, whitebeam)

across the samples. Yew (*Taxus baccata*) and ash (*Fraxinus excelsior*), for example, both occurred in only four samples, but in both cases one was middle Neolithic and the others late Neolithic/early Bronze Age. *Prunus* (cherry/blackthorn) was present in only small quantities, but occurred in nine samples encompassing all three of the phases represented.

The only species confined to one phase was maple (*Acer campestre*) which occurred in very small quantities only in two late Neolithic/early Bronze Age samples.

The late Neolithic/early Bronze Age samples contained a notably wider range of species than those from earlier phases. Since, however, the earlier phases were represented by smaller numbers of samples, it is difficult top attach much significance to this contrast.

Charred plant remains

Samples of charred plant remains from six middle Neolithic pits, six late Neolithic pits and five Neolithic pits which could not be attributed to a more precise phase were analysed, as well as one sample from a middle Bronze Age ring ditch and three from Roman quarry pits (Table 3.38).

In the middle and late Neolithic pits hazel (*Corylus avellana*) nutshell fragments were by far the most frequently occurring item. They occurred in larger quantities in the middle Neolithic pits than in the late Neolithic examples. Three of the middle Neolithic samples, in particular from pits 3091, 3508 and 3327, contained very large groups. Even larger groups were, however, recovered from some of the unphased Neolithic pits. Although the numbers in the late Neolithic pits were smaller, they still occurred in most samples, and hazel was still the most frequently occurring species.

Other wild, edible species were rare and occurred only in middle Neolithic pits. They consisted of a single crab apple/pear pip (*Malus/Pyrus*) and two sloe stones (*Prunus spinosa*).

Remains of cereals occurred in much small numbers than those of hazelnuts, and, in contrast to

1105	1100	1078	1079	1080	1081	1134	1160
3461	3332	3328	3328	3328	3329	3507	3543
30	44	24	12	4	4	37	40
PH in Pit 3502	Pit	Pit	Pit	Pit	Pit	Pit	Pit
3	3a	3b	3b	3b	3b	3c	3e
LN/EBA	LN/EBA	LN/EBA	LN/EBA	LN/EBA	LN/EBA	LN/EBA	LN/EBA
2	10						
3s	15hs	6s	6	12hs	4s	16hs	74hs
64	80	68	77	54	90	69r	12
4		2	2			4	
		2				1	
3					1	1	
25	42	29	17	34	4	9	21
	2				1	2	1
2						1	
5	1					1	
111	153	115	104	100	100	106	108
3	3	8	2	4	4	3	2

Table 3.38 Summary of charred plant remains

		1007	1018	1080	1078	1079	1081	1082	1134	1077	1107	1122	1123
Sample No		1007	1018	1080	1078	1079	1081	1082	1134	1077	1107	1122	1123
Context No		3043	3090	3328	3328	3328	3329	3331	3507	3326	3444	3419	3417
Sample vol. (litres)		20	40	4	24	12	4	20	37	41	40	37	40
Feature type		Pit	Pit	Pit	Pit	Pit	Pit	Pit	Pit	Pit	Pit	Pit	Pit
Period		MN	MN	MN	MN	MN	MN	MN	MN?	MN?	LN	LN	LN
Cereal grain													
Triticum sp.	free threshing wheat grain									1		1	3
Triticum sp.	wheat grain											1	3
Hordeum vulgare grain	cf. hulled, twisted									3			
Hordeum sp.	hulled barley grain												
Hordeum sp.	cf. hulled barley grain												1
Hordeum sp.	barley grain								3				
cf. *Hordeum* sp.	cf. barley												
Avena/Bromus	oat/brome grass												1
Cereal indet.	indeterminate cereal							1	1		1F	1F	4F
Cereal chaff													
Triticum cf. *spelta*	cf spelt glume base												
Triticum dicoccum/	emmer/spelt glume												
Triticum cf. *aestivum*	cf. bread wheat rachis											1	2
Triticum sp.	wheat rachis												1
cf. *Hordeum* sp.	cf. barley rachis							1					
Cereal indet.	indet. cereal rachis												
Edible plants													
Corylus avellana	hazelnut shell fragments	14F 1F	369F	35F	97F	82F	18F	119F	350F	398F	240F	1F	11F
cf. *Corylus*	tiny nutshell Fs - all cf. hazel								c.100				
Malus/Pyrus	pip				1								
Prunus spinosa	fruit stone								1				
Prunus sp.	fruit stone								1F				
Wild plants													
Vicia/Lathyrus	vetch/tare (<2 mm)												1
Fabaceae - Trifolieae	small legumes												
cf. *Viola* sp.	cf. violet												
Raphanus raphanistrum	wild radish capsule												
Brassicaceae undiff.	cabbage family		1										
Polygonaceae undiff.	knotweed family		1										
Veronica hederifolia	ivy-leaved speedwell												
Plantago laceolata	ribwort plantain												
Prunella vulgaris	selfheal												
Apiaceae undiff.	carrot family												
Poaceae undiff.	grass family, small grain												
Poaceae undiff.	small culm node												
Indeterminate	seed/fruit/nut	1	3	3F	2F			2		1	2	2	
Indeterminate	tiny charcoal Fs - cf root wood												
Indeterminate	small tubers												

Key: F - fragment(s)

1125 3414 2 Pit LN	1126 3433 40 Pit LN	1127 3432 20 Pit LN	1125 3390 2 Pit LN	1055 3254 20 Pit LN	1056 3255 20 Pit LN	1104 3460 40 Pit LN?	1100 3332 44 Pit MN-EBA	1101 3404 40 Pit MN-EBA	1137 3505 37 Pit MN-EBA	1105 3461 30 PH MN-EBA	1106 3463 30 PH MN-EBA	1109 3471 6 PH MN-EBA	1136 3511 20 Pit MN-EBA	1225 3390 40 Ring ditch MBA	1180 3119 20 Quarry Roman	1186 3551 40 Quarry Roman	1187 3551 39 Quarry Roman
	1		1											1		8	3
	1		2											2		3	1
			1			1								1			barley
			2											2			
										1				6	1		
			5										1				
														1F			
4	1	1	3	2F			1	1F		2F	1F			3	1	2F	1
			1											1			1
			3											2 + Fs	*spelta*	base	1
																	1
																	1
			1											1			
3F	24F	7F		152F	95F	108F	1019F	162F	30F	517F	450F	53F	9F		1F		
			2.5											2			
															7		
															1		
														1F			
			1														
							1									1	
															2		
															4		
															1		
			1						1						4	3	
														1	c.50		
			2	1			1F		2	1	1F			2	2	1	2
															150+F		
															10		

115

the hazelnuts, were more common in the late Neolithic pits than the middle Neolithic. The middle Neolithic samples contained just a single grain of wheat. This grain, however, resembled standard bread wheat (*T. aestivum*) rather than the small, compact/spheroid bread wheat (*T. aestivo-compactum*) grains, seen sporadically on British sites during the Neolithic period (cf. Palmer and Jones 1991; Fairweather and Ralston 1993). It is possible that this grain was intrusive. The remaining cereals from the middle Neolithic pits consisted of six grains of hulled barley (*Hordeum* sp.) and two unidentifiable fragments. A single fragment, probably of a barley rachis, was also recovered from a middle Neolithic pit.

Although the numbers of specimens was again low, cereals occurred in a much larger number of the late Neolithic samples. They included, again, several grains which resembled standard bread wheat (*T. aestivum*), as well as small numbers of grains of barley (*Hordeum* sp.), including a specimen of the six row species (*H. vulgare*), a single specimen of oat or brome grass (*Avena/Bromus*), and unidentified fragments.

The late Neolithic pits also contained four wheat glume bases, of which one was identified as spelt wheat (*Triticum spelta*), the others as emmer or spelt (*T. dicoccum/spelta*). A small number of fragments of wheat rachis were also recovered, including one resembling bread wheat (*T. aestivum*).

The Neolithic pits that could not be more precisely dated contained few cereals, and all of those that could be identified were barley (*Hordeum* sp.).

A small number of seeds from other wild plants were also recovered from the Neolithic pits. In the case of the middle Neolithic pits these consisted of just two specimens from the same context, one from the cabbage family (Brassicaceae) and one from the knotweed family (Polygonaceae). One of the late Neolithic pits, which produced one of the largest groups of cereals, contained a quite large number of vetch or tare (*Vicia/Lathyrus*) seeds. A single example of vetch or tare was also found in another late Neolithic pit, which also contained a relatively large group of cereals.

In contrast to the pits, the charred plant remains from the middle Bronze Age ring ditch were dominated by cereal remains, including one spelt wheat (*Triticum spelta*) glume base, free threshing wheat (*Triticum* sp.), hulled barley (*Hordeum* sp.) and oat/brome grass grains (*Avena/Bromus*). No hazel nutshells were present, the only wild specimens being rare examples of vetch/tare (*Vicia/Lathyrus*) and wild radish (*Raphanus raphanistrum*) seeds and a grass (Poaceae) culm node.

The Roman quarry pits contained a similar range of species, although one sample was marked by the presence of a much richer range of wild species. Although they did not occur in large numbers, the cereals were dominated by free threshing wheat (*Triticum* sp.) and only a single specimen of barley (*Hordeum* sp.) was recovered. The cereal remains included a small amount of chaff: wheat glume bases and rachis fragments, including one glume base identifiable as spelt. The wild plants included a number of grass culm nodes, small tubers, small legumes, self-heal (*Prunella vulgaris*) and ribwort plantain (*Plantago lanceolata*), amongst others (Table 3.38).

Discussion: woodland and land use at Ridgeway Hill

Wood charcoal

The range of large and small trees and shrubs, and mix of heartwood and sapwood in the pits point to consistent access to a good range of woody resources from the middle Neolithic to the early Bronze Age. As at Maiden Castle, the main woodland surrounding the site seems to have been oak, possibly with ash. Again there was probably an understory of hazel (Gale 1991). The presence of large numbers of hazelnuts and some ash suggest lighter woodland, or glades; hazel requires sunlight in order to fruit. Woodland margins would have supported hawthorn, cherry and blackthorn, as well as the other Pomoideae – pear, crab apple and *Sorbus* species. Most of these produce seasonal fruits, some of which (eg crab-apple, hazelnut) can be dried and stored. Hazel also may have grown in copses, and hawthorn and blackthorn in more open, scrubby terrain, particularly where this was cleared by burning. All three are useful for wattle work. Hawthorn and blackthorn do not make good fuel woods but their spiny twigs make them useful as barriers against livestock or for defence (Edlin 1949; Gale 1991).

Field maple and yew are other trees native to the chalk downs, where yew can form natural groves (Edlin 1947). Field maple has traditionally been used for fencing, turning, and to make bowls and plates. Nevertheless, the first appearance of field maple in charcoal assemblages often coincides with more open woodland conditions and a general diversification of fuel sources or other activities on site (cf. Gale 1991). Oak, ash, hazel and field maple all coppice readily, for example, after woodland has been cleared but the tree stumps left. Oak and ash are superior fuel woods, so the dominance of hazel in the Ridgeway samples must reflect in part a local abundance.

Charred plant remains

The cereal remains identified in some Neolithic samples from Ridgeway Hill should be regarded with some caution, as they may be intrusive, and reflect Bronze Age or later activity. They do not differ greatly to the Roman quarry samples. Spelt wheat (*Triticum spelta*) and the non compact form of free threshing wheat (*T. aestivum* s.l.), are very unusual for the Neolithic, especially in the absence of clear finds of emmer wheat (*T. dicoccum*), which together with (hulled or naked) barley (*Hordeum* sp.) would be expected to dominate the early samples. Interestingly, bread wheat and spelt have been identified by Clapham, in early Bronze Age deposits at nearby Castle Hill on the A30, East Devon, although emmer wheat and barley were more common (Clapham, in Fitzpatrick *et al.* 1999: 51ff). Flax (*Linum usitatissimum*) and peas (*Pisum sativum*) were also present in the Castle Hill samples from the Middle Bronze Age. Additional Neolithic-Bronze Age wild edible foods from the A30 sites include bramble (*Rubus fruticosus*), haws (*Crataegus* sp.) and pignut (*Conopodium majus*) tubers (Clapham ibid.; also see Moffett *et al.* 1989).

The smaller seeds of wild plants at Ridgeway Hill may represent weeds of the cereals or possibly accidentally charred material. The numbers are generally too low and identifications too broad to provide information about agricultural practices or activities taking place on site. The exception is the Roman quarry sample (1180), which produced large numbers of tiny (probable root) charcoal fragments and grass culms, plus tubers and seeds of species associated with grasslands (eg *Prunella vulgaris* and *Plantago lanceolata*). These remains suggest burnt turf material, possibly from a local fire, or amongst rubbish material dumped in the quarry.

Conclusions

The analysis of 31 samples from Neolithic and early Bronze Age deposits from Ridgeway Hill has produced some insights into the local and regional woodland and its use during these periods, and into a range of economic activities taking place in this part of the South Dorset Ridgeway. Wood charcoal, pollen, mollusc and insect evidence from other sites point to considerable variation in the woodland around sites, even over quite short distances, and over quite short time periods. Sizeable pockets of mature/regenerated woodland do seem to have been retained into the Bronze Age and, on the basis of work at Southdown Ridge, into the Iron Age period. The range of cultivated plants present in Neolithic

samples, though narrow, was quite surprising. Further sizeable finds of bread wheat and spelt in better sealed Neolithic deposits should certainly be investigated via AMS dating.

LAND SNAILS *by Elizabeth Stafford*

Introduction

Palaeoenvironmental samples consisting almost entirely of bulk samples of 10-40 litres, primarily for the retrieval of charred remains, bones and artefacts, were taken from a variety of features. Very few small incremental samples were retrieved specifically to recover land snails due to the poor preservation levels indicated by the evaluation. However, the large volumes of sediment processed concentrated the shells in the flots that may not otherwise have been present in the smaller (1-2 litre) samples usually retrieved for land snails. Flots were initially scanned in order to assess the potential for providing information regarding the local environmental setting for the various periods represented. Subsequently seven samples from three features dated to the middle Neolithic, the late Neolithic and the early to middle Bronze Age were analysed in detail. The following report includes the results of both the assessment and detailed analysis.

Method

For the assessment the flots from bulk samples were scanned under a binocular microscope at x10 and x20 magnification. Preliminary identifications were made, along with an estimate of the overall abundance of shell, as well as individual taxa (represented by a scale of 1-3 +, 4-12 ++, 13-25 +++, >25 ++++). The results are presented in Tables 3.39 and 3.40. The assessment report recommended that samples from two Neolithic pits (3041 and 3373) containing an abundance of shade-demanding species should be analysed in detail in order to provide a definitive species list. In order to demonstrate a complete clearance sequence it was also recommended that samples from one of the interventions through the early to middle Bronze Age barrow ditch should also be analysed (3032, cut 3157). It was thought unlikely that further detailed work on the remaining samples would add significant data to that in the assessment report due to the similarity of the open country assemblages and variable shell preservation. For the analysis stage whole shells and apical fragments were extracted from seven flots from the three features. Shells were identified with the aid of a modern reference collection and were counted. The results of are presented

Table 3.39 Assessment of molluscs from Neolithic pits

Period	Middle Neolithic						MN?		Late Neolithic								
Intervention	3330				3041	3091	3327	3403	3256		3371					3373	
Sample	1081	1080	1079	1078	1007	1018	1077	1100	1055	1056	1125	1124	1123	1122	1128	1127	1126
Context	3329	3328	3328	3328	3043	3090	3326	3332	3254	3255	3414	3415	3417	3419	3430	3432	3433
Vol. Processed (L)	4	4	12	24	20	40	41	44	20	20	2	20	40	37	40	20	40
Taxa																	
Open-country																	
Vertigo pygmaea		+	+	+	++	+			+			+	+	+	+	+	++
Pupilla muscorum	+	+	++	+++	+++	+	++	+++	+	++	++	++	+	++	++	++	+++
Vallonia spp.	+	+	++	++	++	+	+	++	+		++	++	++	++	+++	++	++++
Helicella itala	+	+	++	+++	++		+++	++		++	+	+	++	++	++	++	+++
Candidula sp.	+	+				+	++		++	+	+	+			+	++	++
Catholic																	
Cochlicopa sp.					+	+	+				+	+	+		+++	++	
Punctum pygmaea				+											+		
Nesovitrea hammonis											+				++	+	
Vitrina pellucida															+		
Trichia hispida	+	+	++	+	+++		+++	+++	++	++	++	++	+	+	+++	+++	+++
Cepaea/Arianta sp.											+				+	+	
Shade-demanding																	
Pomatias elegans															++	+	
Carychium tridentatum									+	+					++++	++	+
Acanthinula aculeata															++	+	
Ena sp.															+		
Discus rotundatus					++					++	+++	+++	+++	++	++++	++++	++
Vitrea sp.					+						++	+	++	+	++++	++	+
Oxychilus sp.					++				+		++	++	+++	+	++++	+++	
Aegopinella sp.												+		+	++++	++	+
Clausiliidae											+		+		++	++	+
Estimated min. no. individuals/sample	13	12	40	40	76	13	60	60	20	30	60	60	55	30	737	170	119

1-3 +, 4-12 ++, 13-25 +++, >25 ++++

in Table 3.41 and Fig. 3.12. Nomenclature follows Kerney 1999 and ecological information derives from Evans 1972.

Results

Middle Neolithic

Pits 3330, 3041 and 3091

Bulk sample flots were examined from the fills of middle Neolithic pits 3330, 3041 and 3091. Pit 3041 was analysed in detail and produced an assemblage of 76 individuals (8 individuals per 2 litres of sediment). Open-country species (*Pupilla muscorum*, *Vertigo pygmaea*, *Helicella itala*, *Vallonia* spp.) predominated at 53% along with catholic species such as *Trichia hispida* at 22%. Some shade-demanding species were present to 25%, mainly *Oxychilus cellarius* and *Discus rotundatus* with some *Vitrea* sp.

Preservation was poorer in the samples from pits 3330 and 3091 (13-40 individuals per sample, 3-7 individuals per 2 litres of sediment) and was restricted entirely to open-country species. The presence of the introduced species *Candidula* indicates some intrusive material (Table 3.39).

Pits 3327 and 3403

Two flots were examined from the fills of pits 3327 and 3403. Shell abundance was *c* 60 individuals per sample (< 3 individuals per 2 litres of sediment). Although undated these features may, by association, be middle Neolithic or late Neolithic/early Bronze Age. The predominance of open country species (eg *Vallonia* spp., *Helicella itala* and *Pupilla muscorum*), along with the catholic species *T. hispida*, similar to pits 3330 and 3091, suggests that the former date is more likely, and is indicative of dry open grassland. Shade-demanding species were entirely absent (Table 3.39).

Table 3.40 Assessment of molluscs from the early to middle Bronze Age barrow ditch 3157

Period	Early to middle Bronze Age										
Intervention		3384			3157			3368		3496	
Sample	1227	1226	1225	1224	1223	1222	1221	1220	1219	1218	1217
Context	3387	3388	3390	3160	3161	3162	3394	3396	3397	3500	3501
Vol. Processed (L)	10	10	40	20	39	40	30	36	38	40	40
Taxa											
Open-country											
Vertigo pygmaea				+	++	+			++		
Pupilla muscorum	++		+	++	++	+++		+++	++++	+	
Vallonia spp.	+			+++	++	+++		++	+++	+	+
Helicella itala	++	+		++		++++		+++	++++		
Candidula sp.										+	+
Catholic											
Cochlicopa sp.						+		+	++		
Punctum pygmaea				+	+						
Nesovitrea hammonis								+			
Trichia hispida			+	+	+	++++		++	++++	+	
Cepaea/Arianta sp.						+					
Shade-demanding											
Carychium tridentatum	+							+			
Discus rotundatus	+										
Vitrea sp.				+				+			
Oxychilus spp.	+										
Aegopinella spp.						+		+	++		
Clausiliidae	+										
Estimated min. no. individuals/sample	40	2	4	77	23	106	0	50	200	4	4

1-3 +, 4-12 ++, 13-25 +++, >25 ++++

Late Neolithic

Pits 3256, 3371 and 3373

Bulk sample flots were examined from the fills of late Neolithic pits 3256, 3371 and 3373. Samples from pit 3373 were previously assessed by Dr M Allen during the evaluation. Shell was moderately well preserved, with the basal fills containing up to 13 species, including shade-demanding species indicative of stable ground conditions and woodland cover (eg *Acicula fusca* and *Ena Montana*). The upper fills in contrast were dominated by open-country species (eg *Vallonia* sp. *Pupilla muscorum* and *Vertigo pygmaea*).

The samples examined during this stage of investigation from pit 3373 produced a large shell assemblage of 737 individuals towards the base of the feature (fills 3430, 37 shells per 2 litres of sediment), similarly dominated by shade-demanding species at 86%. The most abundant species were the zonitids at 53% (*Oxychilus cellarius*, *Aegopinella nitidula* and *Vitrea* sp.) along with *Discus rotundatus* (23%). Clausiliidae were also noted,

along with a fragment of *Ena obscura*. Open-country species were, however, also recorded in the lower fill at 6% (eg *P. muscorum*, *Vallonia* sp., *V. pygmaea* and *Helicella itala*). Again the presence of the introduced species *Candidula* indicates some intrusive material.

Shell was much sparser in pit 3256 (*c* 23-30 shells per sample), but pit 3371 was more productive (*c* 30-60 shells per sample). The results were broadly similar to pit 3373 though due to lower shell numbers species diversity was lower (Table 3.39).

Early to middle Bronze Age

Barrow ditch 3032 (cuts 3157, 3368, 3384 and 3496)

A number of samples from a single intervention through the barrow ditch (Group 3032) were assessed by Dr M Allen during the evaluation. Unfortunately shell preservation was poor (<10 individuals per sample). The silty loam soils in the ditch were derived from relict argillic brown earths that are largely decalcified. The only species recorded were indicative of open country dry grass-

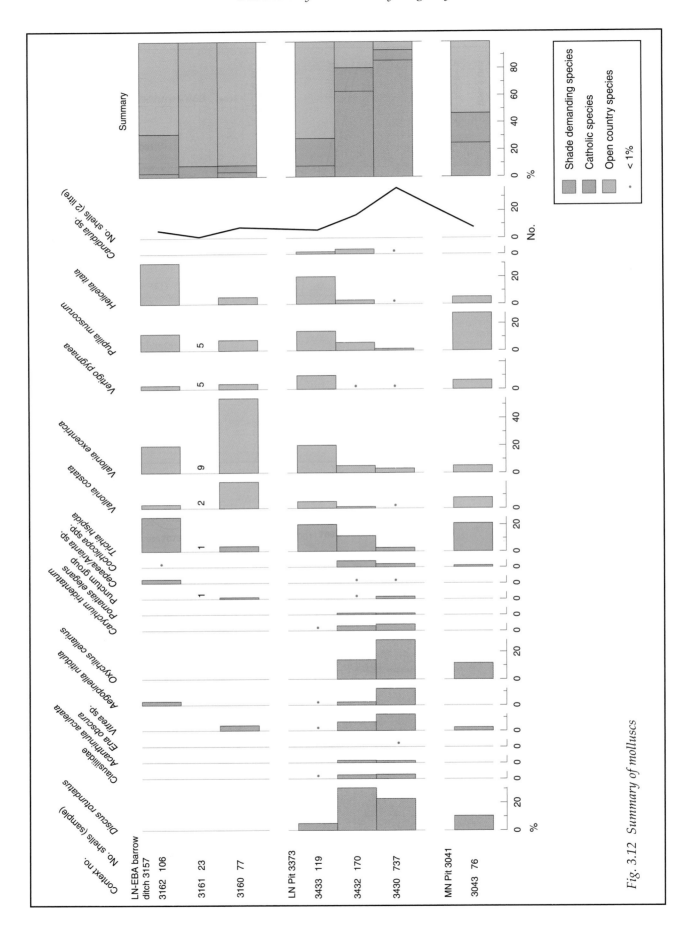

Fig. 3.12 Summary of molluscs

Table 3.41 Molluscan analytical data from Neolithic pits 3041 and 3373 and early to middle Bronze Age barrow ditch 3032, cut 3157

Period	MN		LN			EMBA	
Intervention	3041		3373			3157	
Sample	1007	1128	1127	1126	1224	1223	1222
Context	3043	3430	3432	3433	3160	3161	3162
Vol. Processed (L)	20	40	20	40	20	40	40
Taxa							
Open-country							
Vertigo pygmaea	5	3	1	12	3	5	3
Pupilla muscorum	21	10	10	17	6	5	13
Vallonia costata	6	1	2	6	15	2	3
Vallonia excentrica	4	24	9	24	42	9	21
Helicella itala	4	4	5	24	4		32
Candidula sp.		4	6	2			
Catholic							
Cochlicopa spp.	1	18	8				1
Punctum pygmaea		6			1	1	
Nesovitrea hammonis		6	1				
Vitrina pellucida		2					
Trichia hispida	16	21	20	24	3	1	27
Cepaea/Arianta sp.		1	1				3
Shade-demanding							
Pomatias elegans		8	2				
Carychium tridentatum		35	6	1			
Acanthinula aculeata		11	3				
Ena obscura		+					
Discus rotundatus	8	168	52	6			
Vitrea spp.	2	90	11	1	3		
Oxychilus cellarius	9	211	24				
Aegopinella nitidula		90	4	1			3
Cochlodina laminata		3	2				
Clausilia bidentata		21	3	1			
Min. no. individuals/sample	76	737	170	119	77	23	106
Shell/2L sediment	8	37	17	6	8	1	5
% Open country	52.6	6.2	19.4	71.4	90.9	91.3	67.9
% Catholic	22.4	7.3	17.6	20.2	5.2	8.7	29.2
% Shade demanding	25.0	86.4	62.9	8.4	3.9	0.0	2.8

+ = non apical fragment

land (eg. *Pupilla muscorum, Helicella itala, Vallonia* spp.). Based on the recommendations from the evaluation, samples were retrieved from a number of interventions around the barrow ditch during the detailed excavation to check whether the poor preservation was restricted to one part of the monument and whether the composition of the assemblages varied spatially.

Eleven flots deriving from sediment of between 10 and 40 litres were examined from the upper, middle and basal fills of cuts 3157, 3368, 3384 and 3496. The volumes of sediment are considerably larger than those assessed from the evaluation stage and, although the overall shell numbers were larger (up to 200 individuals per sample), the estimated numbers of individuals per litre of sediment was broadly consistent with the evaluation results. The species composition of the assemblages was also similar, dominated by a few open country species indicative of dry grassland, although occasional shade-demanding species were noted in some of the larger assemblages (eg *Discus rotundatus, Aegopinella nitidula, Oxychilus* sp., *Vitrea* sp., Clausiliidae and *Carychium tridentatum*). In cut 3157 open country species accounted for 91% of the assemblage in the basal fill 3160 (Fig. 3.12). The grass snail *Vallonia excentrica* was most abundant at 55% with *Vallonia costata* at 20%. In the upper fill (3162) *H. itala* becomes more abundant (30%) along with the catholic species *Trichia hispida* (26%).

Roman

A large number of samples was retrieved from the quarry pits scattered around the site, some of which produced very large shell assemblages. After a brief examination of the bulk flots shell appeared to be variably preserved but there was little variation in the composition of the assemblages between samples and features. A selection of samples was scanned in greater detail confirming they were wholly dominated by a few open country species (eg *Pupilla muscorum, Helicella itala, Vallonia* sp. *Vertigo pygmaea*), along with the catholic species *Trichia hispida*.

Discussion

The results of the assessment and analysis indicate shell was variably preserved across the site. Some of the most interesting samples, however, came from the Neolithic pits. Pits dated to the middle Neolithic were dominated by open country species. Apart from pit 3041, shade-demanding species are entirely absent and catholic species are largely restricted to *Trichia hispida*. Although shell abundance was generally low in these features the dominance of open country xerophile species suggests the pits were infilled with soil formed in a dry, open environment, probably low diversity short-turved grassland. However, the presence of a few shade-demanding species in pit 3041, to 25%, may indicate areas of longer rank grassland and/or scrub in the vicinity.

The assemblages from the late Neolithic pits are of a wholly different character. Although open country species were present they were much less abundant. The shade-demanding component in the base of pit 3373 reached 91% and the catholic component was much more diverse. Overall this suggests the pits were infilled with soil formed in a more enclosed environment, probably with some tree cover and leaf litter. It is likely that if woodland was present in the immediate vicinity it was probably regenerated vegetation, as some rarer species indicative of primary undisturbed woodland appear to be absent from the assemblages. The lower but consistent presence of open country species may indicate tree cover was not complete and that more open grassy areas prevailed in the vicinity.

The assemblages from the later features – the early to middle Bronze Age barrow and the Roman quarry pits – produced very similar assemblages dominated by open-country species indicative of an environment of open well established grassland. The very low species diversity suggests that this was probably heavily grazed and perhaps became impoverished.

Chapter 4: Discussion of Ridgeway Hill

by Chris Hayden

NEOLITHIC AND LATE NEOLITHIC/EARLY BRONZE AGE PITS

Introduction: occupation on the Ridgeway in the Neolithic

A total of 21 pits excavated at Ridgeway Hill have been dated to the Neolithic or late Neolithic/early Bronze Age. The pits provide evidence for at least sporadic occupation of the Ridgeway throughout the Neolithic period. Of the more precisely dated pits, one has been attributed to the early Neolithic, three to the middle Neolithic, four to the late Neolithic and four to the Beaker period. A further nine pits could not be dated so precisely, although it seems likely on the basis of their location that they date from either the middle Neolithic or the Beaker period.

Neolithic pits have been excavated at a number of sites in the area around Ridgeway Hill, particularly in and around Dorchester (Poundbury: Green 1987; Thomas Hardye School: Gardiner *et al.* 2007; Middle Farm: Butterworth and Gibson 2004; and Flagstones: Smith *et al.* 1997), but also at Maiden Castle (Wheeler 1943; Sharples 1991), and on the Ridgeway at Rowden (Woodward 1991) and Sutton Poyntz (Farrar 1959). Whilst some of these sites have provided evidence of quite large numbers of pits, such as the group of 34 at Thomas Hardye School, and the adjacent group of seven examples at Middle Farm, the chronological distribution of the pits is uneven. Early Neolithic pits are the most widely represented. The earliest examples are probably the pair of pits at Rowden (associated with Carinated Bowl pottery), but larger numbers are known from possibly slightly later sites, associated with South-Western style pottery, including Maiden Castle, Poundbury, Middle Farm, Flagstones and Sutton Poyntz. Middle Neolithic examples, in contrast, are unknown, although Peterborough Ware has been recovered from the upper fills of probably early Neolithic pits at Poundbury and Maiden Castle.

The worked flint from three pits in Trench 2 at Middle Farm suggests a later Neolithic date. Late Neolithic examples, associated with Grooved Ware are well represented by the large group of pits at Thomas Hardye School, although only eight of the pits contained Grooved Ware. Grooved Ware was also recovered from a small number of pits at Poundbury. The Beaker period and the early Bronze Age are represented by very few examples. Pits containing coarse Beaker pottery are reported as having been found below a barrow (Bincombe 27) just to the east of the Ridgeway Hill site, but otherwise the only evidence consists of Beaker sherds from pits at Poundbury and from the upper fill of two probably early Neolithic pits at Maiden Castle. A Collared Urn was recovered from one of the pits at Thomas Hardye School. Overall, then, whilst the early Neolithic and the late Neolithic are well represented, the middle Neolithic and the late Neolithic/early Bronze Age are not. The length of the sequence of activity associated with pits at Ridgeway Hill is thus unusual.

Whilst the presence of people at Ridgeway Hill, at least sporadically, throughout the Neolithic is thus clear, the character of the activity related to the pits is less so. The interpretation of Neolithic pits has been a subject of some recent interest (eg Anderson-Whymark and Thomas 2012; Garrow 2006; Anderson-Whymark 2008), and the pits at Ridgeway Hill provide examples of many of the issues at stake. Here it will be suggested that the finds from the pits provide only a very partial representation of activity on the site. Whilst the finds from the pits can be seen as no more than domestic waste, there is some structure in the patterns of deposition within them which suggests that the pits were filled on specific occasions. Whilst the small numbers of pits and the generally limited quantities of finds suggest that the pits were related to occupation which was limited in scale and perhaps in duration, the limited representation of activity provided by the pits means that they provide only a very imperfect indication of the way in which the site was occupied. The discussion begins, however, by raising the possibility that the finds recovered from the pits were not related to the primary use of the pits, and that the pits could have been used as temporary stores.

The primary use of the pits

Much of the recent interest in Neolithic pits has been focused upon their contents. It is, however, quite possible that their contents were not related directly to the primary use of the pits, but were deposited only after the pits had otherwise gone out of use. The only evidence, then, for the primary use of the pits may be the form of the pits themselves. Unfortunately, the form of the pits does not provide a clear indication of the way in which they were originally used.

There was some variation in the size and form of the pits at Ridgeway Hill. Most were small, bowl-shaped features of a type recognised as typical of many Neolithic pits (eg Thomas 1999). There were also, however, a number of larger and deeper pits. The early Neolithic pit, and two of the late Neolithic examples in particular, were quite deep and wide. The variation in the size and shape of the late Neolithic pits – three of which formed a group – could be taken to indicate differences in their primary functions. The pits found at sites near to Ridgeway Hill present a similar picture. Most examples are shallow. Most of the large group of pits at Thomas Hardye School, for example, were less than 0.35m deep, and the deepest reached a depth of only 0.5m. Although many of the pits at the other sites near Ridgeway Hill were similarly shallow, there were also a number of deeper examples, especially in the early Neolithic. Examples at Maiden Castle, Middle Farm, Poundbury and Rowden have been reported with depths of 1.2m deep, 1.34m deep, 0.84m deep and around 1m respectively.

The small size and bowl-shaped profile of many Neolithic pits has been used to argue that they were not suitable for the storage of grain. It is, however, possible that the pits were used as temporary stores for other materials. Buttler (1936) describes a number of pits from south-east Europe which were being used to store a range of foodstuffs, more like a fridge or, perhaps more appropriately, a pantry or larder, rather than for long term storage (see also Cunningham 2011 for ethnographic examples, and Cunningham 2005 for experimental data). Whilst most of the pits described by Buttler were quite deep, one example at least appears to have been quite shallow, as is an ethnographic example mentioned by Cunningham (2011). The temporary storage of foodstuffs in pits of the kind described by Buttler and Cunningham does not depend upon the pits being sealed, but rather appears simply to exploit the presumably cooler atmosphere within even quite shallow pits.

It is, therefore, possible that the pits at Ridgeway Hill were used as 'pantry pits'. Although this interpretation perhaps seems most plausible in the case of the deeper early and late Neolithic pits, the stone lining in middle Neolithic pit 3431, one of the smaller pits, could also be taken as an indication that it was used for storage, or at least that it was cut for more than just the one-off disposal of some rubbish. It is, of course, impossible to rule out other possible interpretations of the pits (eg Green 1987) – that they were dug as quarries for chalk, as general rubbish pits or to dispose of some more particular body of material.

Most of the storage pits described by Buttler were associated with above ground structures, some consisting of simple flat roofs or lids over the pits but others of more elaborate gabled structures. It is possible that the holes found in the bases of some of the pits at Ridgeway Hill were associated with structures of this kind. Although comparable features have been noted occasionally at other sites (eg Whitesheet Hill where, however, it was suggested that a pit had truncated some postholes; Rawling *et al.* 2004, 153-4) they are rare, and it seems more likely that the examples at Ridgeway Hill were natural in origin.

The contents of the pits

Although it has been suggested that the contents of the pits were not necessarily related to their primary use, it is of course equally possible that the pits were dug specifically to contain certain material. Recent analyses of pits have suggested that whilst some pits appear to contain carefully placed, deliberately selected, often special objects and others appear to contain random assortments of rubbish, there are also deposits which seem to fall in the middle ground, which appear to be structured in some respects but which do not obviously consist of special objects. The fills of many of the pits at Ridgeway Hill seem to fall into this middle ground.

The finds from the pits at Ridgeway Hill consist predominantly of pottery sherds, worked flint – largely consisting of flakes – fragments of animal bone, marine shells, charred hazelnut shells and small quantities of charred grain. Much of this material consists of waste byproducts (the animal bone, marine shells, charred plant remains and possibly much of the flint) or of broken objects (the pottery). In this sense the finds have the appearance of rubbish.

All of the finds from the pits imply the original presence of other material: the pots would have been parts of whole vessels, the animal bone probably parts of larger joints at least, if not whole carcasses, and the charred plant remains and marine shells presumably represent just small fractions of what were originally larger quantities of the related food (most of which was probably not preserved by being charred).

Overall, the range of finds suggests that in large part the deposits in the pits derive from activities related to the preparation, perhaps storage, and consumption of food. The finds could thus be seen as deriving from a range of domestic activities. It is, however, often impossible to distinguish clearly between the waste that was generated by a ritual and that which derives from quotidian activity. Because of the large quantities of meat they represent, the large deposits of animal bone recovered from two of the Beaker period pits (3544 and 3628) might be seen as the remains of feasting. Even in these cases, however, the animal bone can be interpreted as no more than butchery waste. The other deposits contained quite small assemblages of finds, which are more consistent with activities involving quite small groups of people. There is then, little indication that the pits contain any 'special' deposits.

In their analysis of a number of later Neolithic midden deposits and of Grooved Ware-associated pits at Firtree Field, Cranborne Chase, Dorset, which lay beside the Dorset cursus, Bradley *et al.* (1991, 81-2) found a strong correlation between the overall number of pieces of worked flint and the number of types of worked flint implements. A small number of pits, however, deviated from the usual relationship, and were thus marked out as in some way exceptional. The middle and late Neolithic and late Neolithic/early Bronze Age pits at Ridgeway Hill show a similarly strong correlation (r = 0.86) between the number of pieces of worked flint and the number of types. (The assemblage from pit 3628 is the only group which deviates markedly from this pattern, but the deviation is caused entirely by the presence of a large number of chips. If the chips are excluded this pit too conforms to the general pattern). The flint assemblages from the pits do not, therefore, provide clear evidence for the presence of exceptional deposits.

The range of finds at Ridgeway Hill is generally similar to that recovered from other sites in the surrounding area, although certain contrasts are evident. Compared to the early Neolithic pits at Maiden Castle, in particular, the example at Ridgeway Hill contains a relatively restricted range of finds. The finds from Maiden Castle include, for example, a chalk 'figurine', querns and rubbing stones, pieces of antler, greenstone and other axes, marine shells, and larger groups of animal bone, including dog skeletons. It is possible that the more varied finds at Maiden Castle reflect the pits' association with the causewayed enclosure, just as the exceptional deposits at Firtree Field might be related to their association with the Dorset cursus. The chronological relationship between the pits and

the causewayed enclosure is, however, uncertain. Sharples (1991) suggests that, although clear evidence is lacking, there is no reason to think that were not contemporaneous with the enclosure. In the light, however, of the quite short period over which Bayesian modelling of radiocarbon date suggests the enclosure was in use (Whittle *et al.* 2011), it is worth considering the possibility that the pits could have been in use over a longer period than the enclosure. The early Neolithic pits at Poundbury, Middle Farm, Flagstones and Sutton Poyntz, and the possibly earlier examples at Rowden contain more restricted ranges of finds than those at Maiden Castle, but even in these cases finds of querns, axes and of more or less large groups of animal bone, are not uncommon. The presence of quite large groups of worked flint and pottery, however, is a characteristic shared by many of the early Neolithic pits, as is the presence of small quantities of charred plant remains.

The parallels between the range of finds in the late Neolithic pits at Ridgeway Hill and those at other sites nearby seem to be closer. The large group of late Neolithic pits at Thomas Hardye School, for example, contain quantities of pottery, flint and animal bone which are broadly similar, and seem to vary in a broadly comparable way, to the those from the much smaller number of pits at Ridgeway Hill, although the finds from the Thomas Hardye School pits include a greenstone axe and other worked stone not represented at Ridgeway Hill. The Ridgeway Hill pits, however, seem to have contained richer assemblages of charred plant remains than the Thomas Hardye School pits.

Patterning in the finds assemblages from the pits

Although the Ridgeway Hill assemblages generally appear to consist of samples of waste, there is some indication of patterning. The clearest distinctions are between pits which contained charred plant remains, predominantly hazelnut shells but also including some charred grain, and those which contained animal bone and, in many cases, marine shells. This is particularly striking in the case of the group of three late Neolithic pits, of which one (3371) was associated with plant remains whilst the other two were associated with animal bone. Whatever the source of this patterning, it appears to have been of some longevity. The pattern exists in both the late Neolithic and Beaker period pits, and perhaps in the middle Neolithic examples as well (although the quantity of animal bone in the middle Neolithic pits was very small). Similar patterning is not evident in the large group of late Neolithic pits at Thomas Hardye School, where charred plant remains appear to have been very poorly represented.

In the late Neolithic and Beaker period pits at Ridgeway Hill there appears to have been some patterning in the materials associated with plant and animal remains. Pottery was most strongly associated with plant remains, and worked flint with animal bone. These associations do not, however, characterise the middle Neolithic pits, nor does the early Neolithic pit conform to the later pattern, containing large groups of both worked flint and pottery but no animal bone and just a single hazelnut shell. There was no clear relationship between the kinds of finds in a pit and the form or size of the pit.

The reasons for the existence of the patterning in the finds assemblages at Ridgeway Hill are obscure. If, as is suggested below, the finds derived from a 'pre-pit context', the patterning would imply either that there were different kinds of pre-pit contexts, each associated with different kinds of material, or that the pre-pit context was itself more or less structured (perhaps if it was a midden, it might, for example, have contained more or less distinct dumps of different material). It is possible, alternatively, that the pits were cut after a particular activity in order to dispose of the waste that had been generated. This might explain the consistency in the finds from different layers within pits, ie the fact that where the pits had more than one layer of fill, similar sets of finds were recovered from all of the fills, with the exception of the chalk rubble layers. It would, however, perhaps leave open the question of why the pits appeared to contain only partial remains of what must originally have been larger assemblages. Another possibility is that the finds were related to the primary use of the pits and were deposited in the pits when the pits went out of use, perhaps when the site was abandoned.

It is perhaps worth noting at this point that although the contrast between pits associated with plant remains and those associated with animal bone occurs in both the late Neolithic and the Beaker period, there are contrasts in the size of the animal bone assemblages associated with each phase. The late Neolithic pits contained quite small assemblages of animal bone (the weight of the bone associated with pit 3373 is quite high largely because of the presence of the residual aurochs humerus). The two Beaker pits, in contrast, contained a large assemblage of animal bone, which, as has been discussed above, appears to contain contrasting elements of cattle and pig skeletons. The large assemblage associated with the Beaker pits could be seen as reflecting the occurrence of feasting on the site, and might thus be seen as supporting the idea that the pits were cut after a particular activity to in order to dispose of the waste generated by that activity. In the case of the Beaker pits it could be argued that the remaining elements of the cattle and pig skeletons were removed from the site to be consumed elsewhere.

Whatever the case, the patterning in the finds suggests that the finds from the pits consist of more than just a random assortment of domestic waste. The contrasts in the finds assemblages suggest instead that they were related in some way to a more specific set of activities.

Spatial connections

Although there is little indication that the finds derived from 'special' activity, they nonetheless suggest exploitation of resources from a wide area. Whilst the pottery and flint could have been obtained locally, and the plants and animals represented could have been raised in the vicinity of the site, the marine shells, at least, imply wider contacts, if not direct exploitation. Marine shells are quite widely represented in the pits around Dorchester, occurring in early Neolithic pits at Maiden Castle and late Neolithic pits at Thomas Hardye School. Although the Portland chert might also indicate wide contacts, it is possible that it was obtained from local sources (Woodward and Bellamy 1991). There is little clear indication of consistent changes in the proportion of chert relative to flint in the chipped stone assemblage over time. Overall, the highest proportion of chert occured in the middle Neolithic pits, but the chipped stone assemblage is relatively small compared to those from pits of other periods, and there was a high degree of variation between pits of similar date. The contents of the pits nonetheless provide some indication that the site formed a point at which materials from different locations came together. Although it is, of course, also possible that material was brought to the site from an unknown settlement elsewhere, overall the ranges of materials are consistent with the pits having marked the location of small occupation sites themselves, as has often been suggested (eg Woodward 1991).

The location of the pits

In the absence of extensive open area excavations elsewhere along the Ridgeway it is difficult to assess how widespread was the occurrence of scatters of pits comparable to those at Ridgeway Hill. Although few Neolithic or early Bronze Age pits have been identified on the Ridgeway, examples associated with Beaker pottery have been found nearby under the Bincombe 27 barrow and more distantly, early Neolithic examples have been found at Sutton Poyntz and Rowden. In all of these cases, however, the number of pits was small – one at Sutton Poyntz and two at Rowden.

It is possible that the scatter of pits at Ridgeway Hill reflects the use of the area as a route across the Ridgeway and that the density of pits is exceptional, although comparison with the results of the field-walking which formed part of the Southern Dorset Ridgeway Survey, discussed in more detail below, suggests that the numbers of finds at Ridgeway Hill are not, in fact, that exceptional. That the local topography encourages the use of this particular point to cross the Ridgeway from Maiden Castle or Dorchester is perhaps reflected in the fact that both the Roman and more recent roads run immediately to the west of the site (although it is not the only point where the topography could be seen as encouraging the presence of a route across the Ridgeway). No direct evidence of a prehistoric trackway or path was found in the excavation, but the possibility that such a route was used would be consistent with the spatial connections indicated by the finds from the pits.

The scale and temporality of occupation

Although the presence of pits from all of the conventional divisions of the Neolithic period suggests that the area was returned to repeatedly, the small number of pits, spread over a period of perhaps as much as 2000 years, implies that long periods must have elapsed between episodes of occupation. Healy has noted that the occurrence of such small groups is typical of the early Neolithic. For the late Neolithic, however, the larger group at Thomas Hardye School provides an exception.

The overall scale of the activity associated with the pits at Ridgeway Hill appears to have been limited, both in terms of the size of the social group involved, and in terms of the length of occupation. In the case of the middle Neolithic, to which three pits have been assigned, it is worth noting that at least two of the pits were not contemporaneous, implying that some of the activity on the site in this phase was associated with just a single pit. Some of the later pits appear to form small groups: a group of three in the case of the late Neolithic, and possibly pairs of pits in the Beaker period. It is still possible, however, that each pit or group of pits was related to a distinct episode of occupation, and thus that occupation was always limited in scale.

Although the small number of pits perhaps implies that each episode of occupation would also have been relatively brief, there are certain features of the evidence which suggest that the occupation involved more than very brief stays. One of these features is the presence of pottery. As has often been noted (eg Childe 1951), because of its weight and fragility, pottery is poorly suited to a mobile way of

life. Its presence in the pits thus seems to imply either that occupation at the site was of long enough duration to make the use of pottery worthwhile or that the pottery was brought to the site from elsewhere.

Two further observations suggest that occupation of the site may have been of more than very brief duration and perhaps on a larger scale than the small number of pits implies. As mentioned above, the pottery, animal bone and environmental remains are evidence of the original presence of complete ceramic vessels, larger fractions of animal carcasses than indicated by the surviving bone, and more substantial quantities of food than represented by the charred remains and marine shells. Secondly, since only fragments of objects that were already broken were deposited in the pits, it seems likely that they derived from a pre-pit context of some kind (Garrow 2007; Thomas 2012), perhaps a midden, only part of which became incorporated into the pits.

It is also worth noting that worked flint and chert was recovered from nearly all of the features on the site, much of it residual in Roman, Anglo-Saxon and more recent features. The wide distribution of this material implies that the distribution of activity in the Neolithic was wider than is suggested by the pits, and that much Neolithic activity on the site did not involve the cutting of subsurface features (or at least of features which have survived). The scatter of early Neolithic finds from below the bank at Mount Pleasant (Wainwright 1979) provides an example of the fortuitous preservation of early Neolithic material which had not been deposited in a cut feature. Another example is provided by early Neolithic pottery and lithics recovered from colluvial deposits at Middle Farm (Smith 1997). Any such finds at Ridgeway Hill would have been unlikely to survive or have been recovered. It is, unfortunately, difficult to relate much of the residual worked flint and chert at Ridgeway Hill chronologically to the pits, and impossible to establish that any of it was strictly contemporaneous with the pits. However, the widespread distribution of flint and the likelihood that the finds from the pits derive from a 'pre-pit' context of some kind suggest that the pits provide only a partial picture of activity on the site. Thus whilst the limited number of pits and quantities of artefacts suggest occupation by small groups for short periods, it is impossible to estimate reliably the length and size of occupation from the evidence which survives in the pits alone.

It is perhaps worth noting at this point that, compared to the densities of flint recovered by fieldwalking as part of the South Dorset Ridgeway Survey (Woodward 1991), the quantities of flint recovered at Ridgeway Hill do not appear to be particularly large. There are, of course, numerous difficulties involved in comparing the quantities of lithics recovered by excavation at Ridgeway Hill with those recovered by fieldwalking from the South Dorset Ridgeway Survey (Woodward 1991, chap. 9). It is, nonetheless, striking that the quantities of worked stone recovered from excavated features at Ridgeway Hill are quite small compared to the quantities recovered by fieldwalking in sample areas along the Ridgeway. Fieldwalking by Wessex Archaeology in the area of the excavation and watching brief at Ridgeway Hill (plots 33 and 34: Wessex Archaeology 1993) recovered a total of 242 pieces of flint and chert from an area covering 5.72ha, and noted that whilst there was evidence for activity in more than one period, no significant concentrations were present. The overall density of worked stone recovered from this fieldwalking was 42 pieces per hectare. The fieldwalking during the South Dorset Ridgeway Survey recovered flint with densities of between 147 and 362 pieces per hectare along transects in Sample Area 4, and the densities in the concentrations along these transects were sometimes very much higher – over 1000 pieces per hectare in two cases, and often between 100 and 300 pieces per hectare (data from Woodward 1991, figs 18 to 20). Even the overall density of lithics recovered from the excavations at Ridgeway Hill of 246 pieces per hectare falls within the lower end of this range. Whilst numerous factors, such as the degree of plough damage, the extent to which material was deposited in subsurface features, the conditions during fieldwalking, amongst others, mean that it is difficult to be certain of the implications of these figures, they do suggest firstly, that occupation on Ridgeway Hill may not have been particularly intense or of long duration, and secondly that similar or greater levels of activity occurred reasonably frequently elsewhere.

Conclusions

The evidence from the pits appears in some respects to be contradictory. On the one hand, it indicates that the site was repeatedly visited over a long period extending from the early Neolithic to the beginning of the late Neolithic/early Bronze Age but, on the other, the relatively small number of pits spread across this long period indicates that occupation of the site was sporadic and that episodes of occupation may have been separated by long periods of abandonment. Similarly, although the presence of single pits in some phases and the relatively small assemblages of finds recovered from many of the pits suggest that the occupation was of very limited scale

and duration, the finds from the pits appear to be just a small sample of what must originally have been larger quantities of finds, and the presence of pottery perhaps suggests that occupation was more than temporary. Again, the finds from the pits appear to be little more than domestic debris, which may have derived from a 'pre-pit' context elsewhere (which has not survived), but there is patterning in the finds from many of the pits that suggests that they may have derived from specific sets of activities.

All of this makes it difficult to arrive at a precise characterisation of the pit-related activity. Some of the apparent discrepancies can, however, be reconciled if it is accepted that the pits were only very occasionally cut (or filled) as part of a more extensive occupation, evidence of which has not been directly preserved. The pits would, then, provide only a very partial sample of the wider occupation, of which the residual chipped stone, spread widely across the site, might be evidence. This would account for the partial assemblages of finds, implying originally more extensive debris. The patterning in the finds from the pits could, then, reflect no more than the particular activities occurring at the time the pits were filled or perhaps the proximity of the pits to particular activities. This still, unfortunately, leaves the purpose of the pits, and the extent and duration of occupation to which they were related, unclear.

Whatever the case, the very early radiocarbon date obtained from the Beaker period pit suggests that activity related to the pits may have finished before the area was used for funerary activity in the early Bronze Age, although the single date is, of course, insufficient to establish an end date with any certainty. It seems unlikely that there was any particularly significant relationship between the occupation represented by the pits and the subsequent funerary activity, since the funerary activity clearly formed part of a much wider distribution of barrows which extends well beyond the limits of the early occupation at Ridgeway Hill (Fig. 4.1).

THE EARLY BRONZE AGE BURIALS

The remains of 21 individuals recovered from 15 graves in six groups have been dated to the early Bronze Age. The burials exhibit considerable variation, comprising inhumation and cremation burials, and possibly the interment of groups of human bone which had been buried or kept elsewhere, in large and small pits and cists. Only one group of burials was associated with a ring ditch, but it is suggested below that most of the other groups were probably also originally associated with barrows.

Although the excavations have thus provided a quite large sample of burials of this period from a single site, the evidence suffers from certain deficiencies. All of the burials appear to have suffered from quite severe truncation. Many of the graves survived only as very shallow features in which only fragmentary skeletal remains had been preserved. As a result, it has been possible to determine the sex of only a small number of the burials. Over half of the burials (11 in total) were children or adolescents of which it would probably have been difficult to determine the sex anyway. Furthermore, no direct traces of the barrows which it is suggested covered many of the burials have survived. The site has, therefore, little to contribute to our understanding of the barrows themselves or to the subject of gender.

Despite these deficiencies, it was possible to determine, with more or less precision, the age of all of the burials. Furthermore, radiocarbon dates obtained from 17 of them provide us with a quite detailed chronology. The evidence from Ridgeway Hill thus provides a relatively rich source of evidence with which to address certain questions about the way in which age affected how individuals were buried, questions concerning chronology, including how burial practice changed over time,

and the chronological relationships between burials in sequences and groups.

Although the number of burials recovered was quite large for a single excavation, it is still clearly too small to form the basis for generalisation on its own. The very large number of late Neolithic/early Bronze Age burials excavated in southern England and more widely show that burial practices were extremely varied (Ashbee 1960; Burgess 1980; Woodward 2000) and, although certain more or less clear patterns have been identified, the evidence so far has eluded any straightforward synthesis. Although some attempt has been made here to relate the evidence at Ridgeway Hill to that found more widely, the focus of this discussion is primarily focused upon the patterns at Ridgeway Hill. It is clear, however, even from nearby sites (eg Bellamy 1991), that a wider perspective would reveal more complex and less consistent patterns.

The evidence for the existence of barrows

Before turning to other aspects of the evidence, it is worth briefly outlying the evidence which suggests

Fig. 4.1 General shot of site after excavation, showing Set 6 graves 3147 (with cist) and 3155 (foreground), Roman quarry pit 3110 (centre), Set 2a late Neolithic pits, and other barrows along the Ridgeway

that, despite the absence in all but one case of ring ditches, many of the burials were related to barrows.

The one clear example of a ring ditch that lay within the excavations (3032) was associated with a central burial pit, which contained a deposit of cremated remains and a few uncremated teeth from a child. The pit also contained the tip of a copper alloy dagger. A row of three probably late Roman graves provides evidence which suggests that this ring ditch was associated with a barrow mound. The grave nearest the centre of the ring ditch was the shallowest, measuring just 0.14m deep, and the remaining two burials, which extended across the area enclosed by the ring ditch and cut the ring ditch itself, were progressively deeper, the grave cutting the ring ditch being 1.0m deep. Assuming that all of the graves were originally of the same depth, and allowing 0.3m for the topsoil, would suggest that the barrow still survived to a height of 1.2m in the Roman period, and probably more at its centre, giving some indication of the extent to which the site has suffered from truncation.

The pit associated with the early Bronze Age burials at the centre of the barrow was just 0.1m deep, and the presence of just a few uncremated teeth from an infant, which may originally have formed part of a complete inhumation burial, and just the tip of a dagger, suggests that the burial pit itself has also suffered from truncation, although it seems likely that it was never very deep, unless it was a secondary burial cut through the mound.

In the other groups, many of the burials were equally shallow. These shallow graves comprise small inhumation pits in Sets 4 and 7, the small cremation cist in Set 8, and an inhumation cist in Set 4. Even allowing for 0.3m of topsoil, these would have been very shallow graves, barely deep enough to cover the burials they contained, unless they were secondary burials cut through barrows.

Further support for the idea that at least some of the burials were covered by mounds is provided by the fact that in two cases, deeper graves – large inhumation pits – contained the earliest burials. Such burials occurred in Sets 7 and 6, although in Set 6 the contrast between the depth of the large inhumation pit and the cremation cist which formed the only other burial in the group was not as marked as the contrast between the large and small inhumation pits in Set 7. In the case of Set 4 it is not clear that the large inhumation pit was earlier than other burials in the group, but the dates for the burials in the group were all very similar. The large inhumation pit was, in any case, the shallowest example and perhaps should not have been included in this category. Whatever the case, it is easy to see the large inhumation pits in Sets 6 and 7 as having been

related to primary burials, interred before a barrow was constructed, and the shallow graves as secondary burials, cut through the barrow.

One final piece of evidence that can be taken to suggest the existence of mounds is provided by the fills of the large inhumation pits. Although in the large inhumation pits in Sets 6, 7 and 9 the primary burials were covered with layers of chalk, the remaining fills consisted of silty layers, and it is clear that more chalk was removed from the pits than was put back into them. It is possible that this chalk was used to provide a capping for the mound, as was the case in some of the excavated barrows near to the site.

A number of barrows have been identified in Dorset which were not associated with ring ditches, probably including the Bincombe barrow (Bincombe 24; Payne 1943) which lies adjacent to the site (see also Ashbee 1960, 44, for references to other examples in Dorset). Such mounds may be constructed using turf or soil from surrounding area rather than from a ditch.

Although no traces of such mounds at Ridgeway Hill survived, it is possible, as has long been noted (Ashby 1960, 45), that the white chalk-capped mounds, perhaps surrounded by rings of brown, deturfed soil, set in green grassland on the southern slopes of the Ridgeway, would have been visually striking when seen from the south.

On this basis, then, it is suggested that the graves in Set 7 were related to a barrow, and very probably those in Sets 4 and 6. The case for Sets 8 and 9 is less clear. Set 8 consisted of just a small cremation cist, the depth of which (just 0.1m) suggests it may also have been covered by a mound. The two graves in Set 9, however, were both deeper features (0.4 and 0.5m deep), and if any of the graves were not associated with a barrow, it seems most likely that it was these. It is then, not possible to exclude the possibility that some of the early Bronze Age burials on Ridgeway Hill were not associated with barrows (ie formed flat graves), but there is evidence which suggests that many of them were associated with barrows.

The argument for the existence of barrows based upon the relative depth of the graves, and the consequent division of the graves into primary and secondary burials, also of course implies that, at least in the case of Set 7, the barrow mound was constructed after the primary burial was made, and before the subsequent secondary burials were interred. The mound would thus have marked the primary burial, and may have served as a focus for later burials, rather than marking the closure of the site to burials (cf. Fitzpatrick 2011, 199; Last 2007). Needless to say, it is impossible to prove this point with the evidence from Ridgeway Hill.

Fig. 4.2 Barrow landscape

The distribution of the graves in each set gives little indication of how large any such mounds might have been. If the large inhumation pit in Set 7 was at the centre of a barrow, which is not always the case (eg Last 1998), the barrow would only have had to be around 6m across to cover all of the other burials. A similar calculation in the case of Set 4 suggests the mound would have been at least 11m across, but it is less certain in this case if the large inhumation pit was a primary burial, and all of the burials could have been contained in a mound 7m across. The two graves in Set 6 would imply a mound at least 8m across if the large inhumation pit were at the centre.

Numbers of barrows

Although the details of the possible barrow mounds are a matter for speculation, the discovery of so many burials which were not associated with ring ditches in such a small transect across the Ridgeway does have one significant implication. The Dorset Ridgeway probably contains the densest concentration of barrows of any area in Britain (RCHM(E) 1970, 426-7), and yet the results of the Ridgeway Hill

excavations suggest that the original number would have been even higher than current records suggest.

It is worth stressing, at this point, how difficult groups of burials like those at Ridgeway Hill are to detect without excavation. The South Dorset Ridgeway has been subject to intensive archaeological examination, and, although much of the earliest work went unreported, more recently the barrows have been well documented (eg Grinsell 1959; 1982; Woodward 1991; Royall 2011). Given the extent of previous work, it is remarkable that the South Dorset Ridgeway Mapping Project (Royall 2011, 35-6) identified 325 new barrows, producing a total of 883 when added to already recognised sites, in an area centred on the Ridgeway but extending some way to the north, and south to the coast. Most of the new sites were identified because they were associated with ring ditches. The number of new sites on the Ridgeway itself was quite small, most of the new sites lying to the north-east. The results of the Ridgeway Hill excavations suggests that, even in an area which was subject to particularly intensive examination prior to excavation (Dorset County Council 2005), probably small, ploughed-out, ditchless barrows such as those which may have existed at

Ridgeway Hill, may remain archaeologically invisible. Given the extent of previous work, it seems likely that it is specifically barrows of this kind that are likely to be under-represented in current records.

Putting a precise figure on how much higher the original total number of barrows might have been is difficult. In 1971 the RCHM(E) recorded a total of 233 barrows on the Ridgeway itself and a further 205 barrows nearby (largely on spurs running north from the Ridgeway), giving a total of 438 barrows. This total has been increased by later discoveries (eg Grinsell 1982; Sharples 1991; Royall 2011), and Woodward's (1991, chap. 10) analysis of the distribution of the barrows involved a total of 483 barrows. Although this latter figure does not include the latest additions (Royall 2011), since Woodward's analysis provides the best basis for comparison, his figures have been utilised here.

To simply take the number of barrows previously known at Ridgeway Hill and multiply it by a factor determined by the number of additional groups discovered would clearly be simplistic. Just one barrow was known in the Ridgeway Hill site – Set 10, which was identified because of its associated ring ditch – and five further groups of burials, each of which may have been associated with a barrow, were identified. This would imply that the total number of barrows should be increased by a factor of five, giving a total of well over 2000 barrows for the Ridgeway area.

There are several reasons for thinking that this total is an exaggeration. The first of these is the fact that the route of the Relief Road was deliberately chosen so as to minimise the damage to barrows. The number of previously known barrows within the excavation area was thus deliberately minimised. The second is that it is unlikely that all areas of the Ridgeway have suffered from plough damage to the same extent as Ridgeway Hill (Wessex Archaeology 2011). Although a precise consideration of the extent of damage is beyond the scope of this discussion, it seems likely that in some areas barrows similar to those that may have existed at Ridgeway Hill still survive as visible earthworks. The final consideration worth noting is that the numbers of barrows identified as ring ditches varies along the Ridgeway. In Woodward's (1991; fig. 70) analysis of the distribution of barrows along the Ridgeway, all of the barrows surviving as ring ditches lay in Zone C1. The precise implications of this are unclear. It may, for example, reflect differing extents to which the Ridgeway has suffered from ploughing. It also, however, highlights the potential contrasts in the distributions of barrows of particular kinds (which are also apparent in the distribution of fancy barrows), and thus raises the possibility that small, ditchless barrows of the kind that may have

existed at Ridgeway Hill were not distributed uniformly along the Ridgeway, although bowl barrows are the commonest type in almost all areas.

A more credible way of estimating the extent to which small, ditchless barrows may be under-represented is provided by Woodward's analysis of the distribution of barrows along the Ridgeway (1991, 143-6). Woodward plotted the number of barrows in his territorial groups that lie within 0.5km intervals along the Ridgeway. This method avoids the problem of having to define an arbitrary area within which the density of barrows is calculated (cf RCHM(E) 1971, 426-7), which makes any attempt to compare the density of barrows at Ridgeway Hill with other areas problematical. A figure comparable to Woodward's can be extrapolated from the Ridgeway Hill excavations by treating the site as though it was a 75m wide transection across the Ridgeway. The figure of six barrows in this transect implies a total of 22 or 23 barrows per 0.5km. This figure is roughly twice the number calculated by Woodward for the R8-9 group (of which Ridgeway Hill forms a part), the 0.5km transects along which contained between eight and 13 barrows.

Similar figures of between c 10 and 15 barrows per 0.5km occur at several other points along the Ridgeway, but are rarely exceeded. The only notable exception is the Poor Lot group which has 35 barrows in 0.5km (no other area exceeds 18 barrows per 0.5km). Although the figure for Ridgeway Hill is still open to the challenge that it may encompass a very localised area of particular density, and that the figure would be reduced if it was extended to cover 0.5km, it at least appears to gives a more credible indication of the extent to which, at least in some areas, the number of barrows may have been under-represented. Overall, it might be taken to imply that, although bowl barrows already appear to have been the most common form along almost all of the Ridgeway, their number may have been underestimated, in some areas perhaps by as much as a factor of 2. This also marks out the fancy barrows as even more exceptional than they have appeared to be.

In its discussion of the density of barrows in differing areas the RCHM(E) (1971, 426-7) put forward a simple calculation of the number of barrows that were constructed per year. Using their total of 233 barrows on the Ridgeway (and 433 in the wider area) and a period of construction of a millennium, they suggested that, although the total number of barrows was large, it still equated to only one barrow being constructed every four to five years on the Ridgeway, or one every two years in the wider region.

Overall, of course, in suggesting that the total number of barrows may have been underestimated, the results of the Ridgeway Hill excavations suggest that barrows would have been constructed more frequently. The radiocarbon dates also suggest, however, that the chronological pattern of construction may have been much less uniform over time than these simple estimates suggest. Of the six dated sets of burials at Ridgeway Hill, three (Sets 6, 7 and 9) appear to have begun around 2100 cal BC, two (Sets 4 and 8) may have been slightly later (*c* 2000-1900 cal BC) and one (Set 10) may have been much later (*c* 1700 cal BC). It should, of course, be recalled that the sample at Ridgeway Hill does not include all of the types of barrows or burials that occur along the Ridgeway, and that a wider sample would no doubt fill in the gaps in the sequence. Nonetheless, if it is accepted that all of the sets at Ridgeway Hill were related to barrows, and that the barrows were constructed at the same time as the primary burial was interred, then it appears that barrow construction may have been most frequent in the earlier phases, perhaps even specifically in the first part of Garwood's second phase (*c* 2100 cal BC) and that, although burials continued to be made at later dates, barrows were constructed less frequently.

Overall, then, although it is difficult to calculate accurate figures, the results from Ridgeway Hill suggest that small, ditchless barrows, primarily from a relatively early phase of the development of the Ridgeway cemeteries, are under-represented in current records.

The chronology of the barrows

The radiocarbon dates obtained from the burials suggest that, overall, burial at Ridgeway Hill probably extended over a period of between 400 and 650 years, beginning between 2250 and 2090 cal BC and ending between 1730 and 1600 cal BC (at 68.23% probability). Although the very earliest burials in Sets 6, 7 and 9 might have belonged at the very end of the first phase of Garwood's (2007a) periodisation of barrows, most of the earlier burials would fall largely within his second phase (*c* 2100-1850 cal BC), as would all but the latest burials in Sets 6 and 7 and all of those in Sets 4, 8 and 9. The burials in Set 10, however, would fall into the third phase (*c* 1850 – 1500 cal BC).

The evidence at Ridgeway Hill is generally consistent with the sequence of development suggested by Garwood. His Phase 2 is characterised primarily by multiple burials of a 'wide range of age and gender categories'. 'Single inhumation graves predominate in both central and peripheral positions', although cremation burials occur with increasing frequency. Beakers and Food Vessels occur, alongside other items as grave goods. The

burials forming Sets 4, 7 and 6 correspond quite well with this characterisation. In contrast, Phase 1 was characterised by single inhumation graves in central positions, although some burial sequences occurred in central grave pits. Cremation burials were rare. Phase 3 was characterised by a predominance of cremation burials, single central burials and sometimes rich assemblages of grave goods in single phase mounds, of which Set 10 may have provided a modest example.

Adults, adolescents and children

As well as corresponding reasonably well with the phases of development proposed by Garwood, the radiocarbon dates provide a more detailed picture of the way in which burial practices changed over time at Ridgeway Hill. Before looking at these changes, however, it is important to note the significant differences in the ways in which adults, adolescents and children were treated.

The evidence suggests that the age of the individuals provided the basis for significant distinctions that are reflected in differing burial rites. Most of the children appear to have been interred as secondary burials, inserted into the graves of adults, sometimes at dates much later than the primary adult burials were made. Adolescents seem also to have been distinguished as a category. Many of them were buried in small inhumation pits which, in some cases at least, were probably again secondary graves cut into the barrow mounds, and thus also post-date the primary adult inhumations below the mounds.

The precise age at which the distinctions between children, adolescents and adults were made is uncertain. The secondary burials inserted into graves containing primary adult burials range in age from an infant of 1-5 months to children of up to 13 years. The small inhumation pits, however, although they mostly contain adolescents aged between around 10 and 18 years, also contained one child of only 1.25 to 1.75 years and another of 7.5-8.5 years, as well as one adult over 18 years old. The primary adult burials range in age from 20 to 45 years.

Although the details are uncertain, the distinctions at Ridgeway Hill are generally consistent with the results of Garwood's (2007b) wider analysis of the burials of children in Dorset. His survey revealed that burials of children were most common in his Period 2 (*c* 2150-1800 cal BC) – the period to which most of the burials at Ridgeway Hill belong – but were rare in earlier and later barrows. Most of the child burials occurred, as at Ridgeway Hill, as secondary burials. He also noted distinctions in Phase 2 between the burials of children below the age of about 12 and of children above that age,

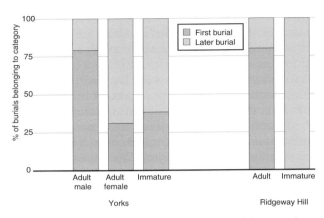

Fig. 4.3 Comparison of the age of first and later early Bronze Age burials in sequences in Yorkshire and at Ridgeway Hill (data for Yorkshire from Mizoguchi 1993; total number of burials: Yorks adult males: 24; Yorks adult females: 16; Yorks immature: 13; Ridgeway Hill adults: 5; Ridgeway Hill immature: 5)

which may correspond to the distinction between children and adolescents at Ridgeway Hill.

Overall, the numbers of burials occurring in sequences, and the order in which they were interred in terms of age, are broadly comparable with figures for Beaker burials in Yorkshire given by Petersen (1972) and Mizoguchi (1993). Amongst the Yorkshire burials, Petersen records an average of 5.1 burials, but this figure is inflated by two sites, and all but a few of the graves contained between two and five burials. The Ridgeway sets of graves contained between two and six individuals, and the sequence of burials within graves all consisted of just two or three individuals. The limited evidence for the sex of the burials at Ridgeway Hill means that the patterning in the sequences of burials can only by compared with Mizoguchi's figures in terms of age. There are two differences between the evidence from Yorkshire and that from Ridgeway Hill (Fig. 4.3). The first is that in Yorkshire as many women as children were interred as secondary burials, whereas at Ridgeway Hill almost all of the secondary burials were of children. The second is

that a small proportion of the primary burials in Yorkshire were of children, whereas no children appear to have been interred as primary burials at Ridgeway Hill. The number of burials at Ridgeway Hill is, however, small, and these differences may just reflect the limited size of the sample.

Change in burial practices over time

Whilst the way in which children and adolescents were treated appears to have been relatively uniform, there is much more variation in the burials of adults. Part of this variation in the adult burials may be chronological, reflecting changes in burial fashions over time.

The radiocarbon dates suggest that there were changes in the kinds of graves over time, and a broad transition from inhumation to cremation (Table 4.1). The earliest graves were the primary burials in large inhumation pits, dating from 2140-2020 cal BC. After around 2020 the first cists were constructed. The early cists include examples containing inhumation burials and cremation burials. The only later example of a cist, falling in the period 1890-1750 cal BC, contained a cremation burial. The latest adult burial , that at the centre of the ring ditch, was a cremation burial placed in a small pit.

In contrast, the radiocarbon dates do not reveal any change in the burials of adolescents over time, all of which were buried in small inhumation pits. The burials of children were all inhumations, and since almost all of them were secondary burials inserted into graves containing adults, the types of graves with which the children were associated follow those of the adults.

One further possible trend suggested by the Ridgeway Hill evidence is a decline in the numbers of burials in each group. Sets 8 and 10, two of the later groups of burials, contain only two burials – one adult and one child in both cases – in contrast to some of the earlier groups – Sets 6 and 7 – which contain larger numbers of burials. This is consistent

Table 4.1 Summary of the chronology of the early Bronze Age burials

2140-2020	2020-1890	1890-1750	1750-1620
Adults in large inhumation pits	(1 adult (Set 4) in a large inhumation pit)		
	Secondary burials of children and adolescents in large inhumation pits (as well as one example in an inhumation cist)		
	Adolescents and older children in small inhumation pits		
	Adult in small inhumation cist		
	Adult in small cremation cist	Adult in cremation cist	Adult in small cremation pit
	Uncremated child with adult cremation burial		

with Garwood's (2007a) chronology, in which Phase 2 is characterised by multiple burials whilst Phase 3 is characterised by single central burials. However, as is discussed further below, the larger number of burials in the earlier groups reflects the continued use of these sets for the burial of children for considerable periods after the primary burial was interred. The final number of burials in each set may well, however, reflect contingent factors which influenced where children were buried, which may in part depend on the particular histories of the related social groups. The extent to which this pattern at Ridgeway Hill reflects wider changes in burial practices rather than the particular circumstances of the social groups involved is uncertain.

Variations in the status of adult burials

Variation in the adult burials was not, however, just related to change over time. There were also contrasts between adult burials made at roughly the same time. Several of the burial groups contained a single primary adult inhumation burial. Most of these burials were placed in large inhumation pits that often contained sequences of later, secondary burials, and were associated with grave goods which consisted usually of just a Beaker vessel and a copper alloy awl. The adult cremation burial at the centre of the ring ditch which was associated with a fragment of a copper alloy dagger provides a comparable later example.

There are two groups of adult remains that contrast with these primary burials. The first consists of the burials in Set 4. This group consisted of three adults and two adolescents, in contrast to the other groups, which consisted almost entirely of single adults and children. Furthermore, most of the burials in Set 4 appear to have been interred over a short period, compared to the other sets of burials, of probably less than 100 years. None of the adult burials in this group was associated with any grave goods, nor did the adult burials here form the start of longer sequences of burials. And, although one of the graves was classified as a large inhumation pit, it differed in form from the other large inhumation pits and was the shallowest example. The adults in this group appear then to have been treated slightly less ostentatiously than the primary burials of adults.

Although it is hard to escape the conclusion that the individuals forming primary burials were in some sense more significant socially, whether as a reflection of their status or of the people responsible for burying them, than some of the other adults, the associated grave goods do not provide clear evidence that any such enhanced status was

reflected in exceptional wealth.

Table 4.2 shows the grave goods of burials associated with Beakers in Dorset and the surrounding counties of Devon, Somerset, Wiltshire and Hampshire, ordered by Social Status analysis. This method of analysis orders artefacts by the mean number of associated types, on the basis that types which are associated with the largest number of other types are likely to be the highest status types, and individual graves by the highest status type they contain (Hodson 1990). The analysis was carried out using the Bonn Seriation package (www.uni-koeln.de/~al001/basp.html). The data for this table was taken from Clarke (1970) and no attempt has been made to update or check Clarke's data, which obviously lacks some significant recent discoveries, such as Fitzpatrick (2011). Nor has any attempt been made to refine the analysis or interpret it in detail.

The results of the analysis suggest that the assumptions underlying Social Status Analysis may not be valid in the case of Beaker burials. Most notably, it is difficult to believe that strike-a-lights, for example, were the highest status object used as grave goods, although their apparent status has been noted before (Case 1977; 1998). An interpretation which goes beyond a simple notion of status is no doubt called for, and possibly one which takes more account of associated sets of tools. The point of the analysis here, however, is simply to show that modest assemblages of grave goods such as those found with the Ridgeway Hill burials are quite typical. Over half of the graves represented in the table contain only one or two types, and there are very few graves with more than five types (cf Fitzpatrick 2011, 209). The analysis also shows that, although overall the range of types is wide, the types represented at Ridgeway Hill are amongst the most common (seven sites with awls, all of the sites have Beakers since that provides the basis for inclusion in the table).

Several points arise from this. The first is that the representation of status in terms of grave goods appears to be more complex than a simple reading in terms of wealth of grave goods would suggest. The distinctions between the burials at Ridgeway Hill suggest that the grave goods did mark distinctions of status of some kind, but the form that status took and the way it was expressed in grave goods was probably complex and is beyond the scope of this discussion. The second is that however the grave goods are interpreted, they do not, prima facie, provide clear evidence to suggest the existence of very marked differences of status.

The reasons for the variation amongst the adult burials at Ridgeway Hill remain obscure. It is, however, noticeable that alongside the adults, Set 4

Table 4.2 Summary of Beaker associated grave goods in Dorset and surrounding counties (data from Clarke 1970)

County	Site	Antler pick	Stone plaque	Battleaxe	Flint dagger	Flint flake	Beaker	Boar's tusk	Bone tanged pommel	Cu alloy awl	Flint core	Shale bead	Cu dagger
Hants	Winchester, St James' Terrace						2						
Som	Brean Down						2						
Wilts	Wilsford						2						
Hants	Winchester St James' Terrace						2						
Wilts	Larkhill						2						
Wilts	Boyton						2						
Wilts	Wilsford				1		1						
Wilts	Brigmerston	1					1						
Som	Stoford Barwick	1					1						
Wilts	Overton West					1	1						
Wilts	Durrington, Woodhenge 1			1			1						
Wilts	Avebury, Beckhampton Grange					2	1						
Dorset	**Ridgeway Hill 3520**					1	1						
Hants	Iford, Sheepwash					2	1						
Dorset	**Ridgeway Hill 3316**						1			1			
Dorset	**Ridgeway Hill 3334**						1			1			
Dorset	Tarrant Lanceston						1			1			
Hants	Stockbridge						1			1			
Dorset	Thickthorn long barrow						1			1			
Wilts	Calne Without						1						1
Som	Wick, Stogursey			1			1						1
Som	Charmy Down						1					1	1
Wilts	Shrewton						1		1				1
Som	Wincanton						1						
Dorset	Worth Matravers						1						
Devon	Langcombe						1						
Wilts	Sutton Veny						1	2					
Wilts	Wilsford						1	1					
Som	Wick, Stogursey					1	1						
Wilts	Winterslow Hut						1						1
Dorset	Tarrant Launceston						1						
Wilts	Figheldean						1						
Som	Corston					1	1						
Wilts	Winterbourne Monkton						1						
Dorset	Blackbush						1				1		
Wilts	Amesbury 54				1		1						
Wilts	Farleigh Wick						2						
Wilts	Amesbury 51						1			1			
Devon	Fernworthy						1						1
Wilts	Mere						1						1
Wilts	Roundway						1						1
Wilts	Winterbourne Stoke 54						1						
Wilts	Winterbourne Monkton						2						
Som	Corston						1						
Wilts	West Overton 6B						1			1			
	Total	2	0	2	2	5	38	2	1	7	1	1	8

Flint scraper	Barbed and tanged arrowhead	Bone belt ring	Stone bracer	Pebble hammer	Flint knife	Flint blade	Gold button caps	Hammerstone	Cu racquet pin	Jet button	Antler/bone spatula	Jet pulley ring	Stone disc	Whetstone	Fe ore nodule	Flint strike a light	No. types
																	1
																	1
																	1
																	1
																	1
																	1
																	2
																	2
																	2
																	2
																	2
																	2
																	2
																	2
																	2
																	2
																	2
																	2
																	3
																	3
																	3
1																	2
1																	2
	3																2
			1														3
		1															3
4				1													4
	2		1														4
					1												2
					1												2
					1												3
	1				2												3
						1											3
								1									3
	4	1				1	1										5
1											1						4
					1					1							4
							2				1						4
	1		1						1								5
						1				1		1		2			5
					1			1		2		1	1				6
3					1									1	1	1	6
					1						1			2	1	1	7
5	5	2	3	1	8	3	2	2	1	3	3	2	1	3	2	2	.

contained two of the three adolescents found at Ridgeway Hill, and that one of the adults in this group was buried in the same way as the adolescents. It seems possible, then, that the differences in status reflected in the variations in adult burials at Ridgeway Hill were related to age. They might, for example, be related to the success of the family of which the deceased formed a part, reflected perhaps in the number of their children. One argument that could be raised against this suggestion, however, is that it might be expected that the success of a family, for example when viewed in terms of number of children related to an individual, would be related roughly to the age of the deceased and, whilst the Set 4 burials consist largely of adolescents and one young adult, they also include a prime adult of 26 to 35 years, whilst the primary burial in a large inhumation pit in Set 6 was of a young adult. It is possible, instead, that there were other ways in which status – such as economic success in farming for example – could be achieved over time, which generally favoured older individuals but which could, nonetheless, vary with age.

Further variation in the burial of adults: stray remains

A possible example of a second, different way of treating adult remains is provided by the small group of adult bone fragments – rib, humerus and femur – discovered in the upper fill of the cist which was constructed within the large inhumation pit (3227) in Set 7. What marks these bones out is the fact that radiocarbon dating shows that they were older than the cremated remains of a child which lay stratigraphically below them. The stratigraphic sequence in this pit is not easy to interpret, and it is possible that these bone fragments simply derived from a secondary burial which was disturbed when the cist was constructed in the grave. It is, however, also possible that they reflect a more complex sequence of events, which could have involved the adult bone fragments having been either buried elsewhere, or otherwise retained and then having been deposited in the grave at a date much later than the death of the individual to which they belonged. Petersen (1972) has documented the occurrence of numerous examples of disarticulated remains in Beaker period graves. The uncertainties surrounding the interpretation of grave 3227 mean that this small group of bones can only be put forward as a possible example of such practices.

Many of the skeletons at Ridgeway Hill were only partially preserved, but almost all came from very shallow graves, and their incomplete preservation is almost certainly a product of the severe truncation that the site has suffered. There is little

reason to think that they did not originally consist of simple, articulated inhumations. If this were the case, it would suggest the existence of a marked contrast between the majority of articulated remains and the single example of disarticulated remains. The significance of this contrast remains unclear, but it is perhaps worth noting that it may have been related to a wider set of contrasts, which involved the closure of sites with mounds, potentially protecting burials below them from further disturbance, and the re-opening of graves.

Social relations and the chronology of the burials

The relatively precise chronology provided by the radiocarbon dates makes it possible to examine certain aspects of the way in which the area covered by the excavations was used as a cemetery over time. The dates indicate that, rather than the burial groups having been formed in succession, several of them were in use over the same period. That is, rather than burial being focused upon one barrow before shifting to a new barrow, burials were made in established barrows even after other barrows had been created. This overlap, however, largely reflects the interment of children as secondary burials at dates more or less distant in time from the associated primary burial. It is quite possible that new barrows were established for each individual deemed worthy of it, and thus that the higher status adults were buried in sequence at different locations, in contrast to the lower status adult burials in Set 4.

Within the sequences of burials there is considerable variation in the periods that elapsed between the interment of the probably primary adult burials and those of the children that followed them. Given the very shallow depth of some of the graves, the possibility that some burials have not survived at all should be noted. The apparently long periods which elapsed between burials in some sets might partly reflect the fact that burials made in the intervening periods have not survived.

In Set 9, the female adult and child burials (which lay in separate graves) could have been interred at similar dates. The adult was between 35 and 39 years old at the time of death, and the child 10 to 13 years old. The adult would thus have been between 22 and 29 years old when the child was born and thus was probably of more or less similar age to the mother of the child, if she was not the mother herself.

In Set 6, however, the primary adult burial was buried at least 10 years (and probably 50 years) before the first child. The child was aged 7-13 years, and thus, whilst it is possible that the child was born when the adult was alive, it is more likely that the adult had died before the child was born. Indeed, given that the gap between the two burials is likely to have been at least 50 years, the adult is more likely to have been the age of a grand- or more likely, a great grandparent with respect to the child.

In Set 7, the gap between the primary adult burial and the first child burial was larger still – at least 120 years, and probably 160 years – although two children were then buried within what was probably a quite short period. The child was 11-13 years old and the adult 36-45 years old, leaving a gap of around five generations between the two, at least.

These more or less long periods raise the question of why the children were buried in these particular graves, when clearly in the case of Set 7 and probably also Set 6, it seems possible that more closely related individuals (in terms of generations) would have been buried somewhere else.

It seems likely, of course, that the location in which children were interred as secondary burials involved in some way the relationship between the child – or the group burying the child – and the individual forming the primary burial. It has been suggested that sequences of burials were intended to 'establish a connection between different generations, emphasising particular lines of descent' (Thomas 1999, citing Barrett 1994, 124; Last 1998; Garwood 2007b). The evidence from Ridgeway Hill suggests that this interpretation should be treated with some caution. Almost all of the secondary burials in sequences at Ridgeway Hill were of children, most of whom were too young to have had their own children. In terms of lines of descent they thus represented dead ends. In the wider evidence, the fact that most of the adults interred as secondary burials in sequences were women should also urge caution. Even where descent is reckoned matrilineally, the relevant line of descent is between sister's son and mother's brother rather than between mother and daughter. A more obvious way of emphasising lines of descent would probably have been to bury sequences of adult men, but this is the least common pattern in Mizoguchi's (1993) data, and it appears from the Ridgeway Hill evidence that men – and especially those of higher status – were more likely to be associated with the construction of a new barrow.

It is possible that the reason why children, in particular, were interred as secondary burials in sequences was related precisely to the fact that they had died too young to contribute to the reproduction of a lineage. It is possible, for example, that children were buried in the graves of certain ancestors so that the ancestors could provide protection for the children. Alternatively, the death of the child might have been attributed to the jealousy or anger of an ancestor, and burial in the same grave might have served as a form of appeasement.

It would be possible to continue multiplying the possible scenarios that could explain why children were buried in particular graves, without it being possible to determine which was the most plausible. One interesting feature which the evidence does highlight, however, is that even though the child burials were in some cases much later than the primary adult burials, the adult burials seem to have been marked out as special even when they were buried, in some cases, long before any secondary burials were added. This is clearest in the case of the primary burials in large inhumation pits, which were not only placed in larger pits than the other burials but were also associated with almost the only grave goods.

Furthermore, whatever the precise circumstances which lead to children being buried in particular graves, the variation in the periods which elapsed between the interment of the primary burials and the subsequent burials of children suggests that there was an element of choice involved. It is possible, then, that the location in which children were buried was used as a means of emphasising certain social relations. In systems in which descent is reckoned cognatically, such choices may form an important element of the way in which the social system functions. Indeed, such systems, where descent can be reckoned through either male or female lines, could provide a context in which it would be useful to single out more or less distant ancestors (although even in unilinear systems, establishing a link with a distant ancestor might have been a way of establishing a link with distant living relatives).

The character of the burial rite: orientations and the positioning off grave goods

The excavations at Ridgeway Hill also provide evidence which suggests that certain aspects of the burial rite were deliberately structured. The orientation of the bodies and the positioning of the grave goods, in particular, appear to be patterned. The significance of this patterning is not clear from the small sample of relevant burials at Ridgeway Hill. It is not, for example, clearly related to age or sex. Wider studies have suggested similar kinds of patterning (eg Mizoguchi 1993; Gibbs 1989; Tuckwell 1975), although when looked at over very wide spatial scales, no universal patterning is apparent.

It is possible that like many elements of other rituals this patterning did not having any great significance, even though it appears that it did. Bloch (2005) has noted that the participants in many rituals may be convinced that the rituals are of great significance despite the fact that they cannot give an easy explanation of what that significance actually is (Humphrey and Laidlaw 1994). In such cases, the conviction that the rituals are significant is maintained by the belief that even if the participants do not know the meaning, ritual specialists, ancestors or other supernatural beings do. Bloch refers to this dependence on the authority of others to guarantee the meaningfulness of rituals using the term 'deference' (see also Sperber's (2010) 'guru effect'). The patterning in the orientation of burials and the positioning of grave goods in the burials at Ridgeway Hill and other sites has the kind of apparently arcane complexity which is consistent with such a scenario. It could be taken to suggest the existence of funerary specialists who could interpret its significance.

Bloch's view of ritual as involving a deference of meaning poses a challenge to the interpretation of any ritual, since it suggests that rituals should not be explained in terms of a set of underlying beliefs which are held to provide reasons for the rites, but rather in terms of the degree to which the participants are convinced of the ritual's significance, and the authority of any ritual specialists involved. It is possible that apparently arcane symbolism of the kind exemplified by the patterning in the positioning of bodies and artefacts in the burials at Ridgeway Hill was one of the elements which convinced the participants of the significance of the ritual, and thus contributed to the perpetuation of the tradition of burial practices of which they formed a part.

Conclusion

Whatever the case, the burials at Ridgeway Hill provide evidence of the way in which several aspects of the social personae of the deceased influenced the way they were buried. Age appears to have been one important determinant of how individuals were buried, but it seems that the form of burial which individuals were given may also have been influenced by some form of achieved status which was only related to age to some extent. The higher status adults formed the focus for burial around which the remains of children in particular were grouped.

Some of the children were interred as secondary burials in graves which contained much older primary burials, the gap in age in one case probably extending up to at least five generations. The reasons for the burial of children in the graves of individuals who had predeceased them by such long periods remain obscure. Rather than directly emphasising lines of descent, the individuals forming the secondary burials may have belonged to categories which had not been able to contribute to the reproduction of a lineage.

The burial evidence seems to imply a gradation from children who were buried as secondary burials in the same graves as adults, to adolescents who were buried in small pits around adults, lower status adults who were given their own graves but lacked their own barrow and grave goods, to the higher status primary burials with grave goods. The form of the burial rite seems then, to reflect the extent to which individuals had successfully reached a full adult social status. The less fully an individual had achieved this status, the closer their burial was spatially to the more successful of their ancestors, but the more different was the form of their burial.

THE ROMAN PERIOD

There is very little evidence for activity on Ridgeway Hill From the middle Bronze Age to the end of the Iron Age. For at least part of this period, and particularly in the earlier part of the Iron Age, occupation may have been focused to the south at Southdown Ridge (see Chapter 5)

The next phase of activity evidenced at Ridgeway Hill dates from the late Iron Age or, more likely, the Roman period, when the area was divided by a series of ditches that may have formed part of a broadly rectilinear field system. Presumably the setting out of this field system formed part of a wider reorganisation of the landscape, perhaps following the Roman conquest. The extent to which this was related to a change in the use of the landscape is unclear. It is quite possible that the land had been used as pasture in the preceding periods and, if that were the case, the field system might reflect a more intensive use of the area rather than a fundamental change in use. The molluscs recovered from the Roman quarry pits suggest that the immediate surroundings consisted of probably heavily grazed grassland, and it thus appears likely that the field system was related to the use of the area as pasture. Furthermore, the fact that the barrow related to ring ditch 3032 seems still to have survived to a height of at least 1.2m in the late Roman period suggests that the area had not suffered from significant plough damage. The purpose of the large features interpreted as quarry pits is uncertain.

Late Roman burials

No direct chronological evidence was obtained for the date of the row of three burials cut across ring ditch 3033. The burials, supine, in rectangular graves, with coffin nails implying the presence of wooden coffins and, in particular, hobnails indicating that they were buried wearing shoes, suggests that they were late Roman (3rd to 4th century AD).

What is perhaps most interesting about these

burials is not so much the typical burial rite, but its context. The depth of the graves indicates that when they were cut the ring ditch was still associated with a barrow, which, the depth of the graves suggests, may have been around 1.2m tall. Roman reuse of prehistoric barrows has been recognised in many parts of Britain. It is particularly common, however, in Dorset (Williams 1997, 79-81; eg), perhaps simply reflecting the large numbers of barrows in the county (Grinsell 1959 and 1982). It is unlikely that the barrow itself retained any definite significance related to its original Bronze Age use since a millennium and a half probably separated the latest Bronze Age burials associated with barrows and the Roman burials. Barrows were, however, also constructed in many parts of the Roman empire (Eckardt *et al.* 2009 with further references), and several examples are known in Dorset (eg Fowler 1965). It is possible then that the positioning of the burials here was an attempt to relate the burials to what may have been a more prestigious form of Roman burial. It is perhaps worth noting that the barrow would probably have been visible from the Roman road which ran to the west of the site, although there us no indication that there was any more extensive Roman road-side cemetery in the area (cf. Eckardt *et al.* 2009).

THE ANGLO-SAXON BURIALS

The most exceptional feature of the three Anglo-Saxon burials, found in two graves, is the reuse of one of the graves. The distribution of the disarticulated remains in the reused grave, found both above and below the articulated burial, suggests that the grave was partially emptied in order to bury the second individual and then backfilled with the same fill, which incorporated much of the remains of the first individual. This implies that the second burial was made at a time when the first burial had at least lost any tissue which might have kept the remains articulated, and that the grave must, in some way, have been marked. There was no clear indication of a recut in the grave, and the emptying of the grave thus seems to have followed the lines of the original cut quite faithfully.

The location of these burials and the reuse of one of the graves suggest that these burials should be seen as deviant, departing significantly from the 'normal' burial rituals prevalent at the time (Aspöck 2008, 17). The reuse of the grave is insufficient on its own to mark out a burial as deviant. The reuse of grave appears to have been quite common in larger Anglo-Saxon cemeteries. In a study of 46 early Anglo-Saxon cemeteries, Stoodley (2002, 105) found that on average 5% of burials were multiple. Furthermore, in almost a third of the 'vertical burials' (in which one burial was interred above another – as opposed to horizontal multiple burials in which the bodies were laid side by side), the burial of the second individual had disturbed the primary burial (ibid., 110; Reynolds 2009, 65). The pattern at Ridgeway Hill is not, then, as exceptional as it might at first appear. It is, however, worth noting that many of the multiple burials include children (Crawford 2007), and the presence of two male adults appears to be unusual.

The location of the burials, however, close to the parish boundary, a location which may have been regarded as liminal and was associated with social outcasts of various kinds -criminals, 'heathens' and suicides (Reynolds 2009) – supports the suggestion that the burial were deviant. A 7th-century burial of a man, apparently mutilated with metal instruments, interred next to a parish boundary in the Neolithic bank barrow at Maiden Castle, provides a nearby example of a deviant burial (Brothwell 1971). The mass burial on the edge of the Ridgeway Hill site (Loe *et al.* 2014) of decapitated Vikings could provide another example of such deviant burial, although it was several centuries later in date than the Anglo-Saxon burials.

The exact circumstances that lead up the burials being made at this particular location, and to two individuals being placed in one grave, inevitably remain obscure. Stoodley suggests that there is no reason to believe that special relationships existed between the individuals in multiple burials. In the case of Ridgeway Hill, however, given the presence of just two Anglo-Saxon graves, and no effective limitations on the space available (Crawford 2007, 83), it is difficult to believe that there was not some reason for the reuse of the grave.

Chapter 5: Later Prehistoric and Romano-British Activity at Southdown Ridge

by Lisa Brown

INTRODUCTION

The Southdown Ridge site was located at NGR SY 673 832 on a spur of land on the southern side of the Ridgeway which rises to approximately 60m aOD (Fig. 1.1). The basal geology is composed of formations of Jurassic date, the Ridge itself representing a narrow band of Corallian Limestone and the underlying geology of Oxford Clays of the lower slope declining to 5-10m aOD to the east of Manor Roundabout. To the south of Southdown Ridge the land falls gently as it approaches the sea (Fig. 5.1), whilst the northern face of the ridge is a pronounced scarp slope.

The evidence recovered from the excavations at Southdown Ridge was dominated by remains of later prehistoric activity, with an emphasis on the early Iron Age and late Iron Age periods. This included remains of an extensive settlement, agricultural enclosures and a Dorset tradition burial ground. There was some limited occupation during the middle Iron Age, as confirmed by a radiocarbon date on a human burial in a pit, but no structural remains could be categorically assigned to this period.

The late Iron Age occupation spanned a period that continued beyond the Roman conquest, as attested by a 1st century AD brooch accompanying a burial, but the conservative character of the pottery used on the site during the 1st century BC-AD, and the endurance of archaic forms, typical for the region, meant that precise dating of archaeological remains from this broad period was difficult. Nonetheless, a few pottery sherds of clearly Roman style, an isolated curvilinear ditch,

Fig. 5.1 View from Southdown Ridge looking south

and three coffined burials with hobnailed foot-wear also confirmed post-conquest activity on the Ridge.

Thereafter, there was apparently little activity on Southdown Ridge that left archaeological traces until the post-medieval period when the scarp edge in the northern part of the site was exploited as a limestone quarry and, elsewhere within the excavated area, field drains and a small collection of post-medieval pottery attested to agricultural use of this location (Fig. 5.2).

LATER PREHISTORIC SETTLEMENT AND LANDSCAPE

Cross-Ridge Dyke

A large linear earthwork, almost certainly the ploughed out remains of a cross-ridge dyke, transected the lower ground of the southern part of the site (Fig. 5.3). It ran on a NNE-SSW alignment, terminating at the pronounced scarp slope near the centre of the excavated area. This feature was still

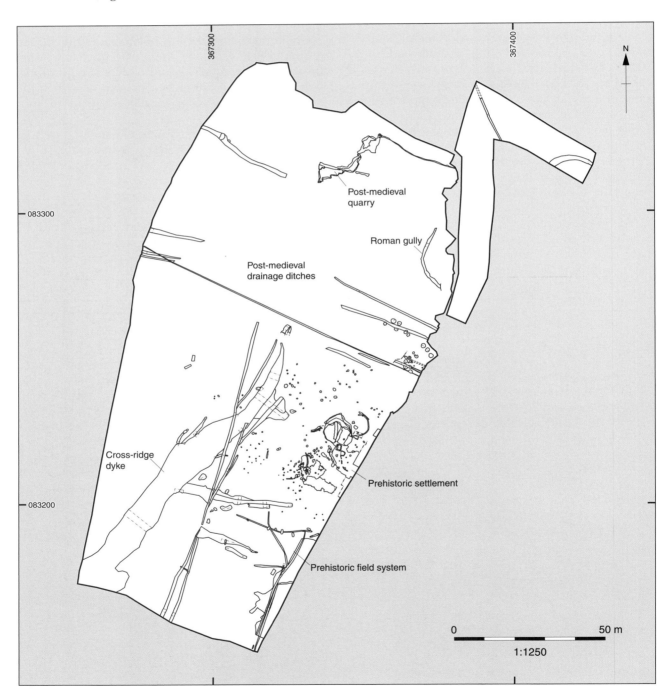

Fig. 5.2 General plan of the Southdown Ridge excavation area

visible as a low depression prior to the machine stripping of topsoil, and the area to the west of it was almost devoid of archaeological activity.

Cross-ridge dykes generally cut across the width of an upland ridge or the neck of an upland spur. A wide degree of variation is exhibited by the linear earthworks included in this class of monument, but they typically consist of one or more ditches running in parallel with one or more raised banks,

and most were constructed at altitudes of over 150m (English Heritage 1990). Research has generally been only regionally based and there is to date no synthesis of this class of monument for England as a whole. In north-west Europe generally, and in southern England in particular, most cross-ridge dykes date to the late Bronze Age or early Iron Age, but examples from Yorkshire (Spratt 1989) and the Welsh Marches have been dated to the medieval

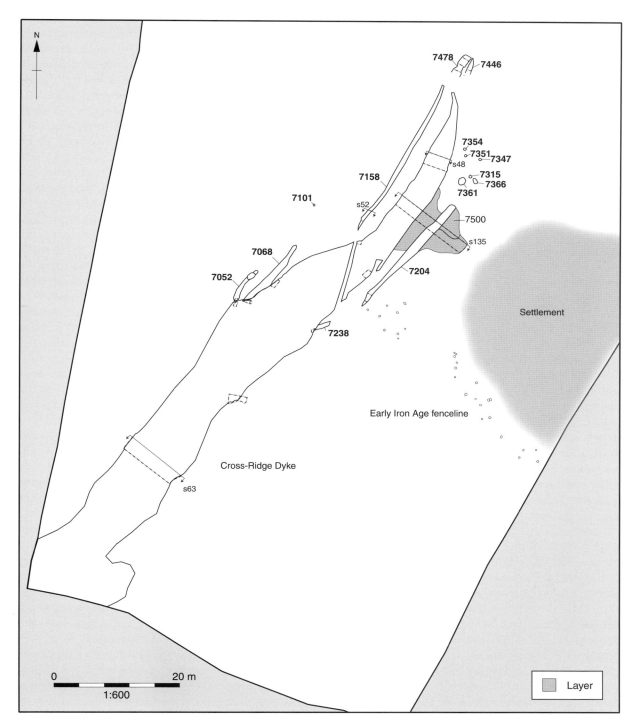

Fig. 5.3 The cross-ridge dyke and Iron Age settlement

period, and some are known to have survived as land divisions into the modern period. The dating of cross dykes tends to have relied on their association with nearby monuments, including Iron Age field systems.

The currently accepted interpretation is that these earthworks were territorial boundary markers or internal boundaries and land allotment markers within agricultural communities. Located as they are on high ground across ridges and spurs, they can constitute substantial monuments and, in some cases, palisades or vegetation may have been used to enhance their visual impact. However, not all cross-ridge dykes seem to have been highly visible or conspicuous, nor were all of them likely to have been sufficiently large to present a physical impediment to movement. The considerable effort expended in the construction of these monuments may not have been justified in strictly economic and agrarian terms. Some may have had a broader role, as territorial boundaries (Fowler 1964; Spratt 1989), as settlement or community boundaries, or as ritual or symbolic structures.

Cross-ridge dykes were usually constructed along significant natural landscape features, including, as the name implies, ridges and spurs, settings also favoured locations for other and earlier monuments, such as round barrows. The significance of the relationship between these natural and man-made features along the Ebble-Nadder chalk ridge has been recently explored by Tilley (2004), who proposes that barrows and dykes were constructed as "material metaphors" within their wider landscapes, serving to encode space "in relation to socially significant ridges, spurs and coombes" (ibid, 197). It is noteworthy in this respect that one of the highest concentrations of round barrows in Britain lies along the Dorset Ridgeway, including those excavated at Ridgeway Hill (this volume) and Bincombe (Dorset County Council and English Heritage 2011).

The Southdown Ridge Cross-Ridge Dyke

The univallate variety of cross dyke, to which the Southdown Ridge example most closely conforms, is characterised by a flat-bottomed ditch, while the ditches of multivallate dykes possess a V-shaped cross-section. In fact, the chief surviving element of the Southdown dyke is a wide flat ditch (Fig. 5.4). Narrow parallel ditches running off either side of the main ditch may have represented ancillary ditches or even hedgerows, but their stratigraphic relationship with the main feature had been affected by truncation and was not clear. The northern end of the monument was not excavated, so it was uncertain whether this was a genuine terminal or simply the extent to which it had survived ploughing in this area, but the ditch certainly narrowed as it ran northwards. It was traced within the excavated area for over 100m, terminating at the scarp that divided the flatter ground of the southern part of the site from the higher northern ground.

No above-ground evidence survived of either a bank or an original ground surface that may have been sealed by a bank. If the dyke had originally incorporated a bank or banks, it was reduced or entirely eroded into the ditch by ploughing, and the ditch and fill then also significantly reduced in depth by further ploughing. The stony fill recorded in the northern stretch of the main ditch may well have represented levelled bank material (Fig. 5.4).

The ditch was of variable width, measuring c 12m at its widest point, narrowing to c 2m wide at the northern end. The southern stretch of the ditch averaged about 10m wide and survived to only 0.70m deep. Four distinct fills (7154, 7155, 7156 and 7157) were observed in Section 63, recorded along this stretch of the ditch (Fig. 5.4). These were silty clays with a yellowish tint, incorporating very little stone, which had formed largely through natural silting, apparently under sometimes wet conditions. Some 202g of pottery recovered from these fills included early Iron Age sherds, but the group was dominated by late Iron Age sandy wares. There was a single early Roman orangeware sherd in the upper fill, along with a few fragments of horse, pig and sheep/goat bone. Single examples of horse and cattle teeth were present in the primary fill.

Section 135 was excavated across the dyke ditch at a point where it cut an earlier natural hollow (7500), close to the northern terminal. The dark clayey fill of the hollow incorporated occupation debris, including almost 100 early Iron Age sherds (1003g), amongst them fragments of red-finished carinated bowls and finger-impressed jars. The fills of the ditch in this location (7395, 7584, 7585, 7586) differed significantly from that at the southern end, having obviously derived in part from the earlier feature. Several limestone blocks averaging 0.15m in size within fill 7395 may have derived from a bank on the western side of the ditch. A Roman sherd, an iron nail (Sf45) and the pin of a copper alloy brooch (Sf27), also found in this deposit, suggest that any such bank had been at least partially levelled during the early Roman period.

The northern end of the ditch (Section 48) was 4m wide and only about 0.25m deep. The single recorded fill (7147) of greyish brown clayey silt incorporated numerous limestone slabs and blocks measuring up to 0.20m across. These were particularly concentrated on the eastern side, but that they were present on both sides of the ditch suggests that the ditch may originally have been flanked by a

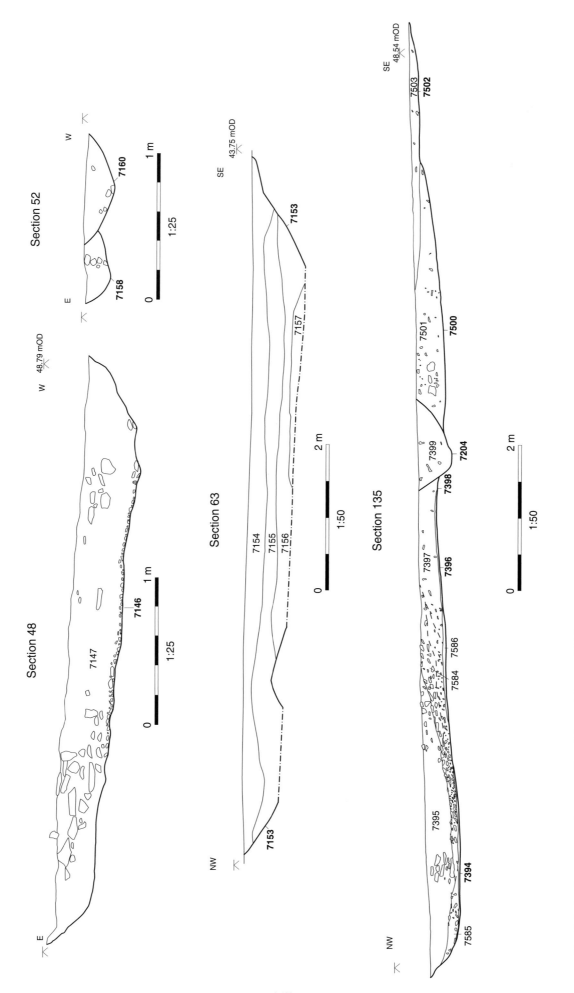

Section 52

Section 48

Section 63

Section 135

Fig. 5.4 Sections across the cross-ridge dyke and feature 7500

147

bank on either side. A single fragment of an early Iron Age slack-shouldered jar in oolitic fabric was associated with a dozen bones of horse, cattle and sheep/goat and dog.

Ancillary ditches

Several small ditches and a cluster of postholes were associated with the dyke ditch. This complex of features may have defined trackways or droveways and access gates, although a stock control function for cross-ridge dykes is sometimes disputed. Equally plausibly, the ditches may have been dug simply to provide material for banks, perhaps hedge banks.

Ditches 7158 and 7204 ran parallel either side of the main dyke ditch, respecting the alignment (Fig. 5.3). Although no clear relationship was established between these features, the fact that they shared a similar orientation suggests that they were once contemporary. The western ditch (7158) was only 0.24m deep, with a flattish base (Fig. 5.4, Section 52). It was traced for a length of 30m but was not visible at the southern end beyond the point that it was cut by a late field drain. The stony fill was flecked with charcoal and produced 10 abraded body sherds of early Iron Age pottery and single teeth of pig, cattle and sheep. In the heavily truncated and disturbed area to the north, two small lengths of ditch (7478 and 7446) may have represented the approximate terminal points of the dyke ditch and ditch 7158.

The eastern ditch (7204) was traced for *c* 23m, and its southern end, like that of 7158, was lost where it was cut by a later enclosure ditch (7220). This small ditch was at most 1.25m wide and 0.45m deep and apparently terminated where it cut across hollow 7500. The fill, which largely derived from the earlier hollow, produced 263g of pottery of early and late Iron Age type and a small fragment of unworked shale, but the eroded silt at the less disturbed southern end of the ditch produced sherds of entirely early Iron Age date.

A cluster of postholes and shallow pits located between the main ditch and ditch 7204 may have supported a gateway or similar structure at the northern end of the putative trackway, suggesting that access by people or livestock (or both) was being controlled at this point. The smallest of these postholes (7351, 7354, 7347, and 7315) were all stone-packed and of similar dimensions, 0.42-0.48m in diameter and 0.25-0.30m deep, strongly suggesting they were contemporary. Three of these features produced a few abraded early Iron Age sherds. Two larger features at the southern end of this group may have been shallow pits or hollows rather than postholes. Feature 7361 was 1.2m wide and only 0.08m deep and filled with grey clayey silt. Feature 7366 was 1.0m across and 0.20m deep, with

a similar silty fill. Both yielded small collections of early Iron Age pottery.

Two smaller ditches (7052 and 7068) projected northwards like spurs from the western side of the dyke ditch. Ditch 7052, laid out on a slight curve, just impinged on the dyke ditch and may have been laid out with respect to it. It was 0.80m long, 0.26m wide and 0.13m deep. The ditch was disturbed by the later insertion of a late Iron Age grave. The clayey silt fill was fairly stony, incorporating small fragments of limestone. A dozen sherds of pottery from the southern end of the ditch include both early and late Iron Age fragments, but 10 early Iron Age sherds from the undisturbed terminal probably provide the most secure date for the feature.

Ditch 7068 was 13m long, 0.36-1.0m wide and 0.40m deep at most, with slightly stepped sides at the southern end. Here it seems to have been cut by the dyke ditch, but this relationship was uncertain due to high levels of disturbance, and there was some indication that the dyke ditch was widened at some stage. The fill was a compact clayey silt with a concentration of small limestone fragments along the base. A dozen sherds of early Iron Age pottery came from the northern terminal fill, but two late Iron Age sherds were present at the junction with the dyke ditch. It seems likely, on balance, that both 7068 and 7052 were originally dug during the early Iron Age, possibly at the same time as the dyke ditch, but that exposure, remodelling and disturbance allowed mixing of later materials in the fills.

A smaller ditch (7238) that projected from the eastern side of the main ditch corresponded in opposition to ditch 7068, and was also cut by the dyke. Only a 0.65m length of this feature survived truncation by a later enclosure ditch. It was 0.40m wide and 0.10 m deep, filled with a stone free grey silt that produced two small early Iron Age sherds.

An isolated feature (7101), of posthole size, but containing only the complete skeleton of a lamb, may have been associated with the ancillary ditches on the western side of the dyke ditch. It lay *c* 8m to the north of ditch 7068 and could have been placed as an offering in this location (see Strid, Chapter 6).

Chronology and significance of the Southdown Ridge dyke

Dating the cross-ridge dyke was problematic. The main ditch appeared to have filled over a long period, and in its partly infilled state would have effectively served as a drain in wet conditions, capturing artefacts from a variety of sources and phases. This could account for the mixed nature of the finds assemblages. The ditch cut two earlier features, the hollow (7500) described above, and a multi-phase east-west aligned ditch (7240/7059/

7601) that may have marked a southern boundary of the earliest Iron Age settlement (see below). The dyke ditch was itself cut only by a post-medieval field drainage ditch (7093), suggesting that it was an important or useful feature, even into the Roman period. The ditch was apparently still filling during the late Iron Age, and possibly the early Roman period. Sherds representing much of a distinctive jar with a squat neck and lattice decoration, produced in the Wareham/Poole Harbour region, were recovered from the fill at the point where it intersected ditch 7238. This type of vessel (Chapter 6, Fig. 6.8, no. 68) was dated at Hengistbury Head to the LIA2 period, represented by typical Durotrigian pottery associated with Dressel 1A amphorae, distributed in the region from the first half of the 1st century BC. The fact that no late Iron Age or Romano-British burials were inserted into this feature during a time when other field ditches were utilised for this purpose emphasises its continued function, perhaps as a drainage channel, into and beyond this period.

In summary it seems that the cross-ridge dyke was an important feature of the early Iron Age agricultural landscape, possibly constructed as a multifunctional monument that served as a boundary of the early Iron Age settlement and agricultural enclosures, possibly with access provided by associated trackways. But it would also have drained water from the high ground of the northern scarp. As was the case with many cross-ridge dykes, it was insufficiently deep to deter access into and out of the settlement, except perhaps by livestock, but may have been a symbolic boundary, recognised both by the local inhabitants and by outsiders.

THE IRON AGE SETTLEMENT

Only the westernmost edge of what may have been a very substantial settlement lay within the excavated area. (Figs 5.3, 5.5). As a result, the potential for establishing the character, evolution and chronology of the settlement were somewhat restricted. This problem was exacerbated by the fact that the settlement had been subject to continual modification, demolition and reconfiguration, followed by consolidation of earlier surfaces during the late Iron Age. Then, at a very late stage of occupation, probably during the 1st century AD, the nucleus of the settlement was levelled using stone robbed from earlier buildings, along with and midden-like material from the earliest phase of settlement, most of which had probably accumulated in areas beyond the excavated area to the east. The midden-like deposit was encountered as a thick and variable, highly organic mass (7002) that almost entirely sealed the remains of the Iron Age buildings and yards. Several late Iron Age burials

inserted within the abandoned agglomeration sometime between the mid 1st century BC-mid 1st century AD were sealed by this mass. Although the purpose of this levelling exercise is unclear, it marked a return of the area to agricultural use.

The Southdown Ridge settlement emerged during the period referred to here as the earliest Iron Age (c 800-600 BC), although the nomenclature of a late Bronze Age to early Iron Age transition is sometimes preferred (Needham 2007, 39-63). During the late Bronze Age in the Wessex region the settlement model was typically one of individual households, probably single family units, practicing mixed farming and engaging in inter-household exchange of goods, labour and marriage partners, on a limited scale (Ellison 1981). The late Bronze Age also saw the emergence of a diversification of site types, including ringworks, early hillforts, timber platforms in wet conditions, and middens (Bruck 2007). Such diversification could be construed as evidence for a corresponding emergence of a settlement hierarchy, and certainly seems to indicate an evolving interest in differentiating certain arenas of social, economic and ritual practice. This is in part reflected in the widening range of items, including worked bone, found on late Bronze Age settlement sites, as compared to that typically recovered from middle Bronze Age sites.

Such differentiation is acutely apparent in the proliferation of ceramic styles during the last part of the Bronze Age, with the replacement in Wessex of the post Deverel-Rimbury styles with the All Cannings Cross and related decorated traditions, as seen at Kimmeridge and Eldon's Seat in Dorset (Cunnington 1923; Davies 1936; Cunliffe and Phillipson 1968). This shift allowed social differences to be expressed in both routine and ritual activities, such as everyday meals and special feasts (Barrett 1989, 312). At about the same time the deposition of Llyn Fawr bronze metalwork appears in the archaeological record (Needham 2007; O'Connor 2007) and the incidence of iron artefacts becomes increasingly commonplace.

The late Bronze Age to early Iron Age transition was also the period when structured midden sites emerge in the archaeological record. Generally considered to be arenas for the conspicuous consumption of both goods and labour in a communal setting, above ground middens are relatively common in the Wessex region, especially Wiltshire and Hampshire. Well known examples are All Cannings Cross (Barrett and McOmish 2004), Potterne (Lawson 2000), East Chisenbury (McOmish 2010), Whitchurch (Sharples and Waddington 2011) and Runnymede Bridge (Needham and Longley 1980; Needham and Sorensen 1988; Needham 1991; Needham and Spence 1996).

Fig. 5.5 The Iron Age settlement at Southdown Ridge

It was within the context of this era of diversification and differentiation that the first settlement was established on Southdown Ridge, and the surrounding landscape of the site arguably epitomises this trend. A late Bronze Age/early Iron Age origin has been mentioned above for a newly emerging type of monument – the cross-ridge dyke. Several early hillforts, amongst them Chalbury Camp, Maiden Castle and Poundbury, were constructed in the vicinity during the early Iron Age. Chalbury Camp was arguably the earliest of these, with a probable late Bronze Age origin. It was constructed on the south side of the South Dorset Ridgeway, overlooking Weymouth Bay, and lies only about 4km to the east of Southdown Ridge, on a similar limestone geology. It is tempting, and perhaps reasonable, to imagine that the Southdown site was being settled as the first ramparts were encircling Chalbury, and as the settlements at Eldon's Seat, Kimmeridge and Rope Lake Hole on Purbeck were engaging in specialised craft industries of shale-working and salt production (Cunliffe and Phillipson 1968; Calkin 1949; Woodward 1986).

The earliest Iron Age: an unenclosed settlement

The earliest settlement at Southdown Ridge, probably established sometime between 800-600 BC, appears to have been unenclosed. The cross-ridge dyke may have already been in existence during this phase of occupation, but the dating evidence is inconclusive. This earliest stage of activity involved the construction of at least one circular structure (7668; Fig. 5.6), although there may have been several more in the unexcavated area to the east of the trench. This structure was badly disturbed, with the entire western side lost to later agricultural activity and, probably, stone robbing during later phases of settlement construction.

Posthole group 7925, 7927, 7929, 7931

A set of four stone-packed postholes sealed by a stone floor associated with structure 7668 may have represented an internal fitting of the building, but it is also possible that it belonged to an earlier structure (Fig. 5.7). On that basis of that possibility this structure is described first.

The four postholes were of similar size and character and lay within the area described by the gullies of 7668. Together they formed a rough rectangle *c* 2m long and 1m wide. The postholes may have supported an internal structure just to the right of the entrance of 7668. They measured 0.20m-0.35m across and 0.20-0.25m deep. The stone packing was set within a brown silty clay with sparse charcoal flecks. Two small pottery sherds from posthole 7925

were not closely dateable, but all of the postholes were sealed by a stone floor (7759) set within a recess (7735) just inside the door of the circular structure.

Circular Structure 7668

Structure 7668 lay at the south-western edge of the settlement. It was represented by discontinuous segments of a curvilinear gully (7739, 7692 and 7075), which together formed a penannular gully describing the south-eastern part of a circular building *c* 13m in diameter (Fig. 5.6). A south-east facing entrance was defined by two large postholes (7609 and 7766) either side of a 2m wide doorway. Several (unexcavated) postholes located outside the entrance (7945, 7947, 7946 and 7948) are likely to have supported porch posts, and a group of postholes (7904, 7650, 7089 and 7091) within the structure represented internal supports or subdivisions.

The two doorposts had been tightly wedged with limestone packing, which had collapsed inwards when the posts rotted or, more likely, were removed during the decommissioning of the building. Had the posts rotted in situ traces of post pipes would probably have survived. The soil component of the fills of these two postholes was so similar that it is obvious the same materials were used to stabilise the posts.

Posthole 7609 was oval in plan, 1.00-0.80m in diameter and 0.60m deep, with vertical sides and a flat base. The lower fill (7619) was a dark greenish-brown gritty soil with large limestone packing stones up to 0.40m in size. The soil was flecked with charcoal and incorporated fuel ash slag, cinder and small pieces of fired clay, along with a few scraps of animal bone and 53g of very fragmented pottery of earliest Iron Age date. The upper fill (7610) was a dark brown silty clay with several more large stones, also flecked with charcoal and yielding fuel ash slag, along with animal bone fragments some 80 sherds (550g) of earliest-early Iron Age pottery. The pottery was very fragmented but many sherds were red-finished and there were several carinated and fingertipped fragments.

A remnant of the posthole construction cut (7611) was preserved on the western side of the feature, aligned with gully segment 7692. Its charcoal-rich fill (7612) included fragments of oak, hazel, blackthorn and ash wood. Small quantities of heat-magnetised waste – cinder, burnt stone and silica spheres (see Keys, Chapter 6) –suggest that industrial activity may have been carried out in the vicinity. A fragment of a shale armlet was also found in this fill, evidence of shale-working on the site during this early phase of occupation (see Shaffrey, Chapter 6, Fig. 6.16, no. 10).

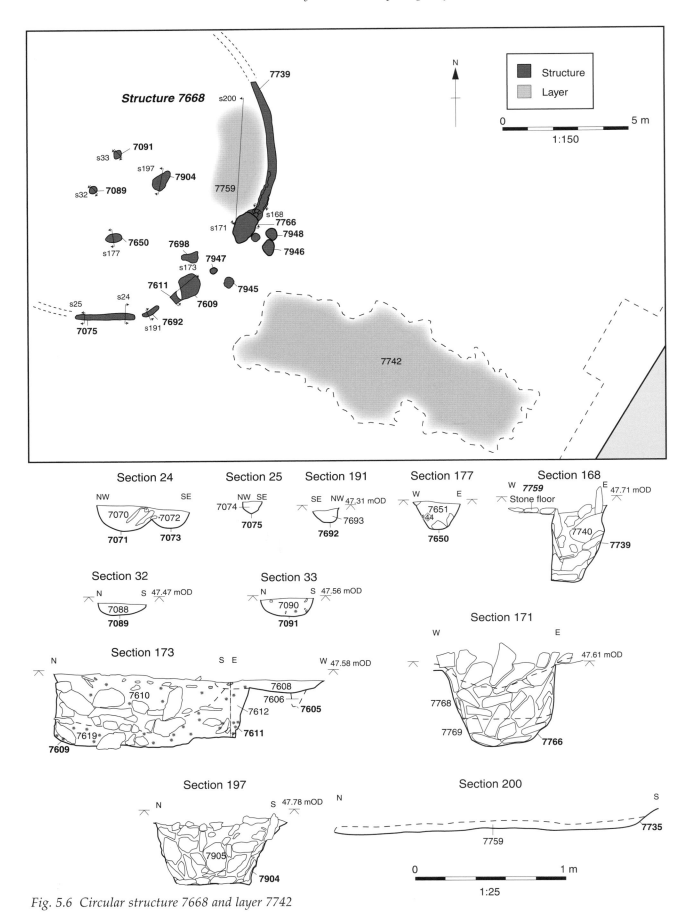

Fig. 5.6 Circular structure 7668 and layer 7742

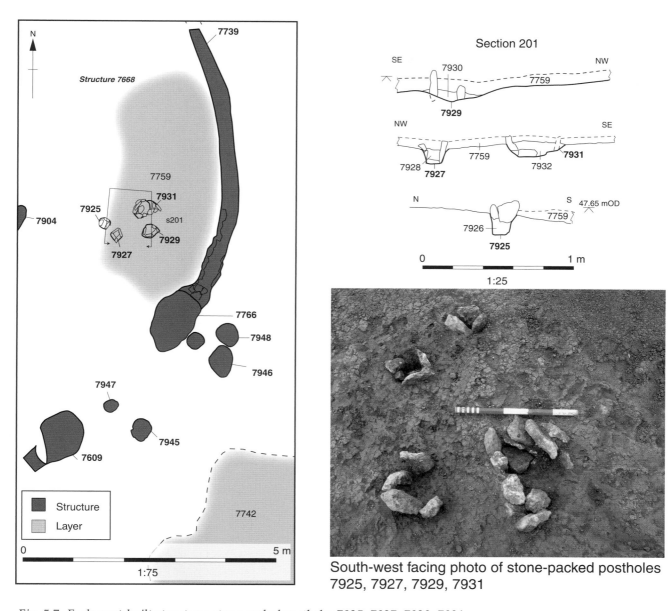

South-west facing photo of stone-packed postholes
7925, 7927, 7929, 7931

Fig. 5.7 Early post-built structure: stone-packed postholes 7925, 7927, 7929, 7931

The northern posthole (7766) was also oval, 1.00-
0.75m in size and 0.60m deep. Collapsed limestone
packing stones up to 0.40m in size (7767) filled most
of the void. The lower fill (7769) was a dark brown
gritty soil tinged with red, blue and yellow flecks
suggestive of organic and heat-affected substances.
Charcoal, fuel ash slag, cinder, fired clay, burnt
stone, animal bone and two sherds of earlier Iron
Age pottery were also present. The upper fill (7768),
also dominated by large stones, had the same
greenish colour as the fill of posthole 7609, was also
charcoal flecked and incorporated fuel ash slag and
cinder. A few pieces of animal bone were present
and 140g of pottery from this fill was dominated by
local oolitic fabrics of earliest or early Iron Age date.

The best preserved stretch of gully (7739)
provided clear evidence of the construction

technique employed in the erection of this structure
(Figs 5.6 and 5.8). The gully was 0.30m wide and
0.50m deep and the base and sides were lined with
slabs of limestone 0.15m-0.40m in size (7785),
packed within a charcoal flecked silty clay (7740).
This deposit produced a small collection of pottery
that included a furrowed bowl fragment, several
carinated fragments and a red-finished sherd. The
stone slab packing would have provided support
for timber wall posts or planks, or both. No traces
of stone lining were seen in gully segments 7692
and 7075, which formed the southern stretch of the
wall, because these features survived to depths of
only 0.08m-0.10m. Nonetheless, seven small
fragments of pottery from the surviving fill also
indicated an earliest Iron Age date. The eastern end
of gully 7075 may have been recut as the profile

shows a double cut (7071/7073; Fig. 5.6, Section 24).

Several postholes lay within the area enclosed by the gullies, but not all were demonstrably associated with the structure. Oval shaped postholes 7904 and 7650 were aligned on the doorposts, positioned about 3.5m within the interior. Postholes 7089 and 7091 lay about 5.5m from the doorway and appeared to align precisely with the putative porch posts. The positions of the internal postholes and porch postholes suggest that the entranceway had been realigned at some stage. Posthole 7904 was a very substantial and clearly weight-bearing feature, very similar in character to the doorposts. It measured 0.85m by 0.53m and was 0.46m deep, tightly packed with angular limestone pieces up to 0.30m in size, some of them burnt. The soil component of the fill (7905) was a grey clayey silt lightly flecked with charcoal, which produced no finds. Postholes 7650, 7089 and 7091 were much smaller features, less than 0.40m in diameter and only 0.10m deep. Their fills (7651, 7088 and 7090) incorporated a scatter of small stone fragments, some pink and possibly burnt, and a little charcoal, along with a few body sherds in oolitic fabrics. A fragment of a shale waste disc was also found amongst the packing material of posthole 7650 and an unworked chunk of shale in the fill of posthole 7091. A simple base fragment in fabric CA1 from posthole 7989 is a rare example of a vessel in calcite-tempered fabric.

A small recessed area (7735) lay just within the arc of gully 7739 (Fig. 5.8). It was paved with limestone pieces (7759) which sealed the post structure described above. The recess was 0.10m deep, 4.20m across and 1.65 wide and the floor was slightly concave, the outer stones curving up to the edge of the terrace (Fig.5.6, Section 200). The paving consisted of randomly placed, unworked, but mostly flat, limestone pieces, the largest *c* 0.30m in size. The fact that this patch of floor was slightly sunken below the natural ground surface no doubt accounted for its preservation in this very disturbed area of the site, but also suggested that its extent had always been restricted. An interesting feature of the floor is that several fragments or complete animal bones had been driven into the ground amongst the stones at the edge of the floor (Fig. 5.8). These included Sf 116 (horse scapula); Sf 118 cattle humerus); Sf 119 (large mammal vertebra); Sf 120 (horse pelvis). The bones may have been used as stakes to secure some sort of lining or cover, perhaps hide or textile, required for whatever activity took place in this sunken area.

Overlying the stone floor (7759) was an occupation-rich deposit (7736) composed of *c* 50% small stones, some burnt to shades of red and grey, set within a matrix of dark greenish-grey gritty silt flecked with charcoal, and described as having the

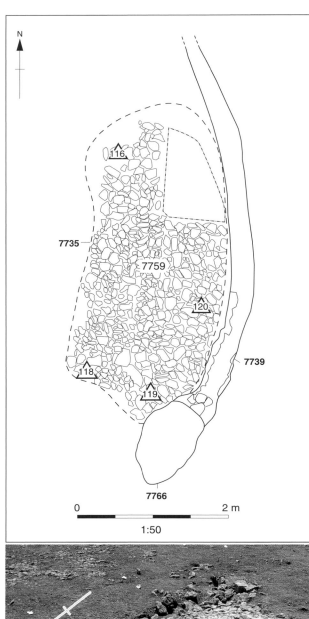

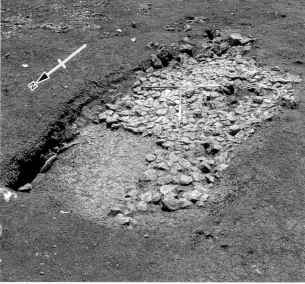

Fig. 5.8 Detail of circular structure 7668: recessed floor 7735 and gully 7739

154

appearance of 'cess'. A 238g collection of pottery recovered from this deposit is dominated by local oolitic fabrics, and includes carinated bowl fragments, one red-finished, all dating to the earliest or early Iron Age. An assemblage of 25 fragments of animal bone from this layer is dominated by pig (including skull and tooth fragments), but includes horse, sheep/goat and cattle. The long bone of a large mammal (Sf 106) found in this fill had been roughly modified, possibly for use as a gouge (see Allen, Chapter 6, cat. no. 5).

Layer 7736 was not confined to the sunken paved area, but spread up to and into the top of gully 7739 and doorpost 7766. This soil may have developed while the building was in use and the walls standing, accumulating up to and spilling over into the exposed packing material that stood proud of the wall and door timbers. Alternatively, the demolition of the building, involving pulling up of posts and walls, may have distributed this material into adjacent features. Another possibility is that the spread of this distinctive material may signify that elements of the building, the recessed floor in particular, represent a modification of the decommissioned structure as an outdoor work space, perhaps for metalworking. A shallow, irregular hollow 0.50m wide (7698) just inside the doorway of the building was filled with heat-magnetised material including burnt clay, cinder and charcoal (Fig. 5.6). This feature appeared to have been a wear hollow rather than a cut feature. A small oval, stone-lined pit (7671), which also lay within the structure (not located on plan), produced a fragment of a smithing hearth (see Keys, Chapter 6). The pit was 0.65 by 0.45m and 0.20m deep, and fuel ash slag and the fragment of a possible smithing hearth bottom were recovered from its fill. The nature of the discoloured soils, heat-affected stone, charcoal and other heat-magnetised materials associated with circular structure 7668 all point to the use of this locale, whether the standing or demolished building, or indeed, a pre-building phase, for metalworking or a related industrial activity. The presence of shale waste in two of the postholes associated with this structure also suggest that shale-working was taking place at an early stage in the occupation of the settlement, and in the vicinity of this structure.

External Yard 7742

A composite compacted, trampled surface (7742) measuring 10m long by 4.5m wide overlay the natural ground surface (7007) just beyond the doorway of structure 7668 (Fig. 5.6). This deposit was rich in occupation material, fuel ash slag, and the same greenish-grey organic clayey silts observed within the structure. In places trampled,

the spread was interspersed with concentrations of sub-angular limestone paving (7713 and 7714). Traces of Poaecae found in samples from this deposit indicated the presence of grassland nearby.

Layer 7742 was stratigraphically one of the earliest surviving occupation layers of the settlement and probably represented a yard contemporary with the construction and/or the use of structure 7668. The layer was very rich in occupation debris, including fuel ash slag, and seemed to have been, at least in part, a deliberately constructed spread that exploited stony soils and occupation-rich material that had accumulated nearby, either within the area of the structure or in an external midden deposit. Intermittent trampling as the deposit was accumulating and as construction, use and modification of the structure advanced, could account for localised areas of compaction that were recorded.

A copper alloy socketed axe (Sf 127; Fig. 5.9) was embedded in this surface. The axe was an unfinished or failed casting, as the fragments are slightly warped and do not precisely join, the loop near the

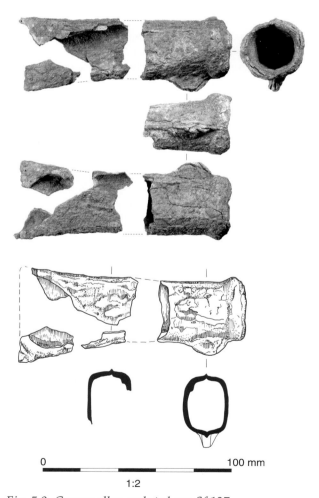

Fig. 5.9 Copper alloy socketed axe Sf 127

socket mouth is blocked by metal, and the surfaces are unfinished (see Scott, Chapter 6). It was identifiable as belonging to the Llyn Fawr period class of linear faceted axes, dated to *c* 800-600 BC (see Northover, Chapter 6). In the absence of other well-dated material, the axe provides the most reliable chronological indicator for the inception of settlement on the site. It is notable as the single piece of metalwork in this primary deposit, and its placement was probably a deliberate act. It may have been a votive offering, marking a location that held some significance on Southdown Ridge, and its imperfection as a failed casting insinuates a recognised practice of deliberate breakage of objects prior to interment noted on other prehistoric sites (Bradley 1998). The location outside the entrance of a roundhouse also bears comparison with the votive hoard of socketed axes of similar type, some of them fragmentary or unfinished, placed close to the entrance of a circular structure at Tower Hill, near the Uffington White Horse in Oxfordshire (Miles *et al.* 2003, 155). A motive for the deposition of that hoard was cited as reflecting a "tradition or ritual of changing times" (Miles *et al.* 2003, 156). During this period, at the transition between the Bronze and Iron Ages, iron was replacing the functional role of bronze axes, and the Southdown axe could reflect the social and practical transformation brought about by the changing role of bronze in society. That this implement was not functional in any utilitarian sense may have been unimportant in the light of its symbolic presence in this place, or may even have enhanced its suitability as an offering.

The deposit also incorporated some 500 sherds (3277g) of earliest Iron Age pottery, highly comminuted fragments with no reconstructable profiles, and with an average sherd weight of only 7g. Nonetheless, it was possible to identify red-finished oolitic wares, furrowed bowls, jars with linear incised decoration and finger-impressed jars. The decorated pottery belongs to the British late Bronze Age to early Iron Age transition (Barrett 1980), with decorated examples that correspond stylistically to forms dated to the 8th–7th centuries BC at Kimmeridge and, more broadly, to the Early All Cannings Cross traditions (Cunliffe 1991, 65), dated at Potterne (Lawson 2000) and other sites in southern Britain to the 10th–7th centuries BC. The relatively large size of this group indicates that it was not incorporated in a developing soil horizon or occupation level through merely incidental processes, but that it was a spread of redeposited occupation or midden debris. The deposit also produced 118 fragments of animal bones representing various species, predominantly cattle and sheep/goat, with lesser numbers of pig and a single dog bone. A wide range of body parts, including skull and mandible, were present.

A flint shale-working hand tool was also recovered from layer 7742. Its occurrence in this stratigraphically early context is interesting, especially as very little other worked flint was found with it. It may have been intrusive, as the records note the possible percolation of material from overlying soils between the stones in this deposit, and no shale objects or offcuts were associated with it here. Most of the shale from the site was subject to a complex history of redeposition, and ended up in mixed secondary deposits with middle and late Iron Age material. However, the settlement may have engaged in shale-working from the outset, and evidence of late Bronze Age shale-working is known elsewhere in Dorset (see below).

The early Iron Age: an enclosed settlement?

Few structural elements associated with the early Iron Age settlement survived the extensive late Iron Age reorganisation. Early Iron Age features and deposits were dated to *c* 600-400 BC largely on the basis of the ceramic evidence because the stratigraphic sequence was compromised by truncation and other disturbance, and therefore very restricted.

The early Iron Age farm could arguably be described as enclosed, not by a surrounding earthwork, but by an arrangement of timber fences that seem to have functioned in conjunction with the cross-ridge dyke and, possibly, at an early stage, with a length of ditch (7059/7061) that ran eastwards from the dyke (Fig. 5.10; 5.17). A pit alignment on the high scarp above the settlement may have marked the northern boundary.

This pattern of enclosure is unusual, but may not have been recognised elsewhere because the individual components – fences, ditch and pits – do not, on initial inspection, form a coherent arrangement. However, these disparate boundaries appear to have been at least broadly contemporary, and must have functioned in concert in some way. The east-west ditch (7059/7061) on the southern side of the enclosure does not appear to have completely surrounded the settlement at any time, in contrast to some early Iron Age sites, such as Gussage All Saints (Wainwright 1979), Old Down Farm and Winnall Down, Hants. (Davies 1981; Fasham, Farwell and Whinney 1989). Nor were the fences at Southdown Ridge replaced during subsequent phases of occupation by earthwork enclosures, as was the case at early Iron Age sites such as Little Woodbury (Bersu 1940; Brailsford 1948, 1949), Swallowcliffe Down (Clay 1925; 1927), Meon Hill

(Liddell 1933; 1935) and Houghton Down (Cunliffe and Poole 2000). This could suggest that the Southdown Ridge settlement activity was not continuous, and that there was a break in occupation of uncertain duration, but probably during the middle Iron Age.

The southern side of the settlement was, at an early stage, enclosed on the southern side by a ditch and, possibly at the same time, by a wooden fence or palisade. A pit alignment along the scarp slope on the northern side of the farm may have served a dual purpose of storage on well-drained ground and as a boundary marker. Another early Iron Age fenceline that ran from the northern end of the cross-ridge dyke to this scarp crest would have controlled access and also may have served as a symbolic border between the settlement, the dyke and the western field.

Southern boundary ditch

There was insufficient stratigraphic and artefactual evidence to establish precisely how the various boundary features functioned in relation to each other. A small section across the dyke ditch and the east-west aligned ditch (7240/7059/7061) (Fig. 5.10) suggests that the dyke post-dated the smaller ditch. However, it is possible that the apparent sequence recorded in the section reflected only that the ditch was in existence when the dyke ditch was recut or widened, as seems to have been the case elsewhere along its length. The ditch and the cross dyke were at least closely contemporary in this area, and both produced only early Iron Age pottery, albeit in small quantities. Alternatively, the east-west ditch may have marked the southern extent of the settlement in its earliest stage, before the cross-ridge dyke was

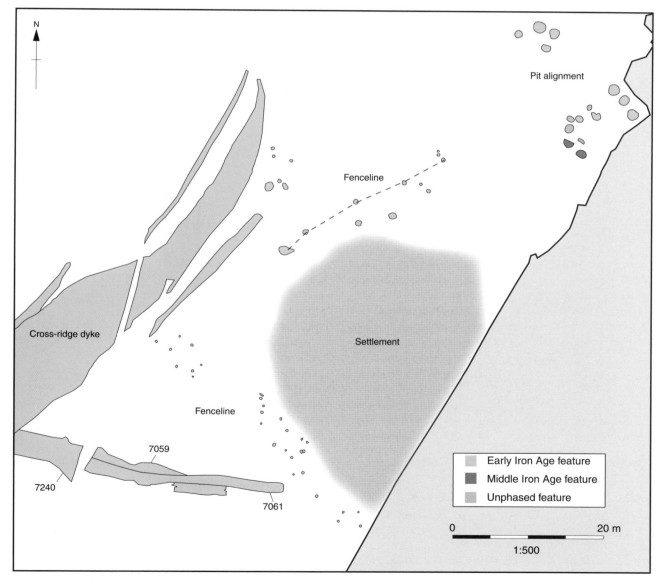

Fig. 5.10 Early Iron Age boundary ditch 7059/7061, fencelines, and pit alignment

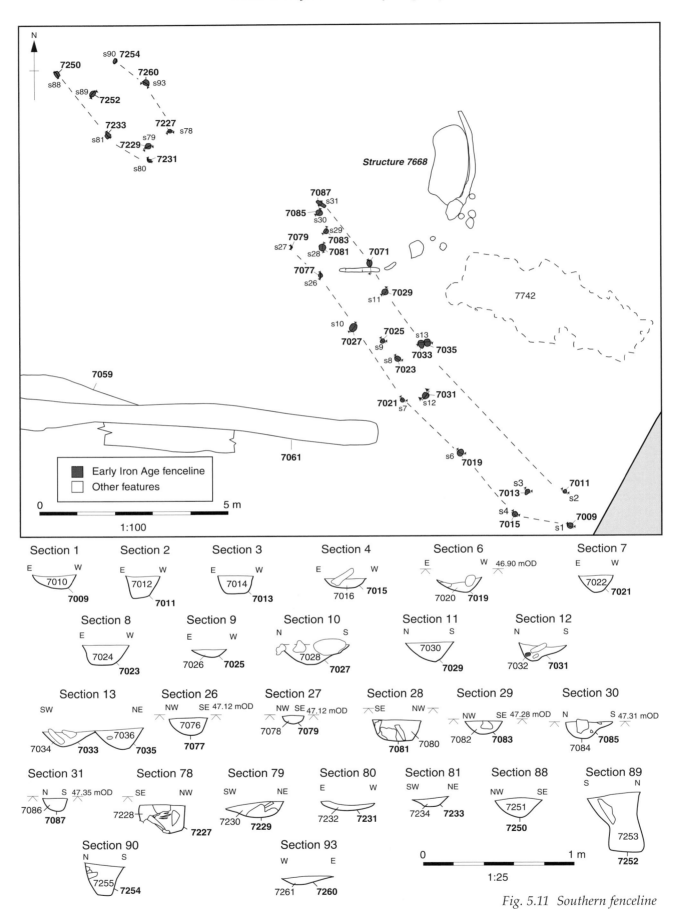

Fig. 5.11 Southern fenceline

constructed. It did not extend west of the dyke but its eastern end terminated close to the southern fenceline, and it is another possibility that the ditch and fence functioned in tandem.

The ditch was shallow and poorly preserved, but it was clear that it had been recut at least once, the earliest version represented by 7059, the later by 7061. The earlier ditch (7059) was only 0.30m deep and the fill of compact greyish clayey silt contained burnt flint, small limestone limestone fragments and a few fragments of animal bone, including pig and sheep/goat. Some 43 sherds of abraded early Iron Age pottery from this fill include a carinated bowl fragment. Along the eastern stretch of the ditch, where the recut was most apparent, the fill of the earlier ditch was a dark silty clay with minimal stone content. It produced a few exclusively early Iron Age sherds, including a fine flint-tempered bowl rim.

The recut (7061) contained a much stonier fill, with burnt flint and limestone, and yielded almost 700g of early Iron Age pottery, including a red-finished carinated bowl and a coarse flint-tempered jar with fingernail-impressed shoulder. A few sherds of late Iron Age Poole Harbour Ware with burnished decoration had collected in the top of the silted up ditch at a late stage.

Southern fenceline

A wooden fence represented by a double row of 28 postholes extended for approximately 20m on a NW-SE alignment along the south side of the settlement, terminating where it met one of the ancillary ditches (7204) associated with the cross-ridge dyke (Figs 5.10-5.11). The alignment of the postholes was somewhat ragged, possibly as a result of various episodes of rebuilding. The fence appeared to post-date circular structure 7668, as one of the fence postholes cut gully 7075 of the building.

The postholes measured on average 0.20-0.25m in diameter. They were severely truncated, and most survived to a depth of only about 0.10-0.15m, an exception being posthole 7252, which was 0.40m deep. These features were strikingly uniform in character, with rounded bases and limestone packing. An entrance gap c 4m wide interrupted the fenceline between postholes 7087 and 7231. Only eight of the postholes contained dating evidence – 7021, 7023, 7027, 7033, 7035, 7077, 7087, 7252 – in all cases a single or few abraded early Iron Age body sherds, almost exclusively in local oolite-tempered fabrics. The only diagnostic sherd was a large fragment of a carinated bowl, from posthole 7027. Four of the postholes (7083, 7229. 7252 and 7254) each produced a single fragment of animal bone of indeterminate species, and postholes 7019 and 7029 yielded single flint flakes.

Northern fenceline

A group of posthole (7540, 7317, 7505, 7577 7531, and double posthole 7514/7517) supported a timber fence that ran north-eastwards from the northern end of the cross-ridge dyke and its ancillary ditch 7398 (Fig. 5.12). The terminal of the fence was marked by a double post setting (7514/7517) sited at the crest of the high ground to the north of the settlement. This feature measured c 0.40m in diameter and 0.30m deep. Displaced packing stones, some burnt, were noted in both sockets. The lower fill of 7514 was a compact mottled orange gritty silt with decayed limestone lumps and a few charcoal fragments, which produced three abraded oolitic sherds. Above this was a brown silty clay that yielded another three abraded sherds and a few scraps of animal bone, including the pelvis of a sheep/goat. The main fill of posthole 7517 was a brown silty clay with decayed limestone lumps, which yielded refitting sherds of a nearly complete early Iron Age carinated bowl (Chapter 6, Fig. 6.7, no. 62), very likely a votive deposit. The construction of the postholes had created a disturbance hollow that, following the removal or rotting of the posts, filled with a friable dark brown silty clay (7520) that incorporated a few bone fragments of cattle and sheep/goat. The double post setting may have marked an important location in the landscape, the break between the low ground of the settlement and the high ground to the north.

Posthole 7540, the southernmost post of the fence, was 0.45m wide and 0.50m deep, and, in common with 7514/7517, was set in shallow disturbance hollow 2.10m wide. The post socket produced 19 sherds (135g) of pottery that included five rims of fineware bowls, also probably deliberately selected for deposition, whilst the hollowed area contained another 16 sherds of early Iron Age pottery, including a carinated bowl fragment.

Postholes 7577, 7505 and 7317 were set at roughly equal intervals of c 6.5m between the two end posts of the fence. If this were a barrier fence, as opposed to a line of marker posts, the spaces between them must clearly have been filled by interval posts or stakes driven in at shallower depths, or by panels of, for example, wattles. The postholes were of similar diameter at c 0.60m, and all were stone packed. Their depths were variable; posthole 7505 was only 0.20m deep, posthole 7577 0.40m deep and 7531 0.36m deep. All produced small abraded early Iron Age sherds in oolitic and shell-tempered fabrics.

Three smaller postholes (7579, 7581 and 7531) which lay close to the fenceline may have been associated with it. Their V-shaped profiles indicated that they supported large stakes with

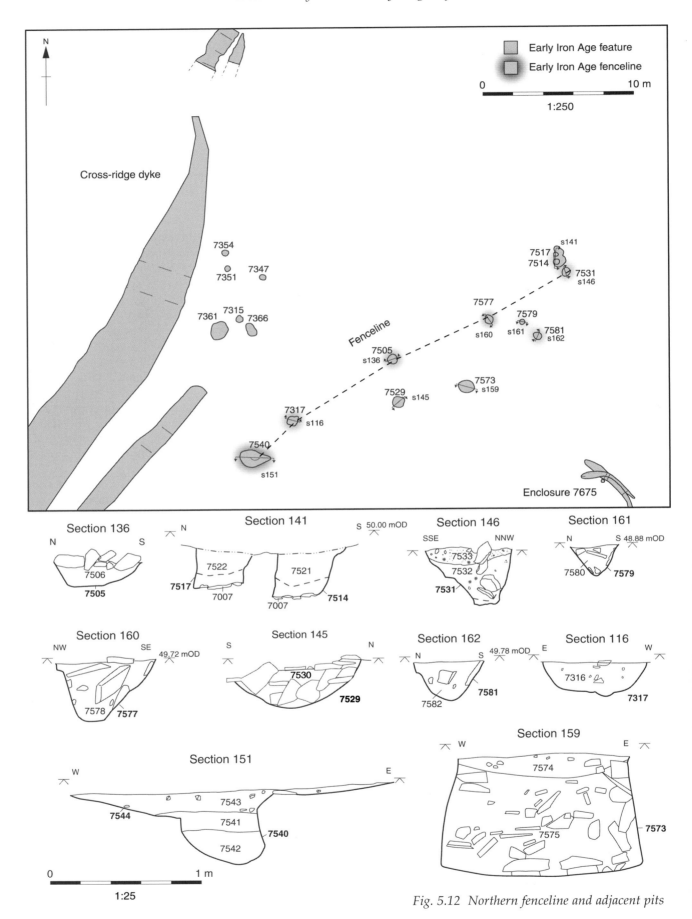

Fig. 5.12 Northern fenceline and adjacent pits

pointed ends that had been hammered in to the ground. Posthole 7531 lay immediately adjacent to double posthole 7514/7517 and contained 57g of comminuted early Iron Age pottery. The position of postholes 7579 and 7581 suggest they could have supported a gate structure.

Two stone-filled pits (7573 and 7529) had been dug just to the east of the fenceline. Pit 7573 was a substantial "beehive" shaped pit, 1.33m by 0.98m and 0.98m deep. The main fill (7575) consisted of limestone rubble measuring 0.10m-0.40m in a friable grey clayey silt. This yielded 10 sherds (99g) of early Iron Age pottery, all body sherds, in a wide variety of fabrics, along with a small quantity of animal bone, including mandibles of pig and sheep and a cattle scapula. A considerable dump of fuel ash slag (1215g) distinguished this pit from those located along the northern scarp, which were entirely lacking in heat-magnetised material (see below). This material may have represented the dumping of the contents of a demolished clay oven during a single backfilling event, a practice observed at Danebury (Poole 1995, 263).

Feature 7529 lay *c* 5m to the west of pit 7573. It may have been a posthole but its large diameter relative to the other postholes in the vicinity and its shallow, bowl-shaped profile suggest otherwise. It was 0.84m in diameter and 0.30m deep and filled with a dump of angular, large limestone rubble within a brownish-red silty clay (7530), which produced a single small, abraded oolitic pottery sherd, five fragments of shale waste and a fragment of a shale armlet.

Northern pit group

The natural slope of Southdown Ridge rises gradually to the north, away from the nucleus of the Iron Age settlement and field system. This relatively high location was selected for the digging of several pits and pit-like features of variable size and shape during the early and middle Iron Age (Fig. 5.13).

Early Iron Age pits

A group of four early Iron Age pits (7327, 7337, 7341 and 7344) and another group of three (7246, 7248 and 7526), separated by a *c* 6m gap, taken together formed part of a pit alignment that respected the crest of the ridge. In the absence of any Iron Age features to the north of this line, their position suggests that they served as a northern boundary to the settlement and its associated agricultural enclosures.

Another group of pits and pit-like features that lay immediately to the south of the alignment included two additional features dated to the early Iron Age on ceramic evidence. A shallow hollow (7296) may have been an unfinished pit or, possibly,

a tree hole. The second was a large posthole (7300). These were surrounded by four undated features (7263, 7305, 7307 and 7553). Two additional shallow pits (7509 and 7555), the southernmost features of the group, produced pottery of middle Iron Age type and are discussed later (see below).

Considering first the western group of four pits of the alignment (7327, 7337, 7341, and 7344), these were clustered quite closely together. Pit 7327, which was slighted by a modern hedge line, was 1.25m in diameter and 0.53m deep with vertical sides and a flat base. The single deliberate fill (7328) was a compacted dark brown silty clay discoloured by comminuted charcoal, with numerous pieces of limestone, few of them larger than 0.30m, and some of which may have collapsed in from the natural limestone bedrock through which the pit was cut. A small collection of 17 sherds of pottery (79g) consisted entirely of abraded body sherds in the range of oolitic, shelly and calcareous fabrics favoured during the earliest and early Iron Age. Five animal bone fragments included a cattle tooth and tibia of a sheep/goat.

Pit 7341 was roughly circular in plan, 1m in diameter and 0.48m deep with vertical sides and a flat base. The single fill (7342) was essentially limestone rubble, the pieces measuring up to 0.40m, in compacted dark greyish-brown clayey silt. Some of the stones were burnt and small quantities of fuel ash slag were also present. A group of 43 sherds (381g) of early Iron Age pottery recovered from the fill is dominated by oolitic fabric and includes three carinated bowls, one red-finished, and a coarse, shouldered jar with elongated flat-topped rim. Nine fragments of animal bone were of pig, sheep/goat and ribs of a medium sized mammal. A worked flake of Portland chert was also recovered.

Pit 7337 was oval in plan, 1.70 by 1.48m and only 0.22m deep, with a reasonably well-cut base. The single fill (7338) was a dark brown clayey silt mottled with yellow limestone grit, containing several limestone blocks up to 0.25m and numerous smaller fragments. Some of this material may have accumulated through collapse of the pit top and sides, and a little occupation debris, including a single fragment of animal bone of indeterminate species and a small lump of fuel ash slag, may have eroded into the pit from the surrounding ground surface. However, an element of deliberate backfill is usual in the case of Iron Age pits, and likely in this case. Six abraded sherds of pottery (44g) include a carinated bowl fragment and a shell-tempered body sherd with incised horizontal line, the group as a whole broadly dated to *c* 8th-5th centuries BC, or thereabouts.

The fourth pit in this goup (7344) lay immediately adjacent to pit 7337. It was 1.50m in diameter and 0.40m deep. In contrast to the others, it had an

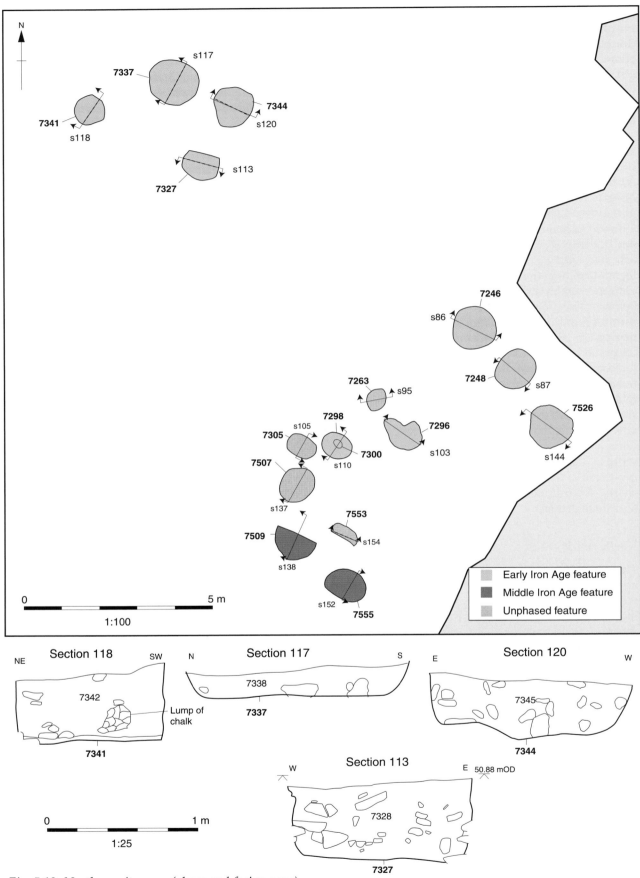

Fig. 5.13 Northern pit group (above and facing page)

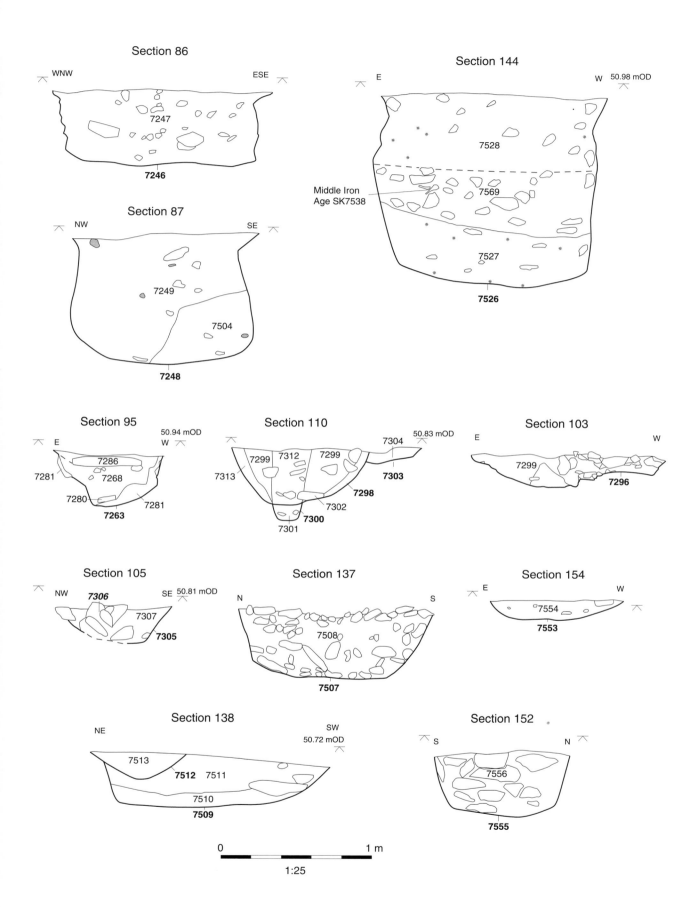

Section 86

WNW   ESE

7247

7246

Section 87

NW   SE

7249

7504

7248

Section 144

E   W   50.98 mOD

7528

Middle Iron
Age SK7538

7569

7527

7526

Section 95

E   50.94 mOD
W

7286

7281   7268

7280   7281

7263

Section 110

7304   50.83 mOD

7299   7312   7299

7313

7303

7298

7302

7301   **7300**

Section 103

E   W

7299

7296

Section 105

NW   *7306*   SE   50.81 mOD

7307

7305

Section 137

N   S

7508

7507

Section 154

E   W

7554

7553

Section 138

NE   SW
50.72 mOD

7513

7512   7511

7510

7509

Section 152

S   N

7556

7555

0   1 m

1:25

uneven base and sloping sides. The fill (7345) was a dark grey clayey silt and small rubble, incorporating sparse traces of fuel ash slag. In common with the other pits in this group, it had been backfilled with limestone blocks, averaging 0.20m in size. A small collection of 18 sherds (111g) of early Iron Age pottery includes a red-finished oolitic jar rim, as well as calcite-tempered and shell-tempered body fragments. The animal bone assemblage consisted of two special deposits. A horse skull lacking mandibular teeth indicates that the jaw bones were disarticulated from the skull prior to deposition. The partial skeleton of a piglet, mostly leg and pelvis elements, in association with the horse skull, suggests that these bones were selected for deliberate placement.

A row of three pits of similar size (7246, 7248 and 7526) lay some 6m to the east. Pit 7246 was 1.50m in diameter and 0.53m deep, with vertical sides and a flat base. It had been filled during a single event with a dark brown, charcoal flecked humic silt (7247) with a scatter of limestone pieces, some burnt, up to 0.20m in size. A group of 15 sherds (117g) includes oolitic fabrics, red-finished fragments, and a shouldered jar sherd in sandy ware QU4. Fragments of a cattle humerus and femur were also present.

Pit 7248 was 1.10m in diameter and relatively deep at almost 1m. The sides belled out slightly and the base was rounded. A wedge-shaped basal fill (7504) that had accumulated on the south-eastern side of the pit probably represented a collapse of topsoil and natural subsoil from the top edge of feature. This was a loose dark greyish-brown loamy silt with occasional small pieces of limestone, and contained no finds. An environmental sample (<54>) containing grains of wheat, barley, emmer/

spelt, vetches, tares, and a single celtic bean, along with remains of grass and rushes provided evidence for contemporary cultivation around the settlement (see Boardman, Chapter 6). The main fill (7249) was a dark brown gritty silt incorporating abundant pieces of limestone 0.05-0.25m in size. Some 222g of early Iron Age pottery included fragments of three bowls in oolitic fabric, two of them red-finished (Fig. 6.7, no. 64) and a jar with squared rim (no. 63). A small collection of animal bones included two sheep/goat metacarpals.

Pit 7526 was relatively large, 1.50m in diameter and 1.30m deep, with near vertical but a slightly bell-shaped profile. Three fills were distinguished. The basal layer (7527) consisted of a mixed accumulation of compacted redeposited natural yellowish clayey silt that incorporated small quantities of occupation debris. It was probably the product of largely natural erosion as the pit lay open, possibly for only a short time. Some large fragments of charcoal lay directly on the base. Seventeen abraded pottery fragments in a wide range of early Iron Age fabrics included the rim of a shouldered jar (JB2). Fragments of a sheep/goat humerus were also present.

Overlying the primary fill was a brownish-grey clayey silt containing c 30% unmodified limestone fragments (7569). A flake of black Portland chert and 176g of abraded pottery sherds in early Iron Age fabrics, the left and right mandibles of a sheep/goat and a cattle horn core were also recovered from this dumped deposit, which reached just halfway up the surviving profile of the pit. The complete skeleton (7538) of an adolescent of uncertain gender, aged 12.5–13.5 years, had been placed on top of this layer (Fig. 5.14). It lay, legs flexed, on the surface of this dumped layer, which reached just

Skeleton 7538

Fig. 5.14 Burial 7538 in pit 7526

over halfway up the pit (Section 144, Fig. 5.13). It bore symptoms of cranial lesions, which could indicate anaemia and deficiency of vitamins B9 and B12. The juvenile also suffered from calculus (mineralised dental plaque) on 23 of its 32 teeth (below and Chapter 6, Gibson and Loe).

A radiocarbon determination on the skeleton produced a date of 380-200 cal. BC (95.4%; SUERC-49472: 2219 ±29), calibrated using OxCal v.4.1 (Bronk Ramsey 2009), using the IntCal09 (Reimer *et al.* 2009) calibration data. This places the burial event firmly in the middle Iron Age. The skeleton was overlain by was a thick deposit of small limestone rubble in dark brown organic soil (7528). The few pottery sherds from this fill include a rounded-profile jar (JC2) in oolitic fabric with a broad date range of early-middle Iron Age. Despite the date of the burial, an early Iron Age date for the pit itself, and its initial filling, cannot be ruled out. It is probable that the pit, along with the others in this alignment, was cut and filled during the early Iron Age and its fill had subsided considerably by the middle Iron Age, producing a visible hollow, which was then used as a convenient location to insert a burial. During this period, two other pits (7509 and 7556) were dug at the southern limit of the pit group (see below)

The popularity of the tradition of pit burial, in central southern Britain particularly, was observed by Whimster (1981, 191) to achieve a peak in the century before the Roman conquest. The extensive Danebury dataset shows that this practice occurred relatively more frequently in the later phases of hillfort occupation, peaking in the late 2nd-early 1st century BC (Walker 1984, 456), but the practice was also common during the middle Iron Age in Wessex. For example, a female adolescent was buried in a middle Iron Age (Phase 2) pit at Gussage All Saints (Wainwright 1979, 24).

Another feature in this early Iron Age group was almost certainly a large posthole (7298/7300). The oval post pit (7298) was 1.06m long, 0.90m wide and 0.36m deep and the post pipe (7300) was 0.28m in diameter and 0.50m deep, the greater depth of the post pipe probably resulting from the weight of a substantial timber pressing downwards. The lower fill of the post pipe was a compact, yellowish-brown gritty silt with a few charcoal flecks and small limestone lumps. Above this the main fill (7312) was a brown silt with a high charcoal content, which may indicate the post was burnt in situ before it was removed or rotted. Ten sherds (48g) of early Iron Age pottery from this fill included a fragment of a finely smoothed bowl in oolitic fabric. A thin layer of eroded natural silt flecked with charcoal (7313) lined the sides of the feature. Limestone packing blocks had been wedged against the post at the base

of the feature, but the main packing material (7299) was a dark brown gritty soil incorporating limestone fragments typically 0.10-0.12m in size, which yielded a single oolitic sherd. The presence of a single large timber upright in this position is interesting and no single obvious explanation can be proposed for its presence. It may have been a marker to signify the location of the zone of pits or to indicate the northern boundary of the settlement.

Undated pits and features

Several less distinctive features shared a location with the pits clustered on the northern ridge (Fig. 5.13). These are described here for convenience, although they are undated, whilst the middle-late Iron Age pits in this group are described below.

To the south of the early Iron Age pit alignment lay feature 7296, a shallow, irregular feature, possibly (but not certainly) a tree hole. It was 1.30m long, 1.04m wide and at its deepest point 0.21m deep. Whilst it is possible that it was a remnant of a hedgeline or other post-medieval boundary, it may well have been contemporary with this northern agglomeration of boundary and storage features on the high ground above the settlement, even if it represented the position of a tree. The fill was a mass of limestone rubble set in compacted greyish clayey silt, with the bulk of the stone concentrated in the shallow western side (Fig. 5.13). Two abraded sherds of pottery from the fill included a fragment of a fine, red-finished oolite-tempered bowl.

Feature 7305 was a small, irregular pit or posthole located immediately adjacent to posthole 7298/7300. It was 0.70m across and 0.45m deep. It was filled with small limestone rubble (7306) within a dark gritty silt flecked with charcoal, which produced a few early Iron Age body sherds.

Feature 7263 was a small oval feature with an irregular profile, measuring 0.62m by 0.82m and 0.38m deep. A thin basal fill was composed of a firm, charcoal flecked eroded natural silt. A lining (7280) of unmodified limestone slabs, most of them heavily burnt to grey and cracked, measuring 0.15-0.30m in size, were set around the south side of the pit edge above 7281. Above this was a main fill of dark brown gritty clay flecked with charcoal (7268). An environmental sample (<44>) from this material yielded charred cereal grains of indeterminate species. The rib of a large mammal was also found but there was no pottery or other dating evidence. The feature was capped by a large, flat and slightly burnt limestone slab (7286) measuring 0.57m by 0.43m and 0.06m thick. Clearly not a conventional storage pit, this feature may have been a storage cist or, as suggested by the burnt stone cap and charred grain, an oven or hearth of some type, although the remnant fill contained little charcoal or ash.

Pit 7507 was 1.30m in diameter, 0.50m deep and contained a single deliberate dump of small limestone rubble in dark grey friable clayey silt (7508). Two animal bone fragments of an indeterminate large mammal were the only traces of occupation material in this somewhat sterile feature.

Pit 7553 was probably originally circular in plan and may have been an early or middle Iron Age pit of standard form, but was largely removed by a post-medieval field drain, leaving only the edge, which measured 0.88m wide and 0.13m deep. The single surviving fill was a clayey silt flecked with decayed limestone, probably an erosion deposit, which yielded only two scraps of animal bone.

The early Iron Age settlement: structural remains

Pavement 7823

The trampled surface (7442) associated with earliest Iron Age structure 7668 was replaced during the early Iron Age by another external surface (7823) (Fig. 5.15). It was composed of small, subangular limestone slabs, rarely larger than 0.15m, set in yellowish-grey clayey silt. The paved area covered an area c 1.20m long and 1.0m wide, but its irregular outline and patchy nature were probably a result of later robbing and disturbance. It spread a little way to the north of earlier surface 7442, and overlapped the northern edge of it, elsewhere overlying the same old ground surface (7007) as 7742. Pavement 7823 appeared to have been a consciously constructed external yard in contrast to the accumulation of mixed materials, consolidated by trampling that characterised 7442.

The pavement produced 139 sherds (645g) of pottery that included a probably residual furrowed bowl (see Cooper and Brown, Chapter 6, Fig. 6.1, no. 3). The other pottery in this group is stylistically somewhat later, corresponding to the early Iron Age tradition in this region, dominated by oolitic fabrics, with rarer shell-tempered, sandy and calcitic fabrics. Forms include carinated bowls, some red-finished and some decorated with incised linear scoring (no. 1) or fingernail impressions (no. 2). No. 4 is impressed above the carination with dart-shaped impressions, and closely resembles the decoration on a bowl from an early Iron Age settlement excavated by Time Team at Waddon, near Weymouth (Brown in Hirst 2000), fig. 9, no. 2).

A fragment of a plain shale armlet (Sf 108; see Shaffrey Chapter 6, Fig. 6.16, no. 8) was also recovered from the pavement, along with some 100 fragments of animal bone, mostly of cattle, pig and sheep/goat, along with two of horse and a dog mandible. None of the bone exhibited evidence of butchery.

The pavement appeared spatially to respect the position of circular structure 7768, and may have been a formalisation and consolidation of the earlier exterior yard by the setting in of paving stones. This suggests that the circular structure remained in use for at least some time during the construction and/or use of the pavement. However, the erection of the wooden fenceline across the position of the

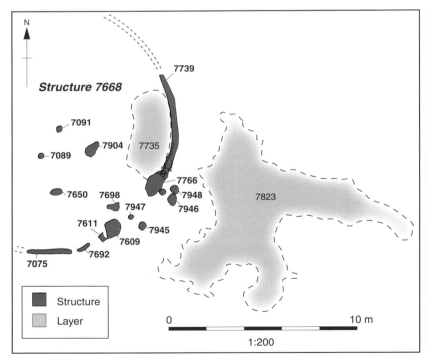

Fig. 5.15 Circular structure 7668 and stone spread 7823

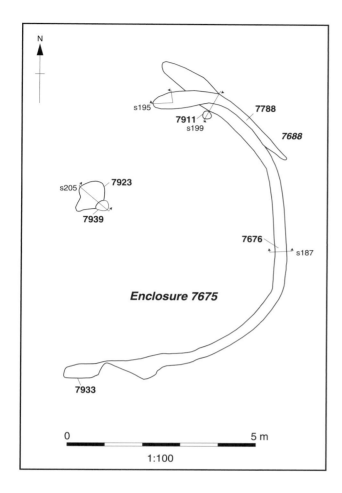

Enclosure 7675

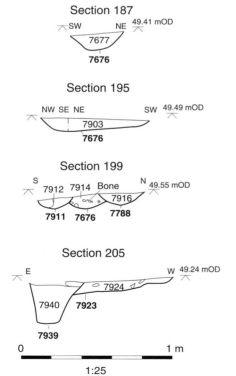

Section 187

Section 195

Section 199

Section 205

Fig. 5.16 Enclosure 7675

building (see above), also during the early Iron Age, means also that the roundhouse must have been abandoned and dismantled sometime during this phase, while the external pavement remained largely in situ.

Enclosure 7675

Enclosure 7675 was represented by a curvilinear gully (7676) that described approximately a half circle with a *c* 9m diameter, open on the western side (Fig. 5.16). Although it is possible that it was a drip gully that surrounded a roundhouse, no obvious supporting structural elements, such as doorposts, beamslots or stone foundations were identified. Although the gully was severely truncated, it was obvious that no gap existed on its southern or eastern side, the position most commonly chosen for doorways of Iron Age roundhouses. However, west-facing entrances were not uncommon and it is not for this reason, but because of the lack of structural features, that an alternative function must be considered for the enclosure gully, perhaps as a stockade.

The gully was 0.45m wide and only 0.10m deep, with a rounded base. The fill (7677/7914) was an organic, charcoal flecked, dark greenish-brown silty clay incorporating small weathered lumps of limestone. It produced only six sherds (20g) of pottery in a range of early Iron Age fabrics, amongst them an oolite-tempered flattened rim fragment of a upright neck jar or bowl. A dozen scraps of animal bone, included pig, cattle and sheep/goat, and also the tooth of a roe deer. A single flint flake was found in the fill of the northern terminal. A short length of gully (7788) that cut across the original northern terminal was the only evidence for modification of the enclosure. The fill of this gully (7903) was only barely distinguishable from that of 7676, and it produced five sherds of similar early Iron Age type.

A large stakehole on the inner edge of the northern curve of gully 7676 could suggest the presence of a stake-built wall within the gully circuit, but this is tenuous as no others were found. A posthole (7939) set centrally within the enclosed area may have held a roof support post, but its small diameter suggests an alternative, such as a tethering post. It was 0.20m in diameter, and about the same depth, and filled with a dark grey charcoal-flecked silty clay. Small limestone pieces had been packed along the southern edge. The posthole was positioned to one side of a shallow hollow (7923), which was probably the product of wear, perhaps animal trampling, rather than deliberate cutting. It produced 25g of highly abraded early Iron Age pottery, including the rim of a fine flint-tempered bowl, along with the broken end of a bone pin or needle (Sf 122).

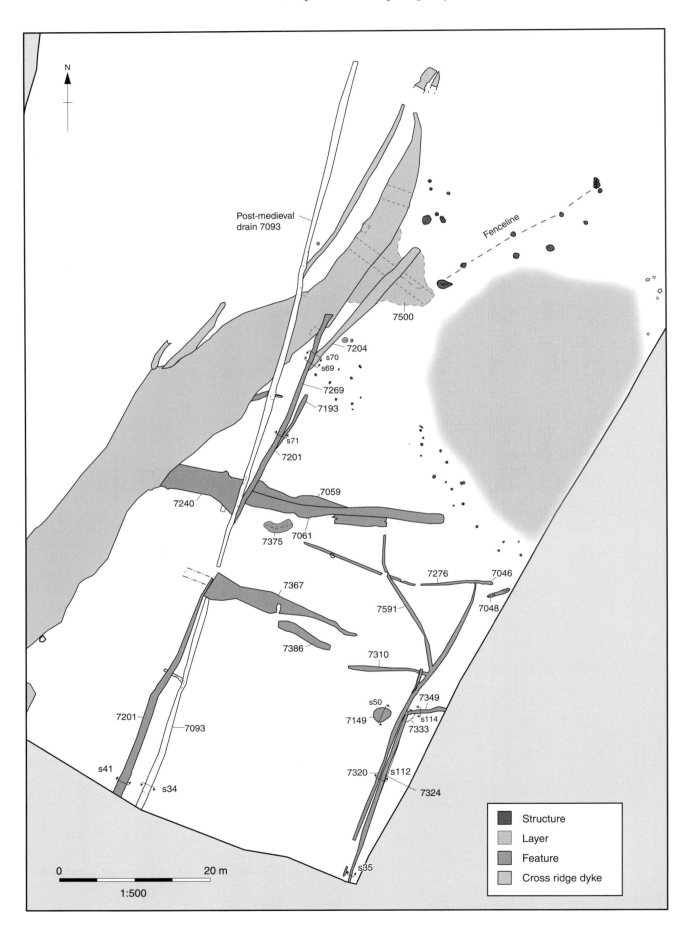

The early Iron Age settlement: field boundaries

A complex of linear ditches transected the area to the south and west of the settlement (Figs 5.17-5.18). These were generally very insubstantial features, heavily truncated, and largely lacking dateable artefacts. On balance it seems that the field system was set out during the earlier part of the Iron Age, possibly at broadly the same time as the cross-ridge dyke and probably at the same time as the fenceline was erected on the southern side of the settlement. Further subdivision may have taken place during the middle or even late Iron Age, but there is no evidence for this. In fact, the evidence for this sequence is poor altogether, and it is difficult to

determine how and whether the various boundaries worked in relation to each other.

Nonetheless, apart from a few occurrences of late Iron Age sherds in the very top fills of some of the ditches, the pottery recovered from them was exclusively of early Iron Age date, a good indication of their date. Further, the stratigraphic sequence demonstrated that the enclosures were laid out with respect to the cross-ridge dyke, a monument that appeared to retain its symbolic and/or functional importance throughout the entire span of the Iron Age and into the Roman period at Southdown Ridge. What is also clear is that the field boundaries and the early Iron Age settlement formed a coherent entity, as none of the ditches impinged on the settle-

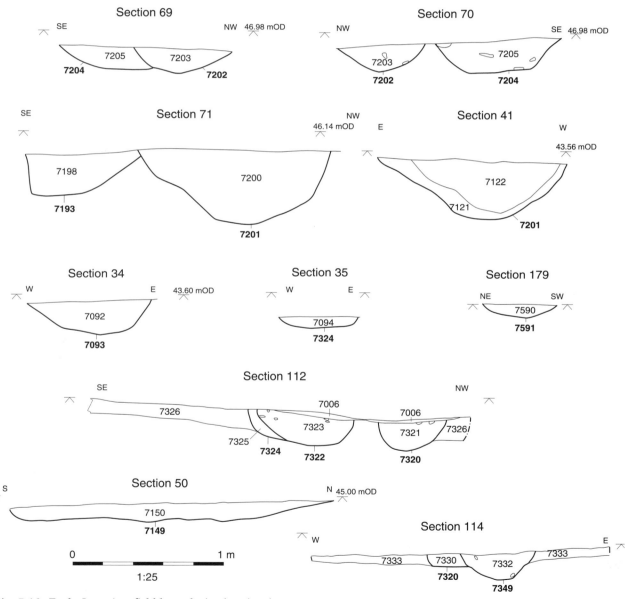

Fig. 5.18 Early Iron Age field boundaries (sections)

Fig. 5.17 (facing page) Early Iron Age field boundaries

ment area. This mutual exclusion of the settlement nucleus and the agricultural hinterland is particularly clear on the southern side of the settlement.

The area to the west of the cross-ridge dyke was evidently not partitioned during the prehistoric period, and there were no entrance gaps observed along the long stretch of the western boundary ditch. The only archaeological features encountered in this large western tract were two Roman burials and post-medieval drainage ditch 7093, so this area was apparently largely unused during the Iron Age, except perhaps as free-range pasture.

Only a small element what was perhaps a very extensive enclosure system was exposed in the excavated area. It consisted of two main parallel ditches (7193/7201 and 7320/7324) running on NNE-SSW alignment and enclosing a strip of land *c* 30m wide. Both of the main ditches were recut at least once, 7193 by 7201 and 7324 by 7320. The western ditch (7201) terminated at the eastern edge of the cross-ridge dyke, suggesting the features were laid out at broadly the same time.

This wide strip was sub-divided by additional ditches running at right angles to the main ditches. A narrow east-west ditch (7046/7276) ran just south of the settlement and a second subdivision was created by another set of east-west ditches (7310, 7367 and 7386), producing a northern enclosure *c* 14m wide and another, southern enclosure of much larger, but uncertain, size.

An entranceway 10m wide at the north-west corner of the small, northern enclosure allowed access from the settlement zone. An irregular feature (7375) which lay within this gap was only 0.20m deep and seemed typical of the churned, muddy hollows left by trampling livestock at the entrance gates of pastures. The function of a small triangular area at the eastern side of the small northern field, formed by ditch 7591, is unclear, particularly as there were no access gaps. This ditch was a very ephemeral feature, 0.08m deep, which cut ditch 7276 and may have been a later, unrelated boundary.

Between the small northern enclosure and the large southern enclosure was a complex staggered entrance gap *c* 4.8m wide, formed by ditches 7310, 7367 and 7386. The short ditch segment (7386) may have served as a baffle for livestock control. This entrance arrangement, and the trampled hollow at the entrance of the field to the north, suggest that a major function of these enclosures was as livestock pasture.

It was possible to establish a broad chronology for the boundary ditches, despite a dearth of dating material. The wide east-west aligned boundary ditch (7240/7059/7601) that possibly predated the construction of the cross-ridge dyke has been discussed above. It did not conform in alignment

and morphology to the ditches of enclosure system and clearly pre-dated it stratigraphically, being cut by the western boundary ditch (7201).

The earliest version of the western ditch (7193) was 0.35m deep and filled with a naturally eroded fine compact silt which yielded 100g of distinctively early Iron Age pottery, along with a few fragments of animal bone, including a dog tooth. It terminated just south of the timber fenceline that enclosed the south-western edge of the settlement, and the two may have functioned together as an entranceway. The recut of this ditch (7201) was 1.3m wide and 0.83m deep at its southern, best-preserved end, narrowing to an average of 0.60m wide and 0.20m deep at its slightest. The character of the clayey silt fill throughout was entirely consistent with natural erosion and alluviation, but was somewhat mixed and mottled at the northern end, where it intercut other features, and more sterile at the southern end. The southern end of the ditch yielded only of a few sandy body sherds, broadly dateable to the early Iron Age. The assemblage from the northern sections was more mixed, dominated by early Iron Age sherds, but including intrusive late Iron Age material and a single unreliably stratified early Roman sherd, a product of intercutting and later disturbance. Fragments of oak charcoal (Sample 49) taken from the fill of this ditch were likely to have come from a structural timber (see Boardman, Chapter 6).

A key relationship investigated was that between ditch 7201 and the dyke ditch. Although superficially it appeared that it cut the dyke ditch it is more likely that they converged and were contemporary, designed as a closed boundary to the field west of the settlement. The excavated section of the dyke ditch at this point produced no pottery and the field ditch only two early Iron Age sherds.

The eastern ditch (7324) had been recut on the same alignment as 7322, probably as part of a routine scouring operation (Section 112, Fig. 5.18). This was then recut on a slightly different alignment as 7320. All of these ditches cut through the accumulated fill (7326) of a natural hollow (7333). A flint scraper (Sf 19) and a few fragments of animal bone were recovered from this spread, but no pottery. Another natural shallow hollow (7149) lay just to the west. The orignal version of the ditch (7324) was very poorly preserved, 0.25m wide and 0.21m deep, shallowing to only 0.06m towards the south. The almost stone free silty fill produced only a single sherd each of middle-late Iron Age Poole Harbour ware and early Roman orange ware, both these are likely to be intrusive as there was clear evidence of severe truncation and general disturbance in this area. Ditch 7320 was 0.30m wide and 0.20m deep, but only 0.05m deep at its northern end, where it intersected ditch 7046/7276. It produced only five sherds (13g) of early Iron Age pottery.

The eastern side of ditch 7320 was cut by an east-west aligned ditch (7349) that marked the southern boundary of an adjacent field, barely exposed in the excavation. This small ditch produced exclusively early Iron Age pottery, but the stratigraphic relationship indicates that the subdivision of the main plots was a later activity, albeit not necessarily very much later.

The east-west aligned ditch (7046/7276) that marked the northern boundary of the small northern enclosure was also poorly preserved, only 0.30m wide and at most 0.20m deep, at its eastern terminal. The section across the shallow main stretch of ditch (7276) produced only eight sherds of abraded early Iron Age pottery. However, the eastern terminal (7046) provided some interesting detail about the later prehistoric practice of selective deposition in boundary features, recognised and described at numerous Iron Age sites across southern England (Gwilt 1997, 153-166; Lambrick and Allen 2004, 489-90; Barclay *et al.* 2003, 37-40). This terminal extended 2.2m beyond the eastern ditch and formed an entrance, in tandem with a short ditch segment (7048), between the settlement and the adjacent eastern field.

The fill of terminal 7046 was a dark brown clayey silt packed with small limestone fragments and a few burnt flints. It contained a small but important collection of 16 sherds (142g) of pottery that included distinctive early Iron Age fragments of oolite-tempered bowls, a shouldered jar and a flint-tempered sherd decorated with incised horizontal lines. Notably, the almost complete skeleton of a dog was also found in this terminal fill. It had bony growths on two vertebrae and an unhealed fractured rib, and so was in poor health and had been injured shortly prior to death (see Strid, Chapter 6). Dog burials have been recorded on other Iron Age sites, most of them in pits (Morris 2008, 114), and have been interpreted as ritual offerings of appeasement of deities, to ward off bad luck or as a safeguard against malevolent spirits (Smith 2006, 12-13).

The other element of this entrance was a gully segment (7048) 3m long, 0.30m wide and 0.20m deep. The fill was similarly dark and organic to that of 7046, but less stony. It contained 31 sherds (121g) of early Iron Age pottery, including thin-walled, fine oolitic ware bowl sherds. The small animal bone collection included a sheep mandible.

It is unlikely to be a coincidence that this east-west ditch was chosen during the late Iron Age as the location for the insertion of six inhumation burials long after the field ditches had silted up. One of these was a double burial (7372) and one

adorned with a necklace of glass beads (7104). Another burial (7017) was placed immediately adjacent to terminal 7046. These and other burials are described in detail below. This enclosure entrance on the southern edge of the settlement, just to the south of the wooden fenceline, was clearly a significant location in the Iron Age landscape of Southdown Ridge. The memory of this place apparently endured from its construction in the early Iron Age until the end of the late Iron Age, a duration of several centuries.

The ditches separating the southernmost field from the small enclosure (7310, 7367 and 7386) may have been a late modification to the field system as, amongst the mere five sherds of pottery recovered from their fills, two are late Poole Harbour ware. However, these very shallow features, with depths as insignificant as 0.06m, were poorly preserved and subject to later disturbance. Ditch 7310 was 0.38m wide and only 0.06m deep and produced no finds. Ditch 7367 was particularly badly affected by plough disturbance but, where best preserved, was 0.55m wide and 0.08m deep, and filled with a charcoal-flecked, gravelly silt, which produced the few sherds of pottery. The short gully (7386) was 1.57m long, 0.45m wide and 0.26m deep and filled with a naturally eroded silt which produced a single early Iron Age sherd.

Evidence of middle Iron Age activity

The most compelling evidence of middle Iron Age activity at Southdown Ridge is the radiocarbon date of 380-200 cal. BC (95.4%; SUERC-49472: 2219 ±29) obtained on bone from the inhumation burial in pit 7526 (Fig. 5.14). Although it has been argued that the pit itself was dug and partly filled during the early Iron Age (see above), the date places the burial event firmly in the middle Iron Age. Additionally, two shallow pits (7509 and 7555) on the southern edge of the pit group produced pottery of middle Iron Age type (Fig. 5.13). It is possible that these were late Iron Age features, contemporary with the late settlement phase, and that the pottery in question represents a continuation of archaic middle Iron Age forms into the late Iron Age, a commonly recognised feature of Durotrigian pottery produced in the Wareham/Poole Harbour area (see Cooper and Brown, Chapter 6). In support of this scenario is the absence of any clear structural evidence for middle Iron Age activity on the site. However, the radiocarbon date from pit 7526 seems sufficient to argue otherwise, and to suggest that any contemporary settlement evidence was either located in the unexposed part of the settlement to the east of the excavation, or was removed wholesale by the extensive reconfiguring of the site during the late Iron Age, leaving only residual middle Iron Age pottery in later deposits.

Pit 7509 was 1.60-1.40m in diameter and 0.38m deep. It was cut by a post-medieval drainage ditch (7512). A primary fill of naturally eroded clayey silt produced no finds. The main fill (7511), a friable dark brown clayey silt with small limestone fragments, contained a few residual early Iron Age sherds and fragments of animal bone, but also a

large fragment of a Poole Harbour ware bead-rim jar (form JC3) of middle-late Iron Age date in a very fresh condition (Chapter 6, Fig. 6.7, no. 67).

Pit 7555 lay immediately adjacent to 7509. It was 1.10m in diameter and 0.45m deep with near vertical sides. The fill was a uniform deposit (7556) of large stone rubble within a greyish-brown clayey silt flecked with decayed limestone. The only pottery recovered was a fragmented lugged jar in

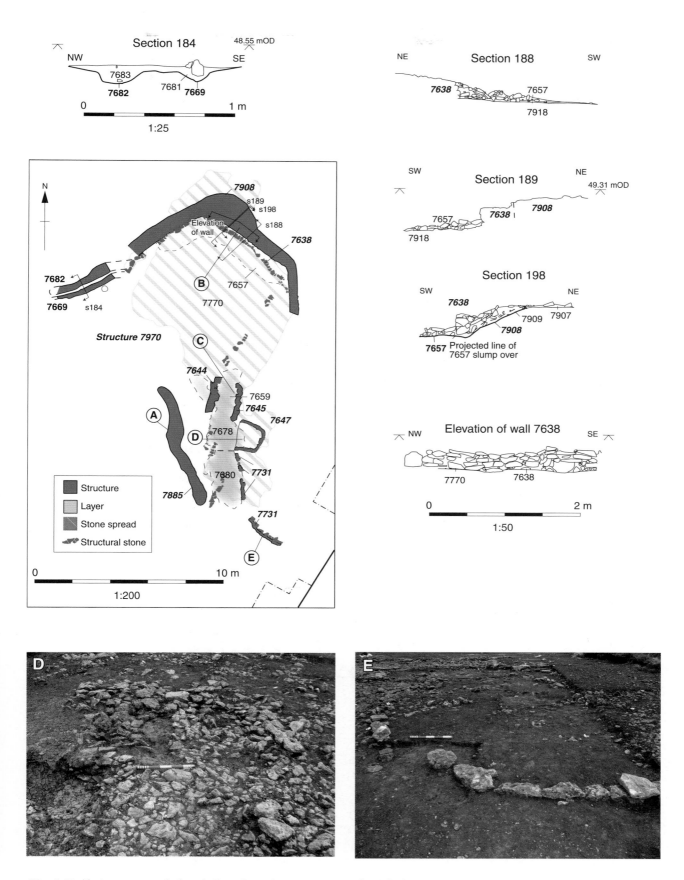

Fig. 5.19 (facing page and above) Late Iron Age terrace complex 7970

Poole Harbour ware (Chapter 6, Fig. 6.7, no. 66), a type dated at Maiden castle to the middle-late Iron Age extended fort Phases 6F-H.

It seems reasonable to propose that the digging of these small features was an event contemporary with the pit burial, but their function is unclear. They were evidently not typical storage pits of the kind typified by early iron Age pits 7526, 7246 and 7248, but were not dissimilar to some of the other features in the vicinity, including the undated pits, which may have been dug at the same time.

Settlement evolution and reorganisation: the late Iron Age

Terrace Complex 7970

During the late Iron Age a terrace (7908) was cut into the scarp slope at the northern end of the settlement (Fig. 5.19). The terrace cut across the earlier pennanular enclosure ditch (7675), signalling its abandonment by this stage. The terrace cut was reinforced by a stone revetment wall (7638) but it seems unlikely that the wall represented the foundation of a building, and it may have been erected to define a space, perhaps for a small building or buildings, subsequently entirely robbed and truncated.

Despite high levels of later disturbance caused by later stone robbing, levelling and rebuilding, it is clear that the terraced area accommodated a complex of features, here referred to as complex 7970. These included the area defined by the wall, a double stone-lined drain (7682/7669) a single drain (7885), and a paved path (7659/7680/7678) lined with low walls (7644/7646/7731), flanked by a small alcove (7647) (Fig. 5.20).

The terrace (7908) was *c* 8.5m wide and c 0.60m high. The revetment wall (7638) was of dry wall construction, 0.50m high and surviving to four courses (Figs 5.19 and 5.20). The wall was of fairly crude construction, made of both roughly shaped and unmodified limestone blocks and slabs, some burnt, measuring between 0.10 and 0.35m in size. Some of the larger slabs were placed directly in front of and on the base of the terrace cut, forming a basic foundation for the successive courses. The coursed face was only one stone deep, the space behind filled with smaller rubble. The interstices between the stones were filled with a yellowish-brown clayey silt, from which a small collection of artefacts was recovered. These included refitting body sherds of middle or late Iron Age burnished vessel in Poole Harbour ware (QU1), but residual sherds more typical of early Iron Age date were also present. Tumbled stone from the revetment wall formed a rubble deposit (7657) in front of the wall

which yielded 553g of pottery dominated by Poole Harbour wares, including a late Iron Age necked jar and a cordoned ovoid jar.

The wall defined a sub-rectangular area paved with limestone metalling (7770), overlain by occupation deposits (7918) (Fig. 5.19, Sections 188-189). These were sealed below tumble (7657) from the upper courses of the wall. The metalled area was made up of several distinct patches, and possibly phases, of limestone 'cobbles' of variable size and shape, averaging 0.10m-0.15m, pressed into the underlying subsoil. (Fig. 5.21). The occupation material overlying the metalled surface contained a few sherds of pottery of middle-late Iron Age type. The terraced area was resurfaced, possibly twice, but it was unclear whether this was wholesale replacement or just patching.

A twin channel (7682/7669) ran westwards from the western end of the terrace wall, and was probably designed to drain water from the terraced area (Fig. 5.19). The direct relationship between the wall and channel was lost to truncation and what remained of the channels was relatively insubstantial. They were 0.20m and 0.25m wide and no more that 0.20m deep. Both were filled with a fine, compact yellowish-brown silty clay, and a number of displaced limestone slabs lying in the fill represent the remnants of a stone lining or capping. The drains were poorly dated as only eight abraded sherds of pottery of indeterminate Iron Age date were found in the fill of 7682.

A larger stone-lined channel (7885), probably a drain, flanked the western side of a stone paved pathway that ran southwards from the terrace floor (Fig. 5.19). Although it was not possible to establish stratigraphically whether the path and drain were contemporary, it is likely that they were associated. The drain may have been a later insertion, a response to a problem with water run-off from the higher ground to the north. The drain was just under 4m long, 0.45-0.60m wide and only 0.25m deep at most, with an irregular but generally rounded base. Flat slabs of limestone, typically 0.15-0.20m in size, lined the base and sides, but the lining had been much disturbed and displaced in some areas and was best preserved at the southern end. A fill of dark brown coarse silt (7884) incorporated small fragments of burnt stone, a few sherds of middle or late Iron Age sandy ware pottery and small fragments of animal bone.

The path that led southwards from the terrace was a paved surface (7678/7680) 1m wide on average and constructed of large limestone slabs 0.20-0.35m in size set in a reddish silty clay. Some of the stones appeared to have been heat-affected, with a pinkish tinge. The only pottery recovered from amongst the paving slabs was a residual early

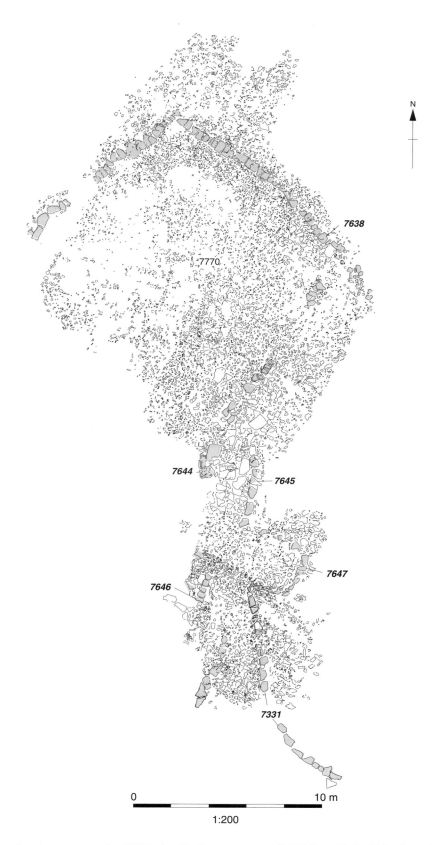

Fig. 5.20 Late Iron Age terrace complex 7970: detail of revetment wall 7638, walls 7644/7645, 7646 and 7331

Fig. 5.21 Photograph showing tumble 7657 from wall 7638 over stone spread 7770

Iron Age flint-tempered sherd. The pavement was laid on a foundation of small stones 0.05-0.07m set in a highly compacted grey silty clay (7691), which directly overlay the subsoil (7007). This consolidation layer produced no dating material, only a few fragments of animal bone, including cattle and horse teeth.

The path was flanked either side by the remnants of a low kerb or wall, of which only a single course was extant, set directly upon the natural subsoil. The kerb or wall that edged the northern stretch of the wall (7644/7645) was constructed of unmodified limestone blocks 0.20-0.30m. A continuation of this wall line (7731) flanked the eastern edge of the southern end of the pathway and then, with a short gap, continued southwards, curving round to the east. Here the path was truncated or robbed and the area adjacent to the wall instead consisted of a deposit of occupation-rich soil (7900) overlain by a discontinuous and diffuse stone surface (7680). The corroded head of a bronze pin, probably dating to the 1st-2nd century AD (Chapter 6, Fig. 6.12, no. 6) was recovered from this surface. The roughly hewn or unmodified limestone blocks used in the construction of wall 7731 were slightly larger than those of the

northern walls, measuring up to 0.40 by 0.30m in size. The difference in construction suggests that this was a later addition. The stones were set directly upon an old ground surface (7627), a greenish-grey clayey silt flecked with charcoal, which produced no finds. The curve of this wall could be taken to suggest a roundhouse foundation, and this cannot be ruled out. However, its position with respect to the other elements of the complex, and the lack of uniformity in size and shape of the stones making up this wall line must leave this in doubt.

The pathway was apparently modified in a successive phase by the addition of a small alcove (7647) on the eastern side of the pathway. This structure consisted of a curved wall footing built of unmodified limestone blocks 0.20-0.30m in size, defining an area *c* 1.5m square. The interior was filled with small angular limestone rubble set in a yellowish clayey silt mottled with greenish-grey patches (7765). The individual stones in this deposit were typically less than 0.15m in size, and it may have been a foundation for a floor within the alcove. This layer produced 30 sherds of pottery in a range of early Iron Age fabrics, but these were associated with a single middle-late Iron Age bead-rim jar fragment in Poole Harbour ware. A spurred hammer flake made from gravel flint was residual in this context. The soil between the stones resembled the organic soils associated with circular structure 7768. This similarity in the soil matrix and the abundance of residual early pottery suggest that this make-up material originated from deposits that derived from earlier settlement debris.

A compacted stony spread (7847) overlay the make-up within the alcove, and spread somewhat beyond this space, probably during post-abandonment dispersal. It was composed of unmodified limestone slabs and fragments 0.05m-0.20m in size set within a matrix of clayey silt. The variable pink, yellow and grey colour may have been the result of exposure to high temperatures, but limestone can tend to degrade naturally under certain conditions to a surprising range of colours. Occupation material recovered from this surface included 87 sherds of pottery (733g), much of it residual early material, but dated to the late Iron Age by burnished round-bodied sandy sherds and a late Iron Age bead-rim in Poole Harbour ware. Over 30 fragments of animal bone, mostly of cattle and sheep/goat, and a large multiplatform flake of Portland Chert were also recovered from this spread.

It is difficult to interpret the date, function and character of complex 7970 in the light of the high levels of truncation, robbing and reorganisation of the area that succeeded its original construction. In fact, it is altogether uncertain whether the terraced area accommodated a structure *per se*, although it was large enough to house a standard Iron Age roundhouse of 8m diameter or so. The terrace might rather have been intended as a level, drained space in which various domestic or craft activities were undertaken, probably during the late Iron Age. The overlying stratigraphy in the terrace complex was patchy, disturbed and complicated, and incorporated artefacts that almost certainly derived from the terrace and pathway localities.

A concentration of a dozen fragments of shale-working waste, including offcuts and bracelet/armlet fragments, was found in the soil layer (7474) that overlay stony spread 7847 (see above). This material probably originated from activity carried out within the alcove or in the near vicinity so it is reasonable to suppose that a shale-working workshop was accommodated somewhere within terrace complex 7970. The fact that some 3kg of shale objects and waste fragments were recovered from the site altogether (much of it unstratified) indicates that shale-working activity was a significant feature of the settlement during the late Iron Age (and perhaps earlier).

Following the abandonment of the terrace complex, the entire area was levelled with material that incorporated the distinctive greenish, organic soils observed elsewhere on the site, particularly around circular structure 7668. Large quantities of redeposited early pottery were also present in this material, suggesting the reuse of material from abandoned buildings, and perhaps middens, to level the area.

Late Iron Age-Romano-British field walls

Wall 7899

Following the abandonment of the structures that occupied the terrace complex, a reasonably well-constructed wall (7899) set on a slight curve was erected over the tumble from wall 7638 (Fig. 5.22). The surviving stretch was 5.95m long and 1m wide and only two courses remained, with no evidence of a construction cut. The two faces were constructed of unmortared, unmodified limestone blocks and slabs averaging 0.20m in size, with a compacted limestone rubble infill between the faces. Considering its size, the wall was likely to have been a field wall rather than part of a building.

The dry bond material filling the spaces between the stones was surprisingly productive of artefacts and occupation debris, likely to have derived from overlying deposits. However, a bone awl, Sf 109 (Chapter 6; Fig. 6.13, no.1) appeared to have been deliberately inserted between the stones, and a heavily utilised flint hammerstone, Sf 13 (Chapter 6, Fig. 6.17, no. 2) was also embedded in the structure. Some 43 sherds (592g) of pottery was of mixed date, with residual early Iron Age sherds, including carinated bowl fragments, associated with late Iron Age bead-rims and lug handles in Poole Harbour wares. A small group of 30 animal bones includes a fragment of antler from a roe deer.

Wall 7825

A length of straight wall (7825), probably also a drystone field wall, constructed after 7899 was demolished, just clipped the eastern side of the earlier wall footing (Fig. 5.23). It was 5.75m long and approximately 0.9m wide, with no trace of a construction trench. The facing walls were unmodified limestone blocks of irregular shape, mostly 0.20 by 0.30m in size, with rubble infill. A collection of 42 sherds (516g) recovered from the soil between the stones was almost entirely of late Iron Age date, with several examples of beaded rims and lugs. Some 24 bone fragments included cattle, pig and sheep/goat.

The area either side of the wall had been consolidated with a compacted, stony soil (7894 and 7897). These two deposits were rich in occupation material, suggesting that the levelling material had

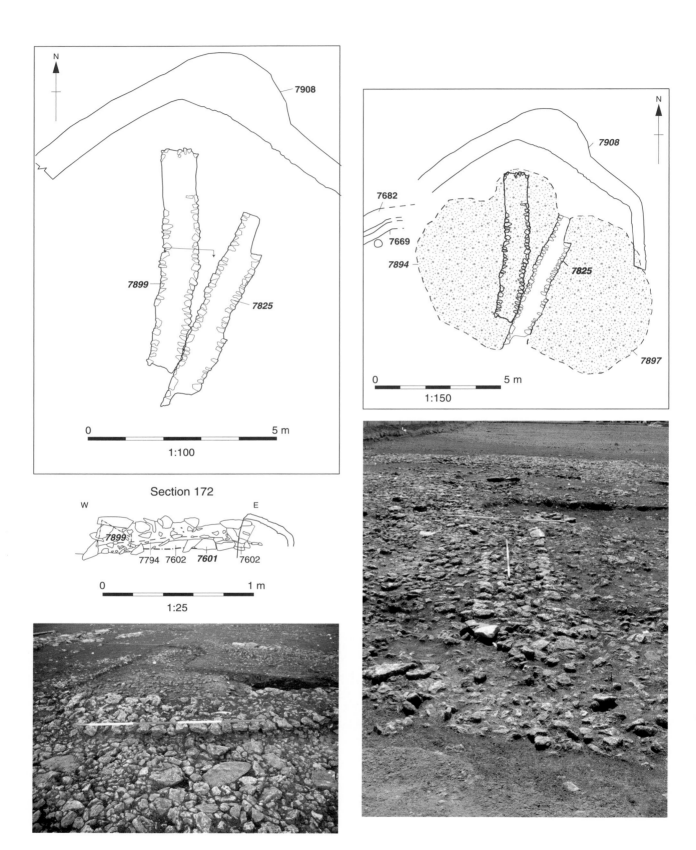

Section 172

Fig. 5.22 *Late Iron Age field wall 7899*

Fig. 5.23 *Late Iron Age field wall 7825 and layers 7894 and 7897*

been quarried from occupation deposits, as this sort of deposit was unlikely to have accumulated against a field wall.

Layer 7894 covered an area approximately 5m by 7m to the west of the 7825, overlying wall 7899. It was a composite stony deposit, with small rubble set in dark brown silts. Most of the stones were limestone but a few pieces of sandstone were identified, some were burnt, and few were above 0.10m in size. The soil component was gritty and mottled with charcoal flecks and degraded stone.

A large assemblage of 218 sherds (2864g) of pottery from this deposit is amongst the best-preserved from the site, with an average sherd weight of 13g (Chapter 6, Fig. 6.4). This group was late Iron in date, with a small residual early Iron Age component. Poole Harbour wares dominated the assemblage and there were numerous examples of fresh, large sherds of burnished necked bowls and bead-rim jars. A tazza type bowl (no. 25) resembles a Poole Harbour ware vessel from Hengistbury Head dated to the LIA2, sometime after 50 BC (Cunliffe 1987, Ill. 179, no. 1762). Another Poole Harbour product (no. 23) illustrated here as a low bowl but which no doubt doubled as a lid, is also closely paralleled within the LIA2 assemblage at Hengistbury (ibid, Ill. 158, no. 1249). The lightly tooled arcading on no. 26 is a common feature of the late Iron Age Durotrigian ceramic style range. Layer 7894 also yielded 180 fragments of animal bone, mostly sheep/goat and cattle, and eight fragments of unworked shale.

Layer 7897 covered an area 4.5m by 7.5m on the eastern side of the wall. It was similar in composition to layer 7894 and probably laid down at broadly the same time, but showed more evidence for wear and patching. In common with 7894, this deposit incorporated a great deal of occupation material, particularly animal bone (112 fragments) and pottery (251 sherds/2365g), along with a residual Neolithic/early Bronze Age end scraper. The pottery is late Iron Age, dominated by Poole Harbour wares (Chapter 6, Fig. 6.3), and includes the necked and bead-rim jars of typical Durotrigian form. A shallow platter (no. 13) is a Romanised vessel copying terra negra forms that were distributed in Britain from the late 1st century BC. A fragment of a bipartite bowl (no. 19) with a faceted carination is a Poole Harbour product dated at Hengistbury Head to the second half of the 1st century BC (see Cunliffe 1987, 212; Ill. 177, nos 1614, 1854).

Abandonment of the settlement

The complex of buildings, stone walls, pathways and drains that occupied the terraced area in the northern part of the settlement was abandoned sometime during the late Iron Age, possibly in the early post-conquest period. The walls were robbed of stone and several crouched burials were set within and alongside pre-existing structures (see below Fig. 5.27). These included two infants buried either side of the gully (7669/7682) that ran westwards from the revetment wall, and a crouched inhumation burial (7624) placed beside stone-lined gully 7885. Another burial (7151) was inserted within the interior of early Iron Age enclosure 7675 and, at a later stage, a Romano-British coffined burial was inserted across gully of enclosure 7675. Two other burials (7124 and 7777) were sited close to the remains of circular structure 7668. The conversion of this western sector of the settlement, previously the focus of domestic and industrial activity, to a burial ground meant either that the settlement had been entirely abandoned or that its nucleus had shifted slightly to a location beyond the limits of the excavation.

Stone spreads 7824 and 7787

After the abandonment of terrace complex 7970, this part of the site was consolidated by the laying of extensive stone spreads (Fig. 5.24). These deposits (7824 and 7787) consisted of distinct patches of stony soil that represented separate dumps of material strewn over the area during a single or very short episode, rather than a long sequence of activity.

Layer 7824 was a relatively cohesive, level surface measuring *c* 20m long, and of variable width. The individual dumps had in common a matrix of dark, occupation rich clayey soil, incorporating unmodified limestone pieces rarely over 0.15m in size, and typically 0.10m. In some areas, the stones were of variegated colour – yellow, pink and white – and some of dark reddish and grey colour may have been heat-affected (Fig. 5.25). Much of the stone making up 7824 had no doubt been robbed from earlier structures and yard surfaces.

Some 16,162g of pottery (909 sherds) and 18 fragments of unworked shale was incorporated in this extensive deposit and, although the assemblage included considerable quantities of residual earliest and early Iron Age material (Chapter 6, Fig. 6.2, nos 8-11), the consolidation event was dated by a roughly equal proportion of late Iron Age pottery (nos 5-7). Much of this was Poole Harbour ware, and bead-rim forms were common. Burial 7624 was sealed by the western edge of the spread, providing further evidence that the levelling activity dated to the late Iron Age or slightly later.

Some 423 animal bone fragments were also recovered from deposits making up this stone spread. Analysis and quantification of species within this assemblage was not appropriate due to the mixed and redeposited nature of the deposit, but a wide range of species was represented, including deer and dog. Notably, one context within this group (7856) produced only a single sherd of early Iron Age pottery but yielded the largest collection of animal bone from any context within the stone spread, some 64 fragments. Assuming that the material making up 7824 was quarried from elsewhere within the abandoned settlement, this may provide evidence, however tenuous, that food refuse was discarded separately from non-organic materials during the early Iron Age.

Also within layer 7824, 20 fragments of unworked shale were found in the same context as a worked bone point, and a shale-working hand tool was also recovered from a context that yielded exclusively early Iron Age pottery, whereas a gritstone saddle quern fragment was associated with late Iron Age sherds.

The stratigraphic relationship between layer 7824 and grave 7624 was important in that it demonstrated that some, at least of the burial activity pre-dated the levelling of this area. The eastern edge of the stone spread may also have just overlapped grave 7777, but the stone was more dispersed in this area so the relationship was not entirely secure.

In the southern part of the settlement more disparate patches of stony soil together constituted

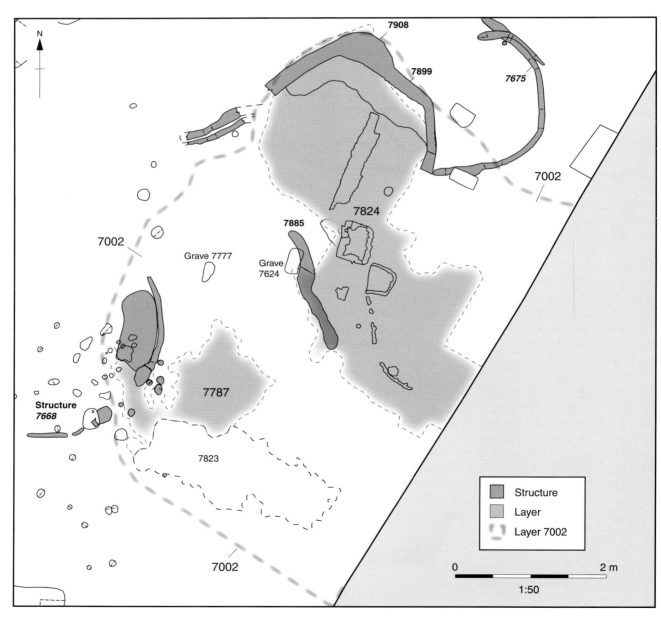

Fig. 5.24 Plan showing extent of stone spreads 7824 and 7787 and overlying composite deposit 7002

Fig. 5.25 Photograph of stone spread 7824 looking south

another consolidation spread (7787). This deposit overlay the northern edge of yard 7823 and spread across the entranceway of structure 7668. The pottery from this layer was more communited than that from 7824 and included a larger component of early material, but late Iron Age pottery was also present.

Redeposited midden 7002

Following the post-abandonment consolidation phase represented by stone spreads 7824 and 7787, the entire area of the settlement exposed in the excavation was finally levelled with a thick deposit of organic soils, interspersed with localised concentrations of small rubble and stone spreads (7002) (Fig. 5.24). The thickness of this deposit was variable, but averaged *c* 0.20-0.25m.

It is likely that the material that made up deposit 7002 was deliberately distributed across the site of the previous settlement during the late 1st century BC – early 1st century AD in order to produce a uniform cultivation soil. Several bronze objects from the northern part of the deposit provide evidence for activity in this location during the 1st century AD.

Much of this large deposit was excavated within a 2m by 2m grid in order to assign finds to a specific context location within it. This produced over 100 separate contexts, which were individually recorded. Most contexts were described as grey, brown or greenish silty clay, some with a highly organic 'cess-like' appearance similar to the soils that overlay structure 7668. These contexts generally incorporated domestic refuse – comminuted pottery, animal bone and, more uncommonly, worked flint, unworked shale and shale-working offcuts. A small number of finished artefacts of metal, worked bone, flint shale-working tools and stone were recovered, but these were rare.

The stone content of these soil-rich areas was typically limestone, with a few pieces of sandstone noted, and constituted 10-15% of the deposit. The stone size was generally smaller than 0.15m. The more stony soils (over 25% stone content) were not apparently laid specifically to create a surface, but were incidental dumps. However, a clear concentration of stone-rich soils noted on the eastern side, close to the eastern limit of excavation, probably reflected the presence of the underlying structures, but may also have indicated the presence of a stone building in the adjacent, unexcavated area.

Most of the grid squares produced pottery and animal bone. Some 1670 fragments of animal bone were recovered altogether, but the spread was quite uniform and relatively sparse, individual grid groups generally numbering 10-20 fragments. The pottery content of the 7002 deposit represented almost 40% by weight of the entire site assemblage – 6696 sherds, weighing 48870g. The quantities were extremely variable across contexts, but groups of fewer than 50 sherds were very uncommon. Two concentrations of pottery yielding context assemblages of over 1000 sherds were noted in the southern part of the settlement, one directly overlying the remains of circular structure 7668, the other some 5m to the east, overlying the area previously occupied by the yard surfaces (7742 and 7823) associated with the structure. Notably, these groups contained almost exclusively sherds of earliest and early Iron Age date, so the make-up may have been obtained from an above-ground midden associated with this early structure. Some 352 fragments of shale waste and broken shale objects, mostly armlets, were also recovered from contexts making up 7002.

Summary analysis of the distribution of materials within deposit 7002 also highlighted a concentration of flint shale-working tools close to structure 7668, but the distribution of shale waste, unworked shale fragments and armlet fragments was broad, covering the entire extent of the deposit. In one grid square (7818) at the northern end of the settlement, three shale-working hand tools were associated with 39 unworked shale fragments, a shale palette or plaque and a shale spindle whorl, indication of some diversity in the range of products being manufactured.

Context 7815, which overlay robbed field wall 7825, produced three objects of early Roman date (Chapter 6, Fig. 6.12) – a glass bead (no. 2), a copper alloy armlet (no. 3) and a Nauheim Derivative brooch (no. 5). This small collection of personal items could have been lost in the vicinity of the wall, but it is equally possible that they represent a small hoard buried beside the wall in a memorable location, which was subsequently exposed by ploughing.

THE LATE IRON AGE AND ROMANO-BRITISH BURIALS

Sometime after the abandonment of the settlement 19 uncoffined inhumation burials were made in a number of locations within the nucleus of the settlement zone and in the silted ditches of the surrounding enclosures (Fig. 5.26). The individuals had been placed in a crouched position and some were accompanied by grave goods, including pottery vessels, shale armlets and joints of meat – all elements of the distinctive south Dorset style of late Iron Age burial practiced by the Durotriges (Whimster 1981). A Nauheim Derivative brooch from one of these burials dates to about the time of the conquest, but the funerary activity may have started well before the conquest and could have taken place over several decades.

The burials of the Maiden Castle 'war cemetery' fall within this funerary tradition, and two of the Southdown Ridge bodies were accompanied by vessels of the 'war cemetery bowl' form described and published by Wheeler (1943). Precise dating of the Southdown graves is difficult, however, as the Durotrigian burial tradition was long-lived. Similar graves at Alington Avenue post-date AD 50, and some individuals may have been buried in this fashion as late as the 2nd century AD (Davies *et al* 2002, 196).

Nine of the individuals were interred within or on the edge of the settlement, the other 10 buried in or next to field boundaries (Fig. 5.26). Two of the graves were shared or later recut to accommodate another body. Grave 7372 was a single feature containing three individuals and grave 7294, which contained one individual, was recut by grave 7264, which also contained a single skeleton.

Six of the individuals were female, five were male and in eight cases, mostly of infants, children and adolescents, it was not possible to determine the sex, due in part to poor preservation and later disturbance. The population of the burials was biased towards infants, children, adolescents and young adults. There were only two mature adults (36-45 years) and six prime adults (26-35 years). The youngest individuals were aged between 2-5 months and 1.5-4.5 months. These infants, along with a child aged 6.5-16 years and a single adult, were the only skeletons that displayed no signs of pathology, although the young adult had suffered from a variety of dental conditions.

The Durotrigian burials

Grave 7546 was located adjacent to the double post setting (7514/7517) that marked the northern end of the early Iron Age fenceline located north-west of the settlement. This burial location may have been selected because of its proximity to a boundary feature, which, although constructed during the early Iron Age, may have maintained its importance for several centuries. The fence may even have been extant at the time of the burial, having been continuously renewed over several centuries, albeit possibly in a form that left no below-ground trace in

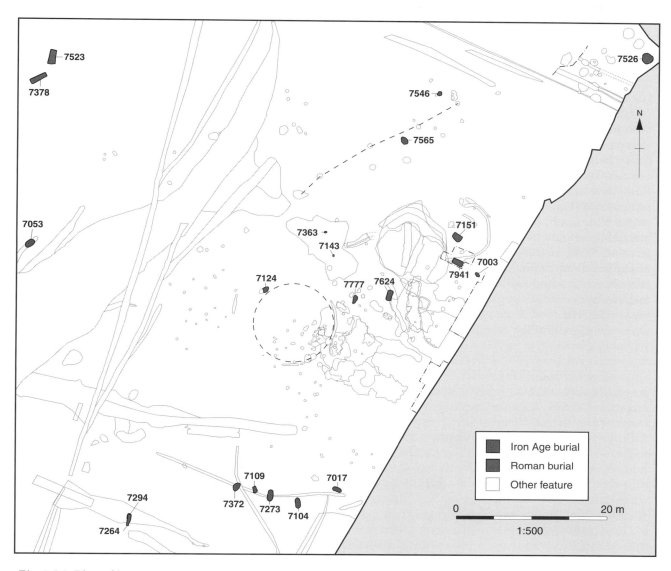

Fig. 5.26 Plan of late Iron Age and Romano-British burials

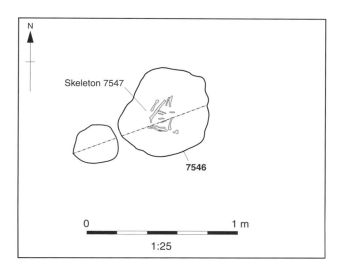

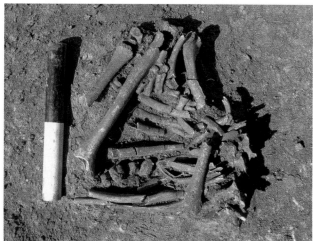

Fig. 5.27 Burial 7546

the later Iron Age. The burial was severely truncated by a modern bridleway and the skeleton (7547) of a child of uncertain sex, aged between 6.5 and 16 years, was less that 25% complete, and lacking the skull. It lay within a sub-rounded grave cut 0.60m across and only 0.05m deep, filled with a bioturbated grey silt (Fig. 5.27). No evidence of pathology was apparent on the bones.

Burial 7565 was made along the line of the same fence, between postholes 7505 and 7577. The grave cut was oval, 1.15m long, 0.80m wide and 0.20m deep, and filled with reddish brown redeposited natural soil (Fig. 5.28). The individual (7570) was a prime male adult, substantially complete, lying in a crouched position with the head to the south-east. Evidence of possible dietary deficiency was apparent, along with a healed hand fracture and several other pathologies, including osteoarthritis, degenerative changes in the spine and tooth plaque. Two 'war cemetery' style bowls in Poole Harbour ware accompanied the burial, one placed close to

the head, the second by the knees. Bones of a juvenile lamb, found near the knees represent an offering of food, typical of South Dorset burial rites. A (by now dated) study of 'Durotrigian' burials found a correspondence between female burials and pig remains and male burials and cattle, but that sheep/goat were equally found in both (Chambers 1978).

Grave 7124 lay at the western edge of the settlement, in a position that would have corresponded precisely with the back wall of circular structure 7668, when it was standing. As in the case of the fence location, this early Iron Age location apparently maintained its significance into the late Iron Age. The grave was 0.85m long, 0.65m wide and 0.28m deep, aligned ENE-WSW, the head facing the east (Fig. 5.29). The tightly crouched skeleton was of a young adult of uncertain sex, again showing possible evidence of dietary deficiency and dental plaque. The grave fill was redeposited natural clayey soil, sparsely flecked with charcoal. A small,

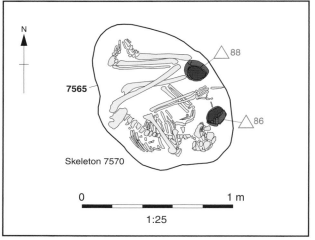

Fig. 5.28 Burial 7565 and ceramic grave goods

Chapter 5

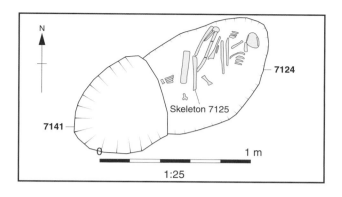

Skeleton 7125

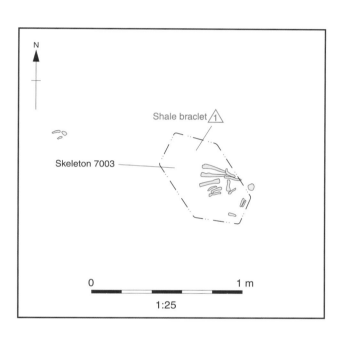

Skeleton 7003

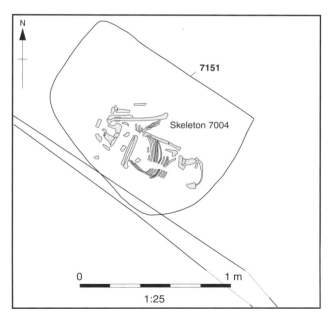

Skeleton 7004

Fig. 5.29 Burials 7124, 7003 and 7151

shallow pit (7141) that cut across the foot end of the grave did not necessarily account for missing elements of the skeleton (7125) as these may have been lost to later truncation, which could also account for the absence of grave goods. The pit may have held a timber post or stone upright to mark the position of the grave.

Another burial (7003) lay within the settlement area, close to the eastern limit of excavation (Fig. 5.29). It was badly disturbed by ploughing and no grave cut was visible. The disarticulated, partial remains, minus the skull, were of a male adult 26-35 years and, at 6 feet tall, the tallest individual from the cemetery. It showed evidence of osteoarthritis in its right hand and spine along with spinal disc disease. The grave fill produced a fragment of a decorated shale bracelet, possibly unfinished, which may have been worn by the individual, but had been displaced by later disturbance (Chapter 6, Fig. 6.16, no. 13). Several bones of cattle and sheep/goat and pig found in close association to the human remains may have been food offerings.

Burial 7151 was cut into the subsoil within the area previously occupied by early Iron Age enclosure 7675, where there was an absence of stratified deposits. The grave was 1.28m long, 0.94m wide and only 0.06m deep, and badly damaged by ploughing (Fig. 5.29). The orientation was NW-SE, the head at the south-east end. The fill of dark brown, charcoal flecked organic clayey silt produced only sherds of residual early Iron Age pottery. The skeleton (7004) was tightly crouched,

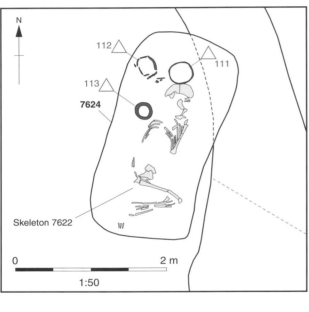

Fig. 5.30 Burial 7624 and ceramic grave goods

lying on its right side, the forearm flexed and one hand by the right knee. The individual was a mature female adult 36-45 years, apparently in relatively poor health. Pathological conditions included a depression fracture of the skull, an ossified hematoma, osteoarthritis and periostitis.

Grave 7624 was 1.46m long, 0.72m wide and 0.12m deep, with animal disturbance at the north end (Fig. 5.30). The grave was orientated NNE-SSW, the head to the north. The fill was a dark reddish mottled clayey silt with small limestone fragments. The skeleton (7622) was of a mature (36-45 years) female, lying flexed on the left side, facing east, legs bent at right angles to the spine and the arms tucked against the chest. The left hand was over the jaw and the right hand next to the face. The individual had possibly suffered from poor diet and anaemia and showed evidence of osteoarthritis, along with some dental caries and plaque. Three complete pottery vessels accompanied the burial, all placed near the head. The forms are parallelled within the late 1st century BC Maiden Castle 'war cemetery' assemblage, two (Sf 112 and Sf 113) with distinctive vertical ribs. A group of vertebrae and a cattle and sheep femur, the latter showing butchery marks, which lay within the fill could represent food offerings or the remains of a burial feast. The position of this burial is noteworthy. It cut across the northern end of the stone-lined gully (7885) that bordered the pathway of the by then demolished building complex 7970, and was partly sealed below stone spread 7824.

One of the best-preserved burials (7777) was partly sealed by a post-abandonment stone spread that was probably contemporary with layer 7824.

The grave was oval, 0.84m long, 0.51m wide and 0.30m deep (Fig. 5.31). The orientation was north-south, the head to the north. The individual (7757) was a male adult 26-35 years old, which lay in a crouched position on its right side, facing west, the arms tucked against the chest and hands beneath the skull. The skeleton exhibited evidence of degenerative changes in the spine and some dental caries. The grave fill incorporated 35 small pottery fragments, including late Iron Age beaded rims in Poole Harbour ware.

Several more burials had been placed within or alongside boundary ditches that defined the enclosures adjacent to the settlement (Fig. 5.26).

Grave 7053 was cut into the fill of ditch 7052 on the western side of the cross-ridge dyke ditch. The grave was 1.74m long, 0.78m wide and 0.17m deep, on a NE-SW orientation, the head to the north (Fig. 5.32). The individual (7054) was a young female 18-25 years which, unusually for this site, bore no signs of pathology. It was in a crouched position, lying on the right side, facing west, with one hand beneath the pelvis. The grave was disturbed but had been stone lined. Two large stones were found at the base of the skull and numerous others lay displaced within the overlying fill (7056). A complete necked jar with burnished wave decoration had been placed close to the head. A fossil shell (Sf 4) found in the fill may have been an offering, but these occur also naturally in limestone geology. Some 111 sherds of pottery from the grave fill, mostly Poole Harbour wares, include a late Iron Age bowl/lid with expanded, grooved rim, a type produced from the mid 1st century BC.

Fig. 5.31 Burial 7777

Skeleton 7757

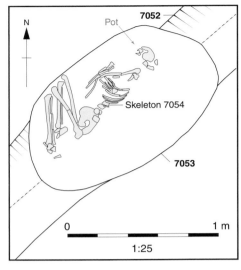

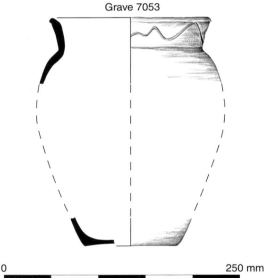

Grave 7053

Fig. 5.32 Burial 7053 and associated pottery vessel

Intercutting graves 7294 and 7264 were cut through the fill of enclosure ditch 7367 (Fig. 5.33). The earliest grave (7294) was north-south aligned, oval in shape 0.99m long, 0.53m wide and 0.34m deep. Vestiges of limestone lining survived on the western edge of the grave and other slabs had collapsed into the fill. The partially preserved skeleton (7262) of a young adult (18-25 years) of uncertain sex was crouched, lying on the left side, head to the north and facing east. The skeleton was so tightly flexed that the body may have been bound prior to burial. The individual may have suffered from dietary deficiency and had spinal disc pathology, vertebral bone spurs and some dental caries. Grave 7294 was recut as a larger grave (7264), 1.61m long, 0.50m wide and 0.20m deep. It was also orientated north-south, but the head was at the south end. Several large stones in the fill (7265) may have come from the underlying grave. The individual (7235) was a young male of similar age to 7262, but in a better state of preservation. The upper body was extended, with the right hand by the pelvis, but the legs were tightly flexed and the lower body had slumped into the void left by the underlying decayed burial. This individual also suffered from vertebral disc problems, possible benign neoplastic disease and non-specific skull lesions. A fragment of an undecorated shale bracelet found in the fill may have been worn by the individual, but was displaced by later activity.

The most common burial location was the east-west enclosure ditch (7276/7046) that defined the enclosure to the south of the settlement. Seven individuals were buried in graves cut along the length of this ditch.

Grave 7017 lay immediately to the north of the ditch terminal (7046) in which a dog had been buried during the early Iron Age (see above). By the time grave 7017 was dug the ditch may have completely filled, but the selection of this location for the burial, at the entrance to an earlier enclosure, is unlikely to have been a coincidence. The grave was on an east-west alignment, 1.23m long, 0.56m wide and 0.15m deep (Fig. 5.34). The skeleton of a female aged 26-35 years (7018) lay on its right side in a tightly crouched position, head to the east, facing north, one hand over the sternum, the other between the femurs. Evidence of kidney or bladder stones, bunions, osteoarthritis and dental caries were identified. The upper fill of the grave produced sherds of early Iron Age pottery and two flint flakes, remnants of earlier activity in the area. A copper alloy Nauheim Derivative brooch (see Scott, Chapter 6, Fig. 6.12, no. 4), a type

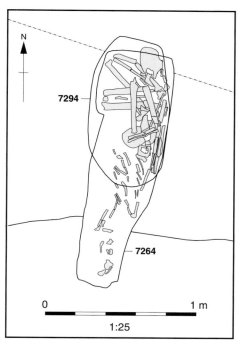

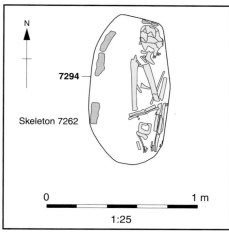

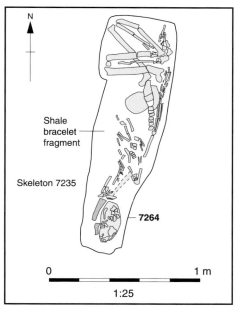

Fig. 5.33 (left and above) Double burial 7294 and 7264

that dated from the mid 1st century AD, lay in the soil above the skull but had probably adorned the body. A small fragment of unworked shale also found in the fill was probably not associated with the burial.

Grave 7104 lay just to the south of ditch 7276. It was roughly oval, 1.40m long, 0.62m wide and 0.13m deep, aligned north-south, head to the north (Fig. 5.34). The skeleton (7105) was of an adolescent 12-14 years old, of uncertain sex, but three small blue glass beads found near the neck indicate that it was probably female. This individual had suffered from septic arthritis in the left hip, and possibly poor nutrition. It lay crouched on its left side, facing east, arms extended downwards, with the hands under the knees. The beads are a type that first reached England as early as the 6th century BC (Guido 1978) but continued in use throughout the Iron Age. They had a wide distribution centring on Dorset and Somerset (Guido 1978; see Scott, Chapter 6). Some 25 sherds of residual early Iron Age pottery and small fragments of animal bone were present in the fill.

Grave 7273 was cut through the fill of ditch 7276. It was oval in shape, 1.56m long, 0.77m wide and 0.08m deep, and aligned north-south, head to the north, (Fig. 5.35). The skeleton (7274) was of a female 26-35 years old, tightly crouched, knees flexed to the left, and hands under the right leg. The greyish clayey silt fill contained a mix of early and late Iron Age pottery. A fragment of a cattle skull and other animal bones were probably not grave goods. The

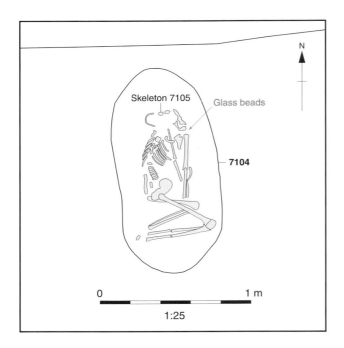

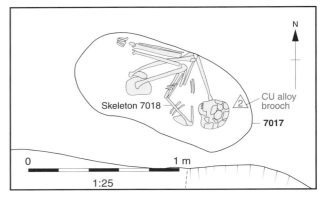

Skeleton 7018

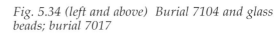

Fig. 5.34 (left and above) Burial 7104 and glass beads; burial 7017

Skeleton 7105

skeleton displayed pathologies including degenerative disease in the spine, disc herniation, child-bearing scars, periostitis and dental caries. In addition, the left arm was smaller than the right.

Grave 7109 also cut the fill of ditch 7276. It was a badly truncated, irregular cut, aligned north-south, 0.92m long, 0.55m wide and 0.10m deep (Fig. 5.35). The bones were disarticulated, the skull at the southeast end, and fewer than 25% of the elements were present. The individual (7111) was a female 18-25 years old who had suffered from spinal osteoarthritis and spinal disc herniations. The grave fill yielded only three residual early Iron Age sherds. Although the records suggest that the body may have been subject to excarnation, the bones did not show any evidence of excarnation (eg cut marks, scavenging and/or burning), and the condition of the burial was most likely due to the same effects of truncation suffered by many of the others.

Grave 7372 cut the ditch at a point where it was intersected by a short NW-SE aligned gully (7591). The grave was roughly oval, aligned NNE-SSW,

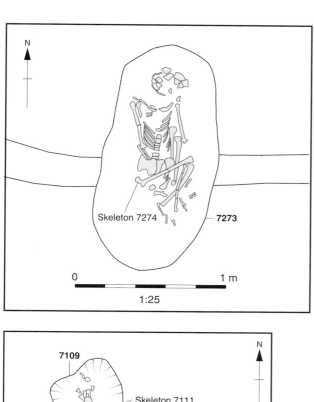

Skeleton 7274

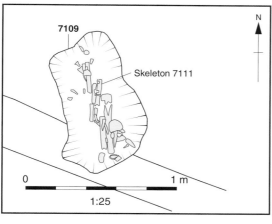

Skeleton 7111

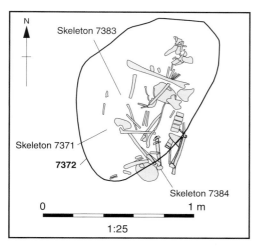

Skeletons 7371, 7383, 7384

Fig. 5.35 Burials 7273, 7109 and triple burial 7372

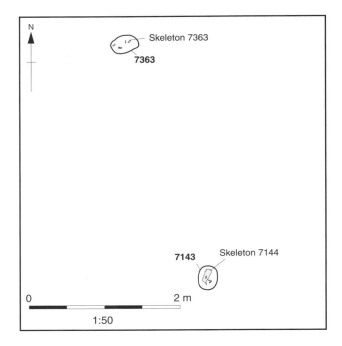

Skeleton 714⟨

Fig. 5.36 Infant burials 7143 and 7363

1.1m long, 0.8m wide and 0.3m deep (Fig. 5.35). It contained the remains of three individuals (7371, 7383 and 7384). Skeleton 7371 was less than 25% complete, only the lower legs and feet surviving. This individual was about 15 years old, of uncertain sex, and showed evidence of periostitis, possibly due to muscle trauma. It seems to have been buried later than 7384 and 7383, and most of the skeleton was removed by later ploughing. Skeletons 7383 and 7384 were probably buried at the same time, but laid out in opposing alignments. Skeleton 7383 was almost complete, an adolescent 12.5-14 years old, also of uncertain sex, and also showing evidence of periostitis, along with a dental anomaly. It lay in a crouched position, on the left side, head to the north and facing east. Skeleton 7384 was also nearly complete, but missing part of the legs and the right arm. It was a male prime adult with vertebral osteo-phytosis and disc herniations. It lay crouched, head to the south, facing west, with the mandible disartic-ulated. The left arm lay below skeleton 7383. There was no osteological evidence to indicate that these individuals were related. An environmental sample (<51>) taken from fill 7385 of this grave produced a range of charred crops and probable weeds, but these suggested that the burial took place in an area that was previously used to dump domestic refuse rather than that the plant material had been deliber-ately placed in the grave.

In the northern part of the settlement the graves of two infants (7363 and 7143) were placed about 3m apart, close to the end of the double gully (7669/7682) associated with building complex 7970 (Fig. 5.36). The stratigraphic evidence, although not entirely secure, suggested that both burials, and

certainly 7362, were cut through redeposited midden deposit 7002. This would almost certainly indicate a burial date in the 1st century AD, possibly contemporary with three coffined graves (below). It seems unlikely that the siting of these burials close to the drain was entirely coincidental, even if the feature had gone out of use. The edges of grave 7143 were not visible due to the similarity between the fill and composite layer 7002. The incomplete skeleton (7144) was of an infant aged two weeks-five months, which bore no traces of pathology. It lay on the right side, the head at the north end, and with no grave goods. The second infant (7362), which had lost most of the left side to truncation, also lay within an ill-defined grave (7363) with undefined edges and a fill resembling 7002 in composition.

The coffined burials

Three Roman inhumation burials were placed in a supine position in wooden coffins (Fig. 5.37). Two of the graves produced hobnails. The presence of hobnails is not necessarily proof that a burial is 'Romanised' in this region, and it is recognised that the South Dorset tradition continued at least into the 2nd century AD. However, the presence of coffins, distinct from the other burials, suggests Roman practice, as found with the coffined burials from Alington Avenue, dated to AD 200–AD 300 (Davies 2002). The supine position, as distinct from the crouched position of 'Durotrigian' burials, is also typical of the Roman period.

Grave 7378 was located in the western part of the site, well away from the Iron Age settlement (Fig.

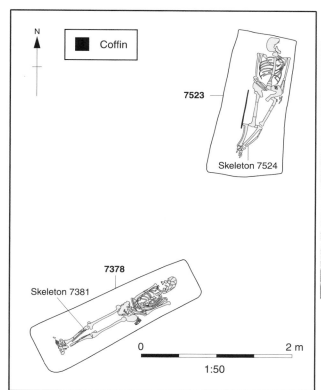

Skeleton 7524   Skeleton 7381

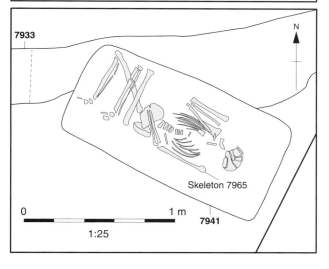

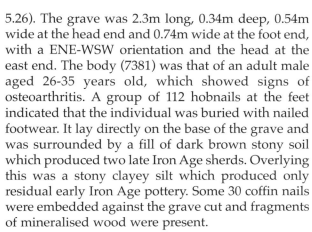

Skeleton 7965

Fig. 5.37 Roman coffined burials 7378, 7523 and 7941

5.26). The grave was 2.3m long, 0.34m deep, 0.54m wide at the head end and 0.74m wide at the foot end, with a ENE-WSW orientation and the head at the east end. The body (7381) was that of an adult male aged 26-35 years old, which showed signs of osteoarthritis. A group of 112 hobnails at the feet indicated that the individual was buried with nailed footwear. It lay directly on the base of the grave and was surrounded by a fill of dark brown stony soil which produced two late Iron Age sherds. Overlying this was a stony clayey silt which produced only residual early Iron Age pottery. Some 30 coffin nails were embedded against the grave cut and fragments of mineralised wood were present.

Grave 7523 lay immediately to the north of 7378. It was 1.92m long, 0.90m wide, 0.46m deep and aligned NE-SW, the head at the north. Staining from a wooden coffin was visible at the legs and 21 coffin nails were recovered from the fill, a greyish-brown clayey silt with fragments of limestone. A group of 76 hobnails was found at the feet. The individual (7524) was a female aged 20-25 years, which showed evidence of anaemia, possibly scurvy, and dental caries.

Grave 7941 lay within the abandoned settlement and cut the southern side of Enclosure 7675. It was 1.50m long and 0.75m wide, orientated SE-NW, the head at the south. The skeleton (7965) was of a male

193

aged 26-35, which lay with right arm flexed at the elbow and the hand by the neck. Although it was supine, the legs were slightly flexed, the knees lying on the right hand side, Fourteen coffin nails were found in the fill of mixed grey soil and redeposited natural, along with 22 residual early Iron Age pottery sherds. This individual had also suffered from anaemia and caries, as well as spinal joint disease.

Chronology of the burials

That seven of the graves (accommodating nine bodies) had been cut through the fills of or close to boundary ditches demonstrated that the enclosure system in its original form had gone out of use by the time the burial activity took place. Within the settlement, grave 7624 was sealed by the stone spread (7824) that also covered building complex 7970 and field walls 7899 and 7825. Grave 7777 was partly overlain by adjacent stony soils that were

probably broadly contemporary with 7824, and both of these deposits were overlain by midden dump 7002. Clearly then, some of the burials pre-dated the major levelling exercise. Seven other burials (7003, 7151, 7124, 7363, 7143, 7546 and 7565) were dug within the settlement and the open area to the north and west. These lay just below the topsoil and were exposed during machine stripping, and so were effectively unstratified. The only closely dateable artefact from a grave was the mid 1st century AD Nauheim Derivative brooch from burial 7017. The pottery vessels, glass beads and shale bracelets that accompanied burials 7053, 7104, 7565, 7624 and 7003 cannot be precisely dated, and could have pre-dated the conquest.

ROMANO-BRITISH DITCH

The only feature of certain Roman date, apart from the three coffined burials, was a curvilinear ditch (7191) at the northern end of the site (Fig. 5.38).

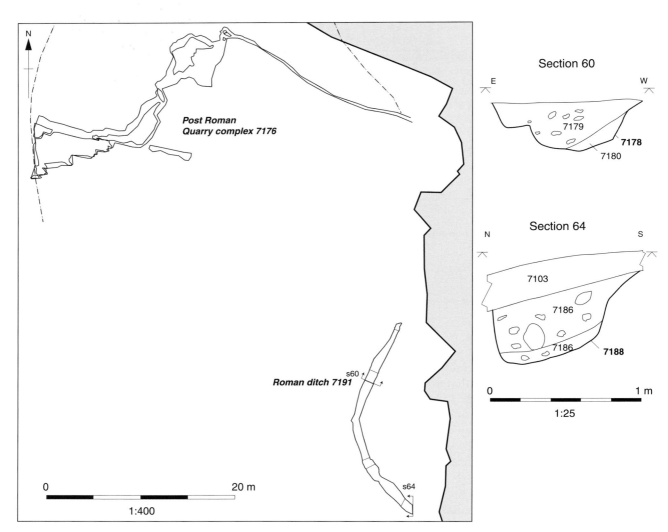

Fig. 3.38 Roman enclosure ditch 7191

194

Only the western segment was exposed in the excavated area but it would have enclosed a circular area *c* 25m in diameter. The ditch was 1.0m wide and 0.35-0.51m deep. A primary fill of yellowish silty clay, at most 0.35m thick, had eroded in from the outer edge of the ditch. A single sherd of early Roman orange ware provided evidence that this feature began to fill during the Roman period. The upper main fill was a dark clayey silt incorporating small fragments of decayed limestone. This produced half a dozen sherds of Poole Harbour ware. That so little occupation material had accumulated in this feature suggests that it was located some distance from domestic activity and was probably a livestock pen.

POST-ROMAN ACTIVITY

Post-medieval field drains

A small assemblage of 308 sherds of unabraded post-medieval pottery recovered from the topsoil and subsoil attests to limited activity in the area during the 17th-18th centuries. Most of this material appears to be from the Donyatt potteries located *c* 30 miles north-west of Weymouth in central Somerset, and later Victorian wares came from a variety of mass-production sites. The pottery was particularly prevalent in the area to the west of the cross-ridge dyke. Sherds were also present in the topsoil in the northern part of the site, an area transected by several WNW-ESE aligned field

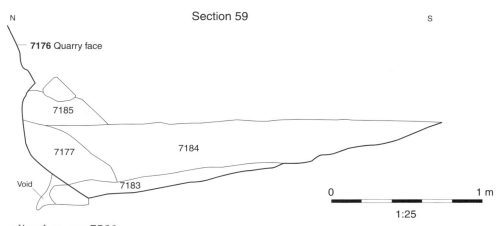

Fig. 5.39 Post-medieval quarry 7586

drains. Several of these cut across the cluster of Iron Age pits described above.

At a late stage, probably during the post-medieval period, a 105m long ditch that transected the entire southern sector of the site, cut across the cross-ridge dyke and the western boundary of the Iron Age enclosure system (Fig. 5.17). The ditch terminated at the crest of the ridge that separated the southern and northern sectors of the site and so was probably intended to drain water off the high ground. The fill of natural clayey silts incorporated two small post-medieval sherds along with a few late Iron Age and a single Roman sherd.

Limestone quarry

Ambiguous evidence of open-cast limestone quarrying was exposed in the northern part of the site, but this was not extensively examined (Fig 5.38). The nature of the geology forming the hill is such that there were layers of strata tipping downs-lope from the crest. The excavation revealed a very slight, irregular east-west aligned ridge of exposed limestone part way down the slope (7586). The quarrying would have involved the removal of this upper layer, leaving the underlying geological deposits intact, rather than working back into the face of the hill upslope. The resulting ridge may mark the point at which sufficient material had been acquired or when works ceased.

The quarry face (7176) was exposed in a machine trench (Fig. 5.39). The fill sequence began with a thin sterile compact yellowish-grey clay with small fragments of abraded limestone (7183). Overlying this was a 0.35m thick sloping fill of collapsed orange-brown clay with a few limestone fragments, some decayed to a dark red colour. Above this a similar deposit (7184) had accumulated as a 0.30m thick horizontal layer, highly root-disturbed, capped at the quarry wall end with collapsed small limestone rubble (7185). No dating material was recovered from these deposits.

Chapter 6: The Finds from Southdown Ridge

LATER PREHISTORIC AND ROMANO-BRITISH POTTERY
by Anwen Cooper with Lisa Brown

Introduction

An assemblage of 17,167 sherds of later prehistoric pottery weighing 136,265g was recovered from Southdown Ridge. Some 17% of the pottery by sherd count (2863 sherds/18763g from 211 contexts) came from cut features (Table 6.1), including six complete vessels which had been placed as grave goods in three late Iron Age inhumation burials. These closed groups represent the few reliably dated context assemblages from the site. The remaining 83% (14,309 sherds/ 117,502g from 256 contexts) of the assemblage derived from a variety of accumulated or deliberately assembled deposits, which included extensive stone spreads and pavements. This material is essentially unstratified. A very large percentage, approaching 40%, of the total assemblage was recovered from a layer of midden-like composition (7002) which was spread across the footprint of the settlement, probably during the early Roman period. The origin of this material could not be established, but it was likely to have been associated with the earliest settlement phase/s.

The pottery spans a period from the earliest Iron Age (*c* 800-600 BC) through to the late Iron Age/ Romano-British transition (*c* 50 BC-50 AD). Within this time-span, the material of earliest Iron Age date is sparsely represented, and much of it was recovered as small, abraded redeposited fragments from the composite levelling deposit (7002). The majority of the collection dates to the early Iron Age (*c* 600–400 BC) and the late Iron Age (100 BC–50 AD). The middle Iron Age (*c* 400–100 BC) is probably poorly represented but much of the pottery imported from the Wareham-Poole Harbour potteries during the middle to late Iron Age cannot be dated precisely because of shared fabric and stylistic traits over several centuries.

A clear divide is apparent in the spatial distribution of the assemblage. The great majority of the material recovered from cut features is of early Iron Age date, while that found in occupation and levelling layers, albeit incorporating a substantial early Iron Age component, dates to the late Iron Age and Romano-British transition.

Methodology

The entire assemblage was examined and all context groups recorded in accordance with guidelines set out by the Prehistoric Ceramic Research Group (PGRG, 1997). The data was recorded on OpenOffice Calc spreadsheet, including the following key fields: context, context type, context group, small find number, form, fabric, sherd count, weight, surface finish, decoration, residue, condition, date. Additional comments were recorded in an open field.

Fabric groups were defined on the basis of macroscopic examination, enhanced where necessary with a hand lens (x 10 and x 20) and binocular microscope. The main fabric groups, together with formal classes and types, are also cross-referenced where relevant with those from major regional assemblages at Maiden Castle (MC) (Brown 1991) and from sites examined as part of the Danebury and Environs Programme (DEP) (Brown 2000a). For each context, an additional summary record presents the principal fabric groups represented, any formal and decorative traits, surface finish, evidence of use, and the overall condition of the sherds. In contexts which were clearly of little informative value (typically those with <50g material, amounting to approximately 5% of the

Table 6.1 Summary of later prehistoric and Romano-British pottery from cut features

Feature type	Contexts	Sherds	Weight (g)	Mean sherd weight (g)
Ring gully	9	56	348	6.21
Posthole	39	246	1496	6.08
Revetment	2	44	497	11.30
Wall	4	87	1170	13.45
Foundation trench	1	7	40	5.71
Ditch	62	1184	7079	5.98
Drain	9	56	299	5.33
Linear feature	14	64	268	4.19
Pit	37	569	4603	6.09
Burial (excluding complete vessels)	22	390	2157	5.53

assemblage), a detailed summary record was not made of each of the fabric groups represented, but any notable features (formal, decorative, etc.) were recorded.

The taphonomic history of over 80% of the pottery assemblage (see above) could not be established due to factors of severe truncation, settlement reconfiguration, robbing and redeposition of occupation and structural material within the settlement area, where most of the pottery was found. For this reason, quantitative and statistical analyses were not considered useful and were kept to a minimum. Instead, key closed groups (most of which are very small) were used to determine the date of specific features and groups of features and, in the cases of large reworked and redeposited spreads of stone and occupation material, the date of the deposition events were determined by the latest material they contained. Frequently, the latest material formed a very small proportion of the total, and residuality was clearly a major factor.

Sherds were selected for illustration on the basis that either they were found in securely dated contexts (but these rarely produced sherds of illustrateable quality); or that they derived from a stratigraphically compromised context which, nonetheless, contained a wide range of diagnostic sherds from all or any periods. An example of this is that the best selection of earliest and early Iron Age pottery came from redeposited midden layer 7002 (Figs 6.5 and 6.6).

Fabrics

Five main fabric groups were identified. With the exception of the predominantly beef calcite, chalk and lignite tempered groups, all fabrics are well represented within other large published assemblages from the region, including Maiden Castle (Brown in Sharples 1991, 185-6) and Hengistbury Head (Brown in Cunliffe 1987, 213-265).

QU Predominantly quartz sand-tempered
[Maiden Castle equivalent Fabric A]

QU1 abundant medium-course quartz grains, with rare-sparse fine-course assorted secondary inclusions including flint, oolite, fossil shell, haematite, rock, and fine mica fragments. Within the *QU1* subgroup it is possible to distinguish between fabrics derived from sources in the Wareham-Poole Harbour area, and those derived from non-Poole Harbour sources. The five complete funerary vessels were produced using clay from sources very similar to those in the Poole Harbour area but located close to Exeter (L. Brown pers. comm.).

QU2 abundant fine quartz sand, with rare-sparse fine-v coarse assorted other inclusions including flint, oolite, fossil shell, haematite, rock, and fine mica fragments

QU3 sparse-common medium-course quartz sand with sparse fine-coarse assorted secondary inclusions including fossil shell, flint, oolite, beef calcite, haematite and rock fragments.

QU4 is a subgroup distinguished by its glauconite content and a general sparcity of other inclusions

FL Predominantly flint-tempered
[Maiden Castle equivalent Fabric B]

FL1 moderate-common medium-course flint inclusions in a sandy matrix with sparse assorted secondary inclusions of medium-coarse beef calcite, haematite, rock fragments, chalk and fossil shell fragments

FL2 sparse fine-medium flint inclusions in a sandy matrix with rare other inclusions (beef calcite, rock *etc.*).

SH Predominantly shell-tempered
[Maiden Castle equivalent Fabric C]

SH1 moderate-common fine-coarse fossil shell in a sandy matrix with sparse, fine-course assorted other inclusions including rock, flint, chalk, beef calcite, haematite and oolite fragments

SH2 moderate-common coarse to very course fossil shell fragments in a sandy matrix with common medium-course assorted other inclusions including oolite, flint, lignite, rock, haematite, chalk and beef calcite fragments

SH3 sparse fine-very coarse fossil shell inclusions in a sandy matrix, with rare other inclusions (usually beef calcite or oolite). Fabrics in this group are closely related to those in the predominantly oolite and chalk-tempered groups and probably derive from similar Jurassic sources.

LI Predominantly oolite tempered
[Maiden Castle equivalent Fabric F]

LI1 sparse-abundant oolite inclusions in a sandy matrix with varying quantities of fine-very coarse assorted secondary inclusions (mainly fossil shell, beef calcite, flint, chalk, haematite, haematite, mica, and organic material). Within this broad group it is possible to identify finer and coarser subgroups (the former generally being sandier with sparser and finer oolite and other inclusions). Fabrics in this group are closely related to those in the predominantly shell and chalk-tempered groups and may well derive from similar Jurassic sources. No specific subgroups, but abundance of oolites is variable.

CA Predominantly beef calcite-tempered

CA1 medium-common, coarse-very coarse beef calcite inclusions with rare-sparse ill-sorted fossil shell, rock, haematite, quartz and oolite fragments

CA2 common-abundant, moderate-coarse crushed beef calcite inclusions with rare-sparse mixed other inclusions

Four additional fabric groups were poorly represented in the assemblage:

CH Predominantly chalk-tempered

Sparse-moderate medium-very coarse chalk fragments in a sandy matrix with sparse-moderate coarse-very coarse fossil shell and oolite inclusions together with rare assorted other inclusions (flint, haematite, rock, etc.). This fabric group is closely related to the oolitic and shelly groups and may derive from similar Jurassic sources. However in this case chalk is clearly the dominant temper.

FC Smooth, fine clay with few visible inclusions
[Maiden Castle equivalent Fabric E]

Compact fine clay with sparse ill-sorted varied other inclusions including quartz, fossil shell, haematite, flint and mica fragments.

LG Lignite inclusions

Common coarse-very coarse lignite inclusions with rare medium-sized flint, fossil shell and stone fragments

MI Mixed composition coarseware
[Maiden Castle equivalent Fabric H]

Mixed sparse-common moderate-very course ill-sorted inclusions in a sandy matrix commonly comprising a variable assortment of flint, fossil shell, haematite, beef calcite, rock fragments and oolite

Key attributes by period

Earliest Iron Age (c 800–600 BC)

Pottery dating to the earliest Iron Age was identified primarily on the basis of distinctive decorative traits, which have close affinities with the 10th-7th century BC Early All Cannings Cross style (Cunnington 1923, Cunliffe 2005, 613) and, in Dorset, the well-

stratified 8th-7th century BC assemblage from Kimmeridge (Davies 1936; Calkin 1949; Cunliffe 1968), two traditions that overlap markedly in form and decoration. A number of important assemblages of the All Cannings Cross tradition have been published in recent years, including those from the Wiltshire sites of Longbridge Deverill Cow Down (Hawkes 2012) and Potterne (Gingell and Morris in Lawson, 2000).

Forms found at Southdown Ridge include furrowed bowls, some with a red finish, and upright or flaring rims, that correspond broadly with the Danebury Environs Programme (DEP) BE form type (Brown 2000a, 89-90), and sherds decorated with a combination of incised lines, and/or impressed circles or dots. The latter mostly belong to large round-shouldered jars with flaring rims that correspond broadly with the DEP JF form type (Brown in Cunliffe 2000, 88). The decoration is commonly inlaid with a white chalk-based paste. These forms are mostly in fabrics that are predominantly tempered with shell (SH1-3) or oolite (LI1) and, as such, show a closer affinity to the often shell-tempered Kimmeridge material than the All Cannings Cross pottery, which is almost invariably sandy.

This material, represented by a small group of mostly very small and abraded sherds that were residual in later, mainly early Iron Age, cut features, occupation layers and levelling deposits, accounts for less than 3% of the total site assemblage. The largest number of sherds of this type was recovered from the extensive redeposited midden deposit (7002) that covered the abandoned settlement (Fig. 6.5, no. 34; Fig. 6.6, nos 43, 46, 59, 60). A few fragments were also present in the underlying limestone consolidation spread (7824) (Fig. 6.2, nos 9 and 10).

The very early pottery derived from deposits, probably including above-ground middens, associated with the earliest phase of settlement activity, but very little was found in primary contexts. The extensive remodelling of the settlement during the early and late Iron Age and subsequent abandonment and robbing activity almost comprehensively destroyed features and occupation layers that belonged to this early phase of activity, at least within the area of archaeological investigation, and it is possible that the focus of domestic occupation during this period lay to the east of the westernmost sector of the settlement exposed in the trench. A possible exception was the external yard (7742), apparently a trampled old ground surface, associated with circular structure 7668, which produced a few highly fragmented sherds of earliest Iron Age type, including a furrowed bowl, along with an 8th century BC copper alloy socketed axe (Fig. 5.9). Although some early Iron Age pottery was also collected from this surface, it may have been intrusive from overlying deposits, and the axe, well-embedded in the surface, is perhaps the best indication of the date of its construction. Also noted was a concentration of residual earliest Iron Age pottery in the contexts belonging to the layer (7002) that overlay circular structure 7768.

Early Iron Age (c 600–400 BC)

The bulk of the pottery from the site dates to the early Iron Age (EIA) period. This includes the vast majority of material from cut features associated with the settlement and the field system, together with a substantial proportion from occupation layers and redeposited levelling material, especially group 7002.

One of the most distinctive traits of the early Iron Age assemblage is a wide variability in the fabrics represented, as outlined below. The assemblage is also characterised by a diverse range of vessel forms and surface treatments, especially noted in the series of fineware bowls, many of which are elaborated with red finishes and/or impressed and incised decoration. The extensive use of fineware bowls, in tandem with coarseware cooking and storage jars, distinguishes the early part of the Iron Age in Dorset (and Wessex generally) from a subsequent trend towards a lack of vessel differentiation, and a preponderance of situlate jars. This stylistic transition from a diverse and ornate to homogenous and unelaborated tradition coincided with the extended hillfort (phase 6) at Maiden Castle (Sharples 1991, 63) and the early part of the middle Iron Age in Wessex. Amongst the explanations offered for this ceramic shift is that it reflected a supression of distinctions in social status that favoured an elite operating within late Bronze Age and early Iron Age communities (eg Barrett 1989), and a move towards an emphasis on activities undertaken by and beneficial to the wider social community.

Fabrics

Many of the early Iron Age fabrics – particularly those predominantly tempered with shell, oolite and chalk – derived from local Jurassic clay sources and were manufactured in the near vicinity, although no evidence of on-site production was identified. However, the presence of quartz sand-tempered sherds from Wareham/Poole Harbour sources and of sherds predominantly tempered with lignite indicates that the assemblage includes a non-local component.

A wide variety of fine and coarseware fabrics are present but overall the early Iron Age assemblage is dominated by sherds predominantly tempered with oolite, as was the case with the earliest Iron Age

pottery. Sherds chiefly tempered with shell, quartz sand and beef calcite make up most of the remainder. Only a small component (c 5%) was made from the clean, compact fine clays of the FC group of fabrics, or are predominantly tempered with lignite (LG) or chalk (CH). Some of the sherds of this date are well-fired and very hard but more typically they are less well fired and extremely friable.

A numerical bias in favour of a red-orange spectrum surface colour seen in the Southdown Ridge early Iron Age assemblage, and typical of many early Iron Age assemblages, is a result of selective firing techniques (allowing in oxygen during the firing). This may have been a means of achieving a red finish that mimicked the haematite-coating technique popular during this era.

Forms

The early Iron Age assemblage incorporates a broad range of vessels, including fine bowls and coarseware bowls and jars. Numerous distinctive rims and angled body sherds are present, and several contexts include refitting sherds, but there are few complete or near complete reconstructable profiles. Bipartite and tripartite jars with simple rounded or flattened or roughly folded over upright or out-turned rims correspond broadly with the DEP forms JA and JB (Brown 2000a, 86).

The assemblage is marginally dominated by bowls, many of them red-finished or fired to red, and includes bowls with mid-line carinations or otherwise well-defined shoulders or bodies (DEP equivalent BA1). These may have elongated flaring rims or short, out-turned rims. Some tripartite bowls have body angles emphasised with cordons (DEP equivalent form BB). Fragments from bowls with a simpler rounded profile corresponding with the DEP form types BA2 are somewhat less common.

Jars typically have a pronounced shoulder and elongated, upright rim (DEP equivalent JB1-3), sometimes one or both emphasised with fingertip or fingernail impressed decoration. Jars with less well-defined, slacker shoulders and poorly-emphasised rims are also present, but far less common. Most of the jars were produced in limestone- or shell-tempered clays or, in a few cases, in composite fabric MI.

Surface finishes and decorative traits

Many of the early Iron Age sherds (c 18%) have a red finish, whether applied or achieved through firing. Most of these belonged to bowls, but red-finished jars were also recorded, especially those in oolitic fabrics. This finish was achieved in a number of different ways – some sherds show traces of an applied haematite rich slip, others have significant quantities of haematite within the fabric that was brought to the surface by wiping and controlled firing. An example of the latter technique was seen on refitting jar sherds from context 7456 from layer 7002 (Fig. 6.6, no. 53). Some red-finished sherds are also burnished to a high degree.

Some bowls were decorated with horizontal lines or zones of diagonal slashed lines or chevrons, or dart or wedge-shaped shaped impressions, typically located immediately above the shoulder angle or just below the rim (Fig. 6.2, no. 8, Fig. 6.5, nos. 42 and 48, Fig. 6.6, no. 57). There is a close parallel for this design on a sherd from the early Iron Age settlement site at Waddon, north-west of Weymouth (Brown 2000b, fig. 9, no. 2). One sherd has a row of diagonally positioned impressed decoration, possibly achieved by impressing the clay with seeds (Fig. 6.1, no. 4). In several cases the shoulder angle is emphasised with a cordon decorated with diagonal slashed lines or in one case with an unusual fine, feathered decoration (Fig. 6.5, no. 37). Another typical motif is incised or shallow-tooled diagonal lines (Fig. 6.1, no. 1, Fig. 6.5, no. 36, Fig. 6.6, no. 54).

The early Iron Age assemblage includes numerous sherds, mostly very fragmentary, from shouldered jars with rows of fingernail or fingertip decoration, or otherwise rows of diagonal slashed lines along the shoulder angle or on the rim top (Fig. 6.6, nos 45 and 47), a decorative style that evolved from late Bronze Age ceramic traditions traceable across southern England. Many sherds were roughly wiped or pulled, occasionally to a degree amounting to scoring. This finish achieved both an aesthetic and a practical effect in that large vessels with a coarsened, textured finish are easier to grip when moving than those with smoothed, rounded surfaces.

Residue and wear

Traces of soot, carbonised organic material and limescale were identified on fewer than 1% of sherds, the low incidence partly due to the poor condition of sherds, many of which had suffered from exposure to the elements and abrasion through cycles of redeposition. Soot is by far the most common residue present on sherds of this date.

Middle Iron Age (c 400–100 BC)

Pottery dating to the middle Iron Age is poorly, or unceartainly represented, in part because in only a very few cases was it possible to distinguish material of this date from that of late Iron Age date. This was particularly the case since material of possible middle Iron Age date was, with the possible exception of sherds from pits 7509 and 7555, recovered from occupation layers containing

mixed material. Additionally, the fact that many traits that define middle Iron Age pottery from the Dorset region continued into the late Iron Age in a ceramic tradition that was notably conservative (Brown 1991, 192). By the middle Iron Age in this area many settlement assemblages were dominated by products of the Wareham-Poole Harbour production centres, and the fabrics (QU1) are quite uniform.

Nevertheless the presence of occasional sherds suggest that the assemblage does include a small middle Iron Age component. With very few exceptions possible middle Iron Age sherds are in quartz sand dominated fabrics (usually QU1), predominantly from sources in the Wareham/Poole-Harbour area. This material was also commonly burnished. Likely examples are S-shaped jars, jars with slightly irregular pedestal bases corresponding broadly with the DEP form type JD (Brown 2000a, 87), dishes with flattened rims (DEP form type DA1, Brown in Cunliffe 2000, 90), in one case in a predominantly oolite-tempered fabric copying the Poole Harbour products, and crudely executed perforated lugs from round profiled vessels.

A proportion of the sherds from Durotrigian style bowls and jars (DEP form type JC, Brown in Cunliffe 2000, 86-7), best represented regionally by the assemblage from Maiden Castle, particularly those with proto-beaded or short out-turned beaded rims, may date to this period. Similarly, a few sherds with Durotrigian motifs including bosses, waves and dimples belong to a decorative style that orginated during the middle Iron Age, but were produced for an extended period, and into the late Iron Age. One small sherd was tentatively identified as a saucepan pot, but this was from redepositsd layer 7002.

Late Iron Age and Late Iron Age/Romano-British transition (100 BC–50 AD)

It is worth emphasising that it is notoriously difficult to distinguish much of the material dating to the middle Iron Age from of the late Iron Age and late Iron Age/Romano-British transition period (LIA-RB) since there are considerable overlaps in the fabrics and formal traits of ceramics from these periods (Brown 1991, 192). However since many more traits typical of the LIA-RB style rather than middle Iron Age assemblages were identified , it seems likely that most of the later Iron Age material from Southdown Ridge dates to the period from 100 BC onwards.

Fabrics

All of the sherds classed as LIA-RB were produced in quartz sand tempered fabrics (mainly QU1), produced almost exclusively using clays from sources in the Wareham-Poole Harbour area. However it is certainly possible that some of the material, distinguished by a slightly pinkish tinge and a sandwiched appearance in section were made from clay from sources in the Exeter area, which is very similar compositionally to that from the Wareham-Poole Harbour sources (Brown 1997, 41; Holbrook and Bidwell 1991).

Forms

The LIA-RB assemblage incorporates a wide variety of vessels, including beaded-rim and necked bowls and jars, dishes, and lids. Numerous rim, base and diagnostic body sherds are present and many contexts produced refitting sherds.

Six complete vessels had been placed as grave goods in funerary contexts. A necked jar with decorated neck came from grave 7053 (Fig. 6.9, no. 69). Two straight-sided pedestal bowls found in grave 7565 (Fig. 6.10, nos 73-74), are paralleled at Hengistbury Head (Brown 1987, Ill. 157), at Cadbury Castle (Woodward 2000b, 340-1) and from burials at Maiden Castle (Wheeler 1943, fig. 72, 171-181). Two ribbed 'war cemetery' bowls from grave 7624 (Fig. 6.10, 70-71) are so-called due to Wheeler's now discounted interpretation that the burials with which they were associated were the hasty interrment following a battle with Roman troops at the hillfort (Wheeler 1943, fig. 72, 181). These are also relatively common in domestic contexts, as at Cadbury Castle and Hengistbury Head (ibid.). Petrological analysis of these forms has demonstrated that some, at least, were produced in the Exeter area from raw materials closely related to the Wareham-Poole Harbour clays (Holbrook and Bidwell 1991). An uncommon form, sometimes interpreted as a tazza, also accompanied burial 7624 (Fig. 6.10, no. 72). This Romanised form, copied in the Durotrigian assemblage, seems to have been fairly restricted in numbers and distribution, and may have served a specific, perhaps ritual, function. Several were found at Hengistbury Head (Brown 1987, 212, Ill. 179, BD7.0) and a possible example from Maiden Castle is published (Wheeler 1943, fig. 74, 229).

The forms represented in the LIA-RB assemblage correspond fairly well with those from ceramic phases 6G-H and 7A at Maiden Castle (Brown 1991). A large proportion of these sherds derive from bipartite vessels (analogous with the MC/DEP form types JC and BC). This includes sherds from jars both with rounded profiles and with high, rounded shoulders. A particularly fine example of the latter is the broken but near complete decorated vessel recovered from the uppermost fill (7237) of the cross-ridge dyke (Fig. 6.8, no. 68).

Several sherds belonged to bowls with simple rounded profiles and beaded rims. In some examples their rims are grooved or lid-seated. There are numerous finely finished perforated lug fragments from jars with rounded profiles. The assemblage also includes many sherds from necked vessels (corresponding broadly with MC/DEP form types JE and BD), a proportion of which are also decorated with burnished waves or arcading. Occasional angled body sherds from necked bowls have cordons distinguishing the neck and shoulder. The great majority of rim sherds from both jars and bowls are beaded, often everted, and sometimes flaring. On a few sherds from round-profiled vessels the rim is emphasised with moulded decoration or slight cordons. A number of base sherds from jars are slightly accentuated, and several have distinct base rings.

Amongst the most distinctive and common forms present in the LIA-RB assemblage are ovoid jars and bowls and dishes with pronounced beaded and flattened rims, or short necks. These include extremely large, coarseware vessels of a type common from the middle Iron Age onwards (eg Fig. 6.5, no. 33), but at Southdown Ridge these sherds are typically found in contexts with high proportions of LIA-RB material, and so are probably examples of forms that endured in a conservative ceramic tradition. Sherds (often refitting) representing at least five vessels were present, all well-made and burnished (eg Fig. 6.5, no. 27).

Surface finishes and decorative traits

Many of the sherds from the LIA-RB assemblage are burnished or well-smoothed. The most common decorative trait on sherds of this date is lightly tooled incised or burnished decoration. This takes a variety of forms, with narrow lattice decoration and zigzag decoration being the most common. The best example of the former comes from the near complete broken vessel recovered from the cross-ridge dyke ditch (Fig. 6.8, no. 68). Zigzag decoration is commonly associated with necked vessels. Many other sherds are decorated with simple incised horizontal lines, sometimes forming concentric circles around the rim. One possibly later Romano-British sherd is decorated with vertical combed lines. A relatively small collection of sherds is also present with dimples, bosses, and incised wavy line decoration. The use of these decorative devices spans the middle to late Iron Age, and they are also found in post-conquest contexts in the region.

Residue and wear

Traces of soot, and limescale were identified on under 1% of sherds of this date, limescale being by far the most common residue. The condition of the material of this date varies according to context and is discussed in more detail below.

Key attributes by context

Cut features

Structural features (peannular gullies, postholes, revetments, walls, foundation trench)

Iron Age pottery was recovered from 55 contexts associated with a range of structural features (Table 6.1). Many of these groups are very small collections of worn sherds, but a few include assemblages of over 100g. Most of the pottery from the penannular gullies associated with circular structure 7668 and enclosure 7675, and postholes and stakeholes associated with these gullies, was of early Iron Age date but the fill (7740) of the stone-packed wall slot (7739) of structure 7668 also produced a small fragment of a 9th-8th century BC furrowed bowl. Refitting sherds representing a large part of an early Iron Age fineware bowl with a flaring rim (Fig. 6.7, no. 62) had been packed in posthole 7517 (7522), probably as a foundation deposit marking an important boundary fence. Posthole 7540, the southernmost post of this fence-line included an unusually high proportion of fineware rims, possibly deposited selectively. Apart from these examples, most of the earliest and early Iron Age pottery was very fragmented and weathered.

The middle-late Iron Age pottery relating to terrace complex 7970 and later field walls 7899 and 7825 was generally less fragmented and abraded than that recovered from most other structural features, suggesting that these fragments were deposited fairly soon after the vessels were discarded. The pottery from layers 7894 and 7897, which had accumulated against wall 7825 included a high proportion of rim sherds and refitting sherds from two vessels.

Linear features (ditches and drains)

The assemblage recovered from linear features, mostly early Iron Age boundary ditches, typically comprised small collections of small to medium sized, abraded sherds. The material from linear ditches was particularly abraded, and rarely closely dateable. This is typical of field boundary ditches, where material has usually eroded in from the surrounding ground sufaces. No material dating to the earliest Iron Age was recovered from linear features, but several produced early Iron Age sherds and the upper fills occasionally included very worn Romano-British sherds.

Pits and hollows

Hollow 7500 (context 7503) produced a relatively large early Iron Age assemblage, but the fill was disturbed and late Iron Age sherds were also present. Perhaps surprisingly, the early Iron Age pit assemblages were generally quite small and unremarkable, consisting mostly of small to medium-sized, moderately abraded sherds. The great majority of the pits produced small amounts of early Iron Age material, including some with an earliest Iron Age component. Pits 7509 and adjacent pit 7555 produced somewhat larger collections of mixed Iron Age material including some distinctly M-LIA sherds (Fig. 6.7, nos 66-67). Sherds from these later pits were generally larger and less abraded than that from the pits that yielded exclusively early Iron Age material.

Burials

The pottery from the late Iron Age inhumation burials generally consisted of small numbers of fairly worn, residual sherds. The smaller of these groups (<100g) all produced material of exclusively EIA date. Of the five inhumation fills which produced larger assemblages (>100g), two (7152) and (7942) produced pottery dating exclusively to the EIA, while the remaining three (7056), (7623) and (7778) produced material of the MIA-LIA/RB transition.

Four contexts (7629), (7630), (7631), and (7566) produced complete or near complete vessels. Burial 7565 included a near complete but broken vessel, together with a complete, but also fragmented, vessel. Context numbers (7629), (7630) and (7631) were assigned to complete vessels deposited as grave goods with burial 7624, none of which contained animal bone or artefacts (Fig. 6.10). These vessels share affinities with the 'war cemetery' vessels recovered from burial contexts at Maiden Castle (Wheeler 1943).

Composite deposit 7002

Some 39% by sherd count (36% by weight) of the total site assemblage, amounting to 6696 sherds/ 48870g, was recovered from contexts making up redeposited midden 7002. Given that this is stratigraphically one of the latest deposits on the site, it is important to highlight that a substantial proportion of the material from this layer is of earliest and early Iron Age date (Figs 6.5-6.6). The deposit was excavated in grid squares and of the 81 excavated contexts from this layer, 24 contained exclusively EIA material, and most of the others contexts included substantial quantities of EIA sherds. Conversely other contexts from this layer produced large quantities of middle-late Iron Age and

Romano-British transition material as well as a few early Roman sherds.

In view of the stratigraphic position of this deposit, and the fact that it includes a reasonable quantity of LIA/RB sherds, it is clear that this material was deposited at around the time of the Roman conquest. The condition of sherds provides further information regarding how it was formed and came to include such large quantities of EIA material. Unusually, the M-LIA/RB transition material was sometimes more worn than the EIA sherds. Moreover, several refitting sherds of earliest and early Iron Age pottery were found in several contexts making up deposit 7002, suggesting that the primary depositional context for this material had not been substantially disturbed. This could indicate that the deposit represented material from a midden-like structure that was dumped wholesale, along with later material, after the abandonment of the settlement and at the end of the occupation of this site.

Comparative assemblages

The later prehistoric pottery assemblage from Southdown Ridge comprises a small but important earliest Iron Age component, a substantial and significant early Iron Age component, a small middle Iron Age collection of uncertain size, and a reasonable quantity of late Iron Age and Late Iron Age/Romano-British transition material.

Material from the earliest Iron Age is fairly well-represented in Wessex as a whole, although much less so within Dorset. The Southdown Ridge pottery shares close affinities with the Early All Cannings Cross tradition (Cunnington 1923, Cunliffe 2005) which has a very wide geographical distribution (Brown in Cunliffe 1987) and is best represented by the assemblages from All Cannings Cross itself (Cunnington 1923), from Potterne (Gingell and Morris 2000) and from Longbridge Deverill Cow Down (Hawkes 2012). Comparable, although smaller, assemblages have been recovered more locally from Phase 3 contexts at Hog Cliff Hill (Ellison and Rahtz 1987) and from Period I contexts at Eldon's Seat and Kimmeridge (Cunliffe and Phillipson 1968). While material of this date was mostly residual in later Iron Age features at Southdown Ridge, the collection represents an important addition to the relatively sparse current corpus. This is particularly the case since this material shows clear affinities with the Early All Cannings Cross tradition rather than with the plainer south Dorset variation of this tradition which is thought by some to have emerged at about the same time (Sharples 2010, 321).

Early Iron Age material is also well-represented in the region at a broad level and is best characterised by the material from Maiden Castle (Wheeler 1943; Brown 2000) and Cadbury Castle (Woodward 2000). The material from Southdown Ridge conforms fairly well to the Dorset coast tradition for this period which is distinguished by the absence of scratched-cordoned bowls, and the presence of small carinated fineware bowls with upright or flaring upper bodies and a red finish (Sharples 2010, 322). The assemblage also has affinities with those recovered from Phase 2 at Rope Lake Hole (Davies 1986), Period II at Eldon's Seat (Cunliffe and Phillipson 1968), Phase 5 at Maiden Castle (Brown 1991), Site D at Chalbury (Whitley 1943) and from Waddon, located just 6km to the west of Southdown Ridge (Brown 2000b). The fairly extensive use of fingertip and fingernail decoration observed in the Southdown Ridge assemblage is also a feature of the groups from

Group 7823

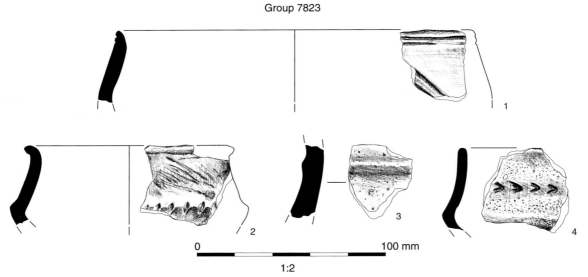

0   100 mm

1:2

Fig. 6.1 Pottery from early Iron Age stone pavement 7823

Group 7824

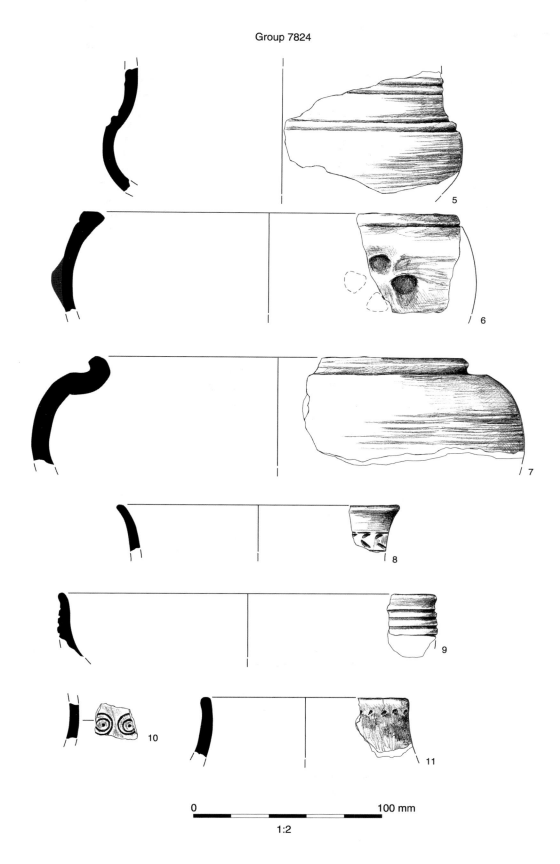

0   100 mm

1:2

Fig. 6.2 Pottery from late Iron Age stone spread 7824

Kimmeridge II (Davies 1936) and Hengistbury Head (Brown 1987). However the Southdown Ridge collection is large and the material sometimes reasonably well-preserved, despite the compromised stratigraphic occurrences in later deposits. Consequently it represents a significant addition to this existing body of material.

The middle Iron Age component is mainly notable for its paucity. This is particularly the case given that middle Iron Age material is extremely well-represented in Dorset generally. Substantial assemblages have been recovered from Gussage All Saints (Wainwright 1979), and from Maiden Castle (Brown in Sharples 2000), situated just 5km to the north of Southdown Ridge. It is also worth noting that a similar hiatus of material of this date was observed in the prehistoric pottery assemblage from Waddon, just north of Weymouth (Brown 2000b). Significant assemblages of LIA-RB transition material have also been recovered widely within Dorset. Key published groups are those from Gussage All Saints

(Wainwright 1979), Hod Hill (Richmond 1968), Maiden Castle (Brown 1991), Poundbury (Green 1986) and Hengistbury Head (Brown 1987). The assemblage from Southdown Ridge is not particularly large but is fairly well preserved and the complete funerary vessels represent an important component of the late Iron Age assemblage.

Illustrated catalogue

Layer 7823 (Fig. 6.1)

1. Carinated bowl with incised diagonal decoration with white inlay in the All Cannings Cross tradition. Fabric FL2. Possibly an import. Ctx 7708. Earliest Iron Age.
2. Carinated bowl with fingernail-impressed decoration. Heavily sooted interior and exterior. Fabrix LI1. Ctx 7708. Earliest-early Iron Age
3. Furrowed bowl fragment. Fabric LI1, Ctx 7708. Earliest Iron Age
4. Carinated bowl with impressed 'dart' decoration. Fabric SH1. Ctx 7708. Early Iron Age

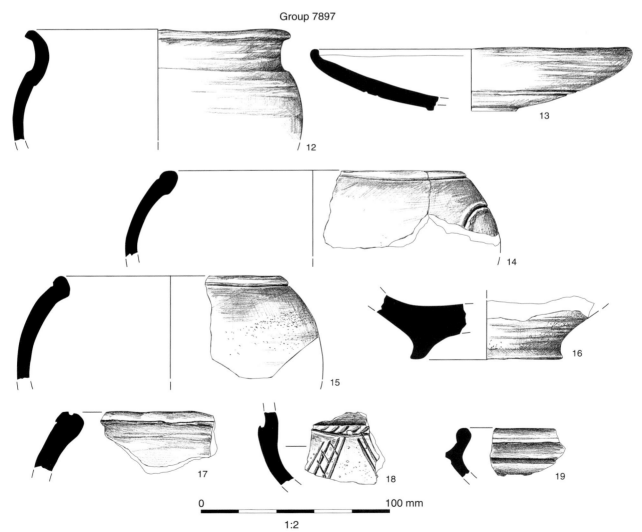

Group 7897

Fig. 6.3 Pottery from late Iron Age layer 7897

Group 7894

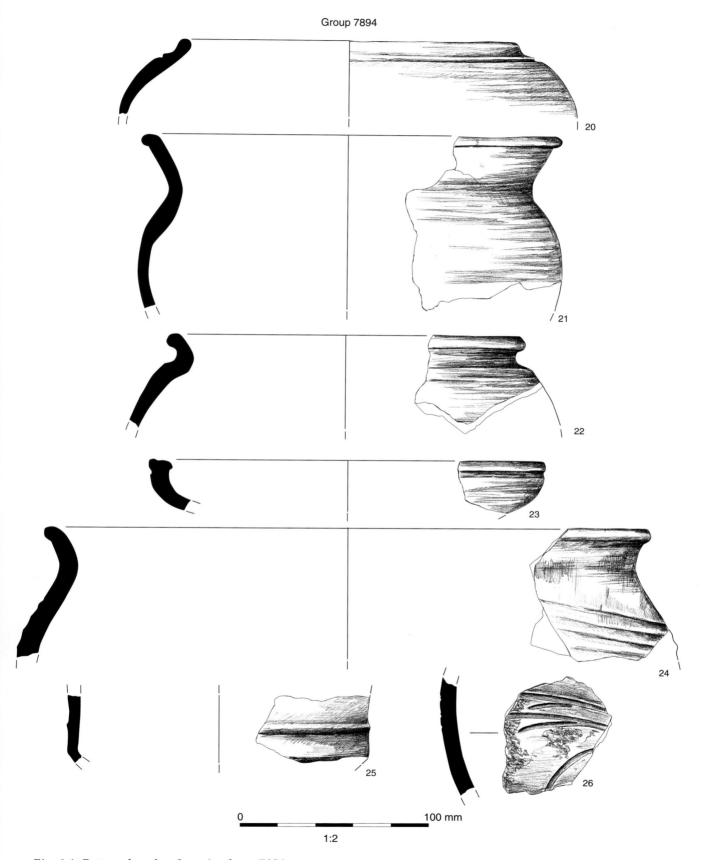

Fig. 6.4 *Pottery from late Iron Age layer 7894*

Group 7002

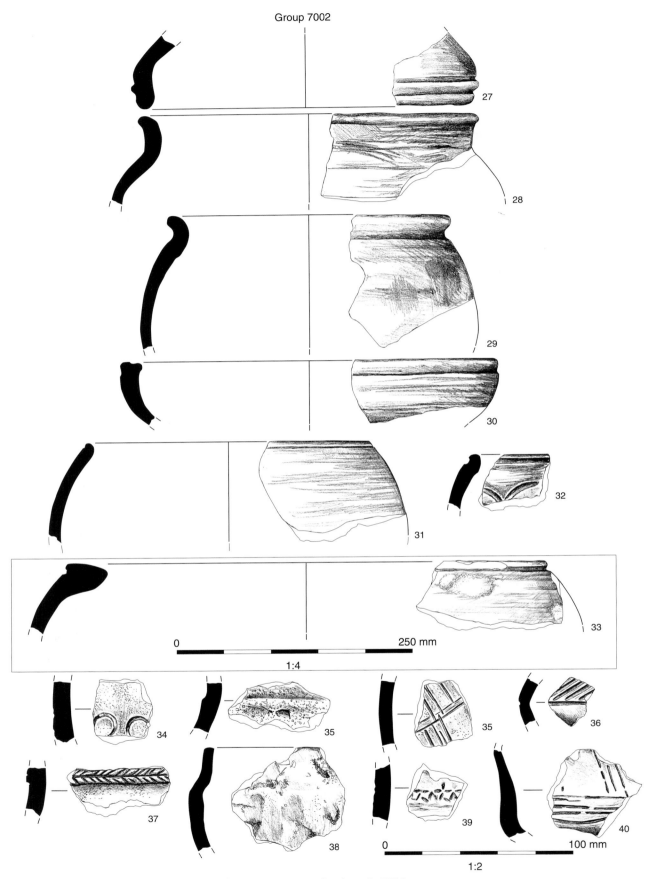

Fig. 6.5 Pottery from late Iron Age-early Roman composite deposit 7002

Group 7002

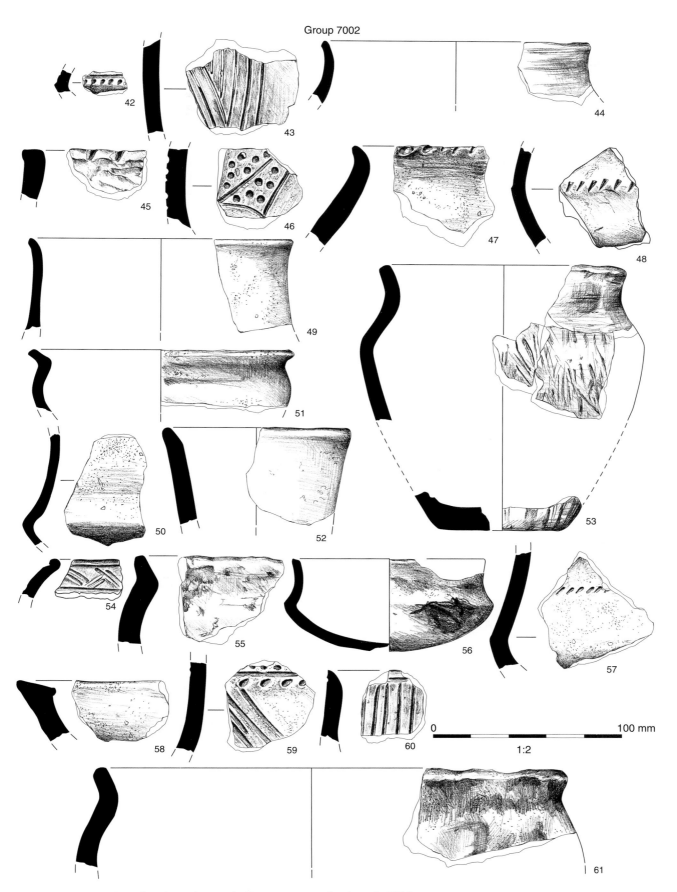

Fig. 6.6 Pottery from late Iron Age-early Roman composite deposit 7002

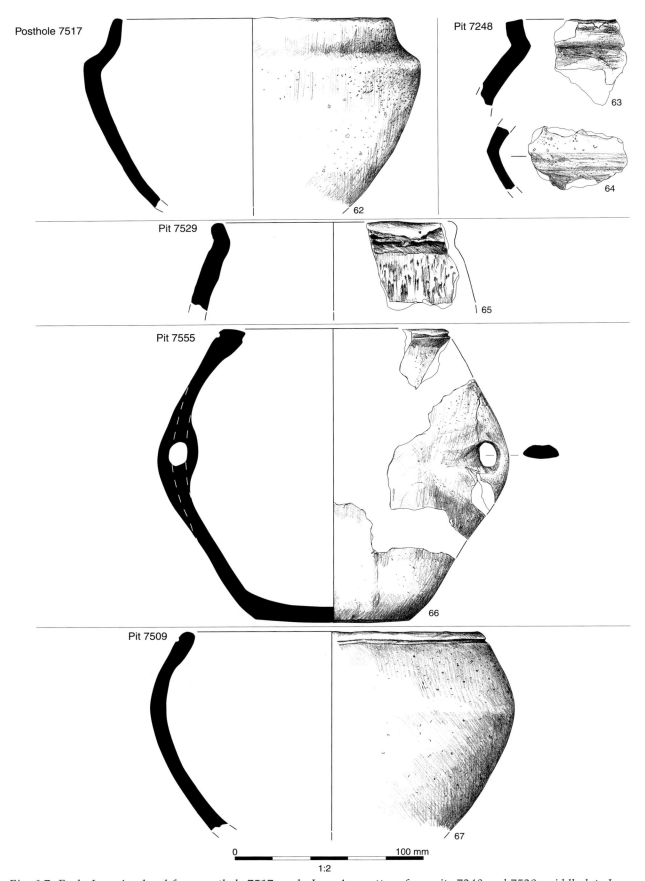

Posthole 7517

Pit 7248

63

64

62

Pit 7529

65

Pit 7555

66

Pit 7509

67

0   100 mm

1:2

Fig. 6.7 Early Iron Age bowl from posthole 7517; early Iron Age pottery from pits 7248 and 7529; middle-late Iron Age pottery from pits 7509 and 7555

Layer 7824 (Fig. 6.2)

5. Cordoned bowl with cordon emphasis at shoulder and neck. Fabric QU1, burnished. Ctx 7829
6. Flat-rimmed bowl with pinched 'flower' decoration. Fabric QU1. Ctx 7829
7. Short-necked jar with high shoulder. Fabric QU1, smoothed. Ctx 7840. Middle-late Iron Age
8. Early Iron Age bowl with impressed 'dart' decoration below rim. Fabric QU2. Ctx 7856. Residual.
9. Furrowed bowl. Fabric FL2. Context 7845. Residual earliest Iron Age
10. Bowl fragment decorated with impressed concentric circles with white inlay in All Cannings Cross tradition. Possible an import. Fabric FL2. Ctx 7856. Residual earliest Iron Age.
11. Early Iron Age bowl with impressed seed decoration below rim. Fabric LI1. Ctx 7845

Layer 7897 (Fig. 6.3)

12. Necked jar. Fabric QU1. Burnished. Ctx 7701/7734
13. Native copy of a terra nigra platter. Fabric QU1, Ctx 7701. Late 1st century BC or later.
14. Bead-rim jar with shallow-tooled arc decoration. Fabric QU1. Context 7701
15. Bead-rim jar or bowl. Fabric QU1, burnished. Ctx 7701
16. Pedestal base. Fabric QU1, burnished. Ctx 7734

17. Bead-rim jar with grooved rim top. Fabric QU1. Ctx 7734.
18. Carinated bowl with incised decoration below and above carination. Fabric CH. Ctx 7734. Residual early Iron Age
19. Shallow bowl with beaded rim and sharply angled shoulder emphasised by a cordon . Fabric QU1, burnished. Corresponds to Hengistbury Head type BD5.2 (Brown 1987, 212); Gussage All Saints (Wainwright 1979, fig. 63, 652). Ctx 7748. 1st century BC/AD

Layer 7894 (Fig. 6.4)

20. High-shouldered jar with moulded bead rim. Fabric QU1, burnished. Ctx 7635/7637
21. Necked jar. Fabric QU1, burnished. Ctx 7635. Late Iron Age
22. Shrt-necked jar. Fabric QU1, burnished. Ctx 7866. Middle-late Iron Age
23. Shallow bowl, reversible as lid, with grooved rim. Fabric QU1, burnished. Hengistbury Head type BC3.42. Ctx 7894. Late Iron Age
24. Necked jar with diagonal grooves on shoulder. Fabric LI1. Ctx 7635. Residual early-middle Iron Age
25. Cordoned bowl /tazza. Fabric QU1, burnished. Hengistbury Head type BD7 (Brown 1987, 212). Ctx 7866. Late Iron Age
26. Jar or bowl sherd decorated with incised arcs. Fabric

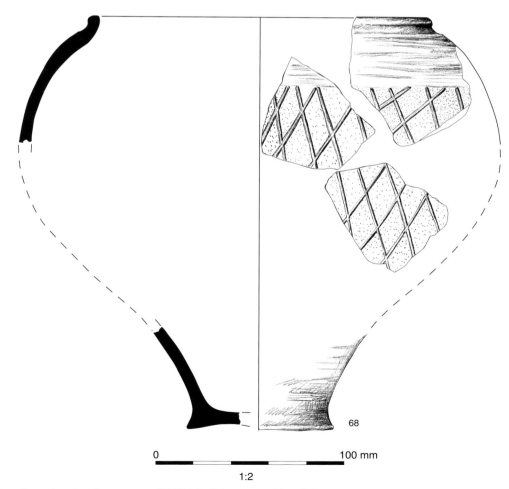

0   100 mm

1:2

Fig. 6.8 Late Iron Age jar from upper fill 7236 of the cross-ridge dyke

QU1. Sooted exterior, limescale interior. Ctx 7866. Late Iron Age

Layer 7002 (Figs 6.5-6.6)

27. Shallow bowl/lid with moulded rim. Fabric QU1, burnished. Ctx 7002. Late Iron Age
28. Necked jar. Fabric QU1, burnished. Ctx 7002. Late Iron Age
29. Short-necked jar. Fabric QU1, smoothed. Ctx 7002. Late Iron Age
30. Shallow bowl/lid with grooved rim. Fabric QU1, burnished. Ctx 7002
31. Bead-rim jar. Fabric QU1, burnished. Ctx 7457. Middle-late Iron Age
32. Bead-rim bowl or jar decorated with incised arcs. Fabric QU1, burnished. Ctx 7436. Middle-late Iron Age
33. Large jar with flartened bead rim. Fabric QU1, smoothed. Ctx 7002. Middle-late Iron Age
34. Sherd decorated with impressed circles with white inlay in All Cannings Cross tradition, but fabric indicates a local copy. Fabric LI1. Ctx 7400. Residual earliest Iron Age
35. Coarse jar with furrow and impressed circles. Heavily abraded . Fabric LI1. Ctx 7400. Residual earliest Iron Age
36. Sherd decorated with incised linear decoration. Fabrix LI1. Ctx 7401. Residual early Iron Age
37. Carinated bowl with incised diagonal lines on upper body. Fabric LI1. Ctx 7002. Residual early Iron Age
38. Bowl sherd with incised linear decoration. Fabric LI1. Ctx 7404. Residual early Iron Age
39. Carinated bowl with upright rim. FabricSH1, roughly smoothed.. Ctx 7404. Residual early Iron Age
40. Fragment of bowl decorated with impressed motif. Fabric LI1. Ctx 7405. Residual early Iron Age
41. Carinated bowl decorated with incised linear decoration. Fabric FL2, smoothed. Ctx 7405. Residual earliest Iron Age
42. Carinated bowl with impressed decoration. Fabric FL2. Ctx 7408. Residual early Iron Age
43. Jar sherd with incised linear decoration with white inlay in All Cannings Cross tradition. Fabric FL2. Ctx 7415. Residual earliest Iron Age
44. Bowl with flaring rim. Fabric LI1, smoothed. Ctx 7419. Residual early Iron Age

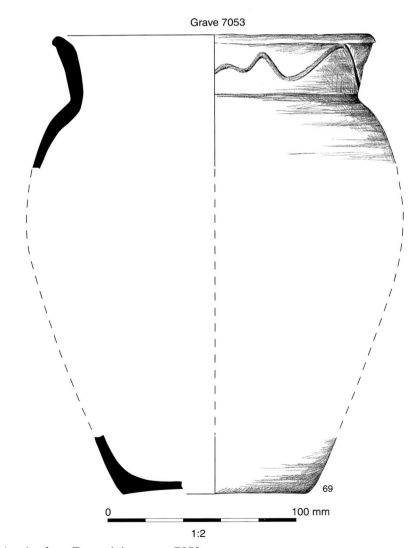

Grave 7053

0   100 mm

1:2

Fig. 6.9 Late Iron Age jar from Durotrigian grave 7053

Grave 7624

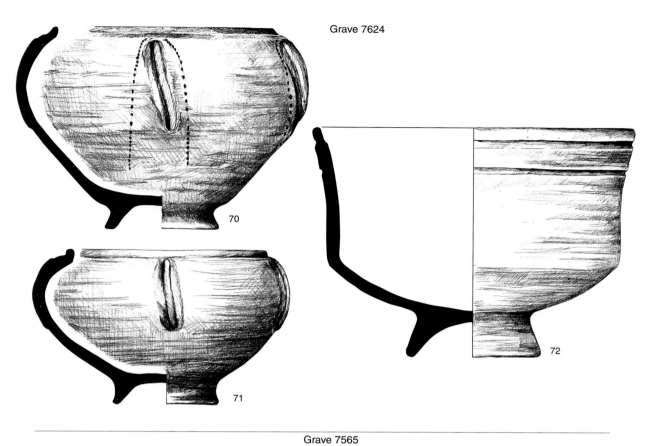

70

71

72

Grave 7565

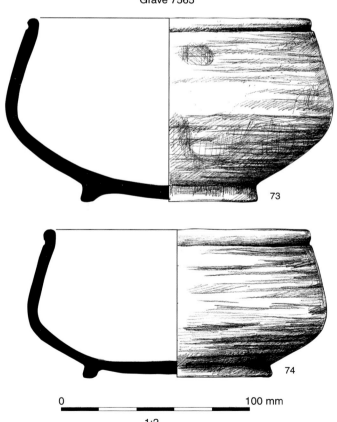

73

74

0   100 mm

1:2

Fig. 6.10 Late Iron Age bowls from Durotrigian graves 7624 an 7565

45. Upright flattened jar rim with fingernail-incised decoration. Fabrix SH1. Ctx 7421. Residual early Iron Age
46. Fragment of jar with impressed and incised decoration in All Cannings Cross tradition. Probably local copy . Fabrix LI1. Ctx 7708/7425/7823. Residual earliest Iron Age
47. Upstanding jar rim with fingernail-impressed decoration. Fabric SH1. Ctx 7425. Residual earliest-early Iron Age
48. Carinated jar or bowl with impressed decoration at angle. Fabric LI1. Ctx 7425. Residual earliest-early Iron Age
49. Bowl with flaring rim. Fabric LI1. Ctx 7433. Residual early Iron Age
50. Carinated bowl. Fabric LI1. Ctx 7436. Residual early Iron Age
51. Bowl with out-turned rim and rounded shoulder. Fabric LI1, smoothed. Ctx 7456. Residual early Iron Age
52. Cup with elongated flaring rim. Fabric QU1. Ctx 7815. Middle-late Iron Age .
53. Shouldered jar with upstanding rim. Fabrix QU2, surface showing pull/smoothing marks. Ctx 7456. Residual early Iron Age
54. Bead-rim bowl with incised chevron decoration. Fabrix QU1. Ctx 7457. Late Iron Age.
55. Jar with slack shoulder and upstanding rim. Fabrix LI1. Ctx 7476. Residual early Iron Age
56. Carinated bowl with flaring rim. Fabric QU3. Ctx 7486. Residual Early Iron Age
57. Carinated bowl or jar, carination emphasised with incised hatched decoration. Fabric LI1. Ctx 7818. Residual earliest-early Iron Age
58. Wide shallow dish with expanded, flattened rim. Resembles Potterne bowl type 11, 9th-8th centuries BC (Lawson 2000, 151, fig. 49, 39). Fabric LI1. Ctx 7814. Residual earliest Iron Age
59. Jar or large bowl with incised and impressed decoration on neck. Fabric LI1. Ctx 7844. Residual early-earliest Iron Age
60. Jar with incised linear decoration in All Cannings Cross style. Fabric FL2. Ctx 7844. Residual earliest Iron Age
61. Slack-shoulded jar with short upstanding rim. Fabric LI1. Ctx 7818. Residual early Iron Age

Posthole 5717 (Fig. 6.7)

62. Large fragment of a carinated bowl with short upright rim. Fabrix LI1. Ctx 7522. Early Iron Age

Pit 7248 (Fig. 6.7)

63. Jar with short, upstanding rim. Fabric LI1. Ctx 7249. Early Iron Age
64. Carinated bowl fragment. Fabrix LI1. Ctx 7249. Early Iron Age

Pit 7529 (Fig. 6.7)

65. Slack profile jar with out-turned rim. Fabric LI1. Extensive sooting on external surface. Ctx 7528. Early Iron Age

Pit 7555 (Fig. 6.7)

66. Lugged jar with flattened bead rim. Fabric QU1. Ctx 7556. Middle-late Iron Age

Pit 7509 (Fig. 6.7)

67. Bead-rim jar. Fabric QU1, smoothed surface. Ctx 7511. Middle-late Iron Age

Cross-ridge dyke (Fig. 6.8)

68. Jar with high, broad rounded shoulder, bead rim and narrow base, decorated with obtuse lattice decoration. Fabric QU1. Ctx 7237 Late Iron Age/early Roman

Grave 7053 (Fig. 6.9)

69. Necked jar with burnished scroll decoration on neck. Fabric QU1. Late Iron Age

Grave 7624 (Fig. 6.10)

70. 'War cemetery' bowl with vertical ribs emphasised by pricking. Fabric QU1, but possibly a Devonian sub-type. For parallels see Maiden Castle (Wheeler 1943, 233, fig. 72, 182) and Exeter Legionary fortress (Holbrook and Bidwell 116, fig. 36, 72), Poundbury (Davies and Hawkes, 1987, 127, fig. 88, 30), Cadbury Castle (Ellison 2000b, 340, fig. 161,1). 1st century BC/AD
71. 'War cemetery' bowl with vertical ribs. Fabric QU1 but possibly a Devonian sub-type. 1st century BC/AD
72. Cordoned, deep open bowl with pedestal foot. Fabric QU1. Similar vessels from Hengistbury Head described as tazze (Brown 1987, 212, Ill. 179, BD7.0). 1st century BC/AD

Grave 7565 (Fig. 6.10)

73. Shallow bead-rim bowl with straight sides and footring base. Fabric QU1. Hengistbury Head form BC3.11 (Brown 1987, 210, Ill.157); Ower Type 102 (Lanceley and Morris 1991, 129, fig. 59, 36); Cadbury Castle Type BC3.2 (Ellison 2000b, 340, fig. 161, 3); very common at Maiden Castle (Wheeler 1943, fig. 72, 171-180). 1st century BC/AD
74. Shallow bead-rim bowl with straight sides and footring base. Fabric QU1. As no. 73. 1st century BC/AD

POST-ROMAN POTTERY *by John Cotter*

Only 308 sherds (6323g) of post-Roman pottery were recovered from Southdown Ridge, most from topsoil and subsoil layers. Most of this group is of post-medieval date (*c* 1600-1925) with one possible late medieval sherd and, generally, ordinary domestic pottery types are represented. Overall the pottery is in a fragmentary condition, although many of the 17th-18th century sherds are quite large and fairly fresh, suggesting nearby occupation at this date. 'Victorian' sherds mixed in with these suggests the earlier post-medieval deposits were disturbed during the 19th and early 20th centuries.

The earliest post-Roman sherd is a medieval-style sagging base probably from a wheel-turned cooking pot in a fine grey fabric similar to the

Donyatt wares. This is probably of 15th or early 16th century date residual in subsoil layer 7006.

The 17th-18th century assemblage is dominated by a good quality pinkish earthenware, usually with an internal olive green, greenish-brown or light brown glaze. The quantity and the range of domestic forms suggest this to be the dominant local earthenware of the area, equivalent to the ubiquitous post-medieval red earthenware tradition found across most of southern England. Dishes and bowls of various sizes are the commonest forms but some small handled bowls (porringers), jars, jugs and a couple of hollow pedestal bases from chafing dishes were also identified, along with a pierced lug handle from costrel (hip flask). A few black or brown glazed sherds may be from globular cups and cylindrical tankards. A pierced base sherd is probably from a dish-like strainer.

In most contexts this plain-glazed ware was associated with a few sherds of slip-decorated earthenware in the same fabric. The distinctive designs on this slipware identify it as Donyatt ware from central Somerset – one of the best known decorative slipware industries of southern England. The similarity of the plainware vessels from this site make it very likely that these are also products of the Donyatt potteries, despite the fact that Weymouth lies *c* 30 miles south-east of Donyatt. This slipware had a wide circulation in south-west England and is fairly common at Exeter and Plymouth in Devon, and Poole, in Dorset.

The plainware is likely to have had a more local distribution but the evidence from this site suggests it was common in the Weymouth area. Although pottery production at Donyatt dates from medieval times, the distinctive post-medieval industry there is dated to the period *c* 1600-1900, with the greatesr output between *c* 1600-1800. A few small sherds of other wares in the assemblage, including imported German Westerwald stoneware and a piece of probable Bristol stoneware, suggest the assemblage of Donyatt wares here could mainly date to *c* 1650-1750.

The Donyatt slipware assemblage comprises only a few dozen sherds, most of them from dishes and a few small bowls or porringers. Some of these have classic Donyatt decoration of closely spaced concentric lines or bands of trailed white slip on the interior, and sometimes sgraffito decoration comprising an incised wavy line cutting through the concentric bands of slip. Some dish rims bear wavy slip lines on the upper flange of the rim while others have slip hoops and pendant crescents. All of these designs can be paralleled in the published corpus of Donyatt slipware (Coleman-Smith *et al.* 1988).

Contemporary, non-Donyatt, wares are rare and include two German Westerwald stoneware sherds and the Bristol stoneware sherd mentioned above, along with two sherds from a single Chinese porcelain dish, probably dating to the later 18th century. The few small Victorian or modern sherds include English porcelain, Staffordshire refined white earthenwares ('Willow pattern') and flowerpots in red terracotta, some of which could be as late as the early 20th century.

The assemblage is of some importance for the study of post-medieval pottery in this part of south-west England as the glazed plainwares appear to be from the same source as the decorated slipwares. Both are probably from the Donyatt potteries located *c* 30 miles north-west of Weymouth in central Somerset. While the presence of Donyatt slipwares is not unexpected in Weymouth, the presence of the plainwares is notable, as their distribution this far afield may not have previously been noted.

FIRED CLAY *by Daniel Stansbie*

A total of 102 fragments (1477g) of fired clay and daub was recovered (Table 6.2). Seven fabric types were identified. Objects were classified where identifiable and thickness recorded. All other material was assigned to one of two categories: structural, deriving from oven superstructures, or wall daub and unidentified. Preservation is moderate to poor and no pieces are complete.

Fabrics

Fabric FC1: Silty clay matrix containing moderate sub-rounded and sub-angular quartz pebbles up to 3mm in size, occasional flint up to 2mm in size and occasional chalk fragments up to 2mm in size.

Fabric FC2: Fine silty clay matrix containing occasional clay pellets <2mm.

Fabric FC3: Silty clay matrix with some organic voids <2mm, containing frequent fossil shell up to 4mm.

Fabric FC4: Silty clay matrix containing frequent elongated voids <2mm.

Fabric FC5: Silty clay matrix with silver mica containing occasional sub-rounded quartz sand <2mm, fossil shell <2mm, chalk fragments up to 9mm, and frequent elongated voids.

Fabric FC6: Silty clay matrix containing frequent sub-angular calcined flint up to 4mm and occasional sub-rounded and sub-angular quartz sand.

Fabric FC7: Silty clay matrix containing occasional sub-rounded and sub-angular quartz <2mm.

Table 6.2 Fired clay by context

Ctx		Ctx Date	Count	Wt (g)	Comments
7034	PH 7015	IA	10	8	Fabric 3 (UNID)
7062	Ditch 7061	modern	1	3	Fabric 7 (UNID)
7397	Ditch 7396	IA	1	15	Fabric 3 (structural)
7399	Ditch 7398 IA	IA	1	14	Fabric 7 (structural)
7406	Layer, group 7002	U/S	2	17	Fabric 4 (structural), fabric 7 (structural)
7413	Layer, group 7002	U/S	1	16	Fabric 7 (structural)
7414	Layer group 7002	U/S	1	17	Fabric 7 (structural 1 wattle impression
7429	Layer group 7002	U/S	2	32	Fabric 3 (structural)
7460	Layer group 7002	U/S	3	110	Fabric 1 (TOB/L frag-thickness 20 mm)
7464	Layer group 7002	U/S	1	28	Fabric 6 spindle whorl? (base dia 40mm top dia 27mm) SF 50
7470	Layer group 7002	U/S	1	16	Fabric 7 (structural)
7472	Layer group 7002	U/S	1	5	Fabric 3 (structural)
7474	Layer group 7002	U/S	1	7	Fabric 1 (structural)
7476	Layer group 7002	U/S	1	5	Fabric 7 (UNID)
7485	Layer group 7002	U/S	3	6	Fabric 3 (UNID), Fabric 7 (UNID)
7486	Layer group 7002	U/S	3	27	Fabric 7 (structural)
7511	Pit 7509	M-LIA	1	32	Fabric 5 (structural?)
7520	Layer	IA	9	19	Fabric 3 (structural/UNID), fabric 7 (UNID)
7527	Pit 7526	EIA	2	3	Fabric 7 (UNID)
7566	Grave 7565	LIA	2	7	Fabric 7 (structural)
7608	Hollow 7607	EIA	1	15	Fabric 5 (structural?)
7615	Rubble layer	M-LIA	2	5	Fabric 7 (UNID)
7618	Stone layer M-LIA	M-LIA	3	8	Fabric 2 (structural)
7623	Grave 7624	LIA	1	8	Fabric 1 (structural)
7734	Stone layer group 7897	M-LIA	2	35	Fabric 3 (structural)
7748	Stone layer group 7897	M-LIA	2	20	Fabric 7 (structural)
7753	Posthole 7752	IA	2	7	Fabric 7
7761	Layer	M-LIA	2	7	Fabric 7 (structural)
7762	Stone layer 7745	EIA	1	27	Fabric 7 (structural)
7764	Stone layer 7745	EIA	1	20	Fabric 3 (fragment of oven plate?)
7769	Pit 7766	EIA	1	13	Fabric 7 (structural)
7771	Rubble layer	MIA-LIA	4	28	Fabric 1 (structural)
7774	Rubble layer	MIA-LIA	1	67	Fabric 1 (structural)
7789	Occupation layer	EIA	1	3	Fabric 3 (structural – poss hearth lining)
7805	Layer group 7002	U/S	3	13	Fabric 7 (structural)
7814	Layer group 7002	U/S	1	13	Fabric 5 (structural)
7816	Layer group 7002	U/S	1	9	Fabric 4 (structural)
7827	Stone surface	M-LIA	1	13	Fabric 5 (structural)
7846	Stone surface 7824	LIA	1	7	Fabric 7 (structural)
7847	Stone surface 7824	LIA	1	3	Fabric 7 (UNID)
7856	Stone surface 7824	LIA	3	31	Fabric 7 (structural)
7857	Stone surface 7824	LIA	1	5	Fabric 3 (UNID)
7865	Layer group 7002	U/S	6	73	Fabric 7 (structural), Fabric 4 (structural)
7866	Stone surface 7894, group 7002	U/S	1	5	Fabric 2 (structural)
7868	Stone surface 7824	LIA	3	26	Fabric 7 (structural)
7875	Stone surface 7824	LIA	1	5	Fabric 3 (structural)
7879	Stone surface	LIA	2	28	Fabric 7 (structural)
7881	Stone surface 7824	LIA	1	533	Fabric 5 (TOB/L frag 69mm thick)
7891	Layer group 7002	U/S	1	8	Fabric 7 (UNID)
7918	Layer	EIA	4	55	Fabric 4 (structural)

Fabric and form

The assemblage is dominated by structural material in fabric 7, most of which probably derives from oven superstructures. This is supplemented by structural material in fabrics 2, 3, 4 and 5. Two fragments of triangular oven bricks or loomweights (TOB/L) from contexts 7460 and 7881 are in fabrics 1 and 5. A spindle whorl from 7464 was made in fabric 6 (SF 50), and a fragment of oven plate from context 7764 in fabric 3.

The fired clay in context

A considerable quantity of the fired clay and/or daub was redeposited, mostly in contexts making up midden-derived deposit 7002, and therefore

0 ————————————— 50 mm

1:1

Fig. 6.11   Fired clay spindle whorl

effectively unstratified. This unstratified group includes fragments of structural clay, an incomplete triangular oven brick/loomweight in fabric 1 and a broken spindle whorl (Fig. 6.11).

Structural clay fragments were also incorporated in late Iron Age stone surfaces 7824 and 7897. This material was also probably residual, as was a second triangular oven brick or loomweight from surface 7824. The small fragments of structural clay found in the fills of graves 7565 and 7624, and ditches 7396 and 7398 were clearly also redeposited.

Only a very small quantity was more reliably associated with phased settlement features and deposits. Doorpost 7766 of circular structure 7668 produced a small fragment of structural clay, and an occupation deposit (7789) associated with this structure yielded a more distinctive, highly fired fragment that may have come from a hearth lining (see Keys). A 20g fragment of fired clay, possibly part of an oven plate, came from the external yard area (7742). A very small piece

of structural daub was found in pit 7509, associated with a middle-late Iron Age jar fragment.

GLASS AND METALWORK *by Ian Scott*

Assemblage composition

Four glass beads were recovered, three as grave goods from a single inhumation burial, the other from redeposited midden layer 7002. The metalwork assemblage numbered 289 iron objects, many of them nails and hobnails from burials, and 21 non-ferrous objects..

Finds from inhumation burials

One of the Late Iron Age graves (7104) produced glass beads and another (7017) a copper alloy brooch. Three coffined Romano-British graves (7378, 7523 and 7941) produced most of the ironwork from the site (Table 6.3).

Nails

Grave 7378 produced 30 nails, 112 hobnails and piece of iron rod or thick wire, and six pieces of mineralised wood. Eight of the nails, are complete and measured 42mm-75mm. Grave 7523 yielded 76 hobnails and 21 nails, of which the 12 complete examples measured 42mm-78mm. Grave 7942 contained 14 nails, and only one complete example 57mm long. The presence of substantial numbers of hobnails in graves 7378 and 7523 indicates that nailed footwear was buried with the deceased, but nailing patterns were not recorded. Table 6.4 shows the lengths of complete nails from inhumation burials.

Beads

The burial (7105) in grave 7104 was accompanied by three small wound annular glass beads in cobalt blue (Chapter 5, Fig. 5.34), all found in fill 7131.

Table 6.3   Summary of small finds from inhumation burials

Grave	Contexts	Glass bead	hobnails	nails	Iron rod or wire	wood fragts	Total	Totals
7104	7131	3						3
	7379				1		1	1
7378	7380		4	27		6	37	37
	7381		108	3			111	111
7523	7525		76	21			97	97
7941	7942			14			14	14
	Totals	3	188	65	1	6	260	263

Table 6.4 Summary of lengths for complete nails from inhumation burials

Context	Length (mm)	Count	Median value	Av. length	Range
Grave 7378					
7380	42	1			
	50	1			
	60	1			
	62	1	63mm	61.13mm	33mm
	64	1			
	66	1			
	70	1			
	75	1			
	incomplete	19	n/a		
	Count	27			
7381	incomplete	3	n/a		
	Count	3			
Grave 7523					
7525	42	1			
	49	1			
	50	1			
	53	1			
	55	2	58.5mm	58.66mm	36mm
	62	2			
	63	1			
	65	1			
	70	1			
	78	1			
	incomplete	9	n/a		
	Count	21			
Grave 7941					
7942	57	1			
	0	13	n/a		
	Count	14			

They belong to Guido's group 6 (ivb) (Guido 1978, 66-7, pl. ii, no. 11), although two examples are close to Group 7 (iv) globular blue beads (ibid., 69-70). Guido argues that beads of Group 6 (ivb) were first imported as early as the 6th century BC, and that they continued in use throughout the Iron Age (ibid, 66). Beads of Group 7 (iv) were also in use over a long period. The distribution of the beads of Groups 6 and 7 illustrated by Guido in 1978 shows a marked concentration in the south of Britain centring on Dorset and Somerset, with some examples in the southern Welsh Marches (Guido 1978, fig. 22).

See Chapter 5, Fig. 5.3 (left to right):

1. Annular glass bead. Undecorated wound bead in cobalt blue metal. D: 6mm; Ht/Th: 2mm. Sample <16> [Inv No 412]

2. Annular glass bead. Undecorated wound bead in cobalt blue metal. D: 5.6mm x 6.5mm; Ht/Th: 3.3mm. Sample <17> [Inv No 410]

3. Annular glass bead. Undecorated wound bead in cobalt blue metal. D: 7mm x 6.5mm; Ht/Th: 3.5mm. Sample <16> [Inv No 411]

Other finds

The finds from non burial contexts are 21 non-ferrous metal objects, 29 iron objects (30 fragts) and 2 pieces of glass including a sherd from a 19th-century bottle. The non-ferrous metal finds comprise 20 copper alloy objects and small fragment of a ring of thin wire, possibly silver (context 7395, Sf 74). The iron objects were almost exclusively nails but two small 20th-century iron artillery shells with lead driving bands were found, one in the topsoil (7000), the other in deposit 7002 (ctx 7008), a possible horseshoe fragment from layer 7002 (context 7405), and an awl from topsoil 7001.

The more interesting finds include fragments of a late Bronze Age socketed axe from layer 7742 (Sf 127, Cat. No. 4; see Northover, below), and a Roman glass bead (ctx 7815, Sf 97, Cat. No. 6) and copper alloy Iron Age coin (ctx 7487, Sf 61, Cat. No. 5), both from redeposited midden layer 7002. One of two Nauheim Derivative brooches of mid 1st-century date may have been a grave good (Sf 2), as it was found in the disturbed fill (7039) of grave 7017, the other from midden deposit 7002 (ctx 7815, Sf 95). The two brooches have narrow flat bows with a central groove (Cat. Nos 7-8). Midden deposit 7002 also produced a hinged pin from a brooch (ctx 7457, Sf 34) and a small plain penannular armlet (ctx 7815, Sf 95, Cat. No. 9). The head of a hair pin (Sf 115, Cat. No 10) was recovered from a stone surface 7860 within late Iron Age building complex 7970, and a plain pin or hair pin (Sf 20, Cat. No. 11) came from midden deposit 7002 (ctx 7430). The other copper alloy items are undateable fragments.

Illustrated catalogue (Fig. 6.12)

Socketed axe (see Chapter 5, Fig. 5.9). The axe is in four pieces that do not quite fit together, it is unfinished and the loop is blocked. L: 96mm. Yard surface 7742, Sf 127. [Inv No 384]. (See Northover below).

1. Uninscribed South-Western struck 'Bronze'. D: 28mm x 27mm. Wt: c 3.6g. Deposit 7002 (ctx 7487), Sf 61. [Inv No.387]. This coin is one of the South-Western series of uninscribed struck 'Bronzes' that start about the middle of the 1st century BC, and seem to continue in use into the 1st century AD, and possibly into the Roman period (Cf. Hobbs 1996, 158-59, esp. pl. 88, nos 2792 & 2794).

2. Globular glass bead. Dark blue, with dirty white almost circular inset. Wound marvered bead, incomplete. D: 11mm; Th: 8mm. Deposit 7002 (tx 7815), Sf 97. [Inv No. 413]. A small Iron Age 'Eye' bead (Class III: Guido 1978, 49-50) which dates from between the 1st century BC and the 3rd century AD.

3. Small plain penannular bracelet of oval cross section with tapered plain terminals. Possibly a child's bracelet? Cu alloy. D: 44mm x 40mm. Deposit 7002 (ctx 7815), Sf 94. [Inv No 393]. This belongs to Cool's Group V of plain penannular bracelets (Cool 1983, 139-40), which seem to occur in contexts ranging in date from the 1st to the 4th century in Britain (ibid., table 5.4). There is a possibility that there are Iron Age examples from Dorset (ibid. 139).

4. Simple sprung wire brooch with narrow flat section tapered bow with central groove and chevron pattern in the groove. Sprung pin with internal chord, part of spring survives. Plain catchplate. Nauheim Derivative. Cu alloy. L: 47mm. Deposit 7002 (ctx 7815), Sf 95. [Inv No 394]. Nauheim derivatives of this form date to the mid 1st-century and their distribution is very much limited to Sussex, Hampshire and Somerset, with few found outside this area.

5. Simple sprung wire brooch with flat tapered bow with grooves. Spring with internal chord. Catch plate largely missing, detached pin survives. Poorly preserved. Nauheim Derivative. Cu alloy. L: 54mm. Grave 7017 (ctx 7039), Sf 2. [Inv No 377]. Similar to no. 4 above.

6. Possible hairpin head, poorly preserved. Decorated head with broad flat circular top, stepped moulding to the stem. Cu alloy. L: 17mm; D: 10mm. Stone spread 7680. Sf 115. [Inv No 396]. Very little of the stem survives. The head may have been recessed on top to take enamel. If this is a hairpin it is most likely to be related to Cool's Group 21 with hollow spherical heads often with evidence of glass or enamel settings in the hollow top. The identification of this pin is uncertain, but if it is related the Cool's Group 21 it may date to 1st or 2nd century (Cool 1990, 170, fig. 11, nos 8-9).

7. Tapering pin, undecorated, with slightly expanded head. Possibly hairpin. Cu alloy. L: 87mm. Deposit 7002 (ctx 7430), Sf 20. [Inv No 381]. This pin fall within Cool's Group 24 of simple pins, which may been used throughout the period of the Roman occupation (Cool 1990, 170, fig. 12, no 7).

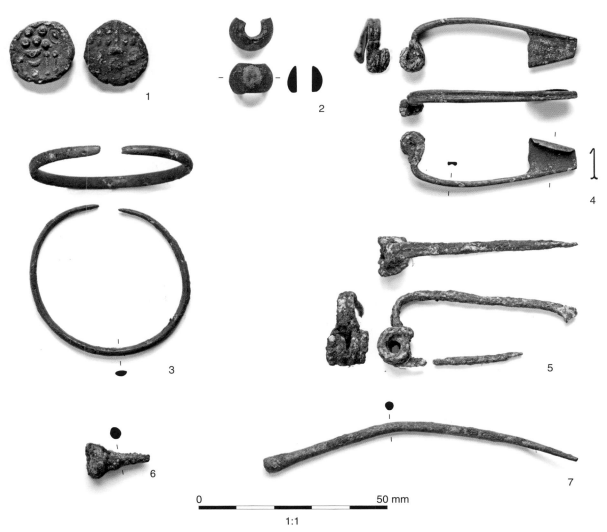

0   50 mm

1:1

Fig. 6.12 Glass bead and copper alloy metalwork

Not illustrated

> Brooch pin fragment. Cu alloy. L extant: 16mm. Ditch 7394 (ctx 7395), Sf 27. [Inv No 378].
>
> Hinged brooch pin, pierced with hole for the pivot. Cu alloy. L: 45mm. Deposit 7002 (ctx 7457) Sf 34. [Inv No 385]
>
> Possible brooch pin fragment, comprising slightly curved thin wire flattened at one end. Cu alloy. L extant: 22mm. Deposit 7002 (ctx 7805) Sf 93. [Inv No 392]

Description of a Fragmentary Socketed Axe
by Peter Northover

The axe (Sf 127; Inv. No 384) referred to above (see Scott, above; Chapter 5, Fig. 5.9) is fragmentary and incomplete. The axe is heavily corroded with thick, light blue-green corrosion products and some earthy encrustation. The overall length is, at a minimum, 96mm and the socket measures 33x33mm. The largest section is the complete upper section of the body with mouth and loop. The cross-section is approximately hexagonal with a single rounded mouth moulding, with the loop set just above it. The corroded state of the axe makes certainty impossible but the loop appears not to have been unblocked when the axe was removed from the mould. There is a prominent line of flash down the centre of each side and also some flash around the mouth, with at least one scar where the sprue was removed. There are traces of a ridge along each angle of the face. One large and many smaller fragments survive from the lower part of the body. The walls are very thin and there is very little depth of metal behind the cutting edge, which appears to be unworked and unexpanded.

A single small fragment, labelled #R4685, was hot-mounted in carbon-filled thermosetting resin, ground and polished to a μm diamond finish. The sample was examined under a metallographic microscope in both as-polished and etched states; the etch used was an acidified aqueous solution of ferric chloride further diluted with ethanol. The structure revealed was an as-cast unleaded or low lead high tin bronze with about 15-18%. The bronze was deeply penetrated by dendritic corrosion with removal of the α phase. The structure is typical for axes of this type and date which are left in the as-cast condition.

The axe falls into the class of linear faceted, non-utilitarian axes of the Llyn Fawr period, the last phase of the Bronze Age in Britain, and broadly contemporary with Hallstatt C on the continent. They have been discussed by O'Connor (1980; 2007) and are shown to have a relatively restricted distribution from Wessex into East Anglia. More recently they have been studied in detail in as yet mostly unpublished research by Boughton (eg Boughton

2013). Specific to the Dorset area are axes with an even higher tin content than that seen here, and with rib-and-pellet decoration, as in the very large Langton Matravers hoard (Roberts *et al.*, forthcoming), and in smaller hoards, for example, from The Verne, Portland and Eggardon (Pearce 1984). The high tin content of many of these axes can give them a corrosion resistent silvery grey surface. These axes may form part of a British tradition of non-utilitarian axes analogous to the Armorican socketed axes across the Channel.

The Southdown Ridge axe has a simpler design and a lower tin content, but the thin casting and the untreated cutting edge with minimal metal behind does put this axe in this category. It may be relatively early in the Llyn Fawr period as it does retain features of more practical tools, such as the Meldreth socketed axes, which can have a moderately elevated tin content.

WORKED BONE
by Leigh Allen (species identification by Lena Strid)

A total of 26 worked bone and three worked antler objects were recovered from the Southdown Ridge excavations. The assemblage is in generally poor condition, with few complete objects, and a majority of pieces surviving only as small fragments. The collection includes tools, points, handles and unidentified fragments displaying some degree of working (Fig. 6.13). The objects are probably all of Iron Age date but most are unstratified as they were recovered from the post-abandonment midden deposit (7002) that covered the settlement.

Methodology

The assemblage was examined and species identified where possible. Objects were categorised using a range of standard reference reports on Iron Age and Roman worked bone. The identifications together with other basic details, including context information, dimensions and a description, were recorded on the finds database, available in archive.

Summary

The range of identifiable objects is fairly limited. The tools include gouges, an awl, a possible scraper and various miscellaneous points possibly from needles. There are also fragmentary remains of handles, possibly from knives. The range includes objects that would have been used for spinning, weaving and the preparation of skins. Several small crude unfinished items suggest on-site working of bone and some pieces appear to have been deliberately split and hollowed for marrow extraction.

All of the objects recovered from Southdown Ridge, apart from Fig. 6.13, no. 2, can be paralleled in the larger assemblages from major Iron Age sites such as Maiden Castle (Wheeler 1943), Dorset, Battlesbury, Wiltshire (Ellis and Powell 2008), and Danebury in Hampshire (Cunliffe 1984).

Illustrated catalogue (Fig. 6.13)

1. Tool, large mammal long bone, incomplete. Long bone split longitudinally, only one edge and the functional end of the tool extant. The surviving edge is worn smooth and flat by wear. The functional end is heavily worn to the extent that it has created a concave wedge shaped working end, and is smooth and highly polished on the inside and outside, ideal for use as a scraping tool, perhaps for cleaning hides. L: 135mm. Deposit 7002 (ctx 7472).
2. Worked object, large mammal long bone, incomplete. A hexagonal sided object cut from a section of long bone. The function is uncertain and no precise parallels have been identified. The bone is hollowed out and cut straight at both ends, a square panel has been removed from the middle of one side and cut marks are visible in the section. L: 52mm. Sf 101. Soil layer 7890 below late Iron Age stone spread 7824.
3. Gouge, sheep/goat tibia, incomplete. Highly polished. The shaft has been hollowed and the proximal end, which forms the butt, has been cut and smoothed. The distal end tapers and has an oblique diagonal cut across the shaft in a longitudinal direction, which exposes the medullary canal, the very tip has broken off. L: 92mm. Middle-late Iron Age pit 7555 (fill 7556).

4. Awl, sheep/goat tibia, complete. Fashioned from the distal end of a sheep/goat tibia. The butt end is complete and unworked, the shaft has been has been cut and shaped to form a slender point. L: 67mm. Sf 109. Inserted between the stones of late Iron Age field wall 7899.

Not illustrated

Gouge

5. Gouge (?), incomplete. Section cut from a large mammal long bone. The cylinder is hollowed out and the butt end cut straight and smoothed. The functioning end is cut obliquely across the shaft in a longitudinal direction exposing the medullary canal. This exposed surface, and presumably the tip had it survived, is worn absolutely flat. L: 102mm. Sf 106, Circular structure 7668, fill 7736 of recessed floor 7735.

Points

6. Point, species unident., incomplete. Broken point, shaft missing. Probably from a gouge, the point tapers to a sharp tip and is polished all over. It has been cut obliquely across the shaft in a longitudinal direction exposing the medullary canal. L: 56mm. Inserted between the stones of late Iron Age field wall 7899.
7. Point, large mammal long bone, complete. A splinter from a large mammal long bone that has been crudely fashioned into a point at each end. L: 65mm. Layer 7900, just below deposit 7002.
8. Point, large mammal long bone, complete. A splinter from a large mammal long bone that has

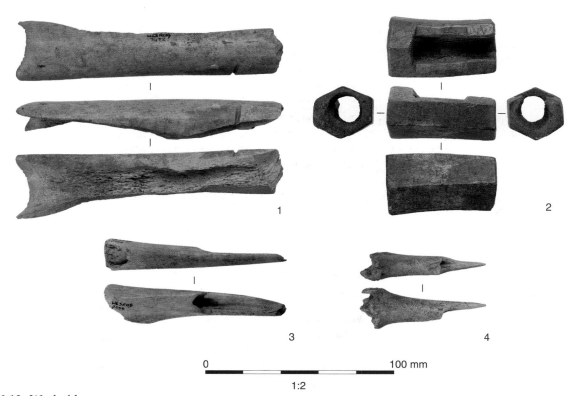

Fig. 6.13 Worked bone

been roughly cut to form a point at each end. The object has a flat back and has not been smoothed or polished. L: 70mm. Sf 72. Deposit 7002 (ctx 7484).

9. Point fragment, species unknown, incomplete. The slender pointed tip from the shaft of a pin or needle. L:28mm. Sf 122, Hollow 7923 (ctx 7924) associated with early Iron Age enclosure 7675.

10. Pin fragment, species unknown, incomplete. A cylindrical fragment from the shaft of a pin. L: 22mm. Early Iron Age stone surface 7823 (ctx 7722).

11. Point, species unident., incomplete. A crude point, fashioned from a quadrant of a long bone tapering towards the tip. L: 28mm. Late Iron Age stone spread 7824 (ctx 7857).

12. Point, antler tine, incomplete. Antler tine that shows evidence of removal on the outside and there is a v-shaped groove cut across the tine towards the tip. L:120mm. Sf 12. Deposit 7002 (ctx 7406).

13. Point, antler tine, incomplete. The upper end of an antler tine, smoothed and highly polished at the tip (although this may be natural) at the base there are traces of a cut and smoothing of the edge. L: 74mm. Sf 17, Deposit 7002 (ctx7425).

Handles

14. Handle ?, horse lateral metapodial, incomplete. Possible handle fashioned from the distal/proximal end of a horse metapodial, the butt end has been shaped and is heavily polished through wear. 55mm. Early Iron Age occupation layer 7745 below stone spread 7823.

15. Handle ?, large mammal long bone, incomplete. Fragment cut from a large mammal long bone, butt end is flat smooth and polished through wear. L: 40mm Deposit 7002 (ctx 7428).

16. Handle, large mammal long bone, incomplete. Section from a large mammal long bone hollowed out and cut straight at the base, the upper edge is broken, the fragment is also broken longitudinally. The surviving fragment is polished and decorated with deeply incised grooves in a chervon pattern. L:46mm. Sf 5. Deposit 7002

Worked fragments

17. Worked fragment, pig tibia, incomplete. A fragment from the distal end of a pig tibia that has hollowed out and is highly polished. The upper edge has been cut and smoothed and there is evidence of a circular perforation through the shaft in the broken edge. L: 48mm. Deposit 7002 (ctx 7436).

18-20. Three perforated bones, two cattle metatarsal and a cattle metacarpal, all incomplete. Fragments from three long bones with longitudinal perforations, possibly to extract marrow.
L: 68mm. Middle-late Iron Age layer 7700.
L: 55mm. Early Iron Age trampled occupation layer 7728.
L: 141mm. Late Iron Age layer 7900.

21. Worked fragment, large mammal long bone, incomplete. Cylindrical section cut from the shaft of a large mammal long bone. The cylinder has been hollowed out and the upper edge has been smoothed and rounded, there is a small circular perforation through the bone. L: 38mm. Early Iron Age posthole 7298 (7299)

22. Worked fragment, horse metatarsal, incomplete. An incomplete horse metatarsal showing evidence of wear, in the form of light polish and striations, running along the length of the shaft. L: 130mm. Late Iron Age stone spread 7896 (ctx 7746), part of 7824.

23. Worked fragment, species unidentified, incomplete. Roughly cylindrical fragment, crudely worked and broken at both ends, possibly from the shaft of a pin. L:30mm Deposit 7002 (ctx 7474).

24. Worked fragment, horse tibia, incomplete. A section from the distal end of a horse tibia with evidence of working. A wide groove has been crudely hacked away at the metaphysis, perhaps in an attempt to remove the distal end, leaving the shank for further work. L: 96mm. Stone spread 7824 (ctx 7881).

25. Worked fragment, antler, incomplete. Fragment of antler cut straight at the base, the sides polished through wear. Possibly a handle. Sf 114. Doorpost 7609 of earliest Iron Age circular structure 7668 (ctx 7610).

26. Worked fragment, large mammal long bone, incomplete. A fragment possibly from a cattle ulna that has been smoothed and polished, the surviving end is rounded and has a small v-shaped notch in it. L:77mm. Deposit 7002 (ctx 7424).

27. Worked fragment, large mammal long bone, incomplete. A small fragment of bone that has been fashioned into a point, smoothed and polished, the tip is missing. L: 33mm. Stone spread 7824 (ctx 7875).

28. Worked fragment, species unidentified, incomplete. Fragment of thin sheet rounded at one end and with a small perforation drilled from both sides. L:24mm. Sf 58. Deposit 7002 (ctx 7474).

29. Bone strip, species unidentified, incomplete. Very slender rectangular section, ands a small circular perforation at one end. L:37mm. Early Iron Age stone surface 7823 (ctx 7722).

WORKED FLINT AND BURNT UNWORKED FLINT *by Michael Donnelly*

Introduction

The excavations at Southdown Ridge produced 423 pieces of flint alongside many natural fragments and 23 (217g) pieces of burnt unworked flint. This material was a mixture of flint from chalk and gravel sources, Portland chert of various qualities, Greensand chert and some other cherts. The assemblage was very unusual in that it included unequivocal Iron Age flints related to shale-working. Unfortunately, as is so often the case with later prehistoric assemblages, there was a high degree of earlier contamination, and some of the pieces attributed to either phase of knapping activity will be incorrectly placed. This is particularly true of less diagnostic components such as preparation and trimming flakes. The fact that shale-working industries often include blade and blade-like forms also has dating implications (Cox and Woodward 1987).

Methodology

The artefacts were catalogued according to OA South's standard system of broad artefact/debitage type (Bradley 1999). General condition was noted and dating was attempted where possible. Unworked burnt flint was quantified by weight and number. The assemblage was recorded directly onto an Open Office (Calc) spreadsheet. During the initial analysis, additional information on condition (rolled, abraded, fresh and degree of cortication), and state of the artefact (burnt, broken, or visibly utilised) was also recorded. Retouched pieces were classified according to standard morphological descriptions (eg Bamford 1985, 72-77; Healy 1988, 48-9; Bradley 1999). Metrical and technological attribute analysis was undertaken and included the recording of butt type (Inizan *et al.* 1993), termination type, flake type (Harding 1990), hammer mode (Onhuma and Bergman 1982), and the presence of platform edge abrasion and dorsal blade scars. Metrical analysis was undertaken using standard methods for recording length, breadth and thickness (Saville 1980). No attempt was made to refit material.

Table 6.5 The flint assemblage

CATEGORY TYPE	Earlier prehistoric	Iron Age	Total
Flake	57	183	240
Blade	11	1	12
Bladelet	8		8
Blade-like	12	5	17
Irregular waste	4	41	45
Chip			
Sieved chips 10-4mm	15	3	18
Sieved chips 4-2mm			
Rejuvenation flake core face/edge	1		1
Core tablet	1		1
Core other blade	1		1
Core single platform flake	1		1
Core multi platform flake	1	5	6
Core on a flake	1	3	4
Core tested module		2	2
Scraper end	2	7	9
Scraper side	2	1	3
Scraper end & side	1		1
Scraper other		2	2
Lathe tool		26	26
Awl		2	2
Spurred piece		2	2
Denticulate		5	5
Burin	1		1
Microdenticulate/serrated flake	1		1
Retouch other		3	3
Retouched flake	4	8	12
Total	124	299	423
Flint	89/124 (71.78%)	158/299 (52.84%)	247/423 (58.39%)
Portland chert	33/124 (26.61%)	129/299 (43.14%)	162/423 (38.30%)
Greensand chert	2/124 (1.61%)	8/299 (2.68%)	10/423 (2.36%)
Other chert		3/299 (1.00%)	3/423 (0.71%)
Burnt unworked flint no./g	?	?	23/217g
No. burnt (exc. chips) (%)	8/124 (6.45%)	32/299 (10.70%)	40/423 (9.46%)
No. broken (exc. chips) (%)	39/124 (31.45%)	78/299 (26.09%)	117/423 (27.66%)
No. retouched (exc. chips) (%)	11/124 (8.87%)	56/299 (18.73%)	67/423 (15.84%)

The Relief Road assemblage

The Southdown Ridge assemblage is quantified in Table 6.5. Most of the 423 pieces originated from occupation or post-abandonment layers in the Iron Age settlement site associated with numerous burials, and more importantly, shale-working. The site also yielded numerous earlier pieces dating from the Mesolithic to the Bronze Age. These were moderately numerous but did not reach the very high levels of residual material encountered along the Ridgeway Hill section of the Relief Road scheme, where individual quarry pits and the mass burial pit (probably a re-used quarry) matched the early prehistoric assemblage from here.

The assemblage taken as a whole was flake-based but with a significant blade component (37 blade-forms to 242 flakes, blade index 13.36%). The earlier component of the assemblage was clearly biased towards blades (35.23%, in large part due to these pieces being far more diagnostic than flakes). The assemblage also has very high levels of breakage at 27.66% (compared to 14.07% for the Ridgeway Hill assemblage), probably due to various factors, including the high levels of residual material (29.31%) and the uncompromising nature of the burial environment, with numerous stone built structures and many stony layers. Perhaps though, the main contributor to the levels of breakage is the lathe tool industry that favoured transversely and laterally snapped flake segments as blanks for its main tool type.

Early prehistoric assemblage

The collection of residual material was mostly fashioned from flint, was blade-based and dates mostly to the Mesolithic or early Neolithic periods. Elsewhere along the scheme, high incidences of blades and blade tools were found in later Neolithic features, but this was largely due to the production of microdenticulates. Southdown Ridge produced only a single example. Patterns in blank morphology are a very good indicator of period and here, the moderately high incidence of narrow pieces and less broad examples than most other Relief Road assemblages (Table 6.6) suggests a mix of ages in the residual material. This is to some extent borne out by late Neolithic-early Bronze Age characteristics, such as faceted platforms, small regular flakes, edge abrasion and an invasively flaked end scraper.

Evidence of blade reduction is further highlighted by a cubic blade-core and a core tablet, while the remaining cores placed in this period exhibit careful platform maintenance. The assemblage includes some well-made end-of-blade and side scrapers on elongated pieces, but a judgement has been made regarding the proficiency of manufacture alongside levels of patination and edge damage to place these objects here. Given the fact that scraper tools and blade forms often form part of a shale working assemblage, a counter argument could also be made that these date to the Iron Age. Other tools include a burin and some thin, regular retouched flakes. Other than retouched flakes, which are fairly ubiquitous, the main tool types associated with the Iron Age assemblage are absent

Table 6.6 Flake morphology Weymouth Relief Road Assemblages

Site / Group	Number	<0.5	%	0.5-1.0	%	1.1-1.5	%	1.5-2.0	%	2.1-2.5	%	2.5>	%
			Broad				Medium				Narrow		
Southdown Ridge	72	1	1.39	16	22.22	20	27.78	18	25	12	16.67	5	6.94
Early prehistory residual	Merged	17	23.61			38	52.78			17	23.61		
Ridgeway Relief Road	317	2	0.63	52	16.40	103	32.49	74	23.34	50	15.77	36	11.36
Early Neolithic pit	Merged	54	17.03			177	55.84			86	27.13		
Ridgeway Relief Road	463	8	1.73	103	22.25	148	31.97	124	28.78	43	9.29	37	7.99
Later Neolithic pits	Merged	11	23.97			272	58.75			80	17.28		
Ridgeway Relief Road	289	2	0.69	71	26.39	115	39.79	54	18.69	28	9.69	19	6.57
Residual groups	Merged	73	25.26			169	58.48			47	16.26		
Ridgeway Relief Road	315	2	0.63	113	35.88	117	37.14	66	20.95	11	3.49	6	1.91
Bronze Age ring ditches	Merged	115	36.51			183	58.09			17	5.4		
Southdown Ridge	191	5	2.62	90	47.12	61	31.94	24	12.57	5	2.62	6	3.14
Iron Age shale-working	Merged	95	49.84			85	44.51			11	5.76		

here and, as will be seen later, the Iron Age examples are far cruder and thicker in nature.

The low levels of early prehistoric material clearly merits discussion. This extensive excavation yielded only as much residual material as Roman quarry pit 3110 and Viking mass burial pit 3358 along the Ridgeway Hill section of the scheme, and two more quarry pits produced similar amounts. It seems that while the Ridgeway section of the relief road ran through an area covered in flint knapping activity, and also probably areas where tools were used and maintained, the Southdown Ridge site, and particularly the Iron Age settlement, saw a markedly lower intensity of activity during these earlier periods. The lack of early features supports this lower intensity, but the area was still visited at least intermittently over many centuries. The obvious reason for a lower level of activity here during early prehistory is that the Ridgeway, around 2km distant, not only served as major route-way but also provided a source for flint. But the addition of other sources of material, in particular Portland chert, complicates the issue and the disparity in intensity may have a far deeper cause, one that may have led to the rich burial and ceremonial landscape along the Ridgeway that we can still see today.

Iron Age assemblage

There is a clear shift between the dominance of flint in the earlier assemblage and a more even split between flint and Portland chert in the shale-working collection. The presence of Greensand chert in the later assemblage is anomalous, and it may be that these pieces are also residual, but since they lack early prehistoric diagnostic attributes placing them there would simply be reinforcing a bias. No shale-working tools were fashioned from Greensand chert but one flake did display lateral edge damage similar to these hafted tools.

This component of the assemblage is dominated by flakes (97.42%), which are often thick (10.26mm compared to 6.77mm for the EPH assemblage) and usually hard-hammer struck (58.10%). The platforms display a lack of abrasion or other forms of preparation and the pieces often display prominent platform spurs. Cores tended to be worked unsystematically and most are small (average 75.6g), although one massive example (393g) skewed these figures greatly, with the remainder averaging just 40.3g. All the cores are related to flake reduction with unmodified platform margins and a tendency for multiple platforms or flaking directions. Many also show deep and broad negative flake scars with step or hinge terminations, and many such removals are present in the assemblage.

There are many snapped flakes, some perhaps relating to taphonomic site processes, but many most likely resulting from the nature of lathe tool production. These snapped fragments are to lathe tools as microburins are to microliths. The flakes show a mix of decortical, trimming and inner flakes indicating that nodules of flint and Portland chert were worked on site and not brought in as shaped cores. The lack of fine knapping waste is more a factor of the site sampling strategy and the difficulty in identifying such shatter amongst very stone rich contexts. The flake morphology is decidedly squat and broad with a high for all Relief Road assemblages of 49.84% compared to 5.76% narrow examples (Table 6.6). Most of these narrow forms are lathe tools or edge trimmed blade-like flakes that may have had a role in the shale industry as shaping and trimming tools. The broad component is greater than even the largely middle-late Bronze Age assemblage found in the ring ditches along the Ridgeway, but those assemblages also include some residual earlier forms that have skewed these numbers.

Lathe tools

The Iron Age tool assemblage is dominated by elongated snapped flake segments chosen for their short sharp chisel-like ends. Due to the specialised nature of the lathe tool industry and the fact that its key component is an intentionally snapped flake segment, the method by which they are measured is different. In these modified forms the length of the piece is generally the former width, while the width is given by the surviving length of the snapped piece. In some instances, the flake segment was a lateral snap and there lengths and widths were as is normal for flint analysis. Some are of a size and form that usually date from Romano-British industries. These pieces are either rectangular or trapezoidal in plan, whereas many of the putative earlier Iron Age tools have a slightly irregular rectangular form with on pointed rhombic end.

The lathe tools average 33.17mm by 22.53mm by 9.70mm and are a mix of Portland chert (15, 57.69%) and flint (11, 42.31%). Despite the similarity in size of many, they are often quite irregular in form, but five are very regular and trapezoidal in shape with very little variety in size. These pieces are identical to Romano-British lathe tools from other sites in Dorset such as Rope Lake Hole (Cox and Woodward 1987) and Kimmeridge (Davies 1936). Interestingly, they also have similar dimensions to the average of the less regular Iron Age examples, as if that size was always attempted but that only in the Romano-British period was the ideal form realised. These five Romano-British forms average 28.2mm (27-30mm) by 11.6mm (9-15mm) by 6.8mm

(4-11) and all are trapezoidal in plan (Fig. 6.14). They display less variability in length than in width or thickness and it seems that the length and shape were the key features of these tools.

Three elongated but irregular flake fragments all display an obvious awl or borer tip to the piece and may represent a tool used for initial perforation, or are an earlier form of the trapezoidal tool. These average 31.33mm by 15.67mm by 8.67mm and have high regular profiles, trapezoidal in cross section. The less regular and probably Iron Age component display heavy wear on their tips and along both lateral margins with less extreme damage along their bases. The Roman-British group display less severe damage in general, particularly along the lateral margins, but also along the flat chisel-edge. It may be that one or more were simply tool blanks or that these very regular forms fit their hafts much more snugly and were less easily damaged as they vibrated/turned in the haft.

A third group of seven lathe tools resemble these idealized forms but display a more rectangular shape in plan, a rhombic shaped end that usually formed the working edge, and which tends to be noticeably smaller than the largest group of irregular snapped flakes. They average 33.43mm (28-38), 20.71mm (16-23) by 9mm (6-14mm) and are fairly flat in cross section. Six of the seven were fashioned from Portland chert. These display very consistent length to width ratios that average 1.62:1, almost identical to the largest groups 1.57:1. In five cases the flat end was utilised while in two others the more rhombic pointed edge was favoured. Three have damage to both lateral margins while four have damage only on one.

The largest group in numbers (10) and size comprise sub-trapezoidal and usually snapped flakes, although two are intact. These could be broadly split between pointed examples (4) and flat ended chisel-like examples (5) with a tenth piece that could have belonged to either group. Most have heavily utilised tips and butts with one (2) or both (7) lateral margins showing damage, presumably from hafting. One piece does not display damage along the margins and some still show an unmodified snapped edge. Despite the morphological variability in tip, the actual size of the pieces is quite constant, averaging 45.5mm by 29.5mm by 12mm. The length varies between 39 and 53mm, the width between 23 and 36mm and the thickness between 8 and 14mm. In each case, however, there is one obvious outlier, particularly in terms of thickness, with dimensions of 12mm on seven, 13mm on two and one example each of 8mm and 14mm. Length to width ratios varies between 1.25:1 and 2.3:1, with most sited around 1.5-1.6 times the width. Again, there are obvious outliers in the group, and these examples may represent tools for very specialised purposes away from the standard lathe tools.

Other retouched forms

The lathe tools are complemented by a large number of other tools, mostly end scrapers as well as several denticulates. These were presumably used for the initial shaping of shale blocks into bracelet preforms. Awls and spurred pieces are also present, and these may have been used for initiating the working hollows on the shale. Finally, there are many simple retouched flakes that probably represent expedient shale-trimming tools. Some of these have blade-like dimensions, and similar tools are also known from other shale-working sites (Cox and Woodward 1987). The quantity of retouched forms is very high (18.73%) and indicates that the assemblage was highly specialised in nature, relating solely to the shale-working and that, despite the apparent simplicity of the reduction strategy, these workers were very skilled in producing the tools they needed.

The scrapers consist of seven end, one side and two other atypical forms, nearly all were formed on thick flakes and they are quite regular in size. Most measure between 40mm and 51mm long but one is on a very squat flake only 20mm long but 28mm wide, and three more are broken. The similarity in size suggests that they were formed to an ideal plan, similar to some of the lathe tools, and with a specific purpose in mind. Most of the scrapers have hard-hammer bulbs, but some are broken and others fashioned on chunks of waste, lacking bulbs. Flint (6) was slightly more preferred than chert (4) for scrapers.

The denticulates are very mixed in form and include one massive example on a secondary flint flake that could arguably belong in any period, but would also be seen as an oddity in most. Two large chunky examples were formed on Portland chert while two smaller pieces in flint may well be unfinished lathe tools. Nearly all aree hard-hammer flakes with large broad plain platforms.

The piercing or boring tools comprise two awl and two spurred pieces. Both awls were fashioned on thick Portland chert flakes, while the spurred pieces were on slightly thinner blanks of flint. Hard-hammer bulbs are present on three of the four pieces, with an indeterminate bulb on the fourth.

The retouched flakes are also mostly hard-hammer struck and are commonly in flint. The flakes are generally thick (average 12mm) with short areas of retouch, occasionally steep and often in odd areas of the piece suggesting that some might be unfinished lathe tools. Reinforcing that possibility was the fact that they were also snapped.

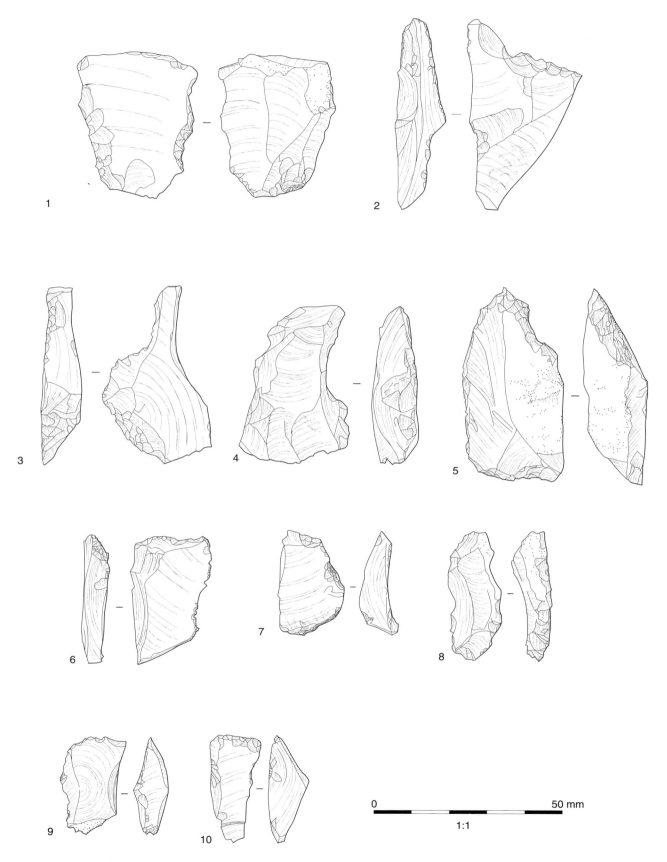

Fig. 6.14 Flint shale-working tools

Discussion

Numerous flint and chert industries are known to be associated with shale-working in the Iron Age and Romano-British periods for many years (Miles 1826). The shift in tool form from the less regular flake-based Iron Age examples to the typical chisel ended tools of the Romano-British period dates back to the 1930s, and Davies excavations at Kimmeridge (1936). Despite this, scant mention was often given to these industries (Cunliffe and Phillipson 1968), though this tendency has been reversed during recent decades (eg Bradley 1987; Errington 1981; Woodward and Cox 1987). Given that there is a still a thorny issue of Iron Age flint working being accepted in much of Britain, these industries give us an unequivocal chance to examine the reduction strategies employed by these Iron Age knappers.

The assemblage from Southdown Ridge is clearly one that was geared towards the production of lathe tools. Large and squat flakes of a a fairly regular form and thickness were produced from a variety of irregular core forms. These were then snapped, retouched and utilised as lathe tools. Other forms were created in order to aid in the shale working and were most likely hand tools. These include the scrapers and denticulates as well as some boring tools and many simple retouched flakes. This industry adhered to many of the characteristics that were believed to typify later prehistoric knapping (Young and Humphrey 1999) even though the industry was itself geared towards the production of a fairly uniform flake blank. These characteristics included the broad squat form of the flakes, hard-hammer technology, small assemblage size, restricted range of tools (dominated here by four types) and simple core typology.

The actual size of the assemblage is surprising, as is the lack of fine knapping waste, and while the tools may have been formed elsewhere, even on another part of the settlement not affected by the road, the presence of cores and preparation flakes suggests otherwise. It is likely that much of the finer knapping debris was missed during excavation, partly due to the difficulty in recognising it amongst the masses of broken stone in a soil rich in natural flint.

As mentioned earlier, the idealised tool form of the Romano-British period is well-documented (Davies 1936; Calkin 1953). However, here at least, similarity in tool form is present throughout the Iron Age material, with a tentative possibility of this tools earlier development being highlighted by the less idealised Iron Age forms. Each piece appears to have a flat chisel end and a pointed end, and often one or both are used, suggesting that a single form could perform a range of tasks dependant on how it was held in the lathe. That these pieces are later replaced by chisels in the Roman-British period may indicate that some of the range of activities performed in flint were later replaced in iron. There may even be evidence of changing tool forms in the Iron age itself with a shift from large and crude examples through to regular and elongated rectangular pieces. Alternatively, and perhaps more likely, these pieces may have represented a range of tools for different tasks or stages in the shale production process.

The limited level of Romano-British activity on site also raises the question of whether these idealised chisel forms were actually a very late Iron Age development or whether there was only a short-lived Romano-British phase of shale-working at Southdown Ridge. If the former is the case, then it is possible that this site represents the earliest use of these chisel tools in southern English shale-working industries.

Illustrated catalogue (Fig. 6.14)

1. (cat 28) Shale-working lathe tool, classic lathe tool, retouched along snap. Light greyish-brown chalk flint. Layer 7008 (below topsoil).
2. (cat 270) Shale-working hand tool. Broad flake deliberately broken to triangular form. Short side has partial abrupt retouch. Strong use wear. More typical of Iron Age than Romano-British tool types. Dark brown gravel flint. Yard surface 7742 (ctx) 7614.
3. (cat 154) Shale-working hand tool. Deliberately fractured twice (?) Dark greenish-grey Portland chert. Deposit 7002 (ctx 7413).
4. (cat 317). Shale-working lathe tool. Dark grey Portland chert. Large retouched flake, convex on one side, concave on the other. Direct parallel with Ower tool (Woodward and Cox 1987, fig. 61, 287). Stone spread 7824 (ctx 7761).
5. (cat 136) Possible shale-working hand tool. Anvil struck. Area of abrupt retouch forming crude point. Heavy wear on one side. (Woodward and Cox 1987, fig. 60, 281). Grey Portland chert. Deposit 7002 (ctx 7404).
6. (cat 38) Shale-working lathe tool. Utilised. Classic snapped rectangular segment with burin spall at point. Good use wear. Grey Portland chert. Early Iron Age ditch 7061 (ctx 7074).
7. (cat 413) Shale-working lathe tool. Blank. Irregular, but similar to pieces from Ower. Grey Portland chert. Deposit 7002 (ctx 7497)
8. (cat 96) Shale-working lathe tool. Blade blank. Heavily backed and worn at distal tip. Grey Portland chert. Grave 7372 (ctx 7385). Residual.
9. (cat 176) Shale-working hand tool. Deliberate break, wedge shape, heavy wear on one edge. Grey gravel flint. Deposit 7002 (ctx 7420).
10. (cat 357) Shale-working lathe tool. Deliberately broken wedge shaped fragment with use wear on blade edge. Classic kite shaped Romano-British lathe tool. Orange-brown gravel flint. Deposit 7002 (ctx 7814).

SHALE *by Ruth Shaffrey*

Introduction

A total of 409 pieces of shale weighing 3kg were recovered from the Southdown Ridge site. This is an assemblage of moderate size containing evidence for shale-working. The material was classified according to a system devised by Cox and Woodward and revised by Mills (Woodward and Cox 1987, 106-107; Cox and Mills 1991, 173; summarised succinctly by Mills 2004, 33). The shale has been recorded by fragment count and shale type using Cox and Woodward's categories in an Access database, accessible in the archive.

Although it is not possible absolutely to distinguish between shale and jet by eye (Allason-Jones 2002, 126) armlets are almost certain to have been made from shale (ibid. 127) and that is the identification ascribed to all the fragments here.

Most of the shale was recovered from deposits that had been extensively mixed and contained a combination of earliest to late Iron Age and Romano-British material. If fact, some 352 pieces, representing 87% of the total site assemblage, came from redeposited midden spread 7002. This made it effectively impossible to analyse changes in shale-working over time. Another 27 pieces (7%) came from the extensive stone spread (7824) underlying 7002, and can also be regarded as redeposited. This leaves only 26 pieces (6%) that have some stratigraphic integrity.

Shale objects

The bulk of the assemblage is likely to be debris from shale-working although most of it does not retain any tool marks, and is classified as type 1 under the Cox and Woodward system.

Evidence for manufacture on site comes from two very fragmentary roughouts, one of a probable spindle whorl and one of a circular item, possibly an armlet, both from redeposited midden layer 7002 (contexts 7800 and 7818, not illustrated). The section of one of these roughouts resembles an example from Norden, Purbeck (Sunter 1987, fig. 18, no 12).

Shale appears to have been worked by hand, as shown by the roughouts and by flint shale-working hand tools (see Donnelly, above). It was also certainly turned on a lathe, as evidenced by those items retaining an internal ridge, a result of lathe use (eg Sf 1, Fig.6.16, no.13, from late Iron Age burial 7003), and also by the identification of several flint lathe tools. Four pieces, each with a singular circular perforation, which could be cores (Fig. 6.15, nos 1-2) were all were recovered from 7002. Circular lathe fittings are typical from the 1st century AD onwards (Cox and Mills 1991, 174). It is also possible, however, that these are small fragments of much larger pierced objects, which cannot now be identified.

The most common objects in the Southdown Ridge assemblage are armlets, all of which are fragmentary, and some unfinished. They vary in internal diameter size from 49mm to 68mm but at least one armlet from 7002 is of a larger diameter at 90mm (Fig. 6.16, no. 7). The section shape is variable and includes triangular, square, and D-shaped (eg Fig. 6.16, nos 8, 10, 14). Four of the armlets were clearly handmade, the roughouts having been partially shaped so that the crude outline of an armlet can be seen (eg Fig. 6.15, nos 3-4). Armlets were also made on a lathe, as evidenced by the resulting ridge inside several (eg Sf 26, Fig. 6.16, no. 5) or tool marks, mostly in the form of fine scratch marks on the inside (Fig. 6.16, nos 11-12). Other examples have well-finished, masking the traces of manufacture, with an oval cross-section and perfectly smoothed surfaces (eg Sf 10, Fig. 6.16, no. 9).

Most of the armlets are plain, but a decorated example recovered from a burial context associated with a male skeleton is decorated with a triangular pattern (Sf 1, Fig. 6.16, no. 13). A internal ridge/lump on this armlet suggests that it was unfinished and that decoration was applied prior to completion. A second, very similar decorated armlet fragment was found in deposit 7002 (context 7430) (Sf 23, Fig. 6.16, no. 14). The similarity in form and decoration suggests they are of comparable date.

A possible spindle whorl and palette were both recovered from deposit 7002 (context 7818). The spindle whorl is very fragmentary and heavily damaged but part of a narrow perforation survives. The pallette is a small fragment of flat shale with one rounded corner. (Neither is illustrated).

Shale from earlier Iron Age contexts

A single unworked shale fragments were found in the fill (7399) of ditch 7204, the eastern ancillary ditch associated with the cross-ridge dyke. Five unworked pieces and a very small, undecorated armlet fragment were recovered from the fill of an early Iron Age pit (7529) which was located close to the northern fenceline that ran alongside ditch 7204. Several features associated with circular structure 7668 also yielded shale. Internal posthole 7091 produced an unworked chunk and posthole 7650 contained three smaller unworked pieces and a disc-shaped offcut. An undecorated armlet fragment was found in the fill of feature 7611, the construction slot of doorpost 7609 (Chapter 6, Fig. 6.16, no. 10).

This small collection provides evidence that shale-working was an activity being undertaken during the early phases of settlement occupation.

0   50 mm

1:1

Fig. 6.15 Worked shale: armlet roughouts and cores

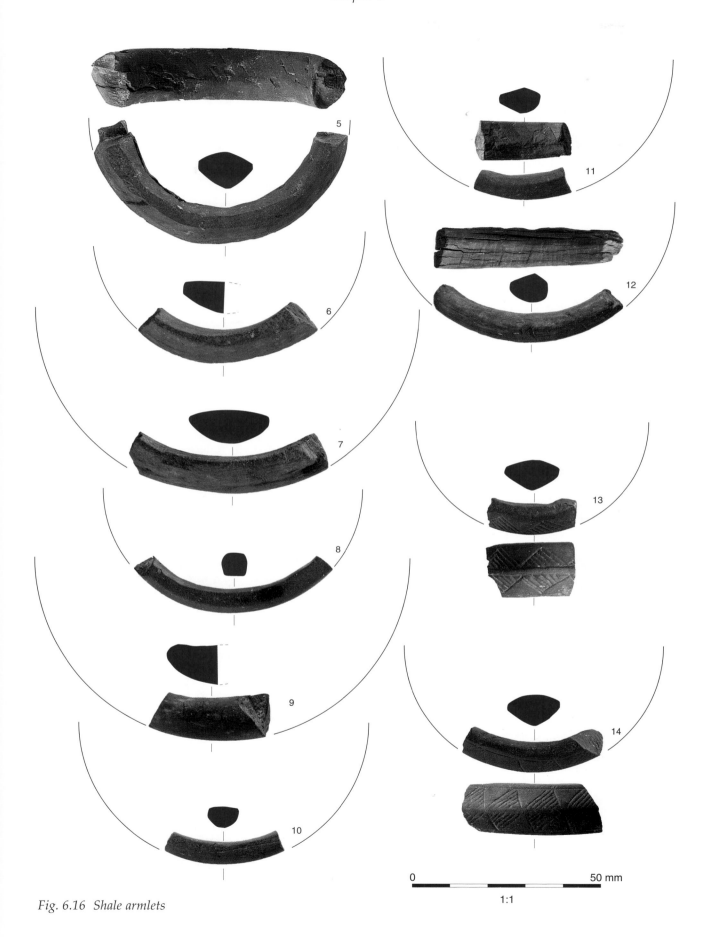

Fig. 6.16 Shale armlets

Undoubtedly, much of the shale recovered from late Iron Age-early Roman stone spread 7824 and deposit 7002, particularly the handmade material, derived from the earlier Iron Age deposits also.

Shale from late Iron Age or early Roman contexts

Discounting the large redeposited collection of unworked shale and shale objects from the late Iron Age/early Roman midden-like deposit 7002, and the 18 fragments of unworked shale from the underlying stone spread 7824, a few more reliably stratified shale fragments and objects were recovered from late Iron Age contexts.

Two of the graves produced fragments of shale armlets and one (7017) a fragment of unworked shale which was no doubt an accidental inclusion in the grave fill. A decorated armlet fragment (Sf 1, Fig. 6.16, no. 13) was found with a partial, disarticulated male skeleton (7003). Clearly, it was not possible to prove that the individual had been wearing the armlet when the burial took place, but it is a possibility, despite the fact that the armlet showed evidence of being unfinished. Another armlet fragment, this one undecorated, was found in grave 7264, close to the arms of skeleton 7235, another male. Again, the association was uncertain, but possible.

Layer 7894, which had accumulated against late Iron Age-early Roman field wall 7825, incorporated eight unworked fragments of shale. It was not clear where the material making up this deposit originated from, and the shale (and other components) may have been residual in this context.

Catalogue of illustrated shale

Fig. 6.15

1. Core. Part of circular edge remains and central circular perforation 4mm diameter. Measures 6mm thick x approximately 50mm diameter but not perfectly circular. Deposit 7002 (ctx 7648).
2. Core. The edges are damaged but there is a circular perforation measuring 5.5mm diameter. Measures 3mm thick x *c* 50mm diameter. Deposit 7002 (ctx 7800).
3. Hand made armlet roughout. Chunk of raw material with partially shaped bracelet. Sf 15. Deposit 7002 (ctx 7422).
4. Hand made armlet roughout. Large chunk, roughly chipped into circular shape of which 1/3 survives. Deposit 7002 (ctx 7401).

Fig. 6.16

5. Armlet fragment. Plain although with lots of fine tool marks running diagonally. Outside face is pointed (cf Sunter 1987, fig. 18 no 12). Measures 50mm diameter x 12mm high x 16 mm wide. Sf 26. Deposit 7002 (ctx 7455).
6. Armlet fragment. Plain with approximately triangular cross section. Measures 49mm internal diameter x 12-12.5mm high x 10.5mm max width. Sf 96. Deposit 7002 (ctx 7822).
7. Armlet fragment. Wide plain example with lots of very fine diagonal scratch marks across the inside. Measures 23 mm wide x 10 mm thick x 90mm internal diameter. Deposit 7002 (ctx 7401).
8. Armlet fragment. Plain slim bracelet with square to sub square cross-section. All surfaces are smooth, there is no ridge along the inside. Measures 5mm wide x 5.5mm high and 58mm internal diameter. Sf 108. Early Iron Age stone spread 7823 (ctx 7764).
9. Armlet fragment. Flattened oval cross section, with all smooth surfaces with no file marks or ridges. Measures *c* 70mm diameter x 10mm thick. Sf 10. Deposit 7002.
10. Armlet fragment. Plain with D-shaped section. Smooth, no tool marks or ridge. Measures approximately 68mm internal diameter x 8mm wide x 5mm thick. Sf 110. Earliest Iron Age circular structure 7668. Posthole construction cut 7611 (ctx 7612).
11. Armlet fragment. Plain with slight ridge along the inside and some 3mm wide blade marks. Measures approximately diameter x 70 mm x 10mm wide x 7mm high. Deposit 7002 (ctx 7472).
12. Armlet fragment. Plain with roughly oval section with slight ridge inside and file marks on internal top half above the ridge. Measures approx 65 mm internal diameter x 10mm high x 7mm wide. Deposit 7002 (ctx 7809).
13. Armlet fragment. Decorated fragment with pointed cross section. Internally there is a vertical ridge/lump suggesting that the armlet was unfinished and that decoration was applied prior to completion. Measures 16mm wide x 8mm high x 60mm diameter. Sf 1. Disarticulated late Iron Age burial 7003.
14. Armlet fragment. Approx 10% survives. Decorated with similar pattern as SF 1 and of same form but from different armlet. Measures 58 mm diameter x 15mm wide x 7 mm high. Sf 23. Deposit 7002 (ctx 7430).

Discussion

Although shale was sometimes imported from a distance, even when local sources were available (Allason Jones 2002, 26), the relatively small scale of the working indicated by the size of the Southdown Ridge assemblage probably indicates a local source either from surface exposures close to the site or on the local beaches. It is important to bear in mind, however, that the material recovered may represent only a small proportion of the total, as so little of the settlement area was excavated.

The evidence indicates that shale was worked on site and that production appears to have concentrated on the manufacture of armlets with a minimum of 20 items represented from all phases of activity. The combination of handmade and lathe-turned armlets may mean that both forms of manufacture operated simultaneously, but the dating is not precise enough to be sure since most of the armlets were residual in late deposits. In addition to the armlets, the presence of a spindle whorl, a small fragment of likely palette or plaque and some perforated fragments hint at some diversity in manufacture. That would seem reasonable given that flint shale-working tools were being made and other materials such as chalk were also being worked. The decorated armlet fragments are of particular interest because decoration on Iron Age armlets is mainly of linear form. Although one of the decorated examples is from an insecure deposit, it is almost identical to the fragment from a late Iron Age burial and is probably of the same date.

No precise matches could be found for the Weymouth decorated examples from any period in the region. The closest parallel of prehistoric date is from a Bronze Age context at Maiden Castle; it is inscribed with a similar, but busier, triangular pattern (Laws 1991, 233; fig. 186.1). It was postulated that this might be from a cup handle rather than an armlet because of the general paucity of decorated armlets of prehistoric date. The Weymouth fragments are both short so could possibly be from handles, but with the emphasis on manufacture of armlets in the rest of the assemblage, that interpretation is still favoured here.

Decorated armlets are more common in Romano-British assemblages than prehistoric ones, although outnumbered by plain specimens (Allason-Jones 1996, 29). The overall effect of the pattern on the Weymouth armlets is similar to that seen on notched armlets in the Yorkshire Museum with a zigzag pattern around the armlet (ibid.). However on the Yorkshire examples the central portion stands proud whereas on the Weymouth examples the central portion is carved. Several examples from Silchester also bear similar decoration – angled decoration either side of a central line (Lawson 1977, fig. 6), as could at least one Dorset example from Rope Lake Hole (Woodward and Cox 1987, fig. 92.124). None of the Roman examples are identical, so there is no reason to doubt an Iron Age date for the armlets.

The level of shale working at Southdown Ridge appears to have been relatively small scale and focussed, but the industry was clearly a significant component of the site economy. The decorated fragments could indicate that it was specialised workshop exporting high quality decorated armlets, but they are a minor component of the assemblage and may have been made as gifts or for personal use. Personal significance of these items would also explain the appearance of one of them in a burial. Armlets are not common finds in inhumation burials and occur more frequently with Romano-British skeletons, as at Tollard Royal (Wainwright 1968). However, an example is known

from a middle Iron Age burial at Winnall Down (Fasham 1985, 84) and a late Iron Age burial at Maiden Castle (Wheeler 1943, 317). Neither of these are examples are decorated. Although the associations between the two armlet fragments and the skeletons are not absolutely certain, both relationships seem likely and they highlight the importance of the industry to these individuals, both male, and those around them.

WORKED AND UTILISED STONE
by Ruth Shaffrey

Introduction

The assemblage of worked stone is small but varied. It includes hammerstones, a cupped stone, a chalk disc, two rubbers, a slab and a fragment of a probable saddle quern (Fig. 6.17). Other utilised but unworked stone was found in the form of small quantities (<1.5kg) of burnt stone and unworked pebbles.

Most of the worked stone came from redeposited midden material 7002 and the underlying stone spread (7824), which was deposited during the late Iron Age or early post-conquest period. Although some of the pieces were probably of early Iron Age date, none were found in situ in contexts of that date.

Five hammerstones, a rubber and a saddle quern probably originated from the early Iron Age settlement activity The rubber (Fig. 6.17, no. 1) had been reused in the construction of a late Iron Age stone-lined gully (7885), part of terrace complex 7970. This and a fragment of likely saddle quern (not illustrated) from stone spread 7824 (7857) represent domestic food preparation. The rubber demonstrates use of quartzite pebbles, but unlike the flint pebbles, has a combination of some percussion wear combined with extensive polish and smoothing, suggesting both pounding and rubbing. The probable saddle quern is a small fragment with a slightly concave and worn surface. It is made of a slightly ferruginous gritstone. Although the precise source has not been identified, quartz grits such as this with are found within the Cretaceous Wealden Beds and as such, the stone might have come from relatively near by such as just along the coast at Swanage.

Most of the hammerstones were recovered from late Iron Age stone spread 7824 (contexts 7813, 7857, 7877) and layer 7002 (contexts 7400, 7426), but one was built into field wall 7899 (Fig. 6.17, no. 2). Two are made of flint and one of quartzite and all demonstrate extensive percussion damage around the edges. Another 17 unworked flint pebbles or cobbles, roughly ovoid and of regular size, probably came from within the natural chalk (Arkell 1947,

Fig. 6.17 Worked and utilised stone

0   100 mm

1:2

197) and could, therefore, have been collected within a mile or two of the site. The easy availability of stones such as these would have made them a popular choice of tool, although there was no concentration in their deposition. Because they were residual in later deposits it is not possible to associate them with specific activity, but they may have been used for manufacturing the flint shale-working tools. The hammerstones and rubbers are comparable to those from earlier phases. All are un-modified except through use and all utilise quartzite pebbles or cobbles. The two hammer-stones from 7002 demonstrate extensive percussion wear and one of the pebbles has some limited signs of polish, suggesting use as a rubber, whilst another from 7824 (context 7877) has extensive wear consis-tent with rubbing as well as some percussion damage, suggesting it was a multi-functional tool,

with rubbing as its main function (Fig. 6.17, no. 5).

The chalk disc, from 7002, has an incomplete perforation towards one edge (Sf 25, Fig.6.17, no. 3). Its function is not clear but the material would probably have been too soft for it to have been a pendant. It may have been intended as some sort of counter or was merely a practice piece. The disc provides some limited evidence that chalk was worked on site.

An object made from Cornish Greenstone, also recovered from 7002 (context 7416) was is certainly residual in that context. The stone has the appearance of a mace-head but without being fully perforated (Fig. 6.17, no.4). The function of these tools, variously identified as incomplete maceheads or cupped tools has not been fully determined but they are generally thought to be Neolithic in origin. Group 1 (Cornish Greenstone) tools (predominantly axes), have a wide distribution, and although items of this precise form are uncommon, a very similar example was found at Beacon Hill, Bulford in Wiltshire (Annable and Simpson 1964, 36).

Catalogue of illustrated worked stone

Fig. 6.17

1. Rubber. Quartzite pebble. Almost perfectly circular pebble, flat with slightly damaged edges but with polish on one face indicating that its main function was as a rubber. One large flake missing from one end. Measures 106 x 103 x 40mm. Weighs 400g. Late Iron Age drainage gully 7885 (ctx 7884).
2. Hammerstone. Flint. Extensively used with lots of damage and flaking. Measures 84 x 76 x 47mm. Late Iron Age-early Roman field wall 7899.
3. Disc. Chalk. Half a disc with partially dug out perforation, started on both sides, but deeper on one side. Perhaps broken during process and thus abandoned. Perforation is close to surviving circumference. Evenly convex faces. Measures 53mm diameter x 9mm thick. Weighs 15g. Sf 25. Deposit 7002 (ctx 7424), LIA-ER
4. Mace head. Group 1 Cornish greenstone. Sf 24. Deposit 7002 (ctx 7416).
5. Rubber. Red micaceous quartzite. Roughly half a spherical rubber. Both faces are really well polished suggesting extensive use. The edges are also slightly damaged suggesting some bashing on them. Evenly convex faces. Measures 100 x >72 x 37mm. Late Iron Age stone spread 7877 (part of 7824).

Catalogue of non-illustrated worked stone

1. Probable saddle quern. Gritstone with some iron cement. Central portion with one slightly concave surface, worn smooth but with some wear patterns. Measures >55mm thick. Weight 617g. Sf 143. Late Iron Age stone spread 7824 (ctx 7857).
2. Hammerstone. Flint. Classic shape with lots of percussion wear on one side. Measures 76 x 67 x 64 mm. Weight 396g. Late Iron Age stone spread 7824 (ctx 7813).

3. Hammerstone. Quartzitic sandstone or possibly quartzite. Flat rounded pebble with low level percussion all around the narrow edge. Measures 71 x 65 x 33mm. Late Iron Age stone spread 7824 (ctx 7841)
4. Rubber. Quartzite pebble. For smoothing something, possibly leather. Not worked / shaped but probably utilised. Deposit 7002.
5. Hammerstone. Quartzite. Large ovoid flat pebble with classic hammerstone percussion wear at both ends and to a lesser degree along both long edges. Also several flakes of damage. Measures 85 x 72 x 44mm. Sf 13. Deposit 7002 (ctx 7400).
6. Hammerstone. Quartzite. Large ovoid flat pebble with classic hammerstone percussion wear at both ends and with some damage along the long edges. Measures 106 x 75 x 44mm. SF 87. Deposit 7002 (ctx 7426).

Discussion

The worked stone assemblage is small but provides evidence for two aspects of life in the settlement – tool making and food preparation. The saddle quern and rubbers indicate that some of the grain produced was being ground into flour on site. The hammerstones suggest that, as well as being used to work shale, flint tools were also being produced nearby. Chalk may have been worked on a small scale alongside the shale. In terms of the shale industry, the site was probably fairly self sufficient with the resources and knowledge to acquire all the raw materials needed. With the exception of the Greenstone cupped stone, all the stone being exploited was either available on or in the vicinity of the site, or, as is the case with the saddle quern, imported only a very short distance.

IRON SLAG AND OTHER HIGH TEMPERATURE DEBRIS *by Lynne Keys*

Much of the 6kg of high temperature debris from Southdown Ridge was fuel ash slag (Table 6.7). Fuel ash slag is a very lightweight, highly porous, light coloured (whitish-grey to grey-brown) residue produced by a high temperature reaction between alkaline fuel ash and siliceous material such as a clay lining or surface. It can be produced by any high temperature activity where these two constituents are present, including domestic hearths, accidental fires (burning down of huts), and even cremations. On its own it does not represent metalworking activity; only when associated with diagnostic evidence can it be said to derive from metalworking.

Although sparse and fragmentary, some material suggests both smelting and primary smithing – smithing of the iron bloom after it is removed from the furnace – but on a limited scale. It is possible this material could have been washed in from elsewhere. Other diagnostic evidence – a smithing hearth

Table 6.7 The slag and other high temperature debris

cxt		^S^	Slag type	Wt g	Comment
7000	Topsoil		charcoal	6	
7000	Topsoil		undiagnostic	140	Irregul.-shaped smithing hearth bottom? 75x60x35
7000	Topsoil		undiagnostic	67	Two fragments
	Post-abandonment deposit				
7002	Midden		cinder	14	
7002	Midden		fuel ash slag	251	
7002	Midden		undiagnostic	19	Weathered
7008	Subsoil		undiagnostic	46	One piece
7400	Midden 7002		fuel ash slag	4	
7401	Midden 7002		run slag	15	
7404	Midden 7002		undiagnostic	57	One piece
7404	Midden 7002		undiagnostic	700	Numerous frags.
7405	Midden 7002		fuel ash slag	9	
7412	Midden 7002		fuel ash slag	25	
7414	Midden 7002		fuel ash slag	7	
7414	Midden 7002		fuel ash slag	10	
7431	Midden 7002		fuel ash slag	21	
7436	Midden 7002		fuel ash slag	20	
7436	Midden 7002		heat-magnetised material	0	Clay & cinder
7440	Midden 7002		fired daub	154	
7440	Midden 7002		fuel ash slag	2	
7440	Midden 7002		undiagnostic	26	
7441	Midden 7002		slag dribble	11	
7441	Midden 7002		undiagnostic	10	
7449	Midden 7002		undiagnostic	70	Slightly run
7452	Midden 7002		fuel ash slag	7	
7452	Midden 7002		undiagnostic	8	
7460	Midden 7002		fuel ash slag	7	
7460	Midden 7002		undiagnostic	5	
7462	Midden 7002		burnt bone	3	
7462	Midden 7002		fuel ash slag	185	
7462	Midden 7002		heat-magnetised material	0	Clay & cinder
7462	Midden 7002		undiagnostic	16	Possible run slag
7463	Midden 7002		fuel ash slag	14	
7464	Midden 7002		fuel ash slag	4	
7464	Midden 7002		undiagnostic	24	
7467	Midden 7002		fuel ash slag	33	
7469	Midden 7002	49	heat-magnetised material	4	
7469	Midden 7002		fuel ash slag	8	
7470	Midden 7002		fuel ash slag	44	
7472	Midden 7002		fuel ash slag	19	
7472	Midden 7002		fuel ash slag	9	
7472	Midden 7002		fuel ash slag	5	
7474	Midden 7002		fuel ash slag	3	
7476	Midden 7002		burnt bone	2	
7476	Midden 7002		fuel ash slag	136	
7476	Midden 7002		undiagnostic	35	Possible run slag
7482	Midden 7002		fuel ash slag	8	
7483	Midden 7002		undiagnostic	8	
7486	Midden 7002		fuel ash slag	4	
7486	Midden 7002		fuel ash slag	5	
7496	Midden 7002		cinder	10	
7496	Midden 7002		fuel ash slag	73	
7496	Midden 7002		heat-magnetised material	0	Clay & cinder
7496	Midden 7002		vitrified hearth lining	3	
7497	Midden 7002		fuel ash slag	1	
7589	Midden 7002		undiagnostic	14	

Table 6.7 The slag and other high temperature debris (continued)

cxt		^s^	Slag type	Wt g	Comment
7803	Midden 7002		undiagnostic	25	
7804	Midden 7002		cinder	6	
7804	Midden 7002		fuel ash slag	49	
7804	Midden 7002		undiagnostic	17	
7804	Midden 7002		vitrified hearth lining	1	
7805	Midden 7002		fuel ash slag	17	
7816	Midden 7002		undiagnostic	29	
7818	Midden 7002		fuel ash slag	63	
7818	Midden 7002		heat-magnetised material	0	Tiny cinder fragments & fired clay
7826	Midden 7002		undiagnostic	4	
7837	Layer under 7002		fuel ash slag	42	
7865	Midden 7002		fuel ash slag	73	
7879	Stone layer part of 7002		fuel ash slag	25	
7615	Rubble part of 7002		fuel ash slag	12	
	Structure 7668				
7610	Doorpost 7609		fired clay	20	
7610	Doorpost 7609		fuel ash slag	4	
7619	Doorpost 7609	130	fuel ash slag	15	
7619	Doorpost 7609	130	fuel ash slag	8	
7619	Doorpost 7609	130	heat-magnetised material	0	
7619 tiny	Doorpost 7609	130	heat-magnetised material	0	Fired clay, cinder & tiny charcoal: all very
7619	Doorpost 7609	130	sample residue	15	Fuel ash slag; some silica microslags
7619	Doorpost 7609		cinder	1	
7619	Doorpost 7609		fuel ash slag	7	
7768	Door post 7766	112	fuel ash slag	6	
7768	Door post 7766	112	heat-magnetised material	11	Fired clay, cinder, burnt stone frags.; larger pieces
7768	Doorpost 7766	112	heat-magnetised material	3	Fired clay, cinder, burnt stone frags; tiny pieces
7768	Doorpost 7766	113	sample residue	17	Fuel ash slag, cinder etc.
7769	Doorpost 7766	113	heat-magnetised material	15	Fired clay, cinder, burnt stone fragments
7769	Doorpost 7766		fuel ash slag	6	
7966	PH 7961	155	heat-magnetised material	8	Fired clay, cinder, burnt stone frags., a few silica spheres; all very tiny
7966	PH 7961	155	fuel ash slag	13	
7612	Gully 7611	131	fuel ash slag	24	
7612	Gully 7611	131	fuel ash slag	9	
7612	Gully 7611	131	heat-magnetised material	36	Fired clay, cinder, burnt stone frags., a few silica spheres
7612	Gully 7611	131	heat-magnetised material	33	Fired clay, cinder, burnt stone frags., a few silica spheres; very tiny frags.
7736	Stone infill terrace 7735	96	undiagnostic	2	
7736	Stone infill terrace 7735	96	sample residue	2	Microslag fragments & one flake hammerscale fragment
7775	Stone infill 7735		fuel ash slag	37	
7789	Organic soil within 7735		fuel ash slag	43	
7699	Hollow 7698 inside door	148	heat-magnetised material	0	Fired clay, cinder & tiny charcoal
7699	Hollow 7698 inside door	148	sample residue	24	Fired clay & cinder - all very tiny
7699	Hollow 7698 inside door		cinder	9	
7699	Hollow 7698 inside door		fired clay	6	
7608	Hollow 7607 cuts doorpost		cindery run	1	
7608	Hollow 7607 cuts doorpost		fired clay	3	
7608	Hollow 7607 cuts doorpost		fuel ash slag	0	
7608	Hollow 7607 cuts doorpost		undiagnostic	1	
7670	Pit 7671	146	fuel ash slag	14	
7670	Pit 7671		fuel ash slag	217	
7670	Pit 7671		undiagnostic	127	One piece; part of smithing hearth bottom?

Table 6.7 The slag and other high temperature debris (continued)

cxt		^s^	Slag type	Wt g	Comment
7730	External yard 7742		fuel ash slag	7	
7743	External yard 7742		fuel ash slag	3	
7762	External surface 7745 over 7742		fuel ash slag	5	
7632	External yard 7823		fuel ash slag	61	
	Structure 7970				
7628	Occupation against wall 7731		fuel ash slag	27	
7758	Stone surface 7896 against 7731		cinder	1	
7885	Drain	51	fuel ash slag	2	
7684	Wall/stone spread		cinder	2	
7684	Wall/stone spread		fuel ash slag	18	
7770	surface		stone	94	Ore?
7873	Localised stone layer 7690 near structure 7675				fuel ash slag 18
	Wall 7825				
7825	Stone wall		fuel ash slag	6	Very white in colour
7635	Rubble 7894 MIA-LIA		fuel ash slag	478	
7776	Rubble 7894		fuel ash slag	5	
7863	Rubble 7894		fuel ash slag	14	
7864	Rubble 7894		fuel ash slag	3	
7866	Rubble 7894		fuel ash slag	19	
7636	Layer Gp 7897 MIA-LIA		fuel ash slag	131	
7700	Layer Gp 7897 MIA-LIA		undiagnostic	9	
7748	Layer Gp 7897 MIA-LIA	108	sample residue	2	Fuel ash slag, cinder etc.
7748	Layer Gp 7897 MIA-LIA		fuel ash slag	127	
	Late Iron Age stone surface 7824				
7829	Stone layer Gp 7824		fuel ash slag	44	
7829	Stone layer Gp 7824		heat-magnetised material	0	Tiny cinder fragments & fired clay
7843	Stone layer Gp 7824		fuel ash slag	19	
7844	Stone layer Gp 7824		fuel ash slag	2	
7854	Stone layer Gp 7824		fuel ash slag	1	
7856	Stone layer Gp 7824		cinder	5	
7856	Stone layer Gp 7824		undiagnostic	19	
	Field system				
7062	Ditch 7061 Field system	61	cinder	1	
7062	Ditch 7061Field system	61	sample residue	0	Cindery microslags
7140	Ditch 7168 Gp 7675 Field system		fuel ash slag	2	
7194	Ditch 7193 Field system	59	fuel ash slag	2	
7200	Ditch 7201 Field system		fired clay	30	Oxygen-reduced fired
7200	Ditch 7201 Field system		fuel ash slag	17	
7332	Gully 7331Field system	63	hammerscale	0	One flake
7336	Ditch 7334 Field system	62	slag dribble	1	
7504	Boundary ditch 7240 EIA	54	heat-magnetised material	3	Includes tiny slag runs, some hammerscale spheres & fuel ash slag spheres (primary smithing?)
	Northern pits and postholes				
7527	Pit 7526 N group	85	fuel ash slag	1	
7293	PH 7292 N group		cinder	6	
7312	PH 7300 N group	49	fuel ash slag	2	
7312	PH7300 N group	49	heat-magnetised material	4	Includes one hammerscale flake
7338	Pit 7337 EIA N group		fuel ash slag	1	
7342	Pit 7341 EIA N group	55	fuel ash slag	2	
7342	Pit 7341 EIA N group		fuel ash slag	3	
7345	Pit 7344 EIA N group		fuel ash slag	12	
7504	Pit 7248 N group	54	fuel ash slag	2	With tiny fired clay fragments
7575	Pit 7573 EIA N group		fuel ash slag	1215	

Table 6.7 The slag and other high temperature debris (continued)

cxt		^s^	Slag type	Wt g	Comment
7575	Pit 7573 EIA N group		heat-magnetised material	0	
7582	PH 7581 N group		fuel ash slag	75	
7582	PH 7581 N group		microslags	0	A few & cindery
	Grave fill				
7145	Grave 7143	25	fuel ash slag	4	
7525	Grave 7523 Roman	93	heat-magnetised material	0	
7570	Grave 7565	86	heat-magnetised material	2	Several microslag runs, fired clay etc.
7570	Grave 7565	87	fuel ash slag	2	
7570	Grave 7565	87	heat-magnetised material	4	*c.* 10% broken flake hammerscale, occasional tiny smithing spheres, fired clay etc.
7570	Grave 7565	87	sample residue	0	Microslag pieces & iron flake

bottom fragment from and very occasional broken hammerscale flake – suggests secondary smithing.

The material in context

Just over one-third of the material (1899g) examined came from the topsoil and redeposited midden layer 7002, and is therefore essentially unstratified, with no information available regarding its origin within the settlement. Just under 100g of fuel ash slag and cinder lying in the interstices between the stone of late Iron Age make-up layer 7824 probably derived from earlier settlement activity. Small quantities of fuel ash slag, slag dribbles and hammerscale were recovered as redeposited material from diches associated with the Iron Age field system (56g) and from grave fills (12g), and could have derived from anywhere in the vicinity of the settlement.

The remainder was distributed within several locations that have some chronological or spatial coherence. The largest group (813g) came from features and layers associated with circular structure 7668. Some 230g of fuel ash slag and heat magnetised material was incorporated in the fills of the doorposts (7609 and 7766) and construction cut 7611 abutting doorpost 7609. Microslag, flakes of hammerscale, burnt clay and stones and cinder from the floor area inside recess 7735 and hollows inside the doorway of the structure highlight at least some limited level of smithing activity, especially considering the recovery of a possible smithing hearth bottom from a feature (7691) within the the structure. The external yard areas 7742 and 7823 also incorporated small quantities of fuel ash slag. Due to the levels of disturbance and truncation to this structure, it is not possible to say how much of this activity, if any, was contemporary with the use of the structure or whether it pre-dated its construction, or indeed post-dated its abandon-ment. The incorporation of fuel ash slag in the doorposts and layer 7742 suggests that at least some heat-related activity predated the construction of the house, and the location may have remained a favoured site for a continuation of such activity during or after the period that the recessed floor (7735) was exposed.

Small quantities of fuel ash slag recovered from features and layers associated with terrace complex 7970 may attest to some heat-related activity in this location also, although there is no evidence for metalworking here, and the debris may be redeposited from earlier activity. The incorporation of some 794g of fuel ash slag in layers associated with late Iron Age-early Roman field wall 7825 provides a better indication of the level of activity that would have generated this material, as it probably derived from the earlier structure.

A number of the pits and postholes located on the higher ground to the north of the settlement nucleus yielded small traces of fuel ash slag, but one early Iron Age pit in particular (7573) produced 1215g of this material. This deep beehive shaped pit also produced other domestic debris – a small collection of early Iron Age pottery and animal bone. The disposal of hearth sweepings, and in fact hearth structure, has been recorded elsewhere, for example at Danebury (Poole 1995, 263).

THE HUMAN REMAINS
by Mark Gibson and Louise Loe

Introduction

One middle Iron Age (7538), 19 late Iron Age (7003, 7004, 7018, 7054, 7105, 7111, 7125, 7144, 7235, 7262, 7274, 7362, 7371, 7383, 7384, 7547, 7570, 7622, and 7757) and three Romano-British (7381, 7524 and 7965) skeletons were recovered from graves excavated on Southdown Ridge (Table 6.8). This was in addition to

Table 6.8 Summary of Iron Age/Roman-British burials

Skeleton no.	C14 date	Grave orientation/ position of skeleton / grave goods	Age category	Age range	Sex	% Completeness
Iron Age						
7003		Disturbed by ploughing; no visible grave cut; remains -of one discernible individual -were disarticulated. Found with jet/slate fragment of bracelet	Prime adult	26-35yrs	M	26-50
7004		East-west, head at east end; crouched on right side head facing North; no finds	Mature adult	36-45yrs	F	26-50
7018			Prime adult	26-35yrs	F	26-50
7054			Young adult	18-25yrs	F	76-100
7105			Adolescent	12-14yrs	/	76-100
7111			Young adult	18-25yrs	F	<25
7125			Young adult	18-25yrs	?	51-75
7144		North-south, head at North end; lying on right side; other orientation/position information could not be determined; no finds	Infant	2wks - 5mths	/	26-50
7235			Young adult	18-25yrs	M	51-75
7262			Young adult	18-25yrs	?	26-50
7274			Prime adult	26-35yrs	F	76-100
7362			Infant	1.5-4.5mths	/	26-50
7371			Adult	15yrs	?	<25
7383			Adolescent	12.5-14yrs	/	76-100
7384			Prime adult	26-35yrs	M	51-75
7538			Adolescent	12.5-13.5yrs	/	76-100
7547			Older child	6.5-16yrs	/	<25
7570		East-west; head at east end facing North; crouched; buried with two pots	Prime adult	26-35yrs	M	76-100
7622			Mature adult	36-45yrs	F	51-75
7757			Prime adult	26-35yrs	M	76-100
Romano-British						
7381			Mature adult	26-35yrs	M	76-100
7524			Young adult	18-25yrs	F	51-75
7965			Prime Adult	26-35yrs	M	76-100

Fragment-ation	Surface condition (McKinley 2004,16)	Skeletal pathology	Dentition				
			No. teeth present	No. sockets present	No. with caries	No. with calculus	No. with enamel hypoplasia
Medium	3	Osteoarthritis, Schmorl's nodes, spinal osteoarthritis, vertebral body osteophytosis	0	0	0	0	-
High	2	Depression fracture on the right parietal, ossified hematoma, spondylosis deformans, spinal osteoarthritis, vertebral body osteophytosis, periostitis	5	12	1	4	-
High	2	Osteoarthritis, spinal osteoarthritis, cribra orbitalia, subluxation of right MT1-pph1 joint due to hallux valgus, kidney or bladder stone	19	18	2	9	-
High	2	None observed	26	23	1	17	2
Low	1	Cribra orbitalia, septic arthritis in the left hip	0	0	0	0	-
High	2	Schmorl's nodes, spinal osteoarthritis	21	19	0	13	-
High	2	Cribra orbitalia, osteochondritis non-dissecans	31	22	2	25	1
High	2	None observed	1	0	0	0	-
High	2	Schmorl's nodes, osteochondritis non-dissecans, undiagnose/button osteoma, endocranial lesions	6	6	0	5	-
High	2	Cribra orbitalia, spondylosis deformans, vertebral body osteophytosis	23	10	2	4	-
Medium	2	Cribra orbitalia, Schmorl's nodes, vertebral body osteophytosis, partuition scar, periostitis, left arm smaller than right	29	29	6	16	-
High	3	None observed	2	0	0	0	-
High	2	Periostitis	0	0	0	0	-
Medium	2	Periostitis, dental anomaly	32	24	0	12	-
High	2	Schmorl's nodes, vertebral body osteophytosis	31	24	0	28	-
High	1	Cribra orbitalia	32	32	0	23	-
High	2	None observed	0	0	0	0	-
Medium	1	Cribra orbitalia, vertebral body osteophytosis, increased porosity on ectocranial vault, hand phalanx fracture, increased vascularity on the endocranial surface, spondylolsis	29	30	0	25	1
High	1	Cribra orbitalia, osteoarthritis, vertebral body osteophytosis	32	26	2	17	-
High	2	Vertebral body osteophytosis, bulging on the endocranial surface	26	24	1	17	-
High	2	Cribra orbitalia, subluxation of Left TMJ with secondary osteoarthritis, spondylosis deformans, spinal osteoarthritis, vertebral body osteophytosis	20	18	5	1	-
High	2	Cribra orbitalia, osteochondritis non-dissecans, linear depression of the left talus, increased porosity on the cranial vault	29	21	5	1	1
Medium	2	Cribra orbitalia, Schmorl's nodes, vertebral body osteophytosis	25	22	2	25	-

a small quantity of disarticulated human bone. Among the late Iron Age skeletons were 14 adults and five juveniles. The middle Iron Age skeleton was juvenile and all of the Roman skeletons were adults. The burial position of five of the Iron Age skeletons could not be ascertained, while the other 16 were in lying in a crouched position.

The skeletons were osteologically analysed and the results are presented below.

Methods

Analysis was undertaken in accordance with published guidelines (Brickley and McKinley 2004). The preservation of each skeleton was recorded with reference to completeness (scored as: <25%, 26-50%, 51-75% or 76-100%), degree of fragmentation (scored as: low – <25% fragmented; medium – 25-75% fragmented; or high: >75% fragmented) and degree of surface erosion (after McKinley 2004, 16).

The sex of adult skeletons was estimated based on observations of the sexually dimorphic traits of the skull and pelvis (Phenice 1969; Bass 1987; Buikstra and Ubelaker 1994). Adults were recorded as either possible female (??F), possible male (??M), probable female (?F), probable male (?M), female (F) or male (M), depending on the level of confidence with which sex could be estimated. For the purposes of this report all probable and possible females and males are counted as females and males. No attempt was made to estimate the sex of juvenile skeletons, in accordance with accepted practice (Brickley 2004, 23). Adult age estimations were based on observations of late-fusing epiphyses (Scheuer and Black 2000), and on the morphological changes of the pubic symphysis (Brooks and Suchey 1990) and auricular surface (Lovejoy et al. 1985; Buckberry and Chamberlain 2002). Juvenile ages were estimated with reference to dental development (Moorees et al. 1963), epiphyseal fusion and long-bone length (Scheuer and Black 2000).

A standard set of measurements was taken (Brothwell and Zakrzewski 2004) where possible. Adult stature was estimated by employing maximum long bone measurements in the regression equations devised by Trotter and Gleser (Trotter 1971). Non-metric traits were scored (Berry and Berry 1967; Finnegan 1978) and pathology and trauma were identified, described and diagnosed

with reference to standard texts (for example, Aufderheide and Rodríguez-Martín 1998; Ortner 2003; Resnick 1995).

Iron Age inhumation burials: articulated skeletons

General descriptions of the graves, orientations and conditions of preservation are provided in the site narrative (Chapter 5).

Completeness and condition

Half of the skeletons were over 50% complete, with all parts of the skeleton surviving to varying degrees (Table 6.9). Skeletons that were 26-50% complete totalled six and were represented by most skeletal regions. This is with the exception of two that had most elements from the left hand side (7362) and lower extremities (7144) missing. Three skeletons were less than 25% complete and comprised lower leg bones (7371), partial bones from the left hand side (7111) and the torso and upper extremities (7547) only.

All of the skeletons were fragmented, with most (15 in total) judged to be highly fragmentary (over 75% of their bones affected). Bone surface erosion resulting from taphonomic alteration was frequent, but it affected skeletons to varying degrees. In two skeletons it was patchy only (consistent with McKinley's grade 1; 2005, 16), but in 14 it was more extensive and showed deeper surface penetration (consistent with McKinley's grade 2; 2005, 16). The most extensively affected skeletons – four in total – had erosion affecting most of their bone surfaces. Although this had masked details on the bones, it had not altered their overall morphology (consistent with McKinley's grade 3; 2005, 16).

Demography

Among the adults there were five males, six females and three skeletons for whom sex could not be determined owing to poor preservation. They were estimated to have been 18-25 (young adult; five skeletons), 26-35 (prime adult; six skeletons) and 36-45 (mature adult; two skeletons) years old when they died (Table 6.10). One skeleton could not be aged more precisely than 'adult' (>18 years of age). The juveniles included three adolescents (12-18

Table 6.9 Completeness and condition of skeletons

| | Completeness | | | | Fragmentation | | | Surface erosion grade | | |
	<25%	26-50%	51-75%	76-100%	Low	Medium	High	1	2	3
Number of skeletons	3	6	4	7	1	4	15	4	14	2

Table 6.10 Age and sex distribution

Age category	Male	Female	Indeter-minate/ NR (%)	Totals
Neonate (birth - 1 month)	-	-	0	0
Infant (1 month – 1 year)	-	-	2	2
Young child (1-5 years)	-	-	0	0
Older child (6-12 years)	-	-	1	1
Adolescent (13-17 years)	-	-	3	3
Young adult (18 – 25 years)	1	2	2	5
Prime adult (26 – 35 years)	4	2	0	6
Mature adult (36 – 45 years)	0	2	0	2
Older adult (>45 years)	0	0	0	0
Adult (unspec.)	0	0	1	1
Totals	5	6	9	20

years), one older child (6-12 years) and two infants (one month to one year).

Metrical analysis

Due to the high level of fragmentation only limited metrical data could be obtained. Stature could be estimated for three males and five females. The tallest individual, Male 7003, was 1.82m (6 ft) tall, but this calculation is based on the maximum length of the radius, one of the least reliable bones for estimating stature with an error margin of 4.32 cm. The other two males, 7570 and 7757, were 1.69 m (five feet six inches) and 1.66 m (five feet five inches) tall respectively. These heights were estimated using the humerus (7570) which, like the radius, has a high margin of error (4.05 cm), and the femur (7757) which is more reliable (error margin: 3.77 cm). Female statures were 1.58m (7054) and 1.59m (7274) (or both five feet two inches), and were both estimated using the femur. According to Roberts and Cox (2003, 103), these results are similar to the averages that have been calculated for Iron Age males and females from several British sites. These are 1.68m (five feet six inches) and 1.62m (five feet four inches) respectively.

In addition to stature, physical attributes were also explored by calculating the platymeric and platycnemic indicies (no crania had survived intact and therefore no cranial indices could not be determined). The platymeric index reflects the degree of anterior-posterior flattening of the femur and concerns values that are 84.9 or lower, which refer to platymeria (flattening) and values that are 85.0 or greater, which refer to roundness (eurymeria). The platycnemic index refers to the medio-lateral flattening of the tibial shaft, where flattening (platycnemia) is indicated by values of 62.9 and lower, and a lack of flattening is indicated by values that are greater than 63 (mesocnemia). In the present sample, there was a tendency towards flattened femoral shafts, but all tibial indices were mesocnemic, reflecting a lack of flattening (see summary, Table 6.12). In general, platymeria and platycnemia are more common among prehistoric populations than more recent populations (Brothwell 1981; Waldron 2007). The reason for shaft flattening is not clear, but it may be an adaptive response to mechanical stress (Brothwell 1981; Wells 1964,32). Squatting, and mineral and vitamin deficiency have also been suggested as other possible factors (Brothwell 1981; Waldron 2007).

Non-metric traits

Non-metric traits are minor anomalies in the morphology of the skeleton and are generally of no pathological significance. They may be present as localised deficiencies of bone (for example, as extra blood vessel openings or foramen), or as extra bones (for example, as wormian bones in the cranial sutures). Non-metric traits may be genetically or environmentally induced (Mays 1998, 110; Tyrrell 2000). Traits which involve variations in joint surfaces tend to be more environmentally influenced and refer to mechanical factors operating on the bones (Mays 1998, 110). Variations in the sutures of the skull (for example, retention of the metopic suture into adulthood and the presence of lambdoid ossicles) are considered to be under significant genetic control (Torgersen 1951a,b, 1954; Sjøvold 1984).

A wide range of non-metric traits was observed on bones form the axial and appendicular regions of the skeletons. Between them, they had four different cranial traits including (in order of most to least

Table 6.11 Cranial non-metric traits within the adult sample (N=13)

Cranial trait	Present		Absent		Total observable		%	
Metopism	2		7		9		20.45	
	R	L	R	L	R	L	R	L
Supraorbital foramen	1	3	7	4	8	7	12.50	42.86
Accessory infraorbital foramen	4	3	3	5	7	8	57.14	37.50
Parietal foramen	3	2	3	2	6	4	50.00	50.00

Table 6.12 Post-cranial non-metric traits within the adult sample (N=56)

Cranial trait	Present		Absent		Total observable		%	
	R	L	R	L	R	L	R	L
Atlas – double facet	1	1	3	2	4	3	25.00	33.33
Atlas – posterior bridge	1	0	0	0	1	0	100	0
Supra-scapular foramen	1	1	2	1	3	2	33.33	50.00
Humerus – septal aperture	0	2	9	8	9	10	0	20.00
Acetabular crease	2	1	5	4	7	5	28.57	20.00
Femur – Allen's fossa	1	1	5	6	6	7	16.67	14.29
Femur – third trochanter	4	3	1	3	5	6	80.00	50.00
Patella – vastus notch	2	1	8	9	10	10	20.00	10.00
Patella – vastus fossa	1	0	9	10	10	10	10.00	0
Tibia – medial squatting facet	3	3	4	4	7	7	42.86	42.86
Tibia – lateral squatting facet	3	3	3	4	6	7	50.00	42.86
Talus – double inferior facet	1	1	9	10	10	11	10.00	9.09
Lateral talar extension	3	3	7	8	10	11	30.00	27.27
Medial talar facet	2	1	8	10	10	11	20.00	9.09
Calcaneus – anterior facet absent	2	0	6	7	8	7	25.00	0
Calcaneus – double anterior facet	3	4	5	3	8	7	37.50	57.14

frequent), accessory infraorbital foramina (R=57.1%; 4/7; L=37.5%; 3/8), parietal foramina (R=50%; 3/6; L=50%; 2/4), supra-orbital foramina (R=12.5%; 1/8, L=42.86%; 3/7) and metopism (20.45%; 2/9) (Table 6.12). The foramina are extra blood vessel openings and metopism is retention of the stuture which divides the frontal bone vertically. Although genetics rather than environment may have greater control over these traits, the present assemblage is too small to explore familial ties.

A total of 16 different post-cranial traits were observed on the first cervical vertebra (atlas), the scaupla, humerus and lower extremities (Table 6.12). There is still limited understanding of some of these traits (for example, the acetabular crease, which is a fold located on the articular surface of the acetabulum of the hip), not least because basic research, on their relationship to age, sex and bone size, is still lacking (Anderson, unpublished). In addition, statistical analysis of the traits seen among the Southdown individuals is limited by the small numbers of skeletons that had observable bones. However, there are a few observations that can be made. For example, the third trochanter, a distinct tuberosity located on the superior aspect of the gluteal ridge on the back of the femur, seems to be related to bone size, being more common on gracile bones and females (Anderson, unpublished). In the present assemblage, they were observed on two females (7054 and 7274), one male (7235) and one unsexed adult (7125). Allen's fossa was also observed on both femora of female 7054 and is a small depression on the anterior superior margin of the femoral head. It may be associated with extreme extension of the hip joint (Anderson, unpublished). Lastly, the vastus notch on the patella and facets on

the tibias may be associated with chronic flexion of the knee and ankle and have been attributed to the adoption of a squatting posture over prolonged periods of time (Capasso *et al.* 1999; Molleson). These traits were found on one female (7111) and two males (7384 and 7757). Interestingly – and perhaps relevant – the femoral shaft index for two of the individuals (7111 and 7384) was platymeric (no data had survived for 7757), which has been linked to squatting (see above).

Dental anomalies

Dental anomalies were recorded on five adults and one juvenile. Skeleton 7235 (18-25 year old male) had a impacted left mandibular third molar which was erupting at a 45 degree angle in an anterior direction into the second molar. Skeleton 7262 (18-25 year old adult) had three roots on their maxillary left first premolar and their mandibular left second molar. Male 7384 (25-35 years) had two dental anomalies; the right maxillary second premolar was rotated 90 degrees clockwise and an additional socket was present between the left maxillary incisors. The tooth from this socket had been lost post-mortem, but its size suggests that it could not have been a full sized adult tooth and was therefore either a retained deciduous tooth or a supernumerary peg tooth. Skeletons 7622 (a 35-45 year old female) and 7757 (a 25-35 year old male) had heavy horizontal wear facets on their anterior dentitions. These could have been the result of the caries that were identified on the molars of both dentitions (second and first respectively), which could have caused them to chew using their anterior teeth. However, the caries were only small or medium in size suggesting that

Table 6.13 Dental pathology: comparison of Southdown prevalence rates with other assemblages – adults only (numbers of affected individuals, or CPR, and numbers of affected teeth or tooth spaces, or TPR. Only the CPR is given for comparative sites)

Site		AMTL	Caries	Periapical cavities	Calculus	Periodontitis	DEH
		(n/N)	(n/N)	(n/N)	(n/N)	(n/N)	(n/N)
Southdown Ridge, Weymouth	TPR	8.84% (22/249)	6.36% (18/283)	0.80% (2/249)	64.31% (182/283)	11.64% (29/249)	1.80% (5/278)
	CPR	53.85% (7/13)	69.23% (9/13)	15.38% (2/13)	100% (13/13)	53.85% (7/13)	30.77% (4/13)
Dorset (Redfern 2008)		36.2%	6.5%	No data	No data	No data	15.6%
East Yorkshire (Stead 1991)		2.11% (175/8290)	2.11% (161/7611)	0.59% (49/8290)	No data	No data	No data
Gussage All Saints, Dorest (Keepax 1990)		24.35% (75/308)	24.54% (54/220)	6.49% (20/308)	18.75% (9/48)*	No data	No data
Mill Hill, Deal, Kent (Anderson 1995)		12.59% (85/675)	12.48% (65/521)	3.70% (25/675)	No data	No data	No data
Suddern Farm, Hants (Cunliffe and Poole 2000)		11.99% (53/442)	7.81% (26/333)	2.04% (9/442)	No data	No data	No data
Yarnton, Oxon (Boyle 2011)		16.31% (39/239)	9.47% (16/169)	1.67% (4/239)	22.72% (5/22)*	No data	0% (0/169)

they would not have affected their chewing habits to this degree. Alternative explanations are an edge to edge bite or extramasticatory wear. Due to fragmentation of the skulls neither skeleton could be assessed for bite and further investigation is required to confirm extramasticatory wear.

An unusual dental anomaly was observed on adolescent 7383 in which a tooth crown was wedged into a gap ('diastema') between the second right premolar and the first right molar. In addition, the second premolar had been displaced anteriorly and was rotated 45 degrees clockwise, and the first right premolar had erupted beyond the occlusal plane, had its root also displaced anteriorly, and its crown angled posteriorly. The wedged crown could be a second deciduous molar which had got stuck during the eruption of the permanent premolar below it. However, the preferred interpretation is that it is the developing left third molar which, as a result of taphonomic processes, had been dislodged from it's tooth crypt and had migrated to its present position.

Palaeopathology

Dental disease

According to Roberts and Cox (2003, 100), overall rates of dental disease during the Iron Age were comparatively lower than the Bronze Age. This may have been due to a variety of factors, an improved diet with lower levels of fermentable carbohydrates, a lower burden of disease and/or increased oral hygiene, being among them (ibid.). It is therefore perhaps surprising that calculus and, to a lesser extent, caries were common among the Southdown skeletons (Tables 6.13).

Calculus, or mineralised dental plaque, was seen on all of the dentitions (182/283 teeth; 64.31%). The condition is consistent with diets high in protein and/or carbohydrate, but it may also refer inadequate oral hygiene practices. Commonly, the prolonged accumulation of calculus in and around the tooth sockets, which irritates and inflames the soft tissues of the mouth (specifically, the gums and periodontal ligament) and alveolar bone, leads to periodontal disease. This was observed on seven individuals (53.85%; 7/13), or 29 tooth spaces (11.64%; 29/249). Besides calculus, there are several other predisposing factors known to this disease, genetics, diet and inadequate levels of oral hygiene, being among them.

Caries was the second most frequent dental condition per number of individuals and involved nine skeletons (69.23%; 9/13) and 18 teeth (6.36%; 18/283). In this condition, the acid in the bacteria in dental plaque destroys the enamel, dentine and cement, resulting in cavities in the crowns and/or tooth roots (Hillson 1996, 269). Severe caries can cause large cavities, which can lead to dental abscesses and, ultimately, tooth loss. It is likely (although impossible to confirm), that caries had contributed to the AMTL seen among the skeletons (53.85%; 7/13), which affected 22 teeth (8.84%; 22/249). Ante-mortem tooth loss may also arise as a result of trauma or deliberate extraction, severe periodontal disease secondary to calculus formation, and pulp exposure and abscess formation secondary not only to caries, but also severe attrition.

Peri-apical cavities were also observed and involved just two individuals who had one tooth space each affected (0.80%; 2/249). These are holes at the apex of tooth sockets that arise as a result of inflammation of the dental pulp, due to trauma, caries or attrition. When they contain a pus-filled sac they are referred to as peri-apical abscesses (Dias and Tayles 1997).

Dental enamel hypoplasia was infrequent; the condition was observed on five teeth (1.80%; 5/278) belonging to four skeletons (30.77%; 4/13), in the form of lines of depressed enamel. These lines are believed to refer to disruptions in enamel development, which can occur in the first six to seven years of life, as a result of episodes of malnutrition or illness lasting at least three weeks (Goodman and Rose 1991, 59-60; Hillson 1996, 165-6; Larsen 1997, 23).

The small number of individuals from Southdown precludes detailed comparison with contemporary assemblages. However, it is useful to note that skeletons from Suddern Farm, Middle Wallop, Hants (Cunliffe and Poole 2000); Yarnton, Oxfordshire (Boyle 2011) and several Iron Age assemblages discussed by Roberts and Cox (2003, 100-101), have lower rates of caries, calculus and periodontal disease than Southdown. The Southdown rates for peri-apical cavities are in keeping with these assemblages and DEH is lower. Finally, less AMTL is present among the Southdown skeletons compared with other assemblages, probably because of their relatively younger age profile and the known tendency for AMTL to be associated with increasing age.

Juvenile dental health

In common with the adults, calculus was prevalent and affected 60.00% (3/5) of all juvenile dentitions and involved 51 permanent teeth (61.45%; 51/83 observable permanent teeth). Only one (1.67%; 1/60 observable teeth) permanent tooth from the entire juvenile assemblage had DEH. No other dental conditions were observed among the juveniles (Table 6.14).

Skeletal pathology

A variety of skeletal manifestations of disease was encountered in the assemblage. In this report, they have been classified according to their primary aetiology as congenital/developmental anomalies; non-specific inflammation/infection; metabolic disorders; spinal joint disease; extra-spinal joint disease; trauma; miscellaneous disease (ie diseases of unknown aetiology) and undiagnosed conditions. No specific infections, circulatory disease or neoplasms were observed. All but five of the skeletons had one or more types of pathology. Unsurprisingly, those without pathology were less than 50% complete (four in total) and/or were infants (two in total), whose bones rarely show disease (Lewis 2007). The most frequent type of pathology observed on the skeletons was spinal joint disease followed by cribra-orbitalia (metabolic disease) and non specific bone inflammation. This differs from other Iron Age assemblages where extra-spinal joint disease is usually the most common (Roberts and Cox 2003).

Congenital/developmental anomalies

This refers to abnormalities in growth or development. They may not become evident until the period of growth or young adulthood, or they may present at the fetal stage or at birth. The most common abnormalities are relatively minor and involve the spinal column (Barnes 1994).

Table 6.14 True and crude prevalence rates for dental pathology in the juvenile Iron Age assemblage

Sk number	No. crowns observable		No. sockets observable	No. crowns/sockets with							
				Caries		Calculus		Dental enamel hypoplasia		Periapiceal cavity	Ante-mortem tooth loss
	Permanent	Deciduous		Permanent	Deciduous	Permanent	Deciduous	Permanent	Deciduous		
7105	27	0	28	0	0	16	0	1	0	0	0
7144	0	1	0	0	0	0	0	0	0	0	0
7362	0	2	0	0	0	0	0	0	0	0	0
7383	28	1	24	0	0	12	0	0	0	0	0
7538	28	0	32	0	0	23	0	0	0	0	0
TOTAL	83	4	84	0	0	51	0	1	0	0	0
TPR %				0.00 (0/83)	0.00 (0/4)	61.45 (51/83)	0.00 (0/83)	1.67 (1/60)	0.00 (0/4)	0.00 (0/84)	0.00 (0/84)
Corrected CPR %				0.00 (0/5)	0.00 (0/5)	60.00 (3/5)	0.00 (0/5)	20.00 (1/5)	0.00 (0/5)	0.00 (0/3)	0.00 (0/3)

The neural arch of the fifth lumbar vertebra of 25-35 year old male 7570 had a bilateral fracture on the pars inter-articularis, which had failed to reunite to the body, indicating spondylosis. This stress fracture may be caused by an underlying congenital weakness in this part of the spine (Aufderheide and Rodriguez-Martin 1998), which is why it is considered here.

Non-specific inflammation/infection

Non-specific bone inflammation/infection included periostitis and skull lesions. Periostitis (increased porosity, striations, plaque like new bone formation and/or swelling on the original bone surface) involved three adults (21.43%, 3/14) and was seen on three tibias and one humerus. This is more frequent than the average (0.68%; 4/591) calculated by Roberts and Cox (2003,93), using data from 19 Iron Age sites. In one of the Southdown skeletons (7004), it was secondary to a fracture involving the tibia. It is not possible to say what had caused the inflammation in the other skeletons.

Periostitis may arise as a result of either a soft-tissue infection extending to the bone; a more generalised disease process; or by involvement from infection (osteitis or osteomyelitis) of the underlying bone (Aufderheide and Rodríguez-Martín 1998, 172). Thus it does not always relate to infection; trauma, neoplastic disease and haemorrhage may all produce periosteal new bone (ibid., 172). Periostitis is frequently observed on the tibia in archaeological material because it is more easily affected by mild recurrent trauma than other bones in the skeleton (Roberts and Manchester 1995, 130).

On the skull, non-specific inflammation was seen on the mandible of one juvenile (7383) in association with a dental anomaly (see above). In addition, young adult male, 7235, had inflammation on the endo-cranial surface of his occipital bone in the form of capillary-like impressions which were focussed around the cruciform eminence, the right transverse sulcus in particular. This may have been caused by many different conditions, trauma, primary and secondary infections of the meninges, tumours, tuberculosis, syphilis and certain vitamin deficiencies being among them (Lewis 2004, 90).

Metabolic disorders

Metabolic disorders may manifest as a disruption of bone formation, bone remodelling and/or bone mineralisation (Brickley 2000, 337). In the present assemblage cribra orbitalia (CO) was the only metabolic disorder that was observed.

This condition is identified on dry bone as small porosities or large interconnected trabeculae on the roof of the orbits. Several hypotheses exist as to the aetiology of these changes, but the most popular, and generally accepted, is iron deficiency anaemia (Stuart-Macadam 1982, 1991). It is thought that the changes are the result of the body's attempt to produce more red blood cells in the marrow, to compensate for the lack of iron (Roberts and Manchester 1995, 167). Similar changes may be observed on the cranial vault, known as porotic hyperostosis (PH), although these changes are far less frequently observed than CO in the UK (ibid., 167). Aside from a diet deficient in iron, excessive blood loss through injury, chronic disease such as cancer, and parasitic infection of the gut, may all have played a significant part in iron deficiency (ibid., 166). Cribra orbitalia and PH are commonly most fully developed in infancy, at which time the mechanism by which marrow expands may result in such lesions of the skull vault or orbits (Aufderheide and Rodríguez-Martín 1998, 349).

The degree of healing may be indicative of ongoing physiological stress into adulthood. The most minimal examples, presenting only as multiple, discrete pinhead-sized perforations may, in older individuals, represent a healing stage of a previously more severe lesion (ibid., 349).

In total, eight out of 14 (57.14%) skeletons with observable orbits from Southdown had CO, involving a total of 14 orbits (60.87%; 14/23). The prevalence is higher than other contemporary sites such as Mill Hill, Deal, Kent (1/41 skeletons; 2.44%) (Anderson 1995), Yarnton (4/33 skeletons; 12.12%) (Boyle 2011) and the calculated average based on several Iron Age assemblages (19.05% of skeletons, or 37.5% of observable orbits) (Roberts and Cox 2003, 103).

Spinal joint disease

Lesions of joint disease in the spine are considered separately from those of the extra-spinal skeleton, due to the greater complexity of joint disease aetiology and the variety of joint types in this region. Spinal joint disease was only seen within the adult assemblage. All but one of the adults (92.86%, 13/14) had one or more observable vertebrae (ie with at least 50% of a body surface and/or at least two apophyseal joint surfaces observable). Vertebrae were systematically assessed for lesions relating to osteoarthritis, spondylosis deformans, marginal osteophytosis and Schmorl's nodes (Table 6.15). Of the individuals with observable vertebrae, 84.62% (11/13) exhibited lesions of joint disease. This calculates as 78.57% (11/14 skeletons) for adults or 55.00% for the population on the whole (11/20). These rates are higher than those observed in East Yorkshire (44.05% 111/252) (Stead 1991),

Table 6.15 TPR's of spinal joint disease, showing distribution by spinal region

Spinal region	Osteoarthritis TPR% (n/N)	Schmorl's nodes TPR% (n/N)	Marginal osteophytosis TPR% (n/N)	Spondylosis deformans TPR% (n/N)
Cervical	9.38 (6/64)	0.00 (0/64)	3.13 (2/64)	12.50 (8/64)
Thoracic	2.25 (2/89)	26.67 (20/75)	46.67 (35/75)	0.00 (0/75)
Lumbar	2.56 (1/39)	28.13 (9/32)	37.50 (12/32)	0.00 (0/32)
Total	4.69 (9/192)	16.96 (29/171)	28.65 (49/171)	4.68 (8/171)

N.B. For OA, N=total number of observable vertebral arches with observable apophyseal joint facets, for all other conditions N=total number of observable vertebral bodies

Yarnton (40.90% 9/22) (Boyle 2011) and Gussage All Saints (4.17% 2/48) (Keepax 1990) and are higher than the average for the period (32.76%) (Roberts and Cox, 2003, 76).

Five individuals had spinal osteoarthritis (OA) involving the apophyseal joints and/or the articular facets for the ribs. This calculates as a 35.71% (5/14 adults), or 38.46% (5/13) of adults with observable vertebrae. The cervical spine was most affected region, followed by the thoracic then lumbar. Osteoarthritis affects any synovial joint in the skeletons and is the most common form of joint disease in both modern and archaeological populations (Rogers and Waldron 1995, 32). The bony manifestations of OA appear in four forms: pitting on the joint surface, as a result of the breakdown of cartilage; reactive bone formation (osteophytes) on or around the joint surface; alteration in the bony contour of the joint; and eburnation – polishing of the joint surfaces as a result of bone on bone contact, due to the destruction of the cartilage (Rogers and Waldron 1995, 35, 44). Eburnation is considered pathognomonic of OA (ibid. 44). In the absence of eburnation, two of the other three bony changes must be present to make a diagnosis of OA (ibid., 44).

Marginal osteophytosis was observed in 8 adults (CPR 57.14% 8/14, or 61.54% 8/13 adults with observable vertebral bodies). The thoracic spine, followed by cervical spine was the region most frequently affected (Table 6.15). 2865% of observable vertebral bodies (49/171) displayed marginal osteophytosis.

Over a quarter of the Southdown adults had Schmorl's nodes (28.57%, 4/14 adults), or 30.77% (4/13) of adults with observable vertebral bodies. Schmorl's nodes are identified on dry bone as indentations, which may be shallow or deep, on the vertebral end plates. They are most commonly observed in the lower regions of the spine. The lesions are essentially 'pressure defects' which arise when the intervertebral disc herniates, allowing the nucleus pulposa to bulge out and place pressure on the underlying bone (Rogers and Waldron 1995, 27). Disc herniation is usually a gradual process in adults, associated with the age-related weakening of the posterior longitudinal ligaments of the spine, but it may also occur as a result of an injury, such as a fall or jump from a height, sending sudden impact through the legs and spine (Lovell 1997, 159). Schmorl's nodes in adolescence are thought most likely to relate to activity or trauma (Jurmain 1999, 165).

In the present assemblage the thoracic spine was the most frequently affected region, followed by the lumbar, which is a commonly observed pattern (Rogers and Waldron 1995, 27). No Schmorl's nodes were observed in the cervical spine. The rate of Schmorl's nodes is higher than that of Yarnton 4.54% (1/22) (Boyle 2011) and of the 11.76% (6/51) average for the Iron Age (Roberts and Cox, 2003, 98).

Spondylosis deformans was observed in the cervical spine of three skeletons, mature adult female 7004, young adult female 7111 and young adult (unsexed) 7262. The condition is identified on dry bone as increased porosity on the surfaces of the vertebral bodies and, as it is mainly caused by degeneration of the intervertebral disc, it is associated with increasing age. That the condition was seen in two young adults from Southdown may suggest that it had resulted from trauma to the neck region in these cases. This may certainly be the case for 7004, who had also sustained a depressed skull fracture and a probable sub-periosteal haematoma to their left tibia.

Extra-spinal joint disease

Extra-spinal OA was observed in three adults, (21.42%, 3/14 of adults or 15.00%, 3/20 of the assemblage) and one juvenile (16.67%; 1/6). These rates are high in comparison with the 4.55% (1/22) of adults with OA in the Yarnton assemblage (Boyle 2011) and the 6.35% and 8.33% of individuals with OA in the East Yorkshire (Stead 1991) and Gussage All Saints (Keepax 1990) assemblages.

In the juvenile (adolescent 7105), the OA was observed in the left hip, which displayed lytic defects from joint cysts, osteophytosis, porosity and bony contour change. All of these changes were secondary to trauma (see below).

Among the adults, a total of six joints (2.63%; 6/228) were affected by OA, including those in the elbow (female 7018), hip (female 7622), knee (female 7018), foot (female 7018) and hand (male 7003 and female 7622). One of the individuals (7622) with hand OA was a 35-45 year old female and this is in keeping with Rogers and Waldron's (1995, 32) observation that hand OA is more commonly seen in middle-aged women. However, the other individual was a prime adult male. The foot OA involved the first right metatarso-phalangeal joint was secondary to hallux valgus ('bunions'). In this condition (not normally considered under joint disease), the proximal phalanx is diverted laterally, exposing the head of the metatarsal. Single or multiple erosions may occur on the medial surface of the metatarsal head (Rogers and Waldron 1995, 82). Painful joint disease may develop in the joint, and in extreme cases, the great toe may cross over, or under, the second toe (Miles *et al.* 2008, 122). Hallux valgus is occasionally found in individuals who do not wear shoes, but it is most commonly associated with footwear with pointed toes (Mays 2005, 139). Females are more commonly affected by the condition in modern, urban populations, probably as the result of ill-fitting, high-heeled shoes (McRae 1999, 181).

In keeping with the fact that OA is strongly linked with increasing age, no individuals within the young adult categories (18-25 years) were found to have extra-spinal joint disease. However, unusually, two of the affected individuals were 25-35 years of age. The third individual was a 35-45 years old. Thus, other causes associated with this multi-factorial disease may have played a greater part in its development in these individuals. Other causes include genetic predisposition, obesity (leading to stress on the joints), activity/lifestyle and environmental factors, such as climate (Rogers and Waldron 1995, 33; Roberts and Manchester 1995, 106).

Trauma

Trauma may be defined as an injury to living tissue inflicted by a force external to the body itself (Lovell 1997, 139; Roberts 2000, 337). Trauma was identified on four skeletons (20.00%, 4/20), four females and one male. They included fractures, an ossified haematoma, a sub-luxation and a parturition scar.

Healed fractures were observed on the cranial vault of 35-45 year old female 7004, and a hand phalanx of 25-35 year old male 7570. A depressed fracture was present on the cranial vault, located on the right parietal bone. Depressed fractures occur when an object of moderate size without a point strikes the vault, but the area of impact does not extend over much of the surface (Galloway 1999,

65). It cannot be said if the striking object was due to interpersonal violence, or even if the object struck the individual, rather than the individual striking the object. The fracture involving the hand phalanx was very well aligned. Fractures involving these bones are often due to direct blows (Galloway, 1999: 156-8). No fractures were observed amongst the juveniles. It is likely that juveniles of the past sustained fractures as frequently as they do today, but they are rarely observed in archaeological bone because they are often incomplete ('greenstick') and remodel rapidly (Brickley *et al.* 2006).

A probable subperiosteal ossified haematoma was present on the left tibia shaft of 35-45 female 7004. This type of lesion is common in archaeological skeletal material (Ortner 2003, 88), manifesting as a generally well demarcated, smooth mass of bone, on the normal bone surface (Aufderheide and Rodríguez-Martín 1998, 310). A haematoma, or blood clot, will form in response to blunt force trauma on the bone. The haematoma is usually resorbed after the initial healing stage is complete, but excessive stress placed upon the periosteum (the fibrous sheath that covers bone) at the injury site may prevent this resorption, and ossification may occur (Lovell 1997, 145).

Adolescent 7105 had suffered trauma to their left hip – probably a compression fracture – which had lead to premature fusion of the innominate and the proximal femoral epiphysis. Secondary to the trauma were OA and disuse atrophy, the latter indicated by a markedly more gracile bone shaft compared with the right femur. Compression fractures result from high impacts such as a fall from a height.

Lastly, one 25-35 year old female (7274) had defect on the dorsal surface of her right pubis bone that is consistent with a parturition scar. Parturition scars may be present as pits or troughs dorsal pubic body or pre-auricular margins of the ilium are are as caused by trauma sustained during child-birth (Cox 2000).

Miscellaneous conditions

Osteochondritis non-dissecans, or pseudo osteochondritis dissecans, was observed on the proximal joint surfaces of the first phalanx of the foot of 7125 (18-25 year old of unknown sex) and 7235 (18-25 year old male). This refers to small pits or porous lesions on the concave surfaces of joints (Rogers and Waldron 1995, 29-30). As the name suggests, they are similar in their appearance to the lesions of osteochondritis dissecans, but their location on concave joint surfaces, instead of convex joint surfaces, differentiates them. It is unclear what causes these lesions, and they could just be normal joint surface variation. Osteo-chondritis dissecans may be caused by low grade chronic trauma or micro-trauma.

Skeleton 7570, a 26-35 year old male, had increased porosity on the ecto-cranial surface of both parietal bones of their skull. Increased porosity on the cranial vault may be seen in porotic hyperostosis (see above), but the present changes were not consistent with this condition because there was no expansion of the diploe and resorption of the outer table. Changes that are similar to the present case are described as having an 'orange peel' appearance by Stirland (2005, 525-6) and are attributed to possible scurvy. Scorbutic lesions can be very subtle in the human skeleton and the disease cannot be diagnosed based on cranial vault porosity alone. It is also possible that the changes are the result of a minor scalp irritation.

The frontal bone of prime adult male 7757 had nodules on the endocranial surface of their frontal bone along the length of the sagittal sinus and up to 17mm lateral to it. The changes are consistent with hyperostosis frontalis interna (HFI), which is associated with obseity and virilism. It may be related to some sort of pituitary gland disorder, its precise cause being unknown (Aufderheide and Rodriguez-Martin 1998).

A somewhat rare discovery was a calculus, or stone, recovered with 25-35 year old female 7018. The calculus was not seen during excavation and therefore its *in situ* location is unknown. It was rounded, smooth, and nodular, was up to 12mm in diameter and was primarily a light, yellowish, brown colour. Its appearance suggests that it is urinary in origin, but without further macroscopic and chemical analysis (the inside of the calculus was not visible), it is not possible to say whether it is from the bladder or kidney. Today, bladder stones are more common among young males from poor agricultural backgrounds, whilst kidney stones are typically seen among adults from affluent industrialised societies (Steinbock, 1989). Poor diet and infection seem to be the primary causes of bladder stones, while a high intake of rich food contributes to kidney stones. Urinary stones have been identified from most time periods, including the Iron Age, but they are infrequently encountered archaeologically because they often go un-recognised (Roberts and Cox 2003; Brothwell 1967).

Undiagnosed conditions

A number of skeletons exhibited lesions for which a confident diagnosis could not be made.

Male 7235 (18-25 years) had a sub-circular, smooth, dense bony mass (*c* 12mm in diameter) on their right parietal bone near lambda. The corre-sponding inner table had a depression that was of a similar size. The bony mass was very similar to a button osteoma, however it lacked the clear circumscribed margin that is typical of this defect. In addition, button osteomas tend to occupy a more anterior position on the cranial vault than was seen in the present case (Aufderheide and Rodríguez-Martín 1998, 375). It is possible that the bony mass is an atypical osteoma which has lost its circumscribed margin as a result of post-mortem modification. Alternatively, it is a morphological or developmental abnormality. Button (or ivory) osteomas are benign tumours and are common among archaeological and living populations. Their cause is unknown, but some have linked them with trauma (Aufderheide and Rodriguez-Martin 1998).

The bones of the left arm of skeleton 7274 (26-35 year old female) were shorter and more gracile than those of the right, but displayed no obvious pathology and no obvious difference in the morphological appearance of muscle attachment sites. Poliomyelitis may cause such limb asymmetry, but in this condition the lower limbs tend to be affected more commonly than the upper limbs (Aufderheide and Rodríguez-Martín 1998, 212). In addition, the limb was not atrophied in the present case, which is common in polio as a result of muscle paralysis (Sissons 1976). Other possible diagnoses are birth trauma or a developmental/congenital defect. During problematic or difficult births an arm of the neonate is sometimes pulled in order to assist the birthing process. This can cause damage to the brachial plexus resulting in an arm of reduced size (Boston pers com).

Skeleton 7570 (26-35 year old male) exhibited increased vascularity and deepening of the meningeal grooves, with some porosity in the largest ones, on the inner table of the skull. The thickness of the diploe had increased but the inner and outer tables had been maintained (the cranium was up to 11mm thick). Thickening and deepening of the meningeal grooves are associated with normal age related changes in the skull (Barber 1993). Thickening is also seen in Paget's disease, a disorder than can result in enlarged bones due to a profound increase in bone resorption and bone formation. The present case did not show the sclerotic and lytic lesions that characterise Paget's disease.

Disarticulated human bone from Iron Age contexts

A small quantity of disarticulated human bone was found in a variety of miscellaneous contexts, some of them non burial contexts (Table 6.16). Bones from one context relate to the fill of grave 7372 and there-

Table 6.16 Disarticulated human bone from Iron Age contexts

Ctx	Context type	Element	Side	Sex	Age	Pathology	MNI	Comments
7498	7002	Mandible (M1)	R	?	Adult		1	
7708								
	EIA layer 7823	Parietal bone fragment	L	?	Adult		1	
		Parietal bone fragment (squamous suture)	L	?	Adult			
7810	7002	TV 11 or 12 (body)		?	Adult	Schmorl's nodes, superior surface	1	
		Mid-lower TV (body)		?	Adult	Schmorl's nodes, inferior surface		
7453	7002	Mts 2-5 (base and shafts)	L	?	Adult		1	
		1st MT (whole)	R	?	Adult			
		Proximal foot phalanx (whole)	?	?	Adult			
7373	Grave 7372 LIA	Ulna (distal third)	L	?	Adult		1	Probably part of
		Radius (midshaft)	R?					7371, although no
		Clavicle (lateral half)	R					no re-fitting could
		Patella (superior half)	L					could be undertaken
		MC3 (base and shaft)	L					
		Tvx9 (arch fragments)						
		Proximal hand phalanx (distal and shaft)	?					
		Distal hand phalanx (whole)	?					
		1 rib head (head and tubercle)	R					
		5 rib fragments (shaft)	?					
		12 skull fragments (vault)	?					
		21 long bone fragments (various)	?					
		1 femur/humerus head	?					
		2 MT/MC head fragments	?					
		X 46 miscellaneous unidentified fragments	?					
7761	Layer 7824–LIA	CV1 (dens facet)		?	Adult?		1	Burnt white/grey, some black. Transverse cracking
7764	EIA deposit/ layer stone	Parietal (where squamous and parietomastoid sutures meet)	L	?	Adult?		1	
7778	Grave 7777 LIA	Proximal tibia (lateral joint surface)	R	?	Adult		1	
		Tibia shaft fragment	?	?	Adult?			
		Tibia shaft fragment	?	?	Adult?			
7779	7002	Proximal tibia joint surface	?	?	Adult		1	
7796	EIA deposit/ layer	Distal femur (both condyles)	L	?	Adult		1	
7810	7002	Fragment rib shaft	L	?	Adult?		1	
7818	7002	Humerus	R	Length= 65 mm; c.40 wks	Neonate		1	
		Humerus	L	?	Neonate			
		Femur	R	?	Neonate			
		Femur	L	?	Neonate			
		Clavicle shaft	R	?	Adult		1	
7829	Layer 7824 LIA	Femur (distal end)	L	?	Neonate		1	
7847	Layer 7824 LIA	Parietal fragment	L	?	Adult?		1	
7848	Layer 7824 LIA	Iliac crest	R	?	Juvenile		1	

Key: Mts=metatarsals; TV=thoracic vertebra

fore probably belong with the uppermost burial (7371). Bones were also recovered from the fill of grave 7777 and probably belong with skeleton 7757. One fragment of burnt bone was found in a late Iron Age general occupation layer, 7761, underlying a stone paving layer 7824, which was one of the latest deposits constructed within the settlement. The mixed nature of the layer meant that nterpretation of the presence of this bone is precluded.

All of the remaining disarticulated bones were not recovered from features and are probably fragments from burials (either already identified above and/or unidentified), disturbed during modern activity. Based on the non-repetition of elements combined with size differences and taking into account contexts, age and sex (Buikstra and Ubelaker 1994), a minimum number of five individuals is represented by these remains, including two neonates (birth to one month), one juvenile (one year to 18 years) and two adults The sex of the individuals could not be determined.

Discussion

The majority of individuals from Southdown Ridge were single inhumations apart from the skeletons found in graves 7372 and 7294. During excavation it was thought that there were four individuals in this grave (adults 7371 and 7376, adolescent 7383, and 26-35 year old male 7384). However osteological analysis determined that fragmentary and poorly preserved adult 7376 comprised the lower legs and feet that belonged with skeleton 7384, reducing the number in the grave to three. Given their relative burial depths it appears that 7383 and 7384 could have been buried at the same time, whilst 7371 may have been added to the grave at a later date. Very little can be said about 7371 (other than that they were over 15 years old when they died), because they comprised a pair of fragmentary lower legs and feet only. No osteological evidence was seen that might suggest that 7383 and 7384 were biologically related. They had no cranial non-metric traits in common (7383 had no non-metric traits at all) and neither did they have any pathology that marked them out from the rest of the assemblage or has a strong genetic component in its aetiology.

It was suggested in the records that one inhumation (7111) may have been excarnated, because the skeleton was disarticulated. However, no cut marks, animal gnawing, burning or other such modifications were observed on the bones. It is possible that the disarticulation had been caused by plough damage instead.

These burials conform to a recognised Iron Age funerary tradition of central Southern England in which simple, crouched inhumations were placed within storage pits, shallow graves and ditches (Whimster 1981). They are among several examples from Dorset, for example, Maiden Castle (Wheeler 1943) and Hod Hill (Richmond 1968), although most are concentrated in Wessex and the Upper Thames Valley (Bryant 1997; Lambrick 2009; Whimster 1981). Like Southdown, the majority appear to be unfurnished. Interestingly, multiple burial and a bias towards young individauls (as seen at Southdown) are uncommon elsewhere, where burials of more senior members of society, in individual graves, seem to be more frequent (Lambrick and Allen 2004). In addition, Southdown is among few examples of the shallow grave type to be associated with a settlement, which is more common to the storage pit and ditch type of burials (Whimster 1981, 191). No dominant burial orientation was observed at Southdown, and this seems to be typical of shallow grave type burials (Whimster 1981, 21). More generally, a north-south orientation was the most common alignment adopted at this time (Lambrick 2009). According to Whimster (1981, 4-36) lying on the right side is less common than lying on the left. Variation in which side the body lies probably refers to differences in local traditions and customs (Wait 1985).

Osteological analysis suggests that the adults had achieved heights that were within the expected range for the Iron Age. Although genetics largely govern potential adult stature, environmental factors encountered during growth can influence actual final height and below average stature is a useful indicator of poor nutrition and physiological stress in childhood (Larsen 1997, 13). This therefore could suggest that the Southdown skeletons had experienced adequate nutrition and low levels of physiological stress during their growing years.

The analysis and interpretation of pathology in the assemblage is hampered by the fact that the number of skeletons is small. The low prevalence of enamel hypoplasia, which indicates low levels of interrupted growth as a result of non-specific health stress, *may* be considered to support the suggestion that the individuals were adequately nourished and their health, un-compromised during childhood. However, the evidence for cribra orbitalia, believed to refer to iron deficiency anaemia during childhood, was prevalent compared to other Iron Age assemblages, implying that this was not the case. Also prevalent among the group was dental disease, non-specific bone inflammation and extraspinal joint disease. The high frequency of extraspinal joint disease is unusual given the predominantly young age profile of the group and this may be related to a combination of poor posture and/or labour intensive activities that placed great strain on the back.

Romano-British inhumation burials

Skeletons 7381, 7524 and 7965 were all recovered from rectangular graves, 7381 and 7524 were north-east to south-west aligned, and 7985 was east west aligned. The skeletons were laid in a supine position with iron nails in the surrounding soil indicating that they was interred within coffins. Skeleton 7524 was also found with hobnails around the feet indicating the presence of boots/sandals.

Skeleton 7381

Skeleton 3481 was lying in an extended, supine, position with both arms folded across the abdomen. It was approximately 76-100% complete, with all regions represented to varying degrees. All bones were fragmentary, but their surface condition was good, with most having patchy surface erosion as a result of root action (consistent with McKinley's (2004, 16) grade 2).

Based on the features of the skull, the sciatic notch of the pelvis and the diameters of the radial and femoral heads, it was concluded that the individual was probably male. A combination of degenerative changes on incomplete auricular surfaces (Lovejoy *et al.* 1990) and dental attrition (Brothwell 1981; Miles 1962) indicated an age at death of approximately 35-45 years.

No metrical data could be gathered from this individual, but several cranial and post-cranial non-metric traits, especially those of the facial region and long bones, could be scored for presence or absence. Among the cranial traits that were present were an accessory infraorbital foramen (an additional blood vessel opening immediately adjacent to the infraorabital foramen) on the right maxialla (not present on the left), and a supraorbital foramen above the left orbit (a bridged vessel opening; the notch remained unbridged on the right). Only one post-cranial non-metric trait was observed and was a double anterior facet on the left calcaneus (right was unobservable). All of these traits are relatively common on archaeological human bone.

Spondylosis deformans (or degnerative disc disease) was present on the superior/inferior surfaces of two cervical vertebrae. The condition is associated with the degeneration of the intervertebral disc and is diagnosed on dry bone by the presence of coarse pitting and associated new bone growth on the superior and/or inferior surfaces of the vertebral bodies (Rogers and Waldron 1995, 27). As with most other joint diseases, there is a general correlation between degenerative disc disease and increasing age (Roberts and Cox 2003, 353; Molleson and Cox 1993, 77). It has been suggested that prolonged labour-intensive physical activities may cause the onset of the condition (Jurmain 1977, 353-356; Lovell 1997). Changes consistent with spinal osteoarthritis were found on the left superior apophyseal joint between the fourth and fifth cervical vertebrae and on the left costovertebral joint of the tenth thoracic vertebra and rib. Marginal osteophytosis was also present on one thoracic and one lumbar vertebra.

Osteophytes and porosity were present on the anterior portion of the temporal facet of the left temporomandibular joint indicating osteoarthritis (OA) in this joint. The osteophyte had formed a pseudo-facet, indicating that in this case the OA may have been caused by a sub-luxation (dislocation) of the joint.

Cribra orbitalia, believed to be the result of iron deficiency anaemia (Stuart-Macadam 1991), was observed on both orbits. They were scored as a type three for the left orbit and a type four for the right orbit after Stuart Macadam (1991,109).

The dentition was incomplete (Table 6.17). Caries, ante-mortem tooth loss and calculus were all present. All of the caries were small except for those on the right mandibular first and second molars, where they were medium-sized. An unusual pattern of dental attrition was noted. Seven anterior teeth were worn down to their roots and the crowns of the remaining five anterior teeth very also heavily worn. It is possible that the anterior dentition had been heavily used to masticate food as a result of the loss of posterior teeth and pain caused by caries in other posterior teeth.

Skeleton 7524

Skeleton 7524 was lying in a extended, supine position with both arms extended beside its sides

Table 6.17 Dentition of skeleton 7381

n/p	n/p	X	X	X	C	RC	R	R		R	R	n/p	n/p	n/p	n/p
8	7	6	5	4	3	2	1	1	2	3	4	5	6	7	8
8	7	6	5	4	3	2	1	1	2	3	4	5	6	7	8
n/p	C	C	R	R	/		n/p	/			/		ca	C	n/p

C=caries; ca=calculus; X= AMTL; /= lost post-mortem; R= root only; n/p=not present

and the right hand on the pelvis. Most regions of the skeleton were represented, which was between 51 and 75% complete. The vertebrae, ribs and skull were highly fragmentary. The surface condition of the bones was good with some erosion from root activity being present on most bones (grade 2 after McKinley 2004,16).

Based on features of the skull, the sciatic notch of the pelvis and the diameter of the femoral head it was concluded that this individual was possibly female. The degree and extent of degenerative changes on the auricular surfaces, coupled with the fused status of the medial clavicle epiphyses indicated that the individual was approximately 20-25 years of age (young adult).

Due to fragmentation only very limited metrical data could be obtained and it was not possible to estimate the individual's stature. Several non-metrical cranial and post-cranial traits could be scored. A supraorbital foramen (blood vessel opening) was present above the right orbit of the cranium. Out of the twenty-one post-cranial non-metric traits that could be scored, none were present.

The left and right parietal bones of the skull exhibited increased porosity on the ectocranial surface, along the saggittal suture. The lesion had an orange peel like texture and there was no expansion of the diploe and resorption of the outer table, consistent with porotic hyperostosis, believed to be caused by iron deficiency anaemia (Aufderheide and Rodríguez-Martín 1998, 348-9). Stirland (2005, 525-6) has linked this lesion with possible childhood scurvy, but on its own this it is not diagnostic of the disease. It is possible that it is inflammation from to a minor scalp irritation only.

Other pathology includes a linear defect on the navicular surface of the left talus bone of the foot. The changes were benign and may refer to old healed trauma, or a developmental anomaly. The joint surface to the calcaneus on the inferior of the left talus also had a sub-circular lytic lesion, approximately 9mm in diameter and 3mm deep, consistent with osteochondritis non-dissecans, described above.

Most of the maxillary tooth locations/sockets and half of the mandibular were present. Twenty-nine teeth were present, only one had been lost

post-mortem, the remaining two were missing along with their sockets (Table 6.18). A left maxillary deciduous canine had been retained. This had caused slight anterior angulation and distal rotation of the permanent canine, which had failed to fully erupt into the occlusal plane. Caries, calculus and DEH were all present. There were six carious lesions on five teeth (one on the retained canine) and most were small or medium in size. This is with the exception of the left mandibular third molar, where entire crown had been destroyed by caries (classified as 'gross' caries). Dental enamel hypoplasia was only present on the left mandibular lateral incisor. Here, the position of the defect (a line) suggested enamel growth arrest between 1.5 and 2.5 years of age.

Skeleton 7965

This skeleton was buried in a supine position with the right arm flexed at the elbow and the hand by the neck. Their left arm was slightly flexed with the hand by their right hip. The skeleton's legs were slightly flexed with their knees lying on their right hand side. Between 75 and 100% of the skeleton was present and all regions were represented. Approximately half of the skeleton was fragmentary. In keeping with the other Romano-British skeletons, bone surface condition was good (grade 2 after McKinley 2004,16).

Based on the features of the skull and pelvis it was concluded that this individual was male. This was supported by measurements taken on the clavicle, humerus, radius and femur. Both the pubic symphyses and auricular surfaces (Suchey-Brooks 1990, Lovejoy et al. 1985, Buckberry and Chamberlain 2002) indicated that this individual approximately 25-35 years old (prime adult). This was was supported by the moderate degree of attrition on the molar teeth (Brothwell, 1981; Miles, 1962)

By employing the maximum length of the right humerus, it was estimated that the individual was approximately 1.76 cm (+/- 4.05 cm), or five feet nine inches tall.

Eighteen cranial non-metric traits could be scored and among those present were a parietal foramen (a small vessel opening near the sagittal suture and

Table 6.18 Dentition of skeleton 7524

n/p		/											caC	C	n/p
8	7	6	5	4	3	2	1	1	2	3	4	5	6	7	8
8	7	6	5	4	3	2	1	1	2	3	4	5	6	7	8
			C						eh				ca	C	CR

C=caries; ca=calculus; eh=enamel hypoplasia; R=root only n/p=not present

254

lambda) on the right (absent on the left); bilateral accessory supraorbital foramina and bilateral extra-sutural mastoid foramina. It was possible to score a standard range of post-cranial non-metric traits and those present included bilateral femoral hypotrochanteric fossae, bilateral vastus notches and a double anterior facet on the left calcaneus (could not be observed on the right).

Scattered foramina and capillary-like impressions were observed in the left and right orbits respectively of the skull and are consistent with cribra orbitalia (types two and one respectively, after Stuart-Macadam, 1991,109), believed to reflect iron deficiency anaemia (ibid.,109). Evidence of spinal joint disease was seen in the form of Schmorl's nodes which were present on the superior and inferior surfaces of six cervical and two lumbar vertebrae. There were marginal osteophytes on two cervical vertebrae and spondylosis deformans on two cervical vertebrae.

Calculus, periodontal disease, caries and AMTL were observed on the dentition. Caries, seen on two teeth, presented as small lesions only (Table 6.19).

Discussion

East-west orientated inhumations became a common burial rite in Roman Britain from the second century AD, replacing the earlier tradition of cremation. While this could be interpreted as the adoption of Christian ways, there is no evidence of Christianity in Britain until the fourth century (Millet 1995, 115). Although only one of the burials from Southdown had been buried on a definite east-west alignment, the other two occupied a similar orientation to this (ie north-east to south-west).

Osteological analysis identified three adults, two males (a prime and a mature adult) and one young adult female. Only the stature of the prime adult male 7965 could be estimated (1.76m) and this was found to be higher than the average male stature of 1.69m, calculated by Roberts and Cox (2003, 163) using data from several Romano-British assemblages.

Pathological lesions were present on all of the individuals and the majority of these related to spinal or extra spinal joint disease. Cribra orbitalia

was also frequent, but is not an unusual or rare condition to see in archaeological human bone. However, it may be worth noting that, according to Roberts and Cox's (2003, 141) national survey, only 9.64% of Romano-British individuals exhibit this lesion.

THE ANIMAL BONE *by Lena Strid*

Introduction

The Southdown Ridge animal bone assemblage consisted of a total of 7466 refitted hand collected fragments from securely dated contexts. The majority derived from Iron Age deposits, but faunal remains from the early Roman period were also present. A small number of bones from the medieval, post-medieval and modern periods have been excluded from the analysis. The small number of identifiable bones from sieved soil samples yielded little information pertaining to animal husbandry practices, butchery or ritual deposits and are therefore also not included in this analysis. A full record of the assemblage can be found in the site archive.

Methodology

The bones were identified at OA South using comparative skeletal reference collections, in addition to osteological identification manuals. All animal remains were counted and weighed, and where possible identified to species, element, side and zone. Sheep and goat were identified to species where possible, using Boessneck *et al.* (1964) and Prummel and Frisch (1986). They were otherwise classified as 'sheep/goat'. Ribs and vertebrae, with the exception of atlas and axis, were classified by size: 'large mammal' representing cattle, horse and deer; 'medium mammal' representing sheep/goat, pig and large dog; 'small mammal' representing small dog, cat and hare; and 'microfauna' representing animals such as frog, rat and mice. The great northern diver was identified by Joanne Cooper at the Natural History Museum, Tring.

The condition of the bone was graded on a 6-point system (0-5). Grade 0 equating to very well

Table 6.19 Dentition of skeleton 7965

X	ca C	X	ca p	ca p	ca	ca	ca	/	ca	ca	ca	/	X	n/p	caC
8	7	6	5	4	3	2	1	1	2	3	4	5	6	7	8
8	7	6	5	4	3	2	1	1	2	3	4	5	6	7	8
n/p	ca	ca	ca	ca	ca	pca	pca	ca	ca	ca	ca	ca	ca	ca	Cca

C=caries; ca=calculus; p=periodontitis; X= AMTL; /= lost post-mortem; n/p=not present

Table 6.20 Bone preservation grading methodology

Grade 0	Excellent preservation. Entire bone surface complete
Grade 1	Good preservation. Almost all bone surface complete
Grade 2	Fair preservation
Grade 3	Poor preservation. Most bone surface destroyed
Grade 4	Very poor preservation. No original bone surface remaining
Grade 5	Extremely poor preservation. Unlikely to be able to identify element

preserved bone, and grade 5 indicating that the bone had suffered such structural and attritional damage as to make it unrecognisable (Table 6.20).

The minimum number of individuals (MNI) was calculated based on the most frequently occurring bone for each species, using Serjeantson's (1996) and Worley's (Strid 2012) zoning guides and taking into account left and right sides, as well as epiphyseal fusion and tooth wear. For the calculation of the number of identified fragments per species (NISP) all identifiable fragments were counted, although bones with modern breaks were refitted. The weight of bone fragments has been recorded in order to give an idea of their size and to facilitate an alternative means of quantification.

For ageing, Habermehl's (1975) data on epiphyseal fusion was used. Three fusion stages were recorded: 'unfused', 'in fusion', and 'fused'. 'In fusion' indicates that the epiphyseal line is still visible. Tooth wear was recorded using Grant's tooth wear stages (Grant 1982), and correlated with tooth eruption (Habermehl 1975). In order to estimate an age for the animals, the methods of Halstead (1985), Payne (1973) and O'Connor (1988) were used for cattle, sheep/goat and pig respectively.

Sex estimation was carried out on morphological traits on cattle pelves and pig canine teeth, using data from Schmid (1972) and Vretemark (1997). Further, the presence/absence of antler was used to sex roe deer remains.

Measurements were taken according to von den Driesch (1976), using digital callipers with an accuracy of 0.01 mm. Withers' height of dog was calculated according to Harcourt (1974).

The assemblage

Bone preservation

The bones were generally in fair condition, regardless of time period (Table 6.21). The relatively large quantity of very well preserved fragments in the early Roman assemblage is not indicative of different bone disposal practices, as these fragments are exclusively teeth and enamel is far more resistant to taphonomic destruction than bone.

Gnaw marks from carnivores, probably mainly dogs, were found on bone from almost all periods. While they were more common in the early Iron Age and middle Iron Age/late Iron Age assemblages, they comprised less than 6% of all bones from these two periods. Gnaw marks from rodents were only observed in the early Iron Age and middle Iron Age/late Iron Age assemblages. Burnt bones, ranging from partially charred to calcined, were recovered in relatively small numbers from all periods.

Overview of the assemblage

The faunal assemblage contained bones from the early Iron Age, middle Iron Age/late Iron Age, late Iron Age, late Iron Age/early Roman periods, as well as bones from unspecified Iron Age and Roman periods. The majority of the assemblage is early Iron Age and middle Iron Age/late Iron Age. In all phases most bones were recovered from layers which were found close to the gully of enclosure 7676 (contexts 7675 and 7913), and represent abandonment material. Features used for depositing bones were overwhelmingly ditches and gullies, with exception for the early Iron Age, where more bone fragments were found in pits (Table 6.22). Analyses from Iron Age and Roman chalkland sites in Hampshire suggest that ditches are more often dominated by cattle bones and pits by sheep and pig bones (Rielly 2009, 206). This hypothesis has not been verifiable for the Southdown Ridge assemblage since the total number of bones from cattle and sheep/goat found in ditches and pits from each

Table 6.21 Preservation level for bones

Phase	n	0	1	2	3	4	5	Gnawed bones	Burnt bones
EIA	3624	7.3%	14.0%	66.7%	1.8%	0.3%		156	16
MIA/LIA	3072	6.3%	21.4%	70.2%	2.0%	0.1%		181	19
LIA	494	4.5%	21.5%	70.4%	3.0%	0.6%		20	6
LIA/ER	245	8.6%	8.6%	75.5%	6.1%	1.2%		7	1
ER	41	22.0%	7.3%	68.3%		2.4%			1
IA	349	6.9%	18.9%	62.5%	11.2%	0.6%		14	6
Roman	1				100.0%				

Table 6.22 Assemblages per phase and feature type

Phase	N	Ditch/Gully	Pit	Post hole	Burial	Layer	Hollow	Natural feature
EIA	3624	189	234	85		2673	30	53
MIA/LIA	3072	110	47			2915		
LIA	494	153	8		152	181		
LIA/ER	245	28				217		
ER	41					41		
IA	349	120	35	47		147		
Roman	1				1			

period is very small. In the early Iron Age and in the middle Iron Age/late Iron Age assemblages pig is the only animal where the bones appear differentially distributed within these two feature types, the vast majority of the pig remains being found in pits. It is not clear if this difference is a real reflection of differential disposal practice. Ditches are often less deep than Iron Age storage pits and are more likely to be recut, thus exposing the bones to scavengers and increased chemical and microbial destruction.

When the types of bones deposited in cut features are compared with those deposited in layers there appears to be little difference in the distribution of species.However the difference in sample sizes is a concern since there were comparatively few speciable bones deposited in features. Nevertheless, when comparing the bone assemblages from layers and features chronologically, no differences in species frequency could be discerned between the two groups. An analysis of the zoned elements recovered from layers indicated that cattle bones were slightly less fragmented in early Iron Age layers than in the middle Iron Age/late Iron Age ones. The degree of fragmentation of sheep and horse bones varied within

Table 6.23 Number of identified bones/taxon by chronological phase

	EIA	MIA/LIA	LIA	LIA/ER	ER	IA	Roman
Cattle	339 (10)	388 (9)	60 (3)	26 (1)	6 (1)	39 (2)	
Sheep/goat	420 (24)	491 (21)	60 (4)	32 (1)	9 (1)	52 (3)	1 (1)
Sheep	49*	10	2	2		1	
Goat		1					
Pig	145 (7)	102 (5)	15 (2)	8 (1)		14 (1)	
Horse	75 (3)	60 (3)	13 (1)	4 (1)	1 (1)	3	
Dog	98** (3)	13 (1)	1 (1)	1 (1)		2	
Cat		1 (1)					
Red deer	2 (1)						
Roe deer	4 (1)	1 (1)	1 (1)				
Deer sp.	2	5					
Domestic fowl		1 (1)					
Duck		1 (1)					
Gull sp.	1 (1)						
Great northern diver				1 (1)			
Indet. bird	1	4	1				
Rodent	2						
Frog		2 (1)					
Toad		4 (2)		1 (1)			
Amphibian		4					
Microfauna		3					
Small mammal	1	5	2	2		2	
Medium mammal	600	553	95	60	9	69	
Large mammal	407	410	56	35	1	46	
Indeterminate	1118	1063	188	73	15	121	
TOTAL	3264	3072	494	245	41	349	1
Weight (g)	35263	28957	5700	1705	347	2842	5

MNI within parenthesis   *: including 37 bones from articulated lamb skeleton   **: including 82 bones from articulated dog skeleton

the different periods, whereas there was no difference for pig. The number of zoned elements recovered from cut features was too small to form a suitable dataset for an analysis of the fragmentation degree. This general picture suggests that the frequency and methods of waste disposal and butchery techniques, including marrow extraction, was essentially similar throughout the Iron Age at Southdown Ridge.

The species present include cattle (*Bos taurus*), sheep (*Ovis aries*), goat (*Capra hircus*), pig (*Sus domesticus*), horse (*Equus caballus*), dog (*Canis familiaris*), cat (*Felis sp.*), red deer (*Cervus elaphus*), roe deer (*Capreolus capreolus*), domestic fowl (*Gallus gallus domesticus*), duck (*Anatinae/Aythyinae*), gull (*Laridae*), great northern diver (*Gavia immer*), and frog/toad (*Rana sp./Bufo sp.*). The assemblage also included remains from red/roe deer, unidentified bird and mouse-sized rodent (Table 6.23). Sheep are more common than goats in the assemblage, which is typical for other Iron Age assemblages from southern England (Hambleton 1999, 14) and it is therefore likely that most of the sheep/goat remains are from sheep. They will therefore be discussed as sheep in the report, except where circumstances warrant a more precise identification.

Early Iron Age and middle Iron Age/late Iron Age

The assemblages dated to the early Iron Age and middle Iron Age/late Iron Age periods comprise the majority of the faunal remains from Southdown Ridge. The two assemblages are similar in species representation and livestock frequency. The ageable and sexable remains are, however, too small in number to clearly state whether there were any chronological changes in animal husbandry strategies at the settlement.

Livestock

Sheep is the most common livestock animal, particularly if using Minimum Number of Individuals (MNI) as a base for comparison (Table 6.23). The MNI figures doesn't change much between the two periods for any taxa, whereas the fragment count (NISP) suggest an increase in the numbers of sheep and a reduction of pigs in the middle Iron Age/late Iron Age. An increase in sheep in relation to cattle from the early Iron Age to the late Iron Age is also verified for several other animal assemblages in Central Southern England, possibly associated with an increase in arable production and consequently reduction of cattle pastures (Hambleton 1999, 87).

There are relatively few ageable remains from livestock, but the dental and epiphyseal data which is present indicates slaughter of young cattle and sheep for meat and older cattle and sheep past their prime as breeders, beasts of burden, dairy and/or wool producers (Tables 6.24-6.25). Sheep were generally not kept to an advanced age, indicating that wool production was not a main feature of sheep husbandry. Pigs were mainly killed as sub adults, ie between 8-20 months of age. A small number of pigs were slightly older, as indicated by small to medium amounts of wear on the third mandibular molar, and might represent breeding animals kept for some more years (Table 6.26).

The epiphyseal fusion data show little difference in the slaughter age of cattle between the early Iron Age and the middle Iron Age/late Iron Age, whereas sheep display a marked increase in animals over 3.5 years of age in the later period (Table 6.27). The sample size for pig is quite small but suggests that there might have been a relative increase in younger pigs slaughtered in the middle Iron

Table 6.24 (all phases): Dental analysis of cattle, using Halstead (1985)

	N	0-1 months	1-8 months	8-18 months	18-30 months	30-36 months	Young adult	Adult	Old adult	Senile
EIA	10			1	1	2			3	3
MIA/LIA	12					4		2	3	3
IA	1									1

Table 6.25 (all phases): Dental analysis of sheep/goat, using Payne (1973). A further 10 loose third mandibular molars in the middle Iron Age/late Iron Age assemblage belong to sheep of 4-8 years

	N	0-2 months	2-6 months	6-12 months	1-2 years	2-3 years	3-4 years	4-6 years	6-8 years	8-10 years
EIA	21		1	2		4	9	5		
MIA/LIA	14			1	3	4	6			
LIA	3					3				
LIA/ER	1					1				
IA	2						1	1		

Table 6.26 (all phases): Dental analysis of pig, using O'Connor (1988).

	N	Juvenile	Immature	Sub-adult	Adult	Elderly
EIA	12		2	8	2	
MIA/LIA	5			4	1	
LIA	1			1		

Age/late Iron Age. It is difficult to discern whether there were any changes in the late Iron Age/early Roman period, as the sample size for all taxa is too small to be reliable.

The sexed remains are few in number and therefore any analysis must be considered tentative. Nevertheless, the remains suggest that there was a predominance of female cattle and sheep throughout the Iron Age (Table 6.28). Such a sex

Table 6.27 Epiphyseal closure of cattle, sheep/goat, pig and horse

	EIA		MIA/LIA		LIA - ER		IA	
CATTLE	N	% unfused	N	% unfused	N	% unfused	N	% unfused
Early fusion	32	3.1%	35	2.9%	3	0.0%		
Mid fusion	26	11.5%	34	8.8%	4	0.0%	5	50.0%
Late fusion	12	33.3%	18	27.8%	1	0.0%	2	0.0%
SHEEP/GOAT	N	% unfused	N	% unfused	N	% unfused	N	% unfused
Early fusion	23	17.4%	41	12.2%	4	25.0%	3	33.3%
Mid fusion	15	53.3%	15	33.3%	5	20.0%	1	0.0%
Late fusion	14	57.1%	14	14.3%	1	100.0%	1	0.0%
PIG	N	% unfused	N	% unfused	N	% unfused	N	% unfused
Early fusion	5	0.0%	5	0.0%	2	50.0%	2	0.0%
Mid fusion	12	25.0%	9	55.6%	2	100.0%		
Late fusion	2	50.0%	1	100.0%				
HORSE	N	% unfused	N	% unfused	N	% unfused	N	% unfused
Early fusion	11	0.0%	8	0.0%	2	0.0%		
Mid fusion			4	0.0%				
Late fusion	1	0.0%	1	0.0%				

Table 6.28 Sexed bones

Phase	Species	Element	Female	Male	Intact male	Castrate
EIA	Cattle	Metacarpal	3			
		Pelvis	6	1		
	Sheep/goat	Pelvis	5			
	Sheep	Horn core		1	1	
	Pig	Maxillary canine	1	1		
	Pig	Mandibular canine	4	4		
	Horse	Maxillary canine		1		
MIA/LIA	Cattle	Metacarpal	1	1		
		Pelvis	4	2		
	Sheep/goat	Pelvis	1			
	Pig	Maxillary canine	1	2		
	Pig	Mandibular canine	5	1		
	Horse	Canine		1		
LIA/ER	Sheep/goat	Pelvis	1			
IA	Cattle	Metacarpal	2			
	Sheep/goat	Pelvis	1			

ratio would imply a herd keeping strategy focussed on secondary products, where most male animals were slaughtered for meat at a young age. The pig remains in the middle Iron Age/late Iron Age assemblage indicate a relative increase in sows. The sexually diagnostic permanent canines erupt at 6-9 months of age and this increase could imply a focus on the slaughter of male pigs below this age, perhaps to enlarge the number of breeding sows.

Since the pre-and post-depositional fragmentation of bones at Southdown Ridge resulted in relatively few measureable bones, an inter-phase comparison is inadvisable due to representative bias. However, the cattle, sheep and horse bones are mostly of similar size to those from contemporary Iron Age sites in southern Britain (Armour-Chelu 1991, 143-144, 146; Hamilton-Dyer 1999, 198-199). Minor variations may reflect different sex ratios, age ratios and/or nutrition related size differences.

Other taxa

The horse remains come exclusively from adult or sub-adult animals, indicating that horses were kept as working animals rather than for meat. While horses were occasionally used for food in the Iron Age, at Southdown Ridge this practice is only indicated by a single middle Iron Age/late Iron Age horse humerus that was split open to facilitate marrow extraction.

The dog remains comprise 30 disarticulated bones from adult or sub-adult dogs, mostly recovered from layers, and a partial adult dog skeleton from early Iron Age ditch terminal (7046). The latter will be discussed with other articulated remains below. The disarticulated dog remains were often fragmented and carnivore gnaw marks on one tibia suggest that the dog remains had been exposed to scavengers, probably by other dogs at the settlement, as well as trampling and redistribution of waste deposits. Most of the dog remains retrieved from layers derive from the head. Animal skulls as foundation sacrifices are known from the prehistoric period up to the modern era (Falk 2008; Grant 1984) and the skull and mandible fragments could therefore indicate one or several disturbed skull deposits, perhaps from a house that had been torn down. Withers' height calculations could only be carried out on the articulated dog, which had a withers' height of 54.4cm (tibia), which is the equivalent of a modern day Labrador retriever. The withers' heights of Iron Age dogs in Britain range between 29-58cm (Harcourt 1974, 163) and the dog from Southdown Ridge would therefore represent a

Table 6.29 Measurements of cattle, sheep/goat, pig and horse

Species	Bone	Measurement	Phase	N	Mean	Min	Max
Cattle	Metacarpal	GL	EIA	3	171.5	170.0	173.5
		GL	MIA/LIA	2	172.5	170.0	175.0
		Bd	EIA	5	51.2	46.8	54.1
		Bd	MIA/LIA	4	54.7	49.3	60.5
	Metatarsal	GL	EIA	1	200.5		
		Bd	EIA	1	47.4		
	Tibia	GL	EIA	2	287.5	287.0	288.0
		Bd	EIA	3	51.0	49.4	51.8
		Bd	MIA/LIA	6	52.7	49.3	59.3
		Bd	LIA	1	54.6		
Sheep/goat	Metacarpal	GL	MIA/LIA	1	121.2		
		Bd	MIA/LIA	1	22.4		
		Bd	LIA/ER	1	21.5		
	Metatarsal	GL	MIA/LIA	2	126.3	123.0	129.6
		Bd	EIA	1	20.5		
		Bd	MIA/LIA	2	21.0	20.6	21.3
	Tibia	Bd	EIA	4	22.1	21.1	22.8
		Bd	MIA/LIA	8	22.0	20.9	22.6
		Bd	LIA/ER	1	22.9		
		Bd	ER	1	23.7		
Pig	Metacarpal IV	GL	EIA	1	73.1		
Horse	Metacarpal	GL	EIA	1	222.0		
	Tibia	Bd	MIA/LIA	1	61.7		

comparatively large dog, possibly used for guarding, herding and/or hunting.

A distal fragment of a cat radius from middle Iron Age/early Iron Age layer (7886, stratified below stone spread 7824) is the only indication of cats in the assemblage. It is unclear whether the cat radius belonged to a domestic cat (*Felis catus*) or the native wildcat (*Felis silvestris*). The evidence for introduction of domestic cat in Britain is ambiguous, but it is believed that they were present in the Iron Age (O'Connor 2010, 92). Wild cat and domestic cat are mainly distinguished by measurements, the wild cat being the larger animal. However, there is an overlap, particularly for neutered domestic cats, which can grow very large. This is the case for the Southdown Ridge cat, which is within the upper size range for modern domestic male cats (Johansson and Hüster 1987, 82) and within the size range for Mesolithic wild cats (Strid 2000).

The middle Iron Age/late Iron Age assemblage also included one tarsometatarsus from domestic fowl. Domestic fowl are rare throughout Iron Age Britain, and only becomes frequent in the Roman period (Poole 2010, 156-158). They were small and therefore probably kept mainly for eggs and feathers/down, with meat being a by-product. However, fowl also has social and symbolic significance. They were common as sacrifices in the late Iron Age and Roman periods and were used for cockfighting (Cool 2006, 98-103; Poole 2010, 158).

Wild animals are represented by remains from red deer and roe deer. Duck and indeterminate gull were also present. Red deer have not been identified in the early Iron Age assemblage, although red deer remains may be included in the indeterminate deer remains from this period. Fragments of antler from red and roe deer suggest that antler working took place at the settlement. No burrs or pedicles were present, and therefore it is not clear whether the antlers came from hunted stags or were collected in winter when the deer shed their antlers. However, hunting of deer is implied by the presence of a first phalanx from red deer and a pelvis, a tooth, a metacarpal and a metatarsal from roe deer.

While the duck tarsometatarsus is likely to be butchery waste, it is uncertain if the seagull humerus represents domestic waste. The lack of butchery marks on the humerus may not mean anything, as a cooked bird carcass can be disjointed by pulling and twisting (Serjeantson 2009, 138). Sea birds have been eaten in historical and earlier times by people living on the north-Atlantic coastline (Serjeantson 2009, 395), but it is not known if gulls would have been considered a normal part of the diet in Iron Age Dorset.

Butchery

Butchery marks occurred on bones from cattle, sheep, pig and horse as well as on indeterminate medium and large mammals. Butchery marks are significantly more common on bones from cattle than on sheep, despite the fact that that sheep/goat bones are more numerous. The butchery marks on cattle consisted mainly of cut marks at the phalanges and at the carpal/tarsal/metapodial joints, indicating skinning and/or disarticulation.

Pathology

Pathological bones were noted only in the early Iron Age and in the middle Iron Age/late Iron Age assemblages. All cattle pathologies in the middle Iron Age/late Iron Age assemblage were connected to joint disorders of pelvis and lower legs, deriving from the use of cattle for traction purposes and/or from age related wear and tear. Two female cattle pelves displayed eburnation in the hip socket, suggesting the possibility that cows were used as beasts of burden. This was not found in the early Iron Age assemblage, where only one metatarsal with minor exostoses around the proximal joint surface could be associated with muscle stress on joints. The pathological sheep remains in the early Iron Age assemblage include smooth bone growths on a tibia and a metatarsal respectively. These are probably haematomas, that is ossified swellings of the membrane covering the bone shaft. Haematomas are mainly caused by blunt impact trauma and are often found on metapodials, as the lack of muscle tissue make these bones vulnerable for impact trauma. One distal humerus had an exostos on the lateral side of the joint. This could be the beginning of a so called "penning elbow", where exostoses occur at the elbow joint, possibly caused by repeated minor impact trauma to the joint. Oral pathologies were found on a single mandible, which displayed bone absorption at the gum and infected molar roots. Oral pathologies were the only pathologies present among sheep in the middle Iron Age/late Iron Age assemblage. These included bone absorption at the gum, buccal swelling of the horizontal ramus and/or widened alveoles. A semi-articulated early Iron Age dog skeleton (see above) displayed exostoses on the first two lumbar vertebrae as well as one fractured rib. A healed fracture of a middle Iron Age/late Iron Age pig scapula was the only other indication of trauma in the animal bone assemblage.

Associated bone groups

Associated bone groups (ABG) occur on many Iron Age sites, often interpreted as ritual deposits or as disposal of carcasses not considered fit for consumption. They commonly fall into three categories: articulate skeletons, complete skulls and articulated limbs – all with little or no signs of butchery (Hill 1995, 27-28). Special animal deposits are usually typified by unusual placement, for example at the base of pits and wells, and by body parts which differ from normal food waste by species and age group composition (Fulford 2001; Hill 1995; Wilson 1992, 342-345).

The ABGs from Southdown Ridge include partial skeletons of one lamb/kid, one piglet and one adult dog, as well as a horse skull. All were found in features dated to the early Iron Age.

The lamb/kid was found in feature 7101, a small isolated pit in the western part of the site. This feature is not associated with any building and contained no dateable material. There were no other bones in the feature, leaving open the possibility that it was dug specifically for depositing the lamb/kid. The feature was distant from the settlement, but close to the cross-ridge dyke. Would a dead lamb be buried or merely left to decompose in the pasture? Did the location of the feature have an significance in the early Iron Age landscape, possibly associated with the cross-ridge dyke, and was the lamb a ritual offering? Without comparative data from similar deposits these questions are hard to answer.

The single fill of pit 7344 contained the partial skeleton of a piglet and 21 loose maxillary teeth from an adult male horse. The teeth are the sole remains of a now destroyed horse skull which was noted during excavation. The lack of mandibular teeth indicates that the jaw bones were disarticulated from the skull prior to deposition. The pit also contained a small amount of slag and pot sherds, which from their composition are believed to be accidental inclusions rather than deliberate deposits of complete pots. The remains of the piglet in close association with the horse skull suggests that this is likely to be a deposit of ritual significance.

The dog skeleton was recovered from the terminal of a boundary ditch (7046) that formed part of the early Iron Age enclosure system. The feature was very shallow and only partly excavated so it was not clear whether the dog bones recovered represented the entire deposit. There are a small number of finds of dog skeletons deposited in Iron Age ditches on other sites, pits being the most common feature type for deposits of this species (Morris 2008, 114). These are often interpreted as ritual, suggesting deposits to appease deities, to ward of bad luck and/or to guard against malevolent spirits (Smith 2006, 12-13).

Late Iron Age – early Roman

The late Iron Age, late Iron Age/early Roman and early Roman assemblages comprised a total of 519 bones, of which 157 were identifiable to species (Table 6.23). These three assemblages were dominated by domestic mammals; great northern diver and toad were the only wild taxa present. The presence of great northern diver in archaeological contexts from southern Britain is unusual. Previous records include Meare (Iron Age), Halangy Down (Roman), Portchester (Roman, Saxon) and Southampton (Saxon) (Yalden and Albarella 2009, 206). The Southampton bone displays cut marks, suggesting that the diver was utilised for meat or plumage (Bourdillon and Coy 1980, 118).

The majority of the faunal remains derives from composite layers, with a few from the top fills of and linear features, suggesting that they represent household waste, and were for the most part redeposited.

The fragment count as well as the MNI calculations indicate that sheep were slightly more common than cattle in the assemblage, comprising 47.7% and 41.8% respectively of the main three livestock taxa. However, this must be considered with caution, as the combined NISP for cattle, sheep and pig falls under 300 fragments, which are considered too few to produce a reliable sample size for inter-species comparison (Hambleton 1999, 39-40). Regardless, due to their greater size, cattle would have provided most of the meat.

The ageing data for livestock is scant (Tables 6.25-6.26), but seems to support the common animal husbandry strategies of keeping pigs for meat and cattle and sheep/goat for a multitude of products. Bones from neonatal and/or juvenile calves, lambs and piglets, could represent either natural mortalities or deliberately slaughtered young animals for meat.

Late Iron Age burials

There were 19 late Iron Age human burials, of which 11 contained faunal remains (Table 6.30). In most cases the faunal remains were more suggestive of accidental inclusions in the grave fill rather than deliberate deposits. However, the faunal remains from inhumations 7003, 7565 and 7624 merit further discussion.

Burial 7003 was heavily disturbed by ploughing activity and no grave cut was observed. Several bones from cattle and a small number of bones from sheep/goat and pig were found in close association to the human remains. The cattle remains include fragments from at least three metacarpals, one metatarsal, one calcaneus, one first phalanx, one femur, two tibiae, one radius, three ulnae, at least one

Table 6.30 Number of identified bones/taxon in the late Iron Age burials

Burial	7003	7017	7054	7104	7124	7151	7273	7385	7565	7624	7777
Cattle	17		7	1			1			1	
Sheep/goat	3		2			1	1		6	2	1
Pig	1		1	1			1				
Horse										1	
Dog						1					
Medium mammal	3			1	1			1	7	17	
Large mammal	6		1	1			3		1	3	
Indeterminate	2	2	20				2			32	
TOTAL	32	2	31	4	1	2	8	1	14	56	1
Weight (g)	1066	1	137	15	3	19	145	1	32	339	11

mandible and one maxillary molar. All bones were fragmented and it is uncertain whether they derive from the burial itself or from overlaying layer (7002).

Burial 7565 contained seven disarticulated bones from a juvenile lamb as well as a small number of bones from adult livestock. The lamb bones and fragments of a sheep tibia and three medium (sheep/goat sized) mammal ribs may represent food offerings or remains from a funeral feast, whereas the other bones were probably accidental inclusions in the grave fill.

Most of the animal remains in burial 7624 were rather small fragments and therefore likely to have been accidental inclusions in the burial fill. However, a fragmented cattle femur, a juvenile femur from a medium (sheep/goat-sized) mammal with cut marks on the shaft, and at least seven vertebrae from medium mammals may represent an offering or the remains of a funeral feast.

Unphased Iron Age context assemblages

In the not further phased Iron Age assemblage sheep/goat is the most numerous taxa (Table 6.25), although this must be viewed with caution due to the relatively small sample size (cf Hambleton 1999, 39-40). The MNI calculations also give a very small dataset and it is not advisable to interpret them as actual inter-species frequency.

The only evidence of butchery was a single cattle humerus which displayed cut marks distally from disarticulation of the joint. Pathologies were found on two bones. One cattle metacarpal had a small swelling mid-shaft on the anterior side. This could be a haematoma, ie an ossification of a swelling of the periosteum after blunt impact trauma, or it could be related to the pathology found on a contemporary sheep metacarpal. The sheep metacarpal had a ridge on the medial part of the posterior side. Similar pathologies, but located on the anterior side, has been noted in several assemblages

from a variety of locations and time periods. The aetiology is unclear, but may be connected to muscle strain or repeated impact trauma from walking on very soft, uneven or hard ground (Brothwell *et al.* 2005; Dobney *et al.* 1995, 43).

Roman

A single sheep tibia fragment was recovered from Roman inhumation grave 7378. It derives from the meat-poor lower part of the tibia shaft and is therefore more likely to be an accidental inclusion in the burial fill than a deliberate offering.

Discussion

In order to carry out a reliable analysis of inter-species frequency of livestock the total number of bones from cattle, sheep and pig should be at least 300, and/or the total MNI at least 30 (Hambleton 1999, 39-40). On this measure, only the early Iron Age and middle Iron Age/late Iron Age assemblages are suitable for such analyses. However, comparing the frequency of livestock at Southdown Ridge with contemporary assemblages from the region is not as straightforward as it might seem. Any analysis of chronological changes in animal husbandry is particularly difficult, since there are no comparative early Iron Age assemblages nearby. The assemblages from Flagstones (Bullock and Allen 1997) and Tolpuddle Ball (Hamilton-Dyer 1999) are dated to the late Iron Age and to the middle Iron Age/late Iron Age respectively. Further, the large assemblage from Maiden Castle (Armour-Chelu 1991) is not divided into sub-phases, rendering it impossible to discuss changes in husbandry strategies over time from this significant assemblage. The relative inflation of the fragment count by the inclusion of several articulated sheep and goat remains is probably of less importance due to the large sample size.

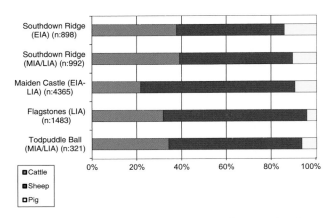

Fig. 6.18 Frequency of cattle, sheep and pig in South-down Ridge and contemporary assemblages in the region

Southdown Ridge differs from the three comparative sites with its larger frequency of cattle and pig and smaller frequency of sheep (Fig.6.18). This is not likely to be entirely due to environmental differences as all four sites lie in the close vicinity of both rivers and Downs, making them suitable for both cattle and sheep rearing. One possibility is that while the landscape was suitable for a variety of animal husbandry strategies, the land was unequally distributed, with some settlements having access to more prime sheep pastures than others. This may be seen in the Flagstones assemblage, where the unusually small size of sheep has been argued to have been caused by poor nutrition and overgrazing, itself ultimately caused by pasture competition (Bullock and Allen 1997, 197).

Analysis of livestock slaughter ages is an important tool for discerning animal husbandry patterns in prehistoric settlements. However, settlements are rarely entirely self-sustaining, and it must be assumed that some trade in animals would have occurred. Nevertheless, before the rise of large urban communities there was no need for largescale livestock movement, and the impact of trade in livestock at Southdown Ridge and at the comparative sites is likely minute compared to the impact of taphonomic loss. The slaughter age pattern for early Iron Age and middle Iron Age/late Iron Age cattle at Southdown Ridge shows two peaks: young cattle slaughtered for prime beef and older cattle past their prime as milkers, breeders or draught animals. The fusion data suggest that two thirds of the cattle were slaughtered when they were skeletally mature, ie after 3.5 years of age (Table 6.27).

The dental dataset from Maiden Castle included three calves and three adult cattle, while the epiphyseal fusion data indicated that 55% of the cattle were 3.5 years or older when slaughtered (Armour-Chelu 1991, 143). The emphasis on adult cattle suggests a cattle husbandry focused on

secondary products, either dairy production or the use of cattle as draught animals. The Flagstones report briefly states that cattle were largely kept for meat (Bullock and Allen 1997, 197), although it is not clear if this is merely a product of bias caused by a small dataset or an indication that the settlement employed a different cattle husbandry strategy than nearby sites.

The slaughter age pattern for sheep on all four sites suggests a sheep economy based on a variety of products. Nevertheless, there are inter- and intra-site differences that warrant discussion. At Southdown Ridge, the dental data suggests that early Iron Age sheep were mainly slaughtered at 2-6 years of age, with a smaller number of surplus young animals slaughtered for meat. This is supported by the epiphyseal fusion data (Table 6.27). The adult sheep from the middle Iron Age/late Iron Age phase were slaughtered at a slightly younger age, none older than 3-4 years. This is in stark contrast to the epiphyseal fusion data, which indicate an increase of sheep older than 3.5 years of age. It has been argued that such differences could imply a taphonomical bias, where late fusing elements from very young individuals are more likely to be utterly destroyed prior to excavation and thus lost from the record. This is less likely to be the case for Southdown Ridge, since neonatal and juvenile bones were not included in the epiphyseal fusion analysis. There is a possibility that the difference may have been caused by small sample size bias, since the total number of ageable mandibles and late fusing bones was not particularly large. Interestingly, the sheep dental data from the middle Iron Age/late Iron Age show a similar slaughter age pattern as Flagstones, where Bullock and Allen argue that this is very unusual for Iron Age sites in southern England (Bullock and Allen 1997, 197). However, Hambleton's study of Iron Age sites in Britain shows that this is a modified truth and that while most sites include remains from sheep older than 3-4 years, there are often relatively few animals in the older age ranges (Hambleton 1999, 70-71). Therefore, considering the relatively small sample size from Southdown Ridge, any older animals present may have been lost due to pre or post-burial taphonomic factors. The number of ageable mandibles from Flagstones has not been published and it is therefore not clear whether the lack of older sheep could be explained by taphonomic loss.

While Amour-Chelu claims that over 50% of the sheep from Maiden Castle survived to at least 5 years of age (Armour-Chelu 1991, 144), a comparison of the Mandibular Wear Stages (MWS) from Maiden Castle to Payne's age stages (cf Hambleton

1999, 64-67) shows that the large peak in MWS (Armour-Chelu 1991, 144) instead represents sheep between 3-6 years of age, similar to the dental data from early Iron Age Southdown Ridge.

At Tolpuddle Ball 55% of the sheep were less than 3 years old when they died (Hamilton-Dyer 1999, 197). This is a higher mortality rate than at Southdown Ridge (14%, 29%), but nearer to the one at Maiden Castle (41%). It might be connected to intra-site and/or inter-site competition for pasture, or to an emphasis on meat production.

Viewing the Iron Age as a whole, Hambleton (1999, 46) argues that animal assemblages from the Wessex and Central Southern England region are rather similar, with a high percentage of sheep/goat ranging from 40-70%, slightly less cattle (20-50%) and very few pigs (0-20%). This implies a predominantly sheep based economy. However, considering the larger size of cattle, beef is likely to have been more common in the diet than mutton. Cattle were also vitally important for agriculture, where they were used for traction.

The ageing data and limited sexing data for Southdown Ridge suggest that the numerically dominant sheep were utilized for variety of products but were not kept for many years beyond reaching their full growth. Cattle would have been the more important animal, used in agriculture, but also yielding large quantities of meat and dairy products. Pigs were kept in small numbers, for meat.

CHARRED PLANT REMAINS AND WOOD CHARCOAL *by Sheila Boardman*

Introduction

Following a detailed assessment of 50 bulk soil samples by Smith and Nicholson (2011), eleven samples were selected for further investigation. These range in date from early Iron Age to mid-late Iron Age. Four of the samples (including three from early Iron Age deposits) were also investigated for wood charcoal. The features investigated include the fills of two early Iron Age pits (7248 and 7263), postholes (7609, 7766) and a gully/construction cut (7611) associated with earlier Iron Age circular structure 7668, fills of

Table 6.31 Charcoal tables

Sample No		132	155	131	49
Context No		7610	7966	7612	7312
Sample vol. (litres)		40	2.1	20	5
Feature		Doorpost 7609 CS7668	PH in CS 7668	Gully CS7668 ditch	Ditch 7201
Dating decision		EIA	EIA	EIA	EIA
Fagaceae	**Common name**				
Quercus	oak	103hsr	102hs	81hs	125h
Betulaceae					
Alnus	alder	2			
Alnus/Corylus	alder/hazel	2	1		
Corylus avellana	hazel	1	2	8	3
cf. *Corylus*	probable hazel	2			
Rosaceae					
Prunus avium/padus type	wild/bird cherry	1		4r	2r
Prunus spinosa type	blackthorn				1
Prunus sp.	cherry/blackthorn	5		5r	5r
cf. *Prunus* sp.	probable cherry/blackthorn			2	2r
Pomoideae* (see key below)	syn. Maloideae	4		3	
Oleaceae					
Fraxinus excelsior	ash	1	13	5h	6
Araliaceae					
cf. *Hedera helix*	probable ivy	1			
Total identified fragments		121	118	108	144
Indet. charcoal		7	1	6	3

Key

Symbols used in fragment counts: h - includes heartwood; s - includes sapwood; r - includes round wood; *Pomoideae (syn. Maloideae) includes: Malus (apple), Pyrus(pear), Crataegus (hawthorn) * Sorbus (rowan, service, whitebeam)

Table 6.32 Charred plant remains

		112	132	131	155	98
Sample No		112	132	131	155	98
Context No		7768	7610	7612	7966	7730
Sample vol. (litres)		30	40	20	2.1	30
Feature type		PH7766 CS7668	PH7609 CS7668	CS 7668	PH of CS7668	Layer 7742
Dating decision		EIA	EIA	EIA	EIA	EIA
Cereal grain						
Triticum sp.	cf. free threshing wheat grain	2		5		
Triticum sp.	wheat grain		5			2
cf. *Triticum* sp.	cf. wheat grain		2	2		
Hordeum vulgare	hulled, twisted barley grain	1	3			
Hordeum sp.	Hulled barley grain	1	5	1		4
Hordeum sp.	cf. Hulled barley grain	1	1	2		
Hordeum sp.	barley grain	3	3	1		2
cf. *Hordeum* sp.	cf. barley	2				
Avena sp.	oat grain	1	6	1		3
cf. *Avena* sp.	cf. oat			3		1
Avena/Bromus spp.	oat/brome grasses	2	3	1F	1F	
Cereal indet.	indet cereal	8	9	7	2	15
Cereal indet.	detached embryos	2				2
Cereal chaff						
Triticum cf. *dicoccum*	cf. emmer glume base			1		
Triticum spelta	spelt glume base	6	4	9		8
Triticum cf. *spelta*	cf spelt glume base	8	3	5	1	12
Triticum dicoccum/spelta	emmer/spelt glume base	13	1	9	2	25
Triticum dicoccum/spelta	emmer/spelt spikelet fork					4
Triticum sp.	wheat rachis					3
Avena sp.	oat awns present					+
Cereal indet.	indet. cereal rachis					2
Cereal indet.	indet. cereal culm node		1			
Pulses, nuts						
cf. *Pisum sativum*	cf. pea					
Vicia cf. *faba*	cf. broad/horse/celtic bean					
Corylus avellana	hazel nutshell frags					
Wild plants						
Vicia cf. *sativa*	cf. common/fodder vetch					
Vicia/Lathyrus/Pisum	vetch/tare/pea (>2 mm)		1			1
Vicia/Lathyrus	vetch/tare (> 2mm)		3			2
Vicia/Lathyrus	vetch/tare (< 2mm)	1F				
Melilotus/Medicago/Trifolium	small seeded legume		2	2	1	2
Fabaceae - Trifolieae	small seeded legume	1	2	1	1	2
cf. *Malva* sp.	cf. mallow					
Brassica/Sinapis	cabbage, mustard, etc					
Raphanus raphanistrum	wild radish capsule (w seed)	2 (2)				
Raphanus raphanistrum	wild radish capsule	1F		1F		8F
Brassicaceae undiff.	cabbage family			1	1F	
Persicaria lapathifolia	pale persicaria					
Polygonum aviculare type	knotgrass		1			
Polygonum sp.	knotgrasses					
Fallopia convolvulus	black bindweed		2			
Rumex acetosella	sheep's sorrel					
Rumex spp.	docks	4	6	1	2	
cf. *Rumex* spp.	cf. docks					
Polygonaceae undiff.	knotweed family					
Stellaria sp.	stitchwort/mouse-ear				1	
Stellaria/Cerastium	stitchwort					

44	54	49	61	51	108
7268	7504	7213	7062	7385	7748
0.3	10	5	40	10	40
Pit	Pit	Ditch	Ditch	Burial	Layer
7263	7248	7201	7061	7372	7894
EIA	EIA	EIA	EIA	LIA	LIA
2	1				1
2	14		7		7
1	1	2		1	1
1	3		3		1
2					1
1	2		4		1
			1		
7	4	2	5	1	7
1F					
5	4	2	6	2	4
11	9	4	12	4	
13	7	8		6	2
14	2	6	1	6	1
22	1	2		5	
				1	
	+				
	1		2		1
	1				
			1F		
1					1
3		2	2	1	2F
5	9			1	2
9	12	2	2	1F	1
6	5		4	1	4
5	7		1	1	2
1					
	1			1	
2 (2)					
1F	4F		3		
2	1		1		
			1		
2	1		1		
	1			1	
			1		
			1		
2	9	1	1		2
			1		
1	3				
	1				1
1					

early Iron Age enclosure ditches 7061 and 7201, a late Iron Age triple grave 7372, and an occupation rich layer (7894, context 7748) that accumulated against a late Iron Age/early Roman field wall (7825).

Methodology

The samples were processed at Oxford Archaeology using a modified Siraf-type water separation machine. The flots were collected in a 250μm mesh and the heavy residues in a 500μm mesh. Flots and residues were sorted using a low power binocular microscope at magnifications of x10 to x20, for cereals grains, chaff, seeds and other quantifiable remains. Wood charcoal greater 2mm in size was removed. Charcoal fragments were fractured by hand and sorted into groups based on features observed in transverse section at x10 to x40 magnifications. The fragments were then sectioned longitudinally along their radial and tangential planes and examined at magnifications of up to x250 using a Metam P1 metallurgical microscope.

Identifications of the wood charcoal were made with reference to Schweingruber (1990), Hather (2000), Gale & Cutler (2000) and Clifford in Godwin (1956, 385). In general, all wood greater than 4mm in size was examined, together with a selection of the material in the 2-4mm size range. Identifications of the charred grains, chaff and seeds were carried out at magnifications of x10 to x40, using standard morphological criteria for the cereals (eg Jacomet 2006) and other plants (eg Berrgren 1969, 1981), and by comparison with modern reference material. Nomenclature of the plant material follows Stace (2010).

Results

Wood charcoal

Wood charcoal results are listed by fragment count in Table 6.31. More than 100 charcoal fragments were identified from each sample and at least seven taxa are represented.. The level of identification reflects preservation condition, the anatomy of the taxa and their bio-geographical range (including whether one or more related species are native to Britain). The most numerous in the four samples were fragments of oak (*Quercus*). Heartwood, sapwood and roundwood were all present. The oak remains are discussed in greater detail below. Fragments of ash (*Fraxinus excelsior*) and hazel (*Corylus avellana*) charcoal were also present throughout. Several *Prunus* species were identified, including blackthorn

Table 6.32 Charred plant remains (continued)

		112	132	131	155	98
Sample No		112	132	131	155	98
Context No		7768	7610	7612	7966	7730
Sample vol. (litres)		30	40	20	2.1	30
Feature type		PH7766 CS7668	PH7609 CS7668	CS 7668	PH of CS7668	Layer 7742
Dating decision		EIA	EIA	EIA	EIA	EIA
Caryophyllaceae undiff.	pink family		1			
Chenopodium album type	fat hen	1	6	4		
Chenopodium sp.	goosefoot	1	2	3	1	1
Chenopodium/Atriplex	goosefoot/orache		1			
Chenopodiaceae undiff.	goosefoot family		1	1		
Chenpodiaceae/Caryophyllaceae	goosefoot/pinks					
Montia fontana cf. ssp. *chondrosperma*	blinks					
cf. *Montia fontana*	cf. blinks					
Galium aparine	cleavers			1		
Galium sp.	bedstraw					1F
Plantago sp.	plantain		1F			
Lamiaceae undiff.	dead-nettle family					2
cf. *Anthemis cotula*	cf. stinking chamomile					
Tripleurospemum inodorum	scentless mayweed		1			
cf. *Tripleurospemum inodorum*	cf. scentless mayweed		1			
Asteraceae undiff.	daisy family		1	1		
Bromus spp.	brome grasses		3			
Poaceae undiff. small	grass family	2	13	6		3
Poaceae undiff. medium	grass family		5			1
Poaceae undiff. large	grass family					
Poaceae undiff.	grass family, culm node					1
cf. Poaceae undiff.	grass family	1F				2
Juncus spp.	rushes	2				
cf *Juncus* spp.	cf. rushes					
Indet seed, etc.			4	7		9
Indet bud				1		
Indet corm				1		
Indet. mericarp/ovary frag						

Key: F – fragments

(*Prunus spinosa*) and wild or bird cherry (*Prunus avium/padus*) but it is not always possible to distinguish between these species groups. Alder (*Alnus*) and hawthorn group (Pomoideae) charcoal fragments were recovered from two samples each. Pomoideae includes crab apple (*Malus*), pear (*Pyrus*), hawthorn (*Crataegus*) and rowan/whitebeam/service (*Sorbus*). A single fragment of possible ivy (cf. *Hedera*) charcoal was recovered from Sample 132.

Charred plant remains

The other charred plant remains are listed in Table 6.32. The counts are for individual grains, seeds, nutlets, etc. unless otherwise stated. F refers to fragments.

The samples were not rich, with *c* 40-150 items each, and they are remarkably consistent in the species and plant parts they contain. Cereal species were mostly spelt wheat (*Triticum spelta*) and hulled barley (*Hordeum* sp.). There were odd grains and/or chaff fragments of free threshing wheat (*Triticum* sp.), six row hulled barley (*Hordeum vulgare*), emmer wheat (*T. dicoccum*) and oats (*Avena* sp., probably the wild species, *A. fatua*, etc.). There were also a number of poorly preserved legumes, including pea (cf. *Pisum*), bean (*Vicia* cf. *faba*) and possible common or fodder vetch (*Vicia* cf. *sativa*). The latter was an important fodder crop in later times. The crop species and wild plant remains are discussed below.

The burial sample (51) did not produce any evidence for plant material deliberately placed in the grave. The mixture of charred crops and probable weeds is very similar the contents of the other samples, so it is discussed with them below.

44	54	49	61	51	108
7268	7504	7213	7062	7385	7748
0.3	10	5	40	10	40
Pit	Pit	Ditch	Ditch	Burial	Layer
7263	7248	7201	7061	7372	7894
EIA	EIA	EIA	EIA	LIA	LIA
2	2		8		
2	4	1	8		
		1			
2					1
1					
	2				
1F					
1		3			1
1F	1	2F			
1					
1	1				
			1	2	
1	1				
9	11	1	3	3	3
2	1		1		
	2				1F
	1				
	1			1	
	2	2	1	2	
			1		
8	5		1	4	1
	1				

Discussion

Wood charcoal

Oak charcoal was the most abundant material. In Sample 155 from an early Iron Age posthole (7966) associated with circular structure 7668, this was a mixture of heartwood and sapwood, and it is possible this material came from a single post. However, the fragments were variable in appearance and ash, hazel and alder/hazel charcoal were also present so, on balance, this material probably represents fuel debris. The oak charcoal fragments from Sample 49 (enclosure boundary ditch 7201) were mostly heartwood and had a very similar appearance, with extremely dense growth rings. This is more likely to have come from a single piece of (heartwood) timber which may have had a structural use originally. Again, the presence of other material

(ash, hazel and blackthorn/cherry roundwood) means this was probably deliberately burnt as fuel.

The other samples (131 and 132) had smaller, less well preserved charcoal fragments and were slightly more mixed in terms of heartwood, sapwood and roundwood, if not species, so they most likely represent what was selected or scavenged from the surrounding countryside for domestic fires. The presence of alder in two samples indicates that some collecting, for a poor fuel wood (Edlin 1949), took place in seasonally damp areas.

The hazel roundwood from Sample 132 did not have large growth rings so there is no hint that local woodlands were being managed via coppicing, although this is possible. It is interesting that mature oak woodland had an apparent continual presence in the region from the Neolithic (Gale, in Sharples 1991; Gale in Fitzpatrick *et al.* 1999, 194-196; Boardman, Chapter 4, this volume) until at least the Iron Age. Mature oak timber and ash are the best fuel woods (Edlin 1949) and important structural timbers, so steps may have been taken to conserve these resources. As compared to nearby Ridgeway Hill, however, the much smaller proportions of hazel charcoal could hint at the loss of some local, mixed oak/hazel woodlands or hazel copses, by the Iron Age. It is possible that some of the probable blackthorn and hawthorn were brought onto site for wattle work rather than fuel.

There is an apparent increase in blackthorn and hawthorn charcoal in assemblages in the region from the middle to late Bronze Age (Gale, in Fitzpatrick *et al.* 1999; 194-196; Gale, in Hearne & Birbeck 1999, 210-213). Blackthorn, sometimes with hawthorn or hazel, can form dense thickets which can rapidly colonise open (including previously grazed) areas, and it is possible that fire was used to control the spread of thorn bushes in the past.

Charred plant remains

A range of cereal species are present in these samples but there were no deposits of cleaned, that is, stored/spoiled grain of any type. The burial seems to have taken place in an area that was previously used to dump domestic refuse. All samples produced some cereal grain, chaff and wild plant species. The most numerous finds were grains and chaff of glume wheats, in particular those of spelt (*Triticum spelta*). Eight samples had more quantifiable glume fragments than glume wheat grains , including the burial sample 51, an indication of lots of small-scale dehusking debris, which in turn suggests that glume wheats were stored in semi-processed form, as whole spikelets (even sheaves) until required (Hillman 1981; Clapham and Stevens, in Fitzpatrick *et al.* 1999, 203-7). The processing of glume wheats in a piecemeal way is typical of many Iron Age and earlier sites in southern Britain, and it allows labour to be spread over the year. The high number of weed seeds to grain in the nine of eleven samples and wide range in weed seed sizes, from the cereal-sized *Avena/ Bromus* grains down to tiny rushes, could suggest whole spikelets (or sheaves) were stored in uncleaned form. This may indicate fairly low (ie household / multi-household) levels of social organisation, with limited resources available for bulk crop processing at busy times of year (Clapham and Stevens, in Fitzpatrick *et al.* 1999, 203ff).

The samples with less cereal chaff generally had quite large numbers of wild plants (samples 132 ad 54) or little plant material overall (108 and 61), so may still represent crop cleaning refuse. Given the number and range in sizes/types of possible weed seeds it was hoped these might shed light on the conditions of cultivation, the possible location of fields and on-site crop processing. Unfortunately, the majority are very general species which grow in a wide variety of open and disturbed habitats, including arable fields and grassland.

Cultivation of heavier soils is tentatively suggested by the probable stinking mayweed (cf. *Anthemis cotula*) seeds in two samples, and damper conditions in or around some fields may be indicated by rushes (*Juncus* spp.) and blinks (*Montia fontana*). Indicators of grasslands include all the small seeded legumes (*Medicago/ Melilotus/Trifolium, Vicia/Lathyrus* & Fabaceae/Trifolieae), plus the grasses and rushes. Some of these could have come onto site with cut grass or animal dung collected to burn as fuel, although the latter is not consistent with the charcoal evidence. The grassland flora may simply reflect the plants that grew at the margins of the cultivated fields; and the latter may have been in previously grazed areas where many grassland plants flora were able to survive.

In the absence of cereal straw, an infrequent survivor on archaeological sites (Boardman and Jones 1991), the presence of small, aerodynamic weeds such as the daisies (Asteraceae), scentless mayweed (*Tripleurospermum inodorum*) and probable stinking chamomile (cf. *Anthemis cotula*) and Aster-

aceae (daisy family), could point to (some) unwinnowed crops reaching the site, and therefore their likely local cultivation (Hillman 1981, 1984; Jones 1984). The numbers of such weeds in this assemblage were very low.

Summary and conclusions

The tree and shrub data indicate mature trees and woodland, and possible hedgerows or scrub, in the vicinity of the site during the Iron Age. There is some evidence from other sites in the region for increasing scrub-type vegetation from the middle Bronze Age onwards, which may be reflected here. The use of small diameter thorny round wood and other non optimal fuel woods, such as alder, hints that there were some pressures on woody resources at some times.

Local farmers living on the Coralian sands overlooking Weymouth Bay appear to have been cultivating spelt wheat and hulled barley from the middle Iron Age, probably with a range of legumes. There are hints from a few weeds that heavier, lower lying ground was used to grow some of the crops, and from the charcoal, that some wood (eg alder) was collected from damper areas. There was no evidence for changes in crop staples through time, which may reflect the fairly narrow time span and small number of samples. The strong presence of plants from grassland habitats may reflect material collected as hay, the cultivation of land previously used as pasture, or that much grassland surrounded the cultivated fields.

The small Southdown Ridge plant assemblage fits into a general pattern of Iron Age crop production for southern England, but it does not add greatly to the emerging local picture for south-west England (see Carruthers in Woodward 1991 106-111; Pelling, in Dinwiddy 2011, 151). Patterns observed at other sites include the early uptake of spelt wheat (which predates this assemblage), the late cultivation of naked barley (not found at Southdown) and the dominance of barley over wheat (spelt wheat was more common here). It will be interesting to see how these intra-regional differences are maintained as further data is collected for the region.

Chapter 7:
Discussion of Southdown Ridge

by Lisa Brown

Introduction

The results of the Southdown Ridge excavation do not offer an ideal opportunity for an examination of later prehistoric settlement in south Dorset. The excavation exposed only a small part of the settlement and did not reveal its full extent, duration and character. Furthermore, the site was affected by a combination of factors that compromised the evidence, including severe levels of truncation across the excavated area. This problem was compounded by the extensive robbing and reworking of deposits over many centuries, culminating in a process of levelling the abandoned settlement with some of the earliest material generated on the site, and ultimately, truncation through agricultural activity during the Roman and succeeding periods. This, in effect, flipped the stratigraphy and then jumbled it, so that the potentially largest and most informative assemblages of artefacts and ecofacts were effectively unstratified, and could then be considered only on their inherent merits.

Despite these constraints, it is worth attempting to address certain questions posed by the evidence, ranging beyond the stratigraphic narrative and results of analyses of the finds as set out in Chapters 5 and 6.

The inception of the Southdown Ridge settlement

The Southdown Ridge settlement emerged sometime during the late Bronze Age/early Iron Age transition (earliest Iron Age). The evidence for this early phase of occupation consists mainly of a relatively small collection of post Deverel-Rimbury decorated pottery, most of which was unstratified within the redeposited mass of midden-like material used to convert the abandoned settlement site to agricultural use at the end of the late Iron Age or early Roman period. This material, and the discovery of a Llyn Fawr type socketed axe in a primary deposit, indicate that settled occupation began sometime between 800-600 BC.

The process of a shifting dominance from funerary and ritual monuments to a period characterised by conspicuous settlement activity and a dearth of burials has been described as a change from 'the dead and the living' to the 'living and the dead' (Barrett, Bradley and Green, 1991). This process is apparent in the contrast between the barrows and burials that dominate the Ridgeway Hill site and the earlier Iron Age settlement and agricultural enclosures at Southdown Ridge.

The settlement model for the late Bronze Age/early Iron Age in Wessex suggests that the early community at Southdown Ridge was one of individual households engaged in mixed farming, with a limited level of exchange of goods and labour between what were probably single family units. As a community it was probably comparable to Rope Lake Hole (Sunter and Woodward 1986) and Eldon's Seat (Davies 1936; Cunliffe and Phillipson 1968). The wider context within which this community emerged was one of an increasingly diverse range of site types, which included ringworks and early hillforts, including nearby Chalbury Camp and, germane to this site, of structured above ground middens.

The impact of such diversification on the economic, social and ritual frameworks can arguably be seen in a widening range of artefacts and a corresponding diversification of activities carried out within settlements. Brück (2007, 25) sees the expanded range of object types as defining new "conceptual boundaries" around specific activities, the fragmentation of previously undifferentiated practices into more precisely defined categories of activities. At Southdown, this trend included shale-working and the specialised production of flint shale-working hand tools, possibly from the very earliest phase of occupation. Bronze Age shale-working sites have been identified elsewhere, both in the area and further afield. A shale workshop was excavated near Kimmeridge during the 1960s (Pitts 2010), and a piece of unworked Kimmeridge shale was found in the Dover boat, built about 1550 BC. At Burnham, near the Medway River in north-east Kent thick deposits consisting of flint shale-working tools and shale debris have been recently found associated with Bronze Age pottery (Pitts 2010).

During the first quarter of the first millennium BC bronze objects had played a significant role in exchange mechanisms and, by extension, in social and political relationships. By the time the Southdown community was established bronze was losing its pre-eminent position to ceramics within these networks. The period from about the 8th century BC saw the development of an expanded range of forms and wide-ranging decorative schema that heralded a patterning of ceramic styles within regionally coherent groups in southern Britain. In the case of Southdown the earliest pottery from the site corresponds most closely to that found at Kimmeridge and Period II at Eldon's Seat in Dorset (Davies 1936; Cunliffe and Phillipson 1968), mirrored in the All Cannings Cross tradition (Cunnington 1923). Most of the pottery of this type was found in the reworked midden-like deposit (7002), which had been quarried from elsewhere on the site.

The deposition of the Llyn Fawr type socketed axe (a probable failed casting, and certainly an unfinished object) close to the entrance of circular structure 7668 may have been an expression of the kind of ritual act of destruction or disengagement from a previously highly valued commodity of exchange seen in the 'potlatch' rituals of the Kwakiutl tribe of north-western America (Rohner and Rohner 1970). This sort of behaviour has been compared to acts of sacrificial transition of material such as the offering of metalwork to wet places, as at Flag Fen (Pryor 1991; 2005) and Runnymede (Longley and Needham and Spence 1996), the breaking or damaging of objects before deposition (Kristiansen 1978; Bradley 1990), and the deliberate burning down of roundhouses, as at Longbridge Deverill (Hawkes 2012) and Brighton Hill South (Fasham *et al.* 1995).

A correlation is often drawn between these forms of conspicuous consumption and that expressed in the construction of above ground middens, which are a feature of some late Bronze Age/early Iron Age communities in parts of southern Britain (Hill, 1996; Brück 2007, 26-8; McOmish 1996). Notable examples of midden sites at All Cannings Cross (Barrett and McOmish 2004), Potterne (Lawson 2000), East Chisenbury (McOmish 2010), Whitchurch (Sharples and Waddington 2011) and Runnymede Bridge (Needham and Longley 1980; Needham and Sorensen 1988; Needham 1991; Needham and Spence 1996) have been mentioned in Chapter 5.

Could Southdown Ridge have been a midden site of the type that served as a focus for communal gathering, feasting and displays of material wealth through the conspicuous disposal of food, pottery and other commodities? The setting certainly could have made the site an attractive location for such activities. It has a prominent aspect, with a view of Weymouth Bay to the south and the Ridgeway to the north, both undoubtedly important locations during the prehistoric period. The cross-ridge dyke may have been a significant landscape feature that served in some way to control or to invite access to the site.

The make-up of the midden-like material, most extensively exposed in layer 7002, was not sampled for environmental remains because it was effectively unstratified and highly mixed, but it produced most of the finds from the site, including much of the animal bone, and most of the early decorated pottery and shale armlets and waste. The earliest Iron Age pottery found in the midden deposits represented a wider production range that the ceramic assemblage of the succeeding early Iron Age, which was almost entirely local oolite-tempered wares. This suggests that some pottery was being brought to the site, and this may have been within the context of communal gatherings. Although the lathe-turned shale pieces were probably late Iron Age, the handmade pieces may have been contemporary with the early shale-working activity at Eldon's Seat.

The conspicuous absence of early metalwork in deposit 7002 (and across the site in general) may have been a reflection of a preference for shale over metal as a commodity through which competitive expression of status was demonstrated in this immediate region. With the natural resources available a short distance away at Kimmeridge, it is reasonable to imagine that a regional enthusiasm for shale could have dominated the competitive order during this period. The scale of craft production at midden sites suggests that raw materials and labour were freely available (McOmish 1996, Needham et al 1996, 242-8), and at Southdown Ridge the easily available raw material would have been shale.

An important function of some midden sites, for example Potterne (Lawson 2000), appears to have to have been livestock control (Locker 2000; Macphail 2000). As such, the ceremonial aspects of midden sites, such as the large-scale feasting activities and conspicuous consumption of commodities, may have been intricately linked adjuncts to seasonal breeding and culling events, with the sites themselves serving to facilitate passage through the wider landscape. The Southdown Ridge site seems to have had a small, permanently resident population, but the scale is uncertain and it is not possible to say whether settlement was episodic.

The early Iron Age settlement

The early Iron Age settlement was probably a relatively small, kin-based community, largely self-sufficient and capable of farming enough land, breeding sufficient livestock and producing sufficient tools and equipment to remain largely independent within the wider framework of the early hillfort community at Chalbury, 3km to the east at Sutton Poyntz and Maiden Castle and Poundbury, 10-12 km to the north near Dorchester.

As discussed above, metals had lost their primacy within exchange networks with the advent of the Iron Age, and the Southdown Ridge settlement of the early Iron Age (c 600 BC) produced no metalwork, with the possible exception of an undated iron awl found in the topsoil. In fact this period in Wessex is characterised by a general rarity of iron objects and a paucity of high quality artefacts overall. Sharples suggests that items that exhibited high quality workmanship and aesthetic qualities did not, by this stage, play a central role in negotiating social and political relationships (Sharples 2007, 176). Most metal artefacts found on early Iron Age sites are functional tools produced on a localised scale, and even these are absent at Southdown Ridge. Admittedly, this absence may be due largely to the small area of the settlement investigated, but even the early Iron Age pits contained no material of this sort.

The early Iron Age site at Southdown Ridge was arguably an enclosed site, although the surviving evidence for boundaries did not take the obvious form of a ditch circuit or continuous palisade. Rather, as has been described in Chapter 5, the enclosing of the settlement was achieved through the construction of a composite arrangement of timber fences and ditches, simultaneously exploiting the presence of a (possibly pre-existing) cross-ridge dyke and a natural break of slope into which a pit alignment was dug. During the Iron Age pit alignments were one of the ways of marking the limits of productive land (Bradley and Yates 2007, 99), and this seems to have been the case at Southdown.

It was not possible to demonstrate that all of these boundary elements were strictly contemporary, and it may be that the circuit, such as it was, had been constructed piecemeal. The very little dating evidence recovered from these features, all of it ceramic, does indicate, however, that at least the pits and the northern fenceline, with its special deposits of pottery, were contemporary.

Boundaries became an increasingly important feature of settlements from the beginning of the Iron Age in Wessex, and were arguably the dominant form of settlement type during this period. The construction of boundary features of any form - palisades, fences, ditches, walls or ramparts - would have required access both to a labour force and to the raw materials, such as stone and timber, required for construction. Whether the settlement at Southdown Ridge could have supplied the labour from within its own population, or whether it would have had to draw upon an external work force is unclear, as the scale of the settlement was not established. Supporting an expanded workforce would have necessitated supplies of food additional to the normal requirements of the permanent occupants. The pits aligned along the northern edge of the settlement, some of them deep enough to have been grain stores, could be evidence of just such agricultural surpluses.

Certainly the quantity of timber required to construct the southern fenceline could have been considerable, and not necessarily available within the settlement itself. This may have involved a reliance on a supply owned or controlled by a wider community, and the access to that resource would have been subject to negotiation. Sharples (2007, 179) proposes that the intake of non-local resources, such as limestone from the Ridgeway for the elaboration of the eastern entrance at Maiden Castle, could represent a means of 'embedding the landscape and its inhabitants into the monument'. By extension, the involvement of a wider populace in the construction of settlement boundaries at Southdown Ridge may have replaced the role played by the communal activities of the earlier Iron Age midden site, becoming the main arena for social and political competition and negotiation.

The charred plant remains offer only limited evidence for the agricultural status of the early Iron Age settlement, as few deposits were appropriate for sampling and much of the animal bone was recovered from the disturbed levelling deposit (7002). However, oak was the most abundant charcoal type and oak timbers were being used for construction while a variety of other species, including ash, hazel and blackthorn/cherry were exploited for fuel (see Boardman, Chapter 6). All samples from early Iron Age deposits produced some cereal grain, chaff and wild plant species, and the most common were grains and chaff of glume wheats, in particular spelt. A dominance of glume fragments over glume wheat grains indicates small-scale dehusking debris, evidence that the glume wheats were stored in semi-processed form, as whole spikelets, or even sheaves, until required, a practice typical of many Iron Age and earlier sites in southern Britain, which allows labour to be spread over the year. A high number of weed seeds relative to grain and a wide range in weed seed sizes could indicate that whole spikelets or sheaves were stored in uncleaned form. This can be evidence that the settlement functioned on a household or multi-household level of social organisation, with small numbers of people available for major bulk crop processing activity.

The faunal remains indicate that sheep were kept for a variety of products but were slaughtered relatively early while cattle were the more important animal, used in agricultural activity but also for meat and dairy products. Pigs were kept in only small numbers, solely for meat.

A middle Iron Age settlement at Southdown Ridge?

The single radiocarbon date obtained on material from Southdown Ridge, from human bone in pit 7526, lay firmly in the middle Iron Age (380-200 cal. BC, 95.4%; SUERC-49472: 2219 ±29). As discussed in Chapter 5, the pit was likely to have been an early Iron Age feature reused as a convenient location for the burial. That the burial was a middle Iron Age event is clear, but the evidence otherwise for middle Iron Age occupation of the site is at best ambiguous.

Pottery generally serves as the most prolific and reliable dating evidence for Iron Age events in southern Britain, bearing in mind the problems posed by the plateau in the radiocarbon calibration curve that affect much of this period. However, pottery production in Dorset during the middle to late Iron Age was dominated by a single industry based in the Wareham-Poole Harbour area, which used a relatively homogenous mix of local sands and clays (Brown 1997). This inhibits the analysis of a progression of fabrics through time that is possible in some regions. In Dorset a conservative adherence to a fairly restricted range of forms and decorative motifs over a long period, and an endurance of archaic forms further complicates the matter. Although this is a somewhat simplistic reprise of the regional ceramic evidence, these factors can make close dating difficult, especially in the absence of well-stratified assemblages, as at Southdown. Although the assemblage of Wareham-Poole Harbour wares recovered from the site is sizeable, the bulk of it cannot be confidently attributed to either the middle or late Iron Age.

An absence of middle Iron Age pottery at several of the hillforts in the vicinity of Southdown Ridge, including Chalbury and Poundbury, suggests that they were abandoned sometime during the early Iron Age, in the wake of the expansion of Maiden Castle. Sharples (1990) has suggested that a system based on communal land-holding centred on Maiden Castle replaced the earlier (fortified) settlements during this time. The number of enclosures in the Wessex area generally seems also to have declined during the middle Iron Age. Sites like Little Woodbury developed larger, more significant boundaries (Bersu 1940), whereas others like Winnall Down were abandoned or had their boundaries filled in (Fasham 1985). Whether the Southdown Ridge settlement fit within this pattern of depopulation in the wake of Maiden Castle's middle Iron Age ascendance is questionable, as the site may have lain too

distant from Maiden Castle to have been subject to this effect. Unfortunately, the lack of definite middle Iron Age stratigraphic or structural evidence for this period, coupled with the ambiguity of the ceramic evidence and a lack of absolute dates (with the single exception cited) has meant that the question of abandonment of the site during the middle Iron Age cannot be definitely resolved.

Chronology of the field boundaries

Depopulation of the settlements surrounding Maiden Castle area during the middle Iron Age has been linked to a corresponding lack of field system evidence (Sharples (1990), 92). As discussed in Chapter 5, it seems most likely that the field boundaries at Southdown were set out during the early Iron Age, but there is no evidence that they were still in use during the middle to late Iron Age. The pottery that accumulated while the ditches were in the process of filling is entirely of early Iron Age date, and the significant collection of early Iron Age sherds from ditch terminal 7046 is especially compelling in terms of establishing the date of the enclosures.

The field boundaries identified near Dorchester at Alington Avenue (Davies 2002) appear, however, to have been set out during the late Iron Age, and boundaries of similar date have been observed at Flagstones (Smith 1997), Poundbury and Fordington Bottom. The late Iron Age boundaries appear to have been directly related to settlements and to have enclosed relatively small areas. The enclosures were clustered together and the clusters were isolated in large areas of unenclosed land. Their function is unclear, but the presence of droveways at Alington Avenue suggests that they were more concerned with livestock management than with crop production. The creation of these enclosure units may reflect an appropriation by small farmsteads of land that had previously been held communally and controlled by the inhabitants of Maiden Castle.

In Dorset there is a tendency, as at Alington Avenue, for inhumation burials to be situated beside these boundary features. This association was also found at Tarrant Hinton, where three inhumation burials were associated with boundary ditches (Graham 2006, 22-5). The circumstances here were somewhat unclear, however, as the ditches were poorly dated and some of them had been recut, apparently after at least one of the burials had been made. Additionally, a radiocarbon date of 400-230 BC from one of the skeletons and the presence of an early first century AD fibula in another grave suggests that the burials were made over a lengthy period.

The morphology of these well-dated late Iron Age field boundaries, and their association with burials, introduces an element of uncertainty into the interpretation of the Southdown Ridge chronological sequence presented in Chapter 5. As mentioned above, the available evidence best places the field boundaries in the early Iron Age, and in fact the ceramic evidence for this could be considered indisputable. However, the burials made alongside and across the boundary ditches and the timber fencelines were obviously late Iron Age. The association between the early boundary markers and the late burials demands that we accept that the late Iron Age inhabitants were conscious of these much earlier boundaries, or that the boundaries were maintained over several centuries. In the case of the ditches, this possibility is not a remote one, as negative features of this sort can remain visible long after they have filled and their fill subsided. As was mentioned earlier, the cross-ridge dyke was still visible as a linear hollow just prior to excavation. The fencelines would clearly not have remained visible in the same way once the timbers had gone but it is possible that the fences were maintained, or their original position recognised, over several generations.

A late Iron Age Durotrigian settlement?

Papworth (2011, 50-60) cites four indicators that are commonly and currently used to define Durotrigian 'culture, reduced from the six originally proposed by Brailsford in the 1950s (1957, 118-121): Durotrigian pottery, Durotrigian farmsteads, Durotrigian burial practices and Durotrigian coinage. The Southdown Ridge evidence meets only one of these criteria. The excavation produced only one coin, one of a South-Western series of uninscribed struck 'Bronzes'. The definition of 'Durorotrigian farmstead' has largely been superseded due to the complexities of classification in the wake of a growing body of settlement data from within and without the Durotrigian zone. In any case, the late Iron Age settlement at Southdown Ridge appears to defy classification on any of the accepted grounds, and no precise parallel has been found for the complex of terrace, stone walls, alcoves, drains and paths exposed at the site. The term 'Durotrigian burial' has also fallen out of favour somewhat because their distribution is restricted even within the tribal area. The term has been replaced by the more general 'Dorset tradition burials' (Haselgrove 1994, 2). The late Iron Age pottery assemblage from the site, therefore, remains the sole incontestable criterion in this exercise.

Whether or not the case can be made for an abandonment of the settlement during the middle Iron Age at Southdown Ridge, the evidence for the re-emergence of a community in this location during the late Iron Age, and the practice of Dorset tradition burials is clear. Whether the Southdown burials reflect the 'independent society of warrior farming families' described by Aitkin and Aitken (1990, 57-94) with reference to the Whitcombe farmstead and cemetery is beyond the scope of the excavated evidence. It is impossible to say also whether the late Iron Age settlement at Southdown reflected the transferral of a framework of communal power over agricultural production to individual control of specialist industries, as seen in the final century of occupation at Maiden Castle (Sharples 1991, 264). The evidence does suggest, however, that Southdown Ridge was a centre for the production of lathe-turned shale armlets during this period, and this may have been a continuation or resumption of the early Iron Age shale-working activity.

As well as the Whitcombe site, several other late Iron Age farmsteads associated with Durotrigian pottery and crouched burials have been found in and around Dorchester, at Max Gate, Poundbury and Fordington Bottom.

Dorset tradition burials

Burials that conform to the Dorset tradition are found almost exclusively in central south Dorset, in the areas around Weymouth and Dorchester. They have been recorded as far west as Burton Bradstock and West Bay near Bridport, so the River Brit may have been the western boundary of this funerary practice (Papworth 2011, 81). They have also been found east of Dorchester at Broadmayne and as far north of Tolpuddle. The distribution pattern indicates that the Piddle Valley lay near the edge of the area where this rite was practiced. Isolated examples have been found in Purbeck and Cranborne Chase to the east of the main distribution zone.

The distinctive Dorset burial tradition is characterised by the (typically) crouched posture of the body, head oriented towards the east, placed in shallow, typically oval graves, and accompanied by a constrained range of grave goods. These normally consist of ceramic vessels, animal bones (probably joints of meat offered as food), ornaments and, more rarely, weapons. The burial tradition evolved from a pre-existing middle Iron Age rite of pit burials and the vessels accompanying the burials also developed from an earlier ceramic tradition, sometimes referred to as the Maiden Castle-Marnhull style (Cunliffe 2005, 107). This new and culturally distinctive burial tradition of south Dorset, in which grave goods were sometimes present, once again reflected an emphasis, as during the early Iron Age, that it was individuals rather than communities that exerted control over the distribution of resources.

The Southdown Ridge burials deviate to some degree from the orientation norm. Some of the burials were incomplete and/or disarticulated, and so the original orientation could not be established. Of the remainder, a north or slightly northeast orientation was more typical (burials 7294, 7273, 7104, 7777) leaving only four (7053, 7124, 7151 and 7017) in the traditional east or ENE orientation. Two were aligned with head to the south (7264 and 7372).

Similar late Iron Age burials have been found at Alington Avenue (Davies *et al.* 2002) and at Gussage All Saints (Wainwright 1979). At Gussage disarticulated human bones recovered from pits and ditches have recently been re-examined alongside the bones from ramparts, ditches and pits at Maiden Castle (Redfern 2008). The study found that the individuals (primarily males) had evidence of peri-mortem blunt force trauma and/or weapon trauma, in addition to ancient modifications indicative of excarnation, secondary burial and curation (ibid.).

The individuals buried at Southdown Ridge show no evidence of such trauma, but this burial population is distinguished by other interesting features, including a relatively high frequency of extra-spinal joint disease and a predominantly youthful age profile. The question of who these people were and where they were living is an interesting one, bearing in mind that parts of the settlement at least were apparently being abandoned as the burials were taking place. These individuals may have been shale-workers and/or or livestock farmers, living within the immediate vicinity, perhaps in the unexcavated part of the settlement to the east of the site. It is also possible that the community was contracting or even being completely abandoned during this time and that the cemetery population had lived somewhere more distant, with the Ridge serving as a dedicated funerary space. Unfortunately, the answers to these questions are beyond the scope of the evidence.

Roman period activity at Southdown Ridge

Few of the excavated features and deposits on the site can be attributed with certainty to the period following the Roman conquest. That there was some occupation during the first century AD is indicated by a handful of pottery sherds of 'Romanised' type, some of them imported fine orange wares, but these number under half a dozen in total, and they were in every case residual, with the single exception of a sherd from cuvilinear ditch 7191 in the northern part of the site, some distance from the Iron Age settlement.

The three coffined burials are not closely dated but were likely to have been post-conquest. Several other Roman burial sites are also known from the area, such as at Greyhound Yard, where human skeletal remains were recovered from 23 contexts (Woodward *et al.* 1993), and to the north of Maiden Castle Road where 23 graves were excavated, incuding a flexed inhumation within a square enclosure (Smith 1997, 56-67). However, those from the late Roman cemeteries at Poundbury have received perhaps the greatest attention to date (Farwell and Molleson 1993). Totalling over a thousand individuals, this is the largest Roman assemblage from the region and is in addition to an isolated Bronze Age burial and a crouched inhumation cemetery also found at the site. The Roman burials at Poundbury observed a variety of rites, evidenced by ditched funerary enclosures, plain earth cut graves, mausolea and stone lined and cist inhumations, some with grave goods and evidence for coffins.

Chapter 8: Excavations and Survey at Redlands and Bincombe Valley

ROMAN ACTIVITY AT REDLANDS
by Chris Hayden and David Score

Introduction

A small excavation was carried out at Redlands as part of the wider archaeological investigations that were carried out prior to the construction of the Relief Road. The site lies at NGR SY 673 823, immediately to the east of the railway line, Greenway Road and the Redlands Sports Centre, and just to the north of Two Mile Coppice (Fig. 1.1).

The area was selected for excavation because the remains of a Roman settlement had been found in the Redlands Sports Ground to the west of the railway (Valentin 1999). These included the remains of a stone building by the side of which lay the burial of an infant, a stone-lined drain, demolition debris and cut features. The associated pottery included imported fine wares as well as local black burnished coarse ware, which suggested activity primarily in the 1st or 2nd century AD. Roof tiles, ironwork and flint shale-working tools were also recovered. Previously, the remains of a metalled surface, Roman pottery, including samian ware, and a sestertius of Trajan had been found during the excavation of a drainage ditch in the same area (Boulter and Squib 1980).

A prior evaluation to the east of the railway, comprising four trenches (1, 2, 3 and 10), had indicated the presence of Roman features and gave some indication of their extent (WA 2004; GSB 2004). Midden-like deposits of Roman date were found in Trench 1, and two Roman ditches, perhaps forming a trackway, were found in Trench 2. Trench 3, however, which lay further to the north, was archaeologically sterile. Trench 10, which lay just to the south of Trench 1, contained only patchy evidence of the midden-like deposits, suggesting that the trench lay near their southern limit.

The excavation results

The Redlands site covered a roughly rectangular area measuring around 37m by 78m, with a total area of 2652m², encompassing Evaluation Trenches 1 and 10 and the southern part of Evaluation Trench 2, as well as extending further to the south of Trench 10 (Fig. 8.1). The site lay in area of gently sloping ground, which falls from 45m OD at the west to 22m OD at the east. The local geology is composed of Kimmeridge and Oxford Clays overlying the Kellaways Formation (http://mapapps.bgs.ac.uk/geologyofbritain/home.html).

The excavation confirmed the chronology and interpretation of the features found in the evaluation, and found only three additional features: two parallel ditches, which lay below the midden, and a third ditch, which lay to the south of the midden-like deposits (Fig. 8.1). The Roman features were covered by topsoil and a silty clay subsoil. A series of three post-medieval land drains were cut through the subsoil.

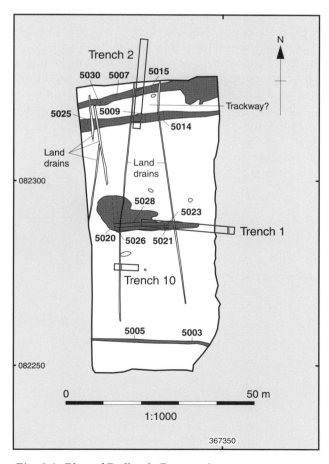

Fig. 8.1 Plan of Redlands Roman site

The trackway

The possible trackway at the northern end of the site was defined by two east-west aligned parallel ditches (5007 and 5009), set between 3.5 and 6m apart, but of different dimensions. The northern ditch (5007) was a shallow feature, only 0.25m deep and 1.9m wide with a rounded base. The southern ditch (5009) was both wider (up to 3.1m) and deeper (up to 0.65m), and in places it had a wide V-shaped profile. Both ditches were filled with deposits of greyish silty clay but, whist the shallower, northern ditch contained only a single deposit, up to four layers of fill, distinguished only by differences in colour from dark grey to yellowish grey were identified in ditch 5009.

Not surprisingly, given its smaller size, ditch 5007 produced far fewer finds than 5009. The pottery from this ditch (24 sherds/149g) suggested a late Roman date, from about AD 240-410. The larger quantity of pottery (516 sherds/1902g) from the ditch 5009 included a significant element that suggested an early Roman date. However, the assemblage recovered from a primary fill (5019) suggests that the ditch was recut, or last cleaned out, after about AD 200. As in most of the other Roman contexts, most of the pottery was Dorset black-burnished ware, although small amounts of Iron Age coarse sand-tempered ware, coarse sandy grey ware and sandy oxidised ware were also present. The pottery from the smaller ditch was also predominantly Dorset black-burnished ware, but included small quantities in a range of other wares, including a single sherd of south Gaulish samian and others in New Forest colour-coated ware, Oxford red colour-coated ware, and sandy oxidised ware.

The other finds from the large ditch included two fragments of Purbeck limestone, a fragment of an unidentified flat iron object, pieces of fired clay, and 79 fragments (744g) of animal bone including cattle, pig, sheep/goat, horse and mouse. The blade of a medieval iron whittle tang knife was recovered from one of the upper fills, indicating later disturbance. The smaller ditch (5007) also contained a fragment of tile in a sandy fabric and a small collection of animal bone (14 fragments/283g), including cattle and horse bone.

A sample taken from ditch 5009 contained an assemblage of charred plant remains, described below.

The midden-like deposit and underlying ditches

A midden-like deposit (5020), which lay around 20m to the south of the trackway, consisted of a mottled greyish-blue and beige silty clay layer, up to 0.2m thick, preserved within a slight natural depression. Overall, it covered an area measuring 27m east-west by up to 10m north-south, although it was narrower over much of its length.

This deposit apparently first accumulated in two other east-west aligned ditches (5023 and 5020), located about 28m to the south of the trackway. Both were very shallow features with U-shaped profiles, 0.25m deep. Ditch 5023 was c 1.1m wide; 5020 narrower at 0.8m wide. Both were filled with similar mottled bluish-grey to yellowish-grey silty clay.

The only find from the ditches was a single sherd of Dorest black-burnished ware from ditch 5023. The midden deposit, in contrast, yielded a much larger assemblage of finds. In total 172 sherds (1725g) of

0   40 mm

2:1

Fig. 8.2 Copper alloy bow brooch from Redlands

278

pottery from this deposit indicated a late Roman date of AD 250-410. The pottery was almost entirely Dorset black-burnished ware but a few sherds in sandy oxidised ware were also identified. The other finds included a copper alloy bow brooch with a flat bow and incised decoration (Fig. 8.2), and nine fragments (72g) of sheep/goat and cattle bone.

The southern ditch

A single east-west ditch, 5005, ran along the southern end of the excavation trench, some 30m to the south of ditch 5020. It was a shallow feature, 0.8m wide and 0.2m deep, with a rounded base, filled with dark grey silty clay. The date of the ditch is uncertain as it yielded only two sherds (21g) of Dorset black-burnished ware and a fragment of (probably) modern glass. Although it shared the orientation of the Roman ditches, it also followed the alignment of a recent fenceline, so could have been either a Roman or a much more recent feature. If it were Roman, it may have defined a field or enclosure to the south of the midden.

The pottery *by Edward Biddulph*

The ceramic assemblage was dominated by Black-burnished ware. Fabrics similar to the sandy fabric produced for Roman-period Black-burnished ware were manufactured in the region through the Iron Age, but all examples from the Redlands site are likely to be Roman. The earliest forms were a lid-seated vessel (cf. Laidlaw 1999, fig. 50.40), a number of bead-rimmed jars and cooking jars with slightly everted rims, all of 1st-century AD type. Some of the jars were associated with plain- or bead-rimmed bowls or deep dishes with curving sides (cf. Seager Smith 1993, fig. 23.1). A straight-sided bowl from ditch 5009, which would typically have a flanged or beaded rim, had a reeded rim instead. Reeded rims are well known on later 1st and 2nd-century vessels from Verulamium, among other sources, but their appearance in this fabric is unusual.

Most cooking jars are late Roman, characterised by their more widely-splayed rims, slimmer bodies, and narrow zone of latticing. A vessel with a warped rim from the midden is probably a second or a waster from a nearby kiln. As in the early Roman period, the jars were sometimes found with dishes or bowls, specifically straight-sided types with dropped flanges. Plain-rimmed dishes were also identified.

Other fabrics were represented by a small numbers of sherds. A sandy fabric is likely to be an oxidised version of Black-burnished ware. Two bead-rimmed jars were recorded in this fabric. Grey wares may have arrived from sources outside the region, although some examples are almost as sandy as the Black-burnished ware and might be non-standard local products. However, without forms it is difficult to be certain. Fine wares more certainly attributed to source include a few sherds of late Roman New Forest and Oxford (F51) colour-coated wares. No rims were found, but an Oxford flanged body sherd is likely to be a hemispherical flanged bowl (Young 1977, type C51). At least two sherds of 1st-century South Gaulish samian ware belonged to a Drag. 27 cup.

Charred plant remains *by Sheila Boardman*

One of the samples collected from southern Roman trackway ditch 5005 proved to be extremely rich in charred plant remains. The sample was processed in the standard OA manner, using a modified Siraf-type water separation machine. Flots were collected a 250μm mesh and the heavy residues in a 500μm mesh. All fractions were dried slowly before examination. Small amounts of wood charcoal were not investigated for this report (see full methodologies in Chapters 3 and 6). Nomenclature follows Stace (2010).

The charred plant remains are listed in Table 8.1. Counts are for individual grains, seeds, fruits, etc., plus glume bases, rachis internodes and culm nodes of cereals. Spikelet forks, each comprised of two glume bases, are counted as two in the glume wheat chaff totals. Fragment counts are suffixed by F. Large numbers of wheat rachis fragments and oat awn fragments have been roughly quantified using asterisks.

The few poorly preserved cereal grains were largely wheat (*Triticum* sp.) and indeterminate cereal, with small quantities of barley (*Hordeum* sp.) and oats (*Avena* sp.). The latter may include wild and/or cultivated species. It was not always possible to distinguish between fragments of oats and those of large grasses such as the bromes (*Bromus* spp.) and rye-grasses (*Lolium* spp.). By far the most numerous finds were glume bases of spelt (*Triticum spelta*), possible spelt (*T.* cf. *spelta*), and emmer or spelt (*T. dicoccum/spelta*). The more complete, better preserved glume bases were all identified as spelt wheat. No definite emmer wheat chaff fragments were found. It is likely, therefore, that spelt was the main species present in this assemblage. Other cultivated plants are represented by single grains of probable pea (cf. *Pisum sativum*) and celtic/horse bean (*Vicia* cf. *faba*), and collected plants by a few hazelnut (*Corylus* avellana) shell fragments. In addition, there was a wide range of wild plant species, which are discussed in greater detail below.

This sample, so dominated by spelt wheat chaff with limited numbers of other remains, is unlikely to

Table 8.1 Summary of charred plant remains

Context No		5033	5033	5033
Sample vol. (litres)		30	30	30
Feature type		Ditch	Ditch	Ditch
Dating decision		Late Roman AD250-400	Late Roman AD 250-400	Late Roman AD 250-400
Fraction		Flot	Residue	Residue
Mesh size(s)		>250μm	0.5-2 mm	0.5-2 mm
Percentage examined		100%	12.50%	87.50%
Detailed sort/scan		Detailed sort	Detailed sort	Rapid scan (see Key#)
Cereal grain				
Triticum sp.	wheat grain	31	1	
cf. Triticum sp.	cf. wheat grain	11		
Hordeum sp.	barley grain	2		
cf. Hordeum sp.	cf. barley	2		
Avena sp.	oat grain	8		**
cf. Avena sp.	cf. oat 4			
Avena/Poaceae spp.	oat/large grasses	2	1	**
Cereal indet.	indeterminate cereal	40	2	**
Cereal indet.	detached embryo	1		
Total (cf.) glume wheat grains		42	1	0
Cereal chaff				
Triticum cf. dicoccum cf.	emmer glume base			
Triticum spelta	spelt glume base	658	29	*****
Triticum spelta	spelt spikelet fork	10		
Triticum cf. spelta	cf spelt glume base	288	9	***
Triticum cf. spelta	cf. spelt spikelet fork 8			
Triticum dicoccum/spelta	emmer/spelt glume base	893	59	*****
Triticum dicoccum/spelta	emmer/spelt spikelet fork	8	2	**
Triticum sp.	wheat rachis (NB. not in totals below+)	5		
Triticum sp.	wheat rachis non quantitifable frags	****	**	**
Avena sp.	oat awns	*****	***	***
Cereal indet./Poaceae	small cereal/large grass culm node	5		*
Total glume wheat glume bases	+NB. 1 spikelet fork = 2 glume bases	1891	101	100's
Pulses, nuts				
cf. Pisum sativum	cf. pea	1		
Vicia cf. faba	cf. broad/horse/celtic bean	1		
Corylus avellana	hazel nutshell fragments	5F		
Wild plants				
Papaver rhoeas/dubium	common/long-headed poppy	1		
Ranumculus acris/repens/bulbosus	meadow/creeping/bulbous buttercup	1		
Vicia/Lathyrus	vetch/tare (> 2mm)	1.5		
Vicia/Lathyrus	vetch/tare (< 2mm)	2		*
Melilotus/Medicago/Trifolium/etc.	small seeded legume	4	2	
Brassica cf. rapa	cf. wild turnip		1	
Raphanus raphanistrum	wild radish capsule (w seed)	3 (3)		
Raphanus raphanistrum	wild radish capsule fragments	10F		
Fallopia convolvulus	black bindweed	1		
Rumex acetosella	sheep's sorrel	2		
Rumex cf. acetosella	cf. sheep's sorrel	2		
Rumex spp.	docks	9		
cf. Rumex spp.	cf. docks	1F		
Polygonaceae undiff.	knotweed family	1		
Stellaria cf. graminea	lesser stitchwort	1		

Table 8.1 Summary of charred plant remains (continued)

		5033	5033	5033
Context No		5033	5033	5033
Sample vol. (litres)		30	30	30
Feature type		Ditch	Ditch	Ditch
Dating decision		Late Roman	Late Roman	Late Roman
		AD250-400	AD 250-400	AD 250-400
Fraction		Flot	Residue	Residue
Mesh size(s)		>250μm	0.5-2 mm	0.5-2 mm
Percentage examined		100%	12.50%	87.50%
Detailed sort/scan		Detailed sort	Detailed sort	Rapid scan (see Key#)
Stellaria sp.	stitchwort/mouse-ear	1		
Stellaria/Cerastium	stitchwort	1		
Caryophyllaceae undiff.	pink family	1		
Chenopodium album type	fat hen	3	1	*
Chenopodium sp.	goosefoot	4		
Chenopodiaceae undiff.	goosefoot family	1		
Montia fontana cf. ssp. *chondrosperma*	blinks	1		
Galium aparine	cleavers	2		
Plantago lanceolata	ribwort plantain	2		
Plantago sp.	plantain	1		
Anthemis cotula	stinking chamomile	1		
Tripleurospemum inodorum	scentless mayweed	1		
Tripleurospemum sp.	mayweed	1		
Asteraceae undiff.	daisy family			*
Juncus spp.	rushes	1		
cf *Juncus* spp.	cf. rushes	1		
Carex sp.	trigonous fruit	1		
Bromus spp.	brome grasses	2		*
Lolium perenne	perennial rye-grass	10		
Poaceae undiff. small (inc. *Poa/Phleum*)	grass family (inc. pos. meadow grasses/cats-tails)	13		
Poaceae undiff. medium	grass family	4	1	*
Poaceae undiff. large (inc. pos *Bromus, Lolium* & *Lolium/Festuca*)	rye-grass, rye-grass/fescue) grass family (inc. pos. brome grasses, rye-grass, rye-grass/fescue)	47	2	***
Poaceae undiff.	grass family, culm node	1	1	*
cf. Poaceae undiff.	grass family	2		
Indet seed, etc.		6 + Fs		**
Indet. mineralised seed		1		

KEY:

F - fragments   * 1-5 items/frags   ** 6-10 items/frags   *** 11-20 items/frags   **** 21-50 items/frags   ***** 51-100+ items/frags

contain mixed age material. Rather, it appears to represent by-products from crop cleaning of one or several spelt crops, probably including refuse from several crop processing stages, plus possibly refuse from other sources (see below). There is little evidence for threshing in archaeobotanical assemblages of all ages, partly because this would have taken place away from settlements, close to arable fields, and because winnowing waste is underrepresented archaeologically. Light cereal chaff, including rachises and awns, and cereal straw are much less likely to survive charring than cereal grains (Boardman and Jones 1990). Here, there is considerable evidence for awns, but of oats rather than spelt,

although oats may have been a weed of the spelt crop. Also, in the absence of cereal straw, the presence of small, aerodynamic weeds such as scentless mayweed (*Tripleurospermum inodorum*) and stinking chamomile (*Anthemis cotula*), may point to unwinnowed crops or winnowing waste reaching the site (Hillman 1981, 1984). There were only a few such weeds, although there were large numbers of small seeds in general, including those of grasses (Poaceae), rushes (Juncus sp.) and other species.

The large quantity of glume bases with few cereal grains is more typical of grain dehusking waste rather than earlier crop processing. A second threshing and winnowing is required to free glume wheat grains from the tightly enclosing spikelets in which they may be stored, traded and sown (Hillman 1981, 1984). This amount of glume wheat chaff would be surprising on a small Iron Age site, where most grain dehusking seems to have taken place day-to-day, as required (cf. Clapham and Stevens in Fitzpatrick *et al* 1999; Boardman in Brown, Hayden and Score 2014). As well as providing protection for the grain, the advantage of piecemeal processing is that labour can be spread throughout the year, rather than huge investments needed at harvest time. It is therefore tempting to link this sizeable deposit to more organised agricultural production and greater labour investment in crop processing during the Roman period. The quantified chaff remains may only point to 40 to 60 whole cereal plants, but there were many thousands of unquantifiable chaff fragments in the sample fractions. Together with probable losses during charring, burial and recovery, this may point to some large scale crop processing at the Redlands site. Furthermore, the presence of earlier crop processing waste (awns, straw, aerodynamic weed seeds), as well as spelt glumes, suggests that a number of crop cleaning operations were carried out simultaneously on the spelt crop(s) before the waste material was burnt and dumped in the ditch.

Spelt wheat is generally the main wheat crop found on sites dating to the Roman period in southern England. In this region, and the southwest generally, the transition from emmer to spelt wheat as staple crops, along with hulled barley, seems to have been largely completed by the late Iron Age, if not earlier (Palmer and Jones, in Sharples 1991; Carruthers in Woodward 1991; Clapham and Stevens in Fitzpatrick *et al* 1999; Pelling in Dinwiddy *et al.* 2011). The other cereal species and pulses are also unsurprising in deposits of this age, and may represent minor contaminants of the main spelt crop or incidental inclusions on domestic fires or in refuse deposited in the ditch.

The majority of wild species present are able to grow in a variety of open and disturbed habitats, including arable fields and grassland. Grassy conditions are particularly well-represented here by grasses, rushes and small seeded legumes (*Medicago/Melilotus/Trifolium* and *Vicia/Lathyrus*). Some of the seeds could have arrived on site with cut grass or animal dung collected to burn as fuel. Perennial rye grass (*Lolium perenne*) was an important fodder crop in the past and its prevalence here may point to more intensively managed grasslands (Clapham *et al.* 1979). The presence of stinking mayweed (*Anthemis cotula*) in archaeological samples is often cited as evidence for the cultivation of heavier soils, and damper conditions in or around cultivated fields also may be indicated by rushes (*Juncus* spp.), blinks (*Montia fontana* ssp. *chondrosperma*) and some smaller grasses (eg many *Poa* spp.). Other species, such as the bromes (*Bromus* spp.), suggest lighter conditions, and sheep's sorrel (*Rumex acetosella*) and rye grass are more common on lighter, mildly acidic soils. The grassland flora may reflect plants that grew at the margins of the cultivated fields and the possible cultivation of areas that were previously grazed. Meanwhile, the range of plants present, associated differing soil conditions, may reflect some of the very diverse geology and soils locally.

On the basis of this sample and evidence from other sites in the region it is clear that spelt wheat was one of, if not the most important of, the crops grown locally during the Iron Age and Roman periods. The evidence from this one sample tentatively points towards more organised agricultural production and processing as compared to the piecemeal, household-level processing seen on many Iron Age sites, but it is not possible to generalise further from a single sample. Cultivation of a wider range of soil types, well underway by the middle Iron Age, also seems to have continued in the later period, and this may have included even more of the previously grazed areas. It is equally possible, however, that the management of grasslands, as agriculture generally, became more intensively managed during the Roman period.

Discussion

The excavations indicate that the Roman settlement found at the Redlands Sports Centre did not extend to the east of the railway line. Instead, the features investigated suggest that the area to the east of the buildings was occupied by a trackway and a system of fields or enclosures. If the southern ditch (5005) was Roman, the ditches defining these enclosure would have been set at quite consistent intervals of around 30m and could have formed part of a quite regular rectilinear system. Given their proximity to the Sports Centre buildings it seems likely that this system was related to that complex. The relatively rich finds recovered from the midden and the largest ditch (5009) were presumably debris from the settlement which had been deposited just beyond its outer limits. The finds from the Sports Ground, however, suggested an earlier Roman date in the 1st-2nd centuries and, although earlier Roman pottery was also recovered from the ditches and midden at the current site, the pottery suggests that they date from the late Roman period (*c* AD 250-400). The apparent discrepancy in the chronology of the Sports Ground (1st-2nd century AD) and the Relief Road excavation (3rd-4th century AD) may simply reflect the limited scale of the work in both areas, or perhaps a change in the spatial focus of activity over time. It is worth noting that, although overall the finds from the Relief Road excavation suggest that the features date from the 3rd-4th century, much of the pottery indicated activity earlier in the Roman period.

The finds provide relatively little further insight into the character of the settlement. The charred plant remains, however, clearly indicate that crop processing, probably on a quite large scale, took place nearby, and thus highlights the agricultural role of the site.

BINCOMBE VALLEY CONTOUR SURVEY AND EXCAVATION *by Chris Hayden, Vix Hughes, John Cotter, Elizabeth Stafford and David Score*

Introduction

A contour survey and two trenches were excavated in the Bincombe Valley as part of the Weymouth Relief Road archaeological investigations The site was selected for investigation because of the presence of two flights of well preserved strip lynchets (RCHM(E) 1999, 23-4). The strip lynchets

in this area had been used as an example by Taylor (1966, 282), who suggested that they might have been of early Anglo-Saxon date. He also suggested that the existence of the strip lynchets in this location was a product of the topography of the land belonging to the medieval settlement of Bincombe. The nature of the topography ensured that any cultivation carried out in strips would have had to have taken the form of strip lynchets.

The area investigated covered an area of 5.9ha, centred at NGR SY 675850 (Figs 1.1 and 8.3). It extended across the Bincombe Valley (Hellwell Bottom) to the south of the Upwey to Bincombe road, and from the railway line at the west to the south of West Farm to the east. The bottom of the valley in this area lies at around 60 m OD, and the land rises towards the Ridgeway to the north and to the Knoll to the south. The land was being used as pasture at the time of the survey.

The area spans the 'Ridgeway Fault' and the underlying geology varies across the valley, crossing bands of mudstone (of the Ridgeway Member), sandstone (of the Portland Sand Formation) and limestone (of the Portland Cherty Member, the Portland Freestone Member and the Mupe Member (which are covered by bands of Wealden and Oxford

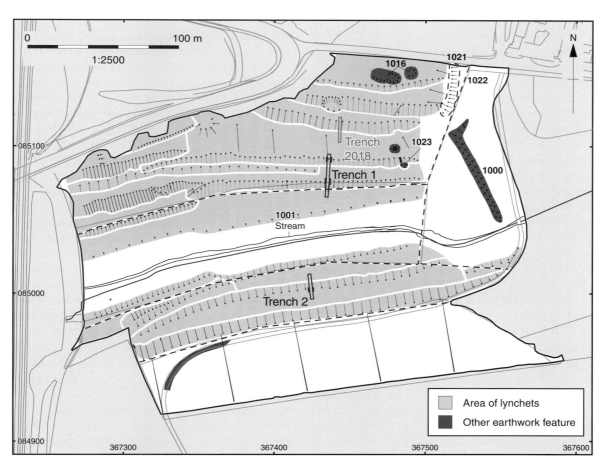

Fig. 8.3 Plan of Bincombe Valley survey site

Clays (http://mapapps.bgs.ac.uk/geologyofbritain/home.html). Some of this variety was revealed in the base of the trenches cut across the lynchets.

The survey was carried out using a combination of Total Station Theodolite (TST) and Global Positioning System (GPS) following English Heritage Metric Survey Specifications (Blake *et al.* 2009) and RCHME specifications (RCHME 1999).

Results of the investigations

A flight of seven lynchets rose from the valley bottom on the northern side of the survey area, although the sequence was slightly different at the eastern and western ends. A further three were present on the southern side. The dimensions of the lynchets varied considerably. On average the treads were around 11m wide and the risers 2m tall, but the treads varied from 4m to 20m in width, and the risers from 0.5m to 5m tall.

Two trenches were cut across the lynchets (Fig. 8.4): Trench 1, which cut across two lynchets on the northern side of the valley, was 29.7m long and 2.1m wide. Trench 2, which cut across a single lynchet on the southern side of the valley, was 17m long and 2.1m wide. A trench had previously been cut to the north of Trench 1 by Wessex Archaeology (1994).

The stratigraphic sequences revealed on both sides of the valley were generally similar. On both sides of the valley the lynchets were overlain by a dark brown clayey silt topsoil.

The positive lynchets were largely formed of mid orange brown silty clay deposits (102, 107 and 205). The front parts of these deposits (ie the part close to the negative lynchet below) generally lay either on bed rock (which varied across the site – 114: limestone, 104, 113 and 207: mudstone), or on relatively thin, natural deposits (208: pale brown clay). The back parts (ie the part close to the negative lynchet above) covered more complex series of deposits, which, however, appeared to have been largely natural. These deposits consisted of mid orange brown (106, 108 and 206), mid brown grey (109, 204), mid and pale brown (202 and 208), and pale brown yellow (103 and 203) clays. Along the negative lynchets the sediments had been cut back to the natural bedrock (114, 113 and 207).

Overall, the sections reveal clearly that the lynchets were formed by the movement of sediment from the negative lynchets downslope to form the positive lynchets. The sequence of deposits which lie below the back of the positive lynchets presumably consist of the original sediments which covered the valley sides, and which have been preserved below the positive lynchets. The fact that the front parts of the positive lynchets overlie bedrock rather than such sequences of deposits suggests that the positive

lynchets have been slowly spread downslope so as to cover parts of earlier negative lynchets. Part of this process may be revealed by deposit 110. This deposit lay above a negative lynchet at the base of positive lynchet 107. It consisted of a dark brown silty clay, very similar to the topsoil, and presumably formed as the result of erosion of topsoil from above positive lynchet 107.

Whilst this general sequence is clear, the sections do not provide any clear indication of whether the creation of the lynchets was deliberate or simply a byproduct of a particular pattern of ploughing. Perhaps the best that can be said is that there is no clear indication of any structures or other kind of deliberate construction. The build up of deposits to form the positive lynchets, however, clearly implies the existence of some kind of boundary that prevented the sediment from continuing downslope. The excavation did not provide any evidence of the form of that boundary.

The only finds recovered from the trenches were four sherds of pottery, one of Donyatt slipware and three of Donyatt plainware, all dating from the 17th-18th centuries. All of this pottery came from topsoil contexts, except one which was recovered from a deposit (107) forming a positive lynchet. Whilst the sherd might be taken to suggest that the lynchets were quite recent features, the RCHM(E) (1970, 23), notes that they remained in use into the 19th century. Furthermore, the evidence described above, indicating that the lynchets have gradually spread, suggests that they may have formed over a period of unknown length. The finds recovered from the trench cut by Wessex Archaeology (1994) also produced post-medieval finds which, again, probably reflect relatively recent activity rather than the original creation of the lynchets. The few finds are clearly insufficient to provide any insight into the overall chronology of the features.

The molluscs from a series of samples taken from the positive lynchet (205) in Trench 2 were analysed. Although the molluscs were moderately well-preserved, species diversity was low, and the samples were dominated by a few open-country species, fairly typical of colluvial and lynchet deposits of the chalk downlands and reflecting, as expected, a very dry and open environment.

Alongside the lynchets, a small number of other features were revealed by the contour survey. These included a slight bank (1000) on the eastern edge of survey area which ran for 70m just off north-south for most of its length before turning to the north-east. Also recorded were a meandering feature (1001) consisting of two uneven banks which followed the course of a stream through the valley bottom, two small banks around a depression (1016) which lay near the northern edge of the survey area,

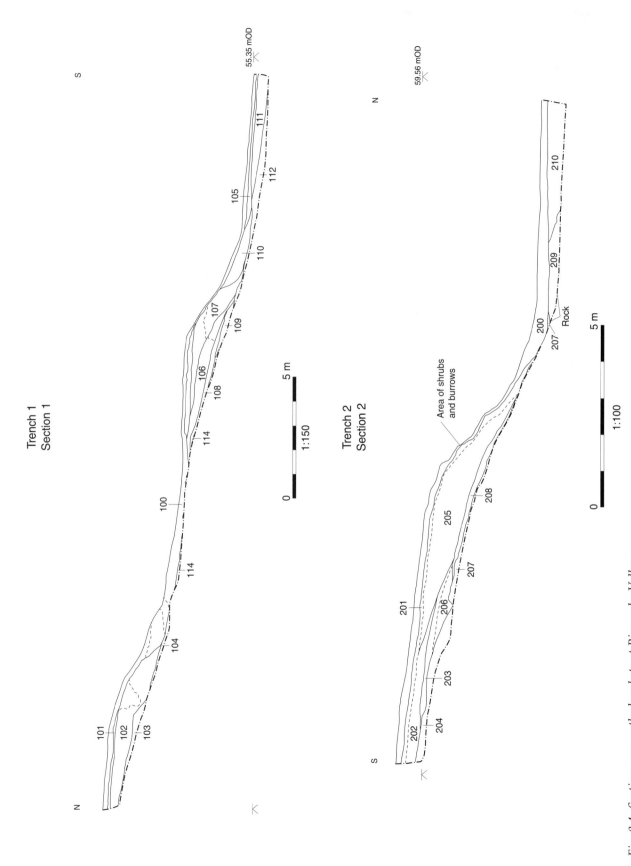

Fig. 8.4 Sections across the lynchets at Bincombe Valley

and a slight mound (1023) associated with a flight of four concrete steps. A small stone crossing point, probably post-medieval in date, had been constructed across the stream near the eastern edge of the survey area. A drystone wall (1022) at the northern edge of the survey area, records of which can be found in the site archive, was recorded before being dismantled. A stone culvert (1021), channelling water below the road, had been constructed within this wall.

Bibliography

AC Archaeology, 1997 *An archaeological evaluation on the site of a proposed all-weather hockey pitch, Redlands Sports Ground, Weymouth*, unpubl rep, AC Archaeology, Hindon

Aitkin, G and Aitken, N 1990 Excavations at Whitcombe, 1965-1967, *Proc Dorset Nat Hist and Archaeol Soc* **112**, 57-94

Albarella, U, and Serjeantson, D, 2002 A passion for pork: meat consumption at the British Late Neolithic site of Durrington Walls, in P Miracle and N Milner (eds), *Consuming passions and patterns of consumption*, Cambridge, 33-49

Allason-Jones, L, 1996 *Roman Jet in the Yorkshire Museum*, York

Allason-Jones, L. 2002 The Jet Industry and Allied Trades in Roman Britain, in P Wilson and J Price (eds), *Aspects of Industry in Roman Yorkshire and the North*, Oxford, 125-132

Allen, M J, 2000 Soils, Pollen and lots of snails, in M G Green, *A landscape revealed: 10,000 years on a chalkland farm*, Stroud, 36-49

Anderson, T 1995 The Human Skeletons, in K Parfitt, *Iron Age burials from Mill Hill, Deal*, London, 114-44

Anderson-Whymark, H, 2008 *The residue of ritualised action: Neolithic deposition practices in the Middle Thames Valley*, BAR Brit. Ser **466**, Oxford

Anderson-Whymark, H, and Thomas, J, 2012 *Regional perspectives on Neolithic pit deposition: beyond the mundane*, Neolithic Studies Group Seminar Papers **12**, Oxford

Annable, F K, and Simpson, D D A, 1964 *Guide catalogue of the Neolithic and Bronze Age collections in Devizes Museum*, Devizes

Arkell, W J, 1947 *The geology of the country around Weymouth, Swanage, Corfe and Lulworth : explanation of sheets, 341, 342, 343, with small portions of sheets 327, 328, 329*, HMSO, London

Armour-Chelu, M, 1991 The faunal remains, in Sharples, 1991, 139-151

Ashbee, P, 1960 *The Bronze Age round barrow in Britain: an introduction to the study of the funerary practice and culture of the British and Irish single-grave people of the second millennium BC*, London

Aspöck, E, 2007 What actually is a deviant burial? Comparing German-language and Anglophone research on deviant burials, in E Murphy (ed.), *Deviant burial practices in the archaeological record*, Oxford, 17-34

Atkinson, R J C, 1946-7, A Middle Bronze Age barrow at Cassington, Oxon., *Oxoniensia* **11-12**, 5-26

Aufderheide, A C and Rodríguez-Martín, C 1998 *The Cambridge Encyclopedia of Human Paleopathology*, CUP, Cambridge

Bailey, C J and Flatters, E, 1972 Trial Excavations of an Iron Age and Romano-British Site at Quarry Lodden, Bincombe, *Proc Dorset Natur Hist and Archaeol Soc* **93**, 135-143

Bamford, H, 1985 *Briar Hill: excavation, 1974-1978*, Northampton Development Corporation Archaeol Monogr **3**, Northampton

Barclay, A and Halpin, C, 1997 *Excavations at Barrow Hills, Radley, Oxfordshire, Volume 1: the Neolithic and Bronze Age monument complex*, Thames Valley Landscapes Monogr **11**, Oxford

Barclay, A, Lambrick, G, Moore, J, and Robinson, M, 2003 *Lines in the landscape, cursus monuments in the Upper Thames Valley*, Oxford Archaeol Thames Valley Landscapes Monogr **15**, Oxford

Barnatt, J, 1994 Excavation of a Bronze Age unenclosed cemetery, cairns and field boundaries at Eaglestone Flat, Curbar, Derbyshire, 1984, 1989-1990, *Proc Prehist Soc* **60**, 287-370

Barrett, J C, 1980 The pottery of the later Bronze Age in lowland England, *Proc Prehist Soc* 46, 297-319

Barrett, J C, 1989, Food, gender and metal: questions of social reproduction, in M L S Sørensen and R Thomas (eds), 1989 *The Bronze Age – Iron Age transition in Europe:Aspects of Continuity and Change in European Societies c 1200-500 BC*, BAR Int Ser **483**, Oxford

Barrett, J C, 1994 *Fragments from antiquity: an archaeology of social life in Britain, 2900-1200 BC*, Oxford

Barrett, J C, Bradley, R and Green, M, 1991 *Landscape, Monuments and Society. The prehistory of Cranborne Chase*, Cambridge

Bass, W M, 1987 (3rd ed.) *Human Osteology. Laboratory Field Manual*, spec publ no. 2, Columbia

Beavis, J, 1974 Excavations at Abbotsbury Castle, *Proc Dorset Nat Hist and Archaeol Soc* **96**, 56

Bell, M, Fowler, P J, and Hillson, S, 1996 *The experimental earthwork project, 1960-1992*, CBA Res Rep **100**, York

Bendrey, R, 2010, The horse, in T O'Connor and N Sykes (eds), *Extinctions and invasions: a social history of British fauna*, Oxford, 10-16

Bennett, K D, 1989 A provisional map of forest types for the British Isles 5000 years ago, *J Quaternary Science* **4**, 141–4

Berggren, G, 1969 *Atlas of seeds, part 2: Cyperaceae*, Swedish Museum of Natur Hist, Stockholm

Berggren, G, 1981 *Atlas of Seeds. Part 3. Salicaceae-Cruciferae*, Swedish Museum of Natur Hist, Stockholm

Bersu, G, 1940 Excavations at Little Woodbury, Wiltshire (1938-39), *Proc Prehist Soc*, **6**, 30-111

Best, M E, 1964 Excavation of three barrows on the Ridgeway, Bincombe, *Proc Dorset Natur Hist and Archaeol Soc* **86**, 102-03

Biddulph, E, Foreman, S, Stafford, L, Stansbie, D, and Nicholson, R, 2012 *London Gateway. Iron Age and Roman salt making in the Thames estuary: excavation at Stanford Wharf Nature Reserve, Essex*, Oxford Archaeol Monogr **18**, Oxford

Biddulph, E, Guest, P, and Manning, W, 2007 Post-Neolithic finds, in D Benson and A Whittle (eds) *Building memories: the Neolithic Cotswold Long Barrow at Ascott-under-Wychwood, Oxfordshire*, Oxford, 319-325

Birks, H J B, 1989 Holocene isochrone maps and patterns of tree-spreading in the British Isles, *J Biogeography* **16**, 503–40

Birks, H J B, Deacon, J and Peglar, S, 1975 Pollen maps for the British Isles 5000 years ago, *Proc Royal Soc London* **B 189**, 87–105

Bjärvall, A, and Ullström, S, 1995 *Däggdjur; alla Europas arter i text och bild*, Stockholm

Blake, B, Bedford J and Andrews, D, 2009 *Metric survey specifications for cultural heritage* (2nd edn), Swindon

Bloch, M, 2005 Ritual and deference, in *Essays on cultural transmission*, 123-38, Oxford

Boardman, S and Jones, G E M, 1990 Experiments on the effects of charring on cereal plant components, *J Archaeol Science* **17(1)**, 1-12

Boast, R, 1995 Fine pots, pure pots, Beaker, in I Kinnes and G Varndall (eds), *'Unbaked urns of rudely shape': essays on British and Irish pottery for Ian Longworth*, Oxbow Monogr **55**, Oxford, 69-80

Boessneck, J, Müller, H-H, and Teichert, M, 1964 *Osteologische Unterscheidungsmerkmale zwischen Schaf (Ovis aries Linné) und Ziege (Capra hircus Linné)*, *Kühn-Archiv* **78**

Boocock, P, Roberts, C and Manchester, K 1995 Maxillary sinusitis in medieval Chichester, England *American J Physical Anthropology* **98**, 483-496

Boughton, D, 2013 The strange case of the bronzes buried in the Vale of Wardour, *British Archaeology* **129**, 62-69

Boyle, A, 2011 Human remains, in G Hey, P Booth and J Timby, *Yarnton: Iron Age and Romano-*

British Settlement and Landscape, Thames Valley Landscapes Monogr **35**, 469-86

Bradley, P, 1997 The worked flint, in Barclay and Halpin 1997, 211-227

Bradley, R, 1987 The worked flints, in N Sunter and P Woodward 1987

Bradley, R., 1998 *The Passage of Arms, An archaeological analysis of prehistoric hoards and votive deposits*, (2nd edn), Oxford

Bradley, R and Yates, D, 2007 After Celtic Fields: the social organisation of Iron Age agriculture, in Haselgrove and Pope 2007 (eds), 94-102

Brailsford, J W, 1948 Excavations at Little Woodbury, part II, *Proc Prehist Soc* **14**, 1-23

Brailsford, J W, 1949 Excavations at Little Woodbury, parts IV and V, *Proc Prehist Soc* **15**, 156-68

Brailsford, J W, 1957 The Durotrigian Culture, *Proc Dorset Nat Hist and Arch Soc* **79**, 118-121

Brickley, M, 2000 The diagnosis of metabolic disease in archaeological bone, in M Cox and S Mays (eds), *Human Osteology in Archaeology and Forensic Science*, London, Greenwich Medical Media, 183-98

Brickley, M, 2004 Determination of sex from archaeological skeletal material and assessment of parturition, in M Brickley and J I McKinley 2004, 23-25

Brickley, M and McKinley, J, 2004 *Guidelines to the standards for recording human remains*, IFA Paper **7**, British Association for Biological Anthropology and Osteoarchaeology and the Institute of Field Archaeologists

Brickley, M, Berry, H and Western, G, 2006 The people: physical anthropology, in M Brickley, S Buteux, J Adams and R Cherrington, *St Martin's Uncovered: Investigations in the Churchyard of St Martin's-in-the-Bull Ring, Birmingham, 2001*, Oxford, 91-151

Brickley, M and McKinley, J, 2004 *Guidelines to the standards for recording human remains* IFA Paper **7**, Southampton

Brodie, N, 2001 Technological frontiers and the emergence of the Bell Beaker culture, Bell Beakers today: pottery, people, culture, symbols in prehistoric Europe, *Proceedings of the international colloquium at Riva del Garda, Trento*, 487-96

Bronk Ramsey, C, 2009 Bayesian analysis of radiocarbon dates, *Radiocarbon* **51**, 337-60

Brooks, S T and Suchey, J M 1990 Skeletal age determination based on the os pubis: a comparison of the Acsádi-Nemeskéri and Suchey-Brooks Methods, *Human Evolution* **5**, 227-238

Brothwell, D R, 1971 Forensic aspects of the so-called Neolithic skeleton Q1 from Maiden Castle, Dorset, *World Archaeology* **3**, 233-41

Brothwell, D R, 1981 *Digging up bones*, Oxford

Brothwell, D, Dobney, K, and Jaques, D, 2005 Abnormal sheep metatarsals: a problem in aetiology and historical geography, in J Davies, M Fabiš, I Mainland, M Richards and R Thomas (eds), *Diet and health in past animal populations. Current research and future directions*, Oxford 75-79

Brown, L, 1987 The pottery, in B Cunliffe, 1987

Brown, L, 1991 Later prehistoric pottery, in Sharples, 1991, 185-203

Brown, L 1997 Marketing and commerce in Late Iron Age Dorset: the Wareham/Poole Harbour pottery industry, in A Gwilt and C Haselgrove (eds), *Reconstructing Iron Age Societies*, Oxford, 40-45

Brown, L 2000a, The prehistoric pottery, in B Cunliffe, 2000

Brown, L 2000b The pottery, in K Hirst, 2000

Brück, J, 2007 The character of Late Bronze Age settlement in southern Britain, in Haselgrove and Pope 2007 (eds), 24-38

Buckberry, J and Chamberlain, A 2002 Age estimation from the auricular surface of the ilium: a revised method, *American J Physical Anthropology* **119**, 231-239

Buckley, L, 1998 Human skeletal report (69-97), in C Mount, Five early Bronze Age cemeteries at Brownstown, Graney West, Oldtown and Ploopluck, Co Kildare, and Stawhall, Co Carlow, *Proc Royal Irish Academy* **98C**, 2, 25-99

Buikstra, J E and Ubelaker, D H (eds), 1994 *Standards for data collection from human skeletal remains*, Arkansas Archaeol Survey Research Series **44**, Arkansas

Bullock, A E, and Allen, M J, 1997 Animal bone, in Smith, Healey, Allen, Morris, Barnes and Woodward 1997, 190-199

Burgess, C, 1980 *The Age of Stonehenge*, London

Burl, A, 1987 *The Stonehenge people: life and death at the world's greatest stone circle*, London

Butler, C, 2005 *Prehistoric flintwork*, Stroud

Butterworth, C, and Gibson, C, 2004 Neolithic pits and a Bronze Age field system at Middle Farm, Dorchester, *Proc Dorset Natur Hist and Archaeol Soc* **126**, 15-25

Buttler, W, 1936 Pits and pit-dwellings in southeast Europe, *Antiquity* **10,** 25-36

Calkin, J B, 1953, Kimmeridge Coal Money. The Romano-British Shale Armlet Industry, *Proc Dorset Natur Hist and Archaeol Soc* **75**, 45-71.

Calkin, J B, and Putnam, W G, 1970 An enlarged Food Vessel from Ridgeway Hill near Weymouth, *Proc Dorset Natur Hist and Archaeol Soc* **91**, 176-77

Carbonell, V M, 1963 Variations in the frequency of shovel-shaped incisors in different populations, in: D R Brothwell (ed.), *Dental Anthropology*, London, 211-234

Case, H J, 1977 The Beaker Culture in Britain and Ireland, in R Mercer (ed.), *Beakers in Britain and Europe*, BAR Int Ser **26**, Oxford, 71-101

Case, H J, 1998 *The Beaker culture in Britain and Ireland: groups, European contacts and chronology*, Bell Beakers today: pottery, people, culture, symbols in prehistoric Europe, proceedings of the international colloquium at Riva del Garda, Trento, 11-16

Chambers, S A, 1978 *An analysis of Iron Age inhumation burials in the Dorset area and an assessment of their value as indicators of social organisation*, unpubl certificate dissertation, Univ Leeds

Champion, T, 1999 The later Bronze Age, in J hunter and I Ralston (eds), *The Archaeology of Britain. An introduction from the Upper Palaeolithic to the Industrial Revolution*, London 95-64

Childe, V G, 1951 *Man makes himself*, New York

Clapham, A R, Tutin, T G, and Moore, D M, 1989 *Flora of the British Isles* (3rd edn), Cambridge

Clarke, D L, 1970 *Beaker pottery of Great Britain and Ireland*, Cambridge

Clarke, D V, Cowie, T G, and Foxon, A, 1985 *Symbols of power at the time of Stonehenge*, Edinburgh

Clay, R C C, 1925 An inhabited site of La Tene I date on Swallowcliffe Down, *Wilts Archaeol and Natur Hist Mag* **43**, 59-93

Clay, R C C, 1927 Supplementary report on the Early Iron Age village on Swallowcliffe Down, *Wilts Archaeol and Natur Hist Mag* **46,** 540-7

Cleal, R M J, 1991 The earlier prehistoric pottery, in N Sharples 1991, 171-85

Coleman-Smith, R, and Pearson, T, 1988 *Excavations in the Donyatt Potteries*, Chichester

Cool, H E M, 1983 *A study of the Roman personal ornaments made of metal, excluding brooches, from Southern Britain*, unpubl PhD thesis, Univ Wales

Cool, H E M, 1990 Roman metal hair pins from Southern Britain, *Archaeol J* **147**, 148-182

Cool, H E M, 2006 *Eating and drinking in Roman Britain*, Cambridge

Cox, M 1996 *Life and Death in Spitalfields 1700-1850*, CBA, York

Cox, M 2000 Assessment of parturition, in, M Cox and S mays (eds) *Human Osteology in Archaeology and Forensic Science*, Greenwich Medical Media, London 131-42

Cox, M, 2000 Ageing adults from the skeleton, in M Cox and S Mays (eds), *Human osteology in archaeology and forensic science*, London, 61-81

Cox, P W, 1987 The flint, in Sunter and P J Woodward (eds) 1987

Cox P W and Mills, J M, 1991 The Kimmeridge Shale, in P W Cox and C M Hearne, *Redeemed from the Heath. The Archaeology of the Wytch Farm Oilfield, (1987-1990)*, Dorset Natur Hist and Archaeol Soc Monogr **9**, Dorchester, 170-175

Crawford, S, 2007 Companions, co-incidences or chattels? Children in the early Anglo-Saxon multiple burial ritual, in S Crawford, and G Shepherd (eds), *Children, childhood and society,* BAR Int Ser **1696**, Oxford, 83-92

Cunliffe, B, 1984 *Danebury: an Iron Age hillfort in Hampshire 2, the excavations 1969-78: the finds,* CBA Res Rep **52**, London

Cunliffe, B, 1987 *Hengistbury Head. Volume 1: Prehistoric and Roman Settlement, 3500 BC–AD 500.* OUCA Monogr **13**, Institute of Archaeol, Oxford

Cunliffe, B, 2000 *The Danebury Environs Programme: The Prehistory of a Wessex Landscape (Volume 1),* OUCA Monogr **48**, Institute of Archaeol, Oxford

Cunliffe, B, 2005 *Iron Age Communities in Britain* (4th edn), London

Cunliffe, B, and Phillipson, D W, 1968, Excavations at Eldon's Seat, Encombe, Dorset, *Proc Prehist Soc* **34**, 191-237.

Cunliffe, B and Poole, C, 2000 *Suddern Farm, Middle Wallop, Hants 1991 and 1996. The Danebury Environs Programme. The Prehistory of a Wessex Landscape,* English Heritage and Oxford Univ Archaeol Monogr **49**, Oxford

Cunnington, M E, 1923 *The Early Iron Age Inhabited Site at All Cannings Cross,* Devizes

Cunningham, P, 2011 Caching your savings: the use of small-scale storage in European prehistory, *J Anthropological Archaeol* **30**, 135-44

Cunningham, P, 2005 Assumptive holes and how to fill them, *euroREA* **2**, 55-66

Curwen, E C, 1918, Covered Ways on the Sussex Downs, *Sussex Archaeol Collections* **59**, 35-75

Curwen, E C, 1951, Cross-ridge dykes in Sussex, in WF Grimes, (ed.), *Aspects of Archaeology,* London, 93-97

Davies, H F, 1936, The shale industries of Kimmeridge, *Archaeol J* **93**, 200-219

Davies, S M, 2002 *Excavations at Alington Avenue, Fordington, Dorchester, Dorset, 1984-87,* Dorset Natur Hist and Archaeol Soc Monogr **15**, Dorchester

Davies, SM, 1987 The coarse pottery, in N. Sunter and P. J. Woodward (eds) 1987, 150-157

Davies, SM, and Hawkes, J W, 1987 The Iron Age and Romano-British coarse pottery, in C J S Green, 1987, 123-127

Dinwiddy, K E, and Bradley, P, 2011 *Prehistoric settlement and a Roman-British Settlement at Poundbury Farm, Dorchester, Dorset,* Wessex Archaeol Rep **28**, Salisbury

Dobney, K, Jaques, D, and Irving, B, 1995 *Of butchers and breeds. Report on vertebrate remains from various sites in the city of Lincoln,* Lincoln Archaeol Studies **5**

Dorset County Council , 2005 *Weymouth Relief Road: environmental statement,* Dorchester

Dorset County Council and English Heritage, 2011, *South Dorset Ridgeway Mapping Project,* English Heritage Project No. 5583, Rep 2011R031

Duray, S M 1996 Dental indicators of stress and reduced age at death in prehistoric Native Americans, *American J Physical Anthropology* **99**, 275-286

Eckardt, H, Brewer, P, Hay, S, and Poppy, S, 2009 Roman barrows and their landscape context: a GIS case study at Bartlow, Cambridgeshire, *Britannia* **40**, 65-98

Edlin, H L, 1947 *Forestry and Woodland Life,* London

Edlin, H L, 1949 *Woodland crafts in Britain: an account of the traditional uses of trees and timber in the British Countryside,* London

Ellis , C and Powell, A, 2008 *An Iron Age Settlement outside Battlebury Hillfort, Warminster and Sites along the Southern Range Road,* Wessex Archaeol Rep **22**, Salisbury

Ellison, A and Rahtz, P, 1987 Excavations at Hog Cliff Hill, Maiden Newton, Dorset, *Proc Prehist Soc,* **53**, 223-70

Eldridge, W M and Holm, G A, 1940 The incidence of hyperostosis frontalis interna in female patients admitted to a mental hospital *American J Roentgenology* **43**, 356-9 EH www.eng-h.gov.uk/mpp/mcd/crossd

English Heritage 1991 *The Management of Archaeological Projects,* London, Historic Monuments and Buildings Commission.

English Heritage 2006 *Management of Research Projects in the Historic Environment: The MoRPHE Project Managers' Guide,* Swindon

Entwistle, R and Bowden, M, 1991 Cranborne Chase: the molluscan evidence, in J C Barrett, R Bradley, and M Hall (eds), *Papers on the prehistoric archaeology of Cranborne Chase,* Oxbow Monogr **11**, Oxford, 20-48

Errington, A, 1981 Flint tools associated with the turning of shale bracelets on lathes, *Bulletin of Experimental Archaeology* **2**, 18-19

Evans, J G, 1972 *Land snails in archaeology,* London

Evans, J G and Jones, H, 1979 Mount Pleasant and Woodhenge: the land Mollusca, in G J Wainwright 1979, 190-213

Fairweather, A D and Ralston, I, 1993 Neolithic plant macrofossils from the Balbridie timber hall, Grampian Region, Scotland: a preliminary note, *Antiquity* **67**, 313-23

Falk, A-B, 2008 *En grundläggande handling. Byggnadsoffer och dagligt liv I medeltid,* Lund

Farrah, R A H, 1958 A Neolithic pit at Sutton Poyntz, Weymouth, *Proc Dorset Natur Hist and*

Archaeol Soc **79**, 112-13

Farwell, D E, and Molleson, T I, 1993, *Excavations at Poundbury 1966-80. II: The Cemeteries*, Dorset Nartur Hist and Archaeol Monogr **11**, Dorchester

Fasham, P J, 1985 *The prehistoric settlement at Winnall Down, Winchester: excavations of MARC 3 Site R17 in 1976 and 1977*, Hants Field Club and Archaeol Society Monogr **2**, Winchester

Fasham, P, Keevill, G and Coe, D, 1995, *Brighton Hill South (Hatch Warren): an Iron Age Farmstead and Deserted Medieval Village in Hampshire*, Wessex Archaeol Rep **7**, Salisbury

Field, N H, Matthews, C L, and Smith, I F, 1964 New Neolithic sites in Dorset and Bedfordshire, with a note on the distribution of Neolithic storage pits in Britain, *Proc Prehist Soc* **30**, 352-81

Finnegan, M 1978 Non-metric variation of the infracranial skeleton *J Anatomy* **125**, 23-37

Fitzpatrick, A P, 1997, A 1st-century AD 'Durotrigian' burial with a decorated IronAge mirror from Portesham, Dorset, *Proc Dorset Natur Hist and Archaeol Soc*, **118**, 51-70

Fitzpatrick, A P, 2011 *The Amesbury Archer and the Boscombe Bowmen: Bell Beaker burials at Boscombe Down, Amesbury, Wiltshire*, Wessex Archael Rep **27**, Salisbury

Fitzpatrick, A P, Butterworth, C A, and Grove, J, 1999 *Prehistoric and Roman sites in east Devon: the A30 Honiton to Exeter Improvement DBFO, 1996-9, volume 1: prehistoric sites*, Wessex Archaeol Rep **16**, Salisbury

Fowler, P J, 1964, Cross-dykes on the Ebble-Nadder Ridge, *Wilts Archaeol and Natur Hist Mag* **60**, 47-51

Fowler, P J, 1965 A Roman Barrow at Knob's Crook, Woodlands, Dorset, *Antiquaries J* **45**, 22-52

Fulford, M, 2001 Links with the past: Pervasive 'ritual' behaviour in Roman Britain, *Britannia* **32**, 199-218

Gale, J, 2003 *Prehistoric Dorset*, Stroud

Gale, R, 1991 The charred wood, in Sharples 1991, 125-129

Gale, R and Cutler, D, 2000 *Plants in Archaeology: Identification manual of vegetative plant materials used in Europe and the southern Mediterranean to c.1500*,

Galloway, A 1999 *Broken Bones: Anthropological Analysis of Blunt Force Trauma*, Springfield, Illinois

Gardiner, J, Allen, M J, Powell, A, Harding, P, Lawson, A J, Loader, E, McKinley, J, Sheridan, A and Stevens, C, 2007, A Matter of Life and Death: late Neolithic, Beaker and early Bronze Age settlement and cemeteries at Thomas Hardye School, Dorchester, *Proc Dorset Natur Hist and Archaeol Soc* **128**, 17-52

Garrow, D, 2006 *Pits, settlement and deposition during the Neolithic and Early Bronze Age in East Anglia*, BAR Brit Ser **172**, Oxford

Garrow, D, 2007 Placing pits: landscape occupation and depositional practice during the Neolithic in East Anglia, *Proc Prehist Soc* **73**, 1-24

Garwood, P, 1999 Grooved Ware in southern Britain: chronology and interpretation, in R Cleal and A MacSween (eds), *Grooved Ware in Britain and Ireland*, Neolithic Studies Group Seminar Papers 3, Oxford, 145-76

Garwood, P, 2007a Before the hills in order stood: chronology, time and history in the interpretation of early Bronze Age round barrows, in J Last (ed.), *Beyond the grave: new perspectives on barrows*, Oxford, 30-52

Garwood, P, 2007b Vital resources, ideal images and virtual lives: children in early Bronze Age funerary ritual, in S E E Crawford and G B Shepherd (eds), *Children, childhood and society*, BAR Int Ser **1696**, Oxford, 63-82

Gibbs, A L, 1989 Sex, gender and material culture patterning in later Neolithic and earlier Bronze Age England, unpubl. PhD thesis, Univ Cambridge

Godwin, H, 1956 *History of the British Flora: A factual basis for phytogeography*, Cambridge

Graham, A, 2006 *Barton Field, Tarrant Hinton, Dorset: Excavations 1968-1984*, Dorset Natur Hist and Archaeol Soc Monogr **17**, Dorchester

Grant, A, 1982 The use of toothwear as a guide to the age of domestic ungulates, in B Wilson, C Grigson and S Payne (eds), *Ageing and sexing animal bones from archaeological sites*, BAR Brit Ser **109**, Oxford, 91-108

Grant, A, 1984 Survival or sacrifice? A critical appraisal of animal burials in Britain in the Iron Age, in *Animals and archaeology. Vol. 4. Husbandry in Europe* (eds C Grigson and J Clutton-Brock), BAR Int Ser **227**, 221-227

Green, C J S, 1987 *Excavations at Poundbury, Dorchester, Dorset 1966-82. Volume I: The Settlements*, Dorset Natur Hist and Archaeol Soc Monog 7, Dorchester

Grimm, J, 2008 Animal bone, Online supplement to Trevarthen, 2008, www.wessexarch.co.uk/ projects/dorset/dorchester_hospital

GSB, 2004 *Weymouth Relief Road, Dorset: geophysical survey report*, unpubl. Rep 2000/54, GSB Prospection Ltd, Bradford

Guido, M, 1978 *The glass beads of the prehistoric and Roman periods in Britain and Ireland*, Soc Antiquaries Res Rep **35**, London

Guilbert, G, 1975, *Rattlinghope/Stitt Hill. Shropshire: Earthwork enclosures and cross-dykes*. Bulletin of the Board of Celtic Studies, 26, 363-373

Habermehl, K-H, 1975 *Die Altersbestimmung bei Haus- und Labortieren* (2nd edn), Berlin and Hamburg

Halstead, P, 1985 A study of mandibular teeth from Romano-British contexts at Maxey, in F Pryor, C French, D Crowther D Gurney, Simpson, G, M Taylor (eds), *The Fenland project: Archaeology and Environment in the Lower Welland Valley, Volume 1*, East Anglican Archaeol Rep **27**, The Fenland Project Committee, Cambs Archaeol Comm, 219-224.

Hamilton-Dyer S, 1999 Animal bones, in Hearne and Burbeck 1999, 188-202

Harding, A F, 1986 *Survey and Excavation on Danby Rigg, 1985*, Univ Durham and Univ Newcastle-upon-Tyne Archaeol Reps for 1985, 20-25

Harding, A F, 1987, *Excavations at Danby Rigg, North Yorkshire, 1986*, Univ Durham and Univ Newcastle-upon-Tyne Archaeol Reps for 1986, 14-16

Harding, P, 1990 The worked flint, in J C Richarde (ed.), *The Stonehenge environs project*, English Heritage, London

Haselgrove, C, 1994 Social organisation in Wessex, in A P Fitzpatrick and E L Morris (eds), *The Iron Age in Wessex: recent work*, Trust for Wessex Archaeology, Salisbury

Haselgrove, C and Pope, R (eds) 2007 *The Earlier Iron Age in Britain and the Near Continent*, Oxford

Hather, J G, 2000 *The Identification of Northern European Woods: A Guide for Archaeologists and Conservators*, London

Hawkes, S C, 1994 Longbridge Deverill Cow Down, Wiltshire, house 3: a major round house of the early Iron Age, *Oxford J Archaeology* **13**, 49-69

Hawkes, S C, 2012 *Longbridge Deverill Cow Down: an Early Iron Age Settlement in West Wiltshire*, Oxford Univ School of Archaeol Monogr **76**, Oxford

Healy, F, 1988 *The Anglo-Saxon cemetery at Spong Hill, North Elmham, part VI: occupation in the 7th to 2nd millennia BC*, East Anglian Archaeology **39**, Gressenhall

Hearne, C M, and Burbeck, V, 1999 *A35 Tolpuddle to Puddletown Bypass DBFO, Dorset, 1996-8, incorporating excavations at Tolpuddle Ball 1993*, Wessex Archaeol Rep **15**

Hearne, C M, and Smith, R J C, 1991 A late Iron Age settlement and black-burnished 1 production site at Worgret, near Wareham, Dorset, 1986–7, *Proc Dorset Natur Hist Archaeol Soc* **113**, 74–89

Hey, G, Mulville, J, and Robinson, M, 2003, Diet and culture in southern Britain: the evidence from Yarnton, in M Parker Pearson *(ed.) Food, culture and identity in the Neolithic and early Bronze Age*, BAR Int Ser **1117**, 79-88, Oxford

Hill, J D, 1995 *Ritual and rubbish in the Iron Age of Wessex. A study of the formation of a specific archaeological record*, BAR Brit Ser **242**

Hill, J D, 1996, Hillforts and the Iron Age of Wessex, in T Champion and J R Collis, (eds), *The Iron Age in Britain and Ireland: Recent Trends*, Sheffield, 95-116

Hillman, G C, 1981 Reconstructing crop husbandry practices from the charred remains of crops, in R Mercer (ed.), *Farming Practice in British Prehistory*. Edinburgh, 123-162.

Hillman, G C, 1984 Interpretation of archaeological plant remains: the application of ethnographic models from Turkey, in W Van Zist and W A Casparie (eds), *Plants and Ancient Man - Studies in Paleoethnobotany*, Rotterdam, 1-41

Hillson, S 1986 *Teeth*, Cambridge

Hillson, S 1996 *Dental Anthropology* (3rd edn), Cambridge

Hirst, K, 2000 *The Excavation of Archaeological remains at Waddon, Dorset*, Time Team unpubl rep, London

Hobbs, R, 1996 *British Iron Age coins in the British Museum*, London

Hodson, F R, 1990 *Hallstatt, the Ramsauer graves: quantification and analysis*, Römisch-germanisches Zentralmuseum Monographien **16**, Bonn

Holbrook, N and Bidwell, P T, 1991 *Roman finds from Exeter*, Exeter Archaeological Rep. **4**

Humphrey, C, and Laidlaw, J, 1994 *The archetypal actions of ritual: a theory of ritual illustrated by the Jain rite of worship*, Oxford

Inizan, M.-L, Roche, H and Tixier, J, 1992 *Technology of knapped stone*, Cercle de Recherches et d'Etudes Préhistoriques, CNRS, Meudon

Jacomet, S, 2006 *Identification of cereal remains from archaeological sites* (2nd edn), Basel

Johansson, F, and Hüster, H, 1987 *Untersuchungen an Skelettresten von Katzen aus Haithabu (Ausgrabung 1966-1969)*. Berichte über die Ausgrabungen in Haithabu **24**, Neumünster

Jones, A M, Marchand, J, Sheridan, A, Straker, V, and Quinnell, H, 2012 Excavations at the Whitehorse Hill cist, Dartmoor, *Past 70*, 14-16

Jurmain, R D, 1999 *Stories from the Skeleton – Behavioural Reconstruction in Human Osteology*, Amsterdam

Keepax, C A, 1990 The human bones, in G J Wainwright, *Gussage All Saints. An Iron Age settlement in Dorset*, Department of the Environment Archaeol Rep **10**, London HMSO, 161-71

Kerney, M, 1999 *Atlas of land and freshwater molluscs of Britain and Ireland*, Colchester

King, A, 1999 Diet in the Roman world: a regional inter-site comparison of the mammal bones, *J Roman Archaeol* **12**, 168-202

Kristiansen, K, 1978 The consumption of wealth in Bronze Age Denmark, in K

Kristiansen and C Paludan-Müller (eds*), New Directions in Scandanavian Archaeology*, 158-190, Lyngby, National Museum of Denmark

Laidlaw, M, 1999 Prehistoric and Romano-British pottery, in C M Hearne and V Birbeck (eds,) *A35 Tolpuddle to Puddletown Bypass DBFO, Dorset, 1996-8*, Wessex Archaeol Rep **15**, Salisbury, 110-127

Lambrick, G and Allen T, 2004 *Gravelly Guy, Stanton Harcourt, Oxfordshire: the development of a prehistoric and Romano-British community*, Thames Valley Landscape Monogr **21**, Oxford

Lanting, J N, and van der Waals, J D, 1972 British Beakers as seen from the Continent, *Helinium* **12**, 20-46

Last, J, 1998 Books of life: biography and memory in a Bronze Age barrow, *Oxford J Archaeol* **17**, 43-53

Last, J, 2007 Covering old ground: barrows as closures, in J Last (ed.), *Beyond the grave: new perspectives on barrows*, Oxford, 156-75

Laws, K. 1991 The shale in Sharples 1991, 233-234

Lawson, A J, 1976 Shale and Jet Objects from Silchester, *Antiquaries J* **105**, 241-276

Lawson, A J, 2000 *Potterne 1982-5: Animal Husbandry in Later Prehistoric Wiltshire*, Wessex Archaeol Rep **17**, Salisbury

Lewis, M E 2004 Endocranial lesions in non-adult skeletons: understanding their aetiology *Internatl J Osteoarchaeology* **14**, 82-97

Lewis, M E and Roberts, C, 1997 Growing pains: the interpretation of stress indicators *Internatl J Osteoarchaeology* **7**, 581-586

Liddell, D M, 1933 Excavations at Meon Hill, *Proc Hants Field Club* **12**, 127-62

Liddell, D M, 1935 Report on the Hampshire Field Club's excavation at Meon Hill, *Proc Hants Field Club* **13**, 7-54

Loe, L, Boyle, A, Webb, H and Score, D, 2014 *'Given to the Ground'. A Viking Age Mass Grave on Ridgeway Hill, Weymouth*, Dorset Natur Hist and Archaeol Soc monogr **22**

Locker, A, 2000 Animal Bone, in A J Lawson 2000, 101-17

Lopez-Duran, L, 1995 *Traumatology and orthopedics*, Madrid

Lovejoy, C O, Meindl, R S, Pryzbeck, T R and Mensforth, R P, 1985 Chronological metamorphosis of the auricular surface of the ilium: a new method for the determination of adult skeletal age at death, *American J Physical Anthropology* **68**, 15-28

Lovell, N, 1997 Trauma analysis in palaeopathology, *Yearbook Physical Anthropology* **40**, 139-70

Lukacs, J R, 1989 Dental palaeopathology: methods of reconstructing dietary patterns, in M Y Iscan and K A Kennedy (eds), *Reconstruction of Life from the Skeleton*, New York, 261-286,

Lynch, A H, Hamilton, J, and Hedges, R E M, 2008 Where the wild things are: aurochs and cattle in England, *Antiquity* **82**, 1025-1039

Macphail R I, 2000 Soils and microstratigraphy: a soil micromorphological and microchemical approach, in Lawson 2000, 47-70

Mays, S, 1998 *The Archaeology of Human Bones*, London

McCormick, F, 1992 Early faunal evidence for dairying, *Oxford J Archaeology* **11(2)**, 210-209

McKinley, J I, 1994a Bone fragment size in British cremation burials and its implications for pyre technology and ritual, *J Archaeol Science* **21**, 339-342

McKinley, J I, 1994b Cremation burial, in J Barnatt, Excavation of a Bronze Age unenclosed cemetery, cairns and field boundaries at Eagleston Flat, Curbar, Derbyshire, 1984, 1989-1990, *Proc Prehist Soc* **60**, 335-40

McKinley, J I, 1997 Bronze Age 'barrows' and funerary rites and rituals of cremation, *Proc Prehist Soc* **63**, 129-145

McKinley, J I, 2000a Cremation burials, in B Barber, B and D Bowsher 2000, *The eastern cemetery of Roman London: excavations, 1983-1990* Museum of London Monogr **4**, London, 264-277

McKinley, J I, 2000b The analysis of cremated bone, in Cox, M and Mays, S (eds) *Human osteology in archaeology and forensic science*, London, 403-421

McKinley, J I, 2000c Funerary practice, in Barber and Bowsher 2000, 60-81

McKinley, J I, 2000d Human bone and funerary deposits, in K E Walker and D E Farwell, *Twyford Down, Hampshire: archaeological investigations on the M3 motorway from Bar End to Compton, 1990-1993*, Hants Field Club Monogr **9**, Salisbury, 85-119

McKinley, J I, 2004a Compiling a skeletal inventory: disarticulated and co-mingled remains, in M Brickley and J I McKinley, *Guidelines to the standards for recording human remains*, IFA Paper **7**, Southampton and Reading, 14-17

McKinley, J I, 2004b Compiling a skeletal inventory: cremated human bone, in Brickley and McKinley 2004, 9-13

McOmish, D 1996 East Chisenbury: ritual and rubbishat the British Bronze Age-Early Iron Age Transition, *Antiquity* **70**, 68-76

McOmish, D, Field, D, and Brown G, 2010 The

Bronze Age and Early Iron Age Midden Site at East Chisenbury, Wiltshire, *Wilts Archaeol and Natur Hist Mag* **104**, 35-101

Meindl, R S and Lovejoy, C O, 1985, Ectocranial suture closure: a revised method for the determination of skeletal age at death based on the lateral-anterior sutures, *American J Physical Anthropology* **68**, 57-66

Meyrick, O, 1946 Notes on Some Early Iron Age Sites in the Marlborough District, *Wilts Archaeol and Natur Hist Mag* **51**, 156-8

Miles A W, 1826 *A Description of the Deverel Barrow, Opened A.D. 1825: Also, a Minute Account of the Kimmeridge Coal Money*, London

Miles, D, Palmer, S, Lock, G, Gosden, C and Cromarty, A M, 2003 *Uffington White Horse Hill and Its Landscape: Investigations at White Horse Hill, Uffington, 1989-95, and Tower Hill, Ashbury, 1993-4*, Thames Valley Landscapes Monogr **18**, Oxford

Millet, M, 1995 *Roman Britain*, London

Mills, J M 2004 The Kimmeridge Shale, in D A Hinton, (ed.) *Purbeck Papers*, Univ Southampton Dept Archaeol Monogr Ser **4**, 33-36

Mizoguchi, K, 1993 Time in the reproduction of mortuary practices, *World Archaeol* **25**, 223-35

Moffett L, Robinson MA and Straker V, 1989 Cereals, fruits and nuts: charred plant remains from Neolithic sites in England and Wales and the Neolithic economy, in A Milles, D Williams and N Gardner (eds) *The beginnings of agriculture*, BAR Int Ser **496**, Oxford, 243–261

Moore, J, and Jennings, D, 1992 *Reading Business park: a Bronze Age landscape*, Thames Valley Landscapes Monogr **1**, Oxford

Moorees, C F A, Fanning, E A and Hunt, E E, 1963 Age variation of formation stages for ten permanent teeth, *J Dental Research* **42**, 1490-1502

Morris, J T, 2008 *Re-examining Associated Bone Groups from southern England and Yorkshire, c. 4000BC to AD1550*, unpubl. PhD thesis, Univ Bournemouth

Needham, S and Longley, D, 1980 Runnymede Bridge, Egham: a Late Bronze Age riverside settlement, in JC Barrett and R Bradley (eds), 1980, *Settlement and Society in the British Later Iron Age*, BAR Brit Ser **83**, Oxford, 123-30

Needham, S and Sorenson, M L S, 1988 Runnymede refuse tip: a consideration of midden deposits and their formation, in J Barrett and I A Kinnes (eds) 1988, *The Archaeology of Context in the Neolithic and Bronze Age: recent trends*, Univ Sheffield, 113-26

Needham, S, *1991 Excavation and Salvage at Runnymede Bridge, 1978: the Late Bronze Age waterfront site*, British Museum, London

Needham, S, and Spence, T, 1996 *Refuse and disposal at Area 16 east Runnymede. Runnymede Bridge research excavations, Volume 2*, London

Needham, S, 2005 Transforming Beaker culture in north-west Europe: processes of fusion and fission, *Proc Prehist Soc* **71**, 171-217

Needham, S, 2007 800 BC, The Great Divide, in Haselgrove and Pope 2007, 39-63

Noe Nygaard, N, 1995 Ecological, sedimentary and geochemical evolution of the late-glacial to postglacial Åmose lacustrine basin, Denmark, *Fossils and strata* **37**, Copenhagen

O'Connor, TP, 1976, The excavation of a round barrow and cross-ridge dyke at Alfriston, E.Sussex, in P L Drewett, (ed.), *Rescue Archaeology in Sussex, 1975*, Bulletin of the Institute of Archaeology of London **13**, 62-66

O'Connor, B J, 1980 *Cross-Channel relations in the later Bronze Age*, BAR, Int Ser **91**, Oxford

O'Connor, T, 1988 *Bones from the General Accident site, Tanner Row*, Archaeology of York Vol. **15/2**, York Archaeol Trust/Council for British Archaeology

Ogden, A 2008 Advances in the palaeopathology of teeth and jaws, in R Pinhasi and S Mays (eds) *Advances in Human Palaeopathology*, Chichester, 283-307

Onhuma, K and Bergman, C A, 1982 Experimental studies in the determination of flake mode, *Bulletin of the Institute of Archaeol London* **19**, 161-171

Ortner, D J 2003 *Identification of Pathological Conditions in Human Skeletal Remains*, London and San Diego

Palmer, C and Jones, M, 1991 Plant resources, in N Sharples, Maiden Castle: excavations and field survey, 1985–6, English Heritage Archaeol Rep **19**, London, 129-139

Papworth, M, *2011 The Search for the Durotriges: Dorset and the West Country in the Late Middle Age*, Stroud

Payne, E H, 1943 The Bincombe barrow, Ridgeway Hill, Dorset, *Proc Dorset Natur Hist and Archaeol Soc* **65**, 35-82

Payne, S, 1973 Kill-off patterns in sheep and goats: the mandibles from Aşwan Kale, *Anatolian studies* **23**, 281-303

PCRG, 1997 *The Study of Later Prehistoric Pottery: General Policies and Guidelines for Analysis and Publication*, Prehistoric Ceramics Research Group Occ Papers 1 and 2, Oxford

Pearce, S M, 1983, The Bronze Age metalwork of south western Britain, BAR, Brit Ser **120**

Petersen, F, 1972 Traditions of multiple burial in later Neolithic and early Bronze Age England,

Archaeol J **129**, 22-55

Phenice, T W, 1969 A newly developed visual method of sexing the os pubis, *American J Physical Anthropology* **30**, 297-301

Pitts, M, 2010 News: Bronze age workshops in Kent used imported shale, *British Archaeology* **114**

Pollard, J, 2006, A community of beings: animals and people in the Neolithic of southern Britain, in D Serjeantson and D Field (eds*), Animals in the Neolithic of Britain and Europe*, Neolithic Studies Group Seminar Papers 7, 135-148

Poole, C, 1995 Pits and propitiation, in B Cunliffe 1995, *Danebury, An Iron Age hillfort in Hampshire: Volume 6 A hillfort community in perspective,* CBA Res Rep 102, 249-275

Poole, K, 2010 Bird introductions, in T O'Connor and N Sykes (eds), *Extinctions and invasions. A social history of British fauna,* Oxford, 156-165

Porter, R W and Park, W, 1982 Unilateral spondylolysis, *J Bone and Joint Surgery* **64B**, 344-8

Prien, E L, 1971 The riddle of stone disease, *J American Medical Association* **45**, 654-672

Prummel, W, and Frisch, H-J, 1986 A guide for the distinction of species, sex and body side in bones of sheep and goat, *J Archaeol Science* **13**, 567-577

Pryor, F, 1991 *English Heritage Book of Flag Fen,* Prehistoric Fenland Centre, Peterborough

Pryor, F, 2005 *Flag Fen: Life and death of a Prehistoric Landscape,* Stroud

Rackham, O, 1983 *Trees and woodland in the British landscape,* London

Rawlings, M, 2007 *Weymouth Relief Road: written scheme of investigation,* RPS, Document ref. no. 262812/027

Rawlings, M, Allen, M J, and Healy, F, 2004 Investigation of the Whitesheet Down environs, 1989-90: Neolithic causewayed enclosure and Iron Age settlement, *Wilts Archaeol Natur Hist Mag* **97**, 144-96

RCHM(E), 1970 *An inventory of the historical monuments in the County of Dorset, vol. 2, south-east,* London

RCHM(E), 1999 *Recording archaeological field monuments: a descriptive specification,* Swindon

Redfern, R 2005 *A Gendered Analysis of Health from the Iron Age to the End of the Romano-British Period in Dorset Mid-to-Late 8th Century B.C. To the End of the 4th Century A.D.,* unpubl PhD thesis, Inst of Archaeol and Antiquity, Univ Birmingham

Redfern, R, 2008 New evidence for Iron Age secondary burial practice and bone modification from Gussage All Saints and Maiden Castle (Dorset, England), *Oxford J Archaeol* **27** (3), 281-301

Reimer, P J, Baillie, M G L, Bard, E, Bayliss, A, Beck, J W, Blackwell, P G, Bronk Ramsey, C, Buck, C E, Burr, G S, Edwards, R L, Friedrich, M, Grootes, P M, Guilderson, T P, Hajdas, I, Heaton, T J, Hogg, A G, Hughen, K A, Kaiser, K F, Kromer, B, McCormac, F G, Manning, S W, Reimer, R W, Richards, D A, Southon, J R, Talamo, S, Turney, C S M, van der Plicht, J, and Weyhenmeyer, C E, 2009 IntCal09 and Marine09 radiocarbon age calibration curves, 0–50,000 years cal BP, *Radiocarbon* **51**, 1111-50

Rielly, K, 1997 Animal bone, in Smith, Healey, Allen, Morris, Barnes and Woodward 1997, 270-273

Rielly, K, 2009 Animal bone, in Trow, James and Moore, 2009, 187-209

Resnick, D, (ed.), 1995 *Diagnosis of bone and joint disorders* (3rd edn), Philadelphia

Reynolds, A, 2009 *Anglo-Saxon deviant burial customs,* Oxford

Richmond, I, 1968 *Hod Hill Volume Two. Excavations carried out between 1951 and 1958,* British Museum, London

Roberts, B W, Boughton, D, Dinwiddy, M, Doshi, N, Fitzpatrick, A P, Hook, D, Meeks, N, Mongiatti, A, Woodward, A and Woodward, P, forthcoming *Collapsing Commodities or Lavish Offerings? Understanding Massive Metalwork Deposition at Langton Matravers, Dorset During the Bronze Age-Iron Age Transition*

Roberts, C and Cox, M, 2003 *Health and disease in Britain from prehistory to the present day,* Stroud

Roberts, C and Manchester, K, 1995 *The Archaeology of Disease,* Stroud

Robinson, M, 2002 *English Heritage review of environmental archaeology: southern region insects,* Centre for Archaeol Rep **39**, London

Rogers, J, 2000 The palaeopathology of joint disease, in M Cox and S Mays (eds), *Human osteology in archaeology and forensic science,* London, 163-182

Rogers, J and Waldron, T, 1995 *A field guide to joint disease in archaeology,* Chichester, New York

Rohner, R P and Rohner, E C, 1970 *The KwakuitlIndians of British Columbia,* New York

Rousham, E and Humphrey, L, 2002 The dynamics of child survival, in H Macbeth and P Collinson (eds) *Human Population Dynamics: Cross-disciplinary perspectives,* Biosocial Society Symposium Series, Cambridge, 124-140

Royall, C, 2011 *South Dorset Ridgeway Mapping Project: results of NMP mapping,* Truro

Saville, A, 1980 On the measurement of struck flakes and flake tools, *Lithics* **1**, 16-20

Scheuer, L and Black, S, 2000 *Developmental juvenile osteology,* Oxford

Schmid, E, 1972 *Atlas of animal bones. For pre-historians, archaeologists and quatrenary geologists*, Amsterdam, London, New York

Schweingruber, F H 1990 *Microscopic wood anatomy* (3rd edn), Birmensdorf, Swiss Federal Institute for Forest, Snow and Landscape Research

Seager Smith, R, 1993 Roman pottery, in R J C Smith, *Excavations at County Hall, Colliton Park, Dorchester, Dorset, 1988, in the north-west quarter of Durnovaria*, Wessex Archaeol Rep **4**, Salisbury, 41-61

Serjeantson, D, 1996 The animal bones, in Needham and Spence 1996, 194-253

Serjeantson, D, 2009 *Birds*, Cambridge

Sharples, N, 1991 *Maiden Castle: excavations and field survey, 1985-6*, English Heritage Archaeol Rep **19**, London

Sharples, N, 2007 Building communities and creating identities in the first millennium BC, in Haselgrove and Pope (eds) 2007, 174-84

Sharples, N M, 2010 *Social Relations in Later Prehistory: Wessex in the First Millennium BC*, Oxford

Shepherd, I A G and Shepherd, A N, 2001 A cordoned urn burial with faience from 102 Findhorn, Moray, *Proc Soc Antiq Scotland* **131**, 101-128

Sibun, L and Start, H 2007 Human skeletal remains, in L Bashford, L and L Sibun, *Excavations at the Quaker burial ground, Kingston-upon-Thames, London (131-139), Post-Medieval Archaeology* **41**, 100-154

Sissons, H A 1976 Osteoporosis and osteomalacia, in:L V Ackerman, H J Spjut and M T Abell (eds), *Bones and Joints*, Baltimore, 25-38

Sjøvold, T, 1984 A report on the heritability of some cranial measurements and non-metric traits, in G N van Vark (ed.) *Multivariate Statistical Methods in Physical Anthropology*, 223-246, Groningen

Sjøvold, T, 1987 Decorated skulls from Hallstatt, Austria: the development of a research project, in G Burenhult, A Carlsson, A Hyenstrand and T Sjøvold (eds) Theoretical approaches to artifacts, settlement and society, BAR Int Ser **366**, Oxford, 5-21

Smith, K, 2006 *Guides, guards and gifts to the gods: domesticated dogs in the art and archaeology of Iron Age and Roman Britain*. BAR Brit Ser **422**

Smith R J C, Rawlings M, and Barnes I, 1992 Excavations at Coburg Road and Weymouth Road, Fordington, Dorchester, *Proc Dorset Natur Hist and Archaeol Soc* **114**, 41

Smith, R J C, Healey, F, Allen, M J, Morris, E L, Barnes, I, and Woodward, P J, *Excavations along the route of the Dorchester by-pass, Dorset, 1986-8*, Wessex Archaeol Rep **11**, Salisbury

Smith, W, 2002 *A review of archaeological wood analyses in southern England*, Centre for Archaeol Rep **75**, Salisbury

Smith, W and Nicholson, R, 2011 Appendix C, Assessment of the Environmental Evidence, C.3. Charred and waterlogged plant remains and charcoal, in Oxford Archaeology, *Weymouth Relief Road, Dorset. Post Excavation Assessment of Project Design, Report to Client*, Feb 2011, 144-159

Sperber, D, 2010 The guru effect, *Review of Philosophy and Psychology* **1**, 583-92

Spratt, D A, 1989, *Linear Earthworks of the Tabular Hills, NE Yorkshire*, Univ Sheffield

Stace, C, 2010 *New Flora of the British Isles* (3rd edn), Cambridge

Stead, S 1991 The human bones, in I Stead *Iron Age cemeteries in East Yorkshire. Excavations at Burton Fleming, Rudson, Garton-on-the-Wolds and Kirkburn*, London, English Heritage Archaeol Rep **22**, 126-39

Steinbock, R T, 1989 Studies in ancient calcified soft tissues and organic concretions, *J Palaeopathology* **3**, 1, 39-59

Stewart, T D, 1953 The age incidence of neural arch defects in Alaskan natives considered from the standpoint of etiology, *J Bone and Joint Surgery* **35A**, 937-50

Stirland, A 2005 Human remains, in: J Gardiner and M J Allen (eds) *Before the Mast, Life and Death Aboard the Mary Rose*, Mary Rose Trust, 516-62

Stoodley, N, 2002 Multiple burials, multiple meanings? Interpreting the early Anglo-Saxon multiple interment, in S Lucy and A Reynolds (eds), *Burial in early Medieval England and Wales*, London, 103-23

Strid, L, 2012 Animal bone, in Biddulph, E, Foreman, S, Stafford, E, Stansbie, D, and Nicholson, R, 2012 http://library.thehuman-journey.net/909/102/15.Animal%20bone.pdf

Stuart-Macadam, P, 1982 *A correlative study of palaeopathology of the skull*, unpubl PhD dissertation, Univ Cambridge

Stuart-Macadam, P, 1991 Anaemia in Roman Britain: Poundbury Camp, in, H Bush and M Zvelebil, *Health in Past Societies, Biocultural Interpretations of Human Skeletal Remains in Archaeological Contexts*, 101-113, BAR Int Ser **567**

Sunter, N, 1987 Excavations at Norden, in Sunter and Woodward, 1987, 9-43

Sunter, N and Woodward , P J, 1987 *Romano-British industries in Purbeck, Dorset*, Dorset Natur Hist and Archaeol Soc Monogr Ser **6**, Dorchester

Taylor, C C, 1966 Strip lynchets, *Antiquity* **40 (160)**, 277-83

Taylor, J J, 1985, Gold and silver, in Clarke, D V,

Cowie, T G and Foxon, A, 1985, *Symbols of Power at the Time of Stonehenge*, National Museum of Antiquities of Scotland, Edinburgh, 182-92

Thomas, J, 1999 *Understanding the Neolithic*, London

Tilley, C, 2004 Round Barrows and Dykes as Landscape Metaphors, *Cambridge Archaeol J* **14** (2), 185-203.

Tinsley, H M, and Grigson, C, 1981 The Bronze Age, in I G Simmons and M Tooley (eds), *The environment in British prehistory*, London, 210-49

Tomber, R and Dore, J, 1998 *The National Roman Fabric Reference Collection: a handbook*, Museum of London Archaeol Service Monogr **2**, London

Torgersen, J H 1951a The developmental genetics and evolutionary meaning of the metopic suture, *American J Physical Anthropology* **9**, 193-205

Torgersen, J H 1951b Hereditary factors in the sutural patterns of the skull, *Acta Radiologica* **36**, 374-382

Torgersen, J H, 1954 The occiput, the posterior cranial fossa and the cerebellar anatomy, in J Jansen and A Brodal (eds) *Aspects of cerebellar anatomy*, Olso, 396-418

Trevarthen, M, 2008 *Suburban life in Roman Durnovaria: excavations at the former County Hospital site, Dorchester, Dorset 2000-2001*, Wessex Archaeology, Salisbury

Trotter, M, 1970 Estimation of stature from intact long bones, in T D Stewart (ed.) *Personal identification in mass disasters*, Washington D.C., 71-83

Trotter, M and Gleser, G, 1952 Estimation of stature from long-bones of American Whites and Negroes, *American J Physical Anthropology* **9**, 427-440

Trotter, M and Gleser, G, 1958 A re-evaluation of estimation of stature based on measurements of stature taken during life and of long bones after death, *American J Physical Anthropology* **16**, 79-123

Trow, S, James, S, and Moore, T, 2009 *Becoming Roman, being Gallic, staying British. Research and excavation at Ditches 'hillfort' and villa 1984-2006*, Oxford

Tuckwell, A, 1975 Patterns of burial orientation in the round barrows of EastYorkshire, *Bulletin of the Institute of Archaeol* **12,** 95-123

Turkel, S J, 1989, Congenital abnormalities in skeletal populations, in M Y Iscan and K A R Kennedy (eds), *Reconstruction of Life from the Skeleton*, 109-27, New York

Tyrrell, A, 2000 Skeletal assessment of non-metric traits and the assessment of inter- and intra-population diversity: past problems and future potential, in M Cox and S Mays (eds), *Human osteology in archaeology and forensic science*, London, 289-306

Valentin, J, 1999 Weymouth, Redlands Sports Ground, *Proc Dorset Natur Hist and Archaeol Soc* **120**, 108

Van Beek, G C, 1983 *Dental morphology: an illustrated guide* (2nd edn), Bristol

von den Driesch, A, 1976 *A guide to the measurement of animal bones from archaeological sites*, Cambridge, Mass.

Vretemark, M, 1997 *Från ben till boskap. Kosthåll och djurhållning med utgångspunkt i medeltida benmaterial från Skara, Skrifter från Länsmuseet Skara 25*, Stockholm

Waddington, K E and Sharples, N M, *2011 The excavations at Whitchurch 2006-2009: an interim report*, Department of Archaeology, School of History Archaeology and Religion, Univ Cardiff

Wainwright, G J, 1968 The excavation of a Durotrigian farmstead near Tollard Royal in Cranbourne Chase, southern England, *Proc Prehist Soc* **34**, 102-47

Wainwright, G. J, 1979 *Gussage All Saints: An Iron Age settlement in Dorset*, Dept Environment Archaeol Rep **10**, London

Wainwright, G J, 1979b *Mount Pleasant, Dorset, excavations, 1970-1971*, Rep Res Comm Soc Antiq London **37**, London

Waldron, T, 2009 *Palaeopathology*, Cambridge

Waton, P V and Barber, K E, 1987 Rimsmoor, Dorset: biostratigraphy and chronology of an infilled doline, in K E Barber (ed*.) Wessex and the Isle of Wight: field guide*, Cambridge, 75-80

Webb, H, 2013 Cremated human bone, in E Biddulph, S Foreman, E Stafford and D Stansbie, 2013

Webster, C J, 2008 *The archaeology of south west England: south west archaeological research framework resource assessment and research agenda*, Taunton

Wells, C, 1977 The human bones, in P Donaldson, Excavation of a multiple round barrow at Barnack, Cambridgeshire, 1974-1976, *Antiquaries J* **57**, 216-25

Wells, C, 1979 Excavations by the late George Rybot on Eggardon Hillfort, 1963-66, *Proc Dorset Natur Hist and Archaeol Soc* **100**, 54-72

Wessex Archaeology, 1994 A354-A353 Dorchester to Weymouth road improvements: archaeological field evaluation - trial trenching, unpubl. Rep W565c, Wessex Archaeology, Salisbury

Wessex Archaeology, 2003 *A354 Weymouth Relief Road, Dorset*, archaeological assessment, unpubl. rep 49715.01, Wessex Archaeology, Salisbury

Wessex Archaeology, 2004 *A354 Weymouth Relief Road, Dorset*, archaeological field evaluation of Orange Route, unpubl. report, Wessex Archaeology, Salisbury

Wheeler, R E M, 1943 *Maiden Castle, Dorset,* Rep Res Comm Soc Antiq London **12**, London

Whitley, M, 1943 Excavations at Charlbury Camp, Dorset, 1939, *Antiquaries J* **23**, 98-121

Whittle, A, Healy, F, and Bayliss, A, 2011 *Gathering time: dating the early Neolithic enclosures of southern Britain and Ireland,* Oxford

Wilkinson, D, *Oxford Archaeology field manual,* unpubl. document, Oxford Archaeology, Oxford

Williams, D F, 1977 The Romano-British black-burnished industry: an essay on characterisation by heavy mineral analysis, in D P S Peacock (ed.), *Pottery and early commerce: characterisation and trade in Roman and later ceramics,* London, 163-220

Williams, H M R, 1997 The ancient monument in Romano-British ritual practices, *Proc Seventh Annual Theoretical Roman Archaeol Conf* **97**, 71-86

Williams-Freeman, J P, 1932, Cross-dykes, *Antiquity,* 6, 24-34

Wilson, B, 1992 Consideration for the identification of ritual deposits of animal bones in Iron Age pits, *International J Osteoarchaeology* **2**, 341-349

Woodward, A B, 2000a *British barrows: a matter of life and death,* Stroud

Woodward, A B, 2000b The late Bronze Age and Iron Age ceramic type series, in J C Barrett, P, Freeman, and A Woodward, 2000 *Cadbury Castle, Somerset: The later prehistoric and early historic archaeology,* London, 325–46

Woodward, A B, and Woodward, P J, 1996 The topography of some barrow cemeteries in Bronze Age Wessex, *Proc Prehist Soc* **62**, 275-91

Woodward, P J, 1986 The excavation of an Iron Age and Romano-British settlement at Rope Lake Hole, Corfe Castle, Dorset, in Sunter and Woodward 1986, 125-180

Woodward, P J 1991 *The South Dorset Ridgeway Survey & Excavation 1977-84,* Dorset Natur Hist and Archaeol Soc Monogr **8**, Dorchester

Woodward, P J, and Cox, P W, 1987 Excavations at Ower and Rope Lake Hole, in Sunter and Woodward 1987

Woodward, P J, and Bellamy, P, 1991 Artefact distributions, in N M Sharples (ed.) 1991, 21-32

Woodward, P J, Davies, S M and Graham, A H, 1993 *Excavations at the Old Methodist Chapel, Greyhound Yard, Dorchester, 1981-1984,* Dorset Hist and Archaeol Soc Monogr **12**, Dorchester

Yalden, D, and Albarella, U, 2009 *The history of British birds,* Oxford

Young, C J, 1977 *Oxfordshire Roman pottery,* BAR Brit. Ser. **43**, Oxford

Young, R and Humphrey, J, 1999 Flint use in England after the Bronze Age; Time for a re-evaluation?, *Proc. Prehist. Soc.* **65**, 231-242.

Index